ART

AN
INTRODUCTION

FIFTH EDITION

ART

AN
INTRODUCTION

FIFTH EDITION

DALE G. CLEAVER
University of Tennessee

HARCOURT BRACE JOVANOVICH, PUBLISHERS

San Diego   New York   Chicago   Austin   Washington, D.C.
London   Sydney   Tokyo   Toronto

COVER PHOTO: © Shostal Associates
BACK COVER PHOTO: G.E. Kidder-Smith

ISBN: 0-15-503434-0
Library of Congress Catalog Card Number:
88-80629
Printed in the United States of America

Preface

The fifth edition of *Art: An Introduction,* like the previous editions, is based on a dual approach to art. Part One discusses the elements of form, design, technique, iconography, and aesthetics. Part Two presents a historical survey in which these elements are utilized for the stylistic analysis of art in its historical context.

The present edition, however, has been changed in several respects. The format of the book is enlarged, and more color and black-and-white illustrations have been added. Black-and-white reproductions of the color plates are now placed within the text for immediate reference. The text and bibliographies have been updated throughout, and substantial additions have been made to the section on photography and motion pictures and to the section on modern art, thus weighting the twentieth-century material very heavily within the historical survey. The aim is to serve the student's need to understand the complexity of art in our century. Finally, a glossary has been added to facilitate the identification and definition of key terms.

As in the previous editions, this book offers generally accepted interpretations of the historically important periods, styles, and artists of Western culture. While basic terms and categories are presented, there has been an effort to use these with caution. Labels, though necessary, can inhibit the user from seeing individual differences. It would be a travesty for an art history or art appreciation course to teach a student to look at a work of art only long enough to assign it to a movement! Now as before, the book is intended to be used in conjunction with other material. To this end, selected bibliographies are provided at the end of each chapter. Many of the books cited here contain additional examples of the periods and artists covered, but further supplements may be desired for such specialized subjects as folk art, Oriental art, and various fields of design.

I would like to express my thanks to teachers of art history across the country for their interest. For their insightful comments on this and previous editions I would like to thank Dr. Clare Martini, Truman College; Dorothy Metzger Habel, James Darrow, and Richard Daehnert, all of the University of Tennessee; Linda Neagley, University of Michigan, Ann Arbor; Bernice Leibowitz, Bergen Community College; David L. Oravez, Boise State University; and Rachel Young, formerly of the University of Tennessee.

It has been most pleasant to work with Julia Berrisford, Helen Triller, Tony Maddela, Vivienne Bennett, and Sheila Spahn of Harcourt Brace Jovanovich. I also thank Merilyn Britt, Maggie Porter and Sarah Randall of the HBJ staff.

Dale G. Cleaver

Contents

ART

AN
INTRODUCTION

FIFTH EDITION

PART ONE

THE PRINCIPLES OF ART

To understand the art of our own time or that of other eras, it is necessary first to consider the nature of art and some of the principles by which it operates. Art has always outgrown the definitions imposed upon it, but for our purposes, a work of art might be defined as an object or event created or selected for its capacity to express and stimulate experience within a discipline. The experience may range from the pity evoked by the face of a starving child to a revelation of order in architecture, from an awareness of the miracle of organic growth to the mystery of ritual, from a call to social justice to defiance of conventional thought. The discipline may vary from the strictest geometrical organization to a spontaneous irregularity that approaches the accidental; yet discipline provides for order, completeness, and intensity.

The basis for the visual arts has usually been visual and tactile experience, although conceptual art in recent years has stressed the manipulation of ideas and mental processes. Of course, not all visual and tactile experiences

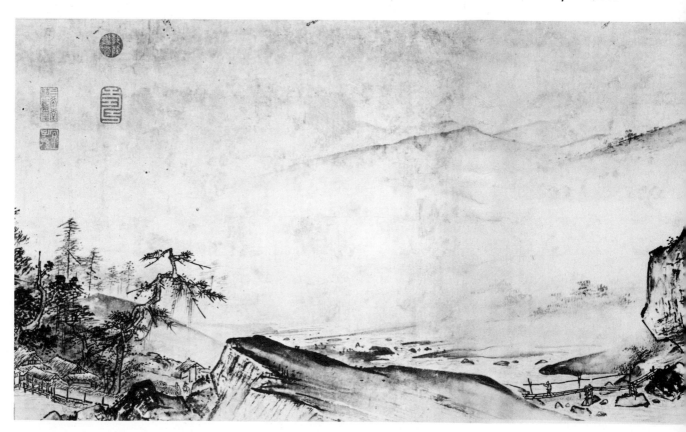

are art; the difference lies in human purpose. The artist arranges an experience for us by selecting and manipulating, within the limits of a discipline, such elements as line, shape, mass, value, texture, and color. The painter or sculptor may use these elements to represent well-known objects from the everyday world and to suggest feelings about them, or he may create an entirely new world for our contemplation. The architect is equally concerned with these elements, although he is rarely inclined to depict objects in his art and must usually consider utilitarian functions such as shelter and useful space. Whatever his field, the artist creates by choosing and composing the basic elements, and the word COMPOSITION is often used to denote a work of art. The individual objects or parts within the work of art are frequently called FORMS, but the word FORM is also used for the total character or structure of a composition. Thus we call the study of how visual and tactile elements function in art FORMAL ANALYSIS.

HSIA KUEI, detail from *River Scenes*, (Sung Dynasty).   Collection of the National Palace Museum, Taipei, Taiwan, Republic of China.

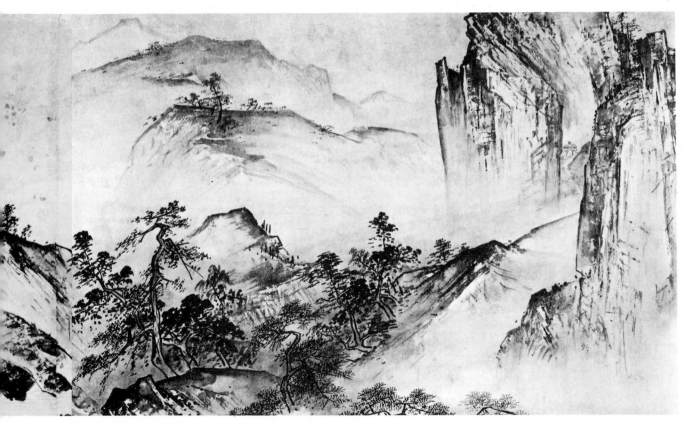

1

Visual and Tactile Elements in Art

LINE

Line may be thought of as the path of a moving point, as the edge of a flat shape, as the axis (dominant direction) of a shape, or as the contour of a solid object. Line may be of even or modulated (varied) thickness, and the range of personality it may express is wide: quick, slow, or still; nervous, majestic, or rigid. It can suggest mass, texture, light, and shadow; it can emphasize form or create mood.

In Picasso's pencil drawing of Dr. Claribel Cone (Fig. 1-1), the lines overlap and are modulated to suggest the roundness and heaviness of the body, but they become light and rippling to depict the ruffles of lace. In contrast, the drypoint (see page 33), *Self-Portrait with Burin*, by Beckmann (Fig. 1-2) expresses a nervous, tense personality by means of its jerky, restless lines and their contrasting angles. Beckmann used *crosshatching* (superimposed sets of parallel lines) for the shadows that define the mass of the head.

Delacroix's painting (Plate 16) evokes line with short, curving brush strokes that occasionally establish the contour of an object but more often blur the separations between the parts, move from the edges into the mass of the forms, and heighten the frenzied activity depicted. In the Chinese scroll painted by Hsia Kuei (pp. 2–3), vast scale is suggested by the contrast between clusters of precise linear details and areas left relatively empty. Men, plants, and surface textures are almost microscopic in a world of towering peaks and infinite, mist-filled space.

Line in sculpture may be seen as the edge of a form considered in silhouette, as incisions in the surface of the mass, or as the general directional thrust of a form. In all three types of line, the horseman carved by a Dogon tribesman of Africa (Fig. 1-3) has tense, straight sections enlivened by abrupt changes of direction. On the other hand, *The Assumption of the Virgin* by Cosmas and Egid Asam (Fig. 1-27) has a Delacroix-like activity in its complex twisting and curling edges.

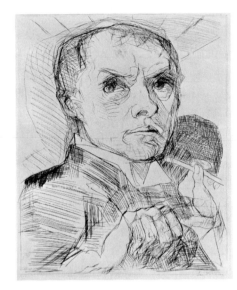

1-2 MAX BECKMANN, *Self-Portrait with Burin,* (1917). Drypoint and etching, printed in black, 11¾″ × 9⅜″. Collection, the Museum of Modern Art, New York. Gift of Edgar Kaufman, Jr.

1-1 PABLO PICASSO, *Dr. Claribel Cone,* (1922). Pencil on paper, 25³⁄₁₆″ × 19½″. The Baltimore Museum of Art: The Cone Collection, formed by Dr. Claribel Cone and Miss Etta Cone of Baltimore, Maryland.

1-3 DOGON TRIBESMAN, *Horseman,* (late nineteenth century ?). Wood, 14¾″ high. Katherine White Collection.

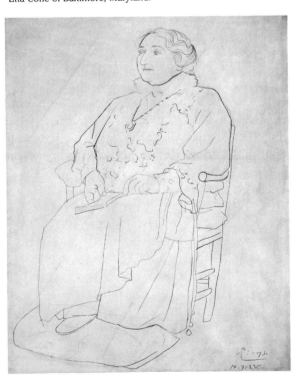

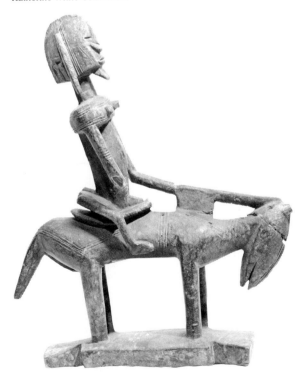

1-4

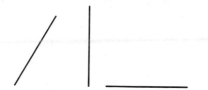

1-5

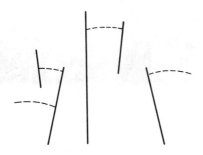

1-6

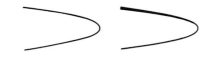

1-7

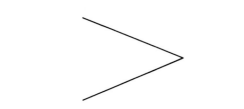

1-8

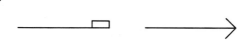

1-9

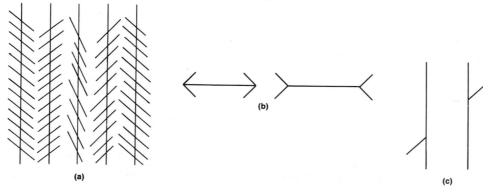

(a)   (b)   (c)

In architecture, line may emphasize rigid simplicity and sharply defined edges, as in Santa Maria delle Carceri (Fig. 1-16). In contrast to the simple balance of vertical and horizontal lines in this church, a powerful upward thrust is provided by the dominant vertical lines of Amiens Cathedral (Fig. 1-29).

Motion in Line

To suggest or emphasize movement, as in the painting by Delacroix or in Amiens Cathedral, line may be used in at least two ways: it may represent or suggest things that we know are capable of motion, such as rippling waves, or it may imply motion by its form or by its relation to other lines. Our experience of gravity causes us to feel that vertical and horizontal lines are stable, whereas unsupported diagonal lines often seem to move in the direction in which they are leaning (Fig. 1-4). Grouped lines may suggest tensions between each other by the degree to which they seem to require or to provide mutual support (Fig. 1-5), an effect often utilized by Cézanne (see Plate 22). Curving lines tend to move in the direction of their greatest thrust; modulating the thickness of a line can accentuate this effect (Fig. 1-6 and Plate 36). An angle often seems to point toward its apex (Fig. 1-7), and a line may suggest motion by drawing the viewer's attention toward one end (Fig. 1-8 and Plate 3). The dynamic effect lines may have on each other is dramatically illustrated by several classic diagrams. The vertical lines in Figure 1-9a are actually parallel but appear not to be because of the pushing forces of the diagonals. The horizontal lines in Figure 1-9b are of equal length but appear to be of different lengths because of the expanding and contracting qualities of the diagonals, whereas the verticals in Figure 1-9c seem to

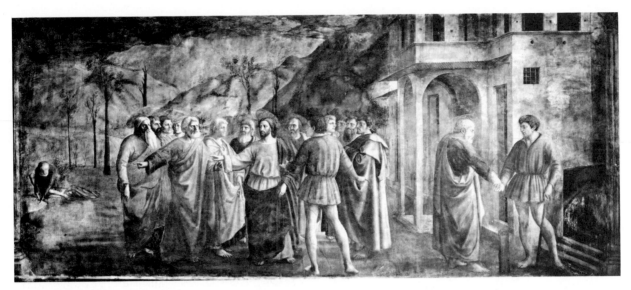

1-10 MASACCIO, *The Tribute Money,* (*c.* 1427). Fresco, approx. 20′ × 8′. Brancacci Chapel, Santa Maria del Carmine, Florence.

push the two diagonals out of alignment. These effects may be exploited deliberately or instinctively by the artist, architect, or designer.

Line and Space

The depth in Masaccio's *The Tribute Money* (Fig. 1-10) is achieved partly by *linear perspective*, one means of creating the illusion of depth on a flat surface. To our eyes, parallel lines in a plane pointing into space appear to converge at a *vanishing point* (V. P.) on the horizon established by our eye level, or on a line perpendicular to the horizon (Figs. 1-11 and 1-12). Frequently, however, intervening objects hide the horizon. In Figure 1-11, the converging lines of Masaccio's building have been extended until they meet, thus revealing the vanishing point, the hidden horizon, and the eye level chosen for us by the artist. Masaccio used linear perspective also to emphasize the major figure in the composition, Jesus, by placing the vanishing point right behind his head. In choosing the eye level and hence the horizon, the artist may give us an ordinary view (Fig. 1-11), a worm's-eye view (Fig. 1-12), or a view from above (Fig. 1-13). When all converging lines focus on a single vanishing point, as in the Masaccio fresco, we call it a *one-point perspective* system (Fig. 1-11). It is often desirable to have more than one vanishing point, as in Figures 1-12 and 1-13; an appropriate term is

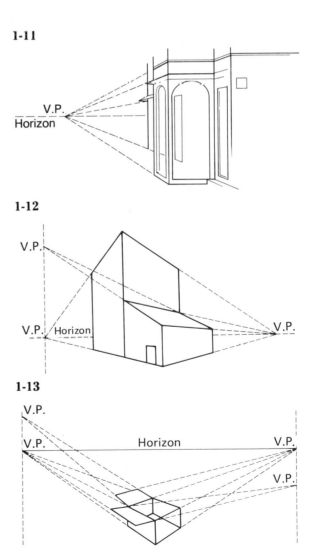

1-11

1-12

1-13

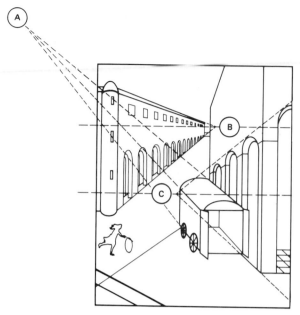

1-14

This diagram of a painting by De Chirico (Fig. 18-31) indicates vastly different eye levels, A, B, and C, for the two buildings and the trailer.

1-15

Diagram of *Decorative Figure on an Ornamental Background.*

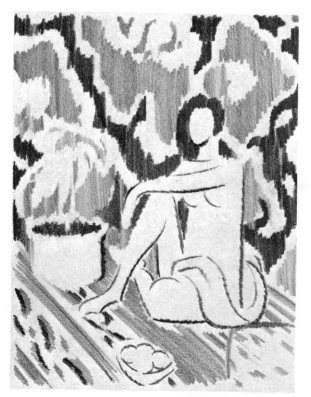

multiple-point perspective. The artist is not bound to restrict himself to a particular system. The various types of perspective—and there are others that have not been mentioned here—are only devices that the artist may or may not wish to use. He may deliberately use two or more different eye levels in the same painting in order to emphasize certain objects or to create for the viewer an unusual experience of space (Fig. 1-14).

SHAPE

A *shape* is an area or a plane with distinguishable boundaries. If we think of shape as having length and width only, then it is a more limited term than *form* and is distinguishable from *mass,* which requires depth as a third dimension (although it is possible to ignore the third dimension of a mass and consider it as a shape if we view it one surface at a time or see it in silhouette). Shape, like line, may have many personalities: rigid, flexible, precise, uncertain, calm, active, awkward, or graceful.

Picasso's *Three Musicians* (Plate 33) has shapes that tip, slide, bend suddenly, break up, and interweave in a staccato fashion; the total effect is one of great activity. In the *Decorative Figure on an Ornamental Background* (Plate 31), Matisse placed a massive, rigidly contoured figure in an environment of shapes that blossom expansively within loose-framing lines (Fig. 1-15). It is the room that is agitated; the woman seems motionless. This unusual effect comes partly from the orientation of the figure along vertical and horizontal lines, which seem stable compared with the diagonals of the floor and the irregular curves on the wall.

As we have seen, it is often necessary to ignore the third dimension when considering shape in sculpture and architecture. Although Egyptian sculpture derives much of its character from mass, it is helpful to consider the nature of shape in *Mycerinus and His Queen* (Fig. 7-8). The clearly delineated shapes present vertical and horizontal elements locked into a static, timeless rigidity. In contrast, the forms of the Asam composition (Fig. 1-27), if considered as shapes, have the restlessness of dried leaves in a wind. Similarly, the simple rigid shapes, organized by line, of Santa Maria delle Carceri (Fig. 1-16) contrast with the lilting and constantly interrupted shapes of San Carlo alle Quattro Fontane (Fig. 15-15), where multiplicity and changes of direction suggest flexibility and even metamorphosis.

Motion in Shapes

Static shapes maintain a rigid equilibrium within themselves and with their environment (Fig. 1-17). Shapes become more dynamic as they draw our attention in a specific direction. The triangle in Figure 1-18 pushes upward more than to the sides. The rectangle is relatively stable, but because of its width our attention is drawn along a horizontal axis. Even the stability of the square may be disturbed if we move it out of alignment with a stable

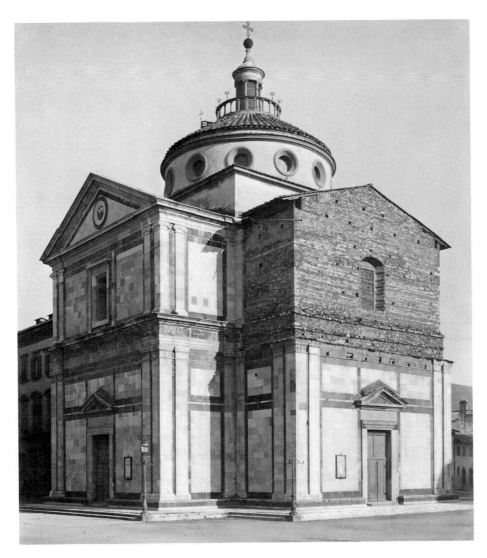

1-16 GIULIANO DA SANGALLO, Santa Maria delle Carceri, Prato, Italy, (1485–92).

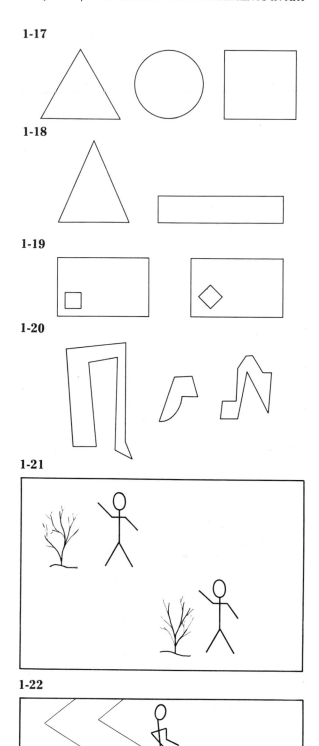

1-17

1-18

1-19

1-20

1-21

1-22

environment (Fig. 1-19). Less regular shapes can suggest much more activity; Figure 1-20 shows several of the shapes in Picasso's *Three Musicians* (Plate 33). Their liveliness comes from irregularly expanding and contracting parts that draw our attention in several directions.

Shape and Space

The illusion of depth on a flat surface may be produced simply by overlapping shapes, as in the Picasso painting and the landscape by Hsia Kuei on pages 2–3. Even the position of shapes on the picture surface can suggest space. In Figure 1-21 the upper figure appears to be farther away even though the two figures are equal in size. The assumption is easily made that the figures are standing on a plane that extends to an unseen horizon outside the picture. Diagonal lines or parallels that do not converge may strengthen the effect of depth (Fig. 1-22), but the illusion of space is strongest when linear perspective is employed. A size difference between similar or recognizable shapes may suggest distance between them because the effect implies linear perspective, as with the figures or the trees in Ghiberti's bronze relief (Fig. 14-19).

MASS

Mass, or three-dimensional solidity, is used directly in architecture and sculpture but must be created by illusion in painting and drawing. The artist can produce the effect of thickness or roundness with highlights and shadows, as in Masaccio's *Tribute Money* (Fig. 1-10); with lines describing some forms pushing in front of others, as in Picasso's drawing of Dr. Claribel Cone (Fig. 1-1); with lines delineating the various sides of a three-dimensional object, either with linear perspective, as in Masaccio's *Tribute Money,* or without it, as in Davis's *Something on the Eight Ball* (Fig. 18-37); and with colors that advance or recede (see p. 16) to pull some parts of an object forward. Mass may express dynamic power, as in Rubens's *Coup de Lance* (*The Crucifixion,* Fig. 1-23), where the vast bulk, foreground placement, and twisting forms emphasize the dramatic violence of the subject (Fig. 1-24). Rembrandt reinforced the quiet equilibrium of his *Supper at Emmaus* (Plate 14) by

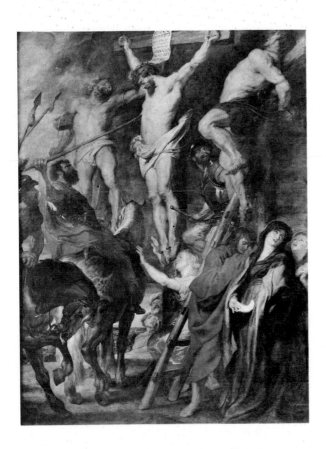

1-23 PETER PAUL RUBENS, *Coup de Lance (The Crucifixion),* (1620). Oil on canvas, 14′ × 10′.
Koninklijk Museum voor Schone Kunsten, Antwerp.

1-24
Diagram of *Coup de Lance.*

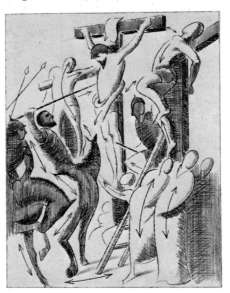

1-25
Diagram of *Supper at Emmaus.*

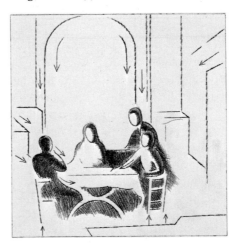

aligning and framing the figure masses with the stable architectural forms and the rigid edges of the painting (Fig. 1-25).

Sculpture may emphasize or deny mass. The term *closed form* is used for sculpture, painting, or architecture that stresses impenetrable mass. The figures of *Mycerinus and His Queen* (Fig. 7-8) have simplified anatomical forms with broad surfaces of blocklike permanence. The mass is not opened up between the two figures or between their legs or their arms and their bodies. For more *open form* and more violent push-pull tensions, consider the Asam sculpture (Fig. 1-27). Some sculptors deny the importance of mass. Gabo, for example, preferred transparent plastics that seem to give order to space without displacing it, as in *Linear Construction* (Fig. 18-46).

Architecture usually employs mass to define interior space, and the character of architectural mass ranges from the quiet symmetry of Santa Maria delle Carceri (Figs. 1-16 and 14-31) to the swooping, turning liveliness of Notre Dame du Haut (Figs. 18-65, 18-66). In the Seagram Building (Fig. 18-64), glass and steel reduce the mass to thin, transparent, membrane walls.

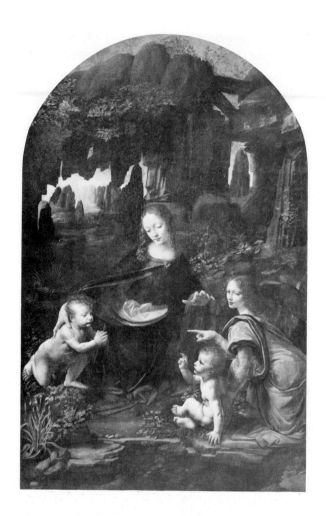

1-26 LEONARDO DA VINCI, *The Madonna of the Rocks,* (*c.* 1485). Oil on wood panel, approx. 6′ × 4′. Louvre, Paris.

VALUE

Variations in lightness and darkness, called variations in *value,* are used to define shapes, to suggest line, to create the illusion of mass and space on a flat surface, to emphasize certain parts, and to express feeling. Value changes define shapes in Picasso's *Three Musicians* (Plate 33). In Rubens's *Coup de Lance* (Fig. 1-23), he *modeled* (molded) solids with light and shadow, focused attention on Christ by floodlighting, and reinforced the dramatic quality of the scene with bold contrasts in value. Holbein clarified details and space relations with light and shadow in his *Ambassadors* (Fig. 14-56); but Rembrandt, in the *Supper at Emmaus* (Plate 14), obscured much of the detail in deep shadow, sacrificing clarity for an effect of soft glowing atmosphere and quiet drama. The light and shadow used to model form, as in the works by Rubens and Rembrandt, are often called by the

Italian term *chiaroscuro*. Leonardo da Vinci employed dramatic chiaroscuro, and often used *reflected light* to separate shaded surfaces. In Figure 1-26, the jaw of the pointing angel acquires solidity and moves out from the neck because the shaded area of the jaw receives reflected light from the lower neck and shoulder.

In sculpture and architecture, value contrasts are produced by different degrees of projection and recession in the masses and by use of different materials and colors, as in *The Assumption of the Virgin* (Fig. 1-27), where the contrasts of colors and of light and dark stone work with the light and shadow produced by bold recessions and deep hollows in the figure groups. The opposition of light and shadow is intensified by windows directly overhead. Value contrasts dramatize the event and acquire Christian content — the Virgin ascends toward the light, which symbolizes God. In Frank Lloyd Wright's Robie House (Fig. 18-55), the hovering horizontals, which suggest shelter and align themselves sympathetically with the ground surface, are stressed by the value contrasts of brick and stone and by highlights and shadows of projecting and receding parts.

Value Relations

Our perception of the value, as well as of the size and color, of a given form may be affected by its environment through the principle of *simultaneous contrast.* Of the two circles of equal white in Figure 1-28a, the top one appears lighter because of its strong contrast with its surroundings. In Figure 1-28b, the white circle tends to appear larger because light areas seem to radiate and expand against darker backgrounds or surroundings. In the *Coup de Lance* (Fig. 1-23), such effects help

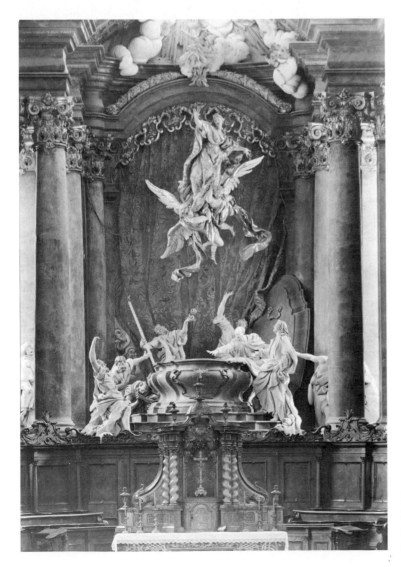

1-27   COSMAS DAMIAN ASAM and EGID QUIRIN ASAM,   *The Assumption of the Virgin,* (1718–25). High altar, monastery church at Rohr, Bavaria.

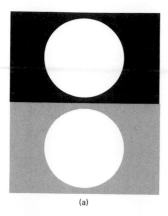

(a)

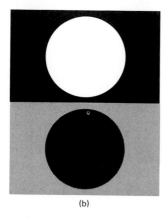

(b)

1-28

create the monumentality of the figure of Jesus, the glowing flesh of Mary Magdalene at the foot of the cross, and the malevolent eye of the warrior who thrusts the lance into the side of Jesus.

Value Contrast and Space

Value contrast can be used in painting to create the illusion of space by defining mass, which implies the space necessary to contain it; by separating planes or edges; and by sharpening or softening details. The illusion of deep space in the Chinese landscape (pp. 2–3) is achieved partly through a carefully adjusted sequence of overlapping masses and planes separated not only by line but also by value contrasts that become softer from foreground to background. *Aerial perspective* (or *atmospheric perspective*) is the term for the softening of value contrasts and details and the muting of colors to give the effect of distance. Aerial perspective is used by Giorgione in his *Pastoral Concert* (Plate 9) and by Masaccio in his *Tribute Money* (Fig. 1-10).

TEXTURE

Texture is the quality of a surface: smooth, rough, slick, grainy, soft, or hard. In painting, it may apply both to the texture of the paint itself and to the textures that are depicted. The painter, the sculptor, and the architect frequently use texture for variety, focus, or unity. In Holbein's *The Ambassadors* (Fig. 14-56), the smooth surface of the paint helps give unity to the work even while the painting gives the illusion of a great variety of textures in the different objects depicted. Delacroix was less interested in depicting a variety of textures in his *Lion Hunt* (Plate 16). He used the rough texture of the paint in undisguised brush strokes to stress the violence of the action and to unify the variety of shapes. In Gabo's *Linear Construction* (Fig. 18-46), space is articulated mainly by nylon strings that produce the illusion of grooved — that is, textured — surfaces. The Asam sculpture (Fig. 1-27) has a multiplicity of textures that increases the complexity of the composition but also helps to separate the figures from their setting. From a distance, the thousands of sculptured details on the surface of Amiens Cathedral (Fig. 1-29) give the cathedral a bristling roughness of texture that has great variety. The countless perforations in the stone façade accentuate the soaring lightness of the structure. Notre Dame du Haut (Fig. 18-65), with its more asymmetrical form, attains some of its unity and massive strength from its relatively uninterrupted surfaces and the overall texture of the concrete.

Textural variation may be used in painting to give the illusion of space. The softening of focus in aerial perspective involves the softening of textural qualities — not only the depicted textures but the actual texture of the paint. In sculpture and architecture, spatial effects may be emphasized by using bold textures in the foreground and softer ones for more distant surfaces.

COLOR

Color is one of the artist's principal means of achieving variety, emphasis, and unity; of creating the effects of mass and space; and of expressing feelings. In Giorgione's *Pastoral Concert* (Plate 9), the focal color of the red hat is set against the cool

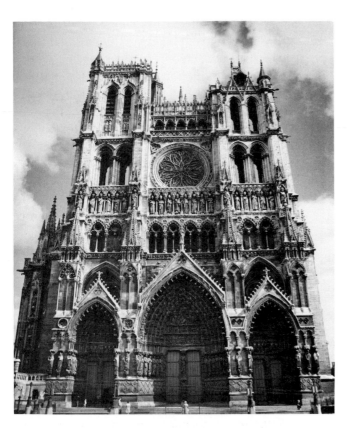

1-29 ROBERT DE LUZARCHES, Amiens Cathedral, thirteenth century with later additions.

light green of the distant meadow; the contrast of warm and cool colors works with the contrast of values and aerial perspective to create depth, and the total effect of serenity and elegance comes partly from the opulent but quiet colors. Monet was fascinated by the shimmer of light and color on the stone façade of Rouen Cathedral (Plate 20). Vibrating contrasts of blue and orange dance backward and forward in accord with their brightness and warmth, denying the mass of the stone and producing a luminous vision. The colors in Matisse's *Decorative Figure on an Ornamental Background* (Plate 31) are heavier and more earthy, but they provide a rich and lively variety as they change in modulations of reds, browns, blues, yellows, and greens.

Color in sculpture and architecture may come from the natural color of the materials or from paint, glaze, or chemical treatment (see Chapter 4). Color may complicate the form, or it may stress the point of central importance and even act as the axis of balance. Color can separate the various parts of a composition or pull the parts together by giving them a common characteristic. Architecture may be united with a landscape through the use of native wood or rock that repeats the colors of the setting, or the building may be separated from its environment by the use of "foreign" colors.

The Nature of Color

Sunlight, or white light, contains the elements of all colors in such a mixture that each color is canceled. White light can be broken into its component colors by projecting it through a prism. An object is seen as a particular color because it absorbs some wavelengths of white light and reflects others. That is, an apple is red when it reflects those wavelengths of light that we have named red and absorbs the others.

The basic color that the artist chooses to give an object is called its *local color*. The artist may emphasize local colors, stress their modifications, or subordinate them to a general effect. The local red of an apple may be modified by reflections from a green tablecloth or by light coming through yellow curtains. By partly subduing local colors, Rembrandt achieved the overall effect of brown-gold light that characterizes many of his works, such as

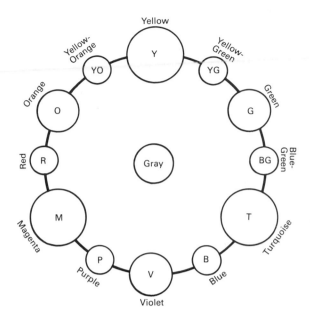

1-30
One form of color wheel. Intervening secondary hues are produced by mixing the primaries. Further mixing can multiply the hues. Opposing complementaries, such as yellow and violet, can be mixed to lower the saturation of one or to produce brown or gray.

the *Supper at Emmaus* (Plate 14). Matisse, in contrast, retained more local colors (Plate 31), although he might change local colors arbitrarily.

The word *color* refers to a combination of *hue, saturation,* and *value. Hue* is the property that distinguishes one color from another, the property that enables us to name the color. Certain *primary* hues can be mixed to produce most other hues. With colored light, the primaries are red, green, and blue-violet. With pigments, red, yellow, and blue have traditionally been cited most often as primaries. More precisely, the pigment primaries might be called magenta-red, yellow, and turquoise-blue. A much richer range of hues can be mixed by using more than just the primaries. Color experts have used slightly different sets of primaries and established *color wheels* and color systems. Our diagram (Fig. 1-30), one of these convenient wheels, shows, between the primaries, the hues obtained by mixing. Colors opposite each other on the wheel are *complementaries.* These dull or neutralize each other when mixed.

Saturation refers to the purity or vividness of a color. A strong red is said to be of high saturation. It is possible to lower the saturation of a color by adding its complement, by diluting it with white, or by darkening it with black.

The *value* of a color is its darkness or lightness. Colors at full saturation can be assigned positions on a value scale ranging from white to black. A bright yellow, for example, would have the value equivalent of light gray, whereas a red would be darker in value. Colors that are greatly diluted with white are called *tints;* colors rendered darker by the addition of black or a complement are called *shades.*

The Effects of Color

For the greatest possible control over his medium, the artist must consider the effects of simultaneous contrast in colors. A neutral gray or white placed near a strong color will appear to take on some of the complementary of the color. This effect also occurs with combinations of colors; for example, red next to yellow will assume a touch of yellow's complement, violet; the yellow will appear to have a tinge of red's complement, blue-green.

Certain colors (yellow, red, orange, and often violet) are considered *warm,* while others (greens and blues) are considered *cool.* This classification is largely based on our association of certain colors with light and heat. Contrasts of warm and cool colors can be especially intense.

For some color phenomena, we do not have adequate experimental data to draw precise conclusions. The considerable variation in response to colors is apparently due to both physiological and emotional differences in observers. Warm colors may make an object seem larger, while cool colors often seem to diminish its size, but value and saturation differences can be manipulated to reverse this effect. For many observers, certain warm colors, especially when light in value and highly saturated, seem to advance toward the eyes. Cool colors often seem to recede. The individual observer's color preferences, however, appear to be important in causing certain colors rather than others to advance. The old rule that warm colors always advance and cool colors always recede is not valid in all cases.

In a given culture, certain colors may be commonly understood as being expressive of particular feelings; we may speak of "seeing red" or "feeling blue." The artist may utilize this expressive potential, but it may not work for an observer from another culture.

Some theorists and researchers have attempted to equate colors with sounds or with tastes *(synesthesia)*, but the results have been inconclusive.

Suggestions for Further Study

Ball, Victoria. "The Aesthetics of Color: A Review of Fifty Years of Experimentation." *Journal of Aesthetics and Art Criticism,* Vol. 23, No. 4 (Summer 1965), pp. 441–52.

Birren, Faber. *Creative Color.* New York: Reinhold, 1961.

d'Amelio, Joseph. *Perspective Drawing Handbook.* New York: Leon Amiel Publisher, 1964.

Fish, Jonathan C. "Colour as Sensation in Visual Art and in Science." *Leonardo,* Vol. 14, No. 2 (Spring 1981), pp. 89–98.

Fisher, Howard T., and James M. Carpenter. *Color in Art.* Cambridge, Mass.: Fogg Art Museum and Harvard University, 1974.

Gerritsen, Frans. *Theory and Practice of Color: A Color Theory Based on Laws of Perception.* New York: Van Nostrand Reinhold, 1975.

Hanes, Randall M. "The Long and Short of Color Distance." *Architectural Record,* Vol. 127, Pt. 2 (April 1960), pp. 254–56 and 348.

Kuehni, Rolf G. *Color, Essence and Logic.* New York: Van Nostrand Reinhold, 1983.

Libby, William Charles. *Color and the Structural Sense.* Englewood Cliffs, N.J.: Prentice-Hall, 1974.

Luckiesh, M. *Visual Illusions, Their Causes, Characteristics, and Applications.* Republication of the original edition of 1922, with a new introduction by William H. Ittelson. New York: Dover, 1965.

Sargent, Walter. *The Enjoyment and Use of Color,* rev. ed. New York: Dover, 1964.

Sloane, Patricia. *Color: Basic Principles and New Directions.* New York: Van Nostrand Reinhold, 1968.

White, Gwen. *Perspective: A Guide for Artists, Architects, and Designers.* London: Batsford; New York: Watson-Guptill, 1981.

2

Functions
of
Design

Among the many sources of satisfaction that works of art offer are the experiences of order and variety. Artists may work consciously or unconsciously to create such experiences. Design is the organization or composition of the visual and tactile elements in a work of art. *Rhythm* may be employed, a recurrence of variations—often in the form of accents and intervals—that have enough similarity to establish continuity and order. Rhythm may be extended indefinitely; it does not require limits. *Balance,* the equilibrium of opposing forces, does involve limits and provides self-sufficiency and unity. Balance may be *axial,* that is, organized on either side of an actual or implied axis that acts as a fulcrum (Fig. 2-1), or *central,* that is, radiating from or converging upon an actual or implied central point (Fig. 2-2). Axial balance may be *obvious* (symmetrical), having very similar or identical elements on either side of

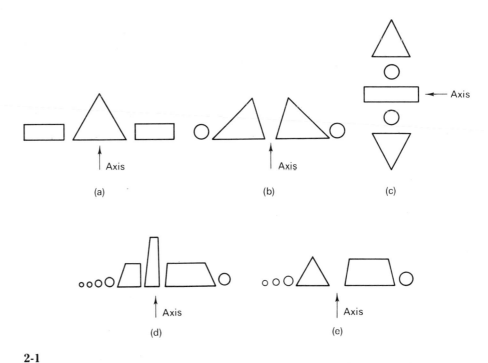

2-1

Types of axial balance: (a), (b), and (c) are in obvious axial balance; (d) and (e) are in occult axial balance.

the axis (Fig. 2-1a, b, c), or it may be *occult* (asymmetrical), having an equilibrium of elements that are dissimilar in size or shape (Fig. 2-1d, e). Central balance may also be obvious with similar elements in equilibrium around a center (Fig. 2-2a, b), or occult, using dissimilar elements (Fig. 2-2c, d). Axial balance and central balance usually become three-dimensional in sculpture, in architecture, and in painting that has the illusion of depth.

Different kinds of rhythm and balance, or the lack of them, can evoke strong reactions in the viewer of a work of art. Such reactions are in part due to the process of *empathy*, by which we identify with an object and tend to respond to it sympathetically. A statue of a man in an unbalanced or awkward pose may cause a sense of physical discomfort. Empathy is especially strong with images of our own species, but it also occurs in response to designs using forms that do not refer to nature.

Both rhythm and balance involve *proportion*, the size relationship of parts. It is partly because of proportion that some schemes of rhythm and balance are more satisfying than others. Throughout history, numerous theories have been proposed as bases for satisfying proportions. One of the most

2-2

Types of central balance.

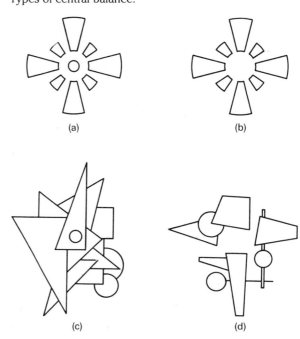

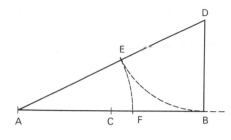

2-3

The Golden Mean. To divide line AB by the Golden Mean, first bisect the line (point C). At B, erect a perpendicular equal in length to AC. Complete the triangle ABD, and on the hypotenuse, AD, locate point E so that DE equals BD. Then locate point F on line AB so that AF equals AE. Line AB is divided by point F according to the proportions of the Golden Mean.

2-4

The Apocalyptic Christ, (twelfth century). 18'8" wide, abbey church of St. Pierre at Moissac, France.

famous is that of the *Golden Mean,* whose mathematical ratio cannot be simply stated, though its proportions are easily found by using geometry (Fig. 2-3).

REPETITION AND VARIATION ON A THEME

Several basic devices are used to achieve order and variety in art. One of these is repetition, the most elementary means of establishing order. We instinctively assume a relationship between similar or identical things. In the visual arts, repetition may appear in line, shape, mass, value, space, color, size, or even directional emphasis. At Moissac (Fig. 2-4), the sculptor used repetition to build an extremely symmetrical composition, or, more precisely, one of obvious axial balance. Such ritualistic formal order adds dignity to the subject. In Matisse's *Decorative Figure* (Plate 31), the scalloped shapes on the wall provide a theme or motif

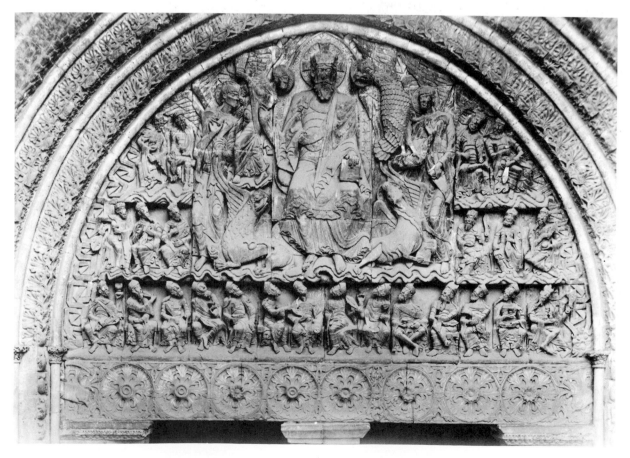

that is repeated with variations in the mirror, the plant, and the floor designs. Even the sturdy figure of the woman is *modulated,* or modified, by curved drapery around the hips to conform to the other curved shapes. The rippling alternation of concave-convex shapes gives rhythmic vitality to the scene. Objects are further related by colors, such as the browns, greens, and yellows that are repeated with variations. Unlike the Moissac

sculpture, Matisse's painting employs an occult axial balance. The figure is opposed by the potted plant and the diagonal floor lines, and the implied axis is a vertical line running through the knees of the figure to the bowl of fruit in the foreground.

In contrast, an obvious axial balance may employ repetition to unify opposing elements and provide focus. For example, in Michelangelo's Tomb of Giuliano de' Medici (Fig. 2-5), the concave

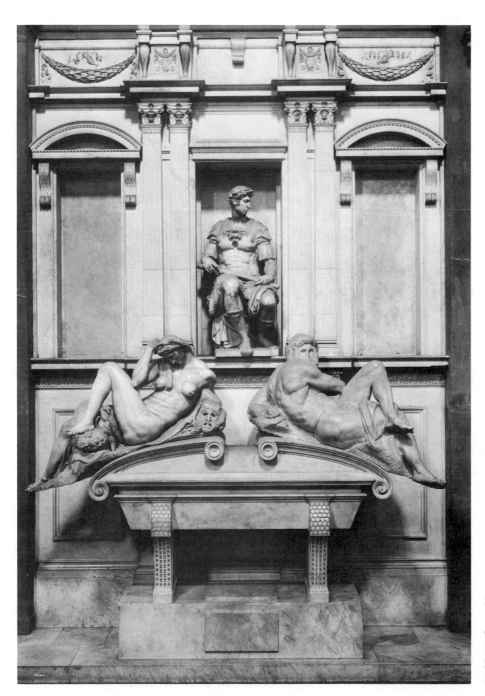

2-5 MICHELANGELO BUONARROTI,   Tomb of Giuliano de' Medici, (1519–34). Marble, central figure approx. 6′ high. New Sacristy, San Lorenzo, Florence.

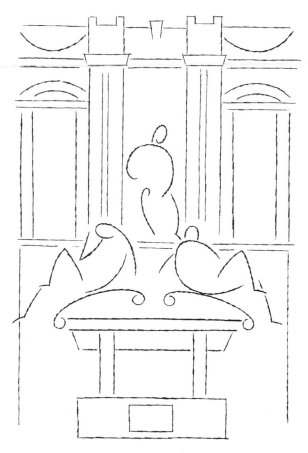

2-6
Diagram of the Tomb of Giuliano de' Medici.

curves of the reclining figures are countered by the convex curve of the sarcophagus (Fig. 2-6). Within the obvious axial balance, symmetrical repetition of alternating curves leads our attention to the figure of Giuliano, who is given added importance by the buildup of repeated architectural forms.

The columns of the Parthenon (Fig. 9-10) create a rhythmic repetition of masses and spaces that adds variety to the rectangular building and enriches its symmetry. Subtle variation in the intercolumnar spaces helps to prevent monotony. The horizontals of the platform on which the temple sits are contrasted with repeated verticals in the columns and are echoed by horizontals in the roof, making an almost static balance with very sharply defined limits. In Amiens Cathedral (Fig. 1-29), a profusion of repeated vertical and horizontal elements frames variations on the theme of the pointed arch. The arches, in turn, frame circular or *foliated* (scalloped) openings and occasional standing figures. Complexity makes the compositional limits fuzzy, but order is achieved by repetition and variations on themes within the obvious axial balance.

CONTRAST

Contrast is basic to variation and important for visual interest. Contrast can be used to clarify or modify form, to create mass and space, to suggest activity, to provide balance, to express feeling, and to focus attention. The lively, aggressive personality of Picasso's *Three Musicians* (Plate 33) depends on contrasts in color, in value, and in shape. Contrast of direction gives the African sculpture (Fig. 1-3) its tense equilibrium, while contrasts of texture, value, and color emphasize the horizontals of brick and concrete masses in the Robie House (Fig. 18-55).

GRADATION AND CLIMAX

Gradation is smooth or step-by-step development that usually suggests direction and builds to a climax. Any of the visual and tactile elements may be treated in this way. In the *Supper at Emmaus*

(Plate 14), Rembrandt developed a gentle gradation from shadow toward a climax of light that emphasizes Jesus. The Asam brothers used gradation and climax in light in the pyramidal buildup of figure groups and in the architectural setting (Fig. 1-27). At Amiens Cathedral (Fig. 1-29), the gradation in the size of the three main doors emphasizes the center one. Each entrance, in turn, is the focus of a funnel-like gradation of arches of decreasing size.

Suggestions for Further Study

Arnheim, Rudolf. *Art and Visual Perception: A Psychology of the Creative Eye,* new version. Berkeley: University of California Press, 1974.

————. *Visual Thinking.* Berkeley: University of California Press, 1969.

Gombrich, Ernst A., Julian Hochberg, and Max Black. *Art, Perception and Reality.* Baltimore: The Johns Hopkins Press, 1972.

————. *The Image and the Eye: Further Studies in the Psychology of Pictorial Representation.* Ithaca: Cornell University Press, 1982.

Hambidge, Jay. *The Elements of Dynamic Symmetry.* Reprint of the original edition of 1919. New York: Dover, 1969.

Kepes, György. *The Language of Vision.* Chicago: Theobald, 1944.

Lowry, Bates. *The Visual Experience: An Introduction to Art.* Englewood Cliffs, N.J.: Prentice-Hall; New York: Abrams, 1961.

Moholy-Nagy, László. *Vision in Motion.* Chicago: Theobald, 1947.

Norberg-Schulz, Christian. *Genius Loci. Towards a Phenomenology of Architecture.* New York: Rizzoli International, 1980.

————. *Meaning in Western Architecture.* New York: Rizzoli International, 1980.

Pepper, Stephen C. *Principles of Art Appreciation.* New York: Harcourt Brace Jovanovich, 1949.

Pope, Arthur. *The Language of Drawing and Painting.* Cambridge, Mass.: Harvard University Press, 1949.

3

Subject Matter

Subject matter is most simply defined as the recognizable objects depicted by the artist; yet subject matter acquires meaning on different levels and can be employed in different degrees.

LEVELS OF MEANING IN SUBJECT MATTER

Factual meaning in subject matter is established through identification of objects. Understanding the significance of the subject matter, however, frequently involves more than recognizing the objects. An inventory of the subject matter in Jan van Eyck's portrait of the Arnolfinis (Plate 5), for example, does not explain why the couple is so formally posed in the privacy of a bedroom; nor does a description of objects in Raphael's *Madonna of*

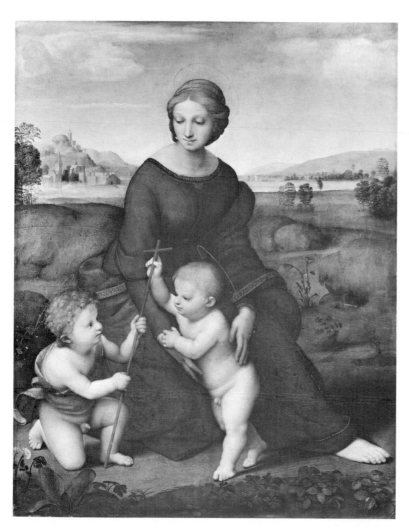

3-1 RAPHAEL SANZIO,
Madonna of the Meadow, (1505).
Panel, approx. 4′ × 3′.
Kunsthistorisches Museum, Vienna.

the Meadow (Plate 6 and Fig. 3-1) convey its content to a person unfamiliar with Christian scripture. Factual meaning is often supplemented or supplanted by meaning on other levels.

Conventional Meaning

Certain objects, actions, and even colors acquire special meaning for a particular culture. In our culture, for example, the cross stands for Christianity, red suggests life or danger, and white is associated with purity. To understand the conventional or generally accepted symbolism of other cultures or historical periods, it is often necessary to do research. In the Van Eyck portrait, a number of symbols would be missed by the casual observer today. The painting is a testament to the marriage vow. The lone candle symbolizes the all-seeing Christ; the fruit on the windowsill refers to the state of innocence before the Fall of Man; the mirror and the crystal beads are symbols of purity; the wooden shoes recall the command of God to Moses on Mt. Sinai to take off his shoes when he stood on holy ground; the dog stands for marital fidelity; and the back of the chair by the bed is carved in the image of St. Margaret, the patron saint of childbirth. The study of such conventional symbols is called *iconography*.

Some of the most pervasive symbols in Western art derive from the Christian tradition. The following are only a few of the hundreds of symbols used in Christian religious art, and for these only the more frequent meanings are included. The iconography of other cultures will be considered in the historical chapters in Part Two.

APPLE   Tree of Knowledge in the Garden of Eden, hence evil. An apple held by Jesus or Mary means salvation from sin.

CARNATION   Red means pure love; pink stands for marriage.

CAT   Laziness, lust.

CHALICE   Last Supper. A chalice with serpent identifies St. John the Evangelist. A chalice with wafer identifies St. Barbara. A broken chalice indicates St. Donatus.

COLUMBINE   Holy Ghost.

CROSS   The Latin cross (tall post with short cross-piece) refers to Jesus; the Greek cross (equal arms) stands for the Christian Church; an X-shaped cross refers to St. Andrew the Apostle.

DOVE   Holy Ghost, peace, purity.

EAGLE   St. John the Evangelist. Resurrection. Generosity.

EGG   Resurrection, source of life.

EWER AND BASIN   Purity, cleanliness.

FISH   Christ, since the five letters for the Greek word for *fish* (ΙΧΘΥΣ) form the initials of the words "Jesus Christ, God's Son, Savior."

FOUNTAIN   Mary, seen as the "fountain of living waters" (Song of Solomon 4:12ff. and Psalms 36:9) because she was the mother of Christ the Savior. Medieval and Renaissance Christian art often interpreted Old Testament passages as predictions of New Testament events.

GARDEN, ENCLOSED   Mary. A symbol of the Im-maculate Conception of Mary (Song of Solomon 4:12).

GLOBE   Earthly or spiritual power, held by God, Jesus, or a monarch.

GRAIN   Body of Jesus (bread in Holy Communion).

GRAPES OR GRAPEVINE   Christ as the "true vine" of which his followers are the branches (John 15:1, 5, 8). Blood of Jesus (wine in Holy Communion).

GRIDIRON   St. Lawrence, who was martyred on a grid over a fire.

HALO   Saintliness. A round halo is most common. A triangular halo reflects the Trinity; a square halo refers to living persons.

HAMMER   Instrument of the Passion, used in the Crucifixion.

INRI   The initials of the Latin words for *Jesus of Nazareth, King of the Jews,* which appear on the Cross of Jesus.

IRIS   Sorrow and purity of Mary. The bladelike leaf is associated with a sword and alludes to the suffering of Mary.

KEY   St. Peter, a reference to Christ's giving the keys of the kingdom of heaven to Peter (Matthew 16:19).

LADDER   Instrument of the Passion, used in the Crucifixion.

LAMB   Jesus, the sacrificial lamb of God. The sinner saved by Jesus the Good Shepherd. St. John the Baptist. St. Agnes. St. Clement.

LAMP   Wisdom.

LIGHT   Christ.

LILY   Purity, Mary.

LION   Jesus. St. Mark the Evangelist. St. Jerome. Majesty.

MANDORLA   Almond-shaped radiation of light surrounding the whole body of Jesus or Mary and signifying divinity.

MOON   Mary, who is identified as the woman with the moon under her feet (Revelation 12:1).

NAILS   Instruments of the Passion.

OINTMENT BOX   Mary Magdalene, a reference to her anointing of Christ.

OLIVE   Peace.

OX OR BULL   St. Luke the Evangelist. The Jewish Nation. Patience.

PALM   Victory.

PEACOCK   Vanity. Immortality, because of the

ancient belief that the flesh of the peacock does not decay.

PILLAR Instrument of the Passion (the pillar to which Christ was tied while he was whipped).

RIVERS The four rivers of Paradise, thought to flow from the same rock, symbolize the four Gospels, which had their source in Jesus.

ROSE Red for martyrdom, white for purity.

SCALES Equality and justice. The Archangel Michael is often shown with scales for the weighing of souls.

SCOURGE Instrument of the Passion.

SHIP The Christian Church, referring to the ark of Noah and the Church as means of salvation.

SKULL The vanity of earthly life (often shown with St. Jerome). A skull at the foot of the Cross refers to Adam and indicates the Cross as a means of salvation from man's original sin.

SPEAR Instrument of the Passion.

SPONGE Instrument of the Passion.

STAR Divine guidance, as in the journey of the Magi. One star is also the symbol of Mary. Twelve stars stand for the Apostles or for the twelve tribes of Israel.

SUN Mary (Revelation 12:1).

SWORD A symbol of martyrdom by the sword, often shown with St. Paul, St. Peter, St. Justina, St. Agnes, and many others.

THORNS Sin, grief. Instrument of the Passion (Christ's crown of thorns).

TOWER Identifies St. Barbara, who was confined in a tower.

WATER OR A WELL Purification, baptism, rebirth.

WHALE A symbol of the Devil or of the story of Jonah.

WHEEL Identifies St. Catherine, who was tortured on a wheel.

XP The Greek letters *Chi* and *Rho,* the first two letters in the Greek word for Christ. They are often superimposed:

A society often modifies its iconography according to changes in the prevailing thought of a period. The study of factors causing changes in iconography and the interpretation of such changes within the history of thought is called *iconology*.

Subjective Meaning

The individual artist may consciously or unconsciously employ a private symbolism based on an association of certain objects, actions, or colors with past experiences, a temporary state of mind, or an adopted world view. Similarly, the observer tends to interpret art according to his own associations, and over this interpretive activity the artist never has complete control. In a sense, therefore, a work of art is re-created anew each time it is experienced by an observer. Mondrian argued that recognizable objects were impurities that distracted the observer from the essential quality in art: a unique equilibrium of line and color (see Fig. 3-2). Thus his work can be described as the most "subjectless," that is, the least encouraging to associational meaning. Dali paints objects in such a way as to encourage a wide range of individual interpretation (see Fig. 3-3). Kandinsky, who felt that painting should make its appeal on the same nonrepresentational basis as nonnarrative music, approached the presentation of objects in the same way (see Plate 32).

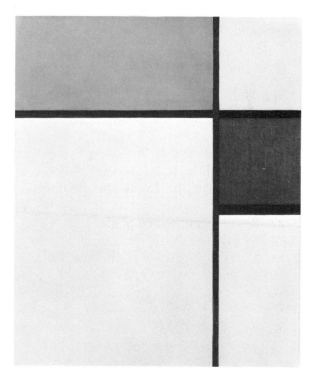

3-2 PIET MONDRIAN, *Composition with Blue and Yellow,* (1932). Oil on canvas, 16¼″ × 13″.
A. E. Gallatin Collection, Philadelphia Museum of Art.

DEGREES OF SUBJECT MATTER

Writers on art generally employ three terms to classify works according to degree of subject matter. These categories overlap somewhat, but the terms are worthwhile if they are used cautiously. *Representational* art has clearly recognizable objects (Fig. 17-8); *abstract* art has a basis in identifiable objects (Plate 33); and *nonobjective* art has no direct reference to such objects—that is, no subject matter (Fig. 3-2). These terms may be applied from either the artist's or the observer's standpoint, with possible disagreement. The artist may work so abstractly that the observer finds no apparent subject matter and assumes the painting to be nonobjective; conversely, the artist may work nonobjectively, but the observer may see recognizable objects in the work and consider it to be abstract. It is important to recall that recognizing objects in representational or abstract art is not necessarily grasping its content. *Content* in both representational and abstract art is an interaction of subject matter with the interpretive qualities of

3-3 SALVADOR DALI,   *The Persistence of Memory,* (1931). Oil on canvas, 9½″ × 13″.
Collection, the Museum of Modern Art, New York. Given anonymously.

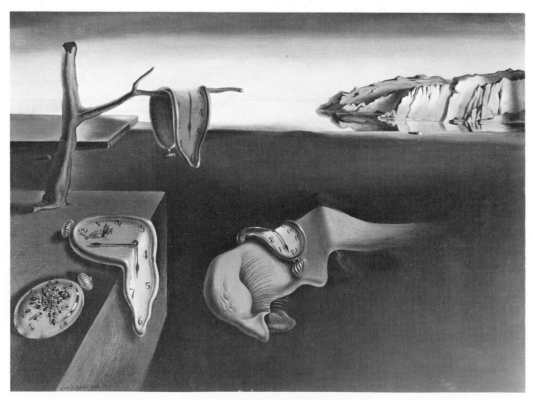

the visual and tactile elements. In fact, subject matter may acquire meaning on different levels if it is present in any degree. For nonobjective art, content is the total effect of the piece.

Suggestions for Further Study

Hall, James. *Dictionary of Subjects and Symbols in Art,* rev. ed. New York: Harper & Row, 1979.

Ogden, C. K., and I. A. Richards. *The Meaning of Meaning.* New York: Harcourt Brace Jovanovich, 1959.

Panofsky, Erwin. *Gothic Architecture and Scholasticism.* New York: Meridian Books, 1957.

————. *Meaning in the Visual Arts: Papers in and on Art History.* New York: Overlook Press, 1974.

————. *Studies in Iconology: Humanistic Themes in the Art of the Renaissance.* New York: Oxford University Press, 1939.

————, and Dora Panofsky. *Pandora's Box: The Changing Aspects of a Mythical Symbol,* rev. ed. New York: Pantheon Books, 1962.

Smeets, René. *Signs, Symbols and Ornaments.* New York: Van Nostrand Reinhold, 1982.

4

Techniques

The content of a work of art depends in varying degrees on its visual and tactile elements, which in turn depend on the materials and techniques used. A particular material, along with the technique appropriate to it, is often called the *medium* (plural, *media*) *of expression*. We can better understand a composition if we know something of the problems and possibilities inherent in the medium. Today artists frequently combine many media in one work; the result is often referred to as *mixed media*.

DRAWING

Though generally identified with line, drawing is a term used so broadly that it often overlaps the realm of painting. A drawing may be a *study,* an investigation of a certain detail of what may become a more extensive work; it may be a *sketch,* the quick notation of the general organization and effect of a composition; or it may be a *cartoon*, a full-size composition meant to be transferred to another surface for a finished work.

In *pencil drawing*, a wide range of values is possible with *leads* (graphite) of differing hardness. Hard lead on a smooth surface is good for a precise light line, such as that in Picasso's drawing of Dr. Claribel Cone (Fig. 1-1); soft lead applied to a rough surface gives a dark line with grainy texture. If the lead is sharpened to a wedge shape, it can be twisted to create a line with considerable modulation.

In *ink drawing*, great variety is possible through the use of colored inks, colored papers, inks of differing degrees of opacity, and different pen points. Formerly pens were made by splitting quills or reeds; nowadays pen points of many shapes and sizes are available in steel. Modulation in line depends on the point's width and on its flexibility, which governs the spreading of the split point. Today pens with felt-tip points add to the range of possibilities.

Charcoal varies in hardness; it can be used directly for crisp lines, or it can be rubbed to produce soft grays. Large areas can be covered quickly in a variety of values characteristic of painting. Charcoal does not adhere well. Soft paper with considerable *tooth* (texture) takes it best, and smearing is minimized if the drawing is sprayed with a *fixative* (thin varnish).

Chalk and *pastel* are made of powdered pigments (coloring matter) mixed with glue and formed into sticks. *Crayon* is made of pigment mixed with wax; it adheres well but does not lend itself to rubbing for soft gradations. Pastels and chalks are more powdery because of their weak glue binder. They have the advantages and disadvantages of charcoal and require a fixative.

Brush drawing — application of ink or watercolor with a brush — is often used in combination with pen-and-ink or pencil. In *dry brush drawing*, ink or watercolor is used dryly, permitting great detail and easy correction. In *wash drawing*, watercolor or ink diluted with water is used for flowing transparent washes, and correction is more difficult. In brush drawing of both types, usually only one or two colors are used. The color limitation differentiates brush drawing from watercolor painting.

PRINTMAKING

A *print* is a work of art produced by a duplicating process. It is considered an original rather than a reproduction because the artist works toward the print as the end product. For this reason the print has been called a multiple original. Many artists perform the whole process themselves; some prepare the printing surface and have special printers make the prints; still others create the composition only and have specialists transfer it to a printing surface and make the prints. In any case, the artist must understand the printing process to be used if he is to exploit its possibilities effectively. The total number of prints is called an *edition*. After the edition is printed, the printing surface is usually destroyed or *canceled* (crossed out with lines). The edition is thus limited, and the prints are more valuable to collectors. Today the artist frequently signs each print in pencil on the margin and uses a fraction to indicate the place of that particular print in the total edition; the notation 6/45 would mean the sixth print in an edition of forty-five. Trial prints made during the preparation of the printing surfaces are called *trial proofs. Artist's proofs* are prints outside the numbered edition intended for retention by the artist. Different stages of the composition (often indicated by trial proofs but sometimes carried out even during the printing of the edition) are called *states*. A composition may have one or many states. An artist might make a number of prints of a landscape and then decide to add a cloud in the sky. Prints without the cloud would be first-state; prints with the cloud would be second-state.

The many processes used in printmaking may be grouped in four broad categories, although the contemporary tendency to mix techniques within each of these general groups sometimes makes it difficult for the observer to know how a print was produced. Photographic images may be transferred to the printing surface and treated to produce prints as part of any of the following processes.

Relief Processes

In a *relief process*, the artist cuts away parts of the printing surface. The surface left raised *(in relief)*

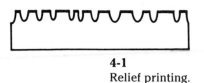

4-1
Relief printing.

is inked and the ink is then transferred to paper (Fig. 4-1).

For *woodcuts,* a piece of wood is cut or gouged to leave the design in relief. Prints may be made with a press or by placing paper over the inked block, and rubbing it with a spoon or other smooth instrument. Color woodcut prints traditionally are made with a separate block for each color. Careful *registration* is necessary to ensure that each color is printed exactly in the proper area. Transparent colors may be overlapped to produce additional colors, and colored paper may be used. Woodcut lends itself to bold lines and large areas of light and dark. Sometimes the grain of the wood or the texture of the paper will be evident in the print.

In *wood engraving,* a hard end-grain (grain at right angles to the surface) block is used, allowing easy cutting in any direction. *Burins* (cutting tools) of various shapes and sizes are employed, and great detail is possible.

For *linoleum cuts,* linoleum mounted on a wood block is cut in the same manner as a woodcut. The surface is soft, and there is no wood grain to exploit. Like a woodcut, the linoleum cut does not encourage great detail.

In a *metal cut,* metal is cut away with engraving tools, or the surface is lowered with punches; or the design may be drawn with acid-resistant material and the rest of the plate eaten *(etched)* with acid, leaving the design in relief.

Intaglio Processes

In *intaglio processes,* the low, rather than relief, parts of the printing surface carry the ink (Fig. 4-2). The lines of the design are cut or eaten into a metal plate (usually copper). Ink is forced into these lines, and the surface of the plate is wiped clean. A high-pressure press forces dampened paper against the surface and into the depressed lines. Often the dried ink can be felt standing in relief on the surface of the finished print. Unless the plate is larger than the print paper, the pressure of the press mashes the paper down around the edges of the plate and makes an indented *plate mark,* which may later be cut away. Since the pressure of the press slowly breaks down the edges or ridges between the intaglio lines, the size of an edition is limited (unless the copper plate is electroplated

4-2
Intaglio printing.

with a firmer metal), and early prints in an edition are generally valued more highly than later ones. As in the relief processes, a separate plate is normally employed for each color.

The sunken lines that hold the ink in an intaglio plate may be produced in several ways. In the *drypoint* process, a sharp point is used to scratch lines into the soft copper plate. Tiny ruffles of displaced metal *(burr)* pile up along the sides of each scratch. The ink held by the burr creates slightly fuzzy lines that can be used very effectively by the artist (Fig. 1-2). The burr quickly wears off, however, and drypoint editions are small.

For *metal engraving,* burins are used to cut out the metal, rather than to push it aside as in drypoint (a drypoint plate with the burr worn off produces the same effect as an engraved plate). Great sharpness and precision are possible. Engraving is often used in combination with etching.

In the process of *etching,* a copper plate is coated with an acid-resistant material *(ground)* through which the lines of the design are easily drawn. The plate is then immersed in acid, which eats into the metal wherever lines have been scratched through the ground. Thus the artist does not fight the resistance of the metal, and lines are produced more easily than in drypoint or engraving. Some lines may be etched a longer time than others to obtain greater depth; these hold more ink and provide greater darkness of line in the print. Etched lines are generally softer and freer than engraved lines. In *soft ground etching,* the ground is so soft that lines drawn on a paper placed on the plate pick up the ground when the paper is pulled away from the plate. The plate is then etched. Fabrics and other materials may be pressed into the soft ground and lifted off. The ground is pulled away where the texture of the material pressed into it, and the texture of the material can then be etched into the plate. *Aquatint etching* produces soft sandy or speckled areas (Fig. 4-3). Resin powder is sifted onto a heated plate. The resin melts partially and sticks to the plate. Acid attacks the metal exposed between the resin particles and produces thousands of tiny pits that hold ink and create speckled areas on the print. The evenness and darkness of the aquatint will depend on the amount of resin sifted onto the plate, the size of the resin particles, and the length of time the plate is

4-3 FRANCISCO GOYA, *Love and Death,* from the *Caprichos* series, (1797–98). Etching with aquatint, approx. 8 ½″ × 6 ⅛″. Clarence Buckingham Collection. Collection of The Art Institute of Chicago.

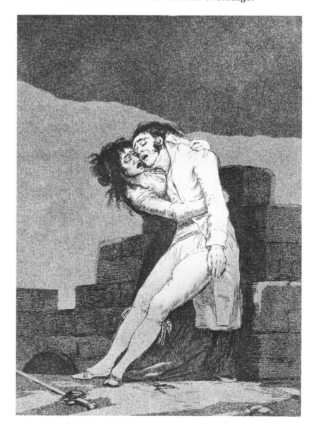

exposed to acid. Although resin is sifted over the whole plate, the aquatint effect is limited to chosen areas by *stopping out* other areas with acid-resistant varnish.

Planographic Processes

As the name implies, these methods print with a level rather than a raised or lowered surface.

The *monotype* process produces only a single print. Inks or paints are brushed, dripped, or rubbed on a smooth glass or metal plate. A paper is laid over the plate and rubbed. Wide varieties of superimposed colors and textures are possible with this procedure.

For *lithography,* the printing surface is traditionally fine-grained limestone, but in commercial lithography metal plates are used. The drawing is done with crayons, pencils, or inks that contain grease; the surface is then treated chemically to make it reject ink except where the greasy substance has established the drawing (Fig. 4-4). Printing is done with a special press.

Stencil Processes

One of the most important stencil processes is *screen printing,* often called *serigraphy.* Many methods are used. Basically, the idea is to fill or cover the pores of a fabric (stretched on a frame), leaving them open only in the shape of the design. Colored inks are then rolled or scraped across the fabric and penetrate to form a print of the design on paper or cloth underneath.

PAINTING

Oil paint, watercolor, crayon, and pastel can all be made from the same pigment. The differentiating factor is the *binder* (the substance that holds the color particles together and makes them adhere to a surface). The word "paint" is normally applied to media that are used in liquid or paste form. The immediate surface that receives the paint is called the *ground* (an entirely different meaning, obviously, from an etching ground). For watercolor,

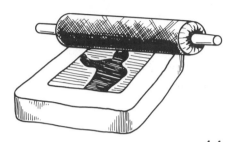

4-4
Lithographic stone being inked
for printing.

the ground is usually the surface of the paper. For many paints applied to wood or canvas, intervening substances such as *sizing* and *priming* must be applied to limit the absorption of the base material. Then the panel or canvas becomes the *support,* and the preparatory coating becomes the ground. Paint may be applied in a single layer *(alla prima)* or in many layers. Transparent layers are called *washes* in watercolor and *glazes* in oil paint. Opaque color can be rubbed or dragged loosely over previous colors to modify them without obscuring them, a process called *scumbling.* Paint applied very thickly is called *impasto.*

Tempera Painting

In *tempera* painting, the binder is an emulsion (a mixture of oil and water) that may include casein, glue, gum, egg, or egg and oil. The advantages of tempera are its short drying time, its potential for precise detail, its resistance to yellowing and darkening with age, its relative insolubility when dry, and—for some types of tempera the convenience of taking a water thinner. The disadvantages are the brittleness of some tempera formulas, the difficulty in blending it smoothly, some change in color and value as it dries, and the impossibility of creating impasto textures.

Watercolor Painting

The binder in watercolor is an aqueous solution of gum. For whites, transparent watercolor depends on the whiteness of the paper, and colors are lightened by thinning with water. The quality of the paper is very important because yellowing can spoil the colors as well as the whites. Advantages of watercolor are the cheapness and lightness of the materials, the quickness with which large areas can be covered with washes, the rapid drying time, and the lively sparkle of transparent washes over the white ground. Disadvantages of transparent watercolor are the difficulty of correction, the change in value during drying, and the necessity of working from light to dark. Opaque watercolor, or *gouache,* sacrifices transparency and quick washes for greater ease of correction and the possibility of using light colors over dark ones.

Oil Painting

The most common binder in oil paints is linseed oil. Most supports (wood, canvas, or synthetic materials) require a ground of oil or synthetic primer. For glazing purposes, complex thinning mixtures are used to increase transparency, to add flexibility, or to speed drying. The advantages of oil paint are its permanence and durability, its range of textural effects from light scumble to heavy impasto, the ease with which it can be manipulated and corrected, and the fact that colors do not change in drying.

Fresco Painting

True fresco, or *buon fresco,* is done with pigments combined with just a water "binder." The ground is wet lime plaster, usually on a wall. The paint becomes part of the ground and is very permanent. The mat, or dull, surface of fresco allows the painting to be seen easily from all angles without disturbing reflections. *Fresco-secco* is painting on a dry plaster surface, and a variety of media—tempera is common—may be used.

Encaustic Painting

The binder used in *encaustic* painting is refined beeswax with additives. Paints are mixed on a heated *palette* (mixing surface) and applied quickly to a rigid surface, usually a wood panel; in classical antiquity, encaustic was sometimes used on sculpture. A heat source (today, an electric coil) is then passed over the surface to "burn in" the wax. The inconvenience of heating is compensated for by the extraordinary range of effects from transparency to impasto, the quick drying time, and the permanence of the colors.

Other Media

Casein paints, with a casein glue binder, harden to a water-resistant but brittle surface, requiring a rigid support. They have the conveniences of taking a water thinner, drying rapidly, and producing a mat finish, which does not create the annoying light reflections of a shiny surface. Modern science has developed synthetic binders such as acrylic resin and polyvinyl acetate that are also fast-drying and have a mat finish. With some such paints, water can be used for thinning and the dried surface is water-resistant. Heavy impasto is not possible with many of these paints unless they are combined with pastes or paints that have been specifically developed for impasto effects.

STAINED GLASS

Designs or pictures in colored translucent glass became especially important in the Medieval period. The basic color of each piece of glass came from chemicals, mainly metallic oxides, added in a molten state. The glass was blown to produce sheets from which pieces were cut for the design. Details were painted on the surface with a mixture of powdered glass and lead or iron oxides and fused by firing (see Fig. 13-26).

SCULPTURE

Sculpture may be freestanding or in relief (projecting from a background). Relief sculpture may be *high relief*, such as Ghiberti's *Sacrifice of Isaac* (Fig. 14-19), with high projections from its background, or *low relief*, with forms projecting only slightly.

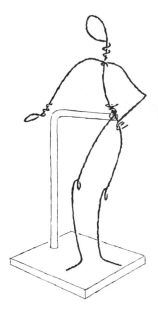

4-5
An armature.

Modeling and Casting

Modeling is an additive process of building up a sculpture from plastic material such as clay or wax. A wire, pipe, or wood *armature* (frame) can be used inside the work to prevent sagging (Fig. 4-5). No tools are necessary for modeling, although wooden spatulas with wire loops at one end are convenient for shaping and cutting. For permanence, natural clay can be *fired* (baked) in a *kiln* (oven), but it then cannot contain an armature, since shrinkage of the clay during firing would cause cracking, nor can it be of vastly different thicknesses. *Ceramic glazes* (a fine clay or glass coating) may be fired on the clay work, making possible a variety of textures and transparent or opaque colors. All fired clay may be called *terra cotta*, but the term refers more precisely to a brown-red unglazed clay.

Another way that clay sculpture may be given permanence is to cast it in plaster. A plaster mold is made while the clay is still wet. The mold is removed and oiled, soaped, or treated in some other way so that new plaster will not stick to it. After the mold has been reassembled and sealed, it is filled with plaster. Small sculptures may be cast solid; larger ones should be hollow. After the plaster has set, the mold is pulled or chipped away. This type of mold is called a *waste mold* because it is usually destroyed to free the cast within; for more than one cast a rubber or gelatin mold may be used. Plaster may be colored to make it resemble metal or stone.

Both cast plaster and fired clay are breakable; for the greatest permanence in sculpture, the traditional materials are stone and bronze. In the *sand mold* process of bronze casting, *French sand* (a mixture of clay, silica, and alumina) is pressed around a plaster cast of the work to form a mold. The parts of the sand mold are fitted into a *flask* (iron holder), and a core of French sand is made to fill the sand mold except for a one-eighth to one-quarter inch air space all the way around. The core is suspended inside the sand mold and flask by metal rods. Holes are made in the mold so that air can escape as molten bronze is poured into the air space between the core and mold. After the bronze has cooled, the mold is removed and the core is dug out. The hollow bronze cast needs much cleaning up before special workers (*pati-*

neurs) can give the cast its *patina* (color) by acid baths and heat treatment. In the *lost max (cire perdue)* method of bronze casting, the following procedure is one of several that may be used. A gelatin mold and a plaster shell to support it are made from the sculptor's plaster cast of the original clay work. On the inside of the gelatin mold, layers of wax are built up to the desired thickness of the bronze. The gelatin is removed, and the hollow wax replica is filled with a core of heat-resistant material. This material is also used to form a mold around the outside of the wax. Metal rods hold the core inside the mold, and vents are made in the mold to allow the melted wax to drain away when the assembly is heated. The air space left between the core and the mold by the removal of the wax is filled with bronze. The mold and core are taken away, and the finishing process begins.

Today the sculptor may do *direct sand casting* by working negatively, that is, creating the mold directly in a special sand mixture. Iron and aluminum are frequently used for the cast.

Another material common today is *cast stone.* A heavy reinforced plaster or gelatin mold is made from the original clay work, and a mixture of stone dust, pigment, sand, and cement is poured or packed into the mold. Sometimes an armature is included to reinforce the cement. After several days of drying, the mold is pulled or chipped away, and the cast can be finished by filing or carving.

Carving

The carver must have foresight, since the subtractive process does not allow for correction if too much is cut away. The most common materials, stone and wood, have different kinds of textures and grains that have aesthetic potential for the sculptor. The stone carver uses hammers, picks, drills, and toothed chisels to rough out the form. Chisels and abrasives are used for finishing. The wood-carver works with chisels, gouges, files, and sandpaper. Frequently the sculptor does the final work from a smaller preliminary model. A *pointing machine* may be used to transfer the proportions of the model to a larger block.

Construction

Constructed sculpture, of which Gabo's *Linear Construction* (Fig. 18-46) and Roszak's *Whaler of Nantucket* (Fig. 4-6) are examples, has become increasingly important during the twentieth century. The sculptor uses any materials or ready-made objects to build a composition, often soldering or welding them. The strength of metals and plastics has made possible very open forms. Different colors are obtained by the use of different metals, by painting, or by controlled oxidation. *Kinetic sculpture*, or mobile sculpture, utilizes air currents or motors to bring actual movement into the composition.

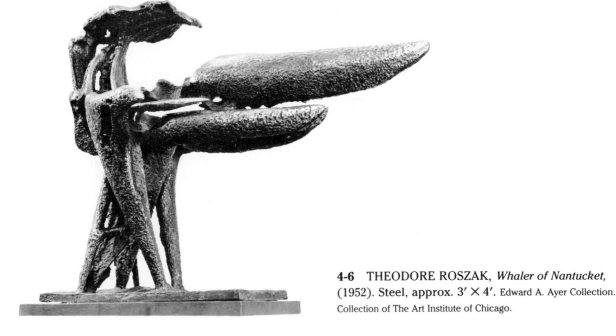

4-6 THEODORE ROSZAK, *Whaler of Nantucket,* (1952). Steel, approx. 3′ × 4′. Edward A. Ayer Collection. Collection of The Art Institute of Chicago.

Art Fabric

This medium includes both constructed fabrics and designs applied to their surfaces. From the early 1950s, fiber artists have employed traditional fabric construction techniques, such as weaving, looping, twining, knotting, plaiting, and felting (compressing), to create forms that are often very untraditional and innovative (Fig. 19-49). Natural fibers are combined with synthetics, with non-fibrous materials, such as metal foil or tree branches, and with ready-made objects ("found objects"). Scale may range from fine filament to massive rope, and forms may be two- or three-dimensional and of architectural scale. Artists working with surface-designed fabric may use traditional methods such as screen printing, block printing, batik (a stencil method using wax), and tie-dying (tying portions of a fabric so that these parts do not absorb dye) or new methods derived from the technologies of photography, computers, or copy machines. Frequently, pieces employ multimedia.

Ceramics

One of the oldest media is *fired* (baked) clay, in the form of pottery, sculpture, or tile. Clay, a plastic kind of earth, occurs in various types, called clay *bodies,* that differ in color, degree of plasticity, and mineral content. Different clay bodies are combined to obtain a desired degree of plasticity for *throwing* a vessel on a potter's wheel (forming a cylindrical vessel from a mass of clay centered on a turntable) and to obtain a certain hardness, color, and texture when fired in a *kiln* (a high-temperature oven). Sand or *grog* (prefired and ground-up clay) may be added to the clay body as *temper* to decrease shrinkage, cracking, or warping. In addition to throwing forms on a wheel, a ceramist may hand-build clay objects with coils or slabs of clay. Clay may also be shaped by presses, molds, or templates, especially in quantity production. To waterproof and decorate clay pieces, ceramic glazes (to be distinguished from the pigment glazes in painting) may be applied. A ceramic glaze is a thin, glasslike coating fused to the clay body by the heat of the kiln. The basic ingredient of glazes is silica, but additives provide colors and change the melting point and hardness of a glaze. Clay bodies and glazes may be low-fired (below 2000 degrees Fahrenheit), and thus somewhat soft and fragile, or high-fired, as in the case of *stoneware* or *porcelain.* The chemistry may become complicated. If the clay body expands or contracts at a significantly different rate than do the glazes, the body and the glaze will crack apart. Glazes may be applied by dipping, spraying, or painting to produce overall color, designs, or scenes on the surface of a clay object. This surface may also be given three-dimensionality by scratching or cutting lines or shapes into the soft clay or by adding clay in relief. The piece is refired, often many times, to fuse the glazes. Some contemporary ceramists use epoxy paint in addition to traditional glazes.

ARCHITECTURE

The basic diagrams of architectural design are *perspective views, plans,* and *elevations.* A perspective view shows how the building will appear in three dimensions. A plan shows the two-dimensional distribution of interior spaces, walls, windows, and doors. An elevation shows the side of a room or a building without perspective distortion. Other kinds of diagrams, such as *cross sections, longitudinal sections,* and *orthographic projections,* are also used to clarify spatial and structural relationships in architecture.

Traditional architectural materials are wood, mud brick, plaster, concrete, stucco, and masonry of stone or fired brick. More recent materials include iron, steel, aluminum, glass, reinforced concrete (ferroconcrete), plywood, and plastics. The strength of reinforced concrete has made it possible for floors, roofs, or ramps to twist, turn, and thrust out into space with very few points of support. Prestressed concrete is particularly strong; here the concrete is allowed to harden around stretched steel cables, or cables are run through the concrete in tubes and anchored under tension at each end. The result is a built-in compression that offsets the weakness of concrete under tension, permitting greater freedom of design.

Post and Lintel

The simplest type of structure is post and lintel, a combination of uprights *(posts)* supporting a crosspiece *(lintel)*. Columns, such as those of the Parthenon (Fig. 9-10), often serve as posts. The span between posts is severely limited by the strength of the material in the lintel. In the twentieth century, steel, reinforced concrete, and prestressed concrete have made possible very wide spans (Fig. 4-7). A lintel that extends beyond its supports (Fig. 4-7b) is called a *cantilever*. Lintels are frequently made in the form of *trusses,* very strong but light frameworks made of small pieces fastened together in such a way that they brace each other (Fig. 4-8). Special strength is provided by the perfect rigidity of a triangle.

Arch

An arch diverts the load — the weight sustained — to the sides as well as down toward the vertical, making possible wider spans than does a post and lintel system in the same material; the arrows in Figure 4-9 show the forces exerted by weight and the tendencies of the arch to fall in and the walls to buckle out. Until the nineteenth century and the development of steel and ferroconcrete, the most common arch was the masonry arch, a structure of wedge-shaped blocks spanning an opening. True arches have several forms. One, the flat masonry arch (Fig. 4-10a), resembles the post and lintel. The steep sides of a pointed arch divert the load more directly toward the ground (Fig. 4-10b) and require less outside *buttressing* (bracing) than the round arch (Fig. 4-10c). A *corbeled arch* (Fig. 4-10d) is not a true masonry arch; it sacrifices strength to avoid the more precise cutting required in the wedge-shaped blocks of the true arch (Fig. 4-10a, b, c). A masonry arch is supported during the course of its construction by a wooden scaffolding called *centering*.

Vault and Dome

Vaulting is arched roofing of stone, brick, or concrete. The *tunnel, barrel,* or *wagon vault* is an extension of a round arch (Fig. 4-11). It requires continuous buttressing along the sides. In Medieval masonry, the common solution to the buttressing problem was thick walls. Windows were infrequent and kept below the level of the *springing* (the beginning of the curve of the arch) to avoid weakening the vault (Fig. 4-12). The interior view of St. Sernin (Fig. 4-13) shows how Medieval

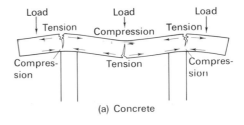

(a) Concrete

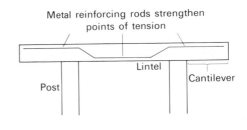

(b) Reinforced concrete

4-7
Post and lintel construction.

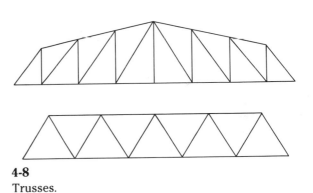

4-8
Trusses.

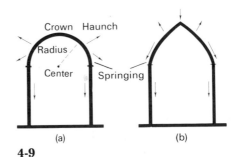

4-9
The dynamics of arches.

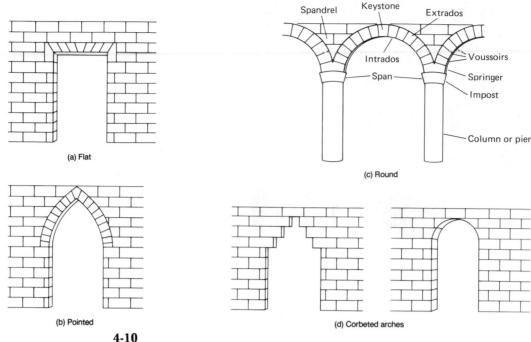

(a) Flat

(c) Round

Spandrel   Keystone   Extrados

Intrados   Voussoirs

Span   Springer

Impost

Column or pier

(b) Pointed

(d) Corbeted arches

4-10
Types of masonry arches.

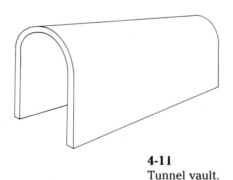

4-11
Tunnel vault.

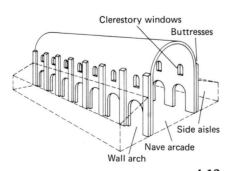

Clerestory windows
Buttresses

Side aisles

Nave arcade

Wall arch

4-12
Tunnel vault on a Romanesque
church.

vaults were often divided into *bays* (sections) by *transverse arches* (arches at right angles to the length of the vault that have the appearance and sometimes the function of reinforcements). The bay division was often continued all the way down to the floor by *engaged columns* (columns partially buried in the wall). In Medieval architecture, vaulting is so important that it is often indicated on floor plans. The plan of St. Sernin (Fig. 13-10) shows the transverse arches in dotted lines.

Greater strength and flexibility are obtained if two vaults are crossed at right angles (Fig. 4-14). The *cross vault*, or *groin vault*, focuses the load on four legs and allows the sides to be opened up. The exterior indentations where the vaults meet are the *groins*. On the interior the groins project as ridges. From directly above or below, the groins form an X-shape between the transverse arches and are so indicated on the plans (Fig. 4-15). When the groins are emphasized by moldings or *ribs* on the interior, the vault is called a *ribbed cross vault*, a series of which can be seen over the nave of Amiens Cathedral (Fig. 13-30). It is thought that in Medieval architecture the ribs were often built first, as a skeleton to shape the vault, and panels of stone were then filled in between ribs and side arches. Since the X formed by the ribs

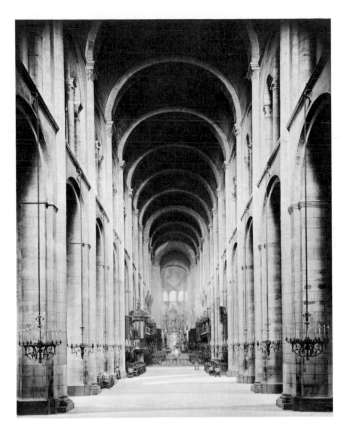

4-13
Interior of St. Sernin, Toulouse, France.

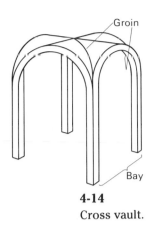

4-14
Cross vault.

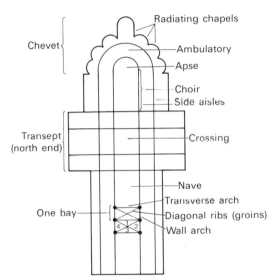

4-15 Robert De Luzarches, plan of
Amiens Cathedral.

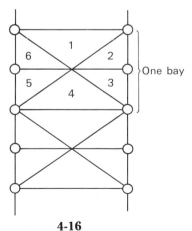

4-16
Plan of sexpartite vault.

divides the vault into four parts, it is called a four-part, or *quadripartite*, vault. Sometimes an additional transverse arch was added in the center of the X, creating a six-part, or *sexpartite*, ribbed cross vault (Fig. 4-16). Figure 4-14 shows the intersecting tunnel vaults, wherein the height of the arches and the ribs is kept level. Semicircular ribs, however, would create a domical form (Fig. 4-17a), since the ribs have a much longer diameter than that of the wall arches. The level *crowns* (tops) of the vaults in Figures 4-14 and 4-17b are made possible by depressing the ribs to less than semicircles, but depressed arches are weaker than semicircular ones. A level effect can be achieved without sacrificing strength if the principle of the pointed arch is applied to the vaulting. The pointed ribs and arches are easily adjusted to different heights by varying the degree of pointedness (Fig. 4-17c), as was done at Amiens Cathedral (Fig. 13-30). The pointed-ribbed cross vault, like the pointed arch, can be built higher with less buttressing. As the height of Medieval vaults became

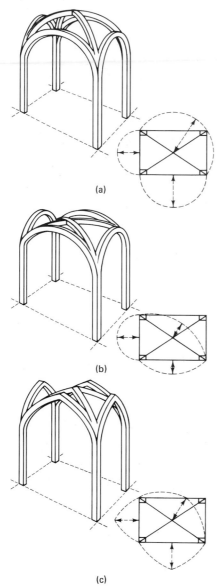

4-17
Ribbed cross vaults.

greater, *flying buttresses* (arched segments carrying the thrust from vaults to vertical buttresses) were developed to help bear the load by transferring the thrust to buttresses along the outer walls (Fig. 4-18).

Domes may be hemispherical, less than hemispherical (like the depressed arch), or pointed. The problem of buttressing varies accordingly. To hold in the outward buckling tendency, large domes may be made of massive thickness or have circling bands of chain or wood buried in the masonry or concrete (modern domes may be made of ferroconcrete). Unlike the arch, the dome is not weakened by an opening in the crown, because the inward leaning only wedges the circular form more tightly together, and the load forces pushing inward are converted to an outward buckling tendency (Fig. 4-19a). Openings in the sides of a dome, however, tend to destroy the circular system of self-support and require special buttressing. The use of a dome over a square room requires a transition to the round base of the dome. Two solutions have been widely used: the *pendentive* and the *squinch.* The pendentive cuts off or fills in the corners of the square with curved triangular fillets (Fig. 4-19b). The squinch provides a more abrupt transition by arching over the corners to form an octagonal base, which is easily accommodated to the circular dome (Fig. 4-19c).

Two of the more striking forms developed in recent years are the *geodesic dome* and the *hyperbolic paraboloid.* The geodesic dome utilizes the geometry of the tetrahedron to create a light struc-

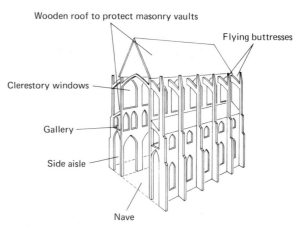

4-18
Section of a Gothic cathedral.

ture of enormous strength (Fig. 4-20). Buoyant spacious effects are possible with the hyperbolic paraboloid, where straight members can be used to construct a curved surface of great integrity (Fig. 4-21).

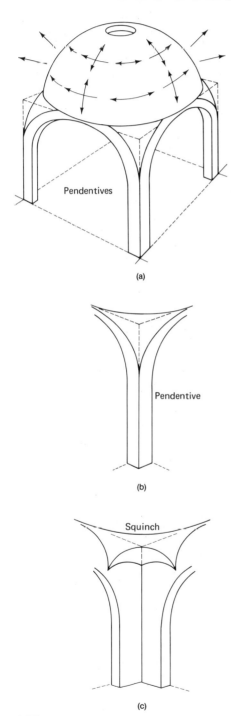

Pendentives

(a)

Pendentive

(b)

Squinch

(c)

4-19
The dome and its supports.

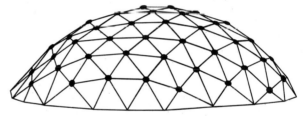

4-20
Geodesic dome.

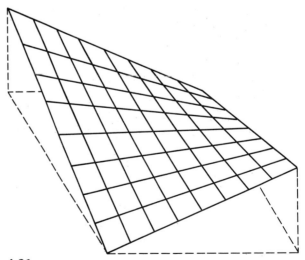

4-21
Hyperbolic paraboloid.

Suggestions for Further Study

DRAWING

Chaet, Bernard. *The Art of Drawing*. New York: Holt, Rinehart & Winston, 1978.

Hayes, Colin. *The Complete Guide to Drawing and Painting Techniques and Materials*. New York: Mayflower Books, 1978.

Mendelowitz, David M. *Drawing*. New York: Holt, Rinehart & Winston, 1966.

Moskowitz, Ira, ed. *Great Drawings of All Time*. 4 vols. New York: Shorewood, 1962.

Nicolaïdes, Kimon. *The Natural Way to Draw*. Boston: Houghton Mifflin, 1941.

PRINTMAKING

Hayter, S. W. *About Prints*. London: Oxford University Press, 1962.

Ivins, William M., Jr. *How Prints Look: Photographs with a Commentary*. Boston: Beacon Press, 1958.

Knigin, Michael, and Murray Zimiles. *Techniques of Fine Art Lithography*, rev. ed. New York: Van Nostrand Reinhold, 1977.

Peterdi, Gabor. *Printmaking*, rev. and expanded ed. New York: Macmillan, 1980.

Ross, John, and Clare Romano. *The Complete Printmaker*. New York: Free Press, 1972.

PAINTING

Mayer, Ralph. *The Artist's Handbook of Materials and Techniques*, 4th ed. rev. and enl. New York: Viking, 1981.

Timmons, Virginia Gayheart. *Painting: Ideas, Materials, Processes*. Dallas: Hendrick Long, 1978.

Wehlte, Kurt. *The Materials and Techniques of Painting*. New York: Van Nostrand Reinhold, 1979.

SCULPTURE

Clarke, Geoffrey, and Stroud Cornock. *A Sculptor's Manual*. London: Studio Vista; New York: Reinhold, 1968.

Gross, Chaim. *The Techniques of Wood Sculpture*. New York: Arco, 1965.

Hale, Nathan Cabot. *Welded Sculpture*. New York: Watson-Guptill, 1968.

Verhelst, Wilbert. *Sculpture: Tools, Materials, and Techniques*. Englewood Cliffs, N.J.: Prentice-Hall, 1973.

ART FABRIC

Constantine, Mildred, and Jack L. Larsen. *The Art Fabric: Mainstream*. New York: Van Nostrand Reinhold, 1973.

CERAMICS

Counts, Charles. *Pottery Workshop: A Study in the Making of Pottery from Idea to Finished Form*. New York: Macmillan, 1973.

Hamer, Frank. *The Potter's Dictionary of Materials and Techniques*. London: Pitman; New York: Watson-Guptill, 1975.

Hamilton, David. *Manual of Pottery and Ceramics*. New York: Van Nostrand Reinhold, 1974.

Nelson, Glenn C. *Ceramics: A Potter's Handbook,* 4th ed. New York: Holt, Rinehart & Winston, 1978.

ARCHITECTURE
Arnheim, Rudolf. *The Dynamics of Architectural Form*. Berkeley: University of California Press, 1977.

Collins, Peter. *Concrete: The Vision of a New Architecture*. London: Faber & Faber, 1959.

Giedion, Sigfried. *Space, Time, and Architecture,* 4th ed. Cambridge, Mass.: Harvard University Press, 1962.

Gropius, Walter. *Scope of Total Architecture* (World Perspectives, Vol. 3). Edited by Ruth N. Anshen. New York: Harper & Row, 1955.

5

Problems of Value Judgment and Approaches to the Study of Art History

PROBLEMS OF OBJECTIVITY AND SUBJECTIVITY

Value judgment in art involves factors of varying degrees of subjectivity. The most obvious objective factors seem to miss the point. Physical permanence — that is, the artist's skill in producing a work that does not deteriorate — can be measured easily but is of little value unless the art object is worth preserving. Some objectivity is possible in measuring the artist's skill in depicting recognizable objects when to do so seems relevant to the work, but such mechanical aptitude alone does not guarantee significant content. We may judge with some objectivity the extent to which an artist has exploited the expressive possibilities of a medium; yet the artist may deliberately limit the range of colors in a painting, the modulation of line in a drawing, or the variety of texture and color in architecture. Furthermore, limitations may have been imposed by time and place. The artist of ancient Egypt did not have the technical knowledge available to the artist of the nineteenth century, but we do not assume that, for this reason, any work produced by a competent nineteenth-century artist is superior to the best work of the older culture. The quality of artistic achievement has not progressed in an ascending spiral, as Western technology has. Clearly, quality means more than technical virtuosity. Art goes beyond the skillful description of facts and feelings to the more subtle and subjective realms of expression and evocation, where artists require not just an imitative facility but a special sensitivity to the visual and tactile elements. They may also need sensitivity to human experience, a capacity for empathy, an agile imagination, and an understanding of the symbols or iconography that will be meaningful to fellow humans. Such things would be hard enough to measure even if they were not colored by the interpretation of individual observers whose capacities to respond may vary widely.

Criteria of formal analysis produce varied judgments because the individual's sensitivity to the visual and tactile elements depends partly on the natural sensitivity of his sensory perceptions and partly on his training. Variations among individuals may therefore lead to disagreement about the total effect of a work of art. The breadth of the observer's experience is important. A person accustomed only to the flowing harmonies of paintings like Raphael's *Madonna of the Meadow* (Plate 6 and Fig. 3-1) might find the relative dissonance and liveliness of Picasso's *Three Musicians* (Plate 33) lacking in unity. The same might be said of the color harmonies in a comparison of Rembrandt and Matisse (Plates 14 and 31). The observer's response also depends upon sensitivity and understanding of human experience. A child might respond with great sensitivity to Rubens's *Coup de Lance* (Fig. 1-23), but more mature experience added to the same sensitivity would deepen the content. Response may be very limited if the observer has no understanding of relevant iconography.

Because of the tremendous stylistic variety encountered in even one medium, such as oil painting, and because of the many subjective factors we have described, the major problem in art criticism is to find measurable standards. Most critical statements might be subsumed under the broad demands for *unity, variety,* and *intensity of experience,* qualities we value because they enable us to experience life more completely by developing the sensitivity and subtlety of our perception, imagination, and understanding. Yet it is obvious that no fixed proportion of these three qualities would make an ideal formula for more than one work of art; nor is it easy to agree upon a measurement for such things in a given work of art.

AESTHETIC THEORIES OF VALUE JUDGMENT

Aesthetics, the branch of philosophy that deals with the nature of beauty, has described many different attitudes toward value judgments. These attitudes may be classed broadly in three overlapping areas.

Objectivism

The most extreme objective attitude assumes unchanging standards by which absolute judgments can be made for the art of any time and place. An example is the "Neoclassic" art theory of the eighteenth and nineteenth centuries, which held that the painting, sculpture, and architecture of any culture should be measured against Greek or Roman art. Such an attitude tends to reject the art of many cultures and to deny variability in concepts of aesthetic value. A more flexible objective position argues that such qualities as unity, variety, and intensity — developed in varying degrees and proportions according to the nature of the art object — give the object aesthetic value not only for its own culture but also for others. The observers' capacity to judge will vary with their sensitivity and understanding, but value resides in the art object itself. Changes in the history of taste therefore do not prove changes in value but only in preference, and preference is not the same as evaluation; a person may prefer one work over another but concede that the second has a higher aesthetic value than the preferred work.

Subjectivism

Subjective theories consider the judgment of art to be purely personal; each individual uses different criteria or different interpretations of criteria, and all criteria are equally valid. The aesthetic value of an art object rests not in the object but in the response of the observer, who may grant or deny such value to any object.

Relativism

Relativist views hold that value arises from an interaction between spectator and art object. According to the relativist position, there are objective standards that can be valid for the members of a particular culture, but each culture forms its own standards. When an observer judges art from a culture other than his own, he should attempt to escape the prejudices of his own culture and judge the work on the basis of the criteria of the culture that produced it. Historical perspective or cultural differences may enable the outsider to comprehend the standards of a foreign culture more objectively than would its own members. Relativist views make value judgments between art objects from different cultures difficult or undesirable. One aspect of relativism is the attempt to understand the artist's intention and then judge to what extent that aim was achieved. One may use *internal* evidence (evidence within the art object or other works by the same artist) and *external* evidence (such as statements by the artist about his own work). However, it is conceivable that the work of art might have high aesthetic value even if the artist did not fulfill his intention; conversely, if the intention was fulfilled, we are left with the need for a decision about the aesthetic value of the intent. Which is better, a superficial success or a magnificent failure?

APPROACHES TO THE STUDY OF ART HISTORY

As with other disciplines, we may explore the history of art from different points of view. Some art historians emphasize iconography, the symbolism of images, and its historical sources. This can be exciting detective work involving the history of ideas from folk traditions to theology. Other scholars stress stylistic changes within a chosen area, such as portraiture or medieval vaulted ceilings, and evaluate how changes occur through mutual influences and original conceptions. A third approach has been the attempt to understand the psychological motivations and meanings, both conscious and unconscious, that are operative within the artist and the public. Today, many art historians emphasize the social context in their interpretations of art. This requires careful study of socioeconomic and cultural climates.

For a particular piece of art, one or all of these approaches may be appropriate. Still, each art historian may have an inherent tendency to favor one aspect over the others.

Suggestions for Further Study

Beardsley, Monroe C. *Aesthetics: Problems in the Philosophy of Criticism*, 2nd ed. Indianapolis, Ind.: Hackett, 1981.

———, and Herbert M. Schueller, eds. *Aesthetic Inquiry: Essays on Art Criticism and the Philosophy of Art*. Belmont, Calif.: Dickenson, 1967.

Bell, Clive. *Art*. New York: Putnam, 1958.

Berenson, Bernard. *Aesthetics and History*. Garden City, N.Y.: Doubleday, 1954.

Boas, George. *Wingless Pegasus: A Handbook for Critics*. Baltimore: The Johns Hopkins Press, 1950.

Fry, Roger. *Vision and Design*. New York: Meridian Books, 1956.

Gedo, Mary Mathews, ed. *Psychoanalytic Perspectives on Art.* Vol. 1. Hillsdale, N.J. and London: Lawrence Erlbaum, 1985

Gilson, Étienne. *Painting and Reality.* New York: Meridian Books, 1959.

Gombrich, Ernst. *Ideals and Idols: Essays on Values in History and in Art.* Oxford: Phaidon, 1979.

Hauser, Arnold. *The Philosophy of Art History.* Cleveland and New York: World Publishing, 1963.

Hertz, Richard. *Theories of Contemporary Art.* Englewood Cliffs, N.J.: Prentice-Hall, 1985.

Heyl, Bernard. *New Bearings in Esthetics and Art Criticism.* London: Oxford University Press; New Haven, Conn.: Yale University Press, 1943.

Kostelanetz, Richard. *Esthetics Contemporary.* Buffalo, N.Y.: Prometheus Books, 1978.

Kubler, George. *The Shape of Time.* New Haven and London: Yale University Press, 1962.

Kuhns, Richard. *A Psychoanalytic Theory of Art.* New York: Columbia University Press, 1983.

Langer, Suzanne. *Feeling and Form: A Theory of Art.* New York: Scribner's, 1953.

Maritain, Jacques. *Creative Intuition in Art and Poetry.* New York: New American Library, 1955.

Pontynen, Arthur. "A Winter Landscape: Reflections on the Theory and Practice of Art History," *Art Bulletin,* Vol. 68, No. 3 (September 1986), pp. 467–79.

Read, Herbert. *The Meaning of Art,* 6th rev. ed. Baltimore: Penguin Books, 1959.

Rosenberg, Jacob. *On Quality in Art: Criteria of Excellence, Past and Present* (Bollingen Series No. 35). Princeton, N.J.: Princeton University Press, 1967.

Tejera, Victorino. *Art and Human Intelligence.* New York: Irvington Publications, 1965.

Venturi, Lionello. *History of Art Criticism.* Translated by Charles Marriott. New York: Dutton, 1936.

Worringer, Wilhelm. *Abstraction and Empathy: A Contribution to the Psychology of Style.* Translated by Michael Bullock. London: Routledge & Kegan Paul, 1953.

PART TWO

THE HISTORY OF ART IN WESTERN CULTURE

The beginnings of art precede written records. The most prolific time for prehistoric art seems to have been the LATE PALEOLITHIC *or* LATE OLD STONE AGE, *which lasted from approximately 35,000 B.C. to 8,000 B.C. Particularly in the period between 15,000 B.C. and 10,000 B.C., humans painted and scratched animals, hunting scenes, and geometric designs on the walls of caves and rock shelters. The artist sometimes painted with charcoal and colored earths, using a binder of animal grease, or sometimes spread the grease on the wall and blew powdered colors against it from a hollow bone tube. Many cave paintings have been found in France and northern Spain; some of the most remarkable are in the caves of Altamira in Spain and Lascaux in France. In these works (see opposite page), modulated contours and modeling in light and dark create the illusion of mass in the bodies of bison, horses, and cows. The artists combined a keen understanding of anatomy with a sensitive expression of an animal's speed, ferocity, or gentleness. Paleolithic artists did not include landscape backgrounds, and each image or group of images is an isolated scene rather than one episode within the time sequence of a story; human figures were shown infrequently and often simplified, with single lines for torso and limbs. The frequent representation of animals pierced by arrows or spears, the casual overlapping of images, and the fact that these paintings were often located in almost inaccessible parts of caves all suggest that the making of these pictures was a magic ritual to ensure success in the hunt. A purely aesthetic impulse might be evidenced by the geometric designs, but these too could have been motivated or rationalized by the need for magic. Paleolithic artists not only painted but also modeled in soft earth and carved bone, tusk, and antler. Animals and the hunt were the preferred subjects in these mediums too, but investigators have found female statuettes that may have been intended to increase the fertility of the clan. Some of the characteristics of these paintings and carvings are found in the art of primitive cultures today.*

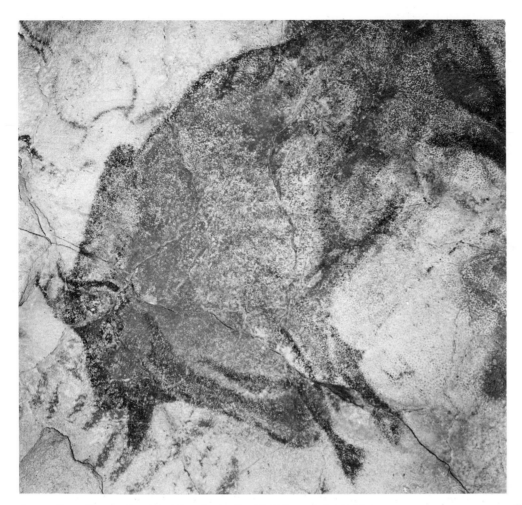

Bison, from the cave at Altamira, Spain, (*c.* 13,500 B.C.). 8 1/4″ long.

While discoveries of prehistoric art were once difficult to authenticate, it is now possible to be more certain. One method used for dating objects relies on STRATIGRAPHY; *an object is dated according to the age of the earth stratum in which it is found. A more precise method is that of* CARBON 14 *measurement. While it is living, each organic substance maintains a known amount of radioactive carbon 14. After the substance ceases to live, the carbon 14 begins to lose its radioactivity at a constant rate. Thus the amount of radioactivity remaining allows us to determine the approximate age of the organic substance.*

The concept of STYLE *is fundamental to an understanding of both prehistoric and later art, for the subtle differences in style reveal man's changing ideas of the beautiful or the significant. Style is a characteristic manner of expression and the kind of content that goes with it. It exists on several levels.* PERIOD STYLE *is the composite of very general characteristics that may be common to much work at a given time or during a given cultural phase. Sometimes, especially in the nineteenth and twentieth centuries, a number of contrasting stylistic tendencies exist simultaneously, making it difficult or misleading to speak of a period style.* REGIONAL STYLE *may be detected in the work of various artists working in the same country or area, if there has not been too much influence from other regions.* INDIVIDUAL STYLE *is seen in the work of a particular artist, and style may change several times in the course of a career.*

6

Ancient Near Eastern Art

4000–330 B.C.

Of all the ancient Near Eastern cultures, that of Egypt has been most thoroughly studied and is best known; yet recent discoveries suggest that the Tigris-Euphrates Valley in Mesopotamia was ahead of Egypt in developing an urban society and a form of writing. Political instability, frequent warfare, a lack of natural boundaries, and a constant mixing of different peoples all complicate our efforts to understand this area.

For a short survey, the developments might be grouped into three successive and overlapping cultures: (1) Sumerian-Akkadian-Babylonian, from about 4000 to 1600 B.C. and 612 to 539 B.C. (Neo-Babylonian); (2) Assyrian, from about 900 to 612 B.C.; and (3) ancient Persian, from about 1000 to 330 B.C. This simplified classification neglects many cultural groups about which we presently know very little, such as the Hittites in Asia Minor, the Mitanni in northern Mesopotamia, and the

Aramaeans and Phoenicians in northern Syria. Persian culture itself was so varied that, for the purposes of this introduction, we will consider only its culmination under the Achaemenian kings (550–330 B.C.), whose era ended with the Persian surrender to Alexander the Great.

The major Sumerian city-states, such as Uruk, Eridu, and Ur, were near the Tigris-Euphrates Delta on the Persian Gulf. Each city had its patron god (represented by the local king), in addition to a common pantheon of nature gods including Enlil, the storm god; Anu, the sky god; Ea, the water god; and Eanna, the Great Mother or Lady of Heaven, who was later known as Ishtar, goddess of love, fertility, and war. The temple was the religious and administrative center for each city-state, handling the distribution of labor and food. The Sumerians eventually came under the domination of a Semitic people from the north, the Akkadians, whose great leader, Sargon of Akkad (c. 2350–2300 B.C.), established a centralized government and the concept of a god-king as central ruler to whom local god-kings were subject. The Akkadians adopted much from Sumerian culture, including the Sumerian script in *cuneiform* (a form of writing employing different combinations of wedge shapes). Akkadian control was broken by the Gutti people, who were, in turn, overthrown by Sumerians. The Neo-Sumerian period (2150–2000 B.C.) was particularly productive during the Third Dynasty of Ur. Invasions by Elamites and Amorites led to the collapse of central government and the rise of another era of independent city-states, the Isin-Larsa period (2150–1763 B.C.). Central control was revived during this period by Hammurabi of Babylon (1790–1750 B.C.). Despite these violent disruptions, there is a discernible cultural continuity.

As the Assyrian Empire expanded from Assur, Nimrud, and Nineveh (c. 1350–612 B.C.) to absorb Mesopotamia, Egypt, Asia Minor, and Persia, the Assyrians also adopted much from Sumerian culture, including a number of gods. The Assyrian state-god, Assur, is a version of Enlil. The Assyrians, however (unlike the Sumerians), thought of their gods as remote from man. Assyrian art shows no confrontation of god and man as portrayed in the earlier cultures. The history of Assyria is one of incessant war, and its art expresses an obsession with physical power.

The Persian Empire grew out of the conquest by the Medes of Nineveh in 612 B.C. and Babylon in 539 B.C. In 550 B.C., Cyrus, a Persian, became king of the Medes and Persians, two related tribes on the Iranian Plateau. From Persian centers at Pasargadae, Susa, Persepolis, and Babylon, expansion swallowed up Syria, Asia Minor, and Egypt. The religion of the Persians evolved from the worship of fire to the worship of Ahura Mazda, god of light. The Persian king was the earthly representative of the god. Impetus came from the religious teacher, Zoroaster.

SUMERIAN (c. 4000–2350 B.C.) AKKADIAN (c. 2350–2150 B.C.) NEO-SUMERIAN (2150–2000 B.C.) ISIN-LARSA, BABYLONIAN (2025–1594 B.C.) NEO-BABYLONIAN (612–539 B.C.) PERIODS

Architecture

Temples and palaces received greatest emphasis. Stone and timber were scarce in the south; the major building material was sun-dried mud brick, the impermanence of which accounts for the scarcity of ruins.

The exterior appearance of the buildings was that of a cubic, closed form. Mass, rather than space, was the major expressive element. Mudbrick walls gained visual interest from the play of light and shadow over alternating niches and buttresses and from whitewash, relief sculpture, and color in the form of inset shells, colored stones, terra cotta cones, and glazed brick. Imported wooden roof beams were covered with reed mats and earth. Arches were used in doorways, and corbeled stone vaults have been found in the royal tombs at Ur. Large brick *piers* (vertical supports, usually square in section and more massive than single columns) and occasional wooden columns provided interior supports.

The major temple was usually placed on a mound of earth, providing either token elevation or considerable height. While such mounds were produced automatically by repeated reconstruction of ancient mud-brick cities (city mounds are called *tells*), it is probable that the temple mounds were deliberately constructed. Sumerian religious thought stressed the mountain as the home of the gods and a link between the earthly and the divine. During the Neo-Sumerian period, the temple mounds evolved into *ziggurats* (Fig. 6-1). In addition to the elevated temples, there were, from the Neo-Sumerian period on, low temples without terraces but with impressive tower-flanked entrances.

Temple plans usually consisted of a rectangular *cella* (sacred room; plural, *cellae*) with a niche for a cult statue at one end, an offering table, and an entrance at one side. There was a long-lasting tendency to use a *bent-axis* approach to important spaces: doors were set off and entries required one or more turns, forcing an indirect approach to the area. In time the bent axis was replaced by a *direct axial* plan, wherein the entrance led directly to the focal point of the interior space. The general evolution of temple building was toward thicker walls and more secluded cellae; anterooms and courtyards lengthened the approach to the place of worship. There was a tendency, especially after the beginning of the Akkadian period, to divide the cella into two parts: the antecella and the main cella. Often the entrance was at the center of a long side and the altar and niche were placed at the center of the opposite wall, producing an oblong cella with stress on the short axis.

Palaces consisted of combinations of a basic unit: rectangular rooms opening onto a courtyard. The dwelling areas and the rooms for official ceremonies were distinctly separated. The houses of the people ranged from reed huts to mud-brick structures having two floors of rooms facing an inner court.

Tombs were modest compared with those in Egypt. The most impressive ones found thus far are the royal tombs at Ur, where stairways of fired brick set in bitumen lead to underground vaulted rooms arranged somewhat like a private house.

ZIGGURAT AT UR (*c.* 2100 B.C.).   The king Ur-Nammu built this, the best preserved of the ziggurats (Fig. 6-1). It is a mud-brick mass with a facing of fired bricks in the form of niches and buttresses. The first level is 50 feet high, and was built with the corners oriented to the points of the compass. The closed form, with its simple masses, obvious axial balance, and gradation toward the summit of the temple, made a striking interruption in the stark plains where it was constructed. Interior space was limited to the gate, which functions as a kind of halfway house on the flights of stairs, and the temple at the top; exterior space was organized by the stairways, which led the worshiper from height to height. A physical pilgrimage and ascent was intended to produce a spiritual parallel. Conversely, the patron god could descend to earth by way of the man-made mountain.

Sculpture

Sculpture served both religious and commemorative purposes. Statues of the gods were apparently used in the niches of the temple cellae, and statues of priests and worshipers were placed in temples to perform as "stand-ins" for their donors, insuring continuous obeisance to the deity. Relief sculpture

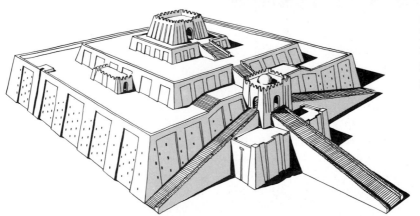

6-1
Reconstruction of the ziggurat at Ur.   Adapted from a drawing at the British Museum, London. Courtesy of the British Museum, London.

was carved or modeled on votive plaques, stone maces, cult vessels, *steles* (upright slabs or pillars), *cylinder seals* (small stone rollers carved to produce a continuous relief design when rolled on soft clay or wax), and walls. Materials include a variety of stone, ivory, shell, clay, gypsum, bronze, gold, silver, and electrum (an alloy of silver and gold), often used in combinations for contrasts of color and texture. Subjects depicted include deities, sacrifices, cult processions, religious epics, military victories, hunts, animals, and hybrid creatures. Generalizations about style must be cautious because of the limited material presently available from excavations.

Throughout Mesopotamian art, a concern for the physical appearance of men and animals runs in contrast to a love of fantasy and lavish abstract ornamentation. Neither relief sculpture nor the few surviving fragments of wall painting show any indications of a desire by the artist to suggest the illusion of deep space. The human body was usually represented by a general type with massive and simplified anatomy. Enlarged inlaid eyes and prominent noses are common, but individual features occur occasionally. In Sumerian figures, the body from the waist to the calf was hidden by a full skirt, often embellished with a surface pattern suggesting fringe and tufts of hair or wool. During the Akkadian period, the clothing fitted more closely and revealed the body, which appeared to be softer and more flexible. Rigidity returned in later periods. Repeated linear motifs in hair, beards, and garments express a love of decorative pattern.

STATUETTES, *from Tell Asmar* (ancient Eshnunna) (*c.* 2900–2600 B.C.). This group of marble figures (Fig. 6-2) was found under the floor of a temple. Identification is uncertain, but the subjects are probably priests and worshipers. The tallest figure may represent the king. The cups that he and the woman beside him hold in their hands may be offerings. The hypnotically intense eyes, closed forms, full skirts, angular elbows, and tensely clasped hands are common to figures from the Sumerian and Neo-Sumerian periods.

Painting

Painting is found on walls, pottery, and sculpture. A dynamic style employing expansive abstract animal motifs and geometric designs enlivens the surfaces of pottery. The fragments of wall painting available to us indicate that painting followed the style of relief sculpture and depicted the same kinds of subjects. Painting was done on mud plaster or gesso (a mixture of plaster and glue) surfaces. There are no examples of the illusion of depth or mass modeled in light and shadow. Instead, flat, outlined shapes form lively geometric designs and figurative scenes.

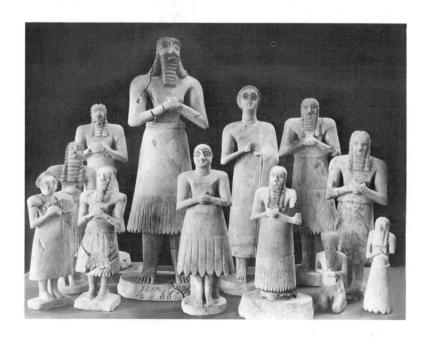

6-2
Statuettes from the Abu Temple, Tell Asmar, (*c.* 2900–2600 B.C.). Marble, tallest figures approx. 30″ high. Iraq Museum, Baghdad, and Oriental Institute, University of Chicago.

ASSYRIAN ART: 900–612 B.C.

Architecture

Assyrian architecture owed much to the Sumerians, Hurrians, and the Hittites. Stone was more plentiful in the north, and the basic mud brick was supplemented by stone blocks in lower walls and around gates. Glazed brick provided color. Wall paintings and reliefs decorated interiors. The power of the empire made possible a new grandeur of scale and elegance expressing the divinity of the monarch and his relation to the other gods. Emphasis continued to be placed on temples and palaces. The ziggurat was sometimes freestanding, sometimes paired, and sometimes built into a temple and palace complex. Temple and palace entrances were centrally placed and flanked by a pair of towers. Typically, temples used oblong antecellae and cellae, and palaces employed combinations of the traditional units of rooms grouped around courtyards. A new motif in planning was a rectangular room with a pillared entrance, actually an enlarged entry to a passageway leading to an interior court. Sargon's records refer to this as a *bît hilani,* a borrowing from Hittite architecture. Its origins seem to be in Syrian architecture of the second millennium B.C., and it bears a striking resemblance to the Greek *megaron* (Fig. 8-2 and p. 81).

CITADEL OF SARGON II *at Khorsabad* (ancient Dur Sharrukin) (*c.* 720 B.C.).   The palace-temple complex (Fig. 6-3) covered 25 acres and was built into the city walls. Tower-flanked gates with relief carvings of human-headed bulls wearing the horned crown indicating divinity opened into the courtyard of the lower level, from which a ramp led to the upper palace. A number of temples were built into the complex, as was a ziggurat with a spiral ramp leading to a summit that was originally about 140 feet high. The 209 rooms and courts of the palace provided a political, military, and religious center for the empire. Like earlier Mesopotamian palaces, the plan is an aggregation of rooms around courtyards. Roofs may have been barrel vaults. Interiors were ornamented with paintings and reliefs glorifying the king as hunter, warrior, and conqueror of evil.

Sculpture

The Assyrians produced a great deal of relief sculpture but apparently had little interest in freestanding statues. Palace walls were covered with reliefs depicting the king participating in sacred rituals, festivals, wars, and hunts. In major palaces, the deeds of the god-king eclipsed those of the other gods, whose images are more plentiful in the provinces. Assyrian art continued the double interest in decorative pattern and physical appearance, but there was an increased study of animal behavior and anatomical detail. Muscle structure was emphasized; physical force was important. Yet even the taut muscles and tendons are reduced to conventional forms and used as motifs in linear patterns. Decorative richness and subtly modulated surfaces produce the effect of opulence,

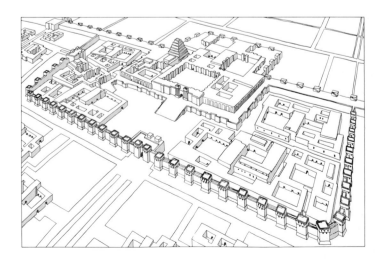

6-3
Reconstruction drawing of the citadel of Sargon II, Khorsabad, (*c.* 720 B.C.).

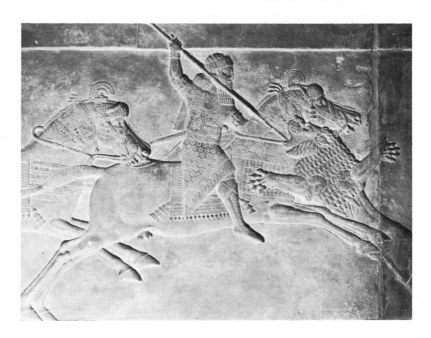

6-4
Assurbanipal Killing a Lion, from Nineveh,
(*c.* 650 B.C.). Gypseous alabaster, approx. 63 1/4″
wide.   British Museum, London.

even in the most brutal battle scenes. Relief backgrounds are usually neutral, and, especially in ritual scenes, cuneiform inscriptions may flow across both raised figures and backgrounds. However, from the ninth through the seventh centuries, there are frequent scenes of battles and hunts with detailed, panoramic landscape settings. Here, the earlier compulsion to attach figures to *ground lines* (the horizontal bottom edge of the composition) eases, and depth is occasionally suggested by the placement of objects one above the other and by increased overlapping of figures.

ASSURBANIPAL KILLING A LION, from Nineveh (**British Museum,** *c.* 650 B.C.).   This section of a *frieze* (a horizontal band of designs) from the palace at Nineveh (Fig. 6-4) demonstrates the combination of violence, admiration for physical power, and love of richly ornamented surfaces that is characteristic of Assyrian art. The king is depicted with conventional body and face. More landscape detail and suggestion of depth are found in some of the other Nineveh reliefs from the reign of the same king.

Painting

The small number of surviving paintings show the same subjects and stylistic character as the reliefs. Pigments were mixed with some fatty binder,

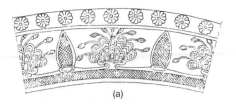

(a)

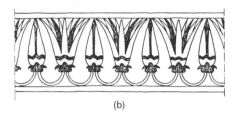

(b)

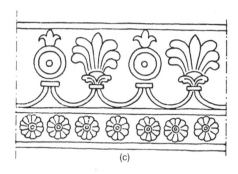

(c)

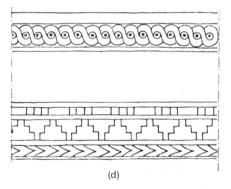

(d)

6-5
Assyrian decorative motifs:
(a) rosettes, palmettes, and pine
cones (b) lotus flowers and buds
(c) rosettes, palmettes, and
pomegranates (d) guilloche,
meanders, and chevrons.

which has now largely decomposed, and were applied in flat shapes to walls that had been mud-plastered and whitewashed. Paintings in Sargon's palace at Khorsabad were done in black, red, brown, blue, and green. Assyrian design motifs (Fig. 6-5) include pine cones and lotus blossoms (derived from Egyptian lotus bud and blossom designs), palmettes (from Egypt), rosettes and guilloches (from Egypt or Chaldea), pomegranates and stepped pyramids (probably Chaldean), and chevrons. Many of these forms occur with variations in Cretan art and, later, in Greek and Roman work.

ACHAEMENIAN PERSIAN ART:
550–330 B.C.

Architecture

Persian architecture during the Achaemenian period found its highest accomplishment in palaces. Though the Persians were eclectic, their borrowings were amalgamated into a distinctive style. Plans tended to be very open, and columns were used more extensively than in previous cultures in the Mesopotamian and Iranian areas. The typically three-part palace plan included a gatehouse, an *apadana* (a rectangular or square *hypostyle* [colonnaded] hall, probably derived from Egypt), and living quarters. These basic parts, as well as necessary storerooms, were often replicated as successive rulers added to a palace (Fig. 6-8). The parts were sometimes widely separated, as at Pasargadae (sixth century B.C.), recalling the tent-cities of the Persian nomads, and sometimes loosely joined, as at Susa and Persepolis (both sixth to fourth centuries B.C.). The buildings were elevated on one or more terraces and often enclosed by a perimeter wall.

The most unusual element was the apadana. It had three to four colonnaded porches and entrances on four sides. The gatehouse was also rectangular or square and stood separately as a monumental entry. It was often given a bent-axis alignment with the apadana, producing a delayed confrontation with the sacred area, or a ritualistic pilgrimage, as is suggested in many Mesopotamian temple plans and in the spiral ramp of Sargon's ziggurat. Columns were made of stone or wood, and wood shafts were often surfaced with plaster and painted with geometric designs. Shafts were both *fluted* (having vertical channels all the way around) and plain. Column designs (Fig. 6-6) reveal the influence of Egypt and of Ionia, the Greek territory in Asia Minor, areas from which the Persians imported skilled carvers. Wall surfaces were decorated with colored and glazed brick reliefs and stone relief sculpture. The Achaemenians worshiped outdoors; temple architecture was not of major importance. Most Achaemenian royal tombs were carved in the face of a cliff and given the form of a Greek cross (equal-armed). The horizontal arm contains a centrally placed door flanked by *engaged columns* (columns emerging from the wall as does relief sculpture) supporting a carved lintel. The upper part of the cross presents several *registers* (bands) of relief sculpture. Interiors are simple shallow spaces probably filled, at the time of burial, with royal furnishings.

PALACE AT PERSEPOLIS (6th–4th cens. B.C.).   The whole palace complex (Figs. 6-7 and 6-8) stands on an irregularly shaped terrace that is 40 feet high, about 900 by 1,500 feet in plan, and set against a mountain range. There is uncertainty about whether or not the whole area was originally surrounded by a high mud-brick wall. The terrace is approached by a stairway at the gatehouse; and,

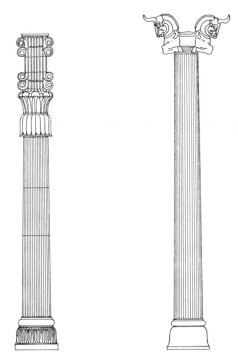

6-6
Fluted columns at Persepolis.

6-7
Stairway to the Royal Audience Hall, Persepolis, (*c.* 500 B.C.).

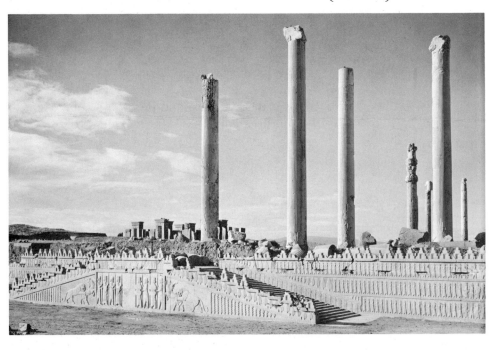

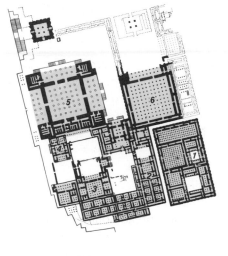

1. Treasury
2. Harem
3. Palace of Xerxes
4. Palace of Darius I
5. Audience hall of Darius I
6. Throne hall of Xerxes
- - - - - Partially excavated
⬜ Originally roofed over (speculative)

6-8
Plan of the palace at Persepolis.

from the gatehouse, a ninety-degree turn is necessary to face the main stairway to the apadana. The apadana, or audience hall of Darius, king of Persia from 521–486 B.C., is 250 feet square and originally had a roof about 60 feet high supported by thirty-six stone columns. These columns are complex, both in form and cultural allusion (Fig. 6-6). The fluted shafts and parts of the base seem to have come from Ionia. The *capitals* (the top or crowning element of the column) often begin with a ring of drooping petals and flaring papyrus blossoms that can be traced to Egypt. Above these is a vertical block with double *volutes* (scrolls) that are found, in various forms, throughout western Asia. These parts were used without additions or with pairs of griffins (winged, eagle-headed lions), bulls, human-headed bulls, or horned lions. Near the audience hall, a hundred-column throne hall was added later by Xerxes and his son, Artaxerxes. Behind the halls were living quarters, treasuries, and storerooms. Massive stone window and door frames survived the destruction of the palace by Alexander the Great, but mud-brick walls have disappeared. Sculptural decoration was concentrated around stairways, gates, and columns; it was used to ornament the architecture rather than for its own sake. The total effect of Persepolis, even in ruins, is an expression of power, wealth, and regal ceremony.

6-9
Procession of Medes and Persians, detail from the eastern stairway to the Royal Audience Hall, Persepolis, (*c.* 500 B.C.). Black limestone, entire relief approx. 268′3″ wide.

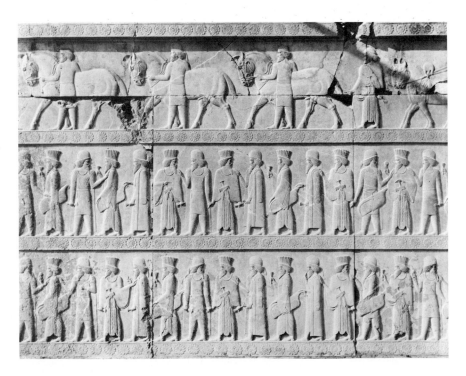

Sculpture

Achaemenian sculpture was primarily the relief embellishment of architecture. Almost no free-standing statues have been found. The Assyrian interest in narration of battles and hunts is absent, although Assyrian influence is evident in the Persian love of linear patterns, and, specifically, in the human-headed bulls at the Persepolis gatehouse, which repeat those at Khorsabad. Assyrian violence is recalled by the motif of a lion biting a bull at Persepolis. Basically, subject matter consisted of real and fantastic animals and processions of retainers, warriors, or subjects. At Susa, relief was executed in richly colored glazed brick; at Persepolis, reliefs were carved in stone and originally painted. The carvings depict processions of soldiers, bearers of tribute from twenty-three nations of the empire, members of the court, guards, and scenes of the king giving audience and offering prayers, all parts of the Achaemenian New Year's festival celebrated at Persepolis. Another outlet for Persian talent in sculptural design was finely wrought gold, silver, and bronze metalwork ranging from cups and vases to jewelry and weapons.

PROCESSION OF MEDES AND PERSIANS, eastern stairway of the audience hall of Darius (Persepolis, c. 500 B.C.).   In this detail of the reliefs outside the audience hall at Persepolis (Fig. 6-9), the *Immortals* (imperial guards) are shown in alternation with Medes, inhabitants of Persia's province of Media, who are clearly indicated by round hats and smooth clothing. Persian costumes are embellished with drapery folds in elegant, symmetrical patterns. The widespread sources of Persian art are revealed by this drapery, influenced by sixth-century Greece, and by the rosettes, taken from Egyptian and early Mesopotamian art. The distinctively Persian quality comes from the combination of repetitive processional compositions, neutral backgrounds, low but round relief modeling, and the love of opulent decorative patterns.

Suggestions for Further Study

Amiet, Pierre. *The Art of the Ancient Near East.* Translated by John Shepley and Claude Choquet. New York: Abrams, 1980.

Frankfort, Henri. *The Art and Architecture of the Ancient Orient* (Pelican History of Art), rev. ed. Baltimore: Penguin Books, 1969.

Ghirshman, Roman. *Iran from the Earliest Times to the Islamic Conquest.* Harmondsworth and New York: Penguin Books, 1978.

Mootgat, Anton. *The Art of Ancient Mesopotamia.* London and New York: Phaidon, 1969.

Parrot, André. *The Arts of Assyria* (The Arts of Mankind). Translated by Stuart Gilbert and James Emmons. New York: Golden Press, 1961.

Porada, Edith. *The Art of Ancient Iran: Pre-Islamic Cultures.* New York: Crown, 1965.

Scranton, Robert L. *Aesthetic Aspects of Ancient Art.* Chicago: University of Chicago Press, 1964.

Sieveking, Ann. *The Cave Artists.* London: Thames & Hudson, 1979.

Strommenger, Eva, and Max Hirmer. *5000 Years of the Art of Mesopotamia.* New York: Abrams, 1964.

7

Egyptian Art

3200 – 30 B.C.

Ancient Egyptian history falls into three major periods, which are further divided into dynasties (ages during which a single family provided the succession of rulers). The *Archaic* period and the *Old Kingdom* may be considered together as the first major period, which began with the unification of northern and southern Egypt, saw the establishment of Memphis as a cultural center, and ended with the decline of central power and an era of confusion and civil war. Order was restored during the *Middle Kingdom,* but in a feudal system that weakened the authority of the *pharaoh* (king). This kingdom eventually collapsed under the burdens of civil war and invasion by the Hyksos (probably Canaanites and Anatolians), who exacted tribute from much of Egypt until they were expelled by princes from Thebes. Thebes became a major center for the *New Kingdom* or *Empire,* the period that brought Egypt to its greatest power. We may group the Empire with the less important periods that followed and with the age of defeats that ended Egypt's leading role in ancient history. She was invaded by Assyrians in the seventh century B.C., by the Persians in the sixth century B.C., and by the Macedonians in 332 B.C.; finally, in 30 B.C. Egypt became a Roman province.

Egyptian civilization began as a series of independent city-states, each with its own patron god. The unity of these parts was always precarious, as Egyptian literature and art reveal; for example, the pharaoh is sometimes depicted wearing the crown (with a flat top and a raised portion at the rear) of northern or Lower Egypt, sometimes wearing the crown (shaped like a bowling pin) of southern or Upper Egypt, and occasionally wearing a combination of both crowns. Life depended on the rhythmic cycles of the Nile River, whose floods enriched the bottomlands but necessitated the frequent resurveying of fields; hence the Egyptians quickly developed a practical mathematics as well as astronomy and a rational calendar.

Egyptian society consisted of the nobility, which owned much of the land; the middle class, which consisted of merchants, artists, civil servants, and — in the Empire — soldiers; and the peasants, who formed the bulk of the population. By the end of the Empire, the power of the nobility had been partially taken over by the growing priesthood and by the increasing number of civil servants.

All Egyptian culture was pervaded by a complex religion that stressed a life after death; therefore, most of the painting, sculpture, and architecture was religious and sepulchral. Egyptian art presents a bewildering variety of gods — male and female human figures and combination animal-human creatures such as the sphinx (a recumbent lion with a man's head). Some of the more important gods were Osiris, lord of the underworld (often shown as a swathed mummy); Anubis, the jackal-god of embalmment; Nut, the sky goddess (a human form arched over the earth); Hathor, the goddess of love and joy (usually shown with cow's horns); Horus, one aspect of the sun god (often shown as a hawk); and Re, or Ra, the sun god who traveled across the sky in his sun-ship during the day and through the underworld at night. The pharaoh himself was believed to be a god. Many of the gods assumed each other's forms or evolved in

form and name during the course of Egyptian history. The most striking development in this history was the effort of the XVIIIth-Dynasty king Akhenaten to establish a monotheistic religion founded on the worship of the sun god.

ARCHAIC PERIOD: 3200–2680 B.C. (DYNASTIES I THROUGH III), AND OLD KINGDOM: 2680–2258 B.C. (DYNASTIES IV THROUGH VI)

Architecture

The palaces of the nobility and the homes of the wealthy were built either of wood frames with walls of colored reed mats or of mud brick with plaster or stucco surfacing decorated with paintings; more modest dwellings were probably made of reed mats plastered with mud. Such impermanent materials have left few remains. The Egyptians concentrated their efforts on tombs and temples, built to serve the deceased or the gods and to defy time and the destructive power of nature. Stone and brick were used for this more permanent architecture, but because the stone and brick sometimes encased only a rubble filling, the wall was not always as permanent as it might have been. The arch was known but rarely used; the basic structural system was post and lintel.

Egyptian architecture emphasizes mass and employs simple, rigid contours. Interior spaces are usually small in proportion to the masses enclosing them and are placed in a mazelike succession, with dead ends or roundabout connections. One of the basic tomb types is the *mastaba* (Fig. 7-1), originally a rectangular block with *battered* (sloping) sides and more mass than enclosed space, though later mastabas are less regular in form and enclose more space. The basic parts are (1) the burial chamber, reached by a vertical or sloping shaft; (2) the statue chamber, a walled-up room containing a statue substitute for the body; (3) a mortuary chapel, where offerings could be left for the deceased; and (4) a false door through which the spirit of the dead was to have access to the offerings. Often the statue chamber has a peephole leading to the chapel. The statue chamber and burial chamber with its entry shaft are often

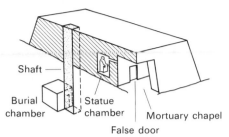

7-1
Cross section of a typical mastaba.

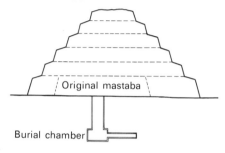

7-2
Step-pyramid of Zoser.

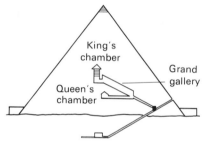

7-3
Cross section of the pyramid of Khufu.

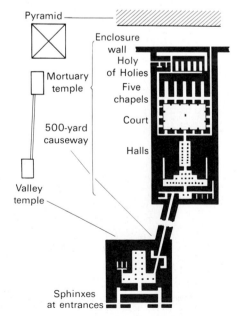

7-4
Pyramid of Khafre, Giza.

encased in hard stone, meant to improve durability and to discourage tomb-robbers, who were attracted by the treasures buried with the dead. The mastaba was thought of as a house for the dead, and groups of mastabas formed cities of the dead *(necropolises)*. It is conjectured that the *pyramid* tomb may have evolved from stacked-up mastabas of decreasing size, as in the tomb of King Zoser (Fig. 7-2), the famous step-pyramid at Saqqara.

Such a step-pyramid could have led to the true pyramid form, which protects its burial chamber and treasures under a mountain of stone (Fig. 7-3). The basic parts of an Old Kingdom pyramid complex (Fig. 7-4) are (1) the pyramid, (2) a mortuary chapel or temple beside or against the pyramid, (3) a causeway leading from the mortuary temple to (4) a valley temple close to the Nile. The huge pyramids only inspired greater efforts by tomb-robbers, however, and in later periods smaller tombs were built. For their post and lintel structures, the Egyptians derived column designs from plants and from construction methods in wood; some columns imitate a papyrus stalk and blossom; others imitate the form of bundles of palms tied together for strength. Polygonal fluted stone columns, like the later Doric columns of Greece, may imitate wooden palm bundles plastered with mud. Capitals atop the columns (Fig. 7-5) resemble lotus buds, papyrus blossoms, palm leaves, or leafy blossoms.

STEP-PYRAMID OF ZOSER (Saqqara, Dyn. III). The first large Egyptian architecture in stone, this 195-foot-high mass (Fig. 7-2) seems to have developed from an original mastaba by added stages. Around the pyramid, a wall originally enclosed a funerary community with chapels, palaces, and temples. Bundle, fluted, and papyrus blossom columns are used. The architect was Imhotep, one of the few Old Kingdom architects whose name is known to us.

PYRAMIDS OF KHUFU, KHAFRE, AND MENKURE (Giza, Dyn. IV).   These largest of Egyptian tombs (Fig. 7-6) are in true pyramid form and were originally encased in polished limestone. The largest of the three, that of Khufu, has a base about 750 feet square and was originally about 475 feet high. The method of construction is not known with certainty; the mammoth stones may have been pulled

7-5
Egyptian column designs.

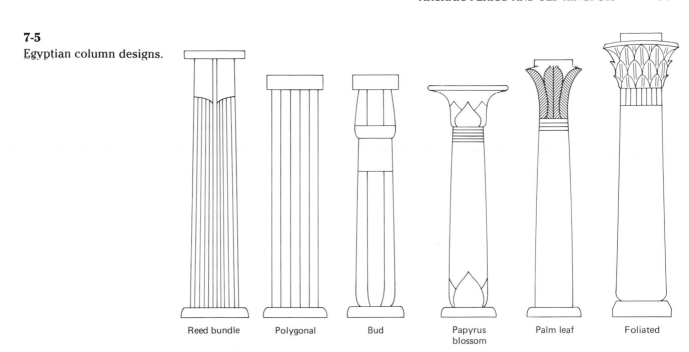

Reed bundle   Polygonal   Bud   Papyrus blossom   Palm leaf   Foliated

7-6
Great pyramids of Giza: Menkure, (*c.* 2460 B.C.); Khafre, (*c.* 2500 B.C.); Khufu, (*c.* 2530 B.C.).

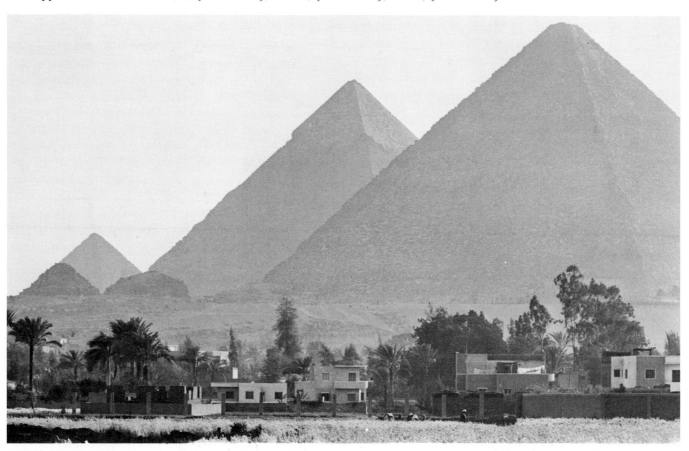

on sledges up ramps of earth that were raised with each level of the structure. The massive, stable geometric form and the simple surfaces are characteristic of monumental architecture in Egypt.

Sculpture

Egyptian sculpture ranges from colossal statues to delicate goldsmith's work. The most significant pieces were done for tombs or temples. For large work, hard stones such as granite, diorite, or basalt were preferred. Softer alabaster was exploited for its translucence, and sandstone, limestone, and wood sculpture was often surfaced with plaster and painted. Small sculpture, or inlay work in large sculpture, might consist of gold, silver, electrum (an alloy of gold and silver), lapis lazuli (a semiprecious, azure-colored stone), and enamel.

Relief sculpture, generally low relief consisting of sharp-edged, relatively flat forms, has some of the abstract symbolic character of Egyptian hieroglyphic writing. The human body is portrayed by conventionalized forms developed early in Egyptian history. A frontally seen eye, for example, is combined with a profile face, frontal shoulders, and profile hips and legs; the artist seems to have thought through an action step by step and shown these steps as in a diagram. The standardized bodies occasionally depict age, but otherwise the passage of time is ignored, for the sharp edges and

angular poses tend to freeze any suggestion of motion. Motion implies time as mass implies space; neither is an element of Old Kingdom relief sculpture. Some overlapping of flat shapes suggests a very shallow space, but massive forms and a perspective illusion of space are not found. As a result, the reliefs do not weaken the mass of the wall or the *stele* that carries them.

In freestanding sculpture, the standard poses are free from the wall, but they may be attached to a supporting back-slab (see Fig. 7-8). Much Egyptian sculpture retains the massive four-sidedness of the block from which it was carved, and the mass contributes to the impression of durability. Closed form is typical. Anatomy is simplified in the direction of geometric shapes, so that the figures assume the rigidity and static permanence of Egyptian architecture. Individuality is concentrated in the face, which is often alert in expression but motionless. It should be noted, however, that the art of the different areas of Egypt varies in its adherence to the conventional forms. The functions of the various statues, as votive images to the gods or as images of servants meant to serve the deceased in his afterlife, also influenced the style of the work.

VICTORY PALETTE OF NARMER (Dyn. I, slate, 25″. Egyptian Museum, Cairo).   The Narmer palette (Fig. 7-7), an elaborate version of the palettes used for mixing eye paints, commemorates the subjec-

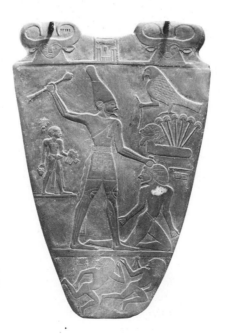
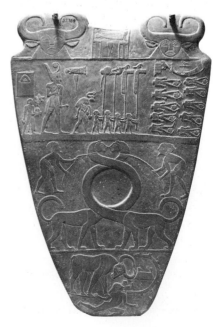

7-7
Victory palette of Narmer, front and back, from Hierakonpolis, (*c.* 3000 B.C.). Slate, 25″ high. Egyptian Museum, Cairo.

tion of northern Egypt by the South. On one side, King Narmer, wearing the tall crown of the South, is about to strike a northerner. A hawk holds captive a plant with a human head, probably the papyrus symbol of the delta region. Above, the hieroglyph for Narmer is framed by a small palace. On either side of this is a human head with cow's horns, the symbol for Hathor. On the other side of the palette, Narmer, wearing the crown of northern Egypt, surveys decapitated enemies. At the bottom, he is seen as a bull knocking down the walls of a city. Typically, the artist shows the figures in "elevation," standing on base lines that establish different registers in the composition, until a different point of view is needed to convey the information he is giving. The artist changes to an aerial view to show the number of slain enemies. Scale expresses importance; therefore, the king acquires giant stature.

MYCERINUS AND HIS QUEEN (Dyn. IV, slate, 54½″ high. Museum of Fine Arts, Boston). The king wears a ceremonial false beard; the queen wears a wig (Fig. 7-8). The individual facial features are somewhat simplified, and yet they contrast with the more generalized treatment of the bodies. The pose is typical for standing figures. Closed form and anatomy reduced to geometric rigidity give a timeless dignity to the couple.

Painting

Papyrus (the pith of the papyrus plant, cut into strips, and pressed to form a material suitable for writing) was occasionally used by the Egyptians for painting, as well as for writing, but the most important paintings are on the walls of tombs and temples. Paint was also often used to enhance relief or freestanding sculpture. Grounds are smoothed stone or a coating of stucco, plaster, or mud and straw. Pigments made from powdered natural substances, such as soot, copper compounds, or earth colors, were mixed with a binder of water and gum and were applied to a dry ground.

Old Kingdom painting, like the sculpture and architecture, shows a preference for rigidly imposed rectilinear order and a limited number of standard forms. During the millennia of Egyptian history, the striking quality of all the arts is not the

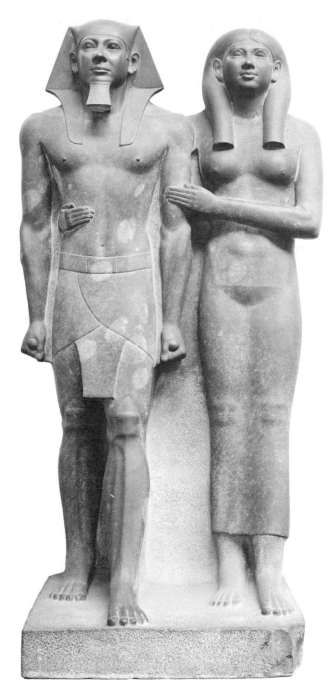

7-8
Mycerinus and His Queen, Kha-Merer-Nebty II, from Giza, (Dyn. IV, 2599–2571 B.C.). Slate schist, 54 1/2″ high. 11.1738, Harvard University-MFA Expedition. Courtesy, Museum of Fine Arts, Boston.

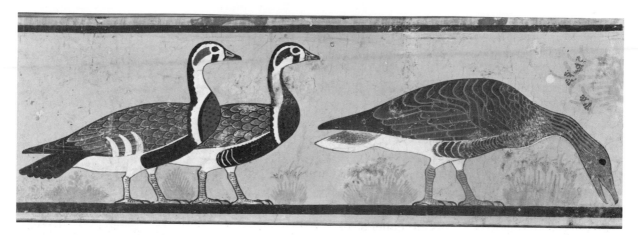

7-9
Detail from *Geese of Medum,* (*c.* 2530 B.C.). Dry fresco, entire fresco approx. 18″ high.   Egyptian Museum, Cairo.

subtle change or occasional rebellion against the standard forms but rather their continuity. Old Kingdom painting was often applied to relief sculpture; it was left to later ages to stress painting as an independent art. Like relief, painting uses sharp-edged flat shapes, and the diagrammatic poses symbolize activity rather than express it. Spaces between figures are often filled with hieroglyphics, which counter any slight illusion of depth that might come from overlapping shapes. Typical forms and actions of animals are keenly observed, but the repetition of shapes and details within shapes imposes a regimented order upon the variety of nature. Subject matter comes from mythology, ritual, biography, or daily activities. Symbolism is pervasive. Many of the activities, such as sowing, reaping, and offering prayers and food, were apparently intended to "serve" the deceased in his afterlife. As in the reliefs, scenes are organized in registers. While overall symmetry was valued, each picture seems to function as an isolated unit, and the accretion of these units gives the painting some of the additive character of the architecture.

GEESE, from the mastaba of Itet at Medum (Dyn. III, approx. 1′ × 6′. Egyptian Museum, Cairo).   Although this is one section from one register in a large wall painting, the composition works effectively as an isolated unit (Fig. 7-9). The colors and the poised strutting of the geese are quite natural, but a typically severe order is evident in the symmetry of the poses and in the crisp patterns of the feathers.

MIDDLE KINGDOM: 2134–1786 B.C. (DYNASTIES XI AND XII)

Architecture

The Middle Kingdom produced smaller tombs and tomb-temple combinations. This resulted in part from a smaller concentration of wealth; it may also be explained by the growth of the Osiris cult, which stressed an afterlife in the underworld rather than in the tomb. Many small stone-faced brick pyramids and mastabas have crumbled, but more permanent tombs, cut into the rock of the cliffs along the Nile Valley at places like Beni Hasan, still remain.

ROCK-CUT TOMB OF AMENEMHAT I (Beni Hasan, Dyn. XII).   The plan and section drawings (Fig. 7-10) illustrate typical features of rock-cut tombs: the courtyard, pillared portico, main room, and the shrine. Of modest size, the main room of these tombs (Fig. 7-11) frequently was supported by fluted columns (sometimes called Proto-Doric because of their resemblance to later Greek Doric columns). These tombs generally contained a simple grave pit for the body. The walls are painted with subjects in the tradition of the Old Kingdom and the ceiling is decorated with geometric designs that probably imitate textiles.

Sculpture

Much Middle Kingdom sculpture was destroyed by the Hyksos and by New Kingdom rulers. What remains varies from crude to highly finished carving. Growing patronage by the middle class and the dispersal of wealth among the nobles seem in many works to have resulted in the sacrifice of quality for quantity. Frequent use was made of the cheaper method of *sunken relief*, in which the outlines of objects are cut into the wall and the form within the outlines is carved so that most of it is below the surface of the untouched background. Its style owes much to the Old Kingdom, although poses are often more affected. Freestanding sculpture developed even simpler bodies than in the Old Kingdom. Forms are either sleek and flowing or heavy, brutal, and blocky. Many seated figures have arms folded over drawn-up knees; such a statue was simply a modified block surmounted by a head and therefore involved a minimum of carving. The most distinctive feature of Middle Kingdom sculpture is the cynicism and careworn weariness in many of the faces, a quality that is echoed in Middle Kingdom writings. This detailed realism is often in striking contrast to the simplified bodies. Middle Kingdom servant statues tend to be of cheaper materials and cruder execution than earlier examples.

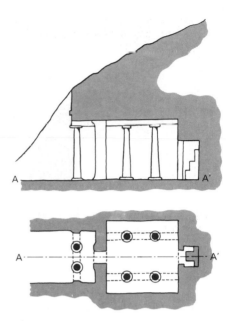

7-10
Plan and section of a rock-cut tomb.
(After Sir Banister Fletcher.)

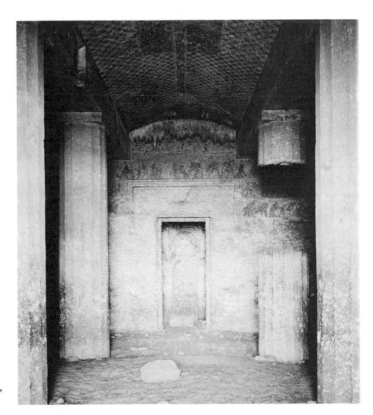

7-11
Interior of the tomb of Amenemhat I,
Beni Hasan, (*c.* 1930 B.C.).

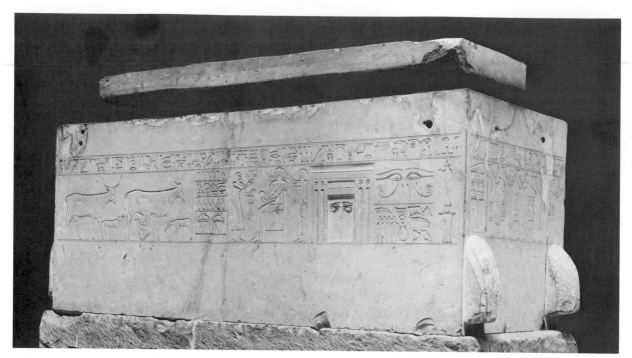

7-12
Relief on the sarcophagus of Mentuhotep's wife,
Kawit, (Dyn. XI).   Egyptian Museum, Cairo.

RELIEF *on the sarcophagus of Mentuhotep's wife,
Kawit* (Dyn. XI, limestone, originally painted. Egyptian Museum, Cairo).   Quite unlike earlier work,
this sunken relief (Fig. 7-12) exemplifies the sleek,
suave contours and rather precious poses characteristic of some Middle Kingdom sculpture.

AMENEMHAT III (?) — identity uncertain (Dyn. XII,
obsidian, 4″ high. Calouste Gulbenkian Museum, Lisbon).   The tired, lined face (Fig. 7-13) illustrates
a Middle Kingdom tendency toward greater detail
and more distinctly individualistic portrait features. The small scale and hard stone demanded
considerable skill.

Painting

The Middle Kingdom employed painting extensively, perhaps partly because painting was
quicker and less laborious than relief. One of the
chief sites for Middle Kingdom painting is the
rock-cut tombs of Beni Hasan. The paintings are
typically done in soft, subtle colors applied to
broad, simple shapes that sometimes contrast with
areas of meticulous detail.

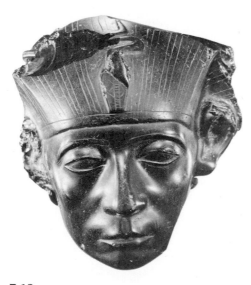

7-13
Sesostris III or *Amenemhat III,* (c.
1850 B.C.). Obsidian, approx. 4″ high.
Calouste Gulbenkian Museum, Lisbon.

DANCING GIRLS, from the tomb of Antefoker
(Thebes, Dyn. XII, approx. 37″ × 67″).   The mild
value contrasts, bland colors, simple shapes, and

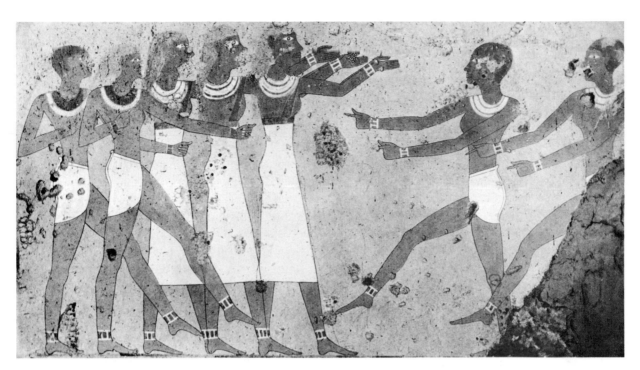

7-14
Dancing Girls, from the tomb of Antefoker, Thebes, (Dyn. XII).

wirelike outlines seen in Figure 7-14 are typical of much Middle Kingdom painting. The costumes are also representative of the period. The outstretched forefingers of the dancers on the right may be ritualistic gestures or a method of counting the steps of the dance. Typical of Egyptian painting is the combination of profile faces with eyes that look straight out at us (frontal eyes).

NEW KINGDOM (EMPIRE) AND LATER PERIODS: 1570 – 30 B.C. (DYNASTIES XVIII THROUGH XXXI)

Architecture

Thebes is the center for the important remains of New Kingdom architecture. In the cliffs on the western side of the river are two desolate rock-strewn valleys: the Valley of the Tombs of the Kings and the Valley of the Tombs of the Queens. Here many of the New Kingdom rulers had themselves buried in hidden mineshaft-like tombs. While these cannot really be considered as architecture, they were lavishly decorated with paintings and sculpture. When the tombs' sites became secret, the mortuary temples occupied more convenient locations near the city. Mortuary temples and temples to the gods became especially large during the New Kingdom and later periods. Both kinds were built in the same general plan: (1) entry through a massive sloping façade called a *pylon* (see Figs. 7-15 and 7-17), (2) an open *courtyard*, (3) a *hypostyle hall* (see Fig. 7-18), and (4) a sacred *inner sanctum*. The basic parts could be multiplied, and temples to more than one god might have several sanctums. From entry to inner sanctum, the progression is from larger to smaller spaces, the plan (see Fig. 7-19) being essentially an elaboration of the Middle Kingdom rock-cut tomb. The temples were often enlarged by a process of accretion over the centuries, and the resulting labyrinthine complexity, which does not lend itself to an easy comprehension of the whole interior, provided effective settings for the processionals so important in Egyptian worship.

Our knowledge of New Kingdom domestic architecture would be greater had not later generations carried away much of the stone from Akhenaten's capital at Amarna. His North Palace has an extensive symmetrical plan organized around a large pool and tightly enclosed behind thick walls.

Typical materials for such architecture were mud brick and stone.

TEMPLE OF AMEN-MUT-KHÔNSU (Luxor, mainly Dyns. XVIII and XIX).   This enormous temple (Figs. 7-15 and 7-16) was not for mortuary offerings but for the glory of the god Amen (whose identity merged with that of Re), his wife Mut, and their son Khônsu. The basic temple parts have been multiplied. From the great pylon and the first court, built under Rameses II (Dyn. XIX), one enters the XVIIIth-Dynasty parts of the building: a double row of 52-foot-high papyrus blossom columns, a second court (bud columns), a hypostyle hall, smaller halls, and two sanctums. Originally, two *obelisks* (tapered shafts with pointed tips) stood in front of the temple. One remains; the other was brought to the Place de la Concorde in Paris. The total length of the structure is about 835 feet.

TEMPLE OF HORUS (Edfu, mainly 237–212 B.C.). The building (Figs. 7-17 and 7-18) comes from the Ptolemaic era, which followed the Macedonian

7-15
Court and pylon of Rameses II (*c.* 1290 B.C.), and court and colonnade of Amenhotep III (*c.* 1370 B.C.), temple of Amen-Mut-Khônsu, Luxor.

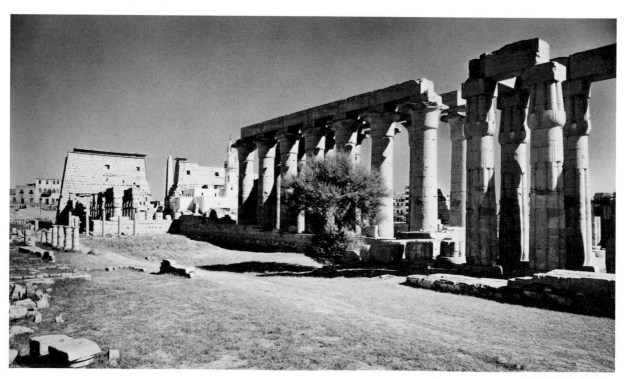

conquest. It is notable for its well-preserved state and for its exemplification of the basic Egyptian temple unobscured by proliferation. The pylon (145' × 250') and massive exterior walls enclose court, vestibule, hypostyle hall, storage rooms, and inner sanctum. The plan (Fig. 7-19) indicates a characteristic axial progression to smaller and darker spaces. The columns typify the late period in the use of a variety of palm and foliated capitals.

Sculpture

Increasing prosperity during the Empire greatly encouraged artistic activity. Tomb statues were often carved in the living rock of the shaft tombs, and quantities of votive statues and reliefs decorated the temples. Sunken relief is common. Middle Kingdom style continued for a time, but the expansion of the Empire brought increased awareness of other peoples, and conventional forms soon relaxed to allow more representation of different racial types. The reign of Akhenaten marked a stylistic change toward more action, greater casualness in pose, increasing complexity in costume and accessory detail, a softening of body

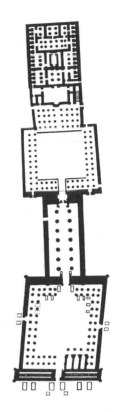

7-16
Plan of the temple of Amen-Mut-Khônsu.

7-17
Pylon at Temple of Horus, Edfu, (mainly 237–212 B.C.).

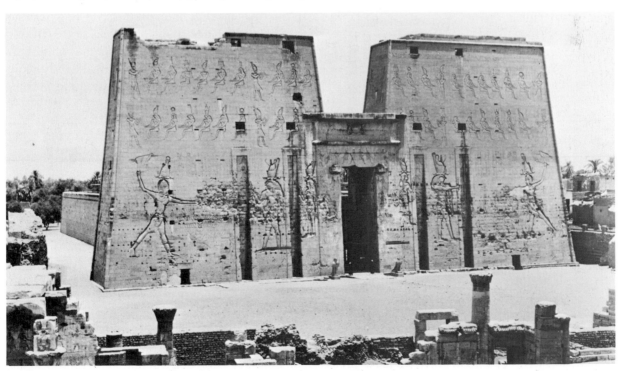

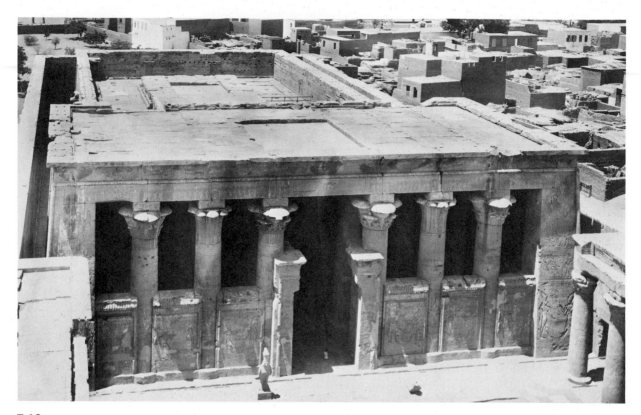

7-18
Temple of Horus, hypostyle hall from the court.

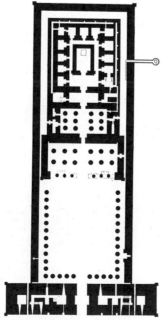

7-19
Plan of the temple of Horus.

forms, and more accurate indication of age. The king's heavy lips, pendulous jaw, long neck, and sagging stomach were stressed to the point of caricature in portraits that he must have encouraged. The royal features soon set the style, and portraits of other people acquired his "ideal" form. The old conventions were modified rather than abolished. Soon after the death of Akhenaten, the old canons returned, but with slightly softer contours in some works and more open form.

AKHENATEN (AMENHOTEP IV) (Dyn. XVIII, sandstone with coloring, 13' high. Egyptian Museum, Cairo).   Although the traditional pose is taken, the features of face and body on this sculpture (Fig. 7-20) make a striking contrast to Old Kingdom statues such as *Mycerinus and His Queen* (Fig. 7-8).

NEFERTITI, wife of Akhenaten (Dyn. XVIII, painted limestone, with eyes—one missing—of inlaid rock crystal, approx. 20" high. Staatliche Museen, Berlin).   This bust (Fig. 7-21), found among the remains of a sculptor's studio, served as a model. Suggestions of fleshy softness under the chin and around the eyes and mouth lend a flesh-and-blood reality to the regal poise of the queen.

Painting

The best-preserved examples of Egyptian painting come from the highly decorated walls of the New Kingdom. Those from the beginning of the period are characterized by stiff poses and vivid opaque colors, with wide use of blue backgrounds. Later came a change to more graceful poses and more delicate transparent colors applied with brushwork that is occasionally loose and sketchy. The reign of Akhenaten produced startling changes in painting as well as in sculpture. When he moved the capital from Thebes to Amarna, he had his palace there decorated with paintings of landscapes and animal life, all done with a new concern for continuity of all the parts. The direct visual experience of nature breaks through the old symbolic concepts. Human forms acquire the casual poses, soft bodies, and elongated faces common to the sculpture of the period. This so-called *Amarna Style* died shortly after Akhenaten, but its influence is seen in the occasional flashes of individuality and naturalism that lighten later art. For the most part, later painting, in answering the demands for ostentatious elegance, tends to be repetitious, garish in color, and technically mediocre.

FOWLING SCENE, *from the tomb of Amenemheb* (Thebes, Dyn. XVIII, 2′10″ high. Fragment in the British Museum, London). The artist gives us considerable information about types of fishes, birds, and plants, as well as methods of hunting — note the hunting cat facing the hunter at knee level (Fig. 7-22). The compositional arrangement of figures, boats, and papyrus is an ancient one for hunting scenes. The small scale of the hunter's companions indicates their lesser importance. The object on the head of the standing woman is a lump of perfumed ointment.

WALL PAINTINGS *in the tomb of Nakht* (Thebes, Dyn. XVIII). Nakht was a priest of the god Amen. The paintings (Fig. 7-23) illustrate offerings made at the painted false door of the chapel, the procedures of farming, and dancers and musicians entertaining guests at a feast. Here also the style

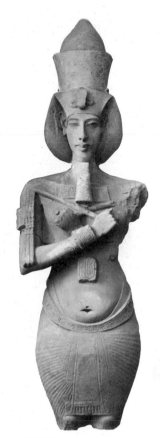

7-20
Akhenaten (Amenhotep IV), from a pillar statue in the temple of Aton, Tell el-Amarna, (*c.* 1375 B.C.). Sandstone, approx. 13′ high. Egyptian Museum, Cairo.

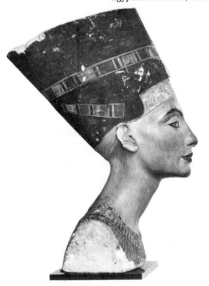

7-21
Nefertiti, from Tell el-Amarna, (*c.* 1360 B.C.). Limestone, approx. 20″ high. Staatliche Museen, Berlin.

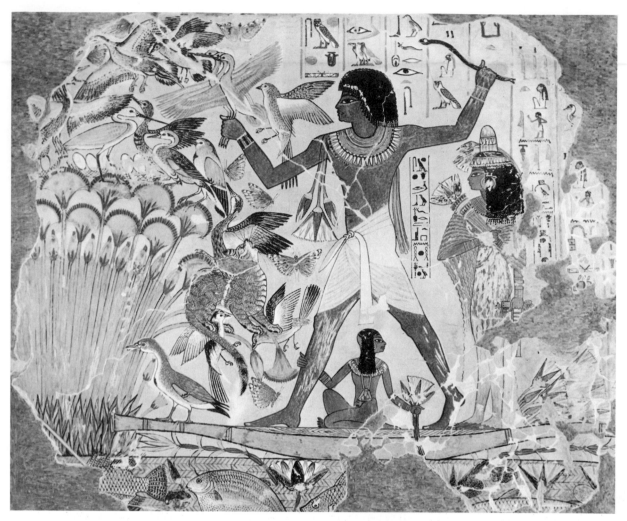

7-22
Fowling Scene, from the tomb of Amenemheb, Thebes, (Dyn. XVIII).   British Museum, London.

indicates the period before Akhenaten, but the freedom of brushwork and the delicate color indicate the period just after the tomb of Amenemheb. Traditionally, men were given a darker skin color than women. The small but well-preserved chapel shows the typically lively decorative effect of the many flat shapes used in Egyptian painting.

Suggestions for Further Study

Aldred, Cyril. *The Development of Ancient Egyptian Art from 3200–1315 B.C.* London: Academy Editions, 1973.

Desroches-Noblecourt, Christiane. *Ancient Egypt: The New Kingdom and the Amarna Period.* Greenwich, Conn.: New York Graphic Society, 1960.

Edwards, I. E. S. *Pyramids of Egypt,* rev. ed. Baltimore: Penguin Books, 1963.

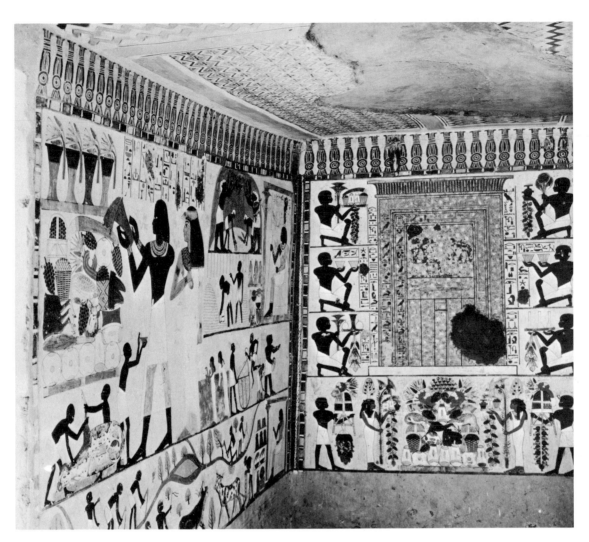

7-23
Wall paintings in the tomb of Nakht, Thebes, (*c.* 1450 B.C.). Rear wall 55″ × 60″.

Frankfort, H. A. G. *Arrest and Movement*. Chicago: University of Chicago Press, 1951.

Lange, Kurt, and Max Hirmer. *Egypt: Architecture, Sculpture, Painting in Three Thousand Years,* 4th rev. and enl. ed. Translated by R. H. Boothroyd, Judith Filson, and Barbara Taylor. London: Phaidon, 1968.

Mekhitarian, Arpag. *Egyptian Painting* (Great Centuries of Painting). Translated by Stuart Gilbert. New York: Skira, 1978.

Smith, E. Baldwin. *Egyptian Architecture as Cultural Expression*. Watkins Glenn, 1968.

Smith, William Stevenson. *The Art and Architecture of Ancient Egypt,* rev. ed. New York: Viking, 1981.

Woldering, Irmgard. *Gods, Men, and Pharaohs: The Glory of Egyptian Art*. New York: Abrams, 1967.

8

Aegean
Art

2800 – 1100 B.C.

Aegean art comes from three main areas: Crete, the Cycladic Islands, and the mainland that later became Greece. On Crete, major sites are Knossos, Phaistos, Hagia Triada, Gournia, Mallia, Palaikastro, and Zabro; of the Cycladic Islands, Melos, Naxos, Paros, and Syros are especially important; on the mainland the many sites include Mycenae, Tiryns, Pylos, Lerna, Orchomenos, and Iolkos. By 2800 B.C., the use of bronze was ending *Neolithic* (New Stone) Age culture and opening the *Bronze Age.* Cretan culture (often called *Minoan,* after the one or more ancient kings named Minos), Cycladic culture, and, on the mainland, pre-Greek culture (referred to as *Helladic*) have been divided chronologically into *early* (2800– 2000 B.C.), *middle* (2000–1550 B.C.), and *late* (1500–1100 B.C.) periods, corresponding roughly to the Old, Middle, and New kingdoms in Egypt. Further subdivisions are used by experts, but because the three geographical areas did not develop technologically at the same pace, the subdivisions are somewhat arbitrary. Dates for Egypt are more certain, and Egyptian artifacts found among the remains of other cultures as a result of trade contacts allow dating by relation to Egyptian chronology.

By 1550 B.C., Cretan art was a dominant influence both on the mainland and in the Cyclades. There is evidence of widespread destruction in Crete about 1700 B.C. (possibly from earthquakes) and of much rebuilding around 1550 B.C. In 1450 B.C., more serious destruction befell the island, probably as a result of the eruption of the volcano on the nearby island of Thera (modern Santorin). After this, the Cretans seem to have been ruled by the Mycenaeans from the mainland until about 1200 B.C., when a period of war and dissolution was followed by the conquest of both Crete and the mainland by the Dorians (later to become the Greeks). It was during this confused period between 1200 and 800 B.C. that the Homeric epics, the *Iliad* and the *Odyssey,* came into being.

Cretan culture grew in the environment of a temperate climate, fertile soil, and a protective sea. The Cretans benefited as well from their position at a trade crossroads; there is evidence of contact with Egypt and Mesopotamia. Notable in Cretan architecture and art is the absence of fortifications and military subject matter. Early hieroglyphic scripts, inspired by Egypt, overlapped the use of two later scripts, Linear A and Linear B. Only Linear B has been completely deciphered; it is a form of early Greek and was used mainly for inventories. Thus far, there are more questions than answers about Cretan government and religion. Government was apparently decentralized, and religion viewed nature as a friendly force. Public worship was held in caves and on mountaintops; private worship was performed in small chapels in houses and palaces. It is not known whether Cretan religion was monotheistic or not. Apparent deities are most frequently female, and it is possible that the various representations are all of a single goddess shown in different forms and functions. Donkey-headed and bull-headed creatures with human bodies (minotaurs) were apparently considered as demons. Sacred objects were special columns, trees, and double-bladed axes. Life in Crete seems to have been colorful, nature-

oriented, and relatively secure, in spite of the occasional devastation apparently caused by earthquakes.

Our knowledge of Cycladic culture is meager. Cretan influence was strong, and the Cyclades prospered from resources of gold, silver, copper, marble, and emery (for shaping stone and sharpening weapons). On the mainland, hilltop fortresses such as Mycenae and Tiryns bespeak a much less carefree life than that of the islands. Graves contain weapons, bodies mummified in the Egyptian manner, and Cretan objects. Mycenae's wealth of gold may have come as payment for mercenary service in Egyptian battles against the Hittites. The art and the tombs reveal influence from Egypt and Crete. Mycenaean power reached its apex between 1400 and 1200 B.C.

Architecture

Cretan architecture took the form of town houses, country villas, palaces, market halls, and tombs. Temples apparently were not needed. Plans for buildings and towns often had a north – south orientation in their long axis. Houses were built of brick, stone, and wood, had symmetrical façades, and consisted of several floors built around an interior courtyard. Palace plans were irregular, labyrinthine, and organized around rectangular inner courts. Royal apartments, storage magazines, and audience chambers have been identified. Although palace entrances were not stressed, the west façade was usually built first, given special ornamental emphasis, and fronted by an exterior courtyard. Walls were of mud brick, rubble masonry, and plaster; stone blocks were used in corners and in frames for doors and windows. Roofs were flat, resting on wooden beams and wooden columns that carried brightly painted cushion-shaped capitals and had shafts that tapered downward. Interior palace floors were of gypsum; exterior floors were made of limestone. Interior walls were often frescoed. Tombs were emphasized only in the early period, when circular stone structures, some probably vaulted, served the whole community.

Our sparse information about Cycladic architecture indicates that it was much like that of Crete, but mainland architecture included fortified citadels, the most famous at Mycenae and Tiryns.

Thick walls of huge stones encircled hilltop clusters of small houses and palaces with plans that developed around the *megaron,* a rectangular hall with central hearth, anteroom, and pillared porch. Such compressed quarters did not compare with the luxury of Cretan palaces, although mainland ruins reveal gypsum floor slabs and plastered walls with painted designs. Pit and shaft tombs in the early period and the first part of the middle period were replaced, at least for royalty, by round conical tombs with corbeled stone domes and ornaments of carved and painted stone as well as attached metal objects. Earth was piled over the tomb exteriors, obscuring everything but the *dromos,* a stone-lined approach to the entrance.

PALACE AT KNOSSOS (*c.* 1600–1400 B.C.).   The ruins of Knossos, the largest of the Cretan palaces, are those of the new palace, built some time after the destruction of about 1700 B.C. The complex, additive, asymmetrical character of the plan (Fig. 8-1) is typical, as are the indirect entrances on each side. The western half of the palace is divided by a long corridor into magazines (storage chambers) on one side and a complex of official rooms, including a throne room, on the other. The eastern half is divided into a northern section of

8-1

New palace at Knossos, (*c.* 1600–1400 B.C.).

1. West porch
2. Corridor of the Procession
3. South propylon
4. Central court
5. "Theater area"
6. North propylon
7. Pillar hall
8. Magazines
9. Throne room
10. Palace shrine and lower verandas
11. Stepped porch
12. Grand staircase
13. Light area
14. Hall of the Colonnade
15. Hall of the Double Axes (principal reception room)
16. Queen's Megaron

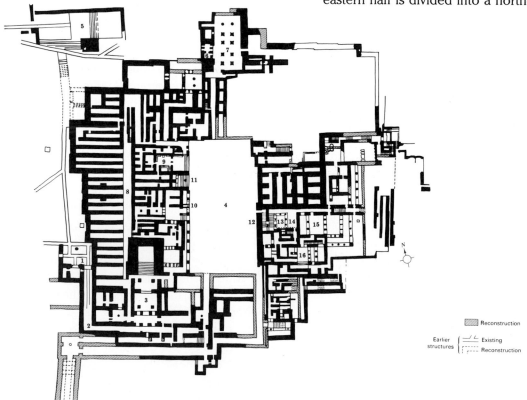

Reconstruction

Earlier structures { Existing
Reconstruction

workshops and a southern section of living quarters and reception rooms. Parts of the structure were three stories high, and interior staircases were built beside light wells (shafts open to the sky). Beneath the palace, terra cotta pipes provided an efficient drainage system. Columns had the typical Cretan cushion capital and downward-tapering shaft. Colorful frescoes showing scenes of processionals and bull games (see p. 83) adorned the walls.

CITADEL AT TIRYNS (Peloponnesus, *c.* 1400–1200 B.C.). This small, heavily fortified hilltop (Fig. 8-2) is better preserved than the fortress at Mycenae. The Greeks believed that Tiryns was the birthplace of Hercules. Although it has none of the expansiveness of Cretan palaces, it suggests more careful planning. The focus is the megaron, which may have its source in Hittite architecture (see p. 56). Huge, rough-cut stones form massive walls that contain passageways with corbeled vaults.

TREASURY OF ATREUS (Mycenae, *c.* 1300 B.C.). Of the nine *tholoi* (round tombs; sing., *tholos*) at Mycenae, this one (Fig. 8-3), mistakenly called the treasury of Atreus (king of Mycenae and father of Menelaus and Agamemnon of Trojan War acclaim)

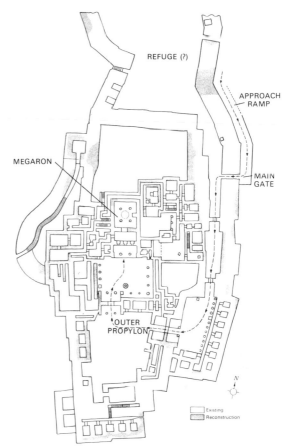

8-2
Plan of the citadel at Tiryns, (*c.* 1400–1200 B.C.).

8-3
Plan and section of the treasury of Atreus, Mycenae, (*c.* 1300 B.C.).

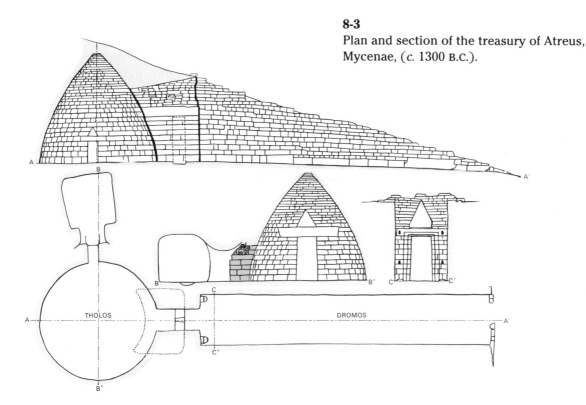

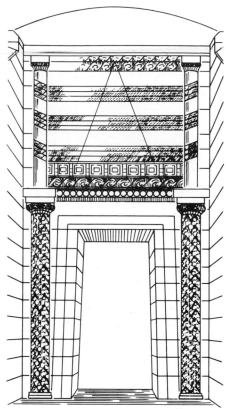

8-4
Relieving arch.

by its discoverer, Heinrich Schliemann, is the most impressive. Its diameter is 47′7″ and the top of the corbeled dome is 43′4″ from the floor. The span of the dome is the largest until the Roman Pantheon in the second century A.D. (see p. 124). The finely cut stones were buttressed and protected by the mound of earth that covered the exterior. The lintel over the door is protected from or relieved of the weight of the dome by a corbeled *relieving arch* (Fig. 8-4), originally filled by a decorated stone slab. Red and green marble embellished the entrance. Designs contained the running spiral, chevron, and petal forms characteristic of Cretan art, but these were used within more rigidly constricted framing shapes. Since the tomb was emptied in antiquity, we may never know who its original occupant was.

Painting

In Crete, the only painting that has been found in any quantity from the early and middle periods is on pottery. Stripes and soft mottled shapes were painted in red-brown or black on a lighter red-brown background. Toward the end of the early period, white designs were applied on a red-brown or black background. In the middle Minoan period (*c.* 2000 – 1550 B.C.), design motifs became bolder in contrast, surer in execution, and more varied. Running spirals, wavy lines, rosettes, lilies, palm trees, fish, seaweed, and net designs in white, red, orange, yellow, and black explode over the surfaces. The best examples are called *Kamares ware,* after the cave on Mt. Ida in which they were found. Late Minoan pottery painting exhibits several trends, some of which (the *Floral Style* and the *Marine Style*) continue the vitality of the earlier Kamares ware. Another style uses the same yellow, red, white, and black for more restrained, tightly grouped, and precisely repeated forms. This trend is also reflected in the so-called *Palace Style,* examples of which have been found only at Knossos and which represent the period of Mycenaean occupation rather than an indigenous Cretan art. Most of the Cretan wall paintings known to us come from the new palace at Knossos (*c.* 1600 – 1400 B.C.), and even these are fragmentary. As with the pottery, exuberance is combined with delicacy in drawing and color. True fresco is used; the images are of Cretans engaged in sports, processions, and ceremonies.

In the Cyclades, the style changes in pottery painting are similar to those of Crete, but they display less variety and sensitivity. Fragments of frescoes portraying plant and animal life in spontaneously painted flowing forms recall the art of Crete.

During the early and middle periods the mainland also developed pottery painting similar in style to that of Crete, but inferior in quality. The late period produced the ornate Palace Style, which the Mycenaeans carried to Crete. Fresco painting on the mainland was strongly influenced by Crete but tended toward rigid and static forms.

BULL GAMES, from the palace at Knossos (*c.* 1500 B.C., fresco, approx. 32″ high including border. Archeological Museum, Herakleion). A small room in the east wing of the palace was decorated with a sequence of scenes (Fig. 8-5) depicting a sport often shown in Cretan art. Male (red-skinned) and female (white-skinned) athletes grasp the horns of a charging bull and somersault over its back. Blue and yellow alternate as background colors. The light colors, supple curves, and wasp-waisted figures are typical of Cretan art.

8-5
Bull Games, from Knossos, (*c.* 1500 B.C.). Fresco, approx. 32″ high including border.   Archeological Museum, Herakleion.

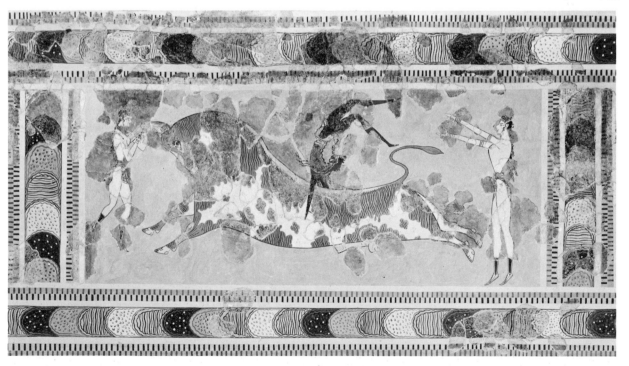

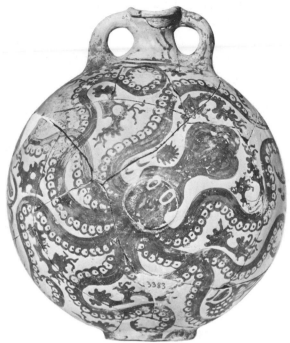

8-6
Octopus Vase, amphora from Palaikastro, (*c.* 1500
B.C.). Approx. 10″ high.   Archeological Museum, Herakleion.

OCTOPUS VASE (Palaikastro, *c.* 1500 B.C., approx. 10″
high. Archeological Museum, Herakleion).   The
lively patterns and references to nature that characterize so much of Cretan art are displayed in this
example of the late Minoan Marine Style (Fig. 8-6).

Sculpture

Although there is some evidence that the Cretans
carved life-sized statues in wood, the only sculpture now known to us is less than three feet high.
Idols, worshipers, children, animals, athletes
vaulting over bulls, and individual limbs used as
ex-votos (votive offerings for cures) were modeled, cast, or carved in terra cotta, glazed clay,
bronze, ivory, or gold. From the early and middle
periods come terra cotta figures found in commu-
nal tombs and mountaintop sanctuaries. These are
severely simplified female images with full, bell-
shaped skirts, and nearly nude males with the narrow waists and broad shoulders depicted in the
later frescoes. As in Egypt, male skin was red and
female skin was white or pale yellow. More anatomical and decorative detail is shown in the figures made of *faïence* (glazed clay) and in those of
ivory with gold fittings. Jewelry and stamp-seal
engravings of subjects ranging from geometric designs to animals and hieroglyphics reveal great
skill in miniature sculpture. The engravings were
made with stamp seals like those of Egypt rather
than cylinder seals like those of Mesopotamia.

Cycladic tombs have yielded up hundreds of
slablike marble statues varying in height from several inches to life size. These so-called *Cycladic
idols* are very simplified human forms with the
main body divisions indicated by grooves or
ridges. In silhouette, many resemble a violin
shape. Chronology is still in question, but most
seem to come from the early period.

On the mainland, there is little life-sized sculpture preserved, but dimensions are more ambi-
tious than in Crete. Gravestones bore geometric
designs and hunting scenes in relief, and architecture apparently carried sculptural reliefs, concentrated at major entrances.

EARTH-GODDESS WITH SNAKES (Knossos, *c.* 1600
B.C., faïence, 11½″ high. Archeological Museum, Herakleion).   This small Middle Minoan figure (Fig.

8-7) is one of two found in stone-lined pits in the palace. Although we are not certain that she is a goddess, her divinity is assumed on the basis of other Cretan art depicting females in control of animals and nature. These may all be different forms of a single mother-goddess. The jackets, bare breasts, and full, ground-length skirts seem to have been standard costume for religious festivals.

LION GATE (Mycenae, *c.* 1300 B.C., limestone, triangular slab approx. 9½' high).   The relief fits within an opening formed by the corbeled relieving arch above and the lintel below (Fig. 8-8). The central column symbolized the strength and unity of My-cenae. The heads of the powerfully modeled lions were attached separately and were turned to confront the visitor approaching the gate from the approach ramp, which lies within the protection of the city wall.

VAPHIO CUPS, from a tholos tomb at Vaphio (*c.* 1500 B.C., gold, approx. 3½" high. National Museum, Athens).   Each of the pair of cups (Fig. 8-9) is made of two sheets of gold, the outer sheet worked in repoussé (hammered out from the back) and lined with a smooth inner sheet. The reliefs depict the trapping of bulls in a net by men with Cretan bodies and costumes. The cups could

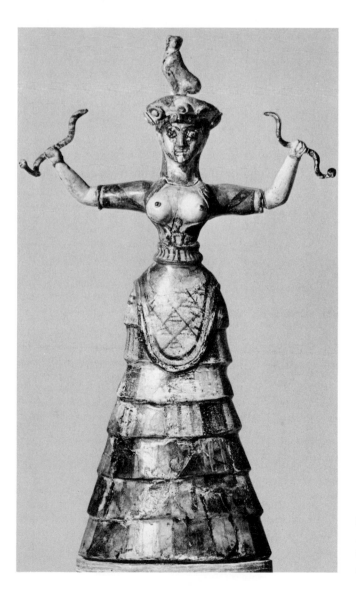

8-7
Earth-Goddess with Snakes, from Knossos, (*c.* 1600 B.C.). Faïence, approx. 11 ½" high.
Archeological Museum, Herakleion.

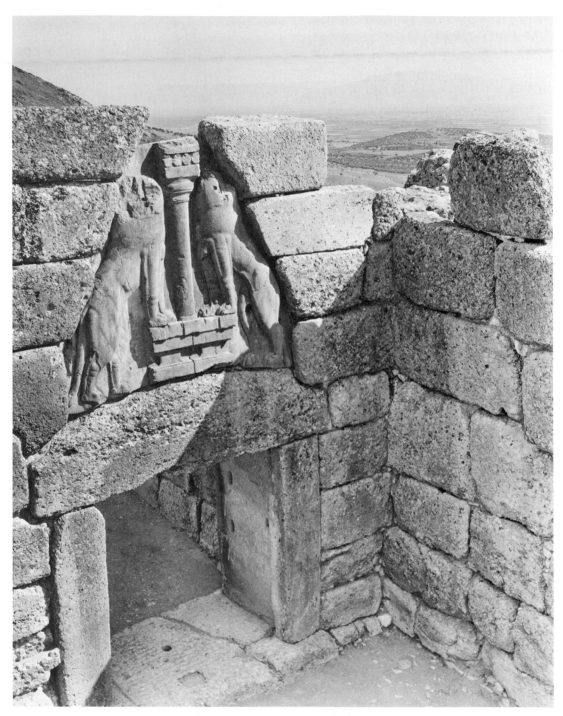

8-8
Lion Gate, Mycenae, *(c.* 1300 B.C.). Limestone, relief panel approx. 9 ½′ high.

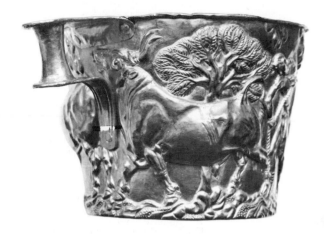

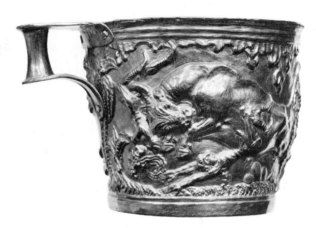

8-9

Vaphio Cups, (*c.* 1500 B.C.). Gold with repoussé decoration, approx. 3 ½″ high.   National Museum, Athens.

be Cretan work or Mycenaean art under the influence of Crete. The action, anatomy, and foliage reveal careful observation of nature.

Suggestions for Further Study

Branigan, Keith. *The Foundations of Palatial Crete: A Survey of Crete in the Early Bronze Age.* New York: Praeger, 1970.

Demargne, Pierre. *Aegean Art: The Origins of Greek Art* (The Arts of Mankind). Translated by Stuart Gilbert and James Emmons. London: Thames & Hudson, 1964.

Hafner, German. *Art of Crete, Mycenae, and Greece.* New York: Abrams, 1968.

Hampe, Roland, and Erika Simon. *The Birth of Greek Art from the Mycenaean to the Archaic Period.* New York: Oxford University Press, 1981.

Hutchinson, Richard Wyatt. *Prehistoric Crete.* Baltimore: Penguin Books, 1962.

Marinatos, Spyridon, and Max Hirmer. *Crete and Mycenae.* New York: Abrams, 1960.

Palmer, Leonard Robert. *A New Guide to the Palace of Knossos.* New York: Praeger, 1969.

Vermeule, Emily. *Greece in the Bronze Age.* Chicago: University of Chicago Press, 1964.

9

Greek Art

1100 – 100 B.C.

About 1100 B.C., the Dorian invasions seem to have been the final step leading to the amalgamation of peoples that became the basis for Greek culture. By 100 B.C., Greece was part of the Roman Empire. In the intervening years, Greek culture's underlying theme was humankind and the rational faculty for understanding and perfecting oneself and nature. The climate favored outdoor activity, influencing architecture directly and painting and sculpture indirectly. The periodic Olympic Games (first recorded in 776 B.C.) reflected the Greek interest in the physical life and the human body. Yet the Greeks grew even more interested in the development of the mind, especially the power of reason, and in the conception of ideal forms for all things. Perfection was sought within carefully chosen limits or rules. That humans are the measure of all things was basic to this culture, and even the gods were seen in human form with few combinations of human and animal like those found in Egyptian religion. For art the most important Greek gods (and their Roman equivalents) are listed in the accompanying table. The most com-

GREEK (AND ROMAN) DEITIES IMPORTANT TO THE STUDY OF ART

Greek god	Roman equivalent	Description
Zeus	Jupiter	Lord of the sky and supreme ruler; wielder of thunderbolts
Hera	Juno	Wife and sister of Zeus and goddess of marriage
Poseidon	Neptune	God of the sea, recognized by his trident spear
Athena	Minerva	Originally a war goddess, but more commonly patroness of civilized life and wisdom
Artemis	Diana	Huntress and patroness of wildlife and the young; often shown with bow and arrows
Apollo	Apollo	God of poetry, music, truth, prophecy, and — in later mythology — god of the sun; sometimes shown with a lyre or bow and arrows
Aphrodite	Venus	Goddess of love and beauty
Hermes	Mercury	Messenger of the gods and patron of commerce; shown with winged sandals and a wand of entwined serpents
Dionysus	Bacchus	God of wine and feasting — a latecomer to Greek mythology
Pan	Faunus	God of shepherds and flocks, a mischievous creature largely in human form but with horns and goat's legs
satyrs	satyrs	Creatures who look like Pan and seek all sensual pleasures
centaurs		Creatures who are half man and half horse and are considered (with the exception of Chiron, a wise and just teacher, who instructed many of the Greek heroes) to be savage

mon idea of life after death was that of a gray world of drifting spirits, and in contrast to the Egyptians, the Greeks emphasized life, an earthly life of balanced attainments, based on the idea that the complete human is governed by reason and enlightened by wide interests. Consequently Greek tombs and burial customs were simple.

GEOMETRIC (900–700 B.C.) AND ARCHAIC (700–500 B.C.) PERIODS

Sculpture

Greek sculpture was mainly religious. Of the works preserved from the Geometric period, many are small bronze votive statuettes dedicated to the gods. During this period, copper and fired clay were also common materials, and it is probable that there were large-scale wooden statues that have disappeared. Some of the metal statuettes were made of sheet metal riveted together; others were cast using a sand mold or the lost-wax process. Divisions between the parts of the body tend to be exaggerated, and some parts are modified according to the sculptor's instinct for design. The result is usually a rigid schematic form that resembles Egyptian art. This strict geometric order is the basis for the name given to the period. The stylistic trend during the Geometric period is toward more flowing transitions between body parts and more natural human form.

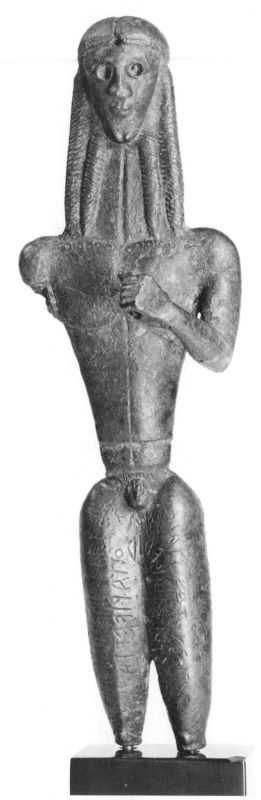

9-1
"Mantiklos Apollo," (*c.* 700 B.C.). Bronze,
approx. 8" high.   03.997, Francis Bartlett Collection.
Courtesy, Museum of Fine Arts, Boston.

After the middle of the seventh century B.C.,
life-sized stone sculpture became more common,
and the geometric rigidity of the earlier period
slowly softened. Nudity, so rare in Egyptian art,
occurs early in Greek sculptures of the male body.
Researchers have found many statues of young
men (*kouroi;* sing., *kouros*) sculpted in the seventh and early sixth centuries B.C.; their frontal
poses, stiff joints, and symmetrical hair and musculature recall Egyptian sculpture. It is rarely clear
whether they were meant to be gods or mortals. A
few works are signed, but little is known of sculptors from the Archaic period. A number of standing maidens (*korai;* sing., *kore*) have also been
discovered. Their pose and clothing (female nudity was not represented until much later) have the
same strict order as that of the male figures. On
many kouroi and korai the corners of the mouth
are turned up in the so-called Archaic smile.

APOLLO (*c.* 7th cen. B.C., bronze, 8" high. Museum of
Fine Arts, Boston).   This Archaic work (Fig. 9-1)
remains Geometric in style and has an inscription
on the thighs dedicating the image to Apollo. The
words ("Mantiklos dedicated me to . . .") imply
that, for the Greeks, each work of art was an independent being.

STANDING YOUTH, from Attica (late 7th cen. B.C.,
marble, 78" high. Metropolitan Museum of Art, New
York).   This Archaic kouros statue (Fig. 9-2) reveals its ancestry in the Geometric style. The frontal pose and the insistent symmetry are similar to
Egyptian work, but there is no back-slab, the arms
are separated from the body, slightly opening up
the form, and the complete nudity is unlike most
Egyptian images.

Painting

Greek Geometric and Archaic painting is known to
us only through vase decoration, but vase painting
was an important medium until the fourth century
B.C. Early Geometric painting consists of geometric shapes in registers. The human body was reduced to sharply divided and simplified parts. The
basic colors were produced by painting red-
brown clay with a thinned mixture of clay that
turned black in firing. Other colors and white were

sometimes added. The technique that employs black shapes on the lighter reddish background is called *black-figure* vase painting.

Black-figure painting continued through most of the Archaic period and into the third quarter of the sixth century B.C., when it began to give way to *red-figure* painting, a technique in which the background is filled in with brown-black, leaving a base color of red-orange or warm tan for the figures. During the Archaic period, the figures became more lifelike, and geometric ornament was reduced. Scenes depict events from mythology, and ornament includes animals and floral motifs. Anatomy acquired more flexibility and naturalness of shape and proportion, but conventional formulas still dominated the forms. Beginning in the second quarter of the sixth century B.C., Athens was the center of great activity in vase painting. Both potters and painters began to sign their work (sometimes one man did both vase and painting).

ATHENIAN GRAVE VASE (8th cen. B.C., 61" high. No. 804, National Museum, Athens).   The geometry of the figures in this funeral scene (Fig. 9-3) places it easily in the large expanse of purely geometric decoration. One of the most common geometric patterns looks like a row of key ends standing upright; this is called the *Greek key* or *fret* and is still in use today. Many grave vases of this type

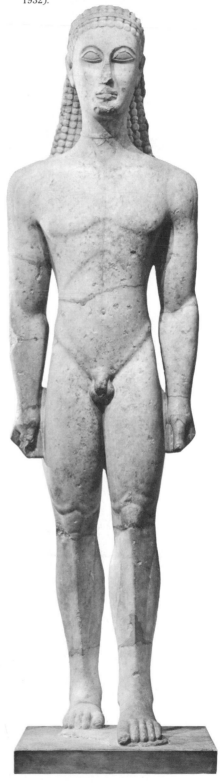

9-2
Standing Youth, kouros from Attica, (late seventh century B.C.). Marble, 78" high.   Metropolitan Museum of Art, New York (Fletcher Fund, 1932).

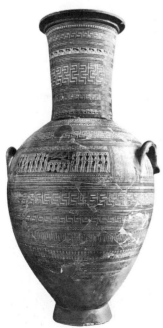

9-3
Dipylon Vase, Geometric amphora, (eighth century B.C.). Approx. 61" high.
National Museum, Athens.

9-4 EXEKIAS, *Ajax and Achilles Playing Draughts,* vase painting, (550–525 B.C.).   Vatican Museums, Rome.

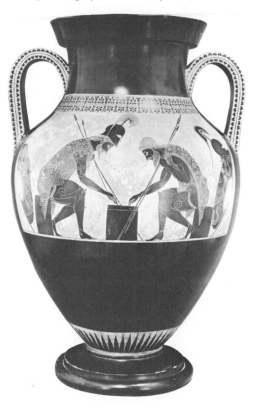

have been found in the Dipylon Cemetery in Athens. They are often from 5 to 6 feet high, and some have perforated bottoms through which liquid offerings could drip onto the grave. Tall vases with two handles were called *amphoras.*

AJAX AND ACHILLES PLAYING DRAUGHTS (550–525 B.C., vase 24″ high. Vatican Museums, Rome). This black-figured scene (Fig. 9-4) decorates an amphora and was done by Exekias, one of the outstanding Archaic vase painters. Geometric ornament is sparse. The frontally seen eye (noted in connection with Egyptian painting, p. 71) is still used with the long-nosed profile of earlier work, and taut, flat shapes seem to bend stiffly at the joints (compare this with Archaic sculpture). Figures are anchored to a common base line; there is no effort to suggest round mass or deep space. The curve of the men's backs repeats the curve of the vase. The diagonals of the spears intensify the focus of attention on the game — the center of the obvious axial balance — and relate the composition to the handles of the vase, which seem to continue the lines of the spears.

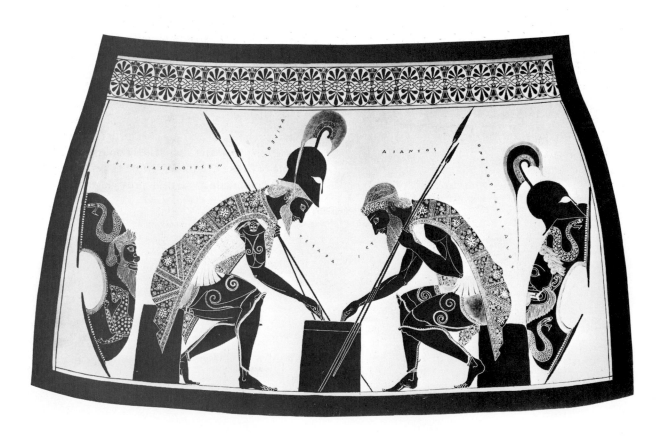

Architecture

Our knowledge of architecture from the Geometric and Archaic periods is incomplete. The most important buildings seem to have been temples to the gods and treasuries to hold offerings. Prior to 650 B.C., the Greeks built with wood and sun-dried brick; hence we have few remains that date from before that time. As the use of stone increased, some of the wooden structural forms were imitated in stone and became decorative rather than structural. Limestone was the usual material, and it was sometimes covered with a white stucco made of marble dust. Roofs were tile, with colored clay ornaments along the tops and edges. The basic structural system was post and lintel. The dominant plan for temples and treasuries was rectangular; from a stepped base, windowless walls rose to enclose one to three cellae (temple rooms) (Fig. 9-5a, c, d, e, f). A *peristyle* (a covered colonnade that surrounds a building or a court) was common. A second type of temple was the *tholos,* which was circular in shape and usually had a peristyle (Fig. 9-5b). The rhythmic alternation of columns and spaces gives the exterior of most Greek temples a lighter, more open form than that of Egyptian architecture. The modest scale, simplicity, and clearly defined limits of Greek buildings focus attention on the proportions and the relationship of the parts of the whole form, which normally uses obvious balance, either axial or central. Two of the three basic types of Greek columns were developed during the Archaic period: the Doric and the Ionic, the latter being more prevalent in Ionia in Asia Minor. These columns each had

9-5

Types of Greek temples. (a) Temple of Hephaistos, Athens: peripteral temple (surrounded by colonnade) with cella in antis (columns set within antae, the projecting walls) at both ends. (b) Tholos, Epidauros: tholos (round temple). (c) Temple B, Selinus, Sicily: prostyle temple (columns in front of antae). (d) Athenian Treasury, Delphi: temple in antis. (e) Temple of Athena Nike, Athens: amphiprostyle temple (prostyle at both ends). (f) Temple of Zeus Olympios, Athens: dipteral temple (double colonnade) with cella prostyle at both ends.

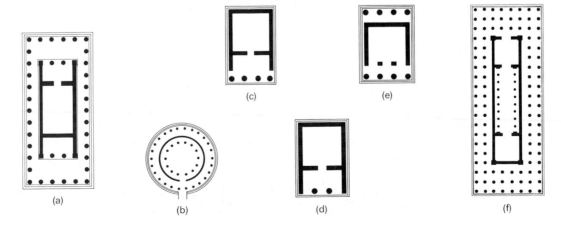

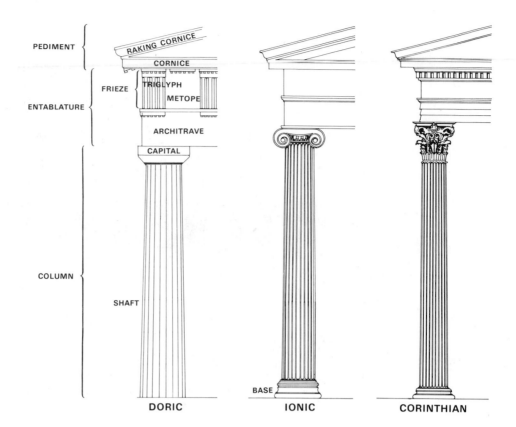

PEDIMENT
RAKING CORNICE
CORNICE
FRIEZE — **TRIGLYPH** **METOPE**
ENTABLATURE
ARCHITRAVE
CAPITAL
COLUMN
SHAFT
BASE
DORIC   **IONIC**   **CORINTHIAN**

9-6
Greek orders.

a special *entablature* to match. The combination of column and entablature is called an *order* (Fig. 9-6).

TEMPLE OF CERES (Paestum, late 6th cen. B.C., limestone, approx. 48′ x 108′).   Only the peristyle remains from this Doric temple (Fig. 9-7) built in the Greek colony at Paestum on the Italian peninsula. The ponderous proportions of the pediment (see Fig. 9-6 and p. 95) and the abrupt mushrooming of the capitals are typical of Archaic temples and indicate some awkwardness on the part of the provincial builders.

FIFTH CENTURY B.C.

Architecture

Despite the wars with Persia, the Athenian struggle for empire, and the Peloponnesian War, the fifth century B.C. showed remarkable activity in the arts. Of the many types of buildings, temples and treasuries continued to be most important. These are often found in sacred precincts such as Delphi,

Aegina, Olympia, and the Acropolis at Athens. Although systematic city planning appeared in the fifth century, vast schemes of axial planning with space and mass were not developed until much later by the Romans; the sacred precincts of the Greeks are, by comparison, more freely arranged. The Athenian Acropolis presents some alignment of parts, however, and contains the most celebrated examples of fifth-century architecture. The major buildings, which owe their beginnings to the statesman Pericles, date from the second half of the century. Marble was used instead of the more economical limestone, and extraordinary efforts were made to achieve the most satisfying proportions and the highest quality of stone carving in both Ionic and Doric temples. The Doric order (Fig. 9-6) received a subtler *entasis* (the slight outward curving of the shaft) than in either the previous or the succeeding century, and the capital became a smoother transition between the vertical shaft and the horizontal entablature. In the most refined Doric temples, the temple platform is slightly domed and all columns lean inward almost imperceptibly, giving the building a more compact, self-contained unity that reinforces the stable

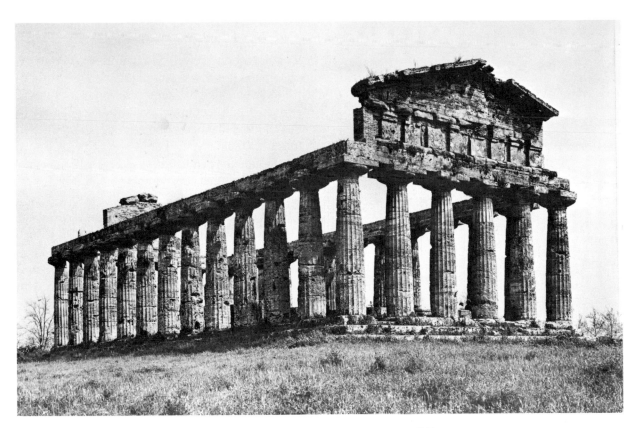

9-7
Temple of Ceres, Paestum, (Late sixth century B.C.).

equilibrium of vertical and horizontal lines. Unlike the Doric, the Ionic order employed a very slender shaft (sometimes with very slight entasis), a base between shaft and floor, a three-part architrave, and usually a continuous frieze instead of the Doric metopes and triglyphs (Fig. 9-6). The third Greek order, the Corinthian, appeared in the second half of the century. It differed from the Ionic only in its leafy capital. The use of two or three orders in the same building became common toward the end of the fifth century. Temples were richly decorated with sculpted moldings (Fig. 9-8) and figure sculpture. Major sculptural compositions were placed in the *pediments* (the triangular gables at the ends of the building), in the frieze area, and sometimes on the outside of the cella walls. As with sculpture, parts of Greek architecture were painted. Blue was common for pediment backgrounds and for Ionic friezes; red was often used as a background for metope sculpture and for capitals and architraves.

PARTHENON, *built by Ictinos and Callicrates* (Acropolis, Athens, 447–432 B.C., marble, approx. 228' x 104' with columns approx. 34' high). The

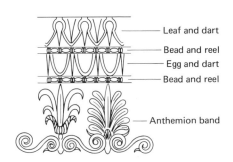

Leaf and dart
Bead and reel
Egg and dart
Bead and reel

Anthemion band

9-8
Greek moldings.

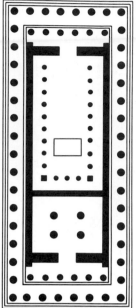

9-9
Plan of the Parthenon.

Parthenon (Figs. 9-9 and 9-10) has the most subtle proportions of all Greek Doric temples and has long been considered the high point of Greek architecture. It is the major building on the Acropolis, was dedicated to Athena, patroness of Athens, and sheltered a colossal gold-and-ivory statue of the goddess that had disappeared by the fifth century A.D. Originally, the Parthenon had sculpture in the pediments, in the metopes (Fig. 9-19), and in a frieze around the outside of the cella wall.

ERECHTHEUM, *built by Mnesicles* (Acropolis, Athens, 421–405 B.C., marble, approx. 80′ x 90′). This irregularly shaped temple (Fig. 9-11) is famous for the subtle proportions and precise carving of its Ionic order and for its porch with *caryatids* (columns in the form of human figures).

Sculpture

For sculpture, as for architecture, the fifth century was a time of brilliant activity. Sculpture was present in public places, in sacred precincts, and on temples. Bronze and marble were the main materials. Subjects were usually taken from mythology, although there are occasional portraits, figures of athletes or heroes, and representations

9-10 ICTINOS and CALLICRATES, Parthenon, Acropolis, Athens, (447–432 B.C.). Marble, approx. 228′ × 104′ with columns approx. 34′ high.

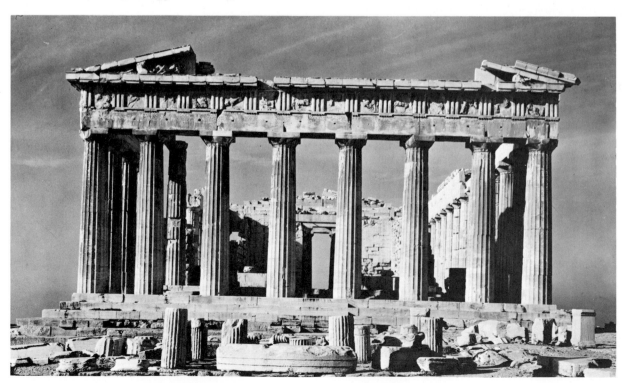

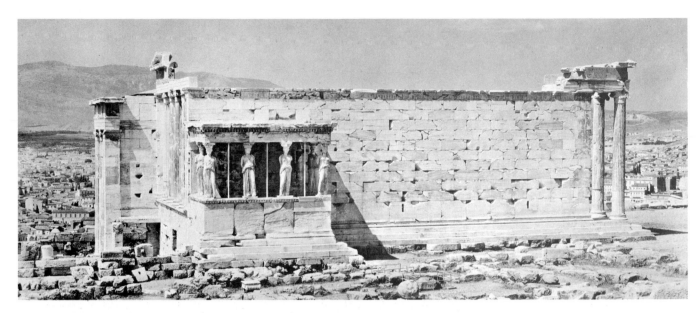

9-11 MNESICLES, Erechtheum, Acropolis, Athens, (421–405 B.C.). Marble, approx. 80′ × 90′.

of animals. Rather than depicting specific historical events, the Greeks used allegory that borrowed themes from mythology. Early fifth-century sculpture represents ideal youthful bodies with simplified, symmetrical anatomy. Proportions are more natural than in earlier work, but action is still slightly stiff, and the musculature is hard. Toward the middle of the century, the work of the great sculptor Myron shows a slight softening and increased flexibility in pose. After mid-century, Phidias started a trend toward more active, flexible poses and greater expression of emotion, only to change in his later work to more restrained action and a calmer, poised equilibrium of pose. His rival, Polyclitus, also concerned himself with ideal form, monumental dignity, and the rhythmic grace of the *contrapposto* pose (in which the body relaxes with the weight on one leg, and the tilt of the hips is countered by the tilt of the shoulders). Late fifth-century sculpture suggested softer flesh and more flexible poses. Throughout the century, however, space remains strictly limited. In reliefs, a blank background restricts action to a shallow layer of depth; in freestanding statues, the form opens predominantly in two dimensions — shallow crates would suffice for packing the works — and there is almost no spiral twisting of the torso.

PEDIMENT SCULPTURES, *from the Temple of Aphaia at Aegina* (marble with traces of paint,

slightly less than life size. Glyptothek, Munich). Three sets of pedimental sculpture were found in debris at the base of the temple, apparently dating from 510 to 490 B.C. Scenes of the Trojan War are depicted, but the exact arrangement of the pediments is not certain. The reconstruction of the east pediment (Fig. 9-12) utilizes obvious axial balance in poses and actions within the triangular pediment. From the tall figure of the goddess Athena, action diverges until it is countered by movements converging from the corners. The poses are more open and active than those in Archaic work, and the anatomy shows more observation of nature; there is, however, still some stiffness of pose and hardness of flesh. The pose of the *Fallen Warrior* (Fig. 9-13), for example, is complex and generally natural; yet some details, such as the misplaced navel, indicate reliance on earlier stylistic conventions rather than on observation of nature.

ARTEMISION STATUE (c. 460–450 B.C., bronze, eyes formerly inlaid, 6′10″ high. National Museum, Athens).   One of the finest of the votive statues that have been found, this work (Fig. 9-14) was discovered in the sea off Cape Artemision. The right hand originally held an object that is now lost, possibly a thunderbolt (indicating Zeus) or a trident (for Poseidon). The musculature and pose show the degree of flexibility, vitality, and poise

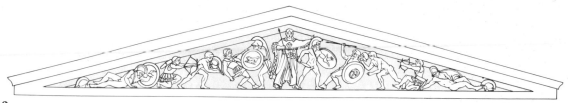

9-12
Reconstruction drawing of the east pediment of the
Temple of Aphaia at Aegina, (*c.* 490 B.C.).

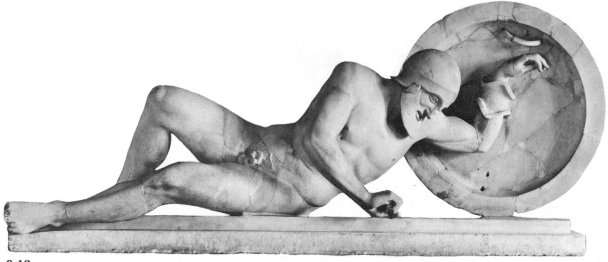

9-13
Fallen Warrior, from the east pediment of the Temple of Aphaia at Aegina. 6′ long.
Staatliche Antikensammlungen, Munich.

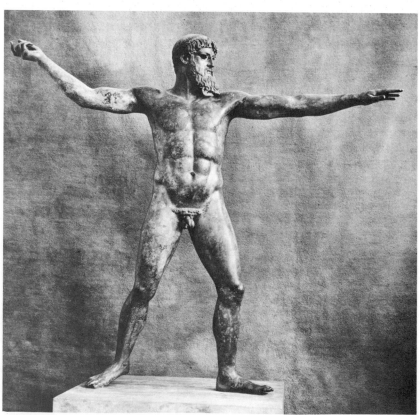

9-14
Artemision Statue, (*c.* 460–
450 B.C.). Bronze, 6′ 10″ high.
National Museum, Athens.

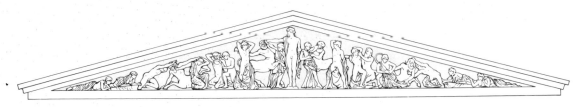

9-15
Reconstruction drawing of the west pediment of the Temple of Zeus at Olympia (465–456 B.C.). Approx. 91′ wide.

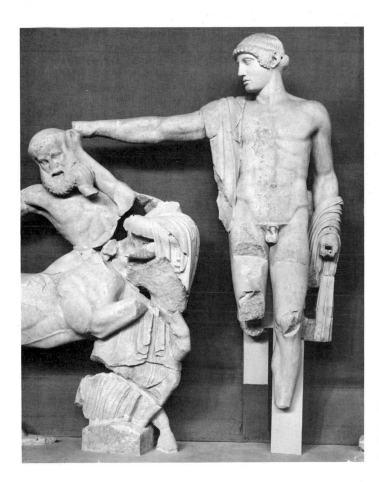

9-16
Apollo, from the west pediment of the Temple of Zeus at Olympia. Marble, over life size.   Archeological Museum, Olympia.

characteristic of work just before mid-century. The composition opens mainly in two dimensions, with severely limited depth.

PEDIMENT SCULPTURES, *from the Temple of Zeus at Olympia* (465–456 B.C., marble, central figures approx. 10′ high. Archeological Museum, Olympia, and Louvre, Paris).   The eastern pediment showed the preparation for the chariot race between Oenomaus and Pelops; the western pediment depicted Apollo observing the battle between the Lapiths and centaurs (Figs. 9-15 and 9-16). Stylistically, the work is close to the *Artemision Statue.*

DISCUS-THROWER, by Myron (c. 450 B.C., reconstruction of a Roman copy, 4′6″ high. Museo delle Terme, Rome).   Myron chose to depict the moment of equilibrium before the forward swing of the throw (Fig. 9-17). The symmetry of the musculature continues to suggest ideal form, and the composition is very limited in depth, but the pose is more complex than that of the *Artemision Statue.*

SPEAR-BEARER, by Polyclitus (450–440 B.C., Roman marble copy, 6′6″ high. Museo Nazionale, Naples). Polyclitus was known for his theories of ideal

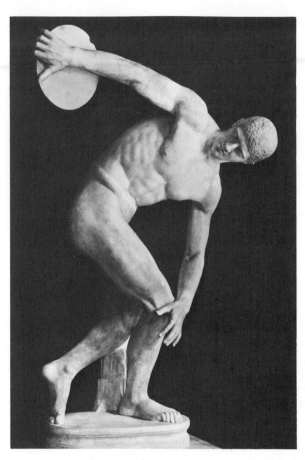

9-17   MYRON, *Discus-Thrower (Discobolus)*, Roman marble copy after a bronze original dated *c.* 450 B.C. Life size.   Museo delle Terme, Rome.

proportions. The muscular figure (Fig. 9-18) attains flexibility through its contrapposto pose even though the hips and shoulders are aligned in the same shallow space. The only strong three-dimensional extension is the forward-reaching arm. The hair is organized in groups of wavy lines, and the face is simplified in broad planes. The musculature is still quite firm in the torso, but increasing softness and detail are evident in the arms, hands, and knees.

LAPITH FIGHTING WITH CENTAUR (447–432 B.C., marble, 4′8″ x 4′8″. British Museum, London). The Parthenon metopes, of which this (Fig. 9-19) is an example, were probably carved under the direction of Phidias. Here the rhythmic curves of the cloak unite and soften the divergent thrusts of the bodies. The blank background, which limits spatial extension, is typical of Greek reliefs. Despite the weathering of the stone, the carving still suggests the softness of skin overlying the bone structure of the ribs and the muscles of the abdomen.

Painting

We must turn again to vases, for the celebrated wall paintings of Polygnotus and Zeuxis are lost. Descriptions by ancient writers indicate that the wall paintings contained some illusion of depth and that theories of perspective had been formulated. The growing interest in depth may have contributed to the decline, after the fifth century, of the importance of vase painting, for depth in vase painting works against the form of the vase by denying its surface. Although red-figure painting continued during the fifth century, there was an increasing tendency to use delicate colors and light linear drawings on vases with white grounds. Figures became rounder, softer, and more flexible as contours overlapped to indicate folds in the flesh. Objects were drawn with more *foreshortening* (diagonal extension into space toward the observer); the eye appears in profile for the first time.

ATHENIAN MIXING BOWL, *from Orvieto* (475–450 B.C., approx. 21″ high. No. G 341, Louvre, Paris). This work (Fig. 9-20) is traditional in its red-figure technique, but it demonstrates the increasing interest in natural anatomy, mass, and space. It

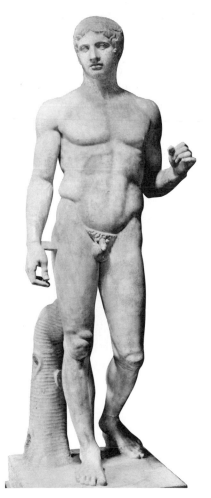

9-18   POLYCLITUS, *Spear-Bearer (Doryphorus),* Roman marble copy after original dated *c.* 450–440 B.C. 6′ 6″ high.   Museo Nazionale, Naples.

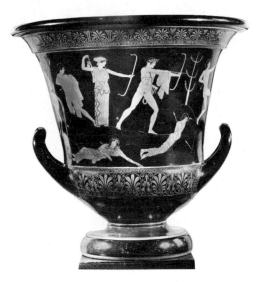

9-20
Athenian mixing bowl from Orvieto, (475–450 B.C.).   No. G 341, Louvre, Paris.

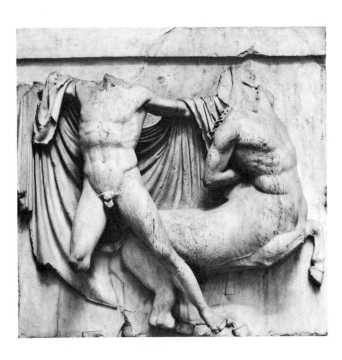

9-19
Lapith Fighting with Centaur, metope from the Parthenon. Marble, 4′8″ high.
British Museum, London.

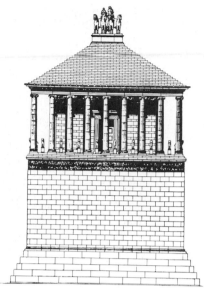

9-21
Reconstruction drawing of the tomb of
Mausolus (Mausoleum) at
Halicarnassus, (353 B.C.).

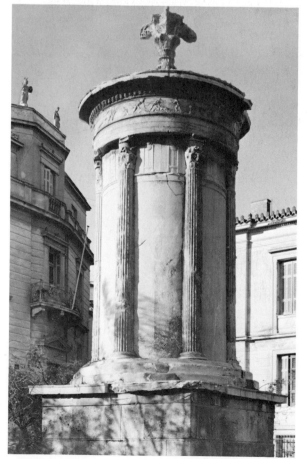

9-22
Choragic monument of Lysicrates, Athens, (*c.* 334 B.C.).

depicts warrior heroes (perhaps the Argonauts) in
casual poses freed from a common base line; the
figures are placed at various levels, suggesting different degrees of depth. Overlapping contours
and foreshortening imply mass in space.

FOURTH CENTURY B.C.

Architecture

Defeat in the Peloponnesian War put an end to
Athens' leadership in architecture. During the
fourth century, many important buildings were
produced in cities like Delphi, Tegea, Epidauros,
and—in Asia Minor—at Priene, Ephesus, and
Halicarnassus. Efforts spread to a wider variety of
types of buildings, many of them secular: *stoas*
(colonnaded, open-fronted sheds used in city
centers as promenades and shopping areas), theaters, council halls, and tombs all received special
attention, although they had prototypes in earlier
centuries. All types of architecture used one or
more of the three orders. The Corinthian capital
shifted from interior to exterior use, and there was
widespread development of the Ionic temple, particularly in Asia Minor. Theaters usually consisted
of a slightly more than semicircular area of tiered
seats set into a hillside, a round central space (or-
chestra), and a structure consisting of a raised
stage and a building that provided an architectural
background and housed dressing rooms and properties. Council halls were oval, square, or rectangular, often with tiered seats around a central altar.
The tholos temple reached a height of subtlety and
richness of design, and tomb architecture acquired monumental scale.

MAUSOLEUM (Halicarnassus, 353 B.C., 136′ high).
The building (Fig. 9-21) is no longer extant, and its
exact form is uncertain, although we have discrip-
tions from ancient literature. Standing on a rectangular base, it had an Ionic peristyle and was
topped by a stepped pyramid and a *quadriga*
(chariot pulled by four horses). The structure
served as a tomb for Mausolus, a satrap of the
Persian kings. In antiquity, it was considered one
of the Seven Wonders of the World.

CHORAGIC MONUMENT OF LYSICRATES (Athens, 334 B.C., limestone and marble, 54′ high). This monument (Fig. 9-22), developed from the tholos form, was built to commemorate a victory in a choral contest. It seems to be the earliest example of the exterior use of Corinthian columns. The small size recalls the decrease in monumental building in Athens after the defeat in the Peloponnesian War in 404 B.C.

Sculpture

Trends that began in the late fifth century grew more evident during the fourth century. Stone and bronze took on the softness of flesh, contrapposto poses became more pronounced, and poses opened up three-dimensionally, with more spiral twisting in the torso. Stone surfaces were polished until the details softened, as though seen through a veil. The famous sculptor Praxiteles led these developments in the mid-fourth century. In some work, the serene poise of earlier Greek art gave way to representations of violent motion; and deep-set eyes and beetling brows created an expression of suffering or consternation.

HERMES WITH THE INFANT DIONYSUS (*c.* 340 B.C., marble, 6′11″ high. Archeological Museum, Olympia). The group (Fig. 9-23) may be an original by Praxiteles. Hermes, whose divine powers were of a particularly intellectual bent, was shown teasing the young god of wine, who often represented human passions, by holding some grapes beyond the child's reach. The cloudlike softness of the modeling, the three-dimensional extension of the arms, the spiral twist of the body, and the relaxed contrapposto pose are typical of later work.

BATTLE OF GREEKS AND AMAZONS, from the east frieze of the Mausoleum at Halicarnassus (*c.* 350 B.C., marble, 35″ high. British Museum, London). Ancient writers say that the east frieze of the Mausoleum was carved by Scopas, one of the most famous sculptors of the time. In the surviving fragments of the frieze (Fig. 9-24) tense poses and contorted faces express a physical and emotional violence quite unlike the characteristic poise and equilibrium of earlier work. Scopas reveals an interest in depicting the inner man; his style is

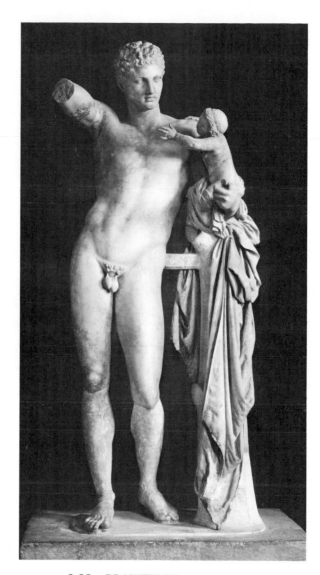

9-23 PRAXITELES, *Hermes with the Infant Dionysus,* (*c.* 340 B.C.). Marble, 6′11″ high.
Archeological Museum, Olympia.

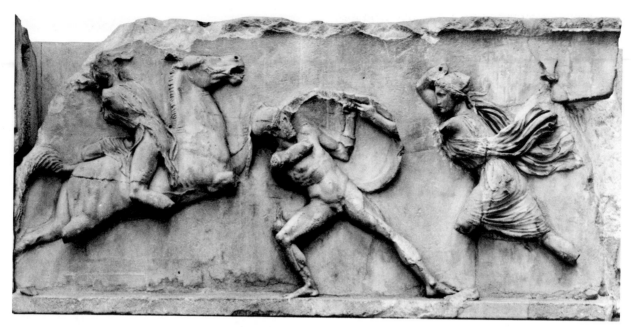

9-24 SCOPAS (?), *Battle of Greeks and Amazons,*
from the east frieze of the Mausoleum at
Halicarnassus, (*c.* 350 B.C.). Marble, 35″ high.
British Museum, London.

characterized by deep-set eyes and expressions
of anguish.

HELLENISTIC PERIOD
323–100 B.C.

The Greeks called themselves Hellenes, and their
culture is often called *Hellenic.* With the conquests
of Alexander the Great, Greek culture, modified by
local cultures, spread over the civilized world. This
international Greek-inspired culture is called *Hellenistic.* Various dates are given for the Hellenistic
period, but 323 B.C., the year of Alexander's death,
and 100 B.C., a year well after Rome had conquered Greece (146 B.C.) and had begun to transform Hellenistic art into Roman art, can be considered the approximate beginning and end dates.

Architecture

The Hellenistic period saw the rise of important art
centers in places far from Greece, such as Pergamon, Rhodes, Tralles, and Alexandria. An increase in the wealth of many cities led to larger
agoras (city centers) with more elegant surrounding stoas. A grid plan of rectangular blocks and
intersecting streets gave order to some cities. As in
the fourth century B.C., there was a wide variety of
building types. Town houses often had two stories

built around a central court, and, in better houses, the court eventually acquired a peristyle. Stone, mud brick, and wood were enhanced by stucco and painted walls. In temple-building, the Doric order became less popular. When it was used, columns were more slender and wall surfaces more ornate; semicircular extensions *(apses)* sometimes emphasized one end of the cella interior. Ionic and Corinthian temples were occasionally raised on high platforms, prefiguring later Roman temples. Some of the Ionic temples were *pseudo-dipteral* in plan; that is, the inner peristyle of the *dipteral* plan (Fig. 9-5f) was omitted, leaving a deep porch around the cella.

ALTAR OF ZEUS AND ATHENA (Pergamon, 180–150 B.C., marble; no longer extant except in reconstruction).   The altar was a U-shaped *peripteral* building (one surrounded by columns, as in Fig. 9-5a) on a base 17′6″ high and about 112′ × 120′ wide (Fig. 9-25). The order was Ionic, and the base was heavily decorated with sculpture, typifying the increasing complexity and variety of architectural shapes and the tendency to cover more of the surfaces with decoration.

9-25 West front of the Altar of Zeus and Athena, Pergamon (restored), (180–150 B.C.).
Antiken-Sammlung der Staatliche Museen zu Berlin Hauptstadt der DDR.

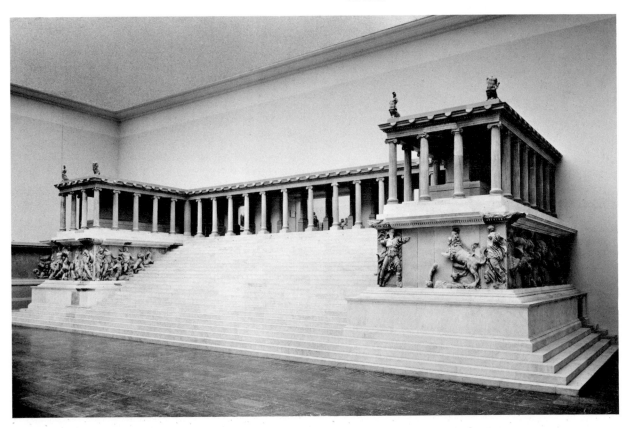

TEMPLE OF ZEUS OLYMPIOS, *by Cossutius* (Athens, marble, begun in 174 B.C. from the designs of the Roman architect Cossutius, and completed in A.D. 132 under the reign of the Roman Emperor Hadrian). The temple (Fig. 9-26), which measures 135' × 354', demonstrates the increasing interest in the ornate Corinthian order. The unusually thick columns are over 55 feet high, and their capitals influenced Roman architecture in Italy. The group of thirteen columns still standing at one corner of the temple is evidence of its original vastness.

Sculpture

Hellenistic sculpture, like Hellenistic architecture, was produced at creative centers far from the Greek mainland. Because artists moved from one center to another, it is hard to assign local styles to the different areas. Most sculpture of this period was not architectural but set in open spaces, in freestanding figures or groups. Portraits and specific historical events were common subjects and encouraged a detailed realism, as did the developing taste for *genre* subjects (scenes from everyday activity), which were sometimes humorous, undignified, or pathetic, and often revealed

9-26 COSSUTIUS, Temple of Zeus Olympios, Athens, (planned *c.* 174 B.C.).

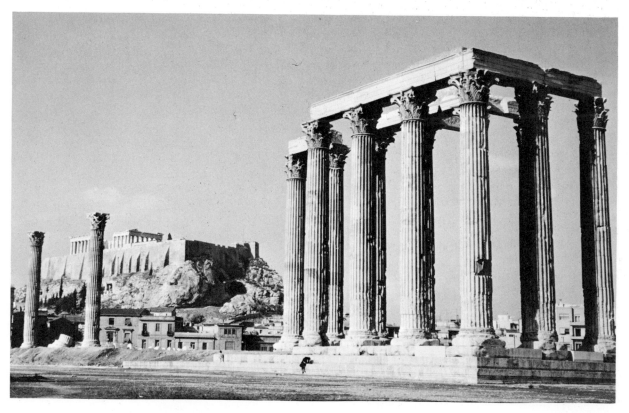

human character. Proportions became more elongated, figures became taller and more slender, poses were restless and required more three-dimensional space, and surfaces were treated with greater refinement than previously.

APOXYOMENOS, by Lysippos (original done *c.* 330 B.C., Roman marble copy 6′9″ high. Vatican Museums, Rome).   Lysippos, court sculptor to Alexander the Great, preferred slender proportions and poses that expand in all three dimensions and consume a comparatively great volume of space. The *Apoxyomenos* (Fig. 9-27) is an athlete scraping the sand of the arena from his body. He is in the process of shifting his weight from one leg to the other, creating a more dynamic version of the contrapposto pose.

WINGED VICTORY, from Samothrace (*c.* 190 B.C., marble, approx. 8′ high. Louvre, Paris).   The goddess (Fig. 9-28) is of the "nike" type; that is, she

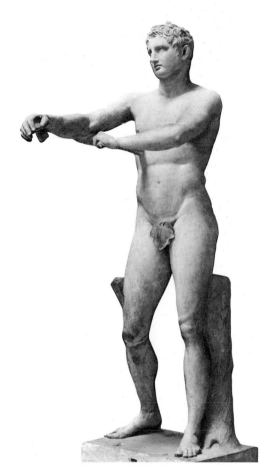

9-27   LYSIPPOS, *Apoxyomenos,* Roman marble copy, probably after a bronze original dated *c.* 330 B.C. 6′9″ high.
Vatican Museums, Rome.

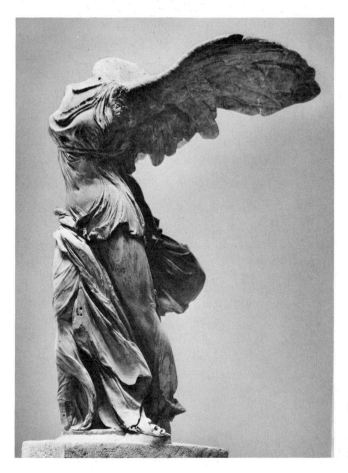

9-28
Winged Victory (Nike) of Samothrace, (*c.* 190 B.C.). Marble, approx. 8′ high.
Louvre, Paris.

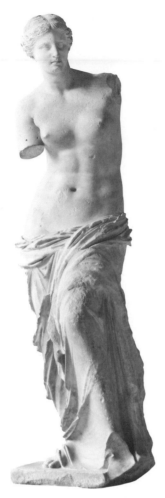

9-29
Aphrodite of Melos, (second
century B.C.). Marble, approx.
6′8″ high.   Louvre. Paris.

commemorates a military victory. The "wet drapery" effect reveals the Greek interest in the body, and the delicate carving of drapery details reveals an interest in the refinement of surfaces. Although the weight is supported by both legs, the body twists in space. The lines of the wind-whipped costume break the large masses into a restless complexity of lights and shadows.

APHRODITE, from Melos (2nd cen. B.C., marble, 6′8″ high. Louvre, Paris).   This statue (Fig. 9-29) is popularly known as the *Venus de Milo*. After the fifth century, Greek sculpture included more female nudes. In the extreme softness of modeling, the proportions of small head, narrow shoulders, and wide hips, and the pose with contrasting diagonals or spiral axes, this is one of the finest examples of Hellenistic work.

LAOCOÖN AND HIS SONS (1st cen. B.C., marble, 8′ high. Vatican Museums, Rome).   Laocoön, with his sons, is being slain by serpents for his disobedience to the gods. The present restoration (Fig.

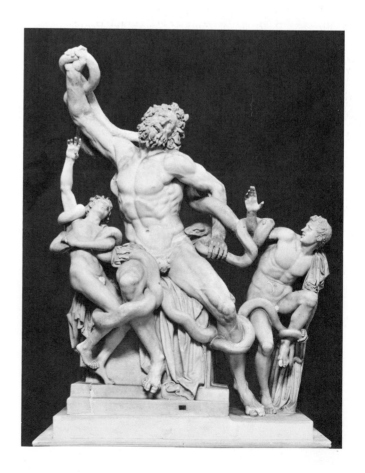

9-30   HAGESANDROS, POLYDOROS, and ATHENODOROS, *Laocoön and His Sons,* (first century B.C.). Marble, 8′ high (partially restored).   Vatican Museums, Rome.

9-30) is probably incorrect; the right hand of Laocoön should be closer to the head, thus completing the oval outline of the group. Although the composition has shallow depth, the intricate, restless, open form, the emphasis on anatomical detail, and the portrayal of mental and physical anguish are typical of late Hellenistic sculpture.

Suggestions for Further Study

Blümel, Carl. *Greek Sculptors at Work*, 2nd English ed. Translated by Lydia Holland. London: Phaidon, 1969.

Boardman, John, José Dörig, Werner Fuchs, and Max Hirmer. *Greek Art and Architecture*. New York: Abrams, 1967.

Charbonneaux, Jean, Roland Martin, and François Villard. *Archaic Greek Art (620–480 B.C.)* (The Arts of Mankind). Translated by Peter Green. New York: Braziller, 1971.

———. *Classical Greek Art, 480–330 B.C.* (The Arts of Mankind). Translated by Peter Green. New York: Braziller, 1973.

———. *Hellenistic Art: 330–50 B.C.* (The Arts of Mankind). Translated by Peter Green. New York: Braziller, 1973.

Havelock, Christine Mitchell. *Hellenistic Art*, rev. ed. New York: W. W. Norton, 1981.

Holloway, R. Ross. *A View of Greek Art*. Providence, R.I.: Brown University Press, 1973.

Lawrence, Arnold W. *Greek Architecture* (Pelican History of Art). Baltimore: Penguin Books, 1957.

Onians, John. *Art and Thought in the Hellenistic Age: The Greek World View, 350–50 B.C.* London: Thames & Hudson, 1979.

Pollitt, J. J. *The Art of Greece, 1400–31 B.C.* (Sources and Documents). Englewood Cliffs, N.J.: Prentice-Hall, 1965.

Richter, Gisela M. A. *Archaic Greek Art Against Its Historical Background: A Survey*. New York: Oxford University Press, 1949.

———. *A Handbook of Greek Art*, 5th rev. ed. New York: Dutton, 1980.

———. *The Sculpture and Sculptors of the Greeks*, 4th rev. and enl. ed. New Haven, Conn.: Yale University Press, 1971.

Robertson, Martin. *A History of Greek Art*. 2 vols. London: Cambridge University Press, 1976.

———. *Greek Painting* (Great Centuries of Painting). New York: Rizzoli International, 1979.

10

Etruscan Art

700–41 B.C.

The origins of Etruscan culture are still unclear. It either arose from an existing *Villanovan* culture (named after a site near Bologna) or was the result of an infiltration and reformation of an older culture by a new people. Greek and Roman authors spoke of the Etruscans as immigrants from Asia Minor. It is clear that Villanovan culture changed suddenly between 700 and 675 B.C. under the influence of new ideas and perhaps the influx of a new population. Tumulus-covered tombs appeared (*tumuli* are earth mounds), some filled with a mixture of Villanovan, Greek, and Near Eastern objects; two different sculptural styles developed, one geometric and one Near Eastern in character; and new wealth is evident. By the late seventh century B.C., the two sculptural styles had fused into one, and a unified culture had formed.

The Etruscan culture existed as a group of independent city-states that generally had republican governments by the late fifth century B.C. In spite of various alliances between the city-states, rivalry prevented any lasting unity. Some of the major cities were Veii, Caere (modern Cerveteri), Tarquinii (modern Tarquinia), Perusia (modern Perugia), and Volsinii (modern Orvieto). Ancient Etruria spread from the areas of Tuscany, Umbria, and Latium as far north as the Alps. The land and sea power of the Etruscans reached its height in the seventh and sixth centuries B.C. Etruria profited as an intermediary in trade between continental Europe and the Mediterranean countries, and the Etruscans' wealth was supplemented by their widely feared piracy. The Tyrrhenian Sea took its name from the ancient name for the Etruscans, the Tyrsenoi; the Adriatic was named after Hadria, an Etruscan colony. Although Rome often warred against Etruscan cities and eventually absorbed them, Rome was ruled by Tarquinian Etruscans from 615 to 510 B.C. Etruscan power declined during the fifth and fourth centuries B.C., and Rome defeated Perusia, the last Etruscan stronghold, in 41 B.C.

The Etruscans borrowed the Greek alphabet and became literate in the mid-seventh century B.C., but only about a hundred words of Etruscan have been deciphered. A considerable literature has been lost; only funerary and ritual inscriptions remain.

Religion was important to the Etruscans. Their gods were of three kinds: those inherited from pre-Etruscan Italic cultures; native Etruscan gods later identified with Greco-Roman deities; and gods adopted from the Greeks.

Although there are different points of view, the major periods of Etruscan art may be classified as follows: *Archaic* (including pre-Etruscan Villanovan geometric styles, the new Near Eastern or Orientalizing elements, and their merger by the late seventh century B.C.), *c.* 900–470 B.C.; *Classic* (with much Greek influence), *c.* 470–300 B.C.; and *Hellenistic* (continuing Greek influence), *c.* 300–41 B.C.

Architecture

Architectural remains are sparse because the Etruscans preferred wood and unbaked brick, and the Romans destroyed or built over much Etruscan work. Houses, known to us chiefly through the forms of cinerary urns, apparently ranged from *wattle and daub* huts (those having walls of woven saplings plastered with mud) to elaborate town houses of the Roman atrium type (see p. 117).

Tombs are the best-preserved remains of Etruscan buildings because they were built of stone blocks or carved from *tufa,* an easily worked stone that hardens when exposed to air. Cemeteries were arranged with grid plans as necropolises, and one tumulus might contain one or several rectangular tombs. The common tomb plan consisted of a rectangular room, with occasional subsidiary rooms, and a pitched roof rising to a ridge beam. When interior supports were used, they had the form of square piers with block capitals into which were incised *volutes* (spirals) that seem to be Asian rather than Greek in origin. Tomb interiors contain the best examples of Etruscan painting — murals depicting mythological scenes, feasting, and sports. Some tomb interiors seem to have imitated house interiors, even to the extent of having household utensils carved on the walls.

Until about 600 or 550 B.C., when temples began to be constructed, Etruscan religious ceremonies were apparently conducted at open-air sanctuaries consisting of platforms within sacred precincts. Although there are no remains that rise much above the stone foundation level, the Roman architect Vitruvius left a description of an Etruscan temple (Fig. 10-1). Its deep porch and three parallel cellae produce an almost square foundation. Widely spaced columns and overhanging eaves offer a topheavy façade. Vitruvius (1st cen. B.C.) probably would have known only late examples. Excavated foundations reveal variations in his plan, one of which may have evolved from the megaron. The decoration of pediments, ridgepoles, cornices, and roof edges with colorful clay sculpture is attested to by numerous fragments found at temple sites. The Etruscans used an occasional corbeled dome in tombs and employed the corbeled arch. Their use of the true arch may have come from the Romans, who, in turn, had taken it from Greece or the East. The Porta Augusta in Perugia is a city gate with a true arch and was probably the result of Roman influence. By the second century B.C., Etruscan architecture had largely been absorbed by Roman and Hellenistic Greek forms.

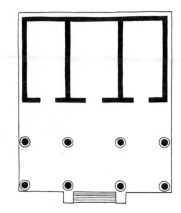

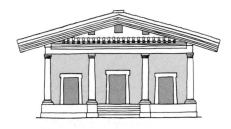

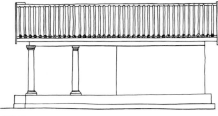

10-1
Plan, section, and elevation of an
Etruscan temple. (After Vitruvius.)

TOMB OF THE PAINTED RELIEFS (Caere, 5th–4th cens. B.C.).   The necropolis at Caere consists of tumuli containing tombs carved and constructed of tufa. This single-chamber tomb (Fig. 10-2) imitates the beamed and pitched roof of a house, although a house would have used supports under the ridgepole, if at all. Here, the piers, carved from tufa left in place, have typically voluted *Aeolic* capitals. The reliefs, both carved and modeled from stucco, depict weapons, household utensils, and even pets.

Sculpture

Etruscan sculpture took the form of cinerary urns, sarcophagus effigies, pottery, reliefs, freestanding statues, architectural ornaments, furniture decorations, bronze mirrors, containers, and jewelry. While they used a wide variety of materials, the Etruscans were especially renowned for their technical skill with clay and bronze. They were less interested in stone and used it principally for funerary sculpture. Villanovan or pre-Etruscan sculpture was geometric in style and had been inherited from Neolithic cultures. Circles, spirals, and triangles are often combined with severely simplified images of men and animals. From 675 to 600 B.C., Oriental or Near Eastern elements appeared in the form of sphinxes, hawks, and other gods from Egypt, and winged lions and fertility goddesses from Assyria. Greek influence is also evident and continued to be important throughout Etruscan history. The geometric patterns in hair and drapery, the almond eyes and straight-ridged nose, and the stiff poses of Greek Archaic sculpture mixed with oriental motifs in Etruria. During subsequent centuries, Etruscan sculpture, like that of Greece, moved toward greater flexibility in pose and naturalness in anatomical detail; yet the Etruscans never lost a suggestion of tenseness in the joints and musculature of the figure, a kind of aggressive awkwardness that is emphasized by large proportions in head, hands, and feet. In spite of Etruscan interest in effigies of the deceased on sarcophagi and cinerary urns, only a specific type of personality and age was expressed until about 300 B.C., when highly individualistic portraiture was imported from Greece.

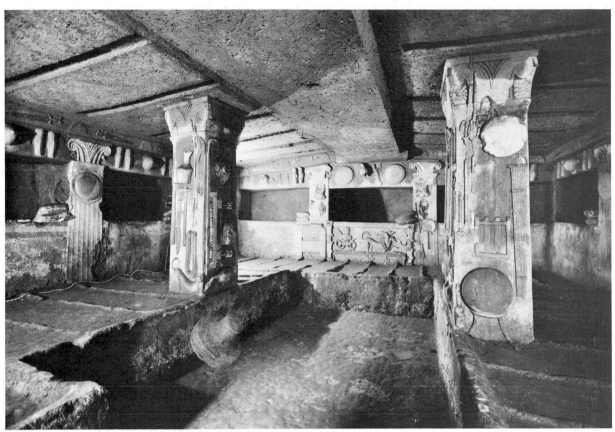

10-2
Tomb of the Painted Reliefs, Caere, (fifth to fourth centuries B.C.).

APOLLO OF VEII (*c.* 510 B.C., clay, 69″ high. Museo di Villa Giulia, Rome).   This life-sized god effigy (Fig. 10-3) was one of four deities originally placed at the ridgepole of the tile roof of a temple at Veii. The figures enacted the contest between Hercules and Apollo for the sacred hind. Greek influence is evident in the Archaic features of face, hair, and clothing. The taut leg muscles and the awkward forward movement are typical of Etruscan art.

SARCOPHAGUS, *from Caere* (*c.* 520 B.C., clay, approx. 6′7″ long. Museo di Villa Giulia, Rome). Etruscan sarcophagi of this sort (Fig. 10-4) provided images of the deceased, just as did many cinerary urns. In this period, the faces, with their abruptly changing planes and Archaic smiles, had little portrait character beyond an indication of age.

Painting

Of the paintings on vases, clay plaques, and tomb walls, the tomb murals are the most rewarding.

10-3
Apollo of Veii, (*c.* 510 B.C.). Clay, approx. 69″ high.
Museo di Villa Giulia, Rome.

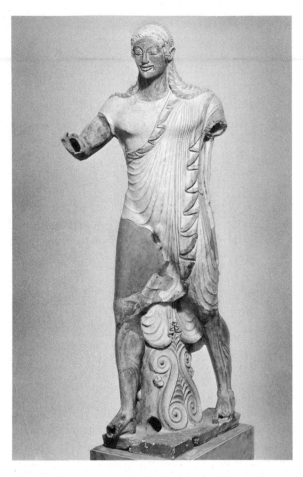

10-4
Sarcophagus from Caere, (*c.* 520 B.C.). Clay, approx.
6′7″ long.   Museo di Villa Giulia, Rome.

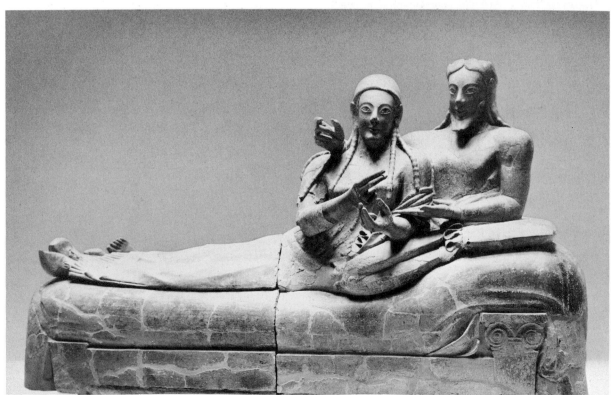

Mineral and vegetable pigments were applied directly on the stone walls or on a plaster ground. Only a few tombs remain from the Orientalizing period. The flowering of tomb painting seems to have come in the second half of the sixth century B.C. Until the mid-fourth century B.C., subjects were generally happy depictions of hunting, feasting, dancing, and funeral games. The flatly painted, unmodeled images are placed on a base line against a neutral background. Human musculature is inflated and tense. By the mid-fourth century, subjects were more somber, depicting underworld scenes or mythical scenes of death and suffering. Proportions and musculature are more natural and mass and depth are suggested by overlapping shapes and outlines. The development parallels that in Greek art, which also expresses a greater awareness of tragedy and of mass in space during the Hellenistic period.

PIPE-PLAYER AND BIRDS, from the tomb of the Triclinium (*c.* 470 B.C. Museo Nazionale Tarquiniense, Tarquinia).   The unmodeled figure, base line, and neutral background (Fig. 10-5) are typical of Etruscan painting of this period, but such delicacy of line, shape, pattern, and movement is unusual. The carefree nature of the subject was to change in the following century. Greek influence is evident, especially in facial profile and drapery.

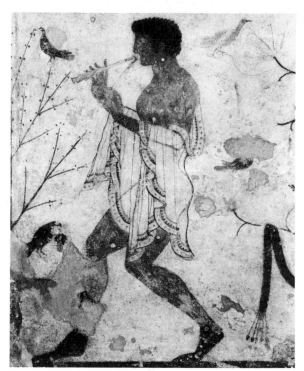

10-5
Pipe-player and Birds, from the tomb
of the Triclinium, (*c.* 470 B.C.).
Museo Nazionale Tarquiniense, Tarquinia.

Suggestions for Further Study

Banti, Luisa. *Etruscan Cities and Their Culture.* Berkeley: University of California Press, 1973.

Bloch, Raymond. *The Ancient Civilization of the Etruscans.* Translated by James Hogarth. New York: Cowles, 1969.

Mansuelli, G. A. *The Art of Etruria and Early Rome* (Art of the World). Translated by C. E. Ellis. New York: Crown, 1965.

Pallottino, Massimo. *The Etruscans.* Translated by J. Cremona. Harmondsworth, Eng.: Penguin Books, 1978.

Richardson, Emeline Hill. *The Etruscans, Their Art and Civilization.* Chicago: University of Chicago Press, 1976.

Spiteris, Tony. *Greek and Etruscan Painting* (History of Painting). Translated by Janet Sondheimer. New York: Funk and Wagnalls, 1965.

11

Roman Art

200 B.C. – A.D. 330

Roman art emerged with distinctive traits during the last two centuries before Christ. In style it persisted until perhaps A.D 500, but its subject matter was reoriented by Christianity long before then. The year A.D. 330, when Constantinople was dedicated as the new capital of the Roman Empire, can thus be considered the end of the Roman period.

The major sources of Roman culture are the Greek and Etruscan civilizations. Like the Greeks, the Romans had little interest in an afterlife; they focused their attention on the organization and exploitation of the physical world, and this is evident in their art. But the Romans considered the manual arts of painting and sculpture less dignified than the arts of music and poetry. Roman art and literature took Greek works for their models, and Greek gods reappeared in Roman culture with Latin names. The Romans, however, were more concerned than the Greeks with historical documentation; Roman historical writings are paralleled by Roman history-recording art.

SECOND AND FIRST CENTURIES B.C.

Architecture

Remarkable engineering skill was applied by the Romans to a variety of building types, most of which received their basic forms in this period. Materials were wood, mud brick and fired brick, stone, stucco, and concrete. The Romans were the first to use concrete extensively; they reinforced it with rubble and often concealed it behind a veneer of stucco, brick, marble, or travertine (a hard, light-colored limestone). The Romans did not limit themselves to the post and lintel system but went far beyond their predecessors in the development of the arch, the vault, and the dome. The semicircular *Roman arch* (Fig. 4-10, p. 40) could be extended in depth to form a *tunnel vault* (Fig. 4-11, p. 40). From this, the Romans created *cross vaults* (Fig. 4-14, p. 41) as early as the beginning of the second century B.C. Roman architecture used elaborated and modified basic Greek forms, including the three orders. Whereas the Greeks used columns as structural members, the Romans frequently added them as decoration without structural function. Greek column shafts are made with drums (cylindrical sections) placed one on top of the other and fastened with interior metal clamps; Roman shafts are generally monolithic.

Round Roman temples were inspired by the Greek tholos. Rectangular temples have the high base, frontal steps, and deep porch of pre-Roman Etruscan temples, but the Romans used Greek columns and modified Greek proportions in the entablature and pediment (see Fig. 11-2). The wider Roman cella often has engaged columns, a device used less frequently by the Greeks. The most common form of Roman monument was the *triumphal arch* (Fig. 11-15 shows a late example), a freestanding structure with inscriptions and relief sculpture describing the event commemorated. One type of Roman building that was very influential for later architecture is the *basilica,* a rectangular structure with an apse at one or both ends and entrances in the sides or at one end (see the basilica part of Fig. 11-9). Columns divided the interior into center and side aisles. The roof (usually wooden) of the center aisle is higher than that of the sides so that *clerestory* windows (windows looking out over a lower roof) provide direct lighting for the center. Basilicas functioned as law courts, public halls, and audience chambers for rulers. The masses of the urban population lived in multistory tenements, usually built of mud brick and wood, but simple or complex private city houses were also built, in accordance with the builder's financial means (see Fig. 11-1). Larger houses occupied the center of a block and were insulated from the street by shops around the perimeter; therefore, all efforts at impressive architecture were concentrated on the interior of the home. The front door opened into a vestibule that led to the *atrium,* a receiving hall. In the center of this room was a pool into which water drained from an opening in the roof (the *impluvium*). The atrium ended in the *tablinium,* where family statues were kept. One then entered the peristyle, a colonnaded walkway around an open court (adapted from Hellenistic houses). Typically, a strong axis from front to back gave order to the progression of interior spaces.

HOUSE OF MENANDER (Pompeii).   The plan (Fig. 11-1) is typical in allowing a spatial vista down the major axis and in its alternation of small and large

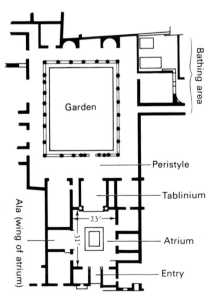

11-1
Plan of the House of Menander, Pompeii. Only the central portion is shown.

spaces. The high ceilings and the free passage of air from garden to front door helped to cool the house.

MAISON CARRÉE (Nîmes, begun A.D. 1–10, 59′ × 117′).   This small provincial temple (Fig. 11-2) is very well preserved. It exemplifies the Roman love of the Corinthian order and the high base, frontal steps, and deep porch inherited from the Etruscans. It is one of the few Roman temples having some of the refinements of proportion found in the best Greek work. The *rinceau* (band of scroll-like vine ornament) in the entablature frieze was widely used in Roman architecture.

Sculpture

Roman sculpture owes much to the Etruscans and the Hellenistic Greeks. In spite of extensive importation of Greek sculpture and the demand for copies of famous Greek originals, the Romans developed certain types of sculpture that are distinctly expressive of Roman culture. The Roman interest in the actual world is reflected in the rise of portraiture as a major field. The custom of making wax images of dead ancestors, the love of factual documentation, and the late Hellenistic tendency toward realism in portraiture all helped to mold the Roman desire for absolute fidelity to physical appearance. Such realism was countered, however, by occasional periods of interest in the idealism of earlier Greek sculpture. Particularly in certain portraits of Augustus as Emperor, the idealistic simplification and strengthening of basic features can be seen. Relief sculpture became the other important form for the Romans and was used chiefly to commemorate events from Roman history. Roman sculpture went much further than Hellenistic sculpture in depicting specific events with specific details in face, costume, and environment. In place of the blank background of earlier Greek relief, the Romans tried for the illusion of infinite space by graduating the relief from high projection in the foreground to fainter projection for distant objects, and by using diagonally receding forms. When occasional allegorical scenes make broader reference to Roman history, more general features reminiscent of earlier Greek art

11-2
Maison Carrée, Nîmes, (begun A.D. 1–10).

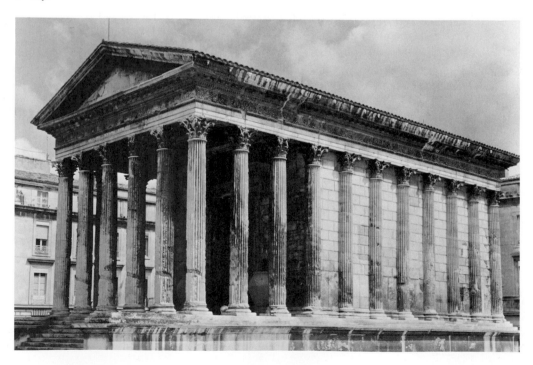

appear. Basic materials of Roman sculpture are wax, terra cotta, stone, and bronze. Parts of stone sculpture were sometimes painted.

AUGUSTUS, from Primaporta (*c.* 20 B.C., marble, 6'8" high. Vatican Museums, Rome).   Individualism is veiled by the interest in ideal form (Fig. 11-3); much detail was omitted in the face, and the large planes are emphasized (note the brows). The visionary stare of the softly carved pupils contrasts with heroic body proportions, a pose of authority, and allegorical scenes on the breastplate referring to the exploits of Augustus. The cupid and dolphin beside the right leg symbolize Aeneas, the half brother of Cupid and the divine source of the Julian family. The statue thus presents the emperor as a divinity.

ARA PACIS or ALTAR OF PEACE (Rome, completed in 9 B.C., marble, processional panels 63" high). The relief sculpture decorates a walled enclosure for the altar. On two walls, a procession of Augustus with his family and retinue is depicted. An end wall shows an allegorical scene in which Tellus (Mother Earth) is surrounded by symbols of the abundance that Augustus brought to the Empire (Fig. 11-4). There is marked contrast between the detailed portraiture of the procession and the

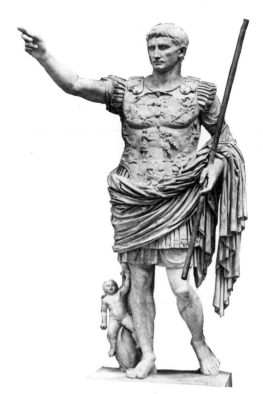

11-3
Augustus, from Primaporta, (*c.* 20 B.C.).
Marble, 6'8" high.   Vatican Museums, Rome.

11-4
Tellus Relief, from the Ara Pacis
Augustae, Rome, (13–9 B.C.). Marble.

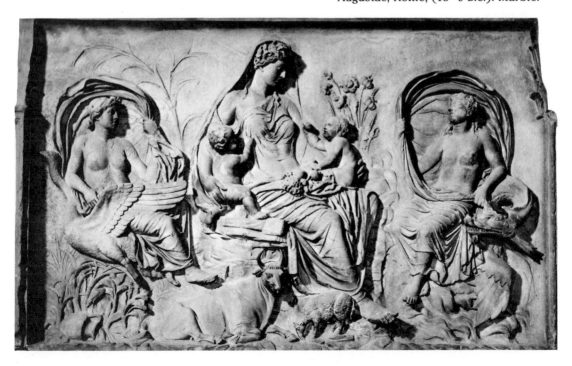

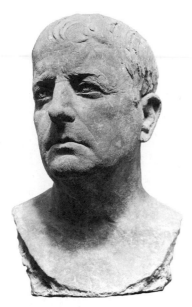

11-5
Portrait of a Roman, (late
first century B.C.). Terracotta,
14″ high.   Museum of Fine Arts,
Boston. 01.8008, purchased by
contribution. Courtesy, Museum of
Fine Arts, Boston.

ideal figures of the allegory, although the latter has
specific details in plants and animals. The illusion
of infinite space is present throughout. The lower
part of the walls is covered with crisply carved
symmetrical vine ornament.

PORTRAIT OF A ROMAN (1st cen. B.C., terra cotta.
Museum of Fine Arts, Boston).   Suffering and disillusionment are nakedly revealed by the sagging
muscles of the eyes and mouth (Fig. 11-5). The
lifeless hair plastered over the wrinkled forehead
gives an added feeling of dejection to the figure.
Such realism reveals the Romans' inclination to
accept and to deal with the physical world.

Painting and Mosaics

Our knowledge of Roman painting comes largely
from wall paintings found in the cities of Pompeii,
Stabiae, and Herculaneum, which were buried by
an eruption of Mt. Vesuvius in A.D. 79. On such a
limited basis, generalization must be tentative. We
may assume probable influence by the lost paintings of the Hellenistic age, however, because imported Greek artists were responsible for some of
the Roman paintings, as is evidenced by Greek

signatures and inscriptions. Wall painting of the
second century B.C. consisted of rectangular
panels of color, often imitating marble. This *First
Style* was succeeded around 60 B.C. by a *Second
Style* depicting landscapes, figures, and architectural vistas. For the illusion of deep space, a make-
shift system of linear perspective was devised,
which consisted of different horizon lines and thus
varying eye levels. Effects of light and shadow,
aerial perspective, and convincing anatomy were
achieved. The wall paintings seem to have been
done in tempera with a binder of lime emulsion.
Encaustic was used for a few colors. The ground
was made with three coats of sand mortar and
three of fine-grained plaster, often mixed with
marble dust. The plaster was polished before the
paint was applied. The permanence of such work
has been remarkable. Sometimes wood panels
were given the plaster ground and utilized as supports for paintings, but most of these panels have
perished. Mosaics were widely used, both on
floors and on walls. In both mosaics and painting,
the style indicates a strong interest in the visual
experience of the physical world.

ODYSSEY LANDSCAPES (*c*. 50–40 B.C. Vatican Library, Rome).   These Second Style paintings
(Fig. 11-6) were discovered in the ruins of a house
on the Esquiline Hill in Rome. Eight episodes from
Books X and XI of the *Odyssey* are shown in a
continuous landscape (44′ × 5′) divided only by a
painted architectural framework. Lively figures are
placed in a world of shimmering light. Shadows
are used to define the ground plane and to locate
objects on it. Aerial perspective creates depth. The
breathtaking effects of color and light seem to be
achieved without effort.

MOSAIC SHOWING STREET MUSICIANS (Museo Nazionale, Naples).   The Greek Dioskourides of
Samos signed this work (Fig. 11-7), probably during the period of the Second Style. The everyday
subject matter, the characterization in faces and
gestures, and the factual treatment of light and
shadow — qualities first developed in late Hellenistic painting — are typical of much Roman painting. The handling of color is particularly subtle,
and shadow areas are enlivened with reflected
lights.

11-6
Ulysses in the Land of the Lestrygonians, from *The Odyssey Landscapes,* (*c.* 50–40 B.C.).   Vatican Library, Rome.

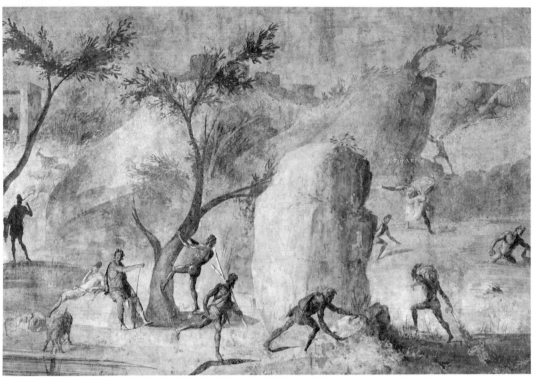

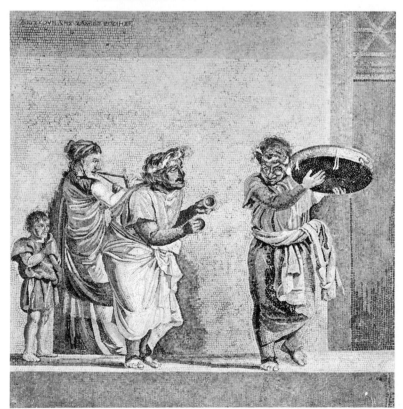

11-7
Mosaic showing street musicians, (probably first century B.C.).
Museo Nazionale, Naples.

FIRST CENTURY TO A.D. 330

Architecture

The Roman Empire reached its height in the second century A.D., and its power and wealth are reflected in architectural design. Vast size and lavish decoration are typical of the period from the first to the fourth centuries. Roman architects tended to impose a scheme of order upon the whole site, arranging landscape as well as spaces and masses to achieve effects of gradation and climax. Plans often used obvious axial balance. Examples may be found in the *forums* (civic centers for Roman towns), where temples, government buildings, and commercial houses were organized around an open space (see Fig. 11-9). The forum has its sources in pre-Roman Etruscan town plans and in the Greek agora. Of the three Greek orders, the Romans preferred the most ornate, the Corinthian. From this they derived the *composite* capital by adding Ionic *volutes* (spirals) to the Corinthian capital. In addition they developed the *Tuscan order,* using a base, an unfluted shaft, a derivation of the Doric capital, and an entablature without frieze ornament. It was Roman architecture that established the system of superposed orders for buildings of several stories.

Doric or Tuscan was used on the ground floor, Ionic on the next, and Corinthian above (see Fig. 11-8 for an example). These post and lintel forms were often combined with the arch, as in the *Roman arch order,* an arched opening framed by engaged columns or *pilasters* (flattened column shapes that project as planes from the wall) and an entablature. The Romans also adopted and elaborated Greek architectural moldings (see Fig. 9-8, p. 95).

For an understanding of Roman culture, it is significant to note that wealth was spent not just on temples but on monuments to Roman leaders, on palaces, and on places of public entertainment such as baths and amphitheaters. For the late period, public entertainment was very important to Roman politics. The amphitheaters (as distinct from theaters, which followed the Greek form) were built for athletic or gladiatorial contests. The tiered seats surrounded an elliptical arena, and the exterior might be banked earth or arcaded galleries. Some of the largest Roman buildings were the public baths *(thermae),* which served as community centers with lecture halls, libraries, lounges, and outdoor playing fields, in addition to housing bathing pools of various temperatures. Planning stressed dramatic axes of interior and exterior spaces. Statues and mosaics decorated the inte-

11-8
Colosseum, Rome, (A.D. 70–82).

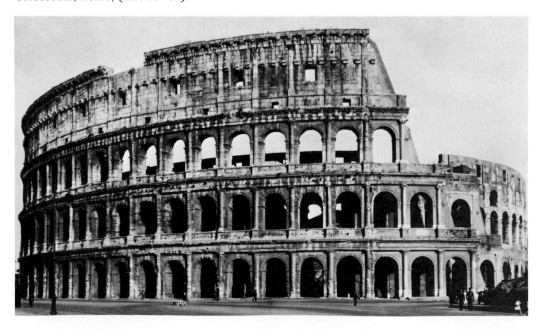

rior; walls and mammoth cross vaults were veneered with sumptuous marble. The populace enjoyed these elegant public facilities and found them a relief from the apartments (mostly of concrete by the first century A.D.) in which many Romans led crowded lives.

COLOSSEUM (Rome, completed *c.* A.D. 84 and frequently restored, elliptical, approx. 620′ × 513′). Rome's vast arena (Fig. 11-8) seated 50,000 spectators. Tunnel and cross vaults were used in corridors and stairways. The core is concrete, and the façade is faced with travertine. The arcades of the façade employ the Roman arch order with engaged columns in the following sequence: Doric, Ionic, and Corinthian. The fourth level has Corinthian pilasters.

FORUM OF TRAJAN, *designed by Apollodorus of Damascus* (Rome, completed *c.* A.D. 113, central square approx. 300′ × 350′).   The Roman preference for grand organization of space and mass is exemplified here (Fig. 11-9). The symmetrical order moves along the axis from the front gate, through the main forum space, into the basilica, past the column dedicated to Trajan's wars (see Fig. 11-17 and text on page 127), and on to the climactic temple of the deified emperor.

PANTHEON (Rome, mainly built A.D. 118–25). The concrete and brick core of this temple (Fig. 11-10) formerly had a marble and stucco veneer. The dome (142 feet in diameter) was the most celebrated in ancient architecture. The concrete ranges in thickness from six to twenty feet, and the interior of the dome (Fig. 11-11) has *coffering* (an excavated grid effect), a device often used in vaulting by the Romans to lighten the structure without weakening it. Aside from the main door, the only light source in the Pantheon is the *oculus* (a round opening in the center of the dome). The dramatic lighting and the vast scale make the much-copied Pantheon one of the supreme examples of effective use of interior space (Fig. 11-12).

BASILICA OF CONSTANTINE (Rome, completed *c.* A.D. 320, after having been started by Emperor Maxentius in 310, 265′ × 195′).   Most basilicas had wooden roofs, but vast concrete tunnel and cross

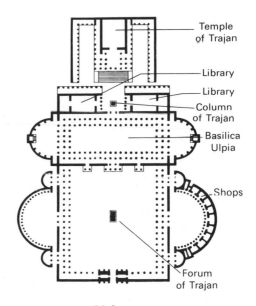

11-9
Plan of the Forum of Trajan.

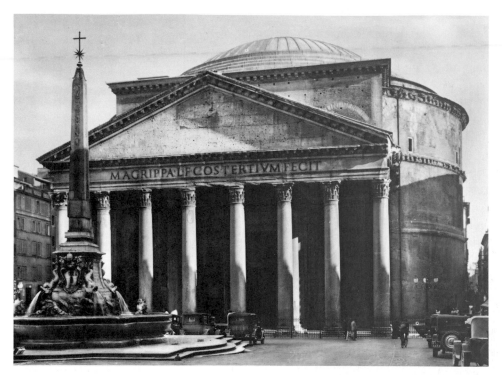

11-10
Pantheon, Rome, (A.D. 118–25).

11-11 GIOVANNI PAOLO PANNINI, *The Interior of the Pantheon,* (*c.* 1740).   National Gallery of Art, Washington, D.C. Samuel H. Kress Collection, 1939.

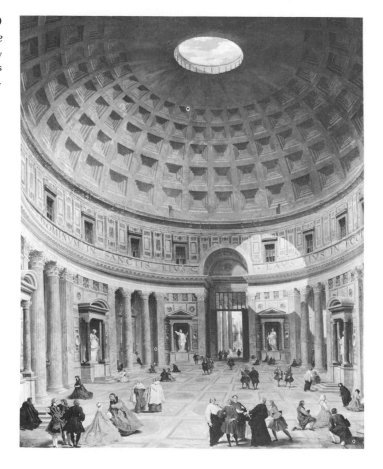

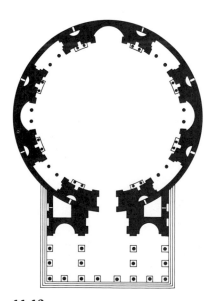

11-12
Plan of the Pantheon.

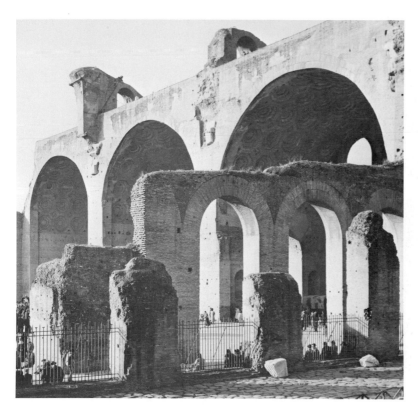

11-13
Basilica of Constantine, Rome,
(*c.* A.D. 310–20).

vaults were used here in one of the largest vaulted interiors of the ancient world (Figs. 11-13 and 11-14). Formerly huge columns were part of the decorative veneer. The effect was more like that of the great hall of a Roman bath than the hall of a basilica. The building provided a grandiose setting for the ritual of Roman government.

TRIUMPHAL ARCH OF CONSTANTINE (Rome, *c.* A.D. 312).   The three arches, the quantity of sculpture (some of it borrowed from earlier monuments), and the decorative Corinthian columns all break up the surfaces and create a sumptuous and dramatic play of light and shadow on the structure (Fig. 11-15). A detail of the sculpture on the frieze and the medallions above one of the outer arches appears in Figure 11-19.

Sculpture

During this period (A.D. 1–330) the otherworldly interests of Christianity began to undermine the Roman world of fact, flesh, and blood. In portrait

11-14
Reconstruction drawing of the
Basilica of Constantine.

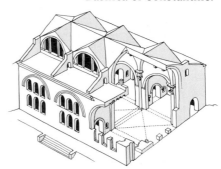

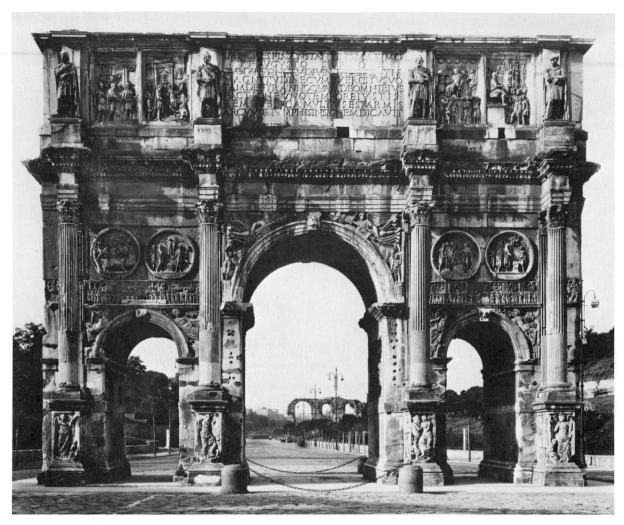

11-15
Triumphal Arch of Constantine, Rome, (A.D. 312–15).

sculpture, the third century brought increased animation in the twist of the head and the turn of the eyes, and the bust-type portrait came to include the shoulders and often one or both arms; but by the fourth century, the eyes had become large and preoccupied, the carving crude or summary, and the forms more stereotyped. Historical and mythological reliefs, used on triumphal arches, commemorative columns, altars, and sarcophagi, became, during the late second and third centuries, more compressed into shallow foreground space, more crowded, and less definite about the climactic centers of the composition. By the fourth century, representations of specific events acquired the effect of scenes staged with dolls; the episode became ritual. The figure functioned somewhat

abstractly as a symbol for man and for his role in a social or divine order. Heads were shown disproportionately large, without much variety in features or expression; costume folds were indicated by quickly carved grooves, poses were more rigid, and abrupt modeling created sudden dark shadows that tended to isolate the many parts.

RELIEFS ON THE ARCH OF TITUS (Rome, A.D. 81, marble).   The arch was built to celebrate the subduing of Jerusalem by Titus. The reliefs (Fig. 11-16) depict a triumphal procession carrying booty (note the seven-branched candelabrum). Diagonal masses and increasingly faint relief suggest atmospheric perspective and deep space. The factual detail expresses the disorder of the event

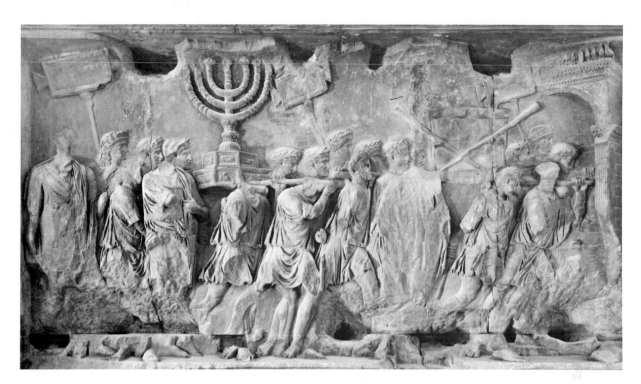

11-16
Spoils from the Temple in Jerusalem, relief on the
Arch of Titus. Marble, approx. 7'10" high.

without the theme and variations of line and shape
that would lend subtle harmony to a Greek interpretation of a similar subject.

COLUMN OF TRAJAN (Rome, completed *c.* A.D. 113,
marble, 128' high).   The column is divorced from
its structural role to become a monument in Trajan's Forum (Fig. 11-9). A spiral relief 625 feet long
and 50 inches high winds from bottom to top depicting Trajan's Dacian Wars (Fig. 11-17). Architecture and landscape are reduced to undersized
stage settings in order for the figures to present
clearly the historical narrative.

JULIA DOMNA, wife of Septimius Severus (early
3rd cen. A.D., marble, 26" high. Metropolitan Museum
of Art, New York).   The animated turn of head
and eyes and the inclusion of the body almost to
the waist are typical of much third-century portraiture. Factual realism is evident especially in the
distinctive nose and mouth (Fig. 11-18).

*CONSTANTINE ADDRESSING THE SENATE, frieze on
the Arch of Constantine* (Rome, early 4th cen.
A.D.).   The style employed in this frieze (Fig.
11-19) reflects the development of late Roman
sculpture, in which the depicted object was

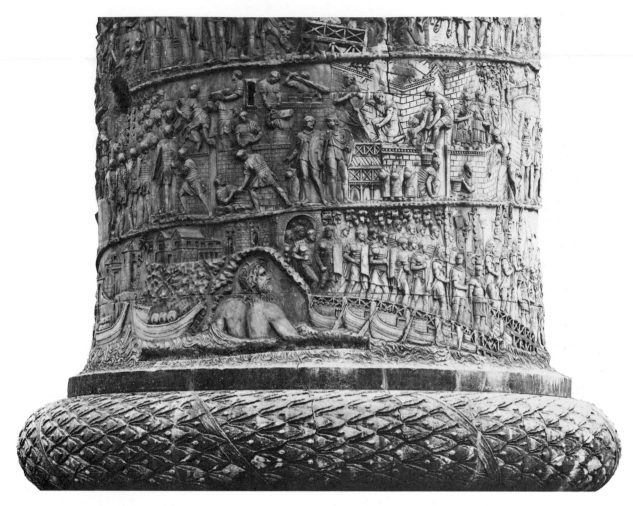

11-17
Reliefs on the Column of Trajan, Rome, (*c.* A.D. 113).

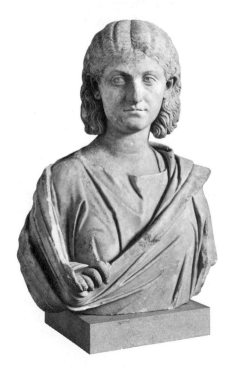

11-18
Julia Domna (wife of Septimius
Severus), (early third century
A.D.).   Metropolitan Museum of Art, New
York, Rogers Fund, 1918.

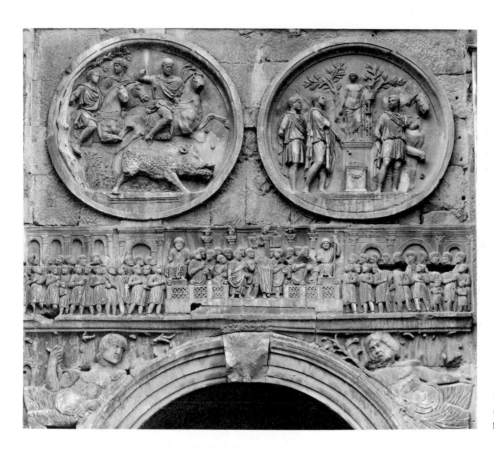

11-19
Constantine Addressing the Senate, frieze on the Arch of Constantine.

becoming an abbreviated symbol. The roughly carved, doll-like figures are shown with enlarged heads and repetitive poses; they provide a striking stylistic contrast with the relief medallions located above them, which are from the second century.

Painting and Mosaics

In wall painting a *Third Style* seems to have prevailed from 20 B.C. to A.D. 60. Here, the wall was treated more flatly but illusional paintings of columns and moldings of delicate proportions were used. Monochrome landscapes were often added to suggest panel paintings hung on the walls. A *Fourth Style,* evident between about A.D. 60 and 79 in Pompeii, again opened up the wall with palatial, theatrical architecture, landscapes, cityscapes, and mythological scenes. This style pushes illusionism even further than before. From Lower Egypt, during the period of Roman occupation, come a number of portraits on panels that have been preserved by the dry climate. These were attached to mummies. The technique is encaustic, and the style is similar to that of some miniature portraits painted on glass medallions during the third century A.D., probably in Italy. There is some evidence that painters (particularly those working for Christians), like sculptors, became less interested in accurate appearance by the fourth century and turned increasingly to flat, schematic shapes whose power lay in their symbolic content rather than in their imitation of physical reality.

THIRD STYLE WALL PAINTING, *with monochrome landscape* (c. 20 B.C.–A.D. 60. Museo Nazionale, Naples).   The scenery is presented as a monochrome panel, emphasizing the flat surface of the wall (Fig. 11-20). Illusionistic space is kept shallow, and the painted columns and moldings are delicate and slender, decorated with plant ornament.

FOURTH STYLE WALL PAINTING, *from Herculaneum* (c. A.D. 60–79. Museo Nazionale, Naples). Delicate motifs from the Third Style are combined with bold architecture and deep space (Fig. 11-21). Curtains and an actor's mask give the effect of stage decoration.

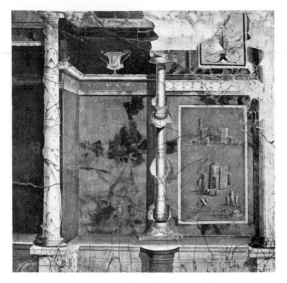

11-20
Third Style wall painting, from Pompeii,
(*c.* 20 B.C. – A.D. 60).   Museo Nazionale, Naples.

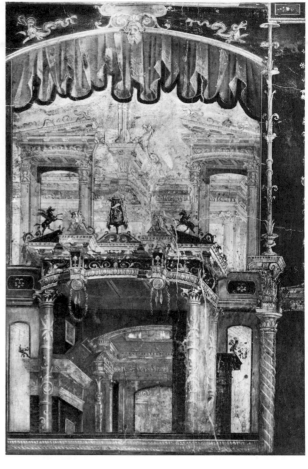

11-21
Fourth Style wall painting, from Herculaneum,
(*c.* A.D. 60 – 79).   Museo Nazionale, Naples.

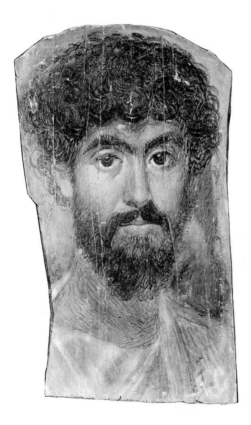

11-22
Portrait of a man, from Faiyum,
(second century A.D.). Encaustic
on wood panel, approx. 13¾″ × 8″.
Albright-Knox Art Gallery, Buffalo (Charles
Clifton Fund).

PORTRAIT OF A MAN, *from Faiyum* (2nd cen. A.D., 13¾″ × 8″. Albright-Knox Art Gallery, Buffalo). Encaustic on wood was used in this example (Fig. 11-22) of the type of portrait that was attached to mummies. Individual features are rendered in somewhat stereotyped forms by an artist accustomed to working quickly and producing in quantity.

Suggestions for Further Study

Andrae, Bernard. *The Art of Rome.* Translated by Robert Erich Wolf. New York: Abrams, 1977.

Boëthius, Axel, and J. B. Ward-Perkins. *Etruscan and Roman Architecture* (Pelican History of Art). Baltimore: Penguin Books, 1970.

Brilliant, Richard. *Roman Art from the Republic to Constantine.* London: Phaidon, 1974.

Hanfmann, George M. A. *Roman Art: A Modern Survey of the Art of Imperial Rome.* New York: W. W. Norton, 1975.

Kähler, Heinz. *The Art of Rome and Her Empire* (Art of the World). New York: Crown, 1963.

Maiuri, Amedeo. *Roman Painting* (Great Centuries of Painting). Translated by Stuart Gilbert. Geneva: Skira, 1953.

Pollitt, J. J. *The Art of Rome, c. 753 B.C.–A.D. 337* (Sources and Documents). Englewood Cliffs, N.J.: Prentice-Hall, 1966.

Richter, Gisela M. A. *Roman Portraits.* New York: Metropolitan Museum of Art, 1948.

Robertson, Donald S. *A Handbook of Greek and Roman Architecture,* 2nd ed. New York: Cambridge University Press, 1969.

Strong, Mrs. Arthur. *Roman Sculpture from Augustus to Constantine.* New York: Scribner's, 1907.

Strong, Donald, and David Brown. *Roman Crafts.* New York: New York University Press, 1976.

Strong, Donald. *Roman Art* (Pelican History of Art). Baltimore: Penguin Books, 1976.

Vermeule, Cornelius C. *Roman Imperial Art in Greece and Asia Minor.* Cambridge, Mass.: The Belknap Press of Harvard University Press, 1968.

Ward-Perkins, John B. *Roman Imperial Architecture.* Harmondsworth and New York: Penguin Books, 1981.

12

Early Christian and Byzantine Art

100 – 1453

One of the most far-reaching changes in Western thought came about through the impact of Christianity upon the Roman world. Late Roman history reveals an increasing interest in foreign religions, such as the worship of Isis (Egypt) or of Mithras (Persia), but Christianity won out and provided the basis for a new world view. For the Christian, reality was the drama within, the struggle of good against evil, the salvation of the soul, and the attainment of life after death; the physical world was inimical, irrelevant, or symbolic of the inner reality. As reality became less materialistic, the role of art became more complex.

Long before the legalization of Christianity by Constantine in 313, paintings with Christian subject matter were done on the walls of *catacombs* (underground passageways with niches used for burial by Christians). Thus the period of Early Christian art overlaps that of Roman art. The term

Early Christian art refers not so much to a certain style as to a period, from about 100 to 500, and to art with Christian subject matter within that period. The term *Byzantine* refers not only to the geographical area of the Eastern Roman Empire, with its capital at Constantinople (the ancient Byzantium), but also to particular stylistic features common to much art of that region from about 500 until the fall of Constantinople to the Turks in 1453. There is, however, no sharp dividing line between Early Christian and Byzantine art. Important art centers were Rome, Constantinople, Antioch, and Alexandria. Much of the Byzantine painting and sculpture was destroyed and its stylistic development affected by *iconoclasm,* a controversy between the *iconophiles,* who wanted religious images, and the *iconoclasts,* who felt that images were idols and that religious art should present symbols rather than images of sacred persons. The battle began with an edict from the Eastern emperor in 726 prohibiting figurative images and ended with the victory of the iconophiles in 843.

EARLY CHRISTIAN PERIOD:
100–500

Architecture

Early Christian architecture inherited the techniques and the forms of Roman building, but aims had changed and form was modified accordingly. Early Christian builders concentrated on churches, *martyria* (buildings marking a martyr's tomb or the site of his or her death, or containing a sacred relic), and baptisteries. They did not seek the earthly grandeur of Roman temples but stressed instead a withdrawal from the physical world and a mystical experience of salvation for the worshiper. Exteriors were left starkly simple; in interiors glittering mosaics and Greco-Roman colonnades, arcades, or masonry piers (often made of columns taken from the ruins of Roman temples) were arranged for effects of gradation and climax that focus on the altar. Plans are of two basic types, the *longitudinal* and the *central,* both having roots in Roman architecture. The longitudinal type was a modified Roman basilica plan and is therefore called a basilica (see Fig. 12-1). From

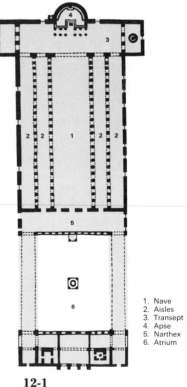

1. Nave
2. Aisles
3. Transept
4. Apse
5. Narthex
6. Atrium

12-1

Plan of Old St. Peter's, Rome,
(fourth century).

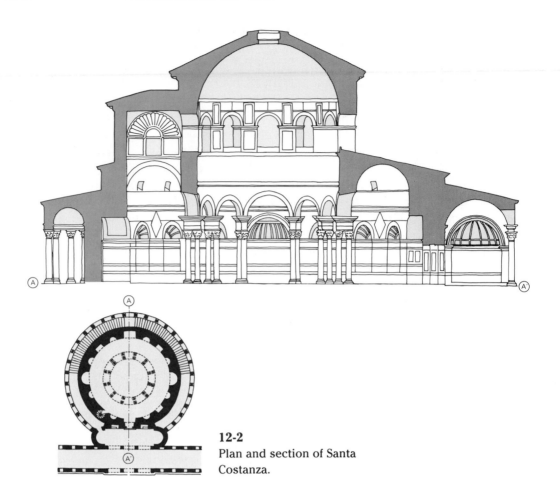

12-2
Plan and section of Santa
Costanza.

an entry gate, one passes through the *atrium* (open court) into the *narthex* (vestibule), where one can see the altar at the far end of the nave. By means of these spaces, which provide progressive degrees of withdrawal from the outside world, the altar gains significance. The longitudinal axis, which lends itself so well to dignified processionals, is sacrificed in the central type of building (see the plan in Fig. 12-2). In the fourth century, the central plan was generally used for martyria, but it soon appeared in churches as well. Although the central space receives the major emphasis, a slight axis may be suggested by placing the altar just off center against an apse. Central plans have a variety of forms, especially in Syria and Armenia, ranging from circular to square or Greek cross (arms of equal length) within a square. Other variations were developed in the Byzantine period. Central churches often had vaulting or domes of stone or brick. Large basilicas were usually roofed with timber, although tunnel vaults were fre-

quently used over side aisles; smaller basilicas, particularly in Syria and Asia Minor, used stone and brick vaulting.

OLD BASILICA OF ST. PETER (Rome).   This old basilica (Fig. 12-1) was destroyed to make room for the Renaissance structure, but the original is known through drawings and descriptions. Built over the tomb of St. Peter between 324 and 354 by order of Constantine, it exemplifies an early but fully developed basilica plan. The structure was apparently roofed with timber. Although in later Christian churches the main entrance was traditionally placed at the west, Old St. Peter's had its entrance at the east end.

SANTA COSTANZA (Rome).   The central building (Fig. 12-2) was ordered by Constantine and was used as a mausoleum for his daughter in about 350. It was converted to a church in the thirteenth century. The central space, about 40 feet in diameter, is covered by a dome on a drum that rests on arcades carried by twelve pairs of columns. Around the central space is a circular side aisle with a tunnel vault and mosaics. The building was originally peripteral. It is an important prototype for later central churches.

Painting and Mosaics

Painting was done on walls and panels and in book illustrations. Tempera, encaustic, and fresco-secco were employed. The earliest Christian painting is found in the catacombs in Rome. These fresco-secco works depict praying figures and episodes of miraculous salvation taken from the Old and New Testaments. The scenes are reduced to the minimum essentials; the figures are sketchily painted and have large heads, staring eyes, and doll-like bodies. There is little interest in landscape or depth, but the abbreviated episodes are sometimes set into painted geometric designs. The effect is that of brief pictorial prayers. Few catacomb paintings were done after the fifth century.

Until the development of the printing press during the Renaissance, books were copied and illustrated by hand. These *illuminated manuscripts* were at first in the *rotulus* form, following the Roman scroll books; rather than using separate pages bound at one side, the text was written on a continuous band held on two rollers, and the reader unrolled one side as he rolled up the other. Between the first and fourth centuries, the rotulus form was slowly replaced by the *codex* form that we use today. Parchment (made from animal skin) was common for centuries; paper was not used until after the eleventh century. The painted illustrations in the Early Christian manuscripts showed varying degrees of naturalness, modified by a tendency to rigidify into conventional shapes that were repeated without direct observation of nature. They are often characterized by flat figures, abrupt modeling, and fanciful colors; the rigid boldness and intensity of these partially abstract and highly symbolic works made them an effective expression of Early Christian theology. A similar stylistic tension between nature and symbol is evident in the mosaics. Generally it is felt that, like Christianity itself, the tendency toward flat symbolic forms had its origin in the Near East.

THE GOOD SHEPHERD and *THE STORY OF JONAH* (Rome, 4th cen.).   This painting is on a ceiling in the catacomb of Saints Pietro and Marcellino (Fig. 12-3). Within a simple geometrical design in obvious central balance, Christ as the Good Shepherd is shown in a landscape with two sketchily painted

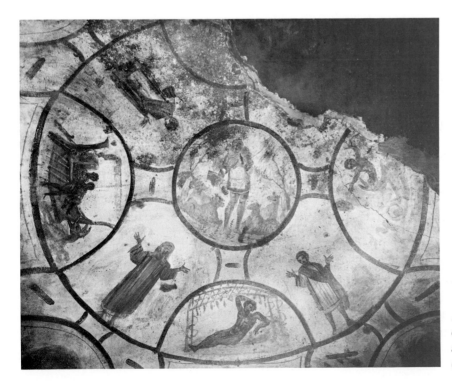

12-3
The Good Shepherd and *The Story of Jonah,* from the catacomb of Saints Pietro and Marcellino, Rome, (fourth century).

trees and several sheep. From the central scene radiate episodes from the story of Jonah done in a quick, abbreviated manner. Between the episodes, praying men hold out their hands to heaven. Some of the contrapposto poses echo pre-Christian Roman art, but the sketchiness and the disregard of scale relationships between Jonah, the ship, and the whale reveal a declining interest in the observation of the physical world.

Sculpture

Sculpture showed a remarkable decline in importance during the Early Christian period, partly because of the Biblical injunction against idols and partly as a reaction against the widespread use of idols in Roman temples. It was generally confined to small-scale works, such as sarcophagi, metal plates and chalices, *reliquaries* (elaborate containers for sacred relics), and ivory carvings. What portraits there were showed less and less interest in specific details of physical appearance. Christian sarcophagi of the fourth and fifth centuries are *frieze-type*, with episodes carved in an unbroken frieze along the sides, or *columnar-type*, with scenes divided by engaged columns. Sometimes double registers were used. As in the catacomb paintings, favorite subjects included such stories as Jonah and the Whale, the Raising of Lazarus, the Sacrifice of Isaac, Daniel in the Den of Lions, the Healing of the Blind, and Moses Striking Water from the Rock.

During the fourth century, sculptural style moved closer to that of the doll-like figures and repetitious poses on the Arch of Constantine. The declining interest in the physical world, the increasing love of flat geometric or floral decoration, and the inclination toward abstract symbols — such as the Cross instead of the figure of Jesus, or the monogram made by superimposing X and P (Chi and Rho, see p. 27), the first letters of Christ's name in Greek — grew from the otherworldly emphasis and the symbolic character of Eastern thought and art. Long before the time of Jesus, Persian art stressed flat patterns and nonfigurative designs. In Constantinople, Christian-Roman culture had been transplanted into the midst of ancient Eastern culture. Thus the more abstract sarcophagi generally come from Constantinople and other Eastern centers or from artists trained in

those areas. The same might be said for the style of the ivory carvings. *Consular diptychs* (two-part ivory plaques celebrating election to the office of consul) from Rome show more interest in anatomy and natural drapery than those carved in Constantinople, even though the Roman work reflects the changes seen in the sculpture on the Arch of Constantine.

SARCOPHAGUS OF JUNIUS BASSUS, *from St. Peter's* (Rome, *c.* 359, marble, 46½″ × 96″).   This fine double-register columnar sarcophagus (Fig. 12-4) mixes Old and New Testament episodes without regard for chronology. Each episode was an abbreviated symbol for the initiate. In the center of the top register, the enthroned Jesus is giving missions to Peter and Paul. The head of Cailus, a Roman sky god, appears beneath a wind-blown canopy at his feet. Directly below, the Entry into Jerusalem is flanked by Adam and Eve and Daniel in the Den of Lions. In the spandrels (see Fig. 4-10, p. 40) of the lower colonnade, lambs are used to represent episodes ranging from Moses Striking the Rock to the Raising of Lazarus. Much natural detail is retained in faces, poses, and costumes, but legs are shortened and heads are enlarged. Compared with earlier sarcophagi, the architecture here is smaller in scale and has more surface decoration.

BYZANTINE PERIOD: 500 – 1453

Architecture

Long before the time of Christ, the dome had been used as a symbol of the heavens and as a covering for sacred places or objects. The domed central plan is particularly characteristic of Byzantine churches; in Constantinople and surrounding regions, however, the central and longitudinal plans are often fused in the form of short, wide, domed basilicas. Domes, usually over square spaces, are supported by pendentives, which were probably developed in Syria, or squinches, which may have originated in Armenia (see Fig. 4-19, p. 43). Domes were sometimes constructed of porous stone or hollow pottery in order to reduce weight and avoid the need for heavy buttressing. Byzantine architecture tends to conceal structural

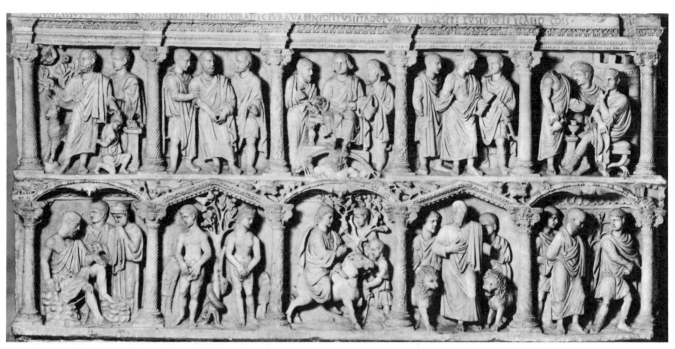

12-4
Sarcophagus of Junius Bassus, (c. 359).
Marble, 46½″ × 96″. Vatican Grottoes, Rome.

masses with flat mosaic decoration and multi-colored marble veneer. Domes and walls appear to be eggshell thin, and capitals of supporting columns are perforated in basketlike designs that make them look hollow and delicate. The supernatural qualities of the sacred place are expressed in the seeming weightlessness and the shimmering color of walls and domes.

SANT' APOLLINARE IN CLASSE (Ravenna, 530–49). The three-aisled basilica (Fig. 12-5) has a characteristically plain exterior (Fig. 12-6) with a tenth-century *campani* (bell tower). Inside (Fig. 12-7), the raised altar receives additional focal emphasis from the framing of the apse and the concentration of the mosaics. Byzantine patronage is evident not only in the mosaics but also in the nave columns; the soft, spongy-appearing capitals are an abstraction from the crisp, leafy, Corinthian form.

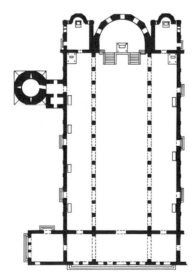

12-5
Plan of Sant' Apollinare in Classe.

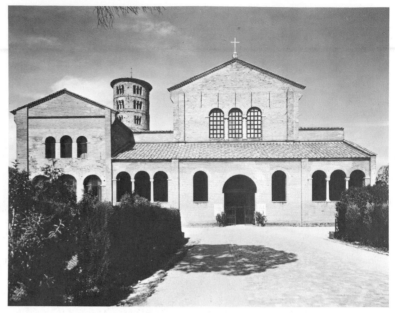

12-6
Sant' Apollinare in Classe, Ravenna, (530–49).

12-7
Interior of Sant' Apollinare in Classe, view toward apse.

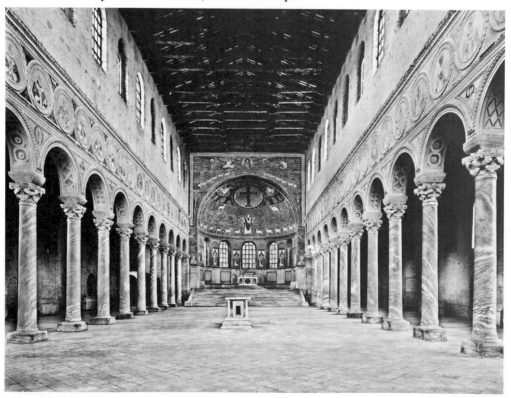

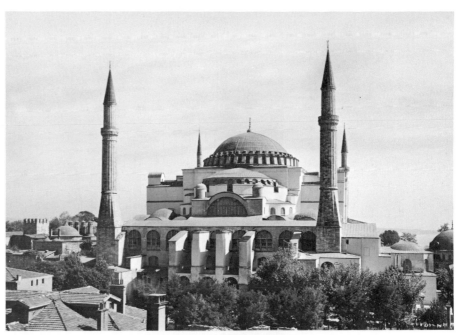

12-8
Hagia Sophia, Constantinople, (532–37).

12-9
Interior of Hagia Sophia.

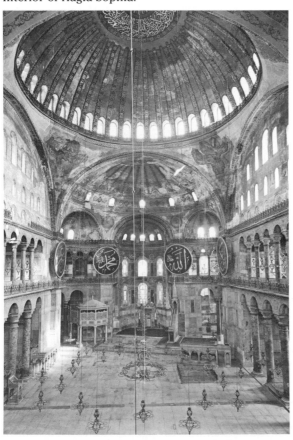

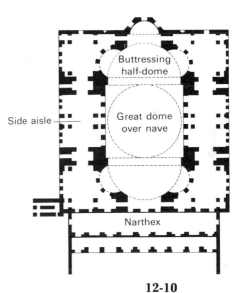

12-10
Plan of Hagia Sophia.

HAGIA SOPHIA (Constantinople, 532–37). Emperor Justinian commissioned this domed basilica (Figs. 12-8 and 12-9) during the first golden age of Byzantine art. A short basilica plan (Fig. 12-10), similar to that of the Basilica of Constantine, is combined with a central dome inspired by the Pantheon; but the effect of this dome (180 feet high) on pendentives is quite different from that of

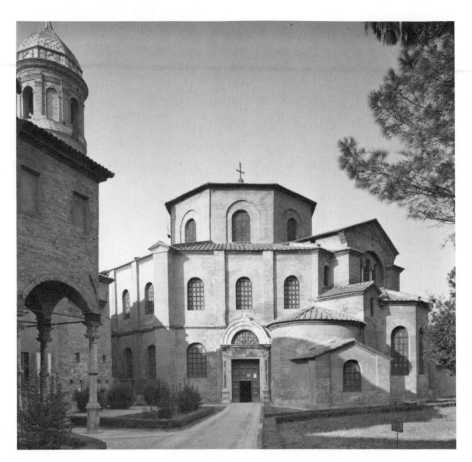

12-11
San Vitale, Ravenna,
(526–47).

its prototype. The blossoming of light from windows around its base makes the Byzantine dome seem to be a hovering canopy. The delicately perforated capitals, the flat shapes in the mosaics, the concealment of the massive supports in the architecture, and the location of the windows all deny the physical weight of the structure and create the effect of a glittering vision, an expressive symbol of heaven.

SAN VITALE (Ravenna, 526–47).   This polygonal central church (Fig. 12-11), built under the patronage of Justinian, shows both the direct influence of Constantinople and its more distant ancestry in buildings like Santa Costanza. The central space is scalloped by semicircular niches in the side aisles and gallery (Figs. 12-12 and 12-13). The lightweight dome is constructed of pottery and mortar, allowing large clerestory windows in the drum. Mosaics cover the interior walls, and the capitals (Fig. 12-14) have intricate Byzantine basketwork weaving.

Painting and Mosaics

By the sixth century, Western (Roman) and Eastern qualities had fused in much of the art produced in and around Constantinople. The resulting style combines frozen figure poses, a disregard for natural scale relationships, and a love of sumptuously decorated flat surfaces. Thus rigid formality is joined with sensuous luxury of design. This style, called Byzantine (after the Byzantine Empire of Constantinople), was not a stable formula, however. Periodic revivals of interest in Greco-Roman art, particularly during the tenth and twelfth centuries, complicated stylistic development between 500 and 1453. Wall paintings and mosaics in Italian churches range from the worldly interests of ancient Roman painting to the symbolism of Byzantine art. Eastern influence is especially strong in the mosaics at Ravenna, one of the main outposts of the Byzantine Empire on Italian soil during the sixth century. The iconoclasm of the eighth and ninth centuries brought to Rome the talents of

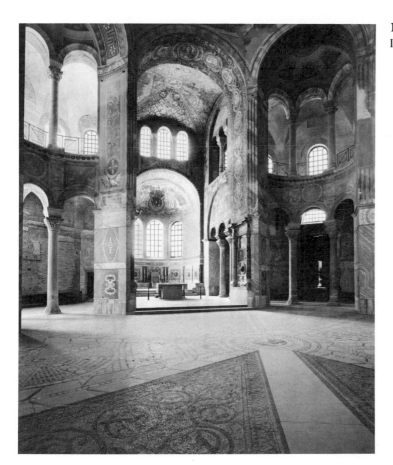

12-12
Interior of San Vitale.

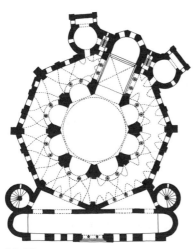

12-13
Plan of San Vitale.

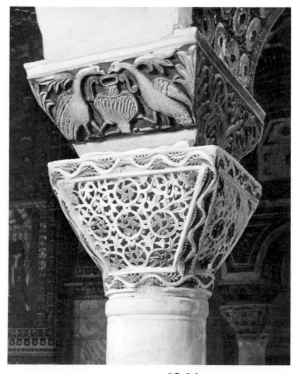

12-14
Capital from San Vitale.

displaced Byzantine artists. Christian painting in Syria and Egypt (except for Alexandria) shows much Byzantine character, although Christian art was interrupted in these areas by Moslem conquests in the seventh century. After the iconoclast period, the second golden age of Byzantine art, lasting roughly from the ninth to the twelfth centuries, brought a number of stylistic changes. More expression of emotion, more massiveness, and more natural anatomy appear, but the formal order of Byzantine art never relinquishes its hold on movement, costume, and figure.

In the decoration of Byzantine churches, subjects tend to be located according to order of importance. The dome was reserved for Christ as Judge, the drum and pendentives for angels and Evangelists, the vault of the apse for the Virgin, and the other regions of the walls for the Twelve Feasts of the Church (Annunciation, Nativity, Presentation, Baptism, Transfiguration, Raising of Lazarus, Entry into Jerusalem, Crucifixion, Harrowing of Hell, Ascension, Pentecost, and Death of the Virgin) and other scenes from the lives of Jesus and Mary. The west wall often showed the Last Judgment.

In manuscript illumination, as in other painting, the anthropomorphic symbolism, landscape interest, mass, space, and natural poses of the old Roman style — sometimes called the Latin style — were affected in varying degrees by the Eastern influence. The stylistic heritage of a painting is sometimes revealed by details; a bearded Christ or one riding sidesaddle into Jerusalem denotes an Eastern background, while a beardless Christ or one riding astride the donkey denotes a Latin source.

ST. APOLLINARIS, apse mosaic from Sant' Apollinare in Classe (Ravenna, 533–49).   This mosaic (Fig. 12-15) is one of the most striking examples of Byzantine art on the Italian peninsula. St. Apollinaris, who was martyred in Ravenna, is shown as

12-15
St. Apollinaris, apse mosaic from Sant' Apollinare in Classe.

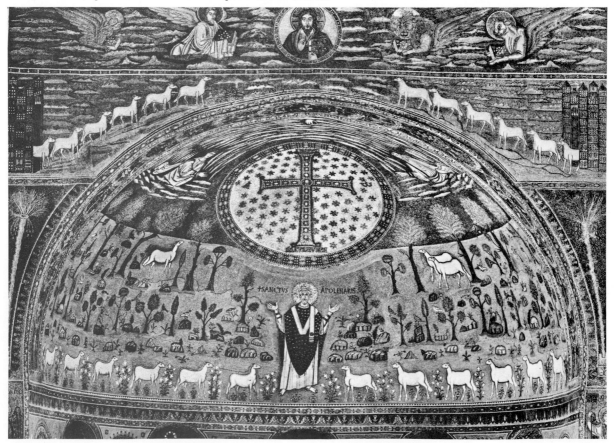

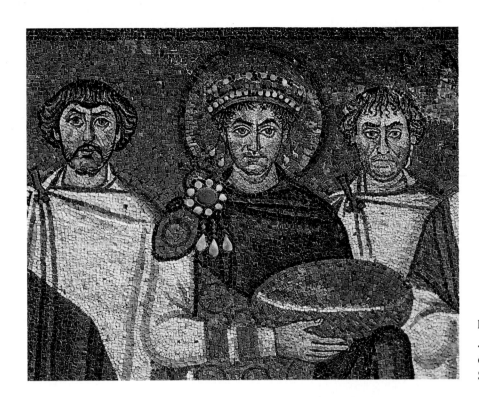

Plate 1

Justinian and Attendants,
detail of an apse mosaic from
San Vitale.

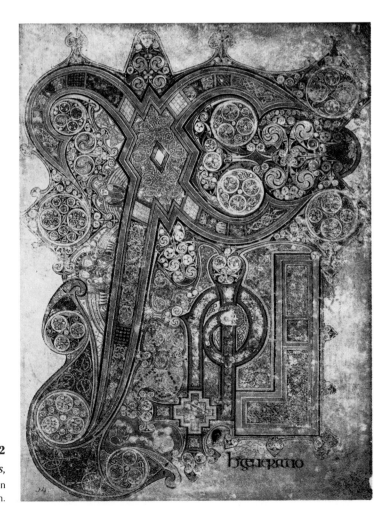

Plate 2
Initial page (XPI) of the *Book of Kells,*
(eighth century).   Reproduced by permission
of the Board of Trinity College, Dublin.

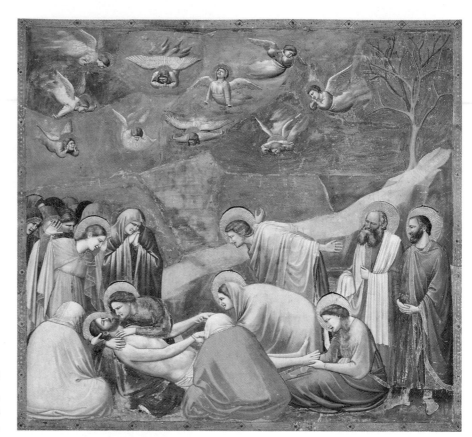

Plate 3
GIOTTO, *Lamentation,*
(*c.* 1305). Fresco. Arena
Chapel, Padua.

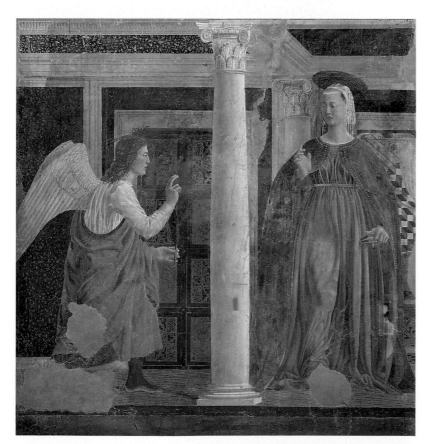

Plate 4
PIERO DELLA FRANCESCA,
The Annunciation, (*c.* 1455).
San Francesco, Arezzo.

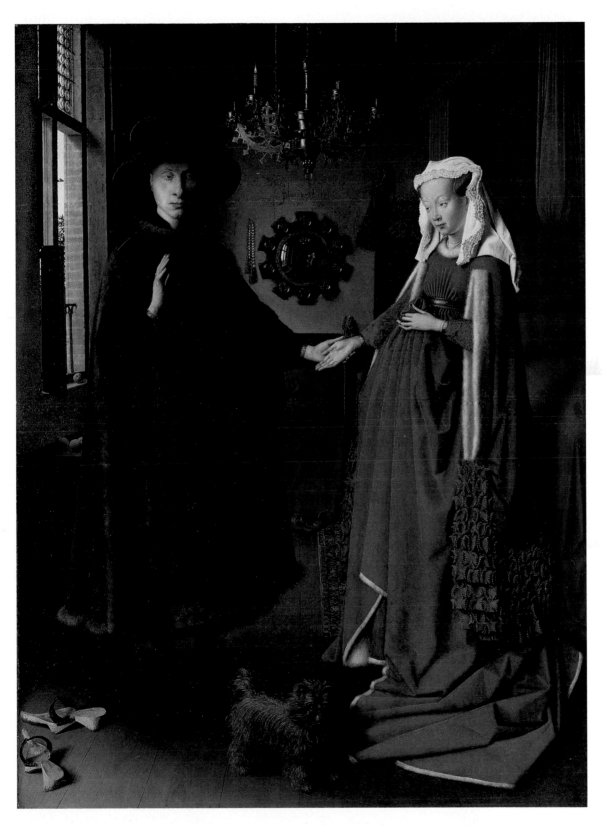

Plate 5

JAN VAN EYCK, *Arnolfini and His Bride,* (1434). Oil on wood panel, approx. 32″ × 22″.

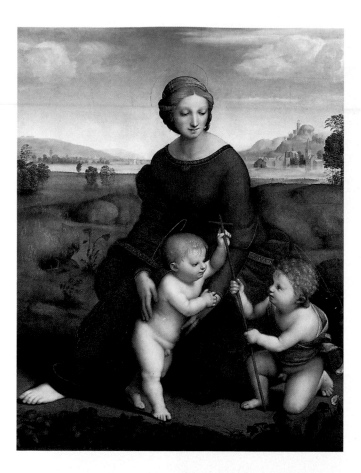

Plate 6
RAPHAEL SANZIO,
Madonna of the Meadow, (1505).
Panel, approx. 4′ × 3′.
Kunsthistorisches Museum, Vienna.

Plate 7
GIOVANNI BELLINI,
St. Francis in Ecstasy, (*c.* 1480).
Panel, 48¾″ × 54″.
Frick Collection, New York.

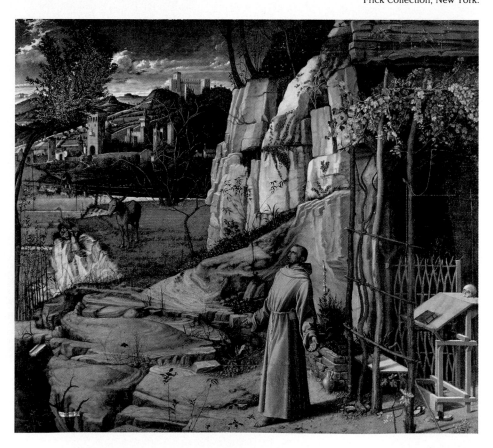

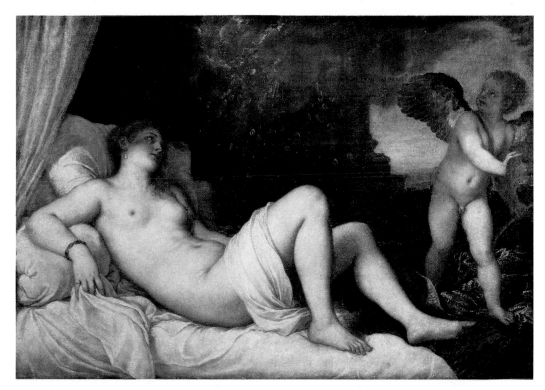

Plate 8

TITIAN, *Danaë, (c.* 1545). Oil on canvas, approx. 4′ × 6′. Museo di Capodimonte, Naples.

Plate 9

GIORGIONE DA CASTELFRANCO, *The Pastoral Concert, (c.* 1508). Oil on canvas, approx. 43″ × 54″. Louvre, Paris.

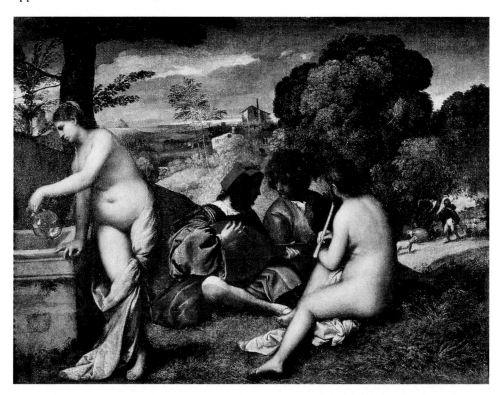

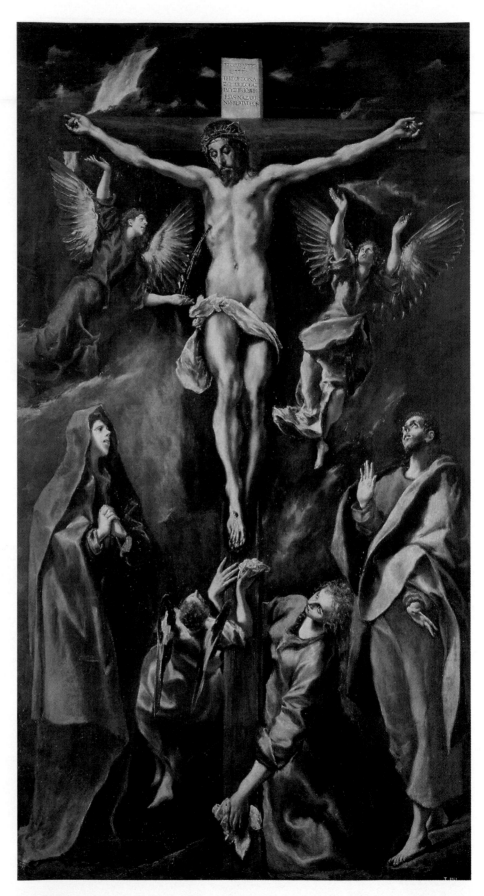

Plate 10

EL GRECO, *The Crucifixion,* (1584–90). Oil on canvas, approx. 10′ × 6′.
Prado, Madrid.

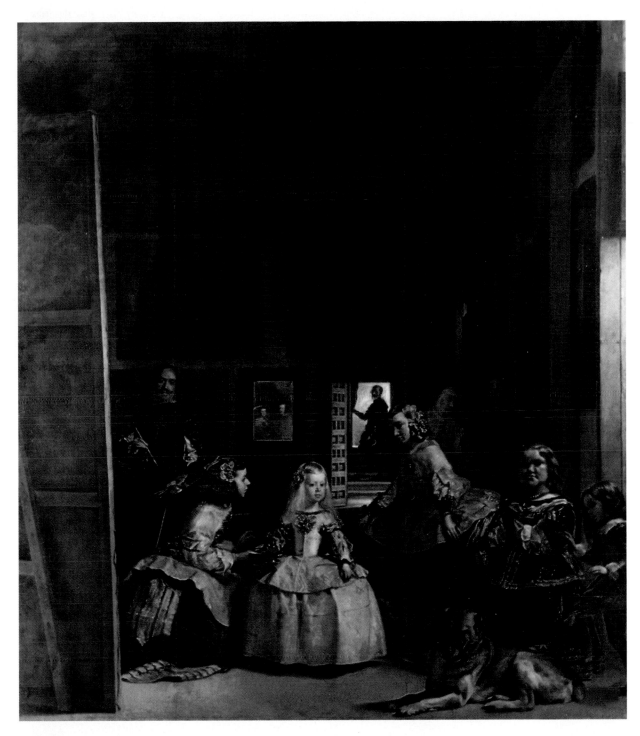

Plate 11
DIEGO VELÁZQUEZ, *The Maids of Honor (Las Meninas),* (1656). Oil on canvas, approx. 10′5″ × 9′.
Prado, Madrid.

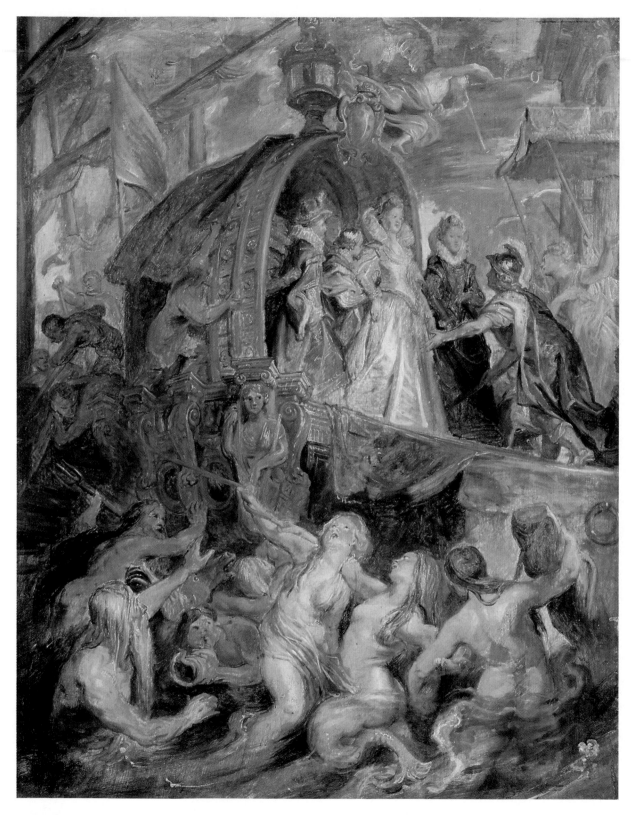

Plate 12
PETER PAUL RUBENS and assistants, study for *The Reception of Marie de' Medici at Marseilles, 3 November 1600,* (1622–25). Oil on wood, approx. 26″ × 19½″.   Alte Pinakothek, Munich.

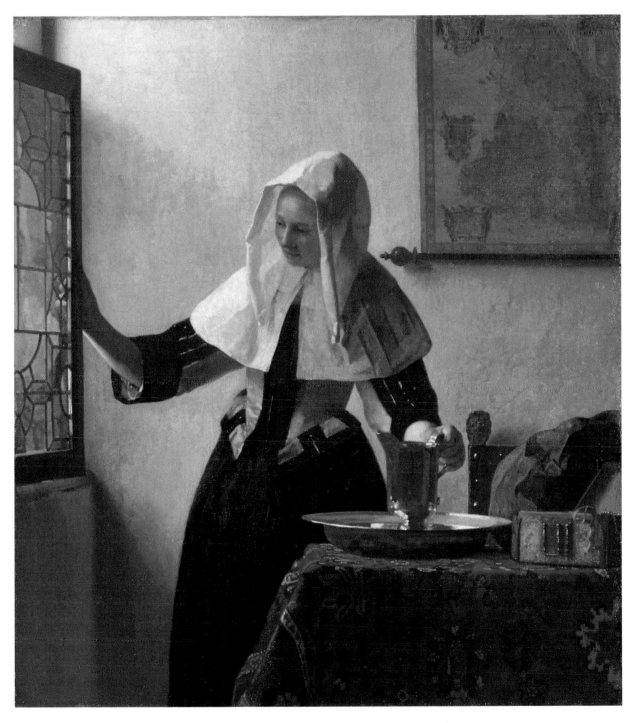

Plate 13

JAN VERMEER, *Young Woman with a Water Jug,* (*c.* 1665). Oil on canvas, approx. 18″ × 16″.
Metropolitan Museum of Art, New York. Gift of Henry G. Marquand, 1889. Marquand Collection (89.15.21).

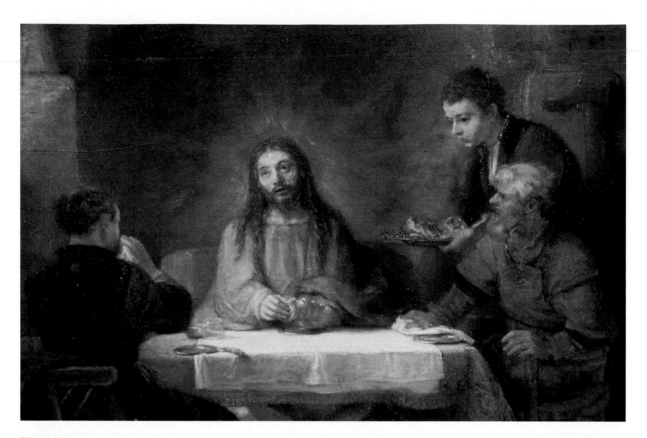

Plate 14
REMBRANDT VAN RIJN, *Supper at Emmaus,* (c. 1648). Oil on panel, approx. 27″ × 26″. Louvre, Paris.

Plate 15

JACOB VAN RUISDAEL,   *Windmill at Wijk,* (1665). Oil on canvas, approx. 2′9″ × 3′5″.

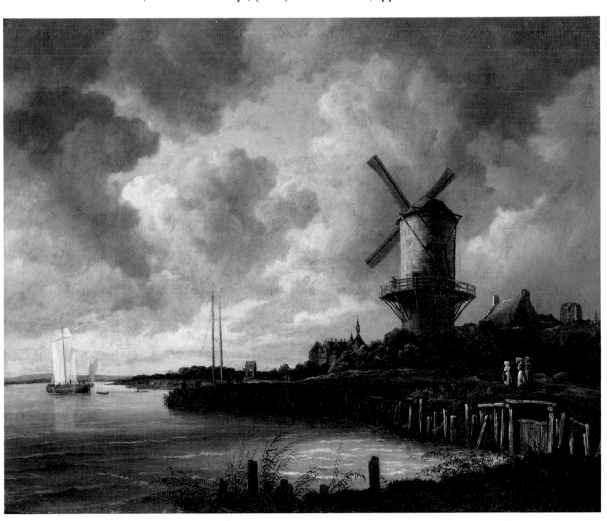

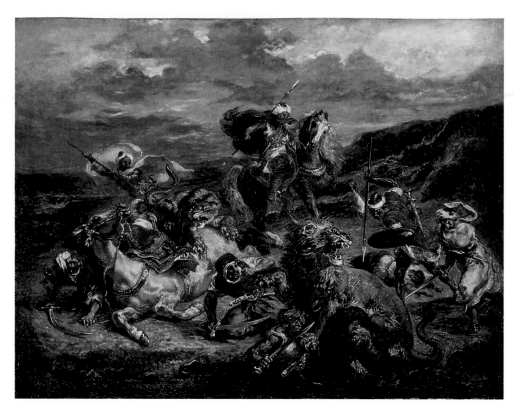

Plate 16

EUGÈNE DELACROIX, *The Lion Hunt,* (1861). Oil on canvas, 30½″ × 38½″.
Collection of The Art Institute of Chicago, Potter Palmer Collection, 1922.

Plate 17

CAMILLE COROT, *Souvenir de Mortefontaine,* (1864).
Oil on canvas, 25¼″ × 34½″.   Louvre, Paris.

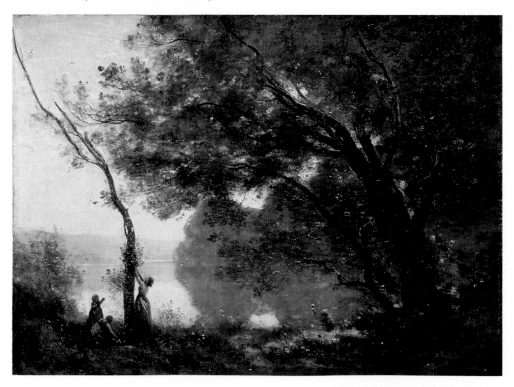

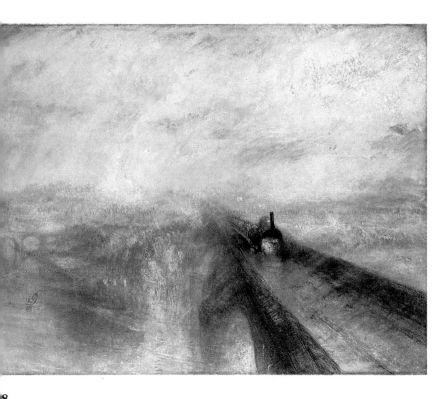

8

H MALLORD WILLIAM TURNER, *Rain, Steam, and Speed,* (1844). Oil on

3' × 4'. Reproduced by courtesy of the Trustees, the National Gallery, London.

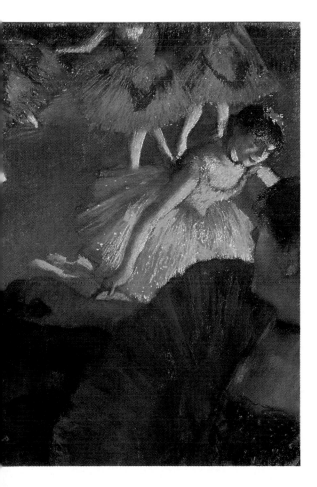

Plate 19

EDGAR DEGAS, *Ballerina and Lady with a Fan,* (*c.* 1885). Pastel on paper, 26" × 20".
John G. Johnson Collection, Philadelphia.

Plate 20

CLAUDE MONET, *Rouen Cathedral,* (1894). Oil
on canvas, approx. 39¼″ × 25⅞″. National
Gallery of Art, Washington, D.C. Chester Dale Collection, 1962.

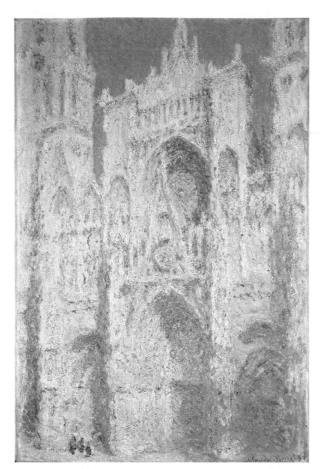

Plate 21

HENRI DE TOULOUSE-LAUTREC,
At the Moulin Rouge, (1892). Oil on canvas,
approx. 48⅜″ × 55¼″.
Helen Birch Bartlett Memorial Collection, Collection of The
Art Institute of Chicago.

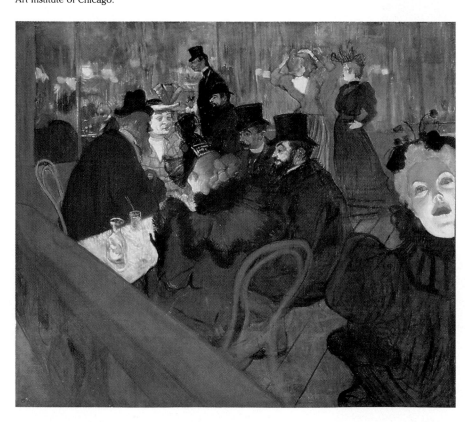

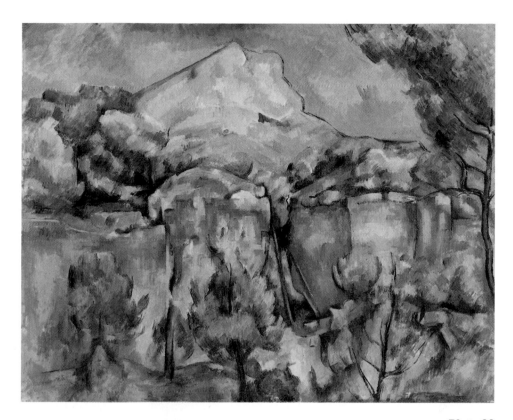

Plate 22
PAUL CÉZANNE,
Mt. Ste.-Victoire from Bibémus Quarry, (*c.* 1898).
Oil on canvas, 25½″ × 32″.   The Baltimore Museum
of Art: The Cone Collection, formed by Dr. Claribel
Cone and Miss Etta Cone of Baltimore, Maryland.

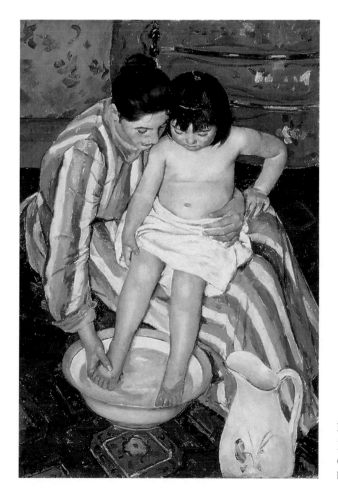

Plate 23
MARY CASSATT,   *The Bath,* (*c.* 1892).
Oil on canvas, 39″ × 26″.
Robert Waller Fund. Collection of The Art Institute of Chicago.

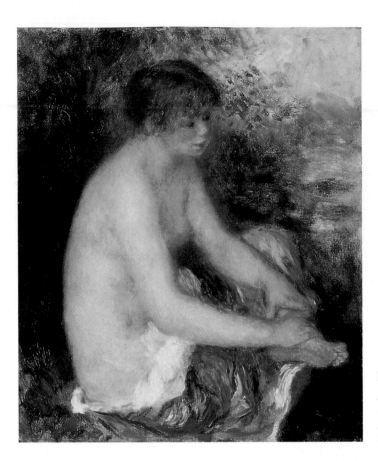

Plate 24

AUGUSTE RENOIR, *Little Blue Nude,*
(*c.* 1880). Oil on canvas, 18¼″ × 15⅛″.
Albright-Knox Art Gallery, Buffalo. Consolidated
Purchase Funds, 1941.

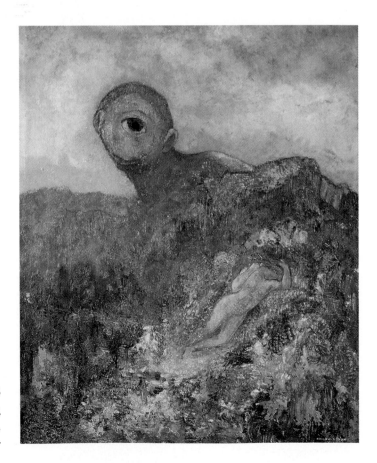

Plate 25

ODILON REDON, *The Cyclops,*
(1900–1905). Oil on panel, 25¼″ × 20″.
Collection: Rijksmuseum Kröller-Müller, Otterlo, Holland.

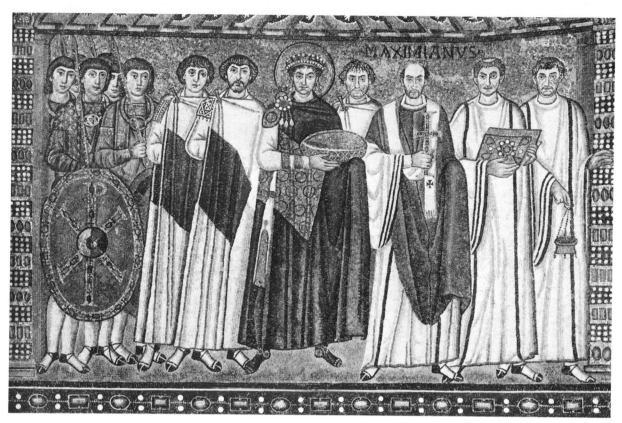

12-16
Justinian and Attendants, mosaic from San Vitale.

an imitator of Christ's martyrdom. Above the saint, the Transfiguration of Christ is symbolized by the vision of the Cross between Moses, Elijah, and three lambs representing disciples. The severe symmetry of the flat shapes and their exotic colors emphasize the symbolic nature of the event.

JUSTINIAN AND ATTENDANTS, mosaic from San Vitale (Ravenna, *c.* 547).   The Emperor, accompanied by his representative in Ravenna, Maximianus, carries a bowl containing the bread of the Eucharist (Plate 1 and Fig. 12-16). The solid, individually detailed portrait heads contrast with the flat shapes of the costumes, and depth is further negated by the brilliant warmth of the gold background. The artist's indifference to weight and space left him free to allow the feet of several figures to stand upon each other. The ritualistic formality of the staring, symmetrically placed images conveys the hypnotic fascination of Byzantine art. A similar composition on the opposite side of the altar shows Justinian's wife, Theodora, carrying the wine for the Eucharist, and her attendants.

12-17
Crossing the Red Sea, a page from the
Paris Psalter, (tenth century).   Bibliothèque
Nationale, Paris.

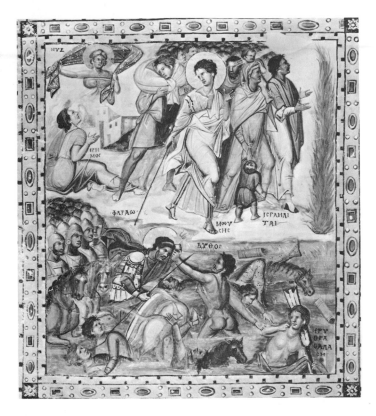

12-18
Madonna and Child on a Curved Throne,
Byzantine school, (thirteenth century).
Panel, 32″ × 19½″.   National Gallery of Art,
Washington, D.C. Andrew W. Mellon Collection, 1937.

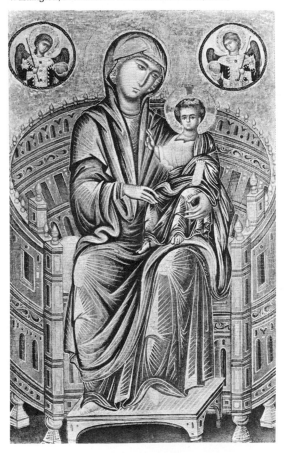

CROSSING THE RED SEA, *a page from the* Paris
Psalter (Bibliothèque Nationale, Paris).   *Crossing the Red Sea* (Fig. 12-17) is one of fourteen
full-page illuminations on parchment in the *Paris
Psalter* (Psalm book). The distortions in scale and
anatomy and the schematic treatment of costume
reveal Byzantine interests. The modeled roundness of some forms, the relatively natural musculature of the nude sea gods and goddesses, and the
landscape setting are debts to earlier Roman art.
The use of human figures for nature divinities, such
as the sea gods and the figure of night (at upper
left with canopy), is also characteristic of earlier
Roman art.

MADONNA ENTHRONED (13th-cen. panel painting,
32″ × 19½″. National Gallery of Art, Washington,
D.C.).   Standard forms are used in the costume
folds and in the flat modeling of the faces in this
painting (Fig. 12-18). Repetition and variation
occur in thematic shapes, such as the radiating
highlights in the clothing. Mass, depth, and natural
effects in proportion and drapery are sacrificed for
stern order and elegant formality. The result is a
symbolic image that stands outside the realm of
the everyday world.

Sculpture

There was very little monumental sculpture in the Byzantine Empire during the Byzantine period; the case is quite different in northern Italy and in Europe, as we shall see in the next chapter. Sarcophagi produced in Constantinople or in its spheres of influence show variations of the Byzantine style. Most of the ivory consular diptychs in the Byzantine style seem to come from the area of Constantinople and to date from the sixth century. Icons or reliquaries combine small-scale relief sculpture, often in gold, with enamel painting. Their portability helped to spread the influence of Byzantine art.

SARCOPHAGUS OF THEODORUS, *from Sant' Apollinare in Classe* (Ravenna, 7th cen., marble, 39½″ × 81″).   The Byzantine tendency to use symbols rather than literal description is well illustrated in this sarcophagus (Fig. 12-19). The peacocks were symbols of immortality; the grapevines referred to the wine of the Eucharist. In the center and on the

12-19
Sarcophagus of Theodorus, from Sant' Apollinare in Classe, (seventh century). Marble.

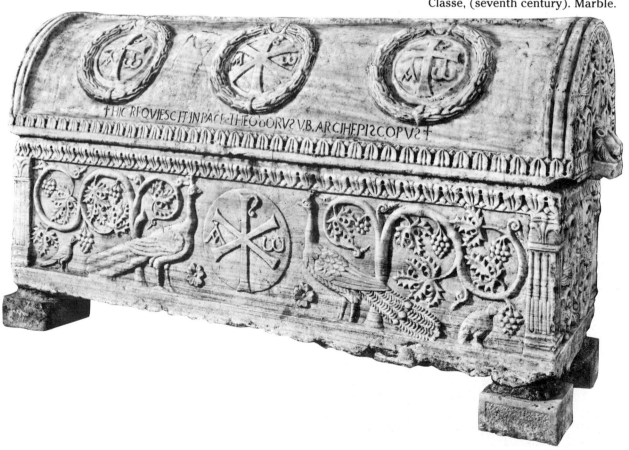

lid, the Chi-Rho symbol is hung with Alpha and Omega, the first and last letters of the Greek alphabet, standing for the all-inclusiveness of Christ. The symbols are framed by wreaths of victory. There is little interest in the natural detail of the vines or animals and no illusion of depth. The forms have little modeling and appear as shallow layers applied to a flat surface.

DIPTYCH OF ANASTASIUS (dated 517, ivory, each leaf 14″ × 5″. Bibliothèque Nationale, Paris).   The two halves of a diptych frequently carried approximately the same scene. In this example (Fig. 12-20), the newly elected consul, Anastasius, is shown in the official act of throwing down the *mappa* (a piece of cloth used as a signal to start the games in an arena). He is surrounded by winged goddesses of victory. At the bottom right, spectators watch a combat of men and wild beasts. The disregard for natural scale relationships between

12-20
Diptych of Anastasius, (517). Ivory, each leaf 14″ × 5″.   Bibliothèque Nationale, Paris.

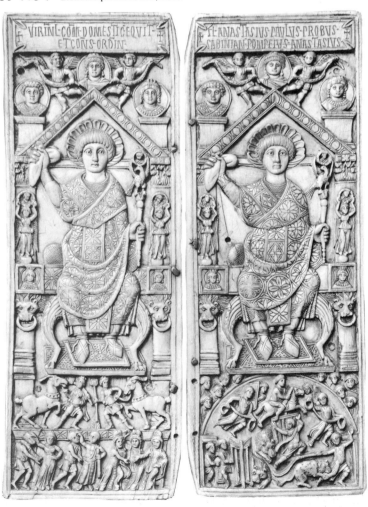

the figures, the preference for flat ornate surfaces rather than mass and the illusion of deep space, the stiff frontal pose, and the masklike faces are all characteristic of Byzantine art.

Suggestions for Further Study

Ainalov, D. V. *Hellenistic Origins of Byzantine Art*. Translated by E. Sobolevitch and S. Sobolevitch. New Brunswick, N.J.: Rutgers University Press, 1961.

Beckwith, John. *Early Christian and Byzantine Art* (Pelican History of Art). Baltimore: Penguin Books, 1980.

Demus, Otto. *Byzantine Mosaic Decoration*. New Rochelle, N.Y.: Caratzas Bros., 1976.

Grabar, André. *Byzantine Painting*. Translated by Stuart Gilbert. New York: Rizzoli International, 1979.

———. *Christian Iconography: A Study of Its Origins* (Bollingen Series). Princeton, N.J.: Princeton University Press, 1980.

Kitzinger, Ernst. *Byzantine Art in the Making: Main Lines of Stylistic Development in Mediterranean Art, 3rd – 7th Century*. Cambridge, Mass.: Harvard University Press, 1977.

Krautheimer, Richard. *Early Christian and Byzantine Architecture* (Pelican History of Art). Baltimore: Penguin Books, 1975.

Mango, Cyril. *Byzantine Architecture* (History of World Architecture). New York: Abrams, 1974.

Mathew, Gervase. *Byzantine Aesthetics*. New York: Viking, 1963.

Volbach, W. F., and Max Hirmer. *Early Christian Art*. Translated by Christopher Ligota. New York: Abrams, 1962.

Von Simson, Otto G. *The Sacred Fortress: Byzantine Art and Statecraft in Ravenna*. Chicago: University of Chicago Press, 1976.

Weitzmann, Kurt. *Illustrations in Roll and Codex: A Study of the Origin and Method of Text Illustration*. Princeton, N.J.: Princeton University Press, 1947.

———. *The Icon*. New York: Knopf, 1982.

13

Medieval
Art
in
the
North

400 – 1400

The art of the Early Christian and Byzantine periods is often considered the Mediterranean branch of Medieval art. *Medieval* and *Middle Ages* are both vague and unsympathetic labels invented by scholars who thought of the years between the decline of Rome and the beginning of the Renaissance as a barren transitional period. Today we are more appreciative of the age, but the labels remain standard terms. The beginning and end dates of the Medieval period vary with different interpretations. This text will follow one widespread practice in using the term Medieval with particular emphasis on Europe north of Rome during the period between 400 and 1400.

While Early Christian and Byzantine cultures were developing in the Mediterranean area, Celto-Germanic cultures developed to the north in areas that now include France, Germany, Scandinavia, the Netherlands, Belgium, and the British Isles.

The Celto-Germanic peoples inhabiting these areas, called Barbarians by the Greeks and Romans, had an indigenous art before their widespread conversion to Christianity during the third to the tenth centuries. Celto-Germanic art slowly changed due to the influence of Early Christian and Byzantine art brought north by missionaries. Art in the northern countries may be divided into at least four periods: *Celto-Germanic art* (400–800), *Carolingian art* (750–987), *Romanesque art* (mainly eleventh and twelfth centuries), and *Gothic art* (overlapping the Romanesque in the twelfth century and extending in some areas into the sixteenth century). The terms Romanesque and Gothic are also misleading and are retained only because of entrenched usage. Romanesque, or "Roman-like," is an inadequate description of eleventh- and twelfth-century art, just as Gothic, originally meant to imply the barbarism of the Gothic tribes, is a pathetic misnomer for such things as the thirteenth-century French cathedrals.

The greatest efforts of Medieval art were in the service of Christianity, the unifying element in a widely divided Europe. The modern distinction between artist and craftsman did not exist; the best talent was often employed to design liturgical equipment, furniture, or jewelry. Since individual identity and originality were not so highly valued as they are today, many works were unsigned and stylistic change was generally gradual. The spread of stylistic influences can be traced along trade routes, the Crusade routes, and pilgrimage routes. From the sixth century on, pilgrims traveled from northwest Europe to three major destinations: Rome, the Shrine of St. James at Santiago de Compostela in Spain, and the Holy Land.

The art of the first three periods developed mainly in the monasteries. Gothic art was more urban and came from the cathedral centers developed by the *secular clergy* (clergy who did not withdraw from lay society to live by rigid rules, as did the regular or monastic clergy). The word *cathedral* comes from the cathedra, the throne of the bishop, placed in the main church of the bishop's diocese.

CELTO-GERMANIC AND CAROLINGIAN ART: 400–987

Metalwork

Many of the earliest remains from the Celto-Germanic period are metalwork of bronze or gold decorated with enamel. Bracelets, brooches, armbands, swords, and purse covers are typical. The style combines lively, intricate, geometric designs with fantastic animal and human forms. Constantly expanding and contracting shapes, sudden changes of direction, and amazing intricacy account for the vitality and richness of the work. There is no illusion of mass or space.

PURSE COVER, *from the Sutton Hoo ship burial* (British Museum, London).   This enamel and gold purse cover (Fig. 13-1) came from the grave goods of an East Anglian king who died in 655. Although it is a fine example of early Celto-Germanic metalwork, the human figures are atypical. The style may have been brought to western Europe by migrating tribes from central Asia; it resembles the abstract animal style of nomadic art from southern Siberia and northern Persia.

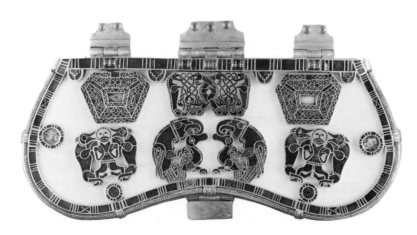

13-1
Purse cover, from the Sutton Hoo ship burial, (before 655). Gold and enamel.   British Museum, London.

Painting

The most significant painting of the Celto-Germanic period that has been preserved from northwestern Europe is in illuminated manuscripts from the British Isles; the style is called *Hiberno-Saxon* or *Celtic* after the Celts of ancient Ireland. Monasteries became centers of learning where the manuscripts, mainly of the Scriptures, were copied and illuminated. Colors with gum, glue, or gelatin binders were used on parchment or *vellum* (calfskin or kidskin). Like the metalwork, the illuminations employ intricate spiral designs, interlaced shapes in *strapwork* (flat bands resembling cut leather), and fantastic animals. The Celto-Germanic style was characteristic of Hiberno-Saxon painting until the ninth century. The style slowly changed, however, under the influence of Byzantine paintings and ivories brought from the south by Christian missionaries, and the Hiberno-Saxon illuminations developed various mixtures of abstract Celto-Germanic design and the relatively more static and representational Early Christian and Byzantine art. During the Carolingian era (750–987), important centers of manuscript illumination were established on the Continent under the patronage of Charlemagne, and different styles evolved in different geographical areas. In the Carolingian Empire, as in the British Isles, Celto-Germanic stylistic traits were increasingly modified by the influence of Early Christian and Byzantine art. In addition, Carolingian painting shows contact with older Roman art; poses, drapery, and landscape sometimes are closer to Roman art than to the Early Christian and Byzantine styles that intervened.

INITIAL PAGE (XPI) *of the* **Book of Kells** (8th cen., 12⅝″ × 9½″. Trinity College Library, Dublin). The manuscript known as the *Book of Kells* was probably made at the monastery of Kells in Ireland or at that of Iona in Scotland. It contains tables of references, prefaces and summaries, the Gospels, and part of a glossary of Hebrew names. Here Celto-Germanic art serves Christianity. Intermingled with the interlaces and spiral designs are human heads and animals. Other pages in the book depict more of the human figure, but this illumination of the sacred initials of Christ (Plate 2 and Fig. 13-2) illustrates the typical shapes and the

13-2

Detail from the initial page (XPI) of the *Book of Kells.*

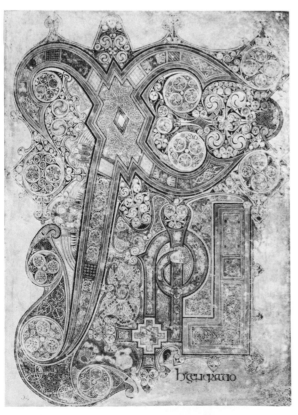

swirling dynamism of line that modified Roman, Early Christian, and Byzantine elements to form Medieval art.

ST. MATTHEW, from the Gospel Book of Archbishop Ebbo of Reims (Épernay, 816–35, 6⅞″ × 5⁹⁄₁₆″).   The so-called Reims School (a regional style) of Carolingian illumination had classicizing tendencies; the pose, costume, massiveness, facial type, and sketchy brush strokes all reflect the influence of ancient Roman art. The Carolingian painter intensified the nervous activity of the lines here (Fig. 13-3), giving the image considerable dramatic vitality.

Architecture

Both Celto-Germanic and Carolingian architecture made extensive use of wood. *Half-timber* wattle and daub construction consisted of a carefully joined wood frame filled in with mud or plaster on reed mats. Sometimes walls were *palisades* (logs planted vertically side by side, as in a stake fence). Norsemen built frame houses around a central pole resembling the mast of a ship. Such *mast construction* was often covered with vertical wood sheathing. Carolingian builders used stone only for important buildings. The little that remains of their architecture reveals a strong interest in longitudinal plans. The basilica plan was elaborated to create more space for altars, reliquaries, and worshipers. An *ambulatory* (aisle around the outside of the apse) was added (for a Gothic example, see Fig. 13-31); secondary chapels were provided by *radiating chapels* around the outside of the ambulatory or by *apses in echelon* (apses placed beside the main apse or on the arms of the transept); and the main apse was separated from the transept by a nave extension called the *choir* (see Fig. 13-31), which allowed space for the clergy choirs. Under the raised choir and apse, a *crypt* provided space for special tombs of local saints and founders of the church or for relics. A Carolingian basilica might be a *double-ender*— that is, it might have an apse at the west end as well as at the east—or it might have a *westwork*, a high, blocklike enlargement giving the effect of a west transept and containing a narthex on the ground level and a chapel above. Carolingian basilicas had timber roofs and many towers; a tower

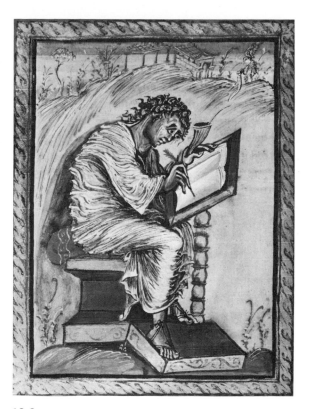

13-3
St. Matthew, from the *Gospel Book of Archbishop Ebbo of Reims,* Épernay, (*c.* 816–35).   Bibliothèque Nationale, Paris.

over a westwork and flanking towers at the sides would be echoed by a tower over the *crossing* (where the transept crosses the nave) with flanking towers at the sides. Central-form churches might be octagonal, with tunnel and cross vaults, or a combination of the apse-buttressed square and cross-in-square, four-column type. Such central churches show Byzantine influence in their form and in the rich, flat patterns of decorative details, which were sometimes imported from Italy.

PALATINE CHAPEL OF CHARLEMAGNE (Aachen, Aix-la-Chapelle).   The major extant example of Carolingian architecture is this central church (Figs. 13-4 and 13-5) designed by Odo of Metz and dedicated in 805. It reveals Charlemagne's admiration for Byzantine culture because the polygonal plan and the general form are similar to those of the church of San Vitale in Ravenna. Marble columns were imported from Italy. The central octagonal space is covered by a domical vault instead of a true dome, and is surrounded by a cross-vaulted side aisle and a gallery with special tunnel vaults. The chapel, which also served as a tomb for Charlemagne, was originally part of a palace complex and contained a throne in its westwork.

ROMANESQUE ART: 1000–1200

Architecture

The Romanesque period produced more buildings, greater variety, and more advanced masonry techniques than the Celto-Germanic and Carolingian periods. The wooden roofing used over the naves of many basilican churches from Early Christian through Carolingian times — a roofing that invited disastrous fires — was slowly replaced by fireproof stone vaulting. Ancient Roman features, such as massive walls, vaults, engaged columns, and pilasters, were used but with significant changes. Romanesque building was of masonry, employing tunnel and groin vaults inspired by Roman and Byzantine architecture. Although dating is controversial, pioneering construction in ribbed groin vaults (see pp. 41–42) appears to have occurred in Durham Cathedral (Anglo-Norman England), in St. Étienne in Caen (Normandy), and in Lombard churches such as Sant' Ambrogio (Milan). The dark, domical, strongly separated nave bays in the Lombard churches contrast with the level vaults and more flowing, continuous nave spaces at Durham. Italian and English characteristics were reconciled by French builders at Caen.

13-4
Interior of the Palatine Chapel of Charlemagne, Aachen, (792–805).

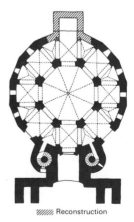

////// Reconstruction

13-5
Restored plan of the Palatine Chapel of Charlemagne.

Despite its variety, much Romanesque church architecture is characterized by (1) fortresslike massiveness; (2) Roman arches; (3) two or more towers; (4) *splayed openings*—doorways or windows formed by layers of increasingly smaller arches producing a funnel effect (for a Gothic example, see Fig. 13-27); (5) *blind arcades*—arcades attached to a wall for decoration or for buttressing rather than to create openings; (6) *corbel tables* (Fig. 13-6)—a *stringcourse* (horizontal band or molding) supported in the Lombard type by a row of continuous, small, blind arches, and in the French type by small brackets projecting from the wall; and (7) *wheel windows*—round windows divided into sections by stone dividers radiating from the center like the spokes of a wheel. The use of *Lombard pilaster strips* (slender pilasters) spreads northward along the trade routes to Germany, as did the exterior arcaded galleries developed in Tuscany and Lombardy, while the Lombard porch, supported by two columns resting on the backs of lions, did not find wide acceptance elsewhere. Tuscan churches employed the Early Christian basilica plan, with the entrance at the west end and the apse at the east; they were often decorated with patterns of different colors in stone veneer. In Germany the double-ender plan was often employed, while in France, in addition to the pilgrimage church type (see p. 154), some basilicas were built in the form of *hall churches,* where the side aisles are as high as the nave, and the nave arcade rises to the springing of the vaults. Some of the most unusual examples of French Romanesque architecture are the domed churches in Aquitania; their source would seem to be Byzantine architecture, perhaps by way of St. Mark's in Venice.

CHURCH OF ST. MICHAEL (Hildesheim). The Church of St. Michael (Figs. 13-7 and 13-8) was built under the direction of Bishop Bernward and completed in 1033, during the period of the Ottonian emperors in Germany. Carolingian architecture had provided all the basic elements. St. Michael's is a double-ender with a second transept, a choir, an apse, a crypt, and a crypt ambulatory in the west end. The nave roof is of wood. The entrances are at the sides of the nave, partly sacrificing the axial emphasis of a basilica plan. Towers over the crossings of both transepts and at their

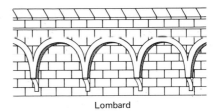
Lombard

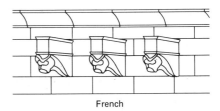
French

13-6
Types of corbel tables.

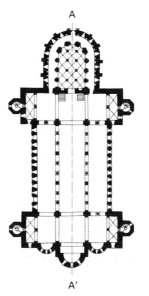

13-7
Section and plan of St. Michael's.

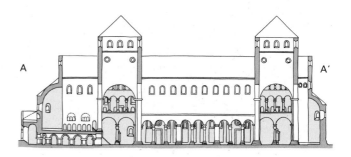

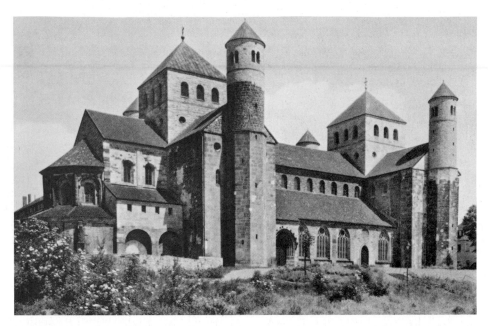

13-8
Abbey church of
St. Michael, Hildesheim,
(*c.* 1001–33). Restored.

ends produce an almost equal exterior balance of east and west. The church was severely damaged in the Second World War.

ST. SERNIN (Toulouse).   The Church of St. Sernin (Fig. 13-9) was begun in the eleventh century and completed in the twelfth, with the exception of the upper part of the crossing tower (built in the thirteenth century) and the west façade, which was never completed. The twelfth-century architect was Raymond Gayrard. St. Sernin is a pilgrimage church and one of the largest surviving Romanesque churches in France. It illustrates the elaboration of the basilica plan by means of choir, ambulatory, apses in echelon, radiating apses, double side aisles, and aisles around the transept (Fig. 13-10). The high nave arcade (Fig. 13-11) rests on *compound piers* (piers of several parts, here having the form of superimposed pilasters and engaged columns) and is topped by a gallery, which provides more room for the congregation. There is no clerestory, for the heavy tunnel vault needs the abutment of the gallery vaults to sustain it. The bays are clearly marked by the transverse arches resting on engaged columns rising all the way from the floor. The columns break through the horizontal lines to establish a vertical emphasis that suggests the Gothic architecture to come. The exterior exhibits round-arched windows, French and Lombard corbel tables, and blind arcades.

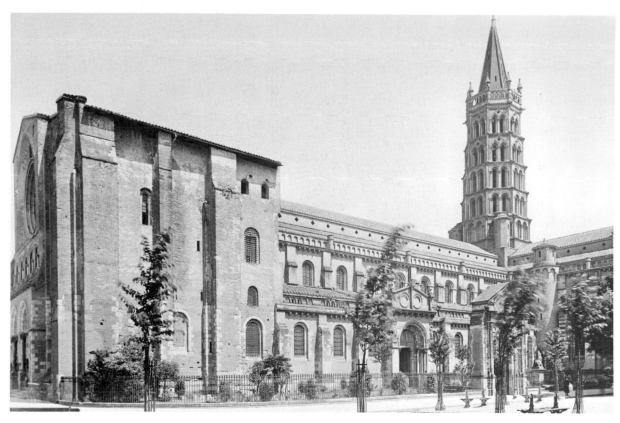

13-9
St. Sernin, Toulouse, (eleventh and twelfth centuries).

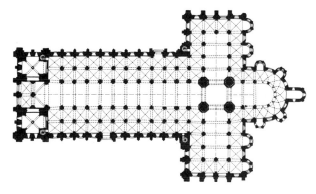

13-10
Plan of St. Sernin.

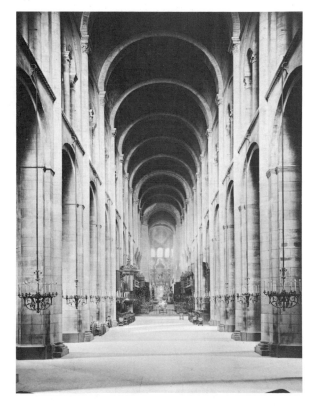

13-11
Interior of St. Sernin (view toward apse).

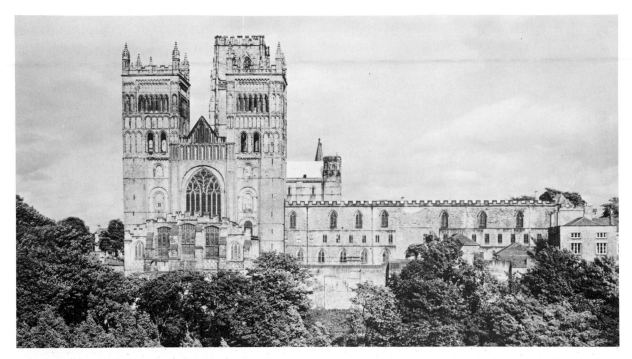

13-12
West façade of Durham Cathedral, (eleventh and twelfth centuries).

13-13
Plan of Durham
Cathedral.

13-14
Nave of Durham Cathedral, (begun *c.* 1093).

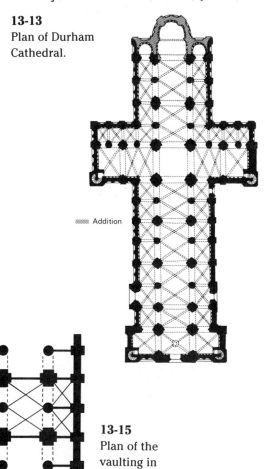

Addition

13-15
Plan of the
vaulting in
Durham Cathedral.

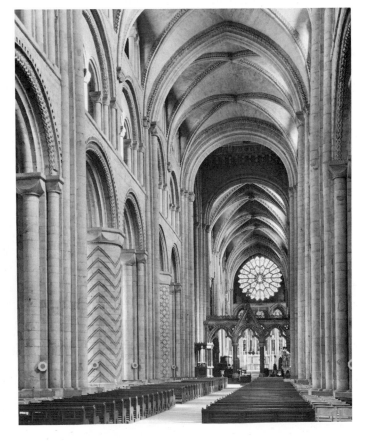

DURHAM CATHEDRAL (England, 11th–12th cens., with later additions such as 13th- and 15th-cen. towers).   Durham Cathedral (Fig. 13-12) is a basilica 469 feet long with a large crossing tower and a square east end (Fig. 13-13). An *alternating system of supports* (here, compound piers alternate with columns) is used, and the heavy round columns that constitute the secondary supports are carved with bold geometric decoration (Fig. 13-14). Two-part bays, with two sets of diagonal ribs between each pair of transverse arches (see Fig. 13-15), a level roof ridge formed by the *crowns* (the highest point in an arch or vault), and light from clerestory windows give an effect of continuous unidirectional space in the nave (the Durham vaults are 73 feet high). The level vaulting is achieved by employing pointed arches in the transverse and side arches so that they reach the height of the semicircular diagonal ribs. (Fig. 4-17c, p. 42, shows how this can be done with the exclusive use of pointed arches.) Durham's nave vaults are distinctive in their use of two sets of

diagonal ribs for each bay (Fig. 13-15). Like the Church of La Trinité in Caen (the sister church to St. Étienne), Durham has flying buttresses that support the wall at clerestory level, although these buttresses are hidden under a shed roof. Both in vaulting and buttressing, Durham provided an important basis for Gothic architecture.

SANT' AMBROGIO (Milan).   The construction of the cathedral extended from the ninth to the twelfth century, with the ribbed four-part cross vaults dating from the twelfth century. The exterior is massive (Fig. 13-16) and simply decorated with pilaster strips and Lombard corbel tables. There are two towers of unequal height beside the narthex and a low polygonal tower over the octagonal domed vault at the crossing. From the atrium, one passes through the narthex to a nave of three low, dark bays (Fig. 13-17). A domical effect comes from the cross vaults because the bays are square, and the ribs and transverse arches are semicircular (Fig. 4-17a, p. 42). An alternating system of piers

13-16
Sant' Ambrogio, Milan, (late ninth to early twelfth centuries).

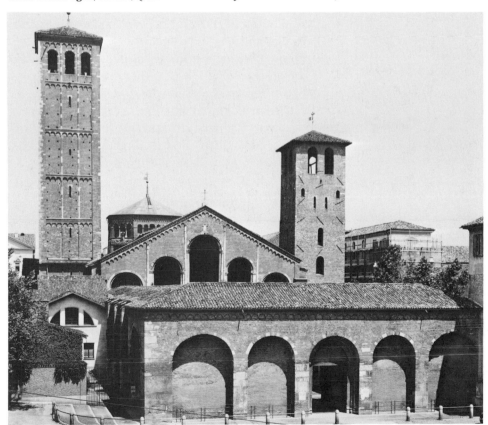

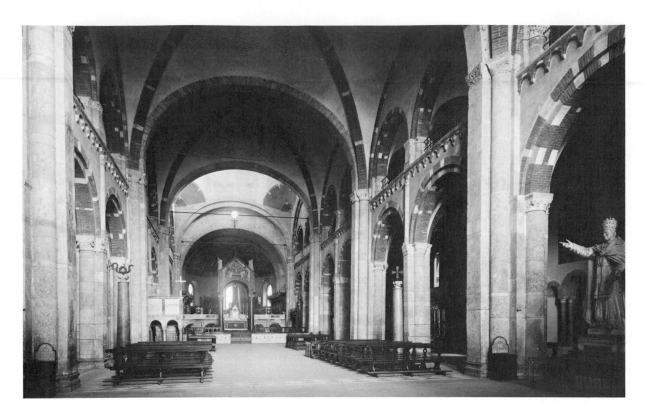

13-17
Interior of Sant' Ambrogio.

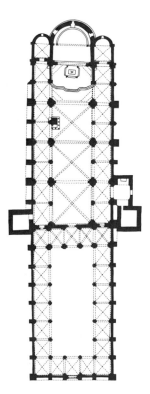

13-18
Plan of Sant' Ambrogio.

divides each bay into two nave arches and two gallery arches. The gallery vaults buttress the nave vaults and leave no room for a clerestory. The side aisles terminate in apses in echelon beside the main apse (Fig. 13-18). There is no ambulatory and only the suggestion of a choir. The nave vaults of such Lombard churches place them beside Durham Cathedral in England (built under Norman occupation) and St. Étienne in France as leaders in Romanesque vaulting.

ST. ÉTIENNE (Caen, 11th–12th cens.).   The west façade (Fig. 13-19) of this Norman basilica has a strong relationship to the interior (Figs. 13-20 and 13-21). The three divisions on the horizontal plane (Fig. 13-19) reflect the interior divisions into nave and side aisles; the three divisions from the bottom to the base of the towers echo the three-part elevation of the nave within. The Gothic steeples must be ignored; the towers were originally flat. An eleventh-century wooden roof over the nave was replaced in the twelfth century by six-part ribbed cross vaults (Fig. 4-16, p. 41). To avoid a domical effect, the diagonal ribs (Fig. 13-20) were depressed to less than a semicircle (Fig. 4-17b,

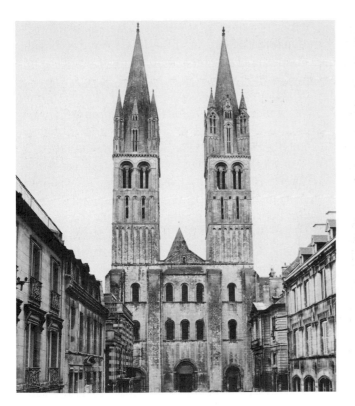

13-19
West façade of St. Étienne, Caen, (begun *c.* 1067).

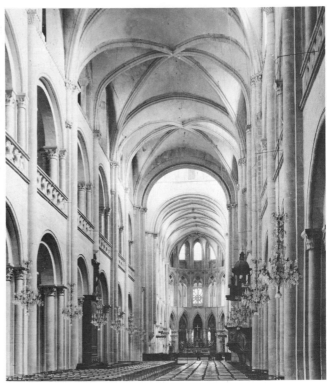

13-20
Interior of St. Étienne, (vaulted *c.* 1115–20).

p. 42). The powerful convergence of the ribs hints at the part-by-part character of Lombard naves, but the level crowns here provide the spatial unity of Durham Cathedral. Every other compound pier is given extra engaged elements that rise to support the ribs and transverse arches, creating an *alternating system* of supports. The *chevet* (the apse, ambulatory, and radiating chapels seen in Fig. 13-21) is thirteenth-century Gothic.

Sculpture

The main sources for Romanesque sculpture are Celto-Germanic art, Roman art, and Early Christian and Byzantine art. The Carolingian period had shared the Byzantine preference for miniature sculpture. The revival of monumental sculpture came with the Romanesque period, although even then many large sculptural compositions were based on small ivory carvings or on manuscript illuminations. Romanesque sculpture is generally found around the entrances to churches — that is, on the *jambs* (layers of the splayed opening) of the door, in the *tympanum* (framed surface over the

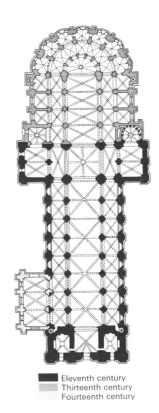

■ Eleventh century
▨ Thirteenth century
□ Fourteenth century

13-21
Plan of St. Étienne.

door), and on the *trumeau* (center post) of a double door; on columns, piers, and capitals; on altars and baptismal fonts; and on tombs. Subjects came from the Old and New Testaments, the Apocrypha, the lives of the saints, the labors of the months (a visual calendar of man's duties in the husbandry of the land), allegorical figures representing the Virtues and the Vices or the liberal arts, and the signs of the zodiac. There are also fantastic animals, which may have personified evil, and geometric or floral designs. Such elements suggest the influence of Celto-Germanic art. The capitals of columns may have been modifications of Greco-Roman forms, geometric ornament, or narrative relief. A number of pre-Christian Roman symbols are woven into the Christian subjects, as in Byzantine art. Romanesque sculpture has considerable regional variation ranging from angular, jerky, stiff figures in crowded linear designs (Fig. 2-4) to relatively massive calm forms. The more massive work is found in southern France and in Italy, where the tradition of ancient Roman art was strong. The beginnings of individual artists' styles can be seen in the works of some of the sculptors whose names have been preserved, such as Gislebertus of

France (Cathedral at Autun), Antelami of Italy (Fidenza Cathedral), and Renier of Huy of Belgium (Baptismal Font at St. Barthélemy, Liège).

ADAM AND EVE REPROACHED BY THE LORD, panel from the doors of Hildesheim Cathedral (bronze, each panel 23″ × 43″).   This example of Ottonian bronze casting (Fig. 13-22), done about 1015, was probably inspired by sculptured doors that Bishop Bernward had seen in Rome; it was originally made for the Church of St. Michael. Each of the two doors is divided into eight panels. The subjects depicted are the advent of sin and the means of salvation; the left door deals with the Fall of Man and the Murder of Abel, and the right door tells the story of Christ from the Annunciation to the Ascension. As in Ottonian manuscripts, the abrupt angularity of the figures, the active poses, and the severely simple backgrounds create dramatic intensity.

THE APOCALYPTIC CHRIST (Moissac, 12th cen., 18′8″ wide).   St. John's vision in Revelation and an illumination in the *Beatus Commentary on the Apocalypse* were the sources for this tym-

13-22 BISHOP BERNWARD, *Adam and Eve Reproached by the Lord,* from the bronze doors of St. Michael's, Hildesheim, (*c.* 1015). Approx. 23″ × 43″.

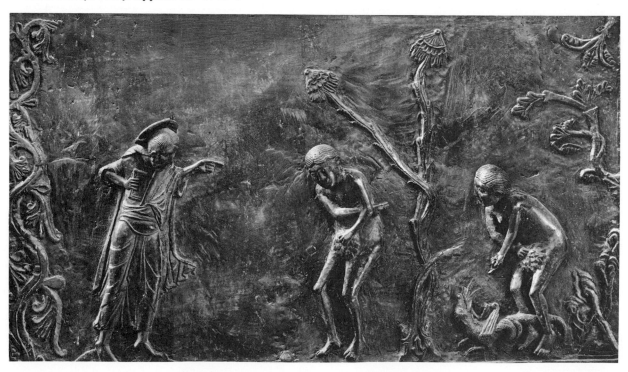

panum composition (Fig. 2-4) depicting Christ surrounded by the symbols of the Evangelists (a man for Matthew, a lion for Mark, an ox for Luke, and an eagle for John), angels, and the Elders (Fig. 13-23). Overlapping layers of *plate drapery* are characteristic of the Languedoc region. The sharp-edged plate folds make linear patterns of repeated and varied shapes that turn and twist with jerky vitality. The scene is framed at the sides by a twisted ribbon design and at the bottom by a lintel carved in delicate *rosettes* (round flower shapes), all having their origins in Greco-Roman architectural ornament. A powerful effect of gradation and climax comes from the enlarged scale of the central figures and their position at the apex of the tympanum and at the center of the obvious axial balance.

SCULPTURE *from the west entrances* ("royal portals") *of Chartres Cathedral* (1145–70). The twelfth-century façade (Fig. 13-24) is attached to a thirteenth-century church because a fire destroyed all but the façade of the twelfth-century structure. The center tympanum shows Christ and the symbols of the Evangelists, while

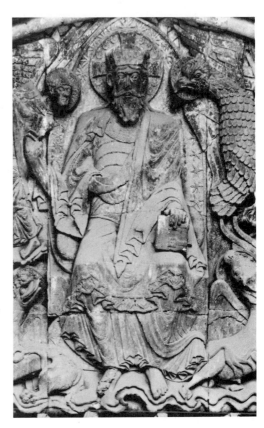

13-23
Detail from *The Apocalyptic Christ* at Moissac.

13-24
West ("royal") portals of Chartres Cathedral, (*c.* 1145–70).

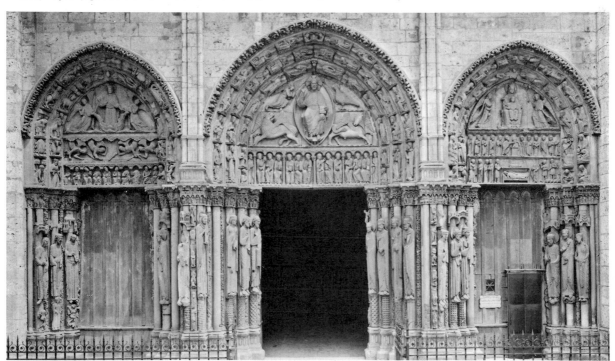

the surrounding arches are carved to represent the Elders. The Apostles are represented on the lintel. The right tympanum contains the Madonna and Child, and the lintel, in two registers, shows the Nativity and the Presentation in the Temple. The arches personify the liberal arts. The left tympanum depicts the Ascension; the lintel contains angels and Apostles. The arches carry the signs of the zodiac and the labors of the months. The jambs beside all three doors carry large figures that seem to portray the kings, queens, and prophets of the Bible. The capitals of the engaged columns have reliefs depicting the lives of Christ and Mary. The sculpture of Chartres-west is sometimes called early Gothic; however, it is much easier to understand as late Romanesque. A new clarity of parts is combined with the rigid poses and linear design of previous work.

Painting

During the eleventh and twelfth centuries, Romanesque painting, like Romanesque sculpture, proliferated in many regional styles, but its geographical bases were more widespread and its subject matter more varied. The term Romanesque was invented with architecture in mind, and it would be unrealistic to attempt a sharp distinction between Carolingian and Romanesque painting. During this period, the general tendency in the north was toward flat shapes and more insistence on line, line that is more active in its twisting and looping than the line in Byzantine art. Later twelfth-century work becomes more sculptural but often less lively. Byzantine influence is frequently evident in geometric drapery panels. Italian painting has Byzantine qualities but often loosens up Byzantine formality by means of more natural poses and more sculpturesque form.

ST. PETER RECEIVING THE KEYS, from the Book of Pericopes of Henry II (Bayerische Staatsbibliothek, Munich, 10⅜″ × 7½″).   This eleventh-century work (Fig. 13-25) is from Reichenau, a school known for illuminations depicting figures with large, dark, staring eyes, bold gestures, and slightly modeled but strongly outlined forms. The bodies here are crowded into spaceless groups and placed against a simple flat background; nothing detracts from the focus on the central action.

13-25

St. Peter Receiving the Keys, from the *Book of Pericopes of Henry II,* (eleventh century). München, Bayerische Staatsbibliothek, Clm 4452 f. 152v.

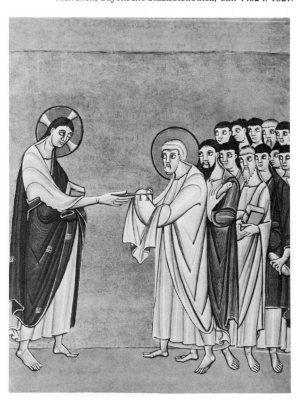

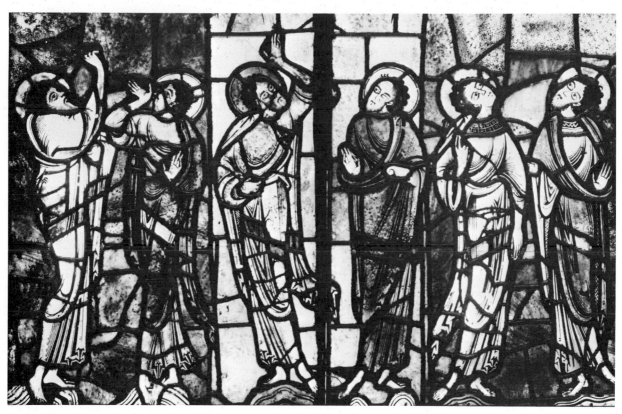

13-26
Detail from the *Ascension* window of Le Mans Cathedral, (*c.* 1150). Stained glass, 45″ × 74″.

SECTIONS FROM AN ASCENSION SCENE, *stained glass in Le Mans Cathedral* (*c.* 1150, 45″ × 74″).   Originally, this Romanesque window (Fig. 13-26) depicted Mary and the twelve Apostles watching the Ascension of Jesus; however, the figure of Christ has been lost, and the proper arrangement of the surviving panels is uncertain. The colors are blue, red, yellow, purple, green, and white. The thin figures and the linear drapery designs link the style to that of sculpture and manuscript illumination of the period.

GOTHIC ART: 1150–1400

Architecture

In the mid-twelfth century, the first churches that are called Gothic appeared in the Ile-de-France region — north-central France, with Paris as its center. From France the Gothic style spread to other countries, where it acquired regional characteristics. The major features of Gothic architecture are height, open walls, and complex linear design, all of which are integrated into a vast system of theological symbolism. The basilica plan attained grand proportions. To its longitudinal focus was added a vertical emphasis achieved through the use of ever higher nave vaults, the pointed arch, and dominating vertical lines in interior and exterior design. The trend toward greater height, complexity, and openness in walls is illustrated by a number of major French cathedrals such as St. Denis, Noyon, Laon, Paris, Chartres, Reims, Amiens, and Beauvais. Late Gothic work of the fifteenth and sixteenth centuries elaborated the pointed arch and the *tracery* (intricate stone carving within a window) in flamelike curves and is therefore known as *flamboyant Gothic*. Examples may be found in the cathedral and the small church of St. Maclou in Rouen. As Gothic architecture developed, Romanesque massiveness disappeared (Figs. 1-29, 13-31, and 13-32); walls became perforated screens for the glowing colored light from stained glass. In Medieval theology, this light was a symbol for God. As walls became more open, mass was further denied by an increase in delicate sculptural detail, which gave a total effect of line rather than mass. On the interior, the stone vaults floated like canopies anchored by engaged columns and thin ribs over the clerestory windows. On the exterior, the openness of the forms, the vertical lines, and the fragile silhouette suggested a weightless vision of soaring splendor. During the Gothic period, the French cathedral became a complex symbol for the City of God; this was expressed not only by architectural form but by the extensive iconography presented in sculpture and stained glass windows.

Early English Gothic stressed length in plan and elevation, the major exception being an occasional tall spire or tower over the crossing. Few flying buttresses were needed. Late English Gothic emphasized height and opened the walls for more glass. It is called *perpendicular* because of the verticality and the use of rectilinear tracery in walls and windows. Typically English is the multiplication of vault ribs into an intricate network. The basilica plan in England tends to be rambling, with several transepts and frequently a square east end.

Germany was slow to turn to Gothic architecture but eventually was influenced by the French style. German Gothic made effective use of the hall church.

CATHEDRAL OF NOTRE DAME (Paris, 1163–1250). The Gothic façade here (Fig. 13-27) has more openings in the wall masses, more elaborately carved splayed openings, and more consistent use of the pointed arch than does earlier architecture. Open arcades and delicate detail soften the limits of the forms. The rose window, with petal-like sections, has evolved from the wheel window. Verticality is more insistent, although the three-part division from side to side and from the bottom to the base of the towers is still evident, as it was at Caen. The west towers are woven into an intricate geometric organization that integrates the sculp-

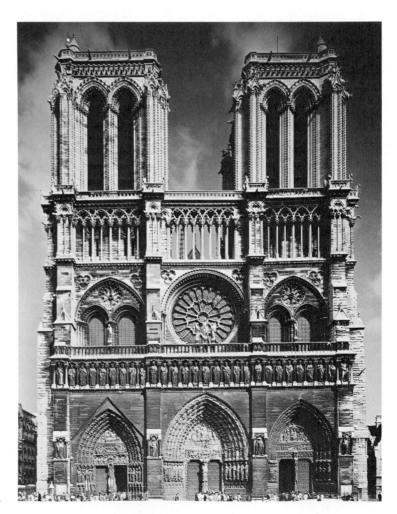

13-27
Notre Dame, Paris, (1163–1250).

ture and the architecture. Over the crossing, the tower used in Norman churches has been replaced by a tall, thin spire. The six-part ribbed and pointed cross vaults (Fig. 13-28) reach a height of 108½ feet and are supported on the outside by flying buttresses. The pointed arch allows the necessary flexibility for level crowns in the vaults (Fig. 4-17c, p. 42). Because of the six-part vaults, a typical bay of the nave elevation would include two arches of the nave arcade, two sets of gallery arches, and two sets of clerestory windows, each set consisting of two *lancets* (bullet-shaped windows) and a rose. The plan (Fig. 13-29) has a long choir, double side aisles, and a double ambulatory.

AMIENS CATHEDRAL, *by Robert de Luzarches* (13th cen., with later additions, such as 14th- and 15th-cen. towers and 16th-cen. rose window in west façade).   Here, the transept of the basilica plan

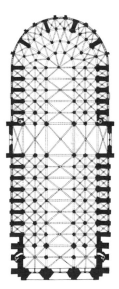

13-29
Plan of Notre Dame.

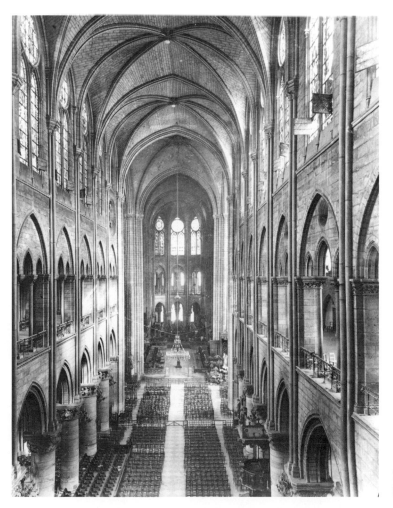

13-28
Nave and choir of Notre Dame.

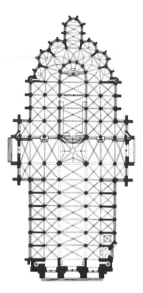

13-30
Plan of Amiens Cathedral.

13-31   ROBERT DE LUZARCHES,   interior of Amiens Cathedral.

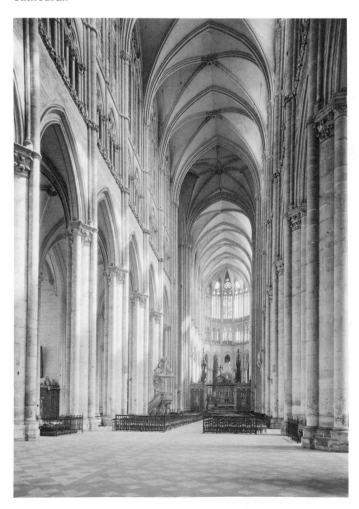

(Figs. 13-30 and 4-15) is almost engulfed by the side aisles, ambulatory, and radiating chapels. The façade (Fig. 1-29) shows a further dissolution of solid wall into superimposed layers of meshlike openings and sculpture. The splayed openings no longer seem to be cut out of the wall; they are extended in the form of porches. Again we find the three-part divisions of the façade, but these have become more complex. The increased perforation and lightness of the walls match the ever-more-insistent vertical emphasis. The interior vaults (Figs. 13-31 and 13-32) reach 139 feet above the floor. From compound piers with leafy capitals, the soaring engaged columns rise through a foliage stringcourse and a plain stringcourse to the four-part vaults above. A typical bay elevation consists of one arch in the nave arcade, two arches (each with three lancets and a trefoil) at the gallery, which has now become a shallow passage, and a clerestory of four lancets and three roses. There is some variation, however, in the elevation in different parts of the church. A forest of flying buttresses provides exterior support. Although Amiens no longer has its original stained

13-32
Choir vaults of Amiens Cathedral.

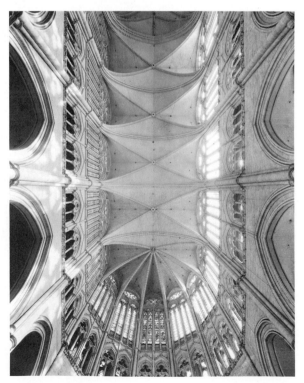

glass, the celebration of light and the double directional emphasis — toward the altar and toward the heavens — are dramatically evident.

SALISBURY CATHEDRAL (begun *c.* 1220).   Verticality is stressed only in the tower and spire over the crossing. The façade (Fig. 13-33), heavily sculpted but with many horizontal lines, does not have the lightness and openness or the three-dimensional complexity of French Gothic. The length is the same as that of Amiens (450 feet), but Salisbury's interior seems much longer because of the narrower nave, lower vaults (about 81 feet), and emphatic horizontal lines. Few flying buttresses are needed. The cathedral has a three-story nave elevation and four-part ribbed and pointed cross vaults (Fig. 13-34). The crossing has an elaborate *star vault* (multiple ribs suggesting superimposed star shapes). The plan (Fig. 13-35) is typical in its square east end and secondary transept.

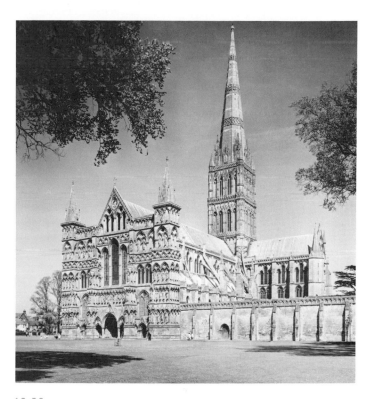

13-33
West façade of Salisbury Cathedral, (begun *c.* 1220).

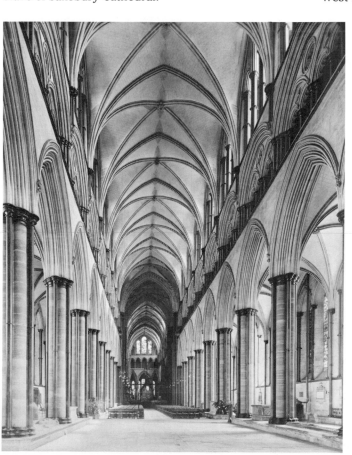

13-34
Nave of Salisbury Cathedral.

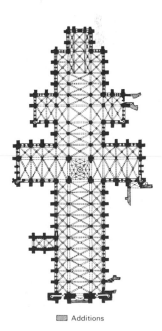

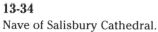 Additions

13-35
Plan of Salisbury
Cathedral.

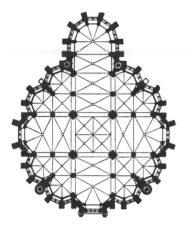

13-36
Plan of Liebfrauenkirche.

LIEBFRAUENKIRCHE (Trier, *c.* 1227–43).   The central plan (Fig. 13-36) is an exception to the predominance of the basilica in German Gothic architecture. Radiating chapels fill in the corners of a Greek cross plan that has an extended choir and apse for some longitudinal emphasis. The exterior (Fig. 13-37) illustrates the German reluctance to leave Romanesque forms; round arches and fortress towers are mixed with large pointed windows. Inside (Fig. 13-38), the arms of the cross have high ribbed and pointed four-part vaults. The elevation is in two levels: a high arcade and a clerestory of two lancets and a rose. Because the clerestory area is partly covered by the roofing of the outside chapels, however, the lancets had to be filled in until only curved triangular windows remained.

13-37
Liebfrauenkirche, Trier, (begun *c.* 1227).

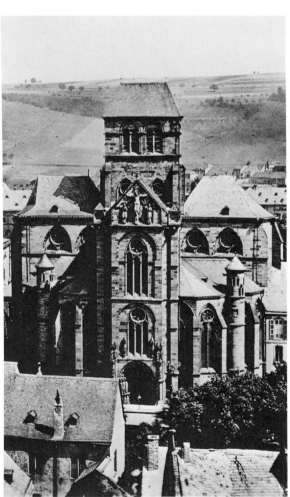

13-38
Interior of Liebfrauenkirche.

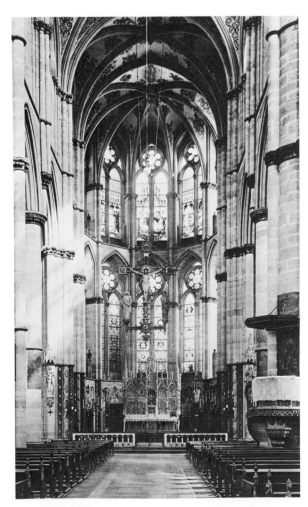

Sculpture

The beginnings of Gothic sculpture may be placed in the second half of the twelfth century. At that time, drapery and poses became calmer, and forms became somewhat less entangled. Figures began to pull away from their architectural backgrounds. In the early thirteenth century, bodies acquired more three-dimensional mass, more flexibility, more natural poses and drapery, and more individual faces. However, faces and figures retained some simplification and emphasis on large planes. Considerable stoniness and restraint of emotional expression are found in the important figures, giving them a more-than-human dignity and permanence. Later thirteenth-century sculpture gave up this monumental power for more specific anatomy, actions, and emotions; the development produced the effect of the superhuman descending to the human level (see Fig. 13-41). Plants and animals were also depicted more naturally and less imaginatively. Late fourteenth-century work continued in the direction of greater mass and more portrait detail in faces. Stylistic development was quite uneven, and considerable variety may often be seen in the sculpture of one church because it was done by traveling sculptors from different regions or in different periods over a wide time span. In Italy, the remains of ancient Roman sculpture fostered an interest not only in mass but in certain facial types, poses, and methods of draping costumes. Classicizing tendencies may be seen in the work of such sculptors as Nicola Pisano.

By the thirteenth century, France had organized the involved subject matter of earlier sculpture into a complete world view including the hierarchy of heavenly beings, the role and duties of man, and the history of the world from events in the Old Testament to the Last Judgment (see Fig. 13-40). Thus equipped with sculpture (and stained glass), the French Gothic cathedral, more than that of any other country, stands as a remarkable monument to its age.

ST. THEODORE (?), from south transept portal of Chartres Cathedral (c. 1215–20). This figure (Fig. 13-39), holding a spear and sheltered under a stone canopy, is quite distinct from its supporting column. The more human presentation is carried

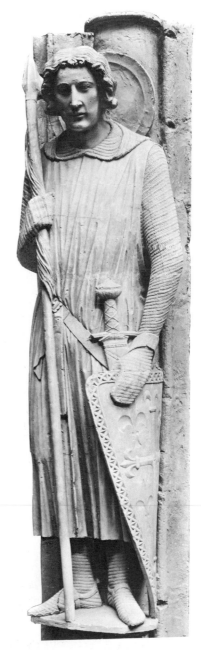

13-39
St. Theodore (?), from the south transept portal of Chartres Cathedral, (c. 1215–20).

through in the naturalistic facial features and body proportions. Large, simple planes in the face and figure provide both a sense of monumental strength and a modification of the earthly reality implied by the image.

THE LAST JUDGMENT, from central portal of west façade of Amiens Cathedral (c. 1220–30).   In the lower register of this portal sculpture (Fig. 13-40), the dead arise from their tombs to be judged on the scales of St. Michael. Above, the Damned and the Elect are going to their respective rewards; and, at the top, Christ is surrounded by Mary, John, and angels bearing the instruments of the Passion. The splayed arches that frame the tympanum depict the Elect with angels, Martyrs and Confessors, the Wise and Foolish Virgins, the Elders, the Tree of Jesse (to represent the genealogy of Christ), and the Patriarchs of the Old Law. On the jambs below are larger-than-life-size figures of the Prophets and Apostles, each identified by

13-40
The Last Judgment, from the central portal of the west façade of Amiens Cathedral, (c. 1220–30).

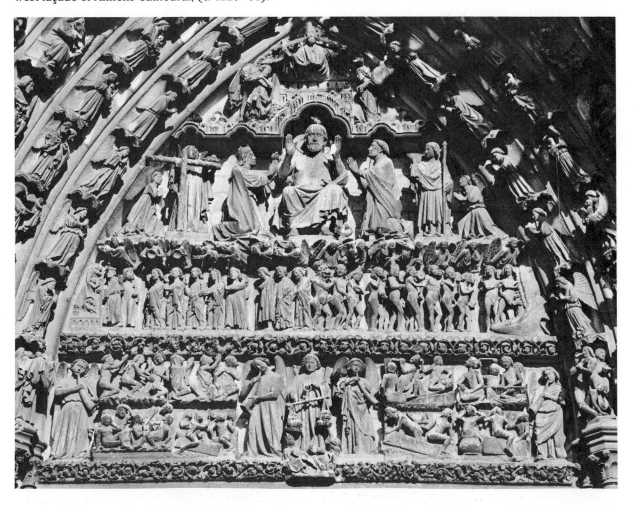

some attribute indicating the instrument of his martyrdom or symbolizing his role as prophet. Below these statues are quatrefoil medallions with relief sculpture depicting prophecies, Virtues, and Vices. The trumeau statue, known as *Le Beau Dieu,* represents Christ. The sizes of the figures in the tympanum and surrounding arches vary according to their importance in the hierarchy. The large scale of the jamb statues and their nearness to entering worshipers give them special grandeur and visually strengthen the supporting columns for the whole portal. Anatomy in faces and nude figures still has austere simplicity, and drapery is arranged in orderly cascades or pleated folds; yet the total effect is so natural that the turning and twisting Apostles and Prophets seem to converse with each other.

VIÈRGE DORÉE (GOLDEN VIRGIN), from south transept trumeau of Amiens Cathedral (c. 1250–70). This popular statue (Fig. 13-41) took its name from the gilt paint originally used in the costume. The austere strength of earlier work is here replaced by extreme gracefulness and human emotion. Although the bulky garment obscures the lower body, the three-dimensional folds seem convincingly activated by a contrapposto pose.

CRUCIFIX (PESTKREUZ), *from St. Marie im Kapitol* (Cologne, 1304, wood, 57″ high). The emaciated body (Fig. 13-42) is shown with harsh angularity and much detail in the bleeding wounds and the sores that suggest that Jesus has suffered from disease and will be sympathetic to the pleas of the sick. The symmetry and orderly repetition of forms in the crown of thorns and the ribs make the wounds and the convulsed hands more shocking by contrast. The hands and arms indicate the increasing study of nature that characterizes much Gothic sculpture.

THE WELL OF MOSES, from former Monastery of the Chartreuse de Champmol (Dijon, 1395–1406, stone, Prophets approx. 72″ high). This work (Fig. 13-43) is the sculpture of Claus Sluter, who came from Holland to the court of the Dukes of Burgundy at Dijon. The well is surmounted by a badly preserved crucifix placed on a base containing the figures of six Prophets from the Old Testament. In accordance with a Medieval passion play,

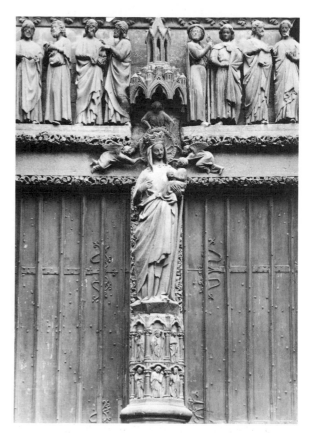

13-41
Vièrge Dorée (Golden Virgin), from the south transept trumeau of Amiens Cathedral, (c. 1250–70).

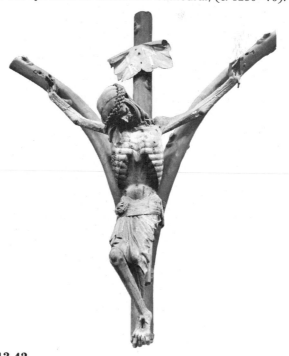

13-42
Crucifix from St. Marie im Kapitol, Cologne, (1304). Wood, 57″ high.

13-43   CLAUS SLUTER,   *The Well of Moses,* (1395–1406). Figures approx. 72″ high. Chartreuse de Champmol, Dijon.

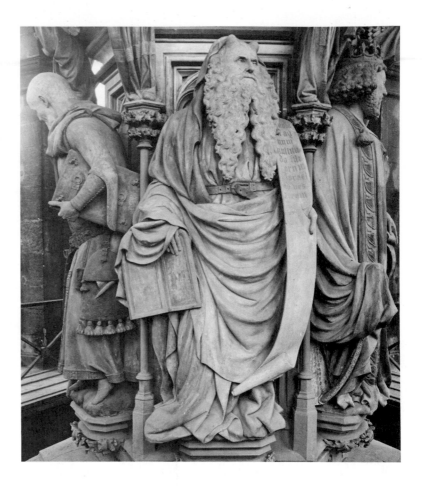

the Prophets are depicted as judges who decide that Jesus must be crucified for the sake of mankind. Each Prophet holds a scroll that contains a quotation from the Old Testament predicting the sacrifice. The massive forms, with their deeply cut depressions, the realism of costume detail, and the individualized faces of Sluter's style forecast the Renaissance, but the slightly exaggerated rhythmic curves in some sections of the drapery relate it to the late Medieval period.

Painting

As walls became more open, Gothic painters in the North had less wall surface on which to work. Their talents were employed in designing stained glass, which in turn affected style in manuscript illumination. Thirteenth-century illuminations often depict slender, willowy figures in gracefully curving and folding costumes, all within the architectural frame of a cathedral window. The modeling of the objects is counteracted by strong, flattened contours. Space around objects is often denied by the use of flat gold backgrounds. By the fourteenth century, illuminations make less use of the window framework and close observation of nature is evident. Jean Pucelle, in Paris, placed paintings at the top and bottom of a page and surrounded the intervening text with elaborate decorative plants, animals, and geometric shapes. The most pioneering Gothic painting was done by the Italian Giotto di Bondone (1267?–1337). Under the influence of thirteenth-century sculpture, Giotto broke with Byzantine traditions to obtain massive bodies and more natural drapery. Landscape, architecture, and figures are severely simple. The directional movements of all his forms give ponderous dignity to the restrained gestures and facial expressions. The massiveness, the more individualized faces, the more natural poses, and the convincing but underplayed emotions all bring a new humanism to Medieval art. Yet Giotto's painting was not fully appreciated by his immediate successors, and it was only with the Renaissance that his interests were developed further.

Duccio de Buoninsegna of Siena (about 1255–1319) made a more gentle break with Byzantine style.

THE *GOOD SAMARITAN* WINDOW, *Chartres Cathedral* (early 13th cen., stained glass). Chartres has one of the best-preserved sets of stained glass windows. The *Good Samaritan* window is a tall lancet contributed by the shoemakers of the town. Three medallions (circular clusters of scenes), one above the other, are separated by sets of three scenes each. The detail here (Fig. 13-44) shows only the central medallion and parts of the scenes above and below it. The compositions are read from the bottom up. The lower third of the window tells the story of the traveler's departure from Jerusalem, of his being robbed, beaten, and left along the road, and of his rescue by the Good Samaritan.

The quatrefoil in our reproduction begins an interpretation of the parable, depicting, in the bottom portion, the traveler in bed receiving care. The other scenes represent the creation of Adam (left) and Eve (right) and God's warning not to eat the fruit of the Tree of Knowledge (top). The top third of the window continues with the story of the Fall of Man and culminates with the figure of Jesus. Thus, Jerusalem represents Eden, the story of the traveler is related to the Fall of Man, and the Good Samaritan for all men becomes Jesus the Savior. The types of figure and drapery patterns, as well as the abbreviated symbols for trees and architecture, are artistic conventions of the time. The theological significance of light is enhanced by the glowing colors of the stained glass, colors that were projected in mottled hues onto the interior columns and floors.

13-44
Detail from the *Good Samaritan* window of Chartres Cathedral, (early thirteenth century). Stained glass.

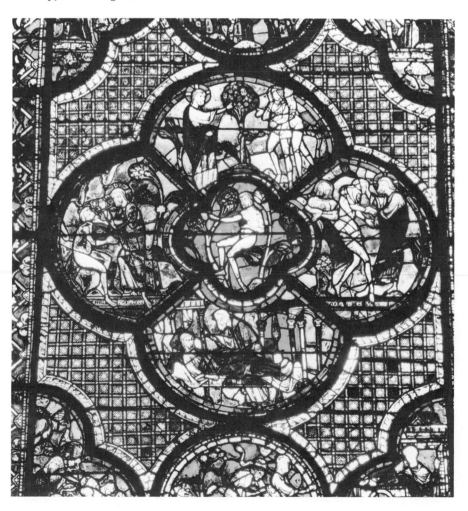

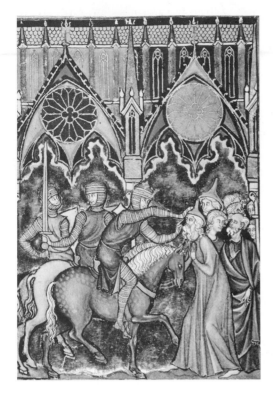

13-45
Nahash Threatening the Jews at Jabesh,
illuminated page (I Kings 11:2) from the
Psalter of St. Louis, (*c.* 1260).   Bibliothèque
Nationale, Paris.

ILLUMINATED PAGE, *from the* Psalter of St. Louis
(Bibliothèque Nationale, Paris, *c.* 1260, approx. 5″ ×
4″).   The illumination (Fig. 13-45) depicts Nahash the Ammonite threatening the Jews at Jabesh. Compared with most Romanesque work, the
human figures here are natural in proportion and
flexible in pose; but less important items, such as
the horses (or architecture in other scenes), are
given a diminished scale. Light and shadow are
used sparingly to create a roundness that is countered by strong outlines. Depth is canceled by the
gilt background. Shapes are filled with strong, relatively unmodulated colors, with blues and reds
predominating. In each illumination in the psalter,
the upper area is treated like a set of stained glass
windows set into a Gothic building.

LAMENTATION, by Giotto (Arena or Scrovegni
Chapel, Padua, fresco, part of a series of paintings done in 1305–1306, 7′7″ × 7′9″).   The significance of the event being interpreted is expressed
here (Plate 3 and Fig. 13-46) not through awe-
inspiring otherworldly images, but through massive human forms whose actions have solemn dignity. The drapery is simplified and used not to

13-46   GIOTTO,   detail from *Lamentation* at the Arena (Scrovegni) Chapel, Padua.

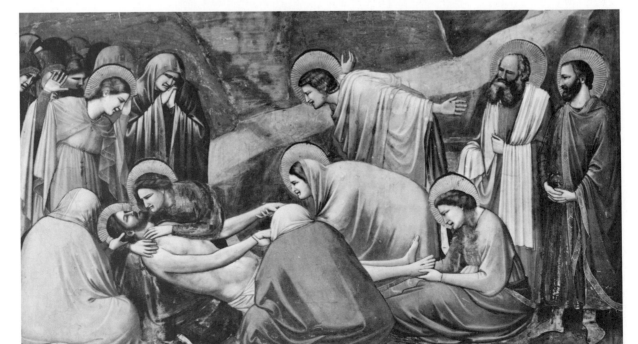

reveal the body but to emphasize the major movement of each figure. As the figures focus on Christ, so does the diagonally descending landscape. Giotto's emphasis on three-dimensional mass and his use of more normal human proportions constituted a new concept of reality in painting and broke with the conventions of Byzantine art. For this reason, Giotto is often seen as a forerunner of the Renaissance. His major frescoes are in Santa Croce in Florence and in the Arena Chapel in Padua.

CHRIST ENTERING JERUSALEM, by Duccio (from the *Maestà Altarpiece*, Siena Cathedral, 1308–11, tempera on wood, detail 40″ × 21″).   The great altarpiece depicts, on the front, a Madonna enthroned and, on the back, scenes from the life of Christ. Compared with Giotto's work, Duccio's use of human proportions and flat shapes (Fig. 13-47) was a much less radical departure from Byzantine traditions. Rigid Byzantine drapery patterns appear in certain cases, especially when Duccio shows Christ in less natural states — during the Transfiguration,

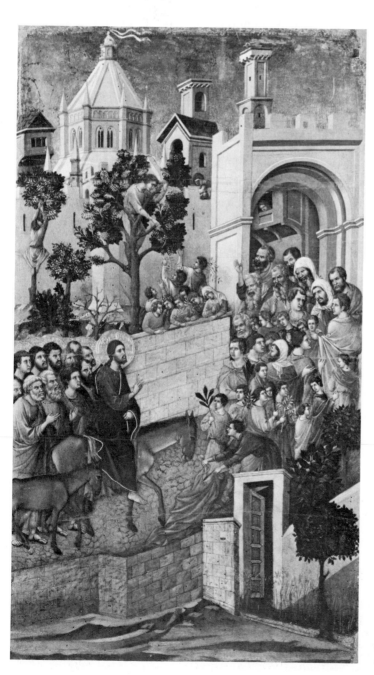

13-47 DUCCIO, *Christ Entering Jerusalem*, detail from the *Maestà Altarpiece*, (1308–11). Siena Cathedral.

for instance, or after the Resurrection. However, the details in gestures and faces have a delicate expressiveness and reflect a keen observation of nature. Duccio did not use a consistent system of linear perspective. The architecture is miniature in scale and may have been influenced by stage sets for religious drama.

Suggestions for Further Study

Conant, Kenneth J. *Carolingian and Romanesque Architecture: 800–1200* (Pelican History of Art), 4th rev. ed. Baltimore: Penguin Books, 1979.

Dodwell, C. R. *Painting in Europe, 800–1200* (Pelican History of Art). Baltimore: Penguin Books, 1971.

Dupont, Jacques, and Cesare Gnudi. *Gothic Painting, 13th–15th Centuries.* Translated by Stuart Gilbert. New York: Rizzoli International, 1979.

Frankl, Paul. *Gothic Architecture* (Pelican History of Art). Translated by Dieter Pevsner. Baltimore: Penguin Books, 1963.

Hubert, J., J. Porcher, and W. F. Volbach. *The Carolingian Renaissance* (Arts of Mankind Series). New York: Braziller, 1970.

Katzenellenbogen, Adolf. *The Sculptural Programs of Chartres Cathedral.* New York: W. W. Norton, 1964.

Landolt, Hanspeter. *German Painting: The Late Middle Ages (1330–1500).* Translated by Heinz Norden. Geneva: Skira, 1968.

Lasko, Peter. *Ars Sacra, 800–1200* (Pelican History of Art). Baltimore: Penguin Books, 1972.

Mâle, Émile. *The Gothic Image: Religious Art in France in the Thirteenth Century.* Translated by Dora Nussey. New York: Harper & Row, 1973.

Meiss, Millard. *French Painting in the Time of Jean de Berry.* 2 vols. New York: Braziller, 1975.

Panofsky, Erwin. *Gothic Architecture and Scholasticism.* New York: Meridian Books, 1963.

Pope-Hennessy, John. *An Introduction to Italian Sculpture,* Vol. 1. New York and London: Phaidon, 1955.

Porter, Arthur Kingsley. *Medieval Architecture: Its Origins and Development.* 2 vols., reprint of the 1909 ed. New York: Hacker Art Books, 1969.

———. *Romanesque Sculpture of the Pilgrimage Roads.* 10 vols. in 3, reprint of the 1923 ed. New York: Hacker Art Books, 1969.

Rickert, Margaret Josephine. *Painting in Britain: The Middle Ages* (Pelican History of Art). Baltimore: Penguin Books, 1965.

Stone, Lawrence. *Sculpture in Britain: The Middle Ages,* rev. ed. New York: Viking, 1972.

Von Simson, Otto G. *The Gothic Cathedral: Origins of Gothic Architecture and the Medieval Concept of Order.* Princeton: Princeton University Press, 1974.

Webb, Geoffrey. *Architecture in Britain: The Middle Ages* (Pelican History of Art). Baltimore: Penguin Books, 1965.

White, John. *Art and Architecture in Italy, 1250–1400* (Pelican History of Art). Baltimore: Penguin Books, 1966.

Witzleben, Elizabeth von. *Stained Glass in French Cathedrals.* Translated by Francisca Garvie. New York: Reynal, 1968.

Zarnecki, George. *Art of the Medieval World* (Library of Art History). New York: Abrams, 1975.

14

Renaissance Art

1400 – 1600

The term Renaissance *implies a rebirth,* and the period is often thought of as a rebirth of the glory of ancient Greek and Roman culture; yet the Renaissance involved much more than imitation of the past. It was a time of emphasis on the importance of the individual, of interest in the physical characteristics of man and nature, and of search for rational order and ideal form in the arts. The period saw widespread geographical exploration, much activity in scholarship, a rapid growth in the sciences, reformation in religion, and broad changes in the arts. These trends had been gathering momentum since the twelfth century, with the exchange of ideas fostered by the Crusades, the emergence of free cities, the rise of the universities, and the developing interests in nature and antique art during the Gothic period. Furthermore, some of the climactic effects of Renaissance trends occurred only afterwards, in the seventeenth century. Thus the beginning and end dates for the period are rather arbitrary markers in the continuous stream of history.

Our concepts of Renaissance art are based primarily on Italy, for it was here that the trends were most distinct. The period from 1400 to 1500 in Italy is called the *Early Renaissance,* the years from about 1500 to 1520 are considered to be the *High Renaissance,* and the remainder of the sixteenth century may be termed *Late Renaissance.* The urbanization that took place in the Gothic period made the cities important centers for the growth of Renaissance ideas and the patronage of art. Artists often joined the courts of nobles and received sustenance and salary in return for painting, sculpture, and design ranging from architecture to theatrical costumes. Florence played the major role in the fifteenth century but was superseded in the sixteenth century by Rome and Venice. Outside Italy, the most productive geographical area for the arts in the fifteenth century was the region of present-day Belgium, with the major centers at Tournai, Bruges, Ghent, Brussels, Louvain, and Antwerp. In Burgundian France, Dijon was an important art center until 1420, when the court of the Dukes of Burgundy was moved to Flanders. Paris continued to be important, along with Fontainebleau in the sixteenth century. In the Germanic areas, Cologne, Nuremberg, Vienna, and Basel were especially significant. London was the center of a tardy development of the Renaissance in England.

During the Renaissance, the Church continued to be an important patron of the arts, but the aristocracy and the growing merchant class commissioned art for themselves as well as for the Church. The powerful Visconti and Sforza families in Milan, the Gonzaga family in Mantua, the Este family in Ferrara, and the Medici family in Florence all earned places in history through their patronage. The new individualism stimulated the quest for renown — for accomplishments in the earthly life — and architecture, painting, and sculpture could be seen as permanent monuments to the patron's importance. The desire to live fully was expressed in the concept of the universal person, the person of many abilities and interests as inspired by Greek thought and described in Baldassare Castiglione's sixteenth-century book, *The Courtier.*

Breadth of interests affected not only the patronage of art but also the attitude of the artist;

Michelangelo was poet, painter, architect, and sculptor, and Leonardo da Vinci was artist, scientist, and engineer. The social status of the artist rose during the fifteenth and sixteenth centuries. By the sixteenth century, the craftsman-artist, trained in a *bottega* (shop) under the apprentice system and the strict rules of a guild, had become the artist-genius, trained in an academy; he was a scholar and a fit companion for princes, a person emancipated from the regulations of the guilds.

During the fifteenth century, the development of the graphic arts in Germany made art in the form of prints available to a larger segment of the population, extending patronage and broadening the artist's audience. Woodcut, wood engraving, and metal engraving were all important media.

THE FIFTEENTH CENTURY

Painting in the North

In the countries north of Italy, fifteenth-century painting is sometimes considered to be late Medieval rather than Renaissance because it shows little interest in ancient Greco-Roman art and does not portray man as heroically in scale, proportions, and action as does the painting of fifteenth-century Italy. Northern painting does intensify the late Gothic study of nature by adding deeper space, more convincing illusion of mass, more flesh-and-blood anatomy, and precise details and textures. Nevertheless, body proportions and drapery effects are conventional. The persistently thin bodies, large heads, narrow shoulders, angular drapery lines, and crowded landscape or architectural settings give much Northern painting of the fifteenth century the total effect of a miniature, no matter how large the actual work (see Plate 5). The intricate physical detail presented was frequently given spiritual meaning by the elaborate symbolism inherited from the Middle Ages. Painters obtained transparent color through the increased use of oil glazes employed alone or in combination with the more traditional egg tempera formulas.

ROBERT CAMPIN, *probably identical with the* **MASTER OF FLÉMALLE** (Flanders, 1378?–1444). Campin, one of the first painters to use oil paint extensively, had his studio in Tournai. He probably

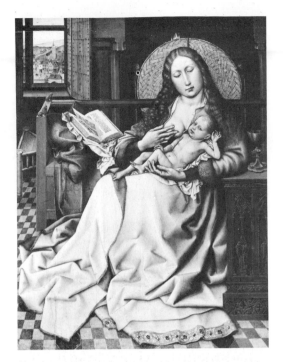

14-1   ROBERT CAMPIN,   *Virgin and Child Before a Fire Screen,* (*c.* 1425). Panel, 24″ × 19¼″.   Reproduced by courtesy of the Trustees of the National Gallery, London.

14-2   JAN VAN EYCK,   *Arnolfini and His Bride,* (1434). Oil on wood panel, approx. 32″ × 22″.   Reproduced by courtesy of the Trustees of the National Gallery, London.

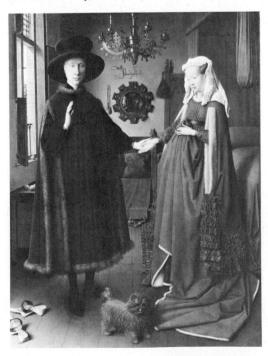

painted works that were formerly credited to an unknown master of the Abbey of Flémalle. The new realism of his style combines deep space created by means of exaggerated linear perspective, crowded objects, the typically rich color and angular drapery of fifteenth-century Northern art, and both private and conventional Medieval symbolism. His *Virgin and Child Before a Fire Screen* (Fig. 14-1), one of the earliest paintings to show a city view outside the window, presents the Madonna in a comfortable contemporary Flemish house. The fire screen suggests the shape of a halo behind her head, and the chalice (probably a later addition) by her elbow suggests the celebration of the Mass and hints at the future sacrifice of Christ.

JAN VAN EYCK (Flanders, *c.* 1390–1441).   This pioneer in Northern painting worked for Count John of Holland and Philip the Good of Burgundy and finally died in Bruges. He was honored by the rulers and sent on a diplomatic mission to Portugal. *Arnolfini and His Bride* (Plate 5 and Fig. 14-2) has typically Northern features, such as the fragile bodies, angular drapery, miniature quality, and pervasive symbolism (see p. 25). The converging lines of the architecture effectively establish depth; but they are instinctive rather than systematic, for they meet at several different horizon levels. Two natural light sources admit a crossing light that shortens the shadows cast so that even the grain of the floorboards at Arnolfini's feet is not hidden. Although the woman's face has the smooth, wide, oval form and tiny mouth found in much Northern painting of the period, the striking individuality of Arnolfini's face is undeniable. The entire painting — from the stubble on Arnolfini's chin to the transparent beads on the wall — demonstrates remarkably careful observation. The round mirror reveals the artist's interest in optical problems: it shows a wide-angle view of the room, the backs of the couple, and two spectators (perhaps including the artist) in the doorway. The mirror frame contains tiny round scenes of Christ's Passion. The most famous work by Van Eyck is the *Ghent Altarpiece* (Fig. 14-3), which carries the names of Jan and his brother Hubert. There is uncertainty about which parts were done by each and whether or not we have any other paintings by Hubert.

ROGIER VAN DER WEYDEN (Flanders, c. 1400–64). Van der Weyden probably studied under Robert Campin at Tournai before becoming the official painter of Brussels. About 1450, he traveled through Italy. Whereas Van Eyck's compositions lead our attention smoothly from foreground to background, Van der Weyden's paintings tend to locate the major figures in a shallow foreground space, and the background serves only as a backdrop. Moreover, the faces in Van der Weyden's paintings convey greater emotional intensity than do the faces painted by Van Eyck. These characteristics are evident in *The Descent from the Cross* (Fig. 14-4), an early work. Other major works attributed to Van der Weyden include *Christ Appearing to His Mother* (c. 1440–45, Metropolitan Museum of Art, New York) and the *Portrait of Lionello* (or *Francesco?*) *d'Este* (c. 1450, Metropolitan Museum of Art, New York).

14-3 JAN and HUBERT VAN EYCK, *God,* a panel from the *Ghent Altarpiece,* (c. 1432). St. Bavo, Ghent.

14-4 ROGIER VAN DER WEYDEN, *The Descent from the Cross,* (c. 1435). Tempera on wood panel, approx. 7′3″ × 8′7″. Museo Nacional del Prado, Madrid.

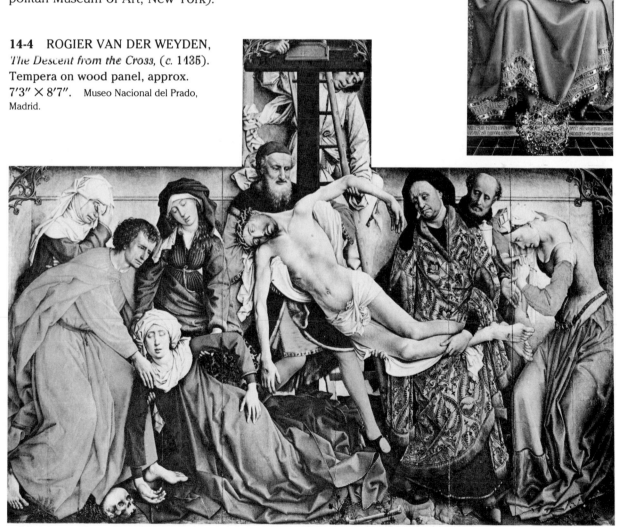

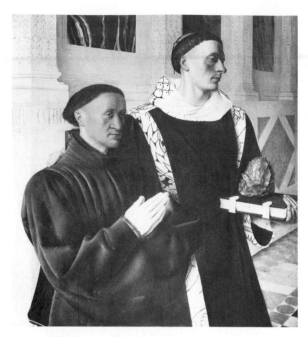

14-5   JEAN FOUQUET,   *Étienne Chevalier and St. Stephen,* (c. 1450). **Tempera on wood, 36½″ × 33½″.**   Staatliche Museen Preussicher Kulturbesitz Gemäldegalerie, West Berlin.

JEAN FOUQUET (France, *c.* 1420–81).   Fouquet was born at Tours, and it is thought that he may have attended the University of Paris, since Parisian buildings often appear in his later book illustrations. If so, he undoubtedly saw there the work of Flemish artists, but his paintings contain Italianate elements, which are best explained by a trip to Rome in 1445. After his return to France, he established himself in Tours, although his activity was not limited to this area. During the period between 1450 and 1460, Fouquet painted the *Portrait of Charles VII* (Louvre, Paris) and the *Pietà of Nouans* (Nouans). The portrait of Charles VII's minister of finance, Étienne Chevalier, with his patron saint, Stephen (Fig. 14-5), originally formed the left wing of the *Diptych* (two-part altarpiece) *of Melun;* the two figures were presented as worshipers of the Madonna and Child depicted in the right wing, which is now in the Antwerp Musée Royal des Beaux-Arts. (The face of the Madonna is thought to be a portrait of Agnes Sorel, the mistress of Charles VII.) The left wing reveals Italian influence in the perspective of the architecture, the amplitude of the massive bodies, and the equivalent scale of man and saint — even though the saint's head is given a traditionally higher position than the head of the man. Having served the court of Charles VII, Fouquet, in 1475, was made court painter to the king by Charles's successor, Louis XI.

HUGO VAN DER GOES (Flanders, 1440–82).   Van der Goes died in a monastery near Brussels after having spent most of his life in Ghent. His work often has a strange tenseness derived from sharp contrasts in directional forces and between sparse and crowded areas, passive and active attitudes, and concentrated and distracted attention. His major work is the *Portinari Altarpiece* (*c.* 1476), done for the Italian representative of the Medici banking interests in Bruges. The central panel of this *triptych* (three-part altarpiece) shows *The Adoration of the Shepherds* (Fig. 14-6). The disparity between the size of the Madonna and that of the angels echoes the Medieval lack of concern for physical reality, while the deep space and realistic detail are characteristically Renaissance. The perspective lines of the architecture converge toward a vanishing point behind the head of the Madonna and emphasize her importance. The foreground

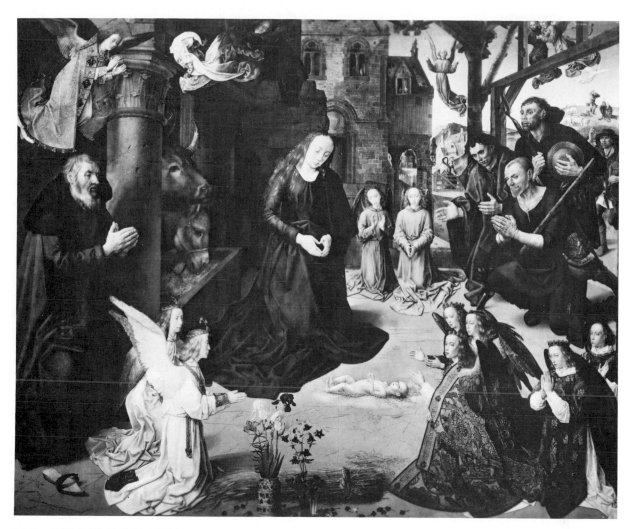

14-6 HUGO VAN DER GOES, *The Adoration of the Shepherds,* central panel of the *Portinari Altarpiece,* (*c.* 1476). 8′3″ × 10′. Galleria degli Uffizi, Florence.

symbols include a cast-off shoe as a sign of a holy event, wheat as a reference to the bread of the Eucharist, scattered anemones as a symbol of sorrow and sacrifice, an iris (sword lily) as a symbol of the Madonna's suffering during the Passion of Christ, a lily as a symbol of sacrifice and chastity, and a cluster of columbine as a symbol of the Holy Ghost. On the basis of the Portinari painting, a number of other stylistically similar works have been attributed to Van der Goes.

HIERONYMUS BOSCH (Holland, *c.* 1450–1516). The extraordinary fantasies of Bosch seem closer to the grotesqueries of the Middle Ages than to the rational order of the Renaissance; yet even the Greeks had their Dionysiac Mysteries, and Bosch painted his visions with a control of deep space that is one hallmark of the Renaissance. His religious scenes and representations of proverbs and fables, which often contain moral lessons, are portrayed through strange combinations of men, plants, and animals. Interpretation is sometimes difficult. Bosch is often cited as a precursor of twentieth-century Surrealism. The much-copied *Temptation of St. Anthony* (Fig. 14-7) is a perfect subject for his imagination. The creatures of hell swarm from earth, sky, and water to torment the saint, whose body is almost lost, even in the very center of the composition. Other notable works by Bosch include *The Garden of Earthly Delights* (*c.* 1500, Prado, Madrid) and *The Hay Wain* (*c.* 1485–90, Prado, Madrid).

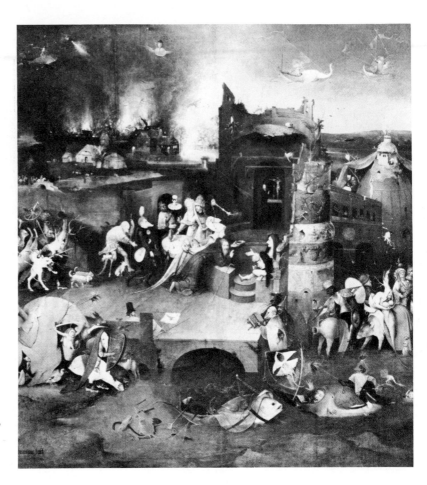

14-7   HIERONYMUS BOSCH,
The Temptation of St. Anthony,
(*c.* 1500).   Museu Nacional de Arte
Antiga, Lisbon.

Painting in Italy

While conservative Italian painting continued the traditions of Byzantine and late Gothic art, the new painting was molded by the major Renaissance interests: individual man, nature, and ancient Greco-Roman art. The scattered remains of antique sculpture had encouraged the love of mass in Medieval Italian sculpture. It was Medieval sculpture that helped shape the art of Giotto, which in turn became a source for young Italian Renaissance painting (Figs. 1-10 and 1-26). Increased efforts were made to duplicate the visual experience of the physical world: linear and aerial perspective were used to create space; natural light (from direct sources and from reflecting surfaces) was studied as a means of suggesting mass; land forms, plant life, and animal and human anatomy were observed in detail; and natural posture as well as convincingly natural movement became important to the new concept of what was "real." For all of this, clarity was considered to be essen-

tial, but, at the same time, the attempt to achieve clarity led to conflicts. Clarity called for sharply outlined edges that contradicted the roundness of the form, and the insistence on mass sometimes made a painted face seem more like stone than flesh. Only late in the century were deep shadows allowed to obscure parts of the composition in the interests of strong focus (Fig. 1-26). Portraiture, nature study, Greco-Roman architecture and mythology, and traditional Christian subject matter were often mixed; an Adoration of the Christ Child might be depicted with ancient ruins or with Roman sarcophagi adorned with mythological reliefs, while portraits of the artist's contemporary patrons might be found among the Three Kings and their retinue. The confidence in human importance and capabilities was expressed by some artists in dignity of pose, emotional restraint, and boldness of masses (Fig. 1-10), all producing a kind of monumentality. Much fifteenth-century Italian painting has a breadth of form and a largeness of scale quite unlike the miniature quality of

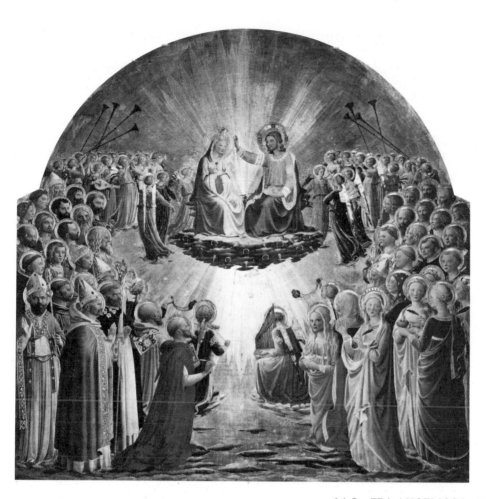

14-8 FRA ANGELICO, *The Coronation of the Virgin,* (*c.* 1435). Panel, 44⅛″ × 45″. Galleria degli Uffizi, Florence.

most Northern work. Flemish painting was admired by Italians, however, and its landscape backgrounds had some influence on Italian art. The major media for the period were fresco, tempera, and occasional oil glazing.

FRA ANGELICO (Florence, 1387–1455).   Guido da Vicchio probably studied under Lorenzo Monaco before joining the Dominican Order and taking the name of Fra Angelico. His early style, which lasted from 1418 into the 1430s and is illustrated by such works as *The Coronation of the Virgin* (Fig. 14-8), was Gothic in its slender figures, delicate textile patterns, and paradisiacal settings. From 1435 to 1445, in such works as the frescoes in the monastery of San Marco in Florence, his figures became more solid, the settings more earthbound, the color more restrained, and the drapery more massive. His late paintings have simpler, more massive bodies and deep perspective vistas framed by grand architecture.

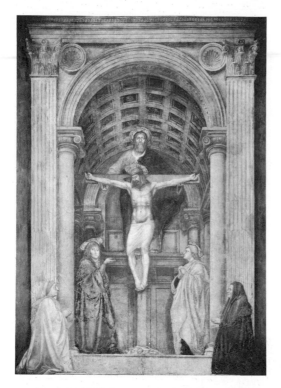

14-9 MASACCIO, *The Holy Trinity,* (1428?).
Fresco, 21′ 10½″ × 10′5″. Santa Maria
Novella, Florence.

14-10 PIERO DELLA FRANCESCA,
The Annunciation, (*c.* 1455).
San Francesco, Arezzo.

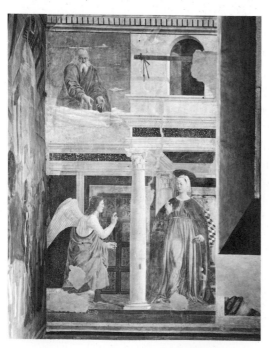

MASACCIO (Florence, 1401–28). *The Tribute Money* (Fig. 1-10) reveals Masaccio's use of aerial and linear perspective (see p. 7) and his modeling with light and shadow to create the illusion of mass. The linear perspective used systematically in *The Tribute Money* was invented by his architect friend Filippo Brunelleschi, who was also an admirer of ancient Roman architecture. Brunelleschi probably encouraged Masaccio to use Roman architecture as a setting for his painting *The Trinity* (Fig. 14-9). The massiveness of Masaccio's figures owes much to the painting of Giotto, and the poses indicate the influence of the sculptor Donatello. Masaccio's greatness lies in the gravity, poise, and depth — the monumentality — he gave to his humanistic vision of man. These qualities stem from his combination of eloquent but restrained facial expressions, a stately rhythmic accord between the lines of poses and drapery, and the suppression of detail where necessary to strengthen the masses. Roman architecture and sculpture were formative influences. There are major frescoes by Masaccio illustrating the life of St. Peter in the Brancacci Chapel in the Church of Santa Maria del Carmine in Florence (see Fig. 1-10).

PIERO DELLA FRANCESCA (central Italy, 1415/20–92). Piero was primarily a painter, but he was also a Renaissance humanist scholar who wrote on perspective and was active as a poet, cosmographer, mathematician, and architect. In painting, his major technical interest seems to have been the effect of light on color and three-dimensional form. His painting often has the quality of bright, diffused luminosity. He brought simple massive figures into alignment with their architectural settings to produce an architectonic stability that reinforces the dignity of the persons portrayed. He owed much to Masaccio's painting and to Donatello's sculpture. Piero's major fresco cycle depicts *The Legend of the Holy Cross* (from the thirteenth-century *Golden Legend* by Jacobus da Voragine) on the walls of San Francesco at Arezzo (*c.* 1458–66). *The Annunciation* (Plate 4 and Fig. 14-10) from San Francesco shows Piero's subtle treatment of color and light in addition to typically Renaissance architecture, perspective, and three-dimensional forms. His fresco work includes *The Resurrection* (1460, Town Hall, Borgo San Sepolcro). His panel paintings of the Duke and Duchess of Urbino (Fig. 14-11) are fine examples of fifteenth-century profile portraiture stressing individual features and meticulous detail.

GIOVANNI BELLINI (Venice, 1430?–1516).   Probably the most significant fifteenth-century Venetian painter, Giovanni was one of three famous painters bearing the Bellini name. He received his early training from his father, Jacopo, and from Andrea Mantegna. Giovanni was also influenced indirectly by Flemish painting, particularly in the use of color. His early style is represented by *St. Francis in Ecstasy* (Plate 7 and Fig. 14-12). Sharp, intricate details reveal a kind of microscopic appreciation of nature. Later, possibly under the influence of his student Giorgione, Bellini's style changed to one using softer light, subordination of detail to large masses, and more emphasis on a general color effect rather than on local color.

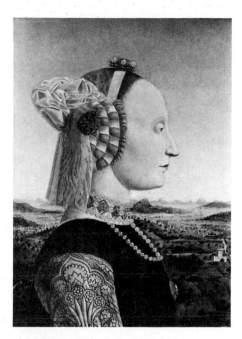

14-11   PIERO DELLA FRANCESCA, *Portrait of Battista Sforza, Duchess of Urbino*, (1470s). Tempera and oil on panel, 18½″ × 13″.   Galleria degli Uffizi, Florence.

14-12   GIOVANNI BELLINI, *St. Francis in Ecstasy*, (c. 1480). Panel, 48¾″ × 54″.   Frick Collection, New York.

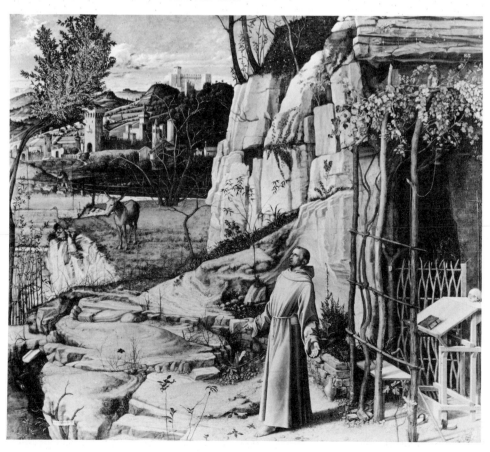

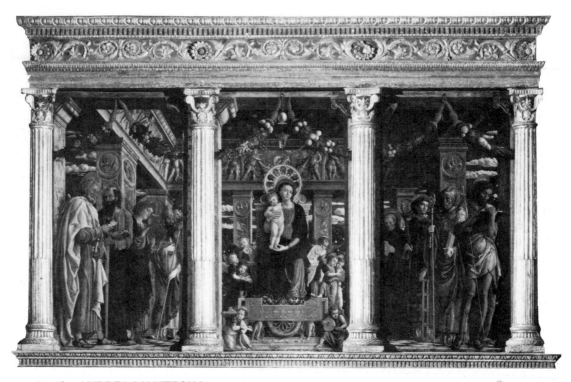

14-13   ANDREA MANTEGNA,
San Zeno Altarpiece, (1456–59).
Each panel, 87″ × 45½″. San Zeno,
Verona.

14-14   ANDREA MANTEGNA,   *The Dead Christ,* (c. 1501).
Tempera on canvas, 26¾″ × 31⅞″. Pinacoteca di Brera, Milan.

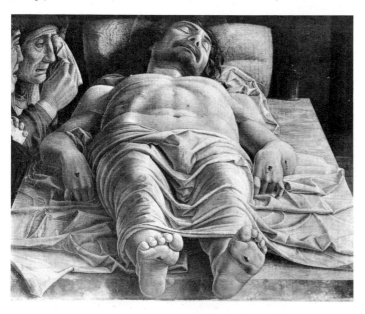

ANDREA MANTEGNA (northern Italy, 1431–1506). Mantegna was apprenticed to Francesco Squarcione in Padua, but it was Donatello's sculpture in Padua that influenced Mantegna's love of statuesque figures with brittle, clinging drapery and highlights of stony or metallic character. Precise detail and settings with architectural reliefs and deep rocky landscapes are typical. In 1459, Mantegna became court painter to the Gonzaga family at Mantua, where he painted wall and ceiling frescoes in the palace. In the *San Zeno Altarpiece* (Fig. 14-13), the traditional triptych format acquires an architectural frame inspired by Roman work. This actual architecture is continued by the illusionistically painted architecture within the panels, architecture covered with reliefs that recall the sculpture of Donatello. The figures of the Madonna and saints reveal the painter's interest in three-dimensional form. *The Dead Christ* (Fig. 14-14) is a dramatic example of Mantegna's interest in spatial illusion; the body is daringly *foreshortened* (the effect of spatial recession obtained by drawing the object as a series of overlapping or successive masses). Mantegna's statuesque figures, his use of Roman architecture and sculpture, and his interest in illusionistic space had wide influence in northern Italy.

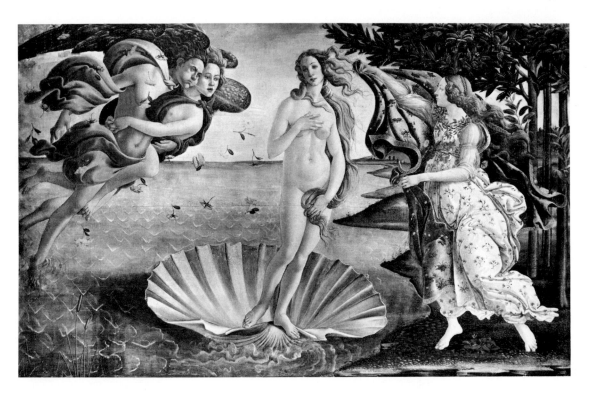

14-15 SANDRO BOTTICELLI,
Venus Landing on the Shore, (*c.* 1482).
Tempera on canvas, approx.
5′8″ × 9′1″.   Galeria degli Uffizi, Florence.

SANDRO BOTTICELLI (Florence, 1444–1510). Under the influence of his teacher Fra Filippo Lippi, Botticelli developed a style of knobby, jointed figures and rippling, linear drapery folds. He was patronized by the Medici family, and his *Adoration of the Magi* (1476–78, Uffizi Gallery, Florence) portrays members of the family as the Magi and their followers. His best-known paintings are *The Primavera* (*c.* 1478) and *Venus Landing on the Shore* (Fig. 14-15), both in the Uffizi Gallery. Both exhibit Botticelli's use of sweeping linear curves and convolutions, his preference for lean figures with enlarged joints, and his use of repetition and variation in richly ornate patterns. In 1481, Botticelli was called to Rome to do three of the frescoes on the walls of the Sistine Chapel. In his later work, Botticelli turned increasingly to religious subject matter, and it is thought that his work was influenced by the emotional preaching of Savonarola. The *Lamentation* (Fig. 14-16) has only traces of his former delicacy of line, now imprisoned within harsh angular forms, and the expressions of the participants convey anguish.

PIETRO VANNUCCI, *called* **PERUGINO** (central Italy, 1445?–1523).   Perugino worked in Perugia in the region of Umbria except for his trip to Rome in the

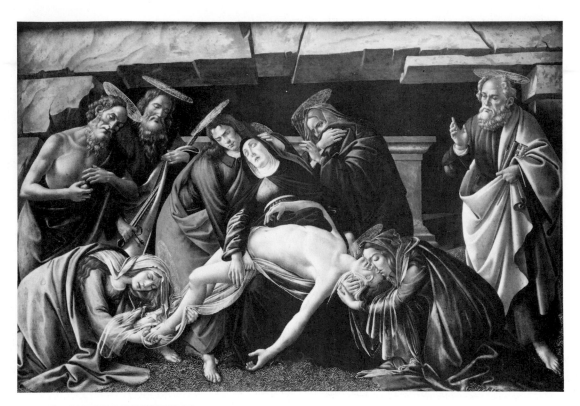

14-16   SANDRO BOTTICELLI,
Lamentation, (*c.* 1500). Tempera on
panel, 55″ × 81½″.   Alte Pinakothek, Munich.

1480s to paint *The Handing of the Keys to St. Peter* (Fig. 14-17) in the Sistine Chapel. Single-point perspective and a symmetrical composition focus on the central event, connect it to the building in the background, and imply that this building is the physical expression of the Church, whose earthly leadership Jesus is entrusting to Peter. Perugino simplified the parts and the action in his compositions, employing serene landscapes, figures and drapery with gently curving rhythmic lines, and passive faces with small, buttonlike eyes and delicate mouths. He was the teacher of Raphael.

LEONARDO DA VINCI (Florence, Milan, and Amboise, 1452–1519).   Leonardo was born near Florence and sent at an early age to be trained in the studio of Andrea del Verrocchio. Leonardo's wide interests ranged from engineering to botany, and his notebooks are famous as records of a many-sided genius. *The Madonna of the Rocks* (Fig. 1-26) reveals not only his interest in anatomy, geology, and botany, but qualities that forecast the sixteenth century: a conscious effort to perfect nature through concepts of ideal form and a desire to go beyond surface appearances to express the work-

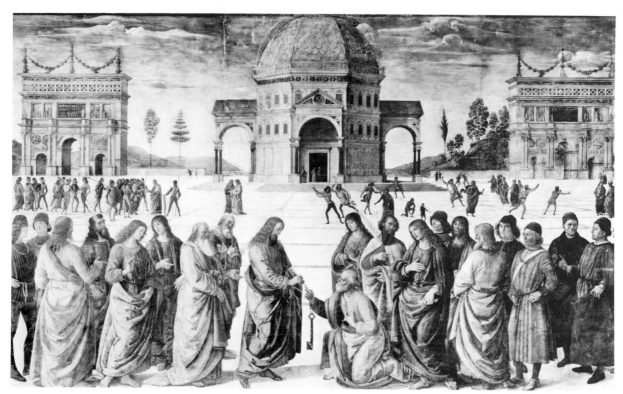

14-17 PERUGINO, *The Handing of the Keys to St. Peter,* (1481–83). **Fresco.**   Sistine Chapel, the Vatican, Rome.

ing of the mind or a condition of the spirit. While Leonardo was not the first to have these concerns, he faced them more deliberately than his contemporaries did and went further in seeking pictorial means for their expression. Sixteenth-century painting was influenced by his triangular figure groupings and his ideal facial type—the softly modeled oval with slender nose and delicately curved mouth. Unlike most fifteenth-century painters, he no longer felt the need for clarity in all parts. His softening of edges produces the effect of an atmospheric veil *(sfumato)* in the *Mona Lisa* (Fig. 14-18). In *The Madonna of the Rocks* (Louvre version), he subordinated local colors to a total color effect and used strong chiaroscuro, leaving parts of the painting in obscurity but providing powerful focus. The highlighted fingers of the Madonna's outstretched hand create a startling illusion of depth; they hover over the head of Jesus and suggest a halo or a crown of thorns. The angel's hand points to the other child, who will become John the Baptist and recognize Jesus as the Christ. The tense concentration of attention between the two children is softened by the meditative gaze of the Madonna, while the angel seems more aware of the spectator. The jagged rocks and

14-18 LEONARDO DA VINCI, *Mona Lisa,* (*c.* 1503–1505). **Oil on panel, approx.** 30″ × 21″.   Louvre, Paris.

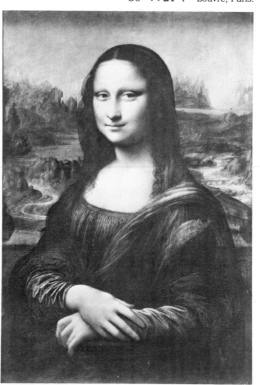

delicate plants do not seem to be included merely to demonstrate technical virtuosity or to establish physical reality, as they do in much fifteenth-century work. Instead, the powerful contrasts of light and shadow, of wild nature and soft flesh create the dramatic intensity of a mystery play or a sacred ritual. In 1481 or 1482, Leonardo moved to Milan, where he enjoyed the patronage of the Sforza family and painted *The Madonna of the Rocks* and *The Last Supper* in Santa Maria delle Grazie. These and the *Mona Lisa* express mental rather than physical drama. Leonardo moved back and forth between Milan, Florence, and Rome until 1517 when he accepted Francis I's invitation and went to Amboise in France. There, he spent the last two years of his life. The variety of Leonardo's interests and his tendency to leave projects unfinished have left us few paintings; his drawings and notebooks contain anatomical and botanical studies and inventions ranging from hydraulic pumps to flying machines. His late painting of John the Baptist (Louvre, Paris) has definite Manneristic traits (see p. 199) and influenced the Mannerist painter Parmigianino.

Sculpture in Italy

Florentine sculpture led the movement toward the consolidation of mass, contrapposto poses, studied anatomical detail, naturalistic drapery, and portraiture, all inspired by the growing interest in Roman art, the physical world, and man. The first freestanding nude figure sculptures since Roman times were produced, and relief sculpture exploited the illusion of depth. As in painting, the desire for clarity often resulted in a linear inscribing of detail on the masses. The range of sculpture widened in subject matter and in function. Human heroes, both contemporary and biblical, were frequently chosen as subjects, and Greco-Roman mythology and secular allegory appeared more often than before. Enthusiasm for small bronze antique statuettes led Renaissance sculptors to take up this art, often borrowing subjects from mythology. Sculptures of the Madonna and of saints acquired portraitlike individuality. Relief sculpture served to emphasize focal points in the church, such as pulpits, *cantorie* (galleries for singers), and bronze doors. The relief on *tabernacles* (devotional

centers ranging in size from small plaques to large wall niches) employed striking single-point perspective views surrounded by elaborate architectural frames using variations of ancient Greco-Roman moldings (Fig. 9-8, p. 95). The Renaissance appreciation of the individual is evidenced in the increased number of portrait busts after the middle of the century. Like old Roman portraits, they contained much detail, yet the sculptor was capable of ennobling the subject by dignity of pose or alertness of expression. The ancient Roman equestrian statue of Marcus Aurelius in Rome inspired similar monuments in homage to fifteenth-century Italians. The desire to perpetuate a name also asserted itself in the Renaissance wall tomb, built into the side of a church. The tombs present Roman pediments, columns, pilasters, moldings, and Roman figure types such as *putti* (cupids or cherubs) and Greco-Roman winged victory goddesses.

LORENZO GHIBERTI (Florence, 1378?–1455). Ghiberti's two sets of bronze doors for the Florentine Baptistery show the transition from late Gothic to early Renaissance style. The *Sacrifice of Isaac* panel, done as an entry in the competition for the first set of doors (1401–1402), is spatially shallow and crowded. The same subject done for the second set of doors (Fig. 14-19), the so-called *Gates of Paradise* (1425–52), is set in a spacious landscape with deep space created by a suggestion of linear perspective in the lines of trees and an effect of aerial perspective in the contrast of high relief in the foreground and faint relief in the background. Typical of the age are the drapery folds that emphasize the flexible poses of the bodies. Ghiberti's freestanding statue of St. Matthew (1420) for Or San Michele adopts the mass, pose, and drapery forms of ancient Greco-Roman statues of orators. In his *Commentaries*, Ghiberti wrote about the lives of great artists and the theory of art, seeking in this way to establish his own place in the history of art.

DONATELLO (Florence, 1386–1466). The most significant fifteenth-century Italian sculptor was Donatello, who learned bronze casting under Ghiberti and traveled to Rome with the architect Brunelleschi to study ancient art. Donatello worked in marble, bronze, and occasionally wood

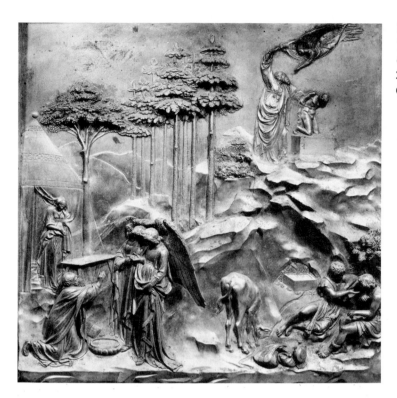

14-19 LORENZO GHIBERTI, *The Sacrifice of Isaac,* from the *"Gates of Paradise,"* (1425–52). Bronze, 21″ × 17½″. Baptistery, Florence Cathedral.

14-20 DONATELLO, *Young John the Baptist,* (c. 1455). Marble, entire figure approx. 6′ high. Museo Nazionale, Florence.

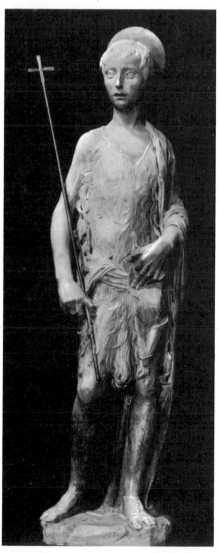

and *stucco* (a fine plaster or cement). His first bronze statue of David (1430–32, Bargello, Florence) appears to have been the first freestanding nude since Roman times. Donatello also did relief sculpture, advancing its illusionistic possibilities by suggesting deep space and a variety of spatial relationships without using high relief for the foreground. He often combined his subtle low relief, called *schiacciato,* with architectural settings in single-point perspective; the effect is much like that of a drawing. Poses are active, and drapery breaks into a complexity of nervously rippling linear folds. Donatello's art reflects the growing importance of the individual not only in the use of specific features and expressions but also in the choice of human heroes such as David, Judith, and "Gattamelata" (Erasmo da Narni, a Renaissance general) as frequent subjects. Most amazing is his ability to express convincingly a wide range of human emotions, from the brutal confidence of a military leader (the *Gattamelata,* Padua) to the contemplative aloofness of *Young John the Baptist* (Fig. 14-20). Realism of form is accompanied by the realism of bared feelings. Strangely enough, Donatello, unlike other sculptors, did not show great interest in the portrait bust.

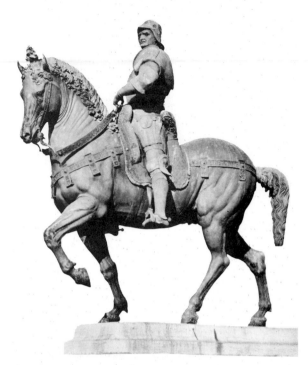

14-21 ANDREA VERROCCHIO,
Bartolomeo Colleoni, (c. 1483–88). Bronze, approx.
13′ high.   Campo dei Santi Giovanni e Paolo, Venice.

ANDREA DEL VERROCCHIO (Florence, 1435–88).
Verrocchio was first trained as a goldsmith and
then may have worked with Desiderio da Settig-
nano. Only one painting, *The Baptism of Christ*
(c. 1472, Uffizi Gallery, Florence), is attributed
with certainty to Verrocchio; his main interest was
sculpture. He worked in terra cotta, stone, and
bronze, with subjects ranging from saints and portrait busts to tomb designs and the equestrian
statue of Bartolomeo Colleoni (Fig. 14-21). The
Colleoni, a monument to a military leader, has
much greater tension in both horse and rider than
does its inspiration, Donatello's *Gattamelata*.
Verrocchio's style is characterized by much hard-
edged detail, bulbous anatomy, and distinct individuality in the faces. He taught Leonardo da
Vinci.

Architecture in Italy

The Renaissance man saw a sharp contrast between Gothic architecture, with its soaring verticals, irregular expansion, and complex geometric
proportions veiled by lavish surface detail, and the
remains of ancient Roman architecture. The
Roman work, long since shorn of its decorative

veneer, revealed a basic symmetry and a logical
clarity in its proportioning that were simple
enough to be quickly felt and comprehended, and
the Renaissance scholar eagerly noted the static
balance of vertical columns and horizontal architraves, the simple curve of the round arch, and the
massive permanence of the walls that related to
the rational structure of Greco-Roman literature
and philosophy. Some fifteenth-century architects
merely applied Roman pilasters, columns, and
moldings in Gothic profusion, but the leaders
sought to understand principles rather than to imitate details, and significant early Renaissance
buildings, such as the Pazzi Chapel in Florence
(Figs. 14-22 – 14-24) and Santa Maria delle Carceri
in Prato (Figs. 1-16, 14-30, and 14-31), display a
severe clarity of plan and elevation. The calculated
simplicity and the linear outlining of each part call
attention to the proportion of the parts to the
whole, and the resulting diagrammatic effect is
reminiscent of the insistence on linear clarity in
much fifteenth-century Italian painting and sculpture. Studies of proportion in Roman architecture
were intensified by the discovery, in a Swiss monastery in 1414, of the writings of Pollio Vitruvius, a
Roman architectural theorist of the first century
A.D., although difficulties in translating the work
somewhat restricted its influence until the sixteenth century.

Florence yielded the first architecture of the
early Renaissance, the Foundlings' Hospital and
the Pazzi Chapel. Other Italian cities, such as
Rimini and Mantua, also became important. In
Venice, the Renaissance came late and was mixed
with strong Gothic and Byzantine traditions. Balconies and arcades kept walls light and open; Venetian politics were less violent than those of Florence, and the massive, fortresslike character of
Florentine palaces was less necessary in Venice.
Rome was also slow in developing the new style,
partly because few buildings were completed during the century. When Renaissance elements appear, the most evident source of inspiration is the
architecture of Leon Battista Alberti.

FILIPPO BRUNELLESCHI (Florence, 1377–1446).
Brunelleschi's aspirations as a sculptor may have
been crushed by his loss to Ghiberti in the competition for the reliefs on the Florentine Baptistery
doors. Brunelleschi turned to architecture and was

the first to make accurate measurements of Roman ruins. He was also the first to use the rediscovered Roman architectural motifs consistently and to combine them with a new sense of spatial unity based on mathematical proportions. For example, his Florentine Church of San Lorenzo (designed in 1421) used a bay in the side aisle as a module that, in different multiples, governs the proportions of all the other spaces in the plan. Although Gothic architecture was often based on mathematical proportions and multiples of a chosen unit of measurement, its complexity does not allow the spectator to sense the relationships of basic proportions as he does in Brunelleschi's buildings. Brunelleschi's design (1418) for a dome on the unfinished Cathedral of Florence revealed his engineering genius. Brunelleschi's surviving buildings include the Foundlings' Hospital (designed in 1419), the Church of Santo Spirito (designed in 1436), and the Pazzi Chapel, all in Florence. In the small Pazzi Chapel (Fig. 14-22), the altar is set into a niche opposite the entry and across the short axis of a simple rectangular plan (Fig. 14-23). Walls and vaults are divided by dark stone pilasters and moldings into distinct geometric areas (Fig. 14-24). The low relief of these

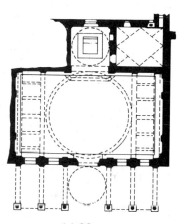

14-23
Plan of Pazzi Chapel.

14-22 BRUNELLESCHI and GIULIANO DA MAIANO, Pazzi Chapel, (c. 1440–61).

14-24
Interior of Pazzi Chapel, Florence.

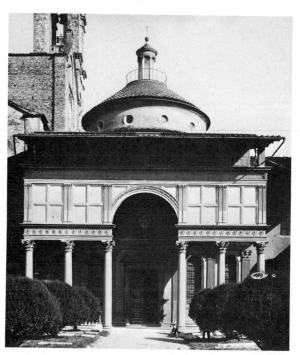

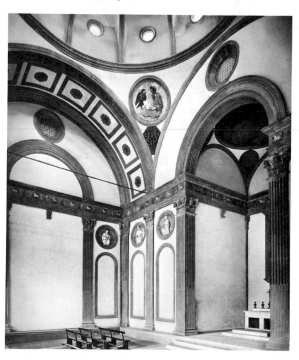

details gives the effect of a linear diagram. A dome covers the center of the space, and the unfinished porch, probably by Giuliano da Maiano, employs the Corinthian order and a *broken architrave* (architrave interrupted by an arch) in the Roman manner. Roman moldings, pilasters, and columns organize mass, planes, and spaces with the self-contained stability and dignity that Renaissance men associated with ancient Roman architecture. Brunelleschi is credited with painting two panels that demonstrated, for the first time, a consistent system of linear perspective, a major step in the Renaissance search for pictorial means of conveying the experience of space.

MICHELOZZO DI BARTOLOMMEO (Florence, 1396–1472).   To his contemporaries, Michelozzo was second only to Brunelleschi as a pioneer in the new architecture. Michelozzo became a favorite of Cosimo de' Medici, and the Medici-Riccardi Palace (Figs. 14-25 and 14-26) is the best-known work by the prolific architect. Roman details compose the arches, moldings, and *cornices* (terminating moldings that project at the top of a wall or building), but the windows of the palace are con-

nected by only a stringcourse, and no attempt was made to proportion the floors with vertical dividers in the form of pilasters or columns. The linear quality of the design is modified by heavy *rustication* (rough stonework) on the ground floor, which changes to boldly jointed but finished stone above and finally to smooth masonry in the top floor. The design is powerful but less subtle and less completely integrated in all its parts than works by Brunelleschi. Michelozzo did restoring and additional building for San Marco and the Palazzo Vecchio in Florence, and he designed the Medici Bank and probably did the drawings for the Portinari Chapel (Sant' Eustorgio), both in Milan. After the death of Brunelleschi, Michelozzo was put in charge of the Cathedral Workshop in Florence. Although occasional use of Gothic arches links his work to the past, Michelozzo helped to spread the basic elements of early Renaissance architecture to Milan and even to Dalmatia.

LEON BATTISTA ALBERTI (Florence, 1404–72). Alberti was born in Genoa to an exiled Florentine family and was educated at the universities of

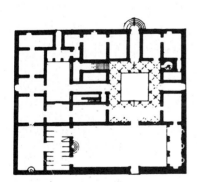

14-25
Plan of Medici-Riccardi Palace.

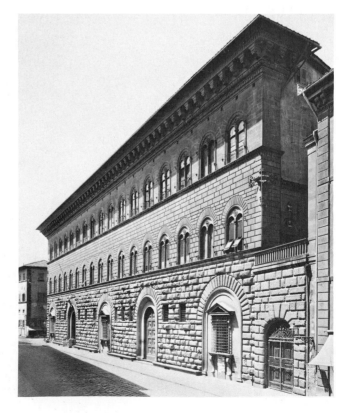

14-26   MICHELOZZO DI BARTOLOMMEO,   Medici-Riccardi Palace, Florence (begun 1444).

Padua and Bologna. He became a universal man of the Renaissance — a humanist scholar, painter, sculptor, mathematician, poet, and architect. His *Ten Books on Architecture*, like the treatises of Vitruvius, had wide influence, and he succeeded Brunelleschi as the leader in Renaissance architecture. The outstanding example of Alberti's church structures is Sant' Andrea in Mantua (Figs. 14-27 and 14-28). The façade combines the forms of a Roman temple and a triumphal arch. The height of the façade equals its width, although to achieve this perfect square, the façade was made lower than the rest of the church. The colossal pilasters on the façade, which rise more than one floor, are the same height as those within, and the nave is as wide as the whole façade. A vast barrel vault intersected by barrel vaults over the chapels on a lower level (Fig. 14-29) recalls the massive scale and structural features of the Basilica of Constantine (p. 123). Alberti maintained that numerical ratios were the source of visual and structural

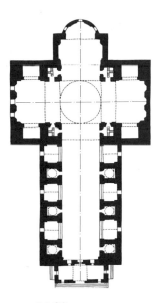

14-28
Plan of Sant' Andrea.

14-27 LEON BATTISTA ALBERTI,
Sant' Andrea, Mantua, (*c.* 1470).

14-29
Interior of Sant' Andrea.

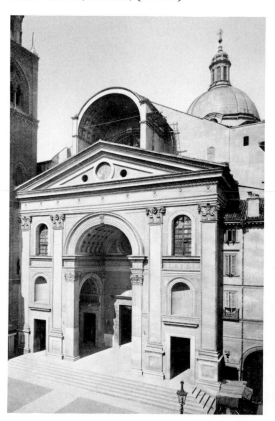

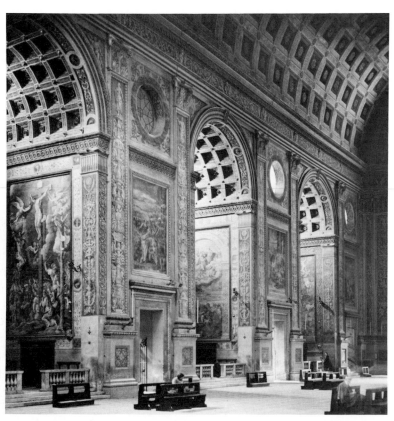

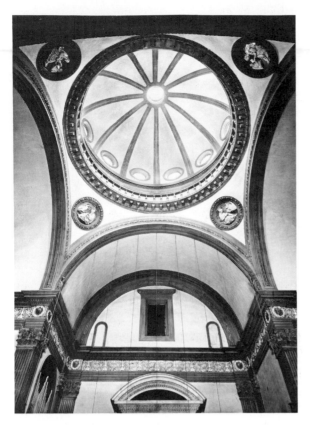

14-30   GIULIANO DA SANGALLO,   interior of Santa Maria delle Carceri, Prato, (1485–92).

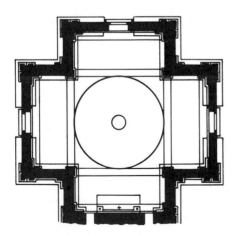

14-31
Plan of Santa Maria delle Carceri.

harmony. Sant' Andrea influenced much later work, including the plans for St. Peter's by Bramante and Michelangelo.

GIULIANO DA SANGALLO (Florence, 1445–1516). Giuliano came from a family of celebrated artists and was trained as a sculptor, engineer, and architect. His sphere of activity extended from Naples to Milan and into southern France, where he served Cardinal Giuliano delle Rovere in Lyons. Giuliano's Santa Maria delle Carceri (Figs. 1-16, 14-30, and 14-31) came late in the fifteenth century; its central Greek cross plan accords with Alberti's argument that the four-sided symmetry of a central plan expressed divine reason in its unity and harmony. Both Sangallo and Alberti forecast the sixteenth-century interest in central plans. The dome over the crossing of Sangallo's church, the linear framing of dark against light, and the low relief of pilasters and moldings all reveal the influence of Brunelleschi. The pilasters and dark bands on the exterior emphasize the proportions and suggest structural framing without destroying the flatness of the wall surface, while the nature of the interior spaces is clearly revealed by the flatness and simplicity of the enclosing walls. Giuliano's career extended into the sixteenth century, and, in later life, he was appointed to serve with Raphael in carrying on the construction of St. Peter's in Rome.

THE SIXTEENTH CENTURY

Painting in Italy

Italian painting of the High Renaissance period (1500–20) developed different aims from those of fifteenth-century art and should therefore not be thought of simply as a culmination of less successful fifteenth-century efforts. The earlier emphasis on the exploration of the physical world was superseded by a general effort to transform and transcend surface appearance without sacrificing its physical qualities. The artist sought to perfect nature according to preconceived ideal forms; faces were generalized to present types of humans rather than individuals, and there was less depiction of contemporary costume and more simplification of drapery folds for broad, sweeping, directional emphasis. The explicit detail and linear clarity of much fifteenth-century work gave way to fuller, simpler masses. Some painters, influenced by Leonardo, used varying degrees of sfumato that contrast with the sharp, airless space of much fifteenth-century painting. Individual actions formed a more flowing, harmonious, rhythmic pattern, and chiaroscuro provided dramatic focus and contrast. All this was part of a concept of the Grand Manner, by which the artist transformed nature and made it expressive of ideal form and inner experience, a concept possible only with the increased tendency to consider the artist as a divine genius rather than a mere craftsman. In the second half of the fifteenth century, many of the High Renaissance qualities had already been developed in the art of Leonardo da Vinci. As a result, he is often considered a High Renaissance painter, even though most of his pioneering works were done in the fifteenth century. It is more helpful to see him as a bridge between the two centuries.

Florence was the seedbed for High Renaissance painting, not only because of Leonardo's work or the intellectually inquisitive and experimental background there, but because Raphael and Michelangelo painted their first mature works in that city. However, the blossoming occurred in Rome with the work of both these artists. In northern Italy, Venetian painting moved away from the sharp detail of the Early Renaissance toward fuller and less detailed masses, and the suppression of local colors for an overall color effect (Plate 9). Soft atmospheric effects were easier to achieve with oil paint, and in the sixteenth century the technique of oil on canvas supplanted the traditional tempera on wood panels that had been used for easel paintings (portable works). Fresco techniques continued to be used for mural painting, although during the sixteenth century use was made of oil on canvas applied to the wall. Venetian painters used oil paint opaquely and in glazes for textural and color effects of great richness.

Italian painting in the Late Renaissance (1520– 1600) manifested several stylistic trends, sometimes within the work of a single artist. While High Renaissance concepts continued to shape the art of some leaders, a second trend, known as *Mannerism*, rejected the clear underlying order of High Renaissance painting and replaced it with ambiguity in spatial relations, mood, and even subject matter. Elongated figures with narrow shoulders, wide hips, tapering hands and feet, and self-consciously affected gestures were composed with a lack of central focus and deliberately inconsistent scale in crowded spaces. A third trend may be called *Proto-Baroque* because it forecasts the violent activity, dramatic lighting, great complexity, and breathtaking illusionism that were to become important devices in seventeenth-century Baroque art.

MICHELANGELO BUONARROTI (Florence and Rome, 1475–1564).   As a youth, Michelangelo was taken from his birthplace, Caprese, to Florence, where he studied painting with Domenico Ghirlandaio and sculpture with Bertoldo di Giovanni. Although his real love was sculpture, papal and financial pressures forced Michelangelo to do painting and architecture as well. The only easel painting that is known with certainty to be his is *The Holy Family* (1504–1506, Uffizi Gallery, Florence); the rest of his painting is mural work done in fresco. One of the greatest monuments of the High Renaissance is his series of frescoes on the ceiling of the Sistine Chapel in the Vatican, done between 1508 and 1512 at the insistence of Pope Julius II. Between 1536 and 1541, he painted *The Last Judgment* on the end wall of the Sistine Chapel, and from 1542 until 1549 he worked in the Pauline Chapel in the Vatican. Michelangelo concentrated on the human figure, often to the near exclusion of setting, and his concept of ideal form led him to paint figures of awesome bulk and musculature in active or restless poses. The Sistine ceiling boils with writhing giants enacting the Creation of the World, the Creation and Fall of Man, the story of Noah, and numerous secondary stories and allegories, all organized within a painted architectural framework. One of the few relaxed figures is that of Adam as he receives life from the outstretched hand of God, whose body ripples with energy. Typically, *The Creation of Adam* (Fig. 14-32) is divided into only two large groupings: that of Adam with the vaguely suggested mound of earth, and that of God and surrounding angels framed by a billowing cloak. The two groupings focus on the almost-touching fingers of God and Adam. In many other scenes, the extraordinary physical power of the bodies is countered by expressions of mental attitudes ranging from contemplation to

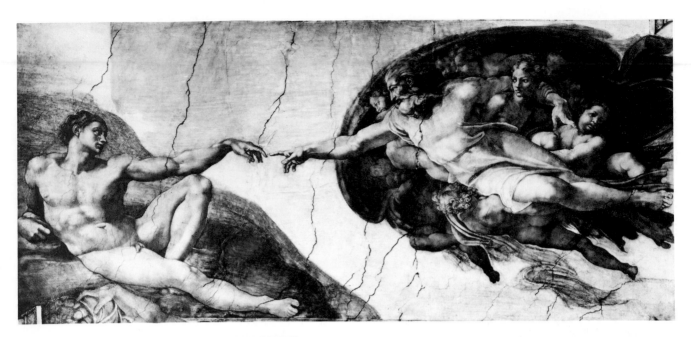

14-32   MICHELANGELO BUONARROTI,
The Creation of Adam, detail from the ceiling of the
Sistine Chapel, the Vatican, Rome, (1508–12).

consternation and anguish. Michelangelo's art
and poetry indicate an increasing disillusionment
with the search for physical beauty. The overpowering scale and activity in his painting forecast the
Baroque art of the seventeenth century.

GIORGIONE DA CASTELFRANCO (Venice, 1478–
1510).   The plague cut short the brilliant career
of Giorgione, one of Titian's fellow apprentices in
the studio of Giovanni Bellini. Scanty documentation has resulted in much discussion about the
identification and dating of authentic paintings by
Giorgione. Generally accepted works are the *Castelfranco Madonna* (Castelfranco), *The Tempest, The Sleeping Venus* (Dresden Gallery), and
The Pastoral Concert, although the latter has
sometimes been questioned. The intended subject
of *The Tempest* (Fig. 14-33) is, thus far, an un-
solved mystery. This work was an innovation in
Italian painting because of the importance of its
landscape elements and its stress on mood. In *The
Pastoral Concert* (Plate 9 and Fig. 14-34) the nude
women may personify the subject of the music
played by the young men. The nude bodies are
painted as heavy three-dimensional forms with
soft edges, generalized anatomy, and delicate
nuances of light and color. The foliage masses and
the lavish costumes have equally full forms and
subtle textures. The painting is organized in alternating areas of light and dark that move back step

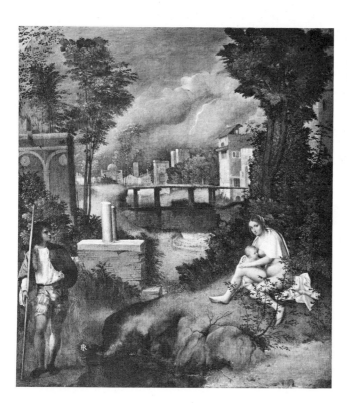

14-33 GIORGIONE DA CASTELFRANCO,
The Tempest (The Soldier and the Gypsy),
(*c.* 1504). Oil on canvas, approx. 30″ × 29″.
Galleria dell' Accademia, Venice.

14-34 GIORGIONE DA
CASTELFRANCO,   *The Pastoral
Concert,* (*c.* 1508). Oil on canvas,
approx. 43″ × 54″.   Louvre, Paris.

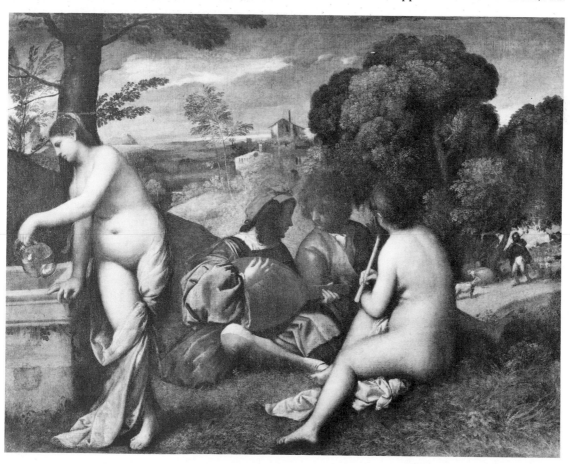

by step from foreground to background; and the colors become cooler and less saturated as they move from the red hat of the central youth into the distance. The forms complement each other in graceful consonance; for example, the tree trunk on the left flows into the vertical arm of the standing woman and also bends to meet the curve of her back, while the leaning position and the rounded forms of the seated woman are echoed in the foliage of the central tree. With his use of soft light, quiet, graceful masses, bold simplification of light and dark areas, and glowing color, Giorgione exemplifies the High Renaissance in Venice. His style may be seen as a bridge between the late work of Giovanni Bellini and the painting of Titian.

TIZIANO VECELLI, *called* **TITIAN** (Venice, *c.* 1490–1576).   As a pupil of Giovanni Bellini and an admirer of Giorgione, Titian acquired a love of soft, light, warm color effects, which subordinated local colors, and massive simplified forms. He enjoyed the lavish textiles and elegant costumes of wealthy Venetian society and incorporated these into his painting. His ideal for the female figure is admirably presented in the Naples *Danaë* (Plate 8 and Fig. 14-35). The breadth of the forms, the

14-35 TITIAN, *Danaë,* (*c.* 1545). Oil on canvas, approx. 4′ × 6′. Museo di Capodimonte, Naples.

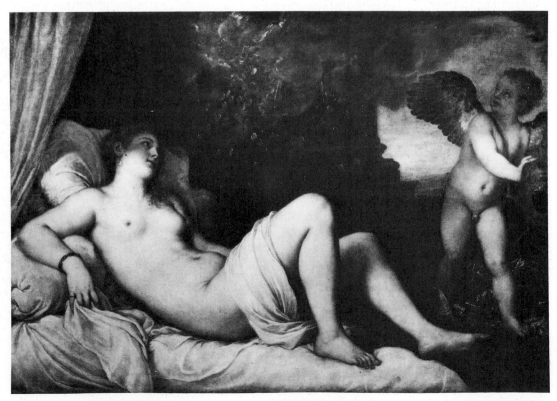

division of the composition into a few large parts, the subordination of details to large areas of light and dark, and the preference for spiral torsion in the poses probably owe something to the art of Michelangelo, but Titian's color is richer and his forms are softer. Titian achieved depth and a variety of subtle textures by building up oil glazes of warm and cool colors along with areas of impasto. His preference for dynamic grouping and powerful chiaroscuro manifests itself in early works, such as *The Assumption of the Virgin* (1516–18) and the *Madonna of the Pesaro Family* (Fig. 14-36), where figures and areas of contrasting value are grouped as counterbalancing diagonals. His late work, such as *Christ Crowned with Thorns* (Fig. 14-37), used heavier impasto and dense sfumato. Titian's fame spread, and his energies were prodigious; in addition to religious subjects and mythological themes, he painted many portraits, including those of Pope Paul III and the Emperor Charles V.

RAPHAEL SANZIO (Florence and Rome, 1483–1520). After studying with Perugino in Umbria and revealing his precocious talent, Raphael went to Florence (1504–1508), where he painted portraits and Madonnas. The *Madonna of the Meadow* (Plate 6 and Fig. 3-1) is typical. The feeling of gentle, sweet serenity is expressed not only through faces and gestures but through the whole compositional structure. The stable triangular group of figures works with the quiet landscape to form an obvious axial balance. The large triangle provides an effect of gradation and climax at the head of the Madonna, while the head of Jesus receives similar emphasis through the triangular shape formed by his body and the cross. The triangular groupings are softened by a modification of bodies and garments to produce variations on ovoid curves. Every part joins the gentle curvilinear harmony and fits into the underlying geometric structure. The face of the Madonna and the use of the triangular grouping owe much to Leonardo. In 1509, Pope Julius II called Raphael to Rome to paint a fresco series in several rooms of the Vatican. *The School of Athens* (Fig. 14-38), in the Stanza della Segnatura, combines Roman architecture on a vast scale, an ideal concept of human form, and individual portraits of the great minds of various ages. The many figures are organized in

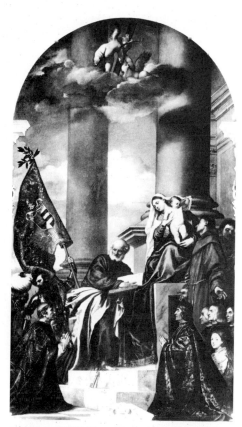

14-36 TITIAN, *Madonna of the Pesaro Family*, (1519–26). Oil on canvas, approx. 16′ × 9′. Santa Maria dei Frari, Venice.

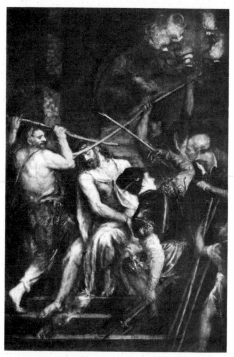

14-37 TITIAN, *Christ Crowned with Thorns*, (c. 1570–76). Oil on canvas, 9′ × 6′. Alte Pinakothek, Munich.

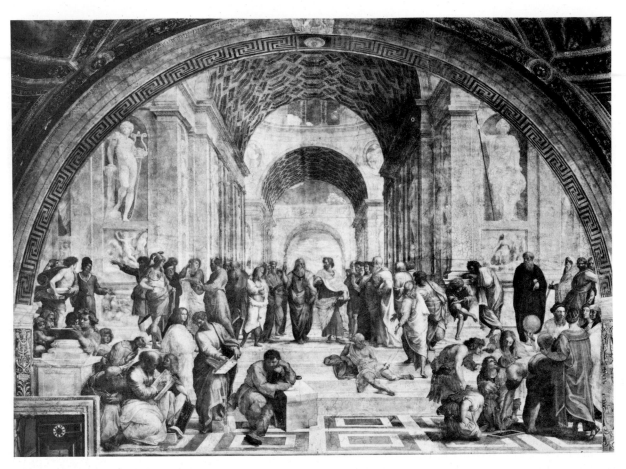

14-38   RAPHAEL SANZIO,   *The School of Athens,*
(1509–11). **Fresco.**   Stanza della Segnatura, the Vatican,
Rome.

large, symmetrically balanced groups by geometric systems of sweeping curves, triangles, and vertical and horizontal lines. Restrained emotions, clear serene order, and exhilarating breadth dignify the grand symbolic program. We seem to witness the apotheosis of man. Some of the bodies in the Vatican paintings suggest the physique and poses of the figures in Michelangelo's contemporary frescoes in the Sistine Chapel. Raphael's earlier Vatican works are the epitome of High Renaissance art; the later ones reveal Mannerist qualities.

ANTONIO ALLEGRI, *called* **CORREGGIO** (Parma, 1494–1534).   Correggio's art indicates an acquaintance with the painting of Leonardo, Michelangelo, and the Venetians. His *Madonna of St. Jerome* (Fig. 14-39), like his frescoes in Parma Cathedral (1526–30), has the spiral poses, fluttering drapery, bold dark and light contrasts, and avoidance of stable verticals and horizontals that forecast much seventeenth-century painting; yet Correggio held the activity within large areas, and the compositions do not figuratively break through their architectural frame. His late work combines saccharine smiles and sensual fleshiness with Manneristic poses.

FRANCESCO MAZZOLA, *called* **IL PARMIGIANINO** (Parma, 1503–40).   Parmigianino, a leading representative of Mannerism, was influenced by Correggio before coming to Rome (1524–27), where he attempted to achieve the dramatic lighting effects of Leonardo, the restless poses of Michelangelo, the rhythmic grace of Raphael, and the sensuality of Correggio. Parmigianino's *Madonna del Collo Lungo* (*Madonna with the Long Neck,* Fig. 14-40) shows the sinuous elongation and the ambiguity in space, scale, and emotions that are typical of the Mannerist aesthetic.

JACOPO ROBUSTI, *called* **TINTORETTO** (Venice, 1518–94).   Tintoretto, one of the giants of Venetian painting, was an admirer of Titian and Michelangelo. His paintings include scenes from the life of St. Mark done for the Guild of St. Mark (1547–66), scenes from the life of Christ done for the School of San Rocco (1560–87), and religious and mythological subjects for the Doge's Palace (1577–78), all in Venice. Tintoretto's series were often elaborate in concept and grand in scale. His powers are summarized in the late painting of *The Last Supper* (Fig. 14-41), which contrasts startlingly with the same subject treated by Leonardo. Tintoretto grouped the active disciples along a table that pushes diagonally back into space. Halfway down the length of the table, the dazzling *nimbus* (glowing halo) around the head of Jesus provides the major light source in the dark room. Small nimbuses glow around the heads of all the disciples, a foreground lamp seems to radiate sparks, and transparent angels swoop down toward Jesus. This remarkably dramatic interpretation did much to inspire seventeenth-century art.

PAOLO VERONESE (Venice, 1528–88).   At the age of twenty-seven, Veronese came from Verona to Venice, where he painted the elegant life style of the Venetians. His selection and interpretation of biblical subjects was governed by his love of lavish costumes, ornate architecture, and elegant table settings. *The Feast in the House of Levi* (Fig. 14-42) is typical in its grand scale. Veronese's interest in decorative details sometimes weakens

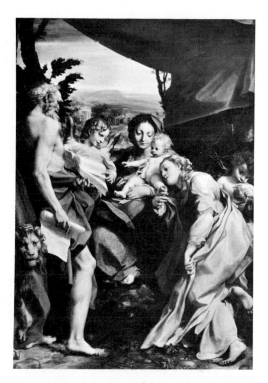

14-39 CORREGGIO, *Madonna of St. Jerome,* (1527–28).   Galleria Nazionale, Parma.

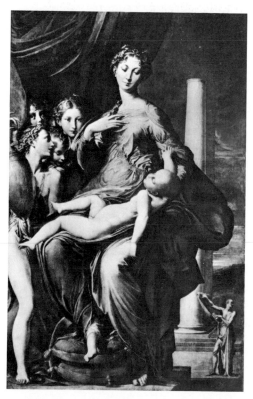

14-40 IL PARMIGIANINO, *Madonna del Collo Lungo (Madonna with the Long Neck),* (*c.* 1535). Oil on canvas, approx. 85″ × 52″. **Unfinished (?).**   Galleria degli Uffizi, Florence.

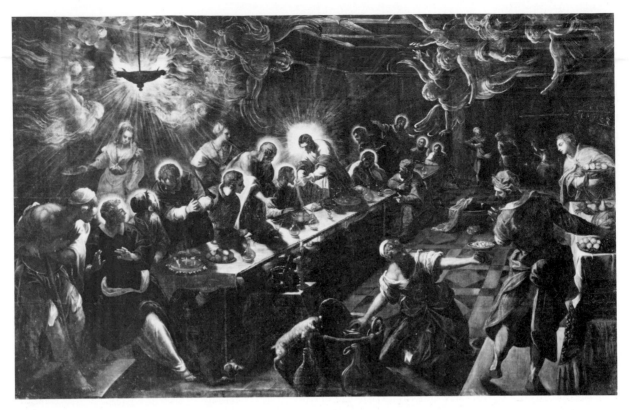

14-41   TINTORETTO,   *The Last Supper,*
(1592–94). 12′ × 18′8″. San Giorgio Maggiore, Venice.

14-42   PAOLO VERONESE,   *The Feast in the
House of Levi,* (1573). Oil on canvas, 18′2″ × 42′.
Galleria dell' Accademia, Venice.

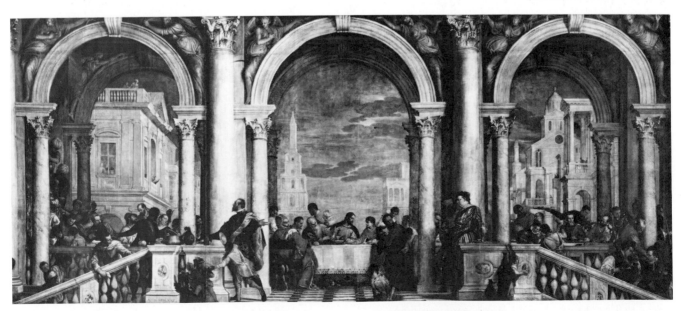

the expressive power of the figures, but his technical facility, his use of silvery color, and the exuberance of his composition compensate for his shortcomings.

Sculpture in Italy

High Renaissance sculpture, like the painting of the period, sought ideal form, the Grand Manner that involved nobility of action and scale, ideal shapes and proportions, and depth of feeling. Some sculptors employed the serene equilibrium and smooth transitions seen in much of Raphael's painting; others chose the twisting poses and more tense vitality of Michelangelo's painting and sculpture. Both these facets of High Renaissance style contributed to the Late Renaissance trends of Mannerism and the Proto-Baroque. The serpentine curves and self-conscious elegance of a Mannerist figure might be derived from Raphael's suave harmonies or might be a softened version of the torsion and heroic musculature in Michelangelo's art. The bold contrast, dramatic action, and powerful focus of Proto-Baroque sculpture were inspired particularly by Michelangelo.

Portrait sculpture tended throughout the sixteenth century to express social position and physical or mental types rather than the sharply individual traits seen in fifteenth-century works. Sixteenth-century wall tombs were often larger and more complex than their fifteenth-century forerunners. The architectural frame developed greater spatial variety in different planes of projecting and receding parts. High Renaissance tombs usually have a smooth integration of figures and architecture, while Late Renaissance tombs may combine Manneristic figures with the lavish materials and bold contrasts that forecast the Baroque. The love of contrast sometimes led the designer to set figures and architecture sharply apart through changes in values, colors, shapes, or scale. The most important source for Late Renaissance tombs was Michelangelo's design for the tombs of the Medici (Fig. 2-5). Only in the Late Renaissance was the fountain developed as a public monument, one that could combine freestanding sculpture, relief sculpture, and water in movement. Fountains tended to become more complex, and relief sculpture gave way to more and more sculpture in the round (freestanding). Mass became more open, and dark and light contrasts became more extreme.

The major centers for the development of sixteenth-century sculptural style were Florence and Rome; Venice, Milan, and Naples were secondary. The sculptors, like the painters, often were active in several cities during the course of their careers.

MICHELANGELO BUONARROTI (Florence and Rome, 1475–1564). Michelangelo's early sculpture, such as *The Battle of the Centaurs*, done under the patronage of the Medici family in Florence, already showed the artist's preference for the nude, muscular body and active intertwining masses. Michelangelo's life was constantly upset by the conflicting demands of various patrons, and many of his sculptural projects remained unfinished or were finished in a compromise with original plans. This is the case with the tombs of Giuliano and Lorenzo de' Medici (Fig. 2-5), which underwent many changes and were left unfinished when Michelangelo departed for Rome. For the tomb of Giuliano, the wall emphasizes the climactic figure of Giuliano seated in a niche above the sarcophagus. Value contrasts stress the framing effect of the architecture, and the triangular grouping of the figures (Fig. 2-6, p. 22) integrates them with the geometry of the wall in spite of their restless poses and precarious positions; they were obviously designed to rest on horizontal surfaces. As in his painting, Michelangelo created muscular giants; he admitted that the central figure bore little resemblance to the face or body of Giuliano. Michelangelo saw his task not as the accurate portrayal of physical appearance but as the creation of a monument expressive of leadership. The female figure of Night and the unfinished male figure of Day seem to be grieving for Giuliano. The torso of *Day* reveals the influence of the *Belvedere Torso*, a fragment of a Roman copy of a Hellenistic Greek work that was known to Michelangelo. In view of his style, it is not hard to understand that Michelangelo's favorite ancient sculpture was the then newly discovered (1506) *Laocoön* (Fig. 9-30, p. 108), whose muscular power and dynamic pose suggest the source of Michelangelo's concept of ideal form. The artist's grandest tomb design, that

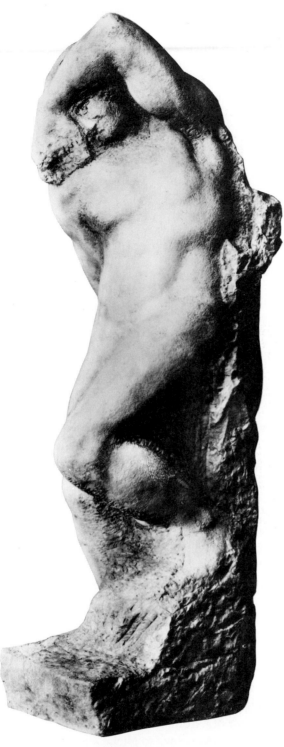

14-43   MICHELANGELO BUONARROTI,
The Young Slave (for the Tomb of Pope Julius II),
(1530–34?). Marble, approx. 8′ high.   Accademia delle
Belle Arti, Florence.

for Pope Julius II (Fig. 14-43), suffered endless changes during forty years of struggle for funds and conflict with other projects. The result, now located in the Church of San Pietro in Vincoli, in Rome, is a sadly heterogeneous collection of parts.

BENVENUTO CELLINI (Florence, Rome, and France, 1500–71).   Cellini was trained as a goldsmith and worked mainly in Rome from 1519 to 1540 as a medalist, that is, doing metal medallions with portraits in low relief. His skill is evident in the gold *Saltcellar of Francis I* (Kunsthistorisches Museum, Vienna), finished during a sojourn in France from 1540 to 1545. It was then that Cellini produced his first large-scale sculpture, using Mannerist proportions that suggest the influence of Francesco Primaticcio, Cellini's rival at the court of Francis I. Cellini's masterpiece was the *Perseus* (Fig. 14-44), done after his return to Florence. The Greek hero holds the severed head of the Medusa and is posed without twisting or violent action, showing more sympathy with Raphael than with Michelangelo. The intricate details reveal the goldsmith's art, and the only Manneristic elements are in the sculpture on the base. Cellini's autobiography is a major sourcebook for the Renaissance.

GIOVANNI DA BOLOGNA (Florence, 1529–1608). Giovanni da Bologna grew up in Flanders, traveled to Rome, and settled in Florence about 1556. Some of his works are Mannerist in their soft anatomy and languid poses. However, the piece called *The Rape of the Sabine Women* (Fig. 14-45) is Proto-Baroque. The complex outline of the open forms, the intertwining organization, and the dramatic pose forecast seventeenth-century art. Giovanni was the first sculptor since the fifteenth century to produce equestrian statues, but his work in this area is very restrained in style and close to its fifteenth-century prototypes. His activity was restricted to the area of Florence, but his influence was widespread.

Architecture in Italy

High Renaissance architecture in Italy used special effects derived specifically from Roman architecture. Closer attention was paid to Roman proportions, and walls were treated more as sculpted

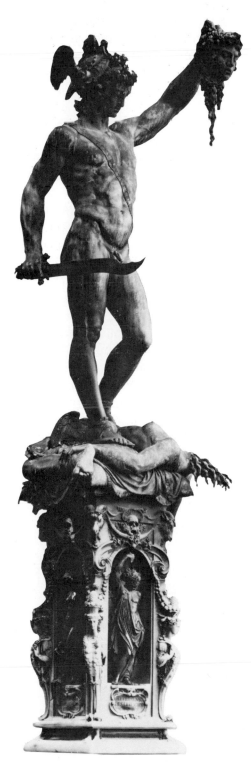

14-44   BENVENUTO CELLINI,
Perseus, (1545–54). Bronze, 10′6″ high
without base.   Loggia dei Lanzi, Florence.

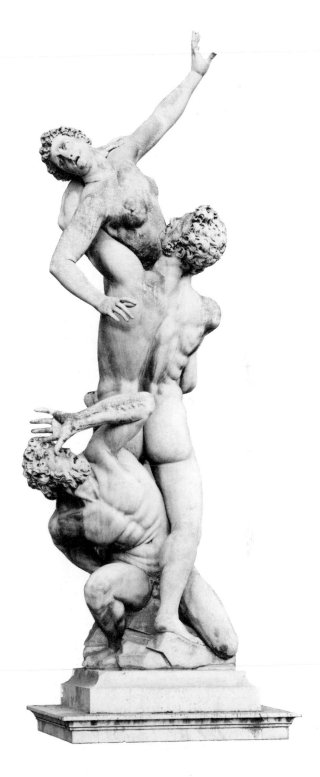

14-45   GIOVANNI DA BOLOGNA,   *The Rape of
the Sabine Women,* (completed 1583). Marble,
approx. 13′6″ high.   Loggia dei Lanzi, Florence.

mass, resulting in stronger contrasts of light and shadow. More intense study of Roman art revealed a concern for shaping not only mass but space, and High Renaissance architects turned to the possibilities of using mass to shape space not only inside but outside, between buildings in a group, for more comprehensive schemes of order. Architecture, like painting, strove for the effects of equilibrium and monumental scale that were so evident in the ruins of Roman architecture. Details were used with restraint in order to stress the largeness of the forms.

Late Renaissance architecture is often characterized by features comparable to Mannerism in painting and sculpture: unexpected contrasts, deliberately crowded forms, fantastic shapes that suggest plants, animals, or men, and ambiguity in structural functions; a column might be robbed of its supporting role by undercutting its base, and an arch might be designed with its keystone slipping precariously out of place. Proto-Baroque tendencies also began to grow in architecture after 1520. Quiet equilibrium and clarity of parts were

sacrificed for powerful focal effects, dramatic contrasts, and dynamic forms, such as concave-convex walls and expanding-contracting spaces. Surfaces were broken up with decorative elements in a great variety of depths.

DONATO BRAMANTE (Milan and Rome, 1444–1514).   Bramante turned to architecture after beginning as a painter. His early works are located in Milan. They include the remodeling of Santa Maria presso San Satiro (begun *c.* 1482), where he used illusionistic perspective relief to make the choir seem deeper, and the choir and dome of Santa Maria delle Grazie (begun in 1493). The early work often shows a typically northern Italian tendency toward rich surface decoration, but there is already some subordination of details to large framing elements, the sign of bolder, grander systems of proportions. Bramante's mature style developed in Rome after 1500, where he was the leader of High Renaissance architecture. The Tempietto (Fig. 14-46), a chapel built on the spot of Peter's crucifixion, is based on the Greco-Roman tholos

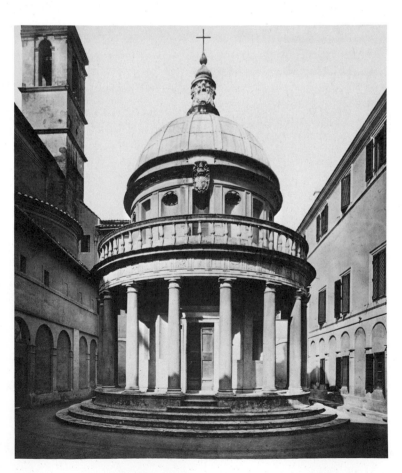

14-46   DONATO BRAMANTE, Tempietto, San Pietro in Montorio, Rome, (*c.* 1511).

temple and typifies the High Renaissance interest in central buildings. The peristyle employs the Roman Doric order with triglyphs and metopes from the ancient Greeks (Figs. 9-6 and 9-10, pp. 94–96), and the dome is a heightened version of the low Roman saucer dome seen on the Pantheon (Fig. 11-10). The wall was treated as a sculptural mass with projecting and receding parts; the light, delicate precision of earlier work has given way to a new monumentality. For the new church of St. Peter's, Bramante aimed at the magnificence of mass and space that still could be seen in the ruins of Roman baths. He turned back to the old Roman material, concrete, and drew a plan based on a Greek cross within a square (Fig. 14-47). The arms of the cross were to terminate in apses and be roofed with barrel vaults. The crossing would be covered with a great dome inspired by the Pantheon. Bramante's death put planning into the hands of a succession of architects, and the present church (see Fig. 14-48b) owes its form mainly to three men: Michelangelo, who planned a Greek cross (see Fig. 14-48a) as Bramante had but made the masses bolder and more active; Carlo Maderno, who lengthened one arm to create a basilica plan and designed the façade; and Gianlorenzo Bernini, who planned the frontal square and its enclosing colonnades. Since Maderno and Bernini did their work in the seventeenth century, St. Peter's can hardly be considered simply as a Renaissance building. Bramante's plan for the Belvedere Court in the Vatican was realized somewhat more fully. Here he used massive walls and grand scale to mold the courtyard space into a focal apse. The boldness of mass, space, and scale set the key for High Renaissance architecture.

MICHELANGELO BUONARROTI (Florence and Rome, 1475–1564). Michelangelo's first major architectural design, the Laurentian Library in Florence (1524), sacrificed the quiet equilibrium and logical clarity favored by Bramante. In the vestibule of the library (Fig. 14-49), the pilasters have an inverted taper, from small base to wide top, and engaged columns seem to deny their supporting role by occupying console brackets extending from the wall. The pilasters, columns, and windows are crowded close together, and a staircase of expansive, curved steps dominates the room. This dramatic intensity disturbed some of

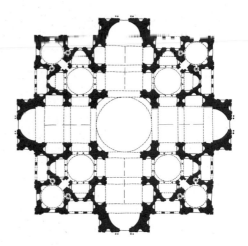

14-47   DONATO BRAMANTE, plan of St. Peter's, Rome, (1505).

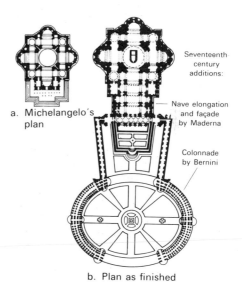

a. Michelangelo's plan

Seventeenth century additions:

Nave elongation and façade by Maderna

Colonnade by Bernini

b. Plan as finished

14-48 Plan of St. Peter's, Rome.

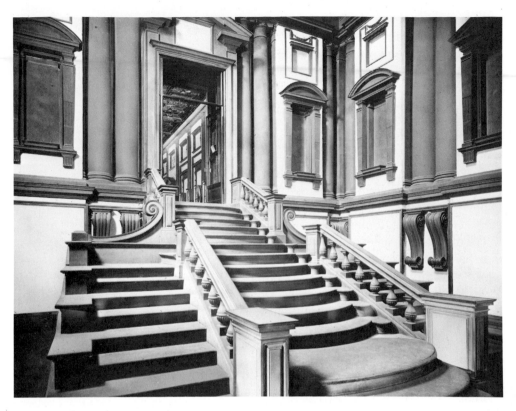

14-49   MICHELANGELO BUONARROTI,
vestibule of the Laurentian Library,
Florence (begun 1524). Stairway designed
1558–59.

Michelangelo's contemporaries, but it is considered today to be a Manneristic quality. In the 1530s, Michelangelo redesigned the Campidoglio (the Capitoline Hill) in Rome. A trapezoidal piazza flanked by two palaces focuses on the Palace of the Senators at the wide end. The piazza is filled by an oval pavement that radiates from the ancient equestrian statue of Marcus Aurelius. This dynamic space is enclosed by façades of strongly three-dimensional design, bold value contrasts, and *colossal orders* (columns or pilasters more than one floor high). Michelangelo's plan for St. Peter's provided walls of alternating angular and curved projections (see Fig. 14-48a and Fig. 14-50), making the form complex to understand, somewhat restless in its movement, and powerful in value contrasts. To avoid weakening and cluttering the great masses of the building, Michelangelo used colossal orders to pull together the levels between base and attic. Such complexity, restlessness, and contrast may be considered Proto-Baroque.

ANDREA PALLADIO (Vicenza, 1508–80). The most influential architect of the second half of the century was Palladio, an admirer of Vitruvius as

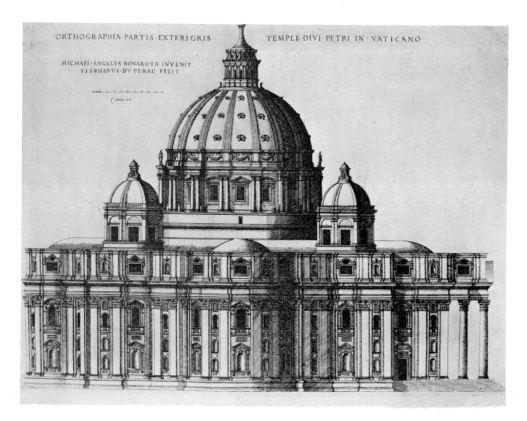

14-50 MICHELANGELO BUONARROTI, south elevation of St. Peter's (1546–64). Engraving by Duperac (*c.* 1569).

well as of Alberti, a student of Roman ruins, and a writer on architectural theory. Palladio's structures were built around his native Vicenza and in Venice, but his influence was international, partly because of his *Four Books of Architecture,* published in 1570. Many of his designs seem conservative in comparison with those of Michelangelo. A Roman dome and identical Ionic porches grace the simple square block of the Villa Rotonda (Fig. 14-51). From any one of the façades, designed in obvious axial balance, one quickly comprehends the whole exterior form. Each part has a beginning, a middle, and an end — that is, a base, a main part, and a termination. Minor parts, such as pediments over windows and doors, build toward focal points such as the pediments on the porches. Proportions are clearly marked by simple moldings. Inside, an equally severe clarity is felt in the obvious central balance of the plan (Fig. 14-52). Such design fits the concepts of High Renaissance architecture. Touches of Manneristic enigma are found in Palladio's Palazzo Thiene, however, where windows are framed by columns imprisoned in large blocks and topped by flat arches, the keystones of which break into a pediment above.

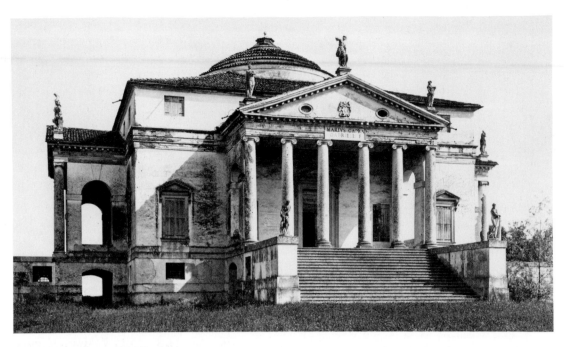

14-51   ANDREA PALLADIO,
Villa Rotonda, Vicenza (begun 1550).

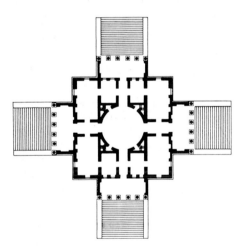

14-52
Plan of Villa Rotonda.

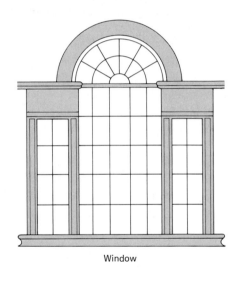

Window

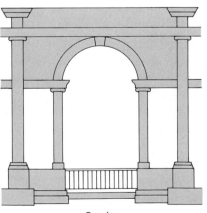

14-53
The Palladian motif.   Opening

And his Loggia del Capitaniato bristles with crowded surfaces and complex three dimensional variations, all heralding the Baroque age to come. One of Palladio's favorite devices, often called the *Palladian motif* (Fig. 14-53), was used frequently in seventeenth- and eighteenth-century architecture. It consists of a three-part opening, the highest part being in the center.

Painting in the North

By 1520, Manneristic Italian elements had begun to appear in the work of many Northern artists. We find imaginative constructions of antique architecture, heroic proportions, broad, full masses, and the occasional use of chiaroscuro and sfumato. In Flanders, Antwerp became a prolific center for paintings in an exaggerated Michelangelesque style imported from Rome. The intricacy of fifteenth-century work was retained in another type of Antwerp painting, produced for export to other European countries: small religious scenes containing weird combinations of Italianate architectural parts and elongated figures in self-conscious poses and fantastic costumes. The term *Antwerp Mannerism* is sometimes applied to both trends. Antwerp and Brussels were both important for landscape and *genre* (scenes from everyday life) painting. Landscapes were panoramic, with delicate detail and subtle color; genre subjects, often including still-life material in the foreground, tended to have sharply defined shapes in complex compositions.

In Germany, Austria, and Switzerland, the Medieval love of intricate active line on the one hand, and flat patterns of clearly edged shapes on the other, modified the ideas that came from Italy. While religious, mythological, and portrait subjects predominated, landscape painting was developed by painters working in the vicinity of the Danube River. Their so-called *Danube Style* created visions of icy peaks, winding valleys, and feathery evergreens or clawlike branches, all in delicate detail.

Sixteenth-century French painting centered on the Palace of Fontainebleau, where Francis I, Henry II, and Henry IV gathered native and foreign artists. The most influential members of this group were Italian Mannerists.

In sixteenth-century England, portraiture was the main interest. Major artists were foreigners such as Hans Eworth of Flanders and Hans Holbein the Younger of Switzerland. Typical stylistic features include brilliant detail in costume and accessories and containment of details within larger areas with sharply defined edges.

MATTHIAS NEITHARDT-GOTHARDT, *called* **GRÜNEWALD** (Germany, 1470/80–1528). Grünewald may have been born in Würzburg; little is known of his life. Between 1508 and 1514, he was court painter to the Archbishop-Elector and then to the Elector of Mainz. Grünewald's major work is the large, many-paneled *Isenheim Altarpiece,* commissioned for a church at Isenheim. The central panel (Fig. 14-54) depicts the torn body of Jesus on the Cross, flanked by the Madonna, John, Mary Magdalene, and John the Baptist. Like many German Medieval artists, Grünewald preferred harsh, jagged, and twisted forms. His sense of deep space and natural light, however, link him with the Renaissance.

ALBRECHT DÜRER (Germany, 1471–1528). Dürer began training as a goldsmith in Nuremberg but turned to painting and studied under Michael Wohlgemuth, a painter of altarpieces in the late Gothic style. Yet Dürer's fame spread more because of his engravings and woodcuts than because of his paintings. His woodcut of *The Four Horsemen of the Apocalypse* (Fig. 14-55) rivals wood engraving in its detail and demonstrates Dürer's love of intricate, boiling line. In an eruption of seething activity, the Four Horsemen—War, Sickness, Famine, and Death—ride down their helpless victims. This print is part of Dürer's *Apocalypse* series, based on the Revelation of St. John. The artist also designed a series of woodcuts on the life of Mary (1504–1505) and others on the Passion of Christ: the *Great Passion* in woodcuts (1500–10), the *Little Passion* in woodcuts (1509–10), and a *Passion* in prints from metal engravings (1508–12). For the woodcuts, Dürer did the drawings, and expert cutters probably prepared most of his blocks. One of the best-known of Dürer's individual metal engravings is the *Adam and Eve,* done between 1504 and 1514. Although he traveled to Italy and the Netherlands, most of Dürer's work retained the gnarled forms and intricate line characteristic of German Medieval art;

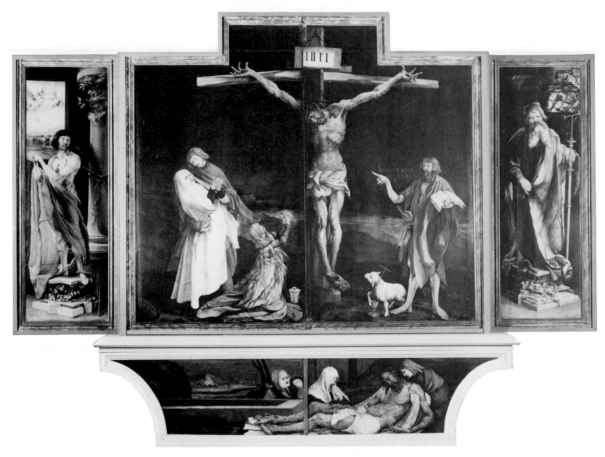

14-54   GRÜNEWALD, central panel of the
Isenheim Altarpiece, (*c.* 1510 – 15). Approx.
8′10″ × 10′1″.   Musée d'Unterlinden, Colmar.

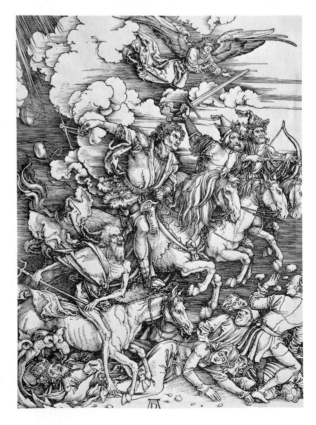

14-55   ALBRECHT DÜRER,   *The Four Horsemen
of the Apocalypse,* (1497 – 98). Woodcut, 15½″ × 11″.
Metropolitan Museum of Art, New York (gift of
Junius S. Morgan, 1919).

but his landscape and anatomical studies, his observation of textures and of light effects, his use of aerial and linear perspective, and his interest in portraiture all link him to the Renaissance. Dürer used the chiaroscuro and sfumato that had been developed in Italy; occasionally he employed simplified massive cascades of drapery that are reminiscent of Italian art.

HANS HOLBEIN THE YOUNGER (Germany, Switzerland, and England, 1497–1543).   Holbein grew up in Augsburg and established himself in Basel as a muralist, woodcut designer, and portraitist, but he found his greatest success as a portrait painter in England at the court of Henry VIII. In *The Ambassadors* (Fig. 14-56), Renaissance interests are apparent in the depiction of individual facial character and in the array of different forms and textures carefully situated in space and rendered in natural light. Like many Italian painters of the preceding

14-56   HANS HOLBEIN THE YOUNGER, *The Ambassadors,* (1533). Oil and tempera on wood, approx. 7' × 7'.   Courtesy of the Trustees of the National Gallery, London.

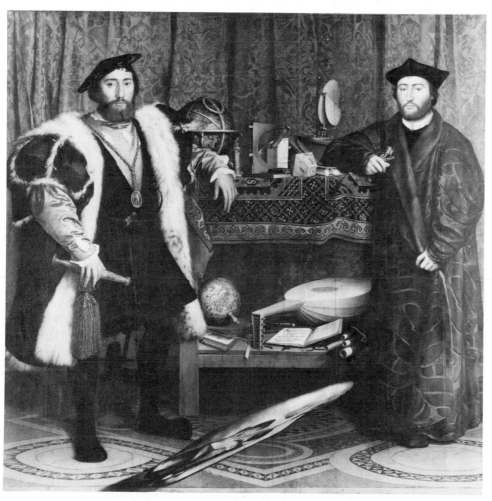

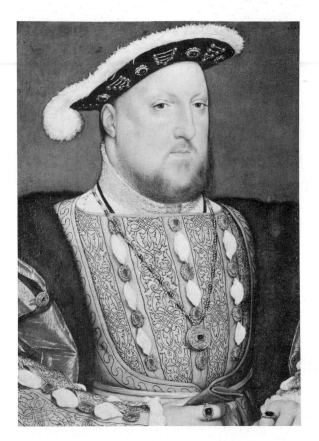

14-57   HANS HOLBEIN THE YOUNGER,
Henry VIII, (1536–37). Oil and tempera on panel,
approx. 11″ × 8″.   Thyssen-Bornemisza Foundation, Lugano.

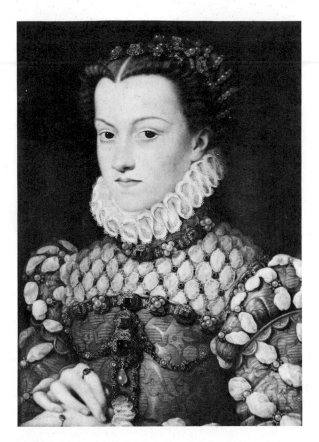

14-58   FRANÇOIS CLOUET,   *Elizabeth of Austria,*
(1571).   Louvre, Paris.

century, Holbein was not above using some illusionistic trickery to display his conquest of the physical world: when the long bony form in the foreground is viewed from the proper angle (hold the page against your face and sight along the length of the object), it becomes a skull. Like many of his contemporaries, Holbein was intrigued by the idea of death, and he designed woodcuts portraying the figure of Death coming to claim men of various social levels. His portrait of Henry VIII (Fig. 14-57) is a remarkably frank expression of luxury and crafty cupidity, yet underlying the bulk of the head and costume are the typically Medieval silhouetted shapes and flat backgrounds.

FRANÇOIS CLOUET (France, 1500?–72).   François was trained by his father, Jean Clouet, and succeeded him as court painter to Francis I. François Clouet's earliest known portraiture shows Italian influence in pose, setting, and massiveness. Later portraits belong to an international portrait style of the second half of the sixteenth century, a style

that owes much to Holbein as well as to Italian painting. Standard poses and accessories are combined with elaborate costume detail, which is treated rather flatly. Clouet's chalk portraits achieve some of Holbein's conciseness of characterization, and his portrait of Elizabeth of Austria (Fig. 14-58) reflects Holbein's ability to depict character as well as an orchestral range of textures.

PIETER BRUEGEL THE ELDER (Flanders, 1525–69).   Although Bruegel may have been born in the Netherlands, his career is part of Flemish art. After registering with the painters' guild in Antwerp in 1551, he traveled in Italy and then returned to Antwerp to work as an engraver. After 1563, Bruegel lived in Brussels. An intellectual, he was a friend of leading humanists in the region. His paintings suggest his philosophical position and often are subtly satirical. *The Wedding Feast* (Fig. 14-59) exemplifies his leadership in genre painting. The rounded, knobby forms, small scale, and

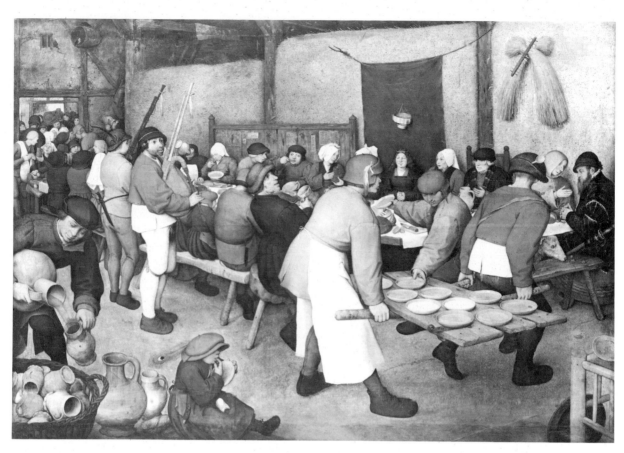

14-59   PIETER BRUEGEL THE ELDER, *The Wedding Feast,* (c. 1565). Panel, approx. 4′ × 5′.   Kunsthistorisches Museum, Vienna.

jerky movements of the countless little people are in jolting contrast to sixteenth-century Italian style, but they are a logical outgrowth of fifteenth-century Flemish art. Although the individual figures are rounded and the space is deep, the contrast of local colors and values gives the effect of a complex, richly varied patchwork of flat shapes. Bruegel's best-known works include a series done in 1565 representing the seasons: *The Harvest* (Metropolitan Museum of Art, New York), *Hunters in the Snow, Dark Day,* and *The Return of the Cattle* (all in the Kunsthistorisches Museum, Vienna).

Architecture in the North

In northwestern Europe, the Gothic style lingered into the fifteenth and sixteenth centuries. Renaissance details slowly infiltrated Gothic detail until at last the basic structure changed and an integrated Renaissance style was formed. The change occurred first in France, the Renaissance influence coming from northern Italy in the early sixteenth century because of French military campaigns there. The importation of Roman moldings, pilasters, columns, arches, and floral ornament is evident in churches such as St. Eustache in Paris and in the châteaux of the Loire Valley, where Medieval forms are given Renaissance decorative details. The Palace of Francis I at Fontainebleau demonstrates various phases of Renaissance architecture during his reign and afterward. Of considerable influence were the writings of the Italian Sebastiano Serlio, who was called to France by Francis I in 1540. Typical sixteenth-century Northern features are steeply pitched roofs and ornate gables. As in painting, the northerners often applied Italian Renaissance motifs in a spirit of fantasy and profusion that suggests the Middle Ages.

PIERRE LESCOT (France, 1510/15–78).   Lescot came from a wealthy family and received a broad education. His architectural style was formed before he traveled to Italy, although he undoubtedly knew the standard sourcebooks for Renaissance and antique architecture. Most of Lescot's work has been changed or destroyed. The most complete remaining structure is the façade of the square court of the Louvre (Fig. 14-60), in which

14-60   PIERRE LESCOT, square court of the Louvre, Paris (begun 1546).

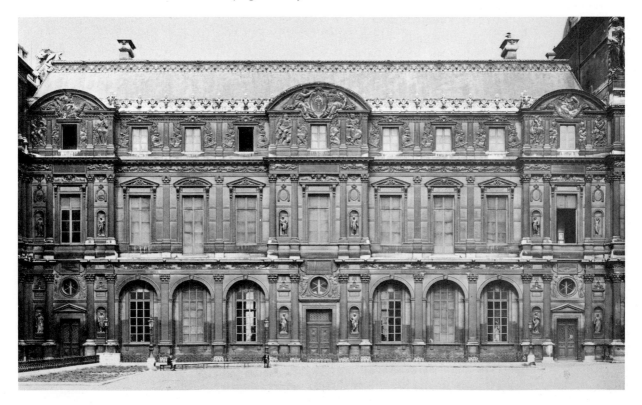

the major horizontal and vertical dividing lines are broken at intervals, and the small size of columns and pilasters, along with the ornamental breakup of the surfaces, creates richness rather than the monumental grandeur of Italian design.

Sculpture in the North

In the North, sculpture, like painting and architecture, clung to the Gothic style until well into the sixteenth century. The fifteenth century had nurtured increasing portraiture in tomb sculpture, the use of standard types for faces portrayed in religious and mythological scenes, and both the smoothly flowing drapery common to late Gothic French art and the crackling angular drapery of the Lowlands and the Germanic areas. Sixteenth-century sculpture produced more portraiture, more anatomical detail, and more interest in landscape and deep space in relief compositions. Countries with the tradition of angular drapery and thin figures turned to fuller masses and curving forms. French sculpture was strongly affected by the Italian Mannerist sculptors serving Francis I, and Renaissance concepts were introduced to England after 1512 by the Italian sculptor Pietro Torrigiano.

14-61 JEAN GOUJON, nymphs from the Fontaine des Innocents, Paris (1548–49).

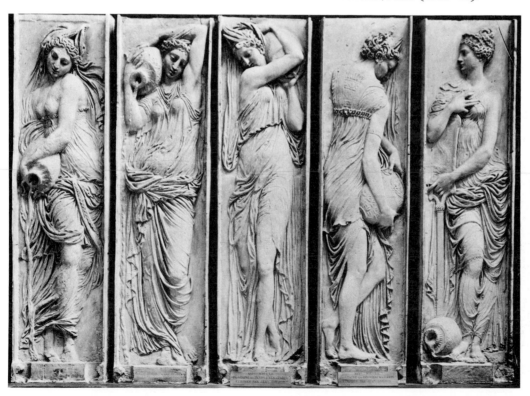

JEAN GOUJON (France, *c.* 1510–1567).   Although Goujon was one of the major sculptors of his day, little is known of his life. By 1540, he had developed a Renaissance style based on a knowledge of both Italian and antique art. His *Pietà* from St. Germain l'Auxerrois (1544–45) reveals Manneristic poses and proportions. Both the *Pietà* and the relief panels of nymphs from the Fontaine des Innocents (Fig. 14-61) have a delicate flowing harmony in the thin linear drapery folds that seems particular to Goujon's style. He provided sculptural reliefs for Lescot's portion of the Louvre (Fig. 14-60).

Suggestions for Further Study

Benesch, Otto. *The Art of the Renaissance in Northern Europe: Its Relation to the Contemporary Spiritual and Intellectual Movements,* rev. ed. London: Phaidon, 1965.

Blunt, Anthony. *Art and Architecture in France: 1500–1700* (Pelican History of Art). Baltimore: Penguin Books, 1977.

———. *Artistic Theory in Italy: 1450–1600.* New York: Oxford University Press, 1956.

Cuttler, Charles D. *Northern Painting from Pucelle to Bruegel.* New York: Holt, Rinehart & Winston, 1973.

De Tolnay, Charles. *Michelangelo.* 6 vols. Princeton, N.J.: Princeton University Press, 1969–70.

Freedberg, Sydney J. *Painting of the High Renaissance in Rome and Florence.* 2 vols. New York: Harper & Row, 1972.

Friedlaender, Walter. *Mannerism and Anti-Mannerism in Italian Painting.* New York: Schocken Books, 1965.

Gilbert, Creighton. *History of Renaissance Art: Painting, Sculpture, and Architecture Throughout Europe* (Library of Art History). New York: Abrams, 1973.

Gombrich, Ernst Hans Josef. *Norm and Form: Studies in the Art of the Renaissance.* London: Phaidon, 1966.

Hartt, Frederick. *History of Italian Renaissance Art: Painting, Sculpture, and Architecture.* New York: Abrams, 1979.

Heydenreich, Ludwig H., and Wolfgang Lotz, *Architecture in Italy, 1400–1600* (Pelican History of Art). Translated by Mary Hottlinger. Baltimore: Penguin Books, 1974.

Müller, Theodor. *Sculpture in the Netherlands, Germany, France, and Spain: 1400–1500* (Pelican History of Art). Baltimore: Penguin Books, 1966.

Murray, Peter. *The Architecture of the Italian Renaissance.* London: Secker and Warburg, 1985.

Osten, Gert von der, and Horst Vey. *Painting and Sculpture in Germany and the Netherlands: 1500–1600* (Pelican History of Art). Baltimore: Penguin Books, 1969.

Panofsky, Erwin. *Early Netherlandish Painting: Its Origins and Character.* 2 vols. New York: Harper & Row, 1971.

————. *Renaissance and Renascences in Western Art.* New York: Harper & Row, 1969.

Seymour, Charles, Jr. *Sculpture in Italy, 1400–1500* (Pelican History of Art). Baltimore: Penguin Books, 1966.

Stechow, Wolfgang. *Northern Renaissance Art, 1400–1600* (Sources and Documents). Englewood Cliffs, N.J.: Prentice-Hall, 1966.

Vasari, Giorgio. *The Lives of the Painters, Sculptors, and Architects.* 3 vols. New York: Abrams, 1979.

Wittkower, Rudolf. *Architectural Principles in the Age of Humanism*, 4th ed. London: Academy Editions, 1973.

Wolf, Robert Erich, and Ronald Millen. *Renaissance and Mannerist Art.* New York: Abrams, 1968.

15

Baroque Art

1600 – 1700

The term Baroque *has dual sources* and has been used with varied meanings. The Italian word *barocco* grew out of the language of Medieval logic and by the seventeenth and eighteenth centuries had come to mean any system of thought that was contorted, irrational, or untrue; in Portugal, the word *barroco* referred to a rough, imperfect pearl. Both words seem to have been sources for the French word *baroque,* which originally meant an imperfect pearl and by extension something irregular or bizarre, and hence was applied to an artistic style that did not conform to accepted rules of proportion but catered rather to individual whim. "Baroque" was used by eighteenth-century writers as a disparaging term for such artists as Giovanni Lorenzo Bernini, Francesco Borromini, and Pietro da Cortona and for writers who showed an appetite for novelty or untraditional forms. In the nineteenth century, "Baroque" was used more objectively to denote a historical period and certain stylistic characteristics. In the narrowest sense, the period was the seventeenth century, but many writers today prefer the broader dates of 1600 to 1750. However, since Baroque qualities persevere in many important works until the end of the eighteenth century, we will use the even broader dating of 1600 to 1800 and treat each century in a separate chapter.

This period developed a wider variety of styles than we have seen in earlier centuries, and it is necessary to consider a broad range of characteristics under the concept of Baroque styles. Complexity, contrasts, bold effects of gradation and climax, overwhelming vastness or unexpected intimacy in scale, deliberate lack of clarity, illusionistic effects, and calculated surprise were used together or in various combinations. The roots of this art are found in the work of Michelangelo, in Mannerism, and especially in the Proto-Baroque.

The seventeenth century was one of bold contrasts within and between ideological systems: the parliamentary system developed in England while absolutism developed on the Continent, particularly in France; Catholicism struggled with Protestantism, and religious truth had to be reconciled with newly discovered scientific truths. Seventeenth-century science replaced the old concept of a finite and fixed universe with the more awesome vision of infinite space and constant motion. The new view was paralleled in art by a preference for vast spaces and the effect of constant movement in much of the architecture, painting, and sculpture of the seventeenth and early eighteenth centuries.

The system of values that sustained much Baroque art was formulated during the sixteenth century by the edicts of the Council of Trent, the Catholic answer to the Protestant Reformation, and by the Accademia di San Luca in Rome. During the seventeenth and eighteenth centuries, the most important artistic institution was the French Royal Academy. Effective at first, the Academy later became dogmatically restrictive, and many artists rebelled against it.

Painting in Italy and Spain

Rome was the international center where the major stylistic trends of seventeenth-century painting were developed. Early seventeenth-century Italian painting reveals three major currents: a continuation of sixteenth-century Mannerism, a reappraisal, led by Annibale Carracci, of High Renaissance styles, and a pioneering trend led by Michelangelo da Caravaggio. The attitude of Carracci and his followers was conservative in that it sought to incorporate selected qualities from certain High Renaissance and Late Renaissance paintings. Clarity in parts, in expressive gestures, and in focus was joined to strong compositional structure and massively solid, ideal human form. The Carracci group was the strongest camp in Rome at the beginning of the century, and its stylistic character — sometimes called *Restrained Baroque* or *Classical Baroque*—was influential during the remainder of the century. The Caravaggio trend sacrificed clarity for dramatic light effects and complex natural detail. As the seventeenth century unfolded, all three trends contributed to full Baroque painting, which exploited illusionistic effects on a grand scale, dramatic value contrasts, active, irregular forms suggesting constant change rather than stability, compositions with a minimum of stabilizing vertical and horizontal lines and a maximum of diagonals or undulating curves, and ideal figures of heroic proportions. It attempted to break through the limits of the frame, making the painted scene a more overwhelming experience because it appears to be a part of the spectator's real world.

The seventeenth century produced a distinct division of painting into different types of subject matter with greater specialization by many artists. During the early seventeenth century, landscape painting in Rome was influenced by German and Flemish painters. Later, landscape art was dominated by two French expatriates, Nicolas Poussin and Claude Lorrain. Genre painting gained popularity with private patrons. Many of the genre subjects, called *Bambocciata*, were painted by Dutchmen living in Rome and were scorned by the critics of the Carracci persuasion, partly because of the commonness of genre subjects and partly because many genre painters rejected ideal form for the realistic detail and bold lighting of Caravaggio. Still-life painting was indebted to Dutch and Flemish art for its intense study of details and textures and to Caravaggio for its lighting.

Several Italian cities, in addition to Rome, were important for seventeenth-century painting.

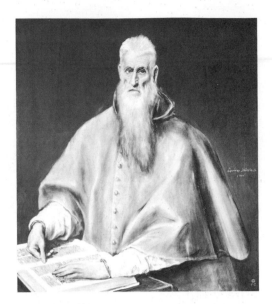

15-1   EL GRECO,   *St. Jerome, (c.* 1595–
1600). Oil on canvas, 43½″ × 37½″.
Frick Collection, New York.

15-2   EL GRECO,   *The Crucifixion,*
(1584–90). Oil on canvas, approx. 10′ × 6′.
Prado, Madrid.

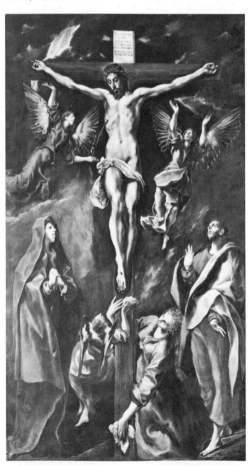

Venice continued in the tradition of its sixteenth-century masters, and Venetian color was a significant influence throughout the century. In Naples, Caravaggio's visits (1606–1607 and 1609–10) and the presence of Ribera after 1616 instilled a stylistic preference for dramatic lighting and descriptive detail. Genoa enjoyed the stimulus of numerous foreign visitors; the Flemish, especially Rubens, were leaders, and both the Caravaggio and the Carracci trends were represented. Bologna was the stronghold of the Carracci Academy, established before Annibale Carracci went to Rome. Florence, however, played a relatively minor role in seventeenth-century Italian painting.

In Spain, Seville and Madrid were the important centers. Early seventeenth-century painting there exhibits strong lighting and intense specificity. By mid-century, there was a tendency toward freer brushwork, soft, silver lighting, and calmer action.

DOMENIKOS THEOTOCOPOULOS, *called* **EL GRECO** (Spain, 1541–1614).   El Greco came from Crete to Spain by way of Italy, working first in Venice, where he was impressed by the chiaroscuro of Titian and the active compositions of Tintoretto, and then briefly in Rome, where he became acquainted with the art of Michelangelo. He settled in Toledo in 1576 or 1577 and received many commissions for portraits and religious subjects (Fig. 15-1). The Prado *Crucifixion* (Plate 10 and Fig. 15-2) is typical in the bold value contrasts, the jagged highlights, and the elongated figures with undulating contours. The crackling, flamelike energy of the stormy sky, the billowing garments, dramatic foreshortening, and the hovering weightless figures all express ecstatic religious experience. While some of his contemporaries sought a physical reality in their art, El Greco revealed the power of the spirit with an electric intensity that seems to illuminate forms from within. Even his portraits seem to transcend the physical world; the bodies, the garments, and the large eyes seem to shimmer like a mirage. In style as in actual chronology, El Greco holds a position between Late Renaissance Mannerism and the seventeenth-century Baroque.

ANNIBALE CARRACCI (Bologna and Rome, 1560–1609).   Annibale's early work included many earthy genre scenes portrayed with frank detail

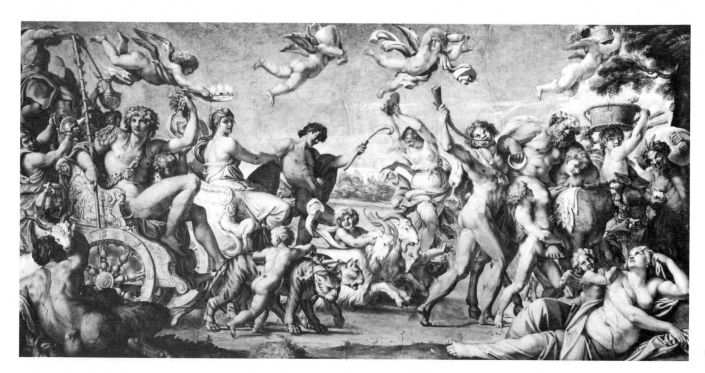

15-3 ANNIBALE CARRACCI, *The Triumph of Bacchus and Ariadne*, central composition on the ceiling of the Farnese Gallery, Rome, (1597–1604).

and inspired indirectly by Netherlandish painters. His mature painting deals with religious and mythological subjects in more idealistic forms. Occasionally, these subjects are shown in small scale within spacious landscapes that, by 1600, had become vistas of an ideal nature.

Carracci began his career as a Mannerist but turned more and more to High Renaissance and Proto-Baroque characteristics. His famous frescoes in the Farnese Gallery in Rome, of which *The Triumph of Bacchus and Ariadne* (Fig. 15-3) is the center, depict the loves of the classical gods and employ the heavy muscular figures seen in the art of Michelangelo and in the late work of Raphael. Carracci used an ideal facial type with full cheeks, straight, flat-planed nose, and broad forehead; his work often has strong value contrasts and compressed compositional activity. For color, his idols were first Correggio and later Titian. Annibale Carracci, his brother Agostino, and their cousin Ludovico opened an art school in Bologna before Annibale went to Rome in the 1590s. The teaching was eclectic, urging a combination of the best qualities from various masters.

MICHELANGELO DA CARAVAGGIO (Rome and Naples, 1573–1610).   Annibale Carracci and his followers led the conservative tendency in early

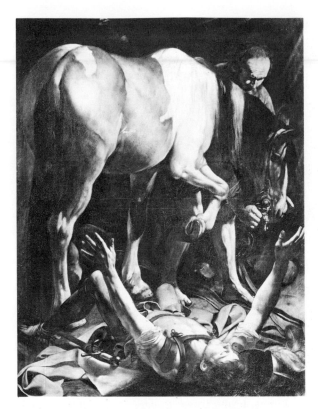

15-4   MICHELANGELO DA CARAVAGGIO,
The Conversion of St. Paul, (1601–1602). Oil on
canvas, 90½″ × 69″. Cerasi Chapel, Santa Maria del
Popolo, Rome.

Baroque painting; Caravaggio represented the
more innovative spirit. He went from Milan to
Rome about 1590 and, at first, earned a precarious
living by painting still lifes with one or two half-
length figures, sometimes with references to classical myths. These works have remarkably precise
details and distinct local colors. About 1597, Caravaggio received his first commission for a church
(Contarelli Chapel, San Luigi de' Francesi), and
from then on his subjects were usually religious.
The style that made Caravaggio well known is evident in his *Conversion of St. Paul* (Fig. 15-4). All
the traditional accessory figures have been omitted. We see an armored man lying on his back with
arms outstretched, while his nervous horse and
mystified companion look on. The scene is pushed
into the immediate foreground so that we have a
startlingly close view. A flesh-and-blood reality is
stressed by precise physical detail, yet there seems
to be something extraordinary about the event.
The strong spotlight that illuminates the objects
against the dark background can hardly be natural
light. Its source is outside the picture and remains a
mystery to us, but its effect is to dramatize rather
than to clarify. The few forms are broken into
many parts by the light and shadow, making the
composition complex and hard to comprehend
immediately. This use of chiaroscuro to transcend
physical reality is typical of Caravaggio's mature
style and forecasts later Baroque painting. *Tenebroso* (murky) is a term often applied to Caravaggio's predominantly dark compositions. His
followers are sometimes called *tenebristi*. Caravaggio's career was cut short by malaria.

PIETRO DA CORTONA (Florence and Rome, 1596–
1669).   Cortona was one of the major seventeenth-century artists in both painting and architecture. He represented the full Baroque rather
than the conservatism of the Carracci school. His
best-known painting, the *Glorification of Pope
Urban VIII's Reign* (Fig. 15-5), contains boiling
masses of clouds and figures soaring up through
the painted illusion of an architectural frame that
seems to surround an opening into the sky. Light
and shadow play over the forms, breaking them
into complex parts. There is a strong focus on the
central figure, Divine Providence, who points
to the Barberini coat of arms. The allegorical-
mythological scenes at the sides of the painting

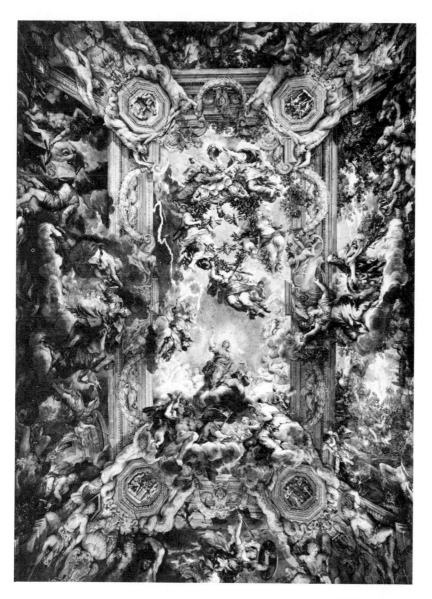

refer to the piety, justice, and prudence of the Barberini Pope. The elaborate program of symbolism was worked out not by Cortona but by a poet in the Pope's circle. Cortona's dazzling production included frescoes for the Pitti Palace in Florence, for Santa Maria in Vallicella in Rome, and for the Palazzo Pamphili in the Piazza Navona in Rome. Unlike some of his contemporaries, Cortona restrained his illusionism to the extent of maintaining a clear division between painted areas and the stucco architectural framework. In his late easel paintings, he stabilized the compositions with firmer vertical and horizontal lines and contained the figures in more rigid groupings, thus rejecting his earlier dynamism.

15-5 PIETRO DA CORTONA, *Glorification of Pope Urban VIII's Reign,* central composition on the ceiling of the Gran Salone, Barberini Palace, Rome, (1633–39).

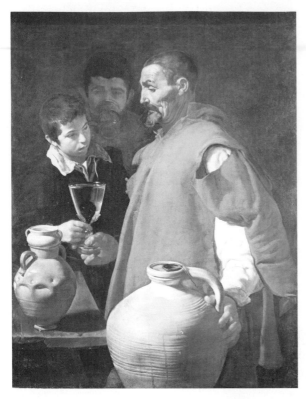

15-6 DIEGO VELÁZQUEZ, *The Waterseller of Seville,* (1619–20). Oil on canvas, approx. 3'6" × 2'8". Courtesy, Wellington Museum, London.

15-7 DIEGO VELÁZQUEZ, *The Maids of Honor (Las Meninas),* (1656). Oil on canvas, approx. 10'5" × 9'. Prado, Madrid.

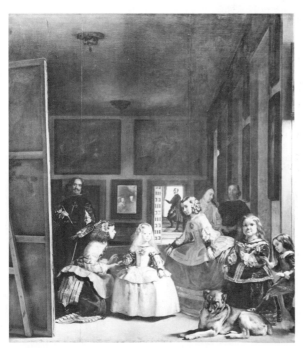

DIEGO VELÁZQUEZ (Seville and Madrid, 1599–1660).   Velázquez's early work, such as *The Waterseller of Seville* (Fig. 15-6), sparkles with the brilliant detail and bold value contrasts that enchanted the followers of Caravaggio. At the age of twenty-three, Velázquez was appointed painter to the court of Philip IV, and he retained this position for the remainder of his life while acquiring other court titles. His mature style exploits glazing and impasto to produce rich color and textural effects. *The Maids of Honor* (Plate 11 and Fig. 15-7) demonstrates his interest in the play of direct and reflected light on a variety of textures. Close observation reveals that details have been softened by brushwork that is much freer than in his early painting, and light bathes the forms like a palpable liquid, suggesting a source of nineteenth-century Impressionism. *The Maids of Honor* presents a highly original court portrait. The Infanta, several of her retinue, and Velázquez, in casual rather than formal poses, look out of the painting toward us. We, in turn, seem to occupy the positions of the king and queen reflected in the mirror at the far end of the room.

Sculpture in Italy

At the beginning of the seventeenth century, sculpture in Italy was dominated by the style of Giovanni da Bologna, with its Mannerist poses and its Proto-Baroque irregularity and openness of form. Full Baroque sculpture developed after 1618, when the expression of greatest vitality was sought in poses, multiple and overlapping planes were employed, and deep undercutting produced dramatic shadows planned to provide gradation and climax from a fixed point of view. The sculpture of this period often breaks through the boundaries of its architectural frame or extends beyond the private spatial environment suggested by the base, so that the composition seems to inhabit the spectator's world of space and action. Such efforts to overwhelm spectators or to draw them into the work of art are analogous to the illusionistic mural and ceiling compositions or to the intimate views found in the painting of the period. Full Baroque sculpture, like painting, used realistic details, complex parts, and lavish color. Varieties of colored stone were combined with bronze, but the leading sculptors did not use colored materials merely to counterfeit nature. Polychrome backgrounds and frames were used for contrast with figures in white stone or bronze. Special lighting, sometimes from hidden windows of colored glass, often intensified dramatic effects. As in painting, there were both full Baroque and conservative trends in sculpture, but the distinction is less clear because the influence of Bernini's full Baroque was so pervasive. After Bernini's death in 1680, the many French sculptors who had come to Rome after the founding of the French Academy in Rome in 1666 made French leadership a significant force in Roman sculpture.

GIANLORENZO BERNINI (Rome, 1598–1680). Bernini, the greatest genius of the Italian Baroque, considered himself to be primarily a sculptor, but he was also an architect, a painter, and a poet. His prodigious abilities as sculptor were demonstrated by an early series of statues done for Cardinal Scipione Borghese between 1618 and 1625. The series included *The Rape of Proserpina, David,* and *Apollo and Daphne,* all in the Borghese Gallery in Rome. The open twisting poses, the complex silhouettes, and the realistic detail make the works intensely alive. Although the Baroque is the antithesis of the serenity of much Greek sculpture, Bernini's admiration for Greek art is evident in such features as the modified Greek profiles used for Apollo and Daphne. From Bernini's middle years came the Tomb of Urban VIII (1628–47, St. Peter's), with its exuberant forms in various marbles and in bronze. In the same period, he did the Cornaro Chapel in Santa Maria della Vittoria, which contains *The Ecstasy of St. Teresa* (Fig. 15-8). The cardinals of the Cornaro family are shown in sculptural relief on the side walls of the chapel, and the space between the walls belongs both to the world of the spectator and to the architectural-sculptural composition, deliberately blurring the boundaries of the work of art. Multicolored marble and lavish architectural details lead to the climactic group within an undulating, concave-convex frame. White marble figures with rippling garments and lively, open silhouettes are

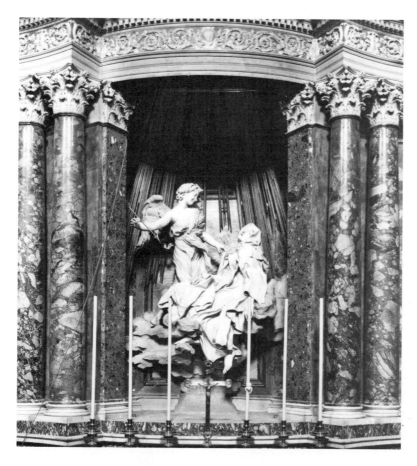

15-8 GIANLORENZO BERNINI, *The Ecstasy of St. Teresa,* (1645–52). Marble, life size. Cornaro Chapel, Santa Maria della Vittoria, Rome.

suspended in space behind the frame and in front of a dark background. A hidden yellow glass window lights the group from above. Bernini's abilities as an organizer enabled him to assemble a large studio with many helpers to develop his ideas for the commissions that were showered on him, and it is often hard to distinguish between works by Bernini and those executed by his assistants.

Architecture in Italy and Spain

Baroque architecture ran the gamut from restrained composition to dynamic complexity. Full Baroque architecture tended to exploit painting and sculpture as well as materials of different colors for a compelling total effect with strong focal emphasis. Masses were composed in complex parts and in many layers of depth; the effect of movement was obtained not only by receding and projecting parts, with their concomitant value contrasts, but also by wall surfaces of concave-convex alternations and by rhythmic variations of spaces, walls, piers, columns, and pilasters. Each layer of a multilayered wall may have a rhythmic scheme of its own, giving a fuguelike complexity to the total effect. Accordingly, architectural space was molded to express dynamic rather than static form. The façade of a major building was often made the climactic focus of converging streets and the funneling walls of adjacent buildings. Interiors reveal a preference for oval plans rather than the more static circular plan, and alternations of expanding and contracting spaces urge the spectator to change position constantly in order to experience the architecture completely. Characteristically, neither the masses nor the spaces have easily or simply perceived limits. Light was manipulated for focus; it often alternates with darkened areas or spaces to create movement or gradation and climax.

In Spain, a special style called the *Churrigueresque* developed in the second half of the seventeenth century; it is characterized by an extraordinary richness of decoration.

PIETRO DA CORTONA (Florence and Rome, 1596–1669).   Cortona's art exemplifies the Baroque tendency to fuse painting, sculpture, and architecture for a powerful total effect. His first major commission in architecture was the Church of San Martina e Luca, which came in 1635 while he was working on the Barbarini frescoes. He gave movement to the façade (Fig. 15-9) in two ways: first, by using a convex center that seems to bulge out in response to the pressure of projecting wings at the sides; and second, by creating an elaborate play of light and shadow through the use of many layers of pilasters, engaged columns, and panels. While the exterior uses the Ionic order below and Corinthian above, the interior (Fig. 15-10) is restricted to the Ionic. The Greek cross plan (Fig. 15-11) is opened up and given flexibility by the interior walls, which are built up in layers of panels, pilasters, and columns that create a rhythm of projecting and receding elements; the wall is transformed into undulating systems of supports. In the vaults and dome, Cortona used much architectural ornament. A unifying feature of the interior is the unusual restriction of color to white. His other church designs include the façades of Santa Maria della Pace and Santa Maria in Via Lata (both in Rome), which exploit deep porches or balconies for dramatic shadows and bold focus. Broken pediments — pediments whose frames have been opened up or cut into projecting and receding parts — are important features of Cortona's architecture and of the Baroque period in general.

GIANLORENZO BERNINI (Rome, 1598–1680). Bernini's activity as an architect began earlier than Pietro da Cortona's. His *baldacchino* for St. Peter's, the canopy shelter over the tomb of St. Peter, done between 1624 and 1633, fuses architecture and sculpture to produce a focal center for the vast interior. Over twisted, vine-covered columns, he placed a canopy of sweeping scroll curves flanked by restless angels and topped by an active receding and projecting entablature. Bernini also designed the keyhole-shaped piazza in front of St. Peter's (see p. 211). The enclosing colonnades shape the piazza into an expanding and contracting space that demonstrates the preference for active spaces in Baroque art. Between 1658 and 1670, Bernini designed the small church of Sant' Andrea al Quirinale in Rome (Fig. 15-12). Concave walls focus upon the convex porch with its rounded broken pediment and ornate coat of arms. Behind the porch, actively curving scroll buttresses support the drum, which, in turn, supports the dome. From the entrance, one looks

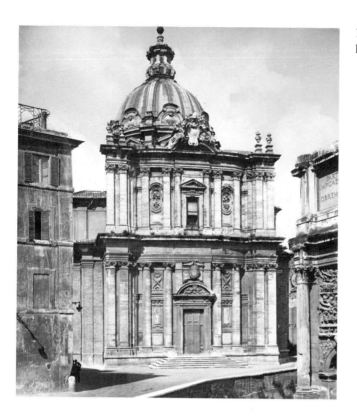

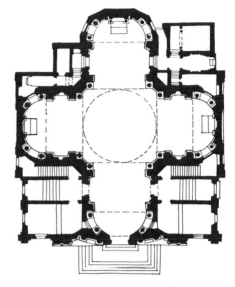

15-9 PIETRO DA CORTONA, San Martina e Luca, Rome, (1635–50).

15-11 Plan of San Martina e Luca.

15-10 Interior of San Martina e Luca.

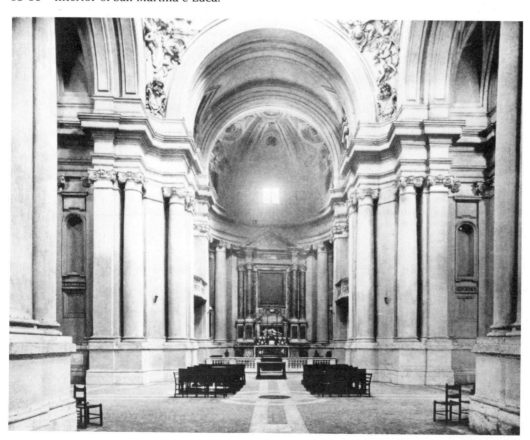

15-12   GIANLORENZO BERNINI, Sant'
Andrea al Quirinale, Rome, (1658–70).

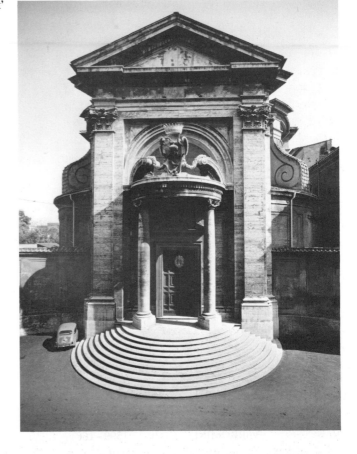

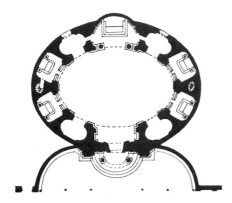

15-14   Plan of Sant' Andrea al Quirinale.

15-13
Interior of Sant' Andrea al
Quirinale.

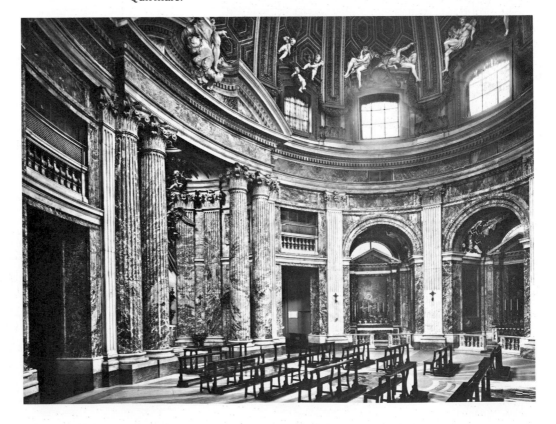

across the width of the oval interior to the high altar set deeply within an architectural frame with a concave, rounded, and broken pediment. Figure 15-13 is a view from one end of the oval space. In the opening of the pediment, the twisting figure of Sant' Andrea is shown ascending into heaven, the irregular white shape of the saint contrasting boldly with its surroundings and creating a powerful focal point. Below, the set-in altar receives dramatic illumination from a hidden window. Elsewhere, the walls are opened to form deep niches and secondary altar spaces (Figs. 15-13 and 15-14) that enrich the lighting and the spatial effect of the interior. Exuberant architectural ornament and multicolored marble complicate the wall surfaces, while the dome achieves its effect through a contrast of white and gold. Bernini's fame led to an invitation from Louis XIV in 1665 to come to Paris to suggest plans for the completion of the Louvre Palace, but the more restrained taste of the French and the jealousy of French architects led to the rejection of all of Bernini's proposals. His architecture did, however, influence the work of French architects.

FRANCESCO BORROMINI (Italy, 1599–1667). From a carver of architectural ornament, Borromini moved to the position of architectural draftsman for Maderno and Bernini and finally became an architect after 1633. His first major work was the dormitory, refectory, and cloisters for the monastery of San Carlo alle Quattro Fontane in Rome (Fig. 15-15). The plan (Fig. 15-16) suggests an intermingling of cross, oval, and octagon shapes, and the interior oval dome is deeply coffered with interlocking hexagonal, octagonal, and cross forms. The interior walls (Fig. 15-17) present convex-concave alternations made more complex by the rhythmic spacing of wall panels, niches, and engaged columns. The entablature has projecting and receding parts that accentuate the active design of the wall and tie together the various parts. The exterior façade (1665–76) was finished after Borromini's death and presents an undulating multilayered composition with engaged columns dividing the concave and convex areas. A frequent motif is the cross within a circle or oval, an apparent symbol for the body of the sacrificed Christ. The plan of the church hints at this symbolic form. In Catholic doctrine, the

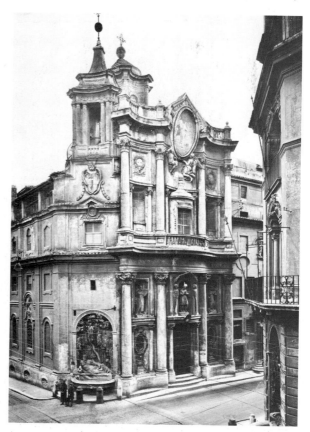

15-15   FRANCESCO BORROMINI, San Carlo alle Quattro Fontane, Rome, (1638–76).

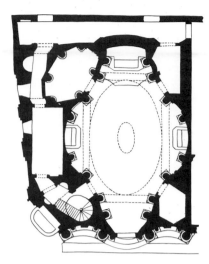

15-16
Plan of San Carlo alle Quattro Fontane.

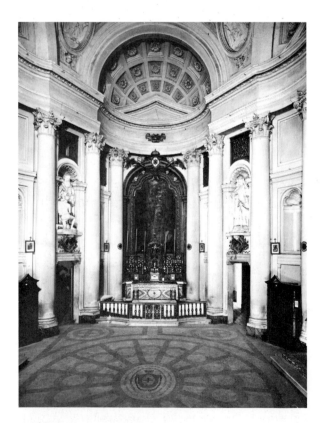

15-17
Interior of San Carlo alle Quattro Fontane (view toward altar), approx. 53′ × 34′.

church itself is identified with the mystical body of Christ. Borromini's other works include Sant' Ivo della Sapienza (begun in 1642, Rome). He frequently used surprising combinations of curves and angles to produce directional forces. His inventive and unorthodox approach led him to squeeze proportions and thereby produce tensions, to create sudden contrasts in shapes and directions, and to provide rapid variations on thematic forms. The source of some of these tendencies is found in Mannerist architecture of the preceding century. Bernini and his followers felt that Borromini went too far, and there was antagonism between these two leaders in full Baroque architecture.

Painting in the North

Seventeenth-century painting in the North was influenced by Italian art, since many Northern artists studied in Italy. For French painting, Caravaggesque lighting and the realism of Bambocciata subject matter were important during the first half of the century. A restrained style, derived from that of Carracci, but emboldened by Caravaggesque lighting, was brought to France when the Frenchman Simon Vouet returned to Paris from Rome in 1627 and acquired a large following. One of his pupils, Charles Lebrun, became director of the French Royal Academy of Painting and Sculpture in 1663. The records of the meetings of the Academy reveal a conflict between advocates of the restrained Baroque and those of the full Baroque; as in Italy, the hero of the conservative attitude was Poussin, while the idol of the full Baroque was Rubens.

In Holland, the prevalence of Protestantism limited the demand for religious subjects, but the merchant class provided a market for portraits, landscapes, cityscapes, interiors, genre painting, and still lifes. A number of Dutchmen returned from Rome to Utrecht and created a center of Caravaggesque painting that reached its height about 1620. In the 1640s, more Caravaggesque influence in the form of Bambocciata painting emanated from Haarlem. There were both Italianate and Flemish strains in seventeenth-century Dutch landscape painting; the first stemmed from Annibale Carracci, Claude Lorrain, and the German Adam Elsheimer; the second came from the tradition of the Flemish painters Joachim Patinir and Pieter Bruegel. Low horizons and vast, cloudy skies are typical of Dutch landscape painting. Still life tends toward lavish displays of colors, textures, and detail in foods and utensils or toward prodigious bouquets of flowers. Sensory experience is dramatized in such work by the intensity and luxury of shapes, colors, textures, and light effects. Flanders also developed outstanding still-life and genre painting, but Roman Catholicism, the dominant religion, encouraged religious subjects. In Holland, the major painter of the century was Rembrandt; in Flanders, Rubens dominated.

Foreigners, particularly Rubens and his assistant Van Dyck, dominated English seventeenth-century painting. German and Austrian painting of the period reveals no school of real national character; there was considerable dependence on Italy and Flanders.

PETER PAUL RUBENS (Flanders, 1577–1640). Rubens, the leading Flemish painter of the seventeenth century, received a broad classical education and was accepted as master painter by the Antwerp Guild in 1598. In 1600, he traveled to Italy and for eight years served the Duke of Mantua as both painter and diplomat. In this capacity, he brought gifts—including many of his own paintings—to King Philip III of Spain. Spanish painting was widely influenced by the Rubens paintings that became part of the royal collections. Rubens was also active in Florence and in Rome, where he copied works by Michelangelo, Caravaggio, and others. By 1608, he was reestablished in Antwerp and was soon appointed court painter to Archduke Albert and the Archduchess Isabella. Rubens's early painting, particularly before 1620, included some relatively quiet compositions, but the majority of his work shows a remarkable assimilation of the violent action and dazzling light of Tintoretto, the massive figures of Michelangelo, the spotlighting of Caravaggio, and the warm color of Venetian painting. The *Coup de Lance* (Fig. 1-23) employs the heroic proportions, the fleshy figures, the dynamic opposition of diagonal forces, the activity, and the intimate view that are characteristic of his Baroque style. Contours tend to twist and undulate; faces tend to have big eyes, delicate flaring nostrils, and small Cupid's-bow mouths; hands and feet are small and tapering.

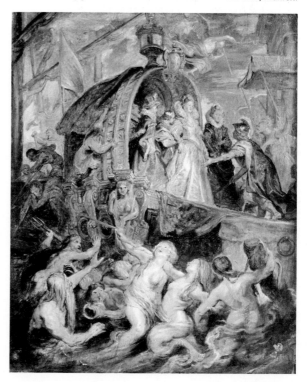

15-18 PETER PAUL RUBENS and assistants, study for *The Reception of Marie de' Medici at Marseilles, 3 November 1600,* (1622–25). Oil on wood, approx. 26″ × 19½″. Alte Pinakothek, Munich.

As his style developed, Rubens later used loose, fluid brushwork and paint textures ranging from heavy impasto to delicate transparent glazes. His international renown brought him many students and a number of large commissions, including the series of allegorical compositions depicting the dramatic life of Marie de' Medici (Plate 12 and Fig. 15-18). Many assistants were necessary, but Rubens's letters to patrons indicate clearly which paintings of a given group were done by his own hand and which were done mainly by helpers. His well-organized workshop made possible enormous productivity in spite of Rubens's time-consuming but historically important diplomatic missions to England and to Spain.

FRANS HALS (Holland, 1580–1666).   Hals was born in Antwerp but is thought of as Dutch because he made his career as a portrait painter in Haarlem. His bohemian life and huge family made him the subject of constant lawsuits for debt and, in his later years, a recipient of assistance from the paupers' fund. From vigorous local colors and a detailed execution, Hals's style changed slowly toward grays and blacks rendered in freer brushwork. *The Banquet of the Officers of St. George* (1616, Frans Hals Museum, Haarlem) exemplifies his early work. Its casual grouping, active poses, and sweeping diagonal forms helped to loosen up the traditionally rigid compositions of Dutch group portraits and prepare the way for Rembrandt's *Night Watch.* Unlike Rembrandt, Hals took care to give almost equal illumination to each face. The *Malle Babbe (Mad Babbe)* (Fig. 15-19) reveals the dazzling impasto brushwork of his late style. The even later *Women Guardians of the Almshouse* (1664, Frans Hals Museum, Haarlem) uses somewhat more restrained execution to express a more contemplative mood. Hals's late painting was less popular than his early work; old age brought him increasing troubles and fewer commissions.

NICOLAS POUSSIN (France and Rome, 1593/4–1665). From a peasant village in Normandy, Poussin traveled to Rouen and then to Paris, seeking instruction in art. In 1624, he carried a Mannerist style with him to Rome, where he worked in the studio of Domenichino, one of the chief pupils of the Carracci. Poussin apparently disliked the large scale required by most major commissions; his

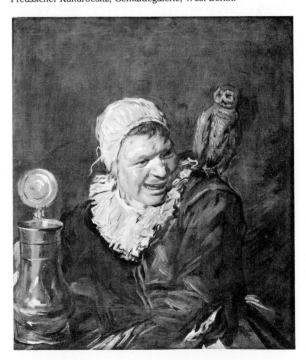

15-19   FRANS HALS,   *Malle Babbe (Mad Babbe),* (*c.* 1650). Approx. 30″ × 25″.   Staatliche Museen Preussicher Kulturbesitz, Gemäldegalerie, West Berlin.

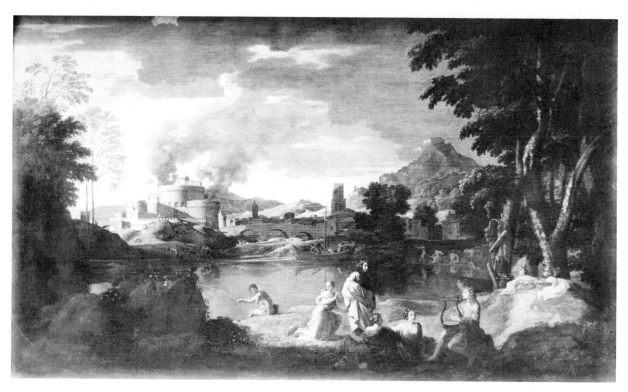

15-20 NICOLAS POUSSIN, *Orpheus and Eurydice,* (1659). Oil on canvas, approx. 4′ × 7′.
Louvre, Paris.

paintings are relatively small, and he depended on a small group of private patrons. His subjects are usually religious, allegorical, or mythological, but the landscape settings often dwarf the subject matter. His early works, in their largeness of mass, dark tree silhouettes, and coloring, reveal the influence of Titian and Veronese. Later, his composition became more formal, with a stable structure of vertical and horizontal elements and an alignment of the main objects with the picture plane. For example, in his *Orpheus and Eurydice* (Fig. 15-20), the groups of trees, the hills, the buildings, and the river are all parallel to each other and to the surface of the painting. Gradation and climax are provided by lighting and by bright color in the foreground figures. Poussin believed that the spectator should read the gestures and symbols in the painting and that the content should be expressed logically and clearly by effective gestures and composition. Painting was to appeal to the mind more than to the senses. Poussin's method consisted of making a rough sketch of the subject and then setting up the composition with little wax figures and linen drapery in a stagelike box in which lighting could easily be controlled. Changes were made with the figures and lighting until the composition was decided on. Poussin said that he did not paint directly from live models because he wanted to preserve idealism in the forms. The sources for his concepts of ideal form were Raphael, Raphael's pupil Giulio Romano, Annibale Carracci, and Greek and Roman sculpture. With the exception of a sojourn in Paris between 1640 and 1642, Poussin made his career in Rome. His work exemplifies the conservative Baroque that started with the Carracci school. His painting was an important source for artistic theory as taught in the French Royal Academy from the mid-seventeenth century until the French Revolution.

CLAUDE LORRAIN (France and Rome, 1600–82).   Claude of Lorraine or Claude Gellée is often linked with Poussin, not only because they were contemporary French expatriates in Italy, but also because they both represent the conservative Baroque. By 1627, Claude had established himself permanently in Rome. His style owed much to German and Flemish landscape painters who had settled there. Landscapes and seascapes provided the real subjects for his paintings; their Christian or mythological subjects were, even more than in Poussin's painting, merely *staffage*—that is, an intellectual or literary excuse for the landscape and a means of establishing scale or providing nostalgia for the past. Claude's major interest was in the poetic qualities of landscapes or seaports seen in late afternoon light. Unlike Poussin's horizontally anchored planes with sharp edges and clear spatial relations, Claude's landscapes suggest no such flat stage-platform base but glide easily along rolling hills and meadows, while the trees shimmer in the breeze and present soft lacy silhouettes against the light. A composition like *A Pastoral* (Fig. 15-21) is less closed in depth than those of Poussin; the vistas give the effect of infinite space. The dazzling, gilt-hued seaport scenes, such as *The Embarkation of St. Ursula* (1641, National Gallery, London), often have the spectator looking directly into a setting sun that dissolves the details of architecture and ships on either side. The great demand for Claude's work encouraged forgery, and he was obliged to make a book of drawings, the *Liber Veritatis*, that recorded all his authentic paintings.

15-21 CLAUDE LORRAIN, *A Pastoral*, (c. 1642). Copper, 15⅞″ × 21⅝″. Yale University Art Gallery, New Haven, Connecticut. Leonard C. Hanna, Jr. Fund.

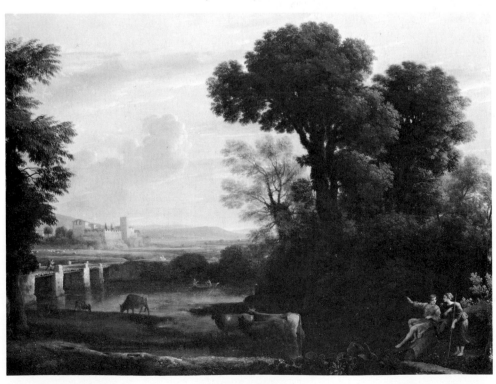

REMBRANDT VAN RIJN (Holland, 1606–69). Rembrandt, the son of a Leiden miller, studied in Leiden and Amsterdam with minor masters. Although he admired Italian art and eventually collected a number of Italian works, he never traveled to Italy. His early style, characterized by theatrical, spotlighted areas and massed shadows, reveals the influence of Caravaggio's lighting, perhaps by way of the Utrecht painters. Rembrandt broke with the conventionally even lighting and formal grouping of Dutch group portraits; his celebrated *Night Watch* (Fig. 15-22), which was originally larger, subordinates some of the company of Captain Frans Banning Cocq to shadowed areas. The dramatic value contrasts, the glowing color, the subtle organization of the active figures into the form of an "M" extending into depth, and the rich variety of personality all help make this painting the outstanding Baroque group portrait in the North. From the 1640s on, Rembrandt's art acquired a deeper gentleness; the drama became less physical and more psychological. The *Supper at Emmaus* (Plate 14 and Fig. 15-23) has the deeper chiaroscuro, the softer light, the suppression

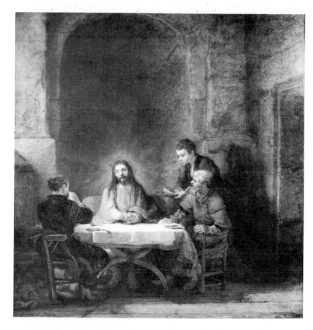

15-23 REMBRANDT VAN RIJN, *Supper at Emmaus,* (c. 1648). Oil on panel, approx. 27″ × 26″.
Louvre, Paris.

15-22 REMBRANDT VAN RIJN, *The Shooting Company of Captain Frans Banning Cocq (The Night Watch),* (1642). Oil on canvas, approx. 12′8″ × 16′6″.
Rijksmuseum, Amsterdam.

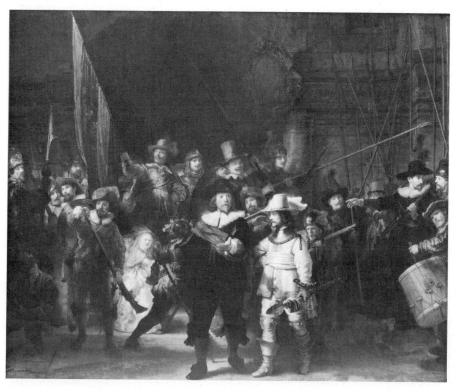

of local color, the reduction of physical movement, and the portrayal of intense human relationships that characterize his later work. Detail has been sacrificed to the fluidity of heavy impasto in the lighted areas and deep glazes in the shadows. Rembrandt produced many of his major etchings between 1650 and 1669. The velvet-rich blacks—often reinforced with drypoint—and the quick, telling character of the lines have made these works masterpieces in the history of printmaking. Although portraits were an important source of income for him, he painted an unusually large number of religious subjects, many of them done, like his self-portraits, for his own satisfaction. Like Caravaggio, but unlike Rubens, Rembrandt visualized biblical events in terms of common people with unheroic proportions and individual features, although he did occasionally use exotic costumes for accessories. Rembrandt's landscape paintings make striking use of stormy skies, areas of luminous foliage, dramatic cloud shadows, and architectural ruins. Rembrandt acquired several students and some wealth, but the death of his wife in 1642 marked the beginning of a period of poor financial management that finally drove him to bankruptcy. His last years were probably unhappy

ones, for his fame had been eclipsed in his own country by the successes of younger men.

JACOB VAN RUISDAEL (Holland, 1628?–82). Within the development of landscape painting in seventeenth-century Holland, Ruisdael's works are among the richest and most varied in technique and emotional depth. His early subjects were views of the coast near Haarlem done in simple compositions with active skies, low horizons, and dark diagonal masses leading from foreground to middleground. Colors are predominantly cool with warm local accents. After a trip to Germany made about 1650, Ruisdael produced, in addition to the flat Dutch landscapes, wild mountainous views with rushing torrents, melancholy skies, and, occasionally, architectural ruins. Some of these works seem to be allegories of mortality and decay. They suggest an analogy to Dutch *vanitas* paintings, still lifes in which a skull or snuffed-out candle may be contrasted with objects of material wealth and luxurious living to point up the homiletic moral of the transience of earthly life. Ruisdael's more violent landscapes were very popular with nineteenth-century Romantic painters. *Windmill at Wijk* (Plate 15 and Fig. 15-24) has

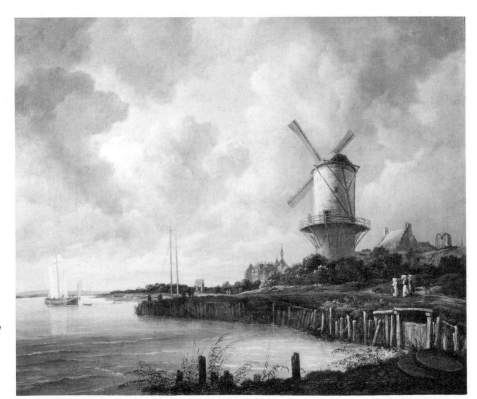

15-24 JACOB VAN RUISDAEL, *Windmill at Wijk,* (1665). Oil on canvas, approx. 2′9″ × 3′5″. Rijksmuseum, Amsterdam.

subtler drama. Towering clouds cast shadows on the land and water, expressing the power of weather. Dark land masses zigzag back into space, and the mill works in tension with the sailboat and the dark clouds on the left. The windy freshness, expansive depth, and grand scale all evoke the excitement of human contact with natural forces.

JAN VERMEER (Holland, 1632–75).   Very little is known about the life of the greatest of the Dutch painters of interiors. He made a precarious living as a painter and picture dealer and left his widow with a large family and numerous debts. Thirty-six paintings or less are now attributed to him, but his limited output seems to have found a ready market. Although Vermeer was a genre painter, he is more readily thought of as a painter of interiors because the quiet human activity in his pictures is usually subordinated to the structure of the composition and to the play of light on colors and textures. As in Poussin's landscapes, most of the larger objects in Vermeer's interiors are parallel to the picture plane, and we experience the picture space in a measured progression from one parallel to another. Occasionally, diagonal forms accelerate the transitions between the parts. The shapes also build a system of interlocking rectangles whose sides are often aligned with the sides of the painting, further emphasizing the static serenity of an all-pervasive order. In such works as *Young Woman with a Water Jug* (Plate 13 and Fig. 15-25), the underlying geometry is given relief by the curves and irregular forms of people and drapery. Light and shadow are used to group objects and to subordinate large areas of a composition in order to focus on others; light seems to wash the spaces and reveal textures and colors with gentle softness. This effect comes from minute pearl-like globules of paint and from the softening of the shadow areas with reflected light. In works such as *Head of a Girl in a Turban* (Fig. 15-26), details never subdivide and weaken the broad surfaces of the basic forms.

Sculpture in the North

France was the major center of seventeenth-century sculpture in the North. During the first half of the century, however, France was represented by men of competence rather than genius. Style in

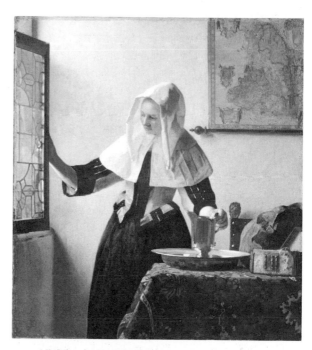

15-25 JAN VERMEER, *Young Woman with a Water Jug*, (*c.* 1665). Oil on canvas, approx. 18″ × 16″. Metropolitan Museum of Art, New York. Gift of Henry G. Marquand, 1889. Marquand Collection (89.15.21).

15-26 JAN VERMEER, *Head of a Girl in a Turban*, (*c.* 1660–65). Oil on canvas, approx. 18″ × 16″. Mauritshuis, The Hague.

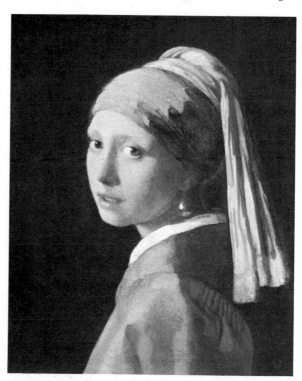

portraiture tended toward much heavy detail, while allegorical, mythological, and religious subjects received some idealization of form. Objects were clearly defined, and drapery was simpler and less active than in Italian full Baroque work. Essentially, the French sculptors were conservative. The second half of the century saw more inspired sculpture, much of it done under the auspices of the French Royal Academy for the enormous palace at Versailles. Bernini was a major influence, but the restraint of French sculptors tempered their borrowings from Italy.

FRANÇOIS GIRARDON (France, 1628–1715). Girardon subscribed to the taste and theory of the French Academy, worked closely with its director Lebrun, and established his career with the commissions for Versailles. Girardon was very interested in ancient sculpture; his famous *Apollo Tended by the Nymphs* (Fig. 15-27) shows the influence of Greek art in the profiles of the faces, the serene poses, and the relatively calm drapery. Originally, the arrangement of the statues was more symmetrical than it is now. Similarly quiet contours and smooth transitions from part to part can be seen in Girardon's tomb of Richelieu (1675–77, Sorbonne, Paris). Girardon represents the restrained Baroque attitude that was shared by such artists as Poussin.

15-27 FRANÇOIS GIRARDON, *Apollo Tended by the Nymphs,* (*c.* 1668). Marble, Park of Versailles.

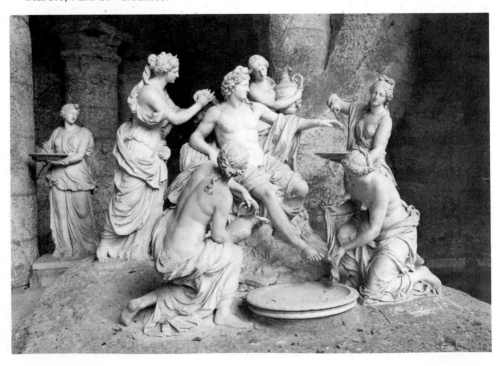

Architecture in the North

France, like Italy, developed city planning as an adjunct to seventeenth-century architecture. Parisian squares and circular places utilized converging avenues for focal emphasis on a special building. The triumph of the age was Versailles, the court palace of Louis XIV, where vast gardens and enormous buildings collaborate in an all-encompassing geometric plan. French churches of the period show the restraint, as well as the Italian influence, seen in French sculpture. The French town house, or *hôtel particulier,* evolved as a central structure with side wings embracing a court and an entrance gate facing the street. Its basic plan goes back to fifteenth-century French châteaux.

English architecture had imported Renaissance details in the sixteenth century, but not until the seventeenth century did the total effect of plan, structure, and detail become Renaissance in attitude, largely through the influence of the sixteenth-century Italian Andrea Palladio. The great fire of London in 1666 allowed a fresh start to be made in city planning and architecture. More squares were created, helping to open up the dense city. The rebuilding of churches provided England's first Baroque architecture; the style was influenced mainly by Renaissance Rome but showed considerable restraint.

In the Low Countries, Holland was inspired by Palladio, but Flanders produced an architecture of strident Italianate Baroque with a special Flemish insistence on fantastically ornate gables.

In German and Austrian architecture, Italy provided the models for churches, while Versailles was the model for palaces. Italian architects were frequently employed, and on several occasions German and Austrian architects were sent to Paris to have their plans approved by leading French architects.

INIGO JONES (England, 1573–1652).   We know little of Jones's background, but he traveled in Italy, gained a reputation in England as a designer of stage sets, accompanied the Earl of Arundel on a European trip, and was appointed to the highest architectural office in England—Surveyor of the King's Works. It was Jones who finally brought to England a classical attitude in the total design of a building. The austere formality of his Queen's House (Fig. 15-28) depends on stark simplicity of plan and elevation, precise symmetry, and a crystalline clarity in all the parts. The rigid equilibrium of quiet, unbroken lines and plain wall surfaces

15-28   INIGO JONES, south front of Queen's House, Greenwich, (1616–35).

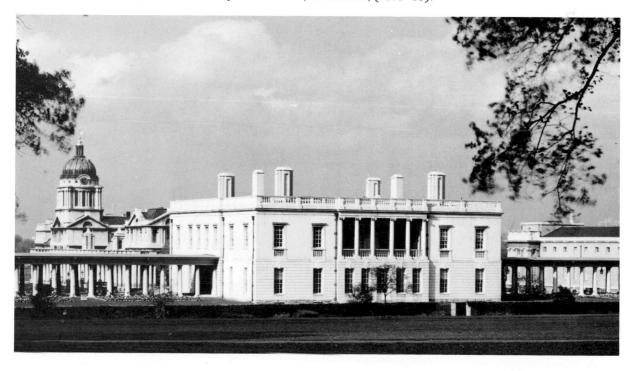

suggests the work of Palladio, Jones's major inspiration. Jones's best-known building, the banqueting hall at Whitehall Palace (1619–22, London), has slightly more activity in its three-dimensional variation and in decorative elements. The interior has ceiling paintings by Rubens. Jones's first ecclesiastical building was the Queen's Chapel, St. James Palace (1623–27, London), where the flat wall surfaces of a rectangular box are broken only by severely simple window frames and limited by sharply defined *quoins* (especially bold stonework used to emphasize the corners of a building), corbeled cornices, and a corbeled pediment. A Palladian window is used at the east end. Jones's architecture inspired a number of followers and was the major source for the eighteenth-century architectural trend in England called the *Palladian movement*.

FRANÇOIS MANSART (France, 1598–1666). Mansart was one of the most competent French architects of the seventeenth century, but his independence and his difficult disposition apparently limited the number of his commissions. Just as Inigo Jones set the key for the general conservatism of English architecture, so Mansart represents the restraint of French designers. The most complete surviving work by Mansart is the Château of Maisons (1642–51), which consists of a rectangular main structure flanked by two wings. The main building has very clear vertical and horizontal lines and a relatively shallow buildup of layered masses around the frontispiece. The classic succession of orders was used. Inside, the crisply carved ornament is unified by the exclusive use of white stone, without color or gilt paint. Mansart also planned the Val-de-Grâce in Paris (Fig. 15-29) and was

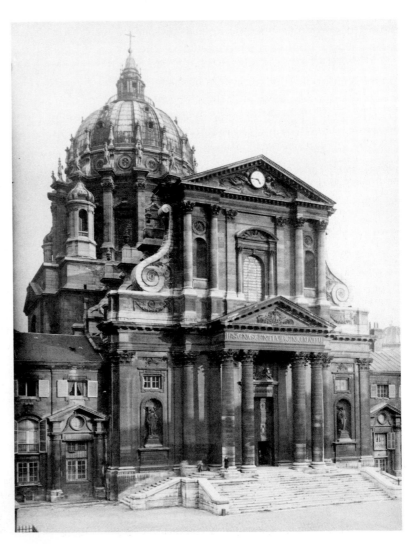

15-29 FRANÇOIS MANSART and JACQUES LEMERCIER, Val-de-Grâce, Paris, (1645–66). 133' high.

responsible for construction up to the second story of the façade and up to the vaults of the nave. The second story, the vaults, and the dome were completed by Jacques Lemercier. The plan (Fig. 15-30) is that of a Latin cross basilica with a chapel added to the rear of the apse, all quite simple and stable compared with plans by an architect like Borromini. The nave is divided from the side aisles by Roman arches and piers with Corinthian pilasters (Fig. 15-31); the entablature is simple, and the richest ornamentation is saved for the vaulting. On the exterior, the façade employs the Corinthian order. On the first level, the façade moves from corner pilasters to engaged columns and then to the freestanding columns of the porch. Above, Lemercier reversed the effect by making the engaged columns at the sides come forward while the center pulls back, taking the horizontal molding of the upper pediment with it. The large scroll buttresses at the sides of the upper level are indebted to Italian architecture.

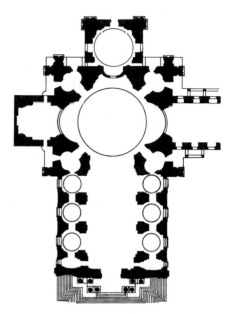

15-30   Plan of Val-de-Grâce.

SIR CHRISTOPHER WREN (England, 1632–1723). Wren started his remarkable career as an astronomer and inventor of practical devices of all kinds. His first architectural work of significance was the Sheldonian Theater at Oxford (1662–63), a design inspired by the Roman Theater of Marcellus as described in one of Serlio's books. In 1665, Wren traveled in France and visited many major works of architecture. His great opportunity came the following year when the London fire destroyed eighty-seven parish churches. As one of the Commissioners for Rebuilding the City of London, and as Surveyor-General of the Royal Works, Wren designed many of the new churches. Like most of the architects of his day, Wren learned much from the designs of the ancient Roman Vitruvius and was aware of seventeenth-century Italian architecture. Nevertheless, the London churches show considerable originality. Their most Baroque qualities are found in the steeples. The best-known example of Wren's work is St. Paul's Cathedral (Fig. 15-32), which developed from an early design in central form to a Latin cross basilica (Fig. 15-33) with Baroque complexity in the many-layered façades. The west façade employs deep porches for dramatic shadow and lavishly ornamented towers echo Sant' Agnese and a Bramante proposal for St. Peter's in Rome. A deep colonnade provides sharp

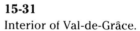

15-31
Interior of Val-de-Grâce.

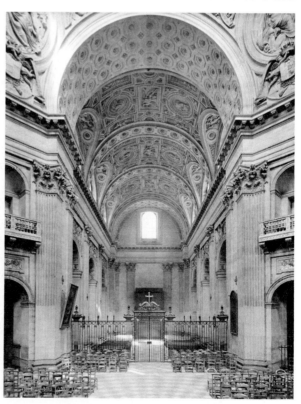

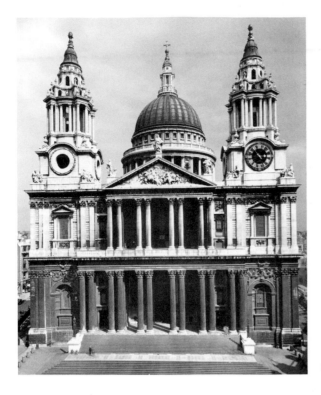

value contrasts at the base of the drum from which the great dome springs. Inside (Fig. 15-34), colors and materials are varied, but the basic form of the interior space is relatively simple. This most Baroque of Wren's churches seems conservative in comparison with full Baroque design in Italy.

15-32   SIR CHRISTOPHER WREN, St. Paul's Cathedral, London, (1675–1710).

15-34   Interior of St. Paul's.

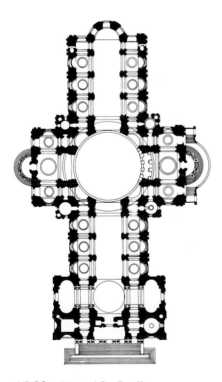

15-33   Plan of St. Paul's.

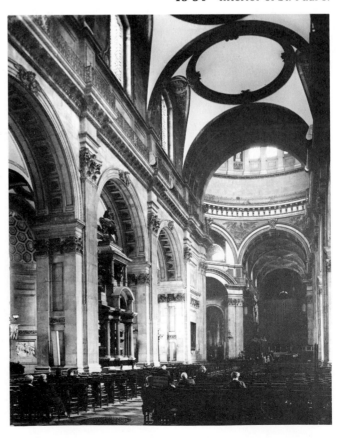

Suggestions for Further Study

Bergström, Ingvar. *Dutch Still-Life Painting in the Seventeenth Century.* Translated by Christina Hedström and Gerald Taylor. New York: Hacker, 1981.

Blankert, Albert. *Vermeer of Delft.* Oxford: Phaidon, 1978.

Blunt, Anthony. *Art and Architecture in France: 1500–1700* (Pelican History of Art), 4th ed. Baltimore: Penguin Books, 1982.

Blunt, Anthony, Alastair Liang, Christopher Tadgell, and Kerry Downes. *Baroque and Rococo Architecture and Decoration.* Cambridge: Harper & Row, 1982.

Brown, Jonathan. *Images and Ideas in Seventeenth-Century Spanish Painting.* Princeton, N.J.: Princeton University Press, 1978.

Downes, Kerry. *English Baroque Architecture.* London: Zwemmer, 1966.

Friedländer, Walter. *Nicolas Poussin: A New Approach.* New York: Abrams, 1964.

Gerson, Horst, and Engelbert H. ter Kuile. *Art and Architecture in Belgium: 1600–1800* (Pelican History of Art). Translated by Oliver Renier. Baltimore: Penguin Books, 1960.

Held, Julius S., and Donald Posner. *Seventeenth and Eighteenth Century Art.* New York: Abrams, 1974.

Hempel, Eberhard. *Baroque Art and Architecture in Central Europe: Germany, Austria, Switzerland, Hungary, Czechoslovakia, Poland* (Pelican History of Art). Baltimore: Penguin Books, 1965.

Kubler, George, and Martin Soria. *Art and Architecture in Spain and Portugal and Their American Dominions* (Pelican History of Art). Baltimore: Penguin Books, 1969.

Lavin, Irving. *Bernini and the Unity of the Visual Arts.* 2 vols. New York: Oxford University Press, 1980.

Martin, John Rupert. *Baroque.* New York: Harper & Row, 1977.

Moir, Alfred. *Caravaggio and His Copyists.* New York: New York University Press, 1976.

Rosenberg, Jakob. *Rembrandt, Life and Work,* rev. ed. Ithaca, N.Y.: Cornell University Press, 1980.

———, Seymour Slive, and E. H. ter Kuile. *Dutch Art and Architecture, 1600–1800* (Pelican History of Art). Baltimore: Penguin Books, 1977.

Stechow, Wolfgang. *Dutch Landscape Painting of the Seventeenth Century.* Ithaca, N.Y.: Cornell University Press, 1981.

Summerson, John. *Architecture in Britain: 1530–1830* (Pelican History of Art), 7th rev. and enl. ed. Baltimore: Penguin Books, 1983.

Waterhouse, Ellis. *Painting in Britain, 1530–1790* (Pelican History of Art), rev. ed. Baltimore: Penguin Books, 1978.

White, Christopher. *Rubens and His World.* New York: Viking, 1968.

Wittkower, Rudolf. *Art and Architecture in Italy, 1600–1750* (Pelican History of Art), 3rd rev. ed. Baltimore: Penguin Books, 1973.

16

Later Baroque, Rococo, and Neoclassic Art

1700 – 1800

Baroque stylistic tendencies continued in much eighteenth-century art; however, two other major trends developed and acquired labels. *Rococo* art retained the complexity of the Baroque but sacrificed power for refined elegance and a delicate, light profusion of forms. *Neoclassicism* was, in part, a reaction against Baroque and Rococo characteristics. Neoclassic theory, promulgated by the German archaeologist and art historian Johann J. Winckelmann, was stimulated by the discovery and excavation of two Roman cities that had been buried by a volcanic eruption in A.D. 79: Herculaneum and Pompeii. The increasing importance of Neoclassic art after 1750 has led some scholars to consider that date as the end of the Baroque period.

One aspect of the Baroque that developed during the eighteenth century was an aesthetic concept called the *sublime*. This was presented in works like Edmund Burke's essay "The Sublime and Beautiful" (1756), which distinguished between the beautiful and the sublime, with Burke stating that the latter could include the ugly. While much eighteenth-century effort sought to unravel nature's systematic order and bring it under human control, lovers of the sublime gloried in the mysterious power of nature over humanity. The sublime could be frightening, painful, or astonishing; it stimulated the emotions and the imagination. The concept of the sublime was fostered by Goethe and the *Sturm und Drang* movement, which emphasized the struggle of the individual against the world. It was the interest in the sublime that provided a basis for the broad nineteenth-century attitude called *Romanticism*.

The eighteenth century saw French art assume the position of leadership that Italian art had enjoyed previously, and French institutions, such as the Royal Academy, were imitated by several other countries.

The late seventeenth and the eighteenth centuries are often called the *Age of Enlightenment*. Major scientific discoveries were made, but the term refers especially to a spirit of rationalism, empiricism, and skepticism in social and political thought. Locke, Voltaire, Rousseau, and Diderot criticized existing society and spread ideas about human rights that laid the basis for the American and French revolutions. Also basic to these revolutions was the rise of the bourgeoisie to a position of power from which it could challenge the aristocracy. Bourgeois power, like the concepts of mercantilism and colonial expansion, developed as a result of accelerating growth of commerce and industry. This social and political environment affected, directly or indirectly, much of the art of the period.

Painting in the North

French painting continued to be dominated by the Royal Academy until the time of the Revolution. The older Academy of St. Luke, which had grown out of the guild system, was held down to a secondary role. No painter could paint and sell pictures without being a member of one of these academies. The Royal Academy acquired a virtual monopoly on exhibitions; its *Salon,* a periodic exhibition named for its location (after 1725) in the Salon Carré of the Louvre, had royal sanction. Until 1748, all members could exhibit in the Salon; after that time, a jury of academicians screened submitted works. Academic teaching used various methods, from apprenticeship under a master to copying accepted masterpieces from sixteenth, seventeenth-, and eighteenth-century painters, drawing from plaster casts of Greek and Roman sculpture, and drawing from live models. Prizes were given for the best work in anatomy, perspective, facial expression, and other categories. The most important prize was the *Prix de Rome,* which since its establishment in the seventeenth century has given selected students the opportunity to study at the French Academy in Rome. Leading academicians gave periodic discourses on theory and principle. In the seventeenth century, a hierarchy was established for subject matter; history painting — religious, historical, allegorical, or mythological subjects — was the highest category, and only painters of history could become professors. Following history painting came portraiture, genre painting, landscape (including seascapes and city views), animal painting, and still life. Early in the century, another category, that of the *fête galante* (an elegant outdoor entertainment), was added to sanction the popularity of Watteau's work. The style of history painting owed much to Rubens and to sixteenth- and seventeenth-century Italian masters. The conflict between *Poussinistes* and *Rubénistes* in the Academy was won by the *Rubénistes* early in the century, but the full Baroque styles gave way increasingly to the lighter colors and playful intricacy of the Rococo. Mythological subjects became more intimate than heroic, more gay than dignified. Genre painting gained in popularity during the period of Louis XV and often shows Rococo characteristics. Portraiture became more casual and livelier in pose and expression. Pastel portraits enjoyed great vogue. Landscape was often combined with battle scenes or with ruins, the style varying from repetitive formulas to the freshness of direct observation from nature. The major source for landscape, animal painting, and still life was seventeenth-century Dutch, Flemish, and Italian painting. The reign of Louis XVI and the revolutionary period that followed reemphasized history painting and introduced the Neoclassic style. Simplicity in accessories, clarity of contours, and rigid organization supplanted the billowing power of the Baroque and the tinkling delicacy of the Rococo. The French leader of Neoclassicism was the painter Jacques Louis David, who will be considered at length in the next chapter.

In England, a royal academy was not founded until 1768. Although its first president, Sir Joshua Reynolds, stressed in his famous discourses the superiority of history painting, he and other English painters found portraiture to be more rewarding financially. The glory of eighteenth-century English painting is its portraiture, ranging from heroic poses, idealized faces, and pompous settings to casual poses, candidly recorded faces, and unassuming environments. Genre painting and satire were also significant in England, and style ran the gamut from caricature to tentative and humble faithfulness to natural detail. Although seventeenth-century Dutch landscape and seventeenth- and eighteenth-century Italian landscape were popular with English collectors, English landscape painters were not given great encouragement at home. In spite of this situation, English painters produced some outstanding landscapes that varied from the delicate detail of John Crome's watercolors to the broadly brushed, sparkling watercolors of Alexander Cozens, and from the deliberately rendered ideal landscape of Richard Wilson to the filmy brushwork of Gainsborough. In the realm of animal painting, George Stubbs's carefully rendered horses appealed to a major interest of the aristocracy. Neither Rococo nor Neoclassic stylistic qualities were developed in England as fully as on the Continent.

In German regions during the eighteenth century, the northern areas were influenced by Holland and France; southern areas were inspired by Italy. Imported painters strengthened such influence, but a vigorous native Rococo style developed in the religious paintings of the German C. D. Asam and in the work of the Austrian Franz Anton Maulbertsch. German painters living abroad, such as Anton Raffael Mengs and Armus Carstens, were influential in the development of Neoclassic art during the second half of the century.

ANTOINE WATTEAU (France, 1684–1721). Of the three major eighteenth-century French painters whose art represents the Rococo style, Watteau is the earliest. He came from the Franco-Flemish city

of Valenciennes to Paris, where he found an international market for his work, partly through the help of several wealthy patrons. His painting was so successful that in order to accommodate it the French Academy created a new category of subject matter: the *fête galante*. Although Watteau painted religious works, portraits, and scenes with soldiers, the majority of his works depict characters or scenes from theatrical comedy or from the French aristocracy at leisure. His procedure was to paint directly on the canvas without elaborate preparatory drawings, but he composed by selecting figures from a large collection of sketches made from life. Thus his compositions are not so much records of a particular event as they are imaginative constructions. The famous *Embarkation for Cythera* (Fig. 16-1) is derived from a play and depicts a gay company about to sail for the legendary island of love. The painting is typical of Watteau in its soft, dreamlike landscape, luxurious costumes, dainty slender figures, and rich silvery colors. Its seeming casualness in composition and its softness in form contrast sharply with the paintings of Poussin. Indeed, the French Academy's acceptance of Watteau in 1717 represents one of the triumphs of the *Rubénistes*. Watteau's idol was Rubens; the delicate pointed noses, small mouths, and tapering hands of Rubens's figures reappear with slender bodies and more restrained sensuality in the art of the Frenchman. Watteau also learned from the Rubenesque painters in Paris and from the art of sixteenth-century Venice. He chose not to portray important historical actions; instead he depended on the spectator's associations or emotional responses to lyrical variations on the themes of theatrical entertainment and a leisurely aristocracy in natural settings. Sometimes it is difficult to distinguish between actor and aristocrat, between theater and *fête galante*.

WILLIAM HOGARTH (England, 1697–1764). The famous eighteenth-century satirist began as an apprentice to a silver-plate engraver but soon turned to painting and produced a number of *conversation pieces* — group portraits posed as an informal gathering with a suggestion of typical activity or anecdote. In 1731, Hogarth painted six works that were engraved and distributed the following year under the general title of *The Harlot's Progress*. The moralizing story of the downfall of a young

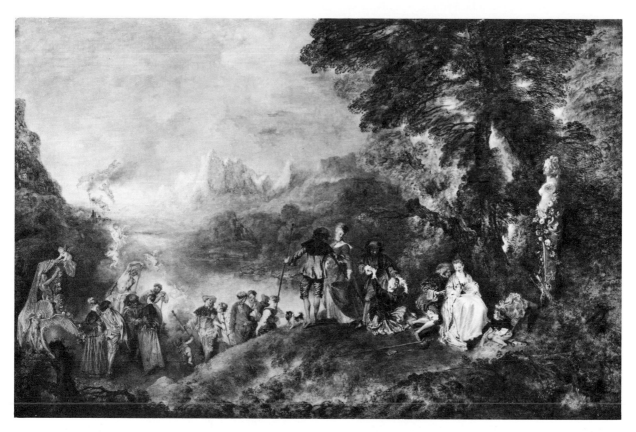

16–1 ANTOINE WATTEAU, *The Embarkation for Cythera,* (1717). Oil on canvas, approx. 4′ × 6′.
Louvre, Paris.

woman in the big city was immediately successful and inspired a number of unauthorized copies. Hogarth then promoted the Copyright Act for Engravers (1735) to secure his market and proceeded to make engravings of a similar series, *The Rake's Progress,* eight scenes portraying the dissolution of a young man. (The third scene is shown in Fig. 16-2.) Such work was far more lucrative than the history painting that was Hogarth's ambition; yet the artist did occasional history paintings and continued with portraiture while he produced paintings for the engravings that were both moralizing and satirical. His satire was aimed at all classes, striking sometimes at topical events, sometimes at specific facets of British society, and sometimes at universal human weaknesses. His remarkable visual memory was aided by a mnemonic system that he devised for remembering the positions and gestures of principal characters in a witnessed event. Hogarth formed the St. Martin's Lane Academy for teaching art and became a governor of the Foundling Hospital, where he arranged for picture exhibitions; he also found time to write a theoretical treatise, *The Analysis of*

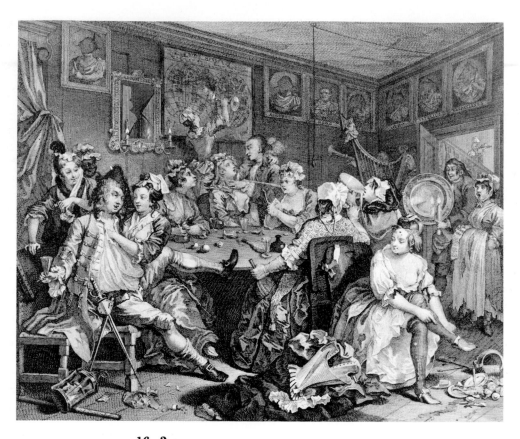

16–2
WILLIAM HOGARTH,
The Orgy, Scene III
from *The Rake's Progress,*
(1735).   Metropolitan Museum of
Art, New York.

Beauty (1753), urging the aesthetic values of asymmetry, intricacy, and the serpentine line. Although the proportions, intricacy, and frequent intimacy of his paintings link him with the Rococo, he was indebted to seventeenth-century Dutch genre painting and to the fifteenth- and sixteenth-century art of Bosch and of Bruegel the Elder. Hogarth was the predecessor of such satirical artists as Goya and Daumier.

JEAN-BAPTISTE SIMÉON CHARDIN (France, 1699–1779).   After working as an assistant to the painter Noël Coypel, Chardin was accepted by the Royal Academy in 1728 as a "genre painter of animals and fruit." In the tradition of seventeenth-century Dutch genre and still life, he painted quiet interiors with single figures or groups and still lifes composed of humble objects, such as *Clay Pipes and Earthenware Jug* (Fig. 16-3). His art is outstanding in its subtlety of color, light, and texture. By 1740, Chardin enjoyed critical acclaim and an international demand for his paintings as well as for the engravings done after them. He spent considerable time copying his own works to satisfy

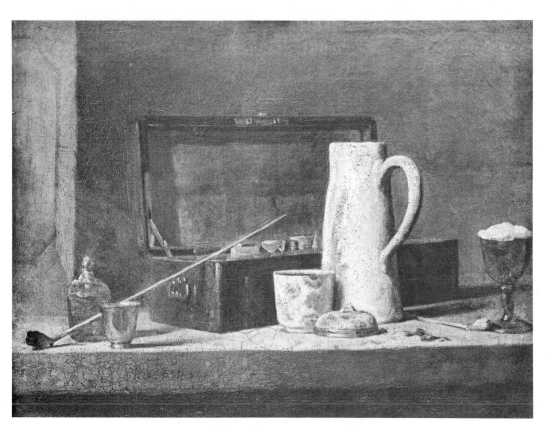

16–3 JEAN-BAPTISTE SIMÉON CHARDIN, *Clay Pipes and Earthenware Jug,* (*c.* 1760–63). Oil on canvas, approx. 12½″ × 16½″. Louvre, Paris.

collectors. By 1755, he was treasurer of the Academy and in charge of hanging exhibits. In his later years, when public favor had shifted from his still-life painting to the more moralizing and anecdotal art of others, Chardin turned to portraiture in pastels, where the crosshatching of color used in his oils is amplified.

FRANÇOIS BOUCHER (France, 1703–70). Boucher was the second major representative of French Rococo art. He was admitted to the Academy in 1734 and became first painter to King Louis XV in 1765. As a favorite of Madame de Pompadour, the mistress of the king, Boucher received many commissions, was named director of the Gobelins Tapestry Works, and designed tapestries as well as figures for the Royal Porcelain Factory at Sèvres. Boucher's subjects ranged from the religious to landscape, but the most frequent are allegory and mythology presented with dainty sensual figures in powder-puff landscapes that suggest stage settings. A typical example is *The Captive Cupid* (Fig. 16-4). The pretty faces, coy poses, sweet colors, delicate accessories, and

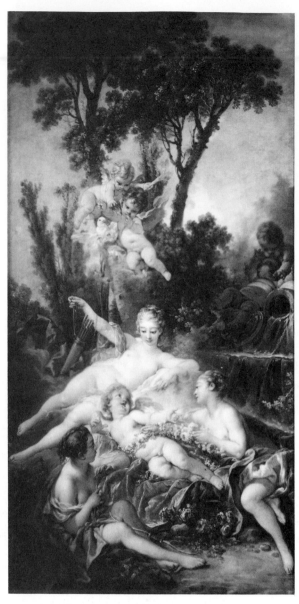

16–4   FRANÇOIS BOUCHER,   *The Captive Cupid,*
(1754).   Wallace Collection, London.

lilting lines all relate Boucher to the Rococo decorations of his early master, François Lemoyne. To appreciate such art, we must not demand depth or monumentality; Boucher's graceful facility was employed to create a pleasant, carefree world that ignores the problems of real life.

THOMAS GAINSBOROUGH (England, 1727–88). Gainsborough started as an assistant to an engraver who had studied under Boucher. As a restorer of seventeenth-century Dutch landscape paintings, Gainsborough acquired a love for landscape but found portraiture more profitable. His landscapes from the Ipswich and Bath periods tend to be detailed and solid in form. In the 1770s, they became softer, more loosely brushed, and more obviously creations of imagination. After his move to London in 1774, his figure paintings had a similar development: from detailed, solid forms to light, freely brushed backgrounds, rather insubstantial bodies, and fairly solid heads, as in *The Morning Walk* (Fig. 16-5). The gauzelike background and the fluffy forms recall Watteau, whose works Gainsborough had copied. Although the full-blown Rococo never found a footing in England, Gainsborough began what has been called English Rococo portraiture. Late in life, he also developed what he called "fancy pictures," genre scenes combining pretty, unsophisticated children and rustic nature. From 1761 on, Gainsborough exhibited with the London Society of Artists, and he was one of the original members of the British Royal Academy at its founding in 1768.

JEAN-HONORÉ FRAGONARD (France, 1732–1806). The third major representative of the Rococo lived through the French Revolution and beyond his own era. Fragonard left Chardin's instruction for the studio of Boucher, where the student copied the master so skillfully that it is sometimes difficult to distinguish between their works. In 1752, Fragonard won the Prix de Rome and, during his stay in Italy, was deeply impressed by the work of Pietro da Cortona and Giovanni Battista Tiepolo. His other idols were Rubens and Rembrandt. Although Fragonard offered a history painting as his acceptance work for the Academy, he chose as his role the development of the subjects and the Rococo style of Watteau and Boucher. His subjects ranged from noble groups and portraits to humble

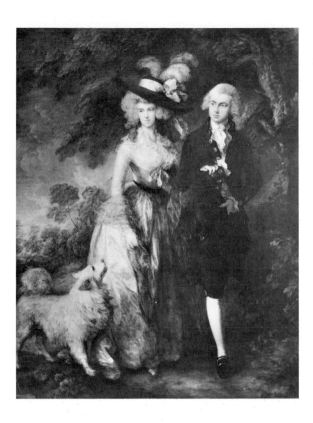

16–5 THOMAS GAINSBOROUGH, *The Morning Walk,* (1785).   Reproduced by courtesy of the Trustees of the National Gallery, London.

16–6 JEAN-HONORÉ FRAGONARD, *The Rendezvous,* (1773).   Frick Collection, New York.

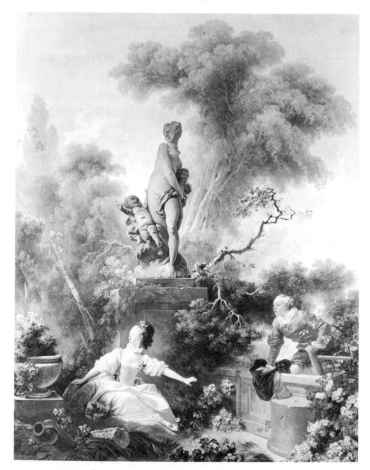

genre scenes and landscapes. With dazzling technical facility, Fragonard endowed the *fête galante* with glowing pools of light and color; glazes are contrasted with impasto. One thinks of Rembrandt, but Fragonard's lightness of touch, the dainty proportions of the figures, the breaking up of the forms, and the fluttery, rippling line are all thoroughly Rococo. Like Boucher, Fragonard often painted panels to be used as part of wall decorations in Louis XV interiors. Well-known examples are the panels on the theme of love (Fig. 16-6), which Fragonard executed for Madame du Barry, the French courtesan who succeeded Madame de Pompadour as the mistress of Louis XV.

Sculpture in the North

As in painting, the three general trends in sculpture were (1) a continuation of the seventeenth-century Baroque, ranging from stereotyped forms to a robust naturalism; (2) a Rococo style, emphasizing lilting, playful curves, intricate details in accessories, and slender proportions; and (3) a Neoclassic tendency toward simplification, quiet equilibrium, and long sweeping curves. Neoclassicism was especially important in the second half of the century. France was the most prolific producer of sculpture, but after the death of Louis XIV in 1715 the number of commissions issued for work at Versailles declined. The nobles were less attached to the court; they built town houses in Paris and furnished them with small sculptures in the Rococo style. Statuettes of porcelain and terra cotta were produced at the Sèvres workshops, a special interest of Louis XV's favorite, Madame de Pompadour. Baroque and Neoclassic styles were preferred for public monuments and other large works. Some sculptors modified their style to suit the commission.

In German areas, demand was greater for small sculpture than for monumental works. Meissen porcelain inspired the manufacture of France's Sèvres; but northern Germany imported French sculptors and French influence, while southern Germany and Austria were influenced by Italian sculpture, particularly in the stucco ornament with which they decorated their ornate Rococo churches.

Sculpture was meager in eighteenth-century England. French Baroque influence was brought to England by the sculptor Louis François Roubillac. Italian influence came from several leading Englishmen who studied in Italy. John Flaxman, for example, sent designs and sculpture from Italy to Wedgwood in England. The resulting Wedgwood ware is Neoclassic in the manner of Robert Adam decoration, that is, with a touch of Rococo delicacy. Otherwise, the Rococo did not take root in English sculpture.

COSMAS DAMIAN *and* **EGID QUIRIN ASAM** (Bavaria, 1686–1739 and 1692–1750).   The Asam brothers were trained by their father, Hans G. Asam, and had the benefit of a year in Rome (1712), where they were impressed by the works of Giovanni Lorenzo Bernini, Giovanni Battista Gaulli, Andrea Pozzo, and Pietro da Cortona. The brothers formed a partnership but also worked separately. Cosmas Damian specialized in fresco painting and Egid Quirin in stucco ornament and sculpture. Their early collaborations include *The Assumption of the Virgin* (Fig. 1-27) above the high altar in the monastery church at Rohr, near Regensburg. In this overwhelming demonstration of Baroque dramatics, the sculpted figures of the gesticulating Apostles are gathered around the sarcophagus,

while Mary ascends toward sculpted clouds and metallic rays that partially eclipse the architecture. The highly colored sculpture of the Madonna and the supporting angels presents a light, active, irregular group that contrasts with a darker curtain suspended in the background. The avoidance of framing and the concentrated lighting from above and from the sides are typically Baroque. The complexity, activity, and richness of the forms indicate a continuation of seventeenth-century sculptural-architectural combinations. The more delicate forms of the Rococo had not yet sapped the boisterous strength of Baroque composition. The later work of the brothers, however, became more Rococo.

JEAN ANTOINE HOUDON (France, 1741–1828). Houdon studied under the Baroque sculptors Jean-Baptiste Pigalle and Michel-Ange Slodtz, won prizes as a youth at the Academy, and spent the years from 1764 to 1768 at the French Academy in Rome. His thorough study of anatomy was demonstrated in the *Écorché* (c. 1766, École des Beaux Arts, Paris), a statue of a man without skin. Copies of this work served as study aids for anatomy classes in art schools. However, Houdon decided early on portraiture as a specialty and received many commissions from the nobility. His portrait style was one of keen characterization and precise detail. He used neither the delicate forms of the Rococo nor the generalization of the Neoclassic. Between 1771 and 1789, Houdon undertook a series of portraits of great men, including Voltaire (Fig. 16-7). His fame spread, and the esteem of Benjamin Franklin and Thomas Jefferson led to the commission for the full-length statue of George Washington (1785) in the State Capitol of Virginia, at Richmond. Houdon adopted a more Neoclassic style in a number of lesser-known works with mythological or allegorical subjects. He lived beyond the Revolution and continued to receive commissions, although he did not enjoy the favor of David, the leader of the Neoclassicists, or the patronage of Napoleon.

Architecture in the North

Eighteenth-century French architecture displayed a very restrained Baroque stylistic tendency that continued through most of the century and received the official sanction of the Academy. During the reign of Louis XV, the Rococo style was popular for interiors; bold surface projections were flattened, and pilasters and engaged columns were replaced by encrustations of dainty floral ornament and fluttering ribbons that break through any restraining geometric frames. Curves obscure, soften, and complicate the straight structural lines. Large halls gave way to small apartments and intimate rooms. Occasionally the Rococo was used for an exterior. The discovery of the buried Roman cities of Herculaneum (found in 1719) and Pompeii (found in 1748) provided inspiration for Neoclassicism, which developed in several directions after 1750. Simpler interiors with uninterrupted lines, rectangular rigidity, and more dependence on Roman ornament appeared in the work of Jacques-Germain Soufflot. With architects like Charles Nicolas Ledoux, however, simplicity and Greco-Roman elements were combined with jolting contrasts, grandiose scale, and surprisingly imaginative forms. The Revolution slowed building but strengthened the preference for the Neoclassic, partly because it was associated with the republican governments of certain periods in Greek and Roman history.

German eighteenth-century architecture developed a variety of styles within the general trends of Baroque, Rococo, and Neoclassicism. Some of the leading architects studied in Italy and France, and designers from these countries were brought to Germany. Churches of the early eighteenth century show the influence of the Italian Baroque. By mid-century, southern Germany and Austria were creating churches with rich Rococo interiors. Palaces were inspired by both Italian and French examples. Exteriors are often quite reserved, with decoration in low relief that does not obscure the basic masses; interiors could be lavishly Rococo. Winckelmann's influence was important in the second half of the century, and Neoclassicism waxed strong, particularly in Berlin. Neoclassic interiors often resemble those by Adam in England and suggest faint echoes of the delicacy of the Rococo.

The eighteenth century in England opened with the reserved Baroque that had developed in the previous century. After 1710, this tendency was challenged by the *Palladian Revival,* a movement espousing a return to the simpler Roman forms of

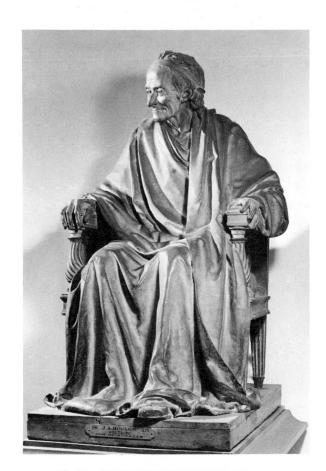

16–7   JEAN ANTOINE HOUDON,   *Voltaire,*
(1781).   Comédie Française, Paris.

the sixteenth-century Italian Palladio. A third tendency is evidenced by the occasional designs in Romanesque or Gothic styles. The ruins of Medieval architecture could be appreciated, as could Roman ruins, for their *picturesque* qualities of rough, irregular, and varied forms, and for their *sublime* qualities, which evoked nostalgic enjoyment of man's smallness and of the transitory character of his achievements in the face of nature's vastness and power. Furthermore, Gothic ornament could be appreciated for having some Rococo qualities. Neoclassic architecture developed in the second half of the century under the leadership of Robert Adam, Sir William Chambers, and Sir John Soane. An architect might work in several of these four trends.

JOHANN BERNHARD FISCHER VON ERLACH (Austria, 1656–1723).   After his training in Rome, Fischer von Erlach returned to Vienna, where he became a leader in seventeenth- and eighteenth-century Austrian architecture. His Church of St. Charles Borromaeus (Fig. 16-8) provides a strong

16-8 JOHANN BERNHARD FISCHER VON ERLACH,   St. Charles Borromaeus, Vienna, (1716–37).

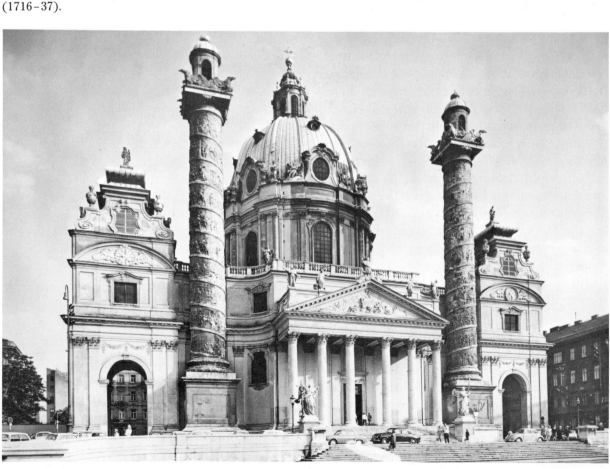

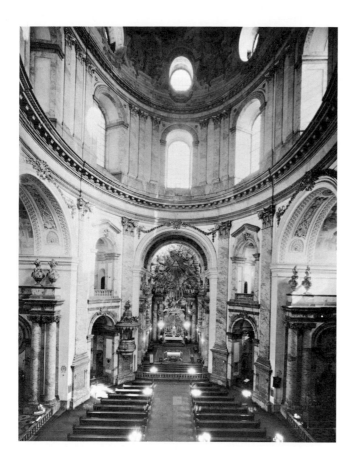

16-9
Interior of St. Charles Borromaeus.

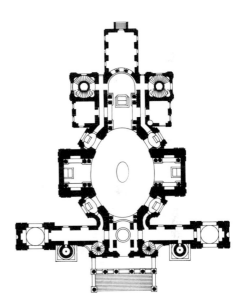

16-10
Plan of St. Charles Borromaeus.

focus on the main altar, which is placed in an extension at one end of an elliptical interior space (Fig. 16-9). At the opposite end, a wide narthex is placed at a right angle to the elliptical center section (Fig. 16-10). The exterior façade of this narthex consists of a Corinthian porch connected by two concave wings to towers at the sides. Within the concave areas at each side of the porch stand two tall columns with spiral reliefs in the manner of the ancient column of Trajan in Rome. Above the impressive façade looms a high dome set over the elliptical interior. The total effect both inside and out is one of dramatic contrasts between parts, but there is greater restraint in ornament than in many Italian Baroque churches.

BALTHASAR NEUMANN (Germany, 1687-1753). Neumann was trained by the Würzburg bronze caster Sebald Kopp, and in addition gained considerable experience as a military engineer-architect. In 1720, he was given responsibility for the building of the Episcopal Residence at Würzburg and, in 1723, was sent to Paris to study French architecture. The Residence, like so many

16–11   BALTHASAR NEUMANN,
Vierzehnheiligen (The Fourteen Saints), near
Banz, (1743–72).

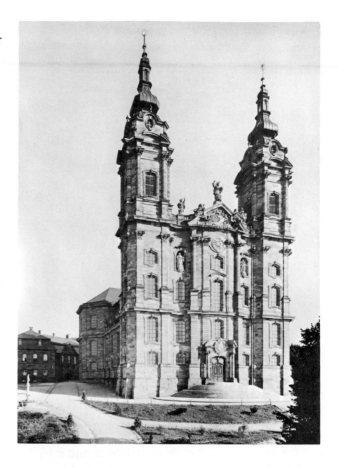

16–12
Interior of Vierzehnheiligen.

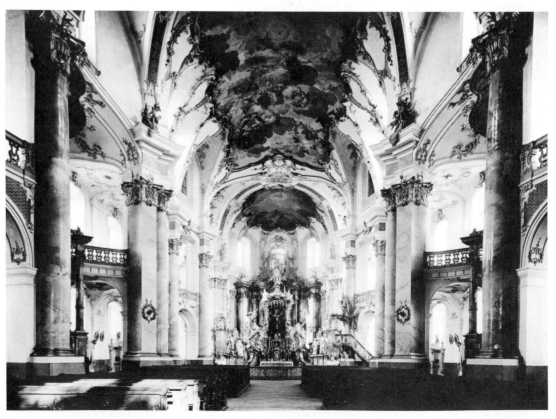

other eighteenth-century palaces, owes much to Versailles. French influences were important in the development of Neumann's Rococo style, which left a strong imprint on the architecture of southern Germany. Of his many buildings, the most celebrated church is that of Vierzehnheiligen (The Fourteen Saints, Fig. 16-11). Here, the façade pushes forward in a convex center framed by engaged columns and broken pediments; the twin towers become more complex and bolder in value contrasts as they rise. Rococo touches can be seen in the lilting curves of pediments and window frames, but the real drama is in the interior (Fig. 16-12). Neumann's basilica plan (Fig. 16-13) was based on ovals and circles, producing even more restless wall planes than those of Borromini's San Carlo alle Quattro Fontane. The activity of the walls is intensified by the profusion of vinelike, irregular ornament that seems to crawl over the surfaces. The lavish colors, the delicate details, and the amazing effervescence of the interior of the church make it an outstanding example of German Rococo.

ANGES-JACQUES GABRIEL (France, 1699–1782). Gabriel came from a family of architects and studied with his father. As architect for Louis XV, he produced both independent buildings and large building groups. His feeling for gradation and climax was expressed with spatial vistas leading to a building, central colonnaded pavilions, and occasional four-sided domes and concentrations of sculpture, as in his Military School (Paris, 1751). Gabriel's typical reserve is better demonstrated in the pair of palaces in the Place de la Concorde (1757–75), formerly the Place Louis XV. Rusticated and arcaded bases support colossal Corinthian orders that carry an entablature, balustrades, and corner pediments. Although the seventeenth-century east front of the Louvre inspired Gabriel's design, he used more three-dimensional variation and value contrast in the base. The simplest of his buildings is the Petit Trianon at Versailles (Fig. 16-14), an almost square structure with a symmetrical arrangement of interior spaces. While the interior has some traces of Rococo decoration, the exterior is remarkably austere. Three façades use slightly projecting pavilions marked by columns or pilasters framing the tall windows of the main floor and the square windows of the attic. The blocky

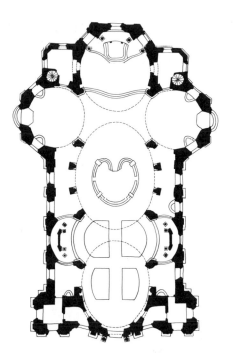

16–13
Plan of Vierzehnheiligen.

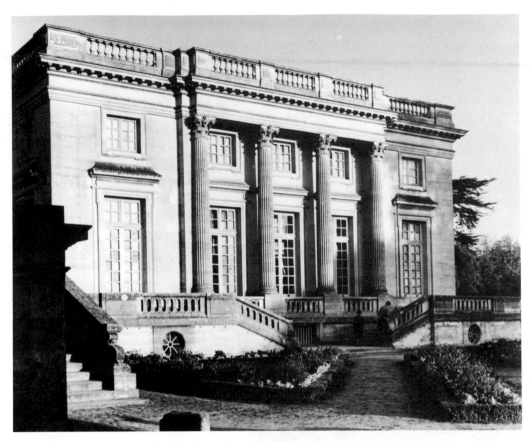

16–14   ANGES-JACQUES GABRIEL,   Petit Trianon, Versailles (façade on the Jardin Français), (1762–68).

form is topped by an entablature and a balustrade. It has been claimed that Gabriel was influenced by the publication, in 1758, of J. D. LeRoy's *Ruins of the Most Beautiful Monuments of Greece,* but the natural reserve of Gabriel's style came basically from the traditional restraint of French architecture in the preceding two centuries.

ROBERT ADAM (England, 1728–92).   Robert Adam was born in Scotland and attended the University of Edinburgh. From 1754 to 1758 he toured Italy, joined the artist's Academy of St. Luke in Rome, became a friend of Piranesi, and measured and drew the ruins of the palace of the Roman Emperor Diocletian at Spalato. Upon his return to England, he formed an architectural office with his brothers James and William. In 1761, Robert Adam was appointed one of the two Architects of the King's Works. He and his brothers designed whole houses, reconstructions, interiors, and furnishings. Stylistically, their work was among the

most significant done in England in the 1760s and 1770s, and their influence was international. The Adam style may be called, with qualification, Neoclassical. Floor plans such as that of Syon House, Middlesex, have balanced symmetry and were inspired by specific Roman or Greek buildings. Façades range from the massive stately south front of Kedleston Hall, Derbyshire, with its Roman triumphal arch motif, to the delicate, crisp, miniature character of the Adelphi Houses in London. The Adams' greatest influence was on interiors. Their preference was for slender pilasters, Grecian urns, and architectural moldings borrowed from Rome and Greece and used with rich profusion in very slight relief with sharp contrasts in value or color. The result has some of the delicacy of the Rococo but much more rigid geometric structure, as shown in No. 20, Portman Square (Fig. 16-15). In speaking of architecture, Robert Adam emphasized "movement," the rise and fall, the advance and recession of parts that is a facet of the Baroque love of strong gradation and climax.

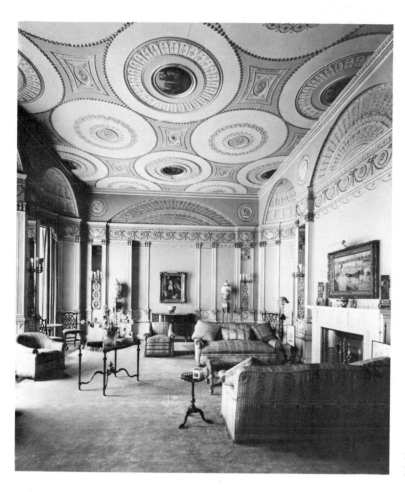

16–15   ROBERT ADAM,   music room of No. 20, Portman Square, London, (1777).

Painting in Italy

Major centers for eighteenth-century Italian painting were Naples, Bologna, Rome, and Venice; many Italian painters also found employment in other countries. As elsewhere, there was increased specialization in subject matter. Style in history painting was based on the work of Carracci, Pietro da Cortona, Rubens, Titian, Tintoretto, and Veronese. The shimmering color of Veronese can be seen as one source for Italian Rococo, which was developed independently by Giovanni Battista Tiepolo. Loose brushwork and ragged, fluttering shapes created light, spacious compositions that maintain more breadth and grandeur of scale than French Rococo. Foreign painters were responsible for Neoclassic work in Italy. Portraiture was abundant in both the Baroque and the Rococo styles. Paintings of city views, ruins, landscapes, and imaginative combinations of all three found a wide market. Not only were many northern Italian palaces decorated with such subjects, but travelers collected them as souvenirs. Style varied from precise, dry detail, natural light, and documentary accuracy to fluid brushwork, dramatic lighting, and exaggerated scale. Genre painting followed the traditions of the Bambocciata and that of the upper-class interiors from seventeenth-century Dutch painting.

GIOVANNI BATTISTA TIEPOLO (Venice, Lombardy, Würzburg, and Madrid, 1696–1770).   Tiepolo's rise to fame began during his study under a secondary master in Venice. Commissions for wall and ceiling frescoes eventually led him from one city to another. The heavy forms and powerful value contrasts of his early work, like *The Sacrifice of Abraham* (1715–16, Church of the Ospedáletto, Venice), show the influence of Titian and of Tintoretto, but Tiepolo then turned to lighter and more open composition. In the Church of the Gésuati in Venice, he did the ceiling painting of *St. Dominic Instituting the Rosary* (1737–39), a composition that recalls the illusionistic architecture in Veronese's *Triumph of Venice.* Yet Tiepolo reduced the proportion of heavy solids and increased the proportion of sky. The thin, fluffy clouds, the fluttering airborne figures, and the light colors and shadow areas produce a buoyant effect. Between 1750 and 1753, he decorated the Episcopal Residence at Würzburg. The ceiling painting of the throne room depicts *Apollo Conducting Beatrice of Burgundy to Barbarossa* (Fig. 16-16) and goes further than earlier work in lightening and opening the composition. Architecture is reduced to a small structure in the lower left, and the figure groups present fluttering irregular shapes reminiscent of leaves blown in the wind. The sweeping clouds are thin overlapping veils with delicately scalloped edges. Around the painting, a gilded stucco frame consists of compound curves and lacy edges, broken in several places by painted forms that seem to spill over it in typical Baroque illusionistic fashion. From 1762 until 1770, Tiepolo worked in Spain, decorating the Royal Palace at Madrid. The jealousy of rivals and the growing preference for Neoclassicism led to a decline in his popularity and may have hastened his death. Tiepolo's painting presents the fullest expression of the Rococo in Italian art.

GIOVANNI ANTONIO CANAL, *called* **CANALETTO** (**Venice, Rome, and London, 1697–1768**).   Canaletto studied first with his father, a painter of theatrical scenery. In 1719, the young artist traveled to Rome, where he saw Giovanni Paolo Pannini's paintings of ruins and the Bambocciata paintings of everyday life in the city. After his return to Venice, Canaletto specialized in painting views of the city *(vedute)* and obtained numerous commissions from Englishmen making the grand tour of

16–16   GIOVANNI BATTISTA TIEPOLO,   *Apollo Conducting Beatrice of Burgundy to Barbarossa,* ceiling of the throne room of the Episcopal Residence, Würzburg, (1750–53).

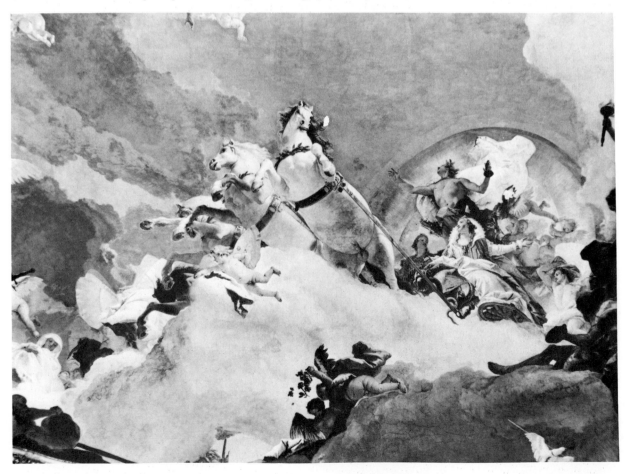

the Continent and wishing to take home souvenirs. Canaletto painted Venice in sharp linear detail, sweeping spaces, and vast gentle skies, as in the *Piazza San Marco* (Fig. 16-17). The popularity of his art led to the publication of a series of engravings of his paintings that was used as a catalogue by his clients and an aid by his imitators. It is probable that he visited Rome again in 1740. Between 1742 and 1743, he painted a series of scenes depicting Roman ruins. Canaletto did not always limit himself to documenting particular spots; he occasionally created imaginary scenes, sometimes containing well-known buildings. Much of the period from 1745 to 1755 was spent in England, where his reputation was already well established. The visit was a great success, although the English collectors were, at first, disconcerted

16–17 CANALETTO, *Piazza San Marco,* (*c.* 1760).   Courtesy of the Trustees of the National Gallery, London.

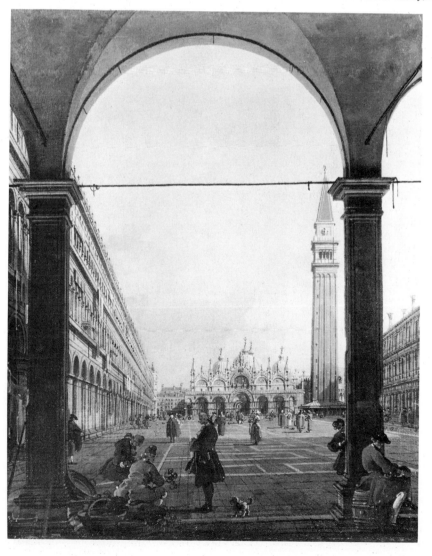

by the *caprices*—imaginary scenes—that the painter produced along with many views of London. Commissions were so plentiful that Canaletto employed assistants. Cityscapes and landscapes were considered inferior subject matter by academic standards, however, and in spite of his international success Canaletto was not accepted into the Venetian Academy until 1763.

GIOVANNI BATTISTA PIRANESI (Rome, 1720–78). Piranesi's engravings and etchings demonstrate the growing eighteenth-century interest in Greco-Roman art and the appreciation of the picturesque. Piranesi began his career in Venice as a student of architecture but established himself in Rome in 1740. There he turned to engraving and etching prints of ruins and views of modern Rome. His etching of the Great Hall of the Baths of Cara-

calla indicates his love of grand scale, often exaggerated by depicting tiny human figures next to ragged, crumbling architecture eaten away by time and vegetation. Etching needles of different sizes made for rich diversity of line. Piranesi's best prints show a wide variation of grays and deep blacks. He documented and interpreted ancient Rome in his views of that city, but the range of his imagination is shown in his *Carceri* series (Fig. 16-18), imaginary interiors of prisons in fantastic scale and structural elaboration based vaguely on Roman architecture. A comparison of the art of Piranesi with that of David indicates the wide range of style that could be inspired by intense interest in ancient Greco-Roman art. In an effort to describe Piranesi's particular attitude and style, some writers have used the rather awkward term *Romantic Classicism*.

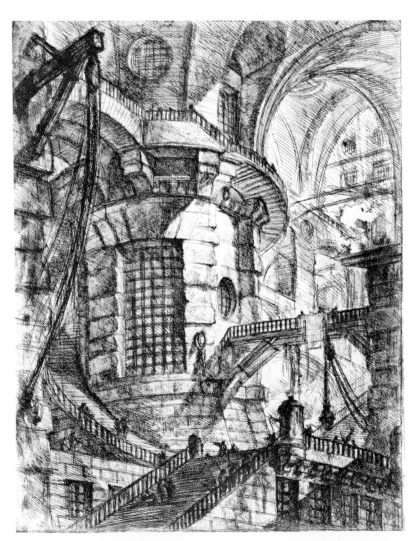

16–18   GIOVANNI BATTISTA PIRANESI,   scene from the *Carceri* series, (1744–45). Etching.   The Metropolitan Museum of Art, Harris Brisbane Dick Fund, 1957.

Suggestions for Further Study

Eitner, Lorenz. *Neoclassicism and Romanticism, 1750–1850* (Sources and Documents in the History of Art). 2 vols. Englewood Cliffs, N.J.: Prentice-Hall, 1970.

Gerson, Horst, and Engelbert H. ter Kuile. *Art and Architecture in Belgium: 1600–1800* (Pelican History of Art). Translated by Olive Renier. Baltimore: Penguin Books, 1960.

Hempel, Eberhard. *Baroque Art and Architecture in Central Europe: Germany, Austria, Switzerland, Hungary, Czechoslovakia, Poland* (Pelican History of Art). Baltimore: Penguin Books, 1977.

Honour, Hugh. *Neo-Classicism* (Style and Civilization Series). Baltimore: Penguin Books, 1978.

Irwin, David. *English Neo-Classical Art.* London: Faber & Faber, 1966.

Kalnein, Wend Graf, and Michael Levey. *Art and Architecture of the Eighteenth Century in France* (Pelican History of Art). Translation of Part II by J. R. Foster. Baltimore: Penguin Books, 1973.

Morassi, Antonio. *Tiepolo: His Life and Work.* New York: Phaidon, 1955.

Rosenberg, Jakob, Seymour Slive, and E. H. ter Kuile. *Dutch Art and Architecture, 1600–1800* (Pelican History of Art). Baltimore: Penguin Books, 1979.

Rosenblum, Robert. *Transformations in Late Eighteenth-Century Art.* Princeton, N.J.: Princeton University Press, 1970.

Summerson, John. *Architecture in Britain: 1530–1830* (Pelican History of Art), 6th rev. ed. Baltimore: Penguin Books, 1971.

Waterhouse, Ellis. *Painting in Britain, 1530–1790* (Pelican History of Art), rev. ed. Baltimore: Penguin Books, 1979.

Wittkower, Rudolf. *Art and Architecture in Italy, 1600–1750* (Pelican History of Art), 3rd rev. ed. Baltimore: Penguin Books, 1973.

17
Neoclassic through Post-Impressionist Art

1800 – 1900

Modern art is often dated from David's rebellion against the Baroque and Rococo styles in the late eighteenth century (see p. 274). Rebellion against tradition, even an immediately preceding one, and the rapid change of form and content are important characteristics of modern art. With these characteristics in mind, we can consider the nineteenth century to be the first major period in the history of modern art. The development of archaeology and art history as disciplines seems to have led to greater self-consciousness about individual style and to an increased awareness of stylistic movements and group identities. For some artists, however, the interest in these disciplines led to more precise borrowing from the art of the past. These divergent tendencies, along with changing ideas in philosophy and science, help to explain why different concepts of artistic "truth" are implicit in the different styles in art and in the writings of art critics during the nineteenth century.

The most important geographical area for developments in painting and sculpture was France. In architecture, England played a significant role, especially since her leadership in the Industrial Revolution encouraged pioneering use of iron and glass as building materials.

During the first half of the nineteenth century, the various styles tended to express one of two major attitudes, Neoclassicism or Romanticism. The distinction between the two is not always sharp since there was considerable overlapping and mutual influence. Nineteenth-century Neoclassicists borrowed more specifically from Greek and Roman art than did their eighteenth-century predecessors. Underlying the many Neoclassic styles is the search for an absolute beauty based on the perfection of nature and in accordance with preconceived ideal types. Clarity of parts, stable equilibrium, and proportions inspired by Greek and Roman art are basic to Neoclassic work. The attitude called Romanticism produced such a wide range of styles that it is more difficult to characterize; generally there is an insistence on the freedom of the individual and the importance of individual experience. Individual characteristics —the unique form rather than the ideal type—are stressed, and restrictive traditions are rejected. In the famous preface to his play *Cromwell* (1827), Victor Hugo provided a manifesto for Romanticism. He attacked academic dogma and argued that the Christian concept of the worth of the individual makes possible a new kind of pity, *melancholy*. He stated that the individual, indeed all of nature, contains the ugly as well as the beautiful, evil as well as good. Art should therefore dramatize the dual nature of reality, stress the worth of the individual, and evoke the profound sentiment of melancholy. Romantic artists found subject matter in the works of Lord Byron and Sir Walter Scott and inspiration in the appeal to emotional and mystical experience by writers like François René de Chateaubriand and Wilhelm H. Wackenroder. Christian pietism frequently reinforced the Romantic attitude and created an interest in the Middle Ages; the Romantic artist could turn to any period in the past, however, since he appreciated the exotic and the remote in time or place.

After the middle of the nineteenth century, the Neoclassic and Romantic attitudes gave way to tendencies that have been described as a *positivistic reaction* and that are reflected in some of the pioneering literature, painting, and sculpture of the period. The continuing desire to upset conventional ideas was joined by an interest in treating all aspects of everyday life in styles that were labeled *Realistic* or *Naturalistic*. Such art was linked with the growing enthusiasm for science, and artists began to investigate even the chaotic incidental nature of human events and the impressionistic character of our experience of the physical world. Toward the end of the century, however, the realization grew that science and progress would not solve all the ills and mysteries of the world. The *Symbolist movement* in literature and art emphasized the enigma of existence and the subjective nature of reality. In the 1890s, symbolism was often expressed in a stylistic trend called *Art Nouveau* in France and *Jugendstil* in Germany. This trend spread across Europe and America, bringing into art and product design a preference for flat shapes and undulating, plant-like contours.

Painting

In France, the late eighteenth and early nineteenth centuries saw the triumph of Neoclassicism under the leadership of Jacques Louis David. During the early years of the nineteenth century, however, Neoclassic stylistic qualities were temporarily supplanted, in the work of many artists, by more irregular masses, deliberate merging and obscuring of some compositional parts, more individualistic details in anatomy, and more specific and contemporary details in accessories. These features, some of which recall seventeenth-century Baroque art, were particularly evident in the painting of Napoleonic history and were further developed, during the years after the fall of Napoleon, in much of the painting that has been called Romantic. The immediate ancestry of Romantic art can be found in the eighteenth-century enjoyment of the picturesque and in the sentimentality of such eighteenth-century painters as the Frenchman Jean Baptiste Greuze. Delacroix was considered to be the leader of Romanticism, while Ingres led academic art in the search to find the ideal truth of

Neoclassicism. The Salon of 1824 provided a confrontation of works by the two leaders, and it is from this date that the conflicting and overlapping attitudes of Neoclassicism and Romanticism assume major importance in French art.

Academically approved "classic landscape" painting, exemplified by Poussin's work, was superseded during the first half of the century by the art of certain French painters who turned to more direct experiences of nature. These *Barbizon painters* did much painting outdoors, in the forest of Fontainebleau near the village of Barbizon. Although the works were usually finished in the studio, they retained the freshness of firsthand experience in more casual, varied, and free compositions than those of academic landscape. The Barbizon painters made their debuts around 1830 but were not widely accepted until the second half of the century. Their delight in sensitive interpretation of the moods of nature, ranging from lyrical reverie to dramatic storm, links them with Romanticism, and their ancestry may be found in seventeenth-century Dutch landscape painting.

The mid-century was marked not only by political revolution but also by a new movement in French painting, *Realism,* which treated all facets of daily life in a style that showed frank enjoyment of the natural shapes, textures, and colors of things and a delight in the manipulation of the paint itself. In comparison with Realist work, the painting of the Barbizon artists and the exotic subjects, grand passions, glowing colors, and dashing brushwork of Delacroix became much more acceptable to conservative critics, and Realism succeeded Romanticism as the rebel of the period. The leader of the Realists, Gustave Courbet, was rebuked for the vulgarity in form and subject matter in his work.

The hegemony of the French Academy suffered a blow in 1863 when the outcry against the severity of the Salon jury caused the emperor to order an exhibition of rejected works, called the *Salon des Refusés.* Although the public tended to agree with the jury's decisions, the artist's right to exhibit outside the Salon was taken more seriously than before.

After about 1860, certain French artists, notably Édouard Manet, began to intensify their pictorial images by using patches of color relatively unbroken by internal modeling. An important inspiration for this trend was the Japanese woodblock print.

The intensification of vision assumed another form in the stylistic movement called *Impressionism,* which made its formal debut in the exhibit of the *Société anonyme des artistes, peintres, sculpteurs, graveurs, etc.* in 1874. The momentary visual impression of a world of light and color in constant change became the major interest of Impressionist leaders like Claude Monet and Auguste Renoir, who went one step further than the Barbizon painters by finishing their paintings outdoors, working directly from the subject. Their patient study of the effects of light and color has been linked with the scientific study of optical phenomena, but they intensified the effects of shimmering light, reflected colors, and simultaneous contrasts, re-forming the visual world into a luminous matrix of small strokes of rich color. Their scientific objectivity seems to have been qualified by sensuous enjoyment of visual experience. By the 1890s, Impressionist work was grudgingly accepted by academic juries and even awarded occasional prizes.

Meanwhile, attitudes in academic painting had undergone changes. The fall of Napoleon had not stopped Napoleonic history painting, and the taste for specific details and local color that had been inspired by Napoleonic history was strengthened by an interest in the developing scientific methods in archaeology and history and by the exactitude of photography. Neoclassic painting was continued by some painters, but after mid-century, academic painters turned increasingly to precise, carefully researched details, and the truth of Neoclassic ideal form was supplanted in academic work by this documentary or archaeological truth.

In the 1880s and 1890s, a number of pioneering young painters who had tried Impressionist painting early in their careers came to feel that Impressionism sacrificed too much solidity of form and compositional structure for the sake of color and light. They therefore turned to very different styles in their mature painting. The most important of these artists were Seurat, Van Gogh, Cézanne, and Gauguin. They have been called *Post-Impressionists,* and their styles forecast significant directions in twentieth-century painting.

German painting at the beginning of the nineteenth century was molded by the doctrines of Winckelmann and the influence of the Frenchman David. Rome was the training ground for many of the leading German painters, just as it had been for

David (see p. 274). A group known as the *Nazarenes* sought new purity of religious content through a self-consciously simple, linear style inspired by Italian Renaissance art like that of Perugino and Raphael. Members of the Nazarene group later obtained positions of leadership in German academics at Düsseldorf, Munich, and Berlin. German Romanticism was expressed in styles that incorporated more precise detail than did those in France; evocations of nostalgia about the brevity of human existence, the mysterious forces of nature, and the secret life of the individual recur frequently in paintings by Philipp O. Runge and by Caspar David Friedrich. Realism developed in the work of several Germans and was inspired either by Courbet or by the concept of documentary truth. Impressionism had a belated emergence in Germany.

In Italy, as in France and Germany, the major academies were dedicated to Neoclassicism in the early part of the century. A Romanticism that rejected Neoclassic ideal form for individualistic details made its appearance in Milan. By mid-century, a group of Roman painters called the *Macchiaiuoli* ("painters of spots") were employing bold patterns of color patches that forecast the style of Manet in France several years later. Documentary history painting became important in the second half of the century.

In England, the opening years of the nineteenth century were dominated by several of the great eighteenth-century portrait painters. As the century unfolded, genre painting found a wide market. Landscape painting was led by Constable, whose free brushwork influenced Delacroix, and by Turner, who exploited dramatic effects of light and color in both real and imaginary landscapes. In 1848, the *Brotherhood of Pre-Raphaelites* united several precocious young painters whose moralizing zeal was combined with a yearning for mystical experience, a love of involved literary symbolism and feverishly bright detail, and a desire to return to the style of art before Raphael. Carefully staged and precisely rendered history painting came from the brushes of academicians. Impressionism did not develop in England as it did in France. Oriental art fascinated the American expatriate James McNeill Whistler, and his muted, misty riverscapes of scenes along the Thames combine the broad patterns of Manet's art with

Impressionistic interest in atmospheric effects. His English student, Walter Sickert, used more *broken color* (see p. 295), but his heavy, earthy style is quite unlike French Impressionism.

During the nineteenth century in the United States, patrons became increasingly more sophisticated and developed interests in a wider range of subject matter and style. Portraiture remained the type of painting in greatest demand, and style ranged from the facile brushwork of Thomas Sully to the sparkling detail of Thomas Eakins. Genre and landscape painting expressed a patriotic enthusiasm for the local customs and natural beauty of a rapidly growing America. The *Hudson River School*, a group of landscape painters dedicated to depicting Arcadian river views, might be compared with the Barbizon painters in France. During the second half of the century, a romantic nostalgia for grandeur and overpowering scale is evident in some landscape paintings. The mystery of nature was expressed in the glowing, somber landscapes and seascapes of Albert P. Ryder; the Impressionistic interest in natural light and color came only in the last decade of the century.

FRANCISCO GOYA (Spain, 1746–1828). While Goya's love of fantasy has led some historians to consider him a Romantic, his expository portrayal of human personality has inspired the term *Realist*. The latter designation seems more accurate in that even his imaginative work stresses the realistic acceptance of the role of the irrational in human experience; yet Goya's art differs considerably from that of the French Realists of the mid-nineteenth century. Goya's teachers were minor masters, who had less influence on his art than did the paintings of Tiepolo and Velázquez. In his mature work, Goya used a dazzling variety of textures; his style ranges from harsh light and simplified forms to soft light and the effect of mass and detail seen through dense air. In *May Third, 1808* (Fig. 17-1), which shows Spanish citizens being shot by Napoleonic soldiers, a harsh style underscores the painting's social comment. The grouping of shapes into simple areas of light and dark intensifies the gestures of the subjects and the total impact of the composition; Goya here forecasts the art of Manet. Social commentary is implicit in some of Goya's portraits as well. *The Family of Charles IV* (1800, Prado, Madrid) candidly reveals

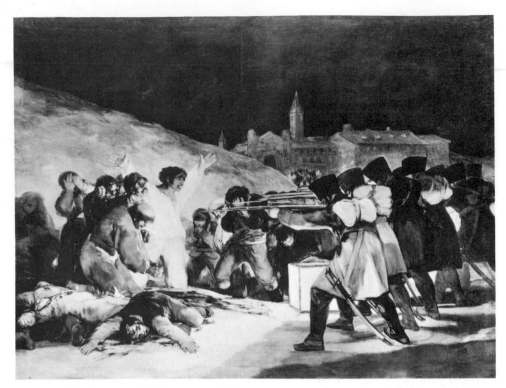

17–1   FRANCISCO GOYA,   *May Third, 1808,*
(1814–15). Oil on canvas, approx. 9′ × 11′.
Museo Nacional del Prado, Madrid.

the homeliness or viciousness of the different personalities and contrasts these with the luxurious costumes. Goya's frankness makes his official success surprising, for he became painter to the king and the head of painting within the Spanish Academy. The most macabre and enigmatic of his works are the so-called *black paintings,* done on the walls of his house in the 1820s. His strongest social commentary and his most unrestrained fantasy are found in his prints. *The Caprichos* (Fig. 4-3), a series of eighty aquatint etchings, depict man as unreasonable, petty, self-indulgent, and sadistic. *The Disparates,* a set of twenty-two aquatint etchings, reveal Goya's extraordinary imagination in a sequence of grotesque visions; they are frequently ambiguous in meaning, but the total effect is one of fascination and horror in the observation of man. Inhumanity and viciousness are the essence of *The Disasters of War,* a series of eighty aquatint etchings presenting a catalogue of barbaric cruelties in Spain during the period of Napoleonic conquest and occupation.

JACQUES LOUIS DAVID (France, 1748–1825). David lived through some of the most violent periods in French history, and his art spearheads one of the most drastic stylistic changes in French

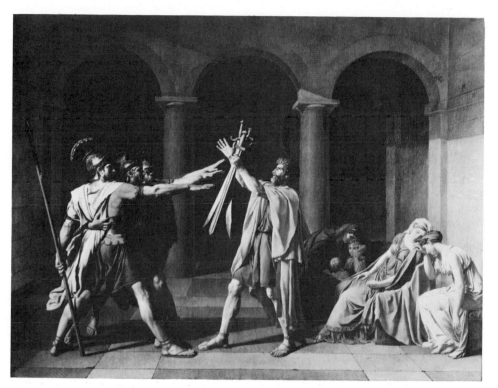

17-2 JACQUES LOUIS DAVID, *The Oath of the Horatii*, (1784).   Oil on canvas, approx. 10′ × 14′. Louvre, Paris.

painting. As a student at the Paris Academy, David won a Prix de Rome in 1774 with a history painting done in the Baroque manner. During his sojourn in Rome, he changed his style in works like *The Oath of the Horatii* (Fig. 17-2), which caused great excitement. This composition is starkly simple; the figures form triangular or rectangular groupings, and the main elements are aligned with stable verticals and horizontals as well as with the picture plane. While the light is dramatic, it does not obscure the rigid structure of the painting. There is no softening effect of sfumato in the sharp contours of the forms. David's inspiration came from certain Greek and Roman works, from his teacher Joseph Vien, and from the theories of Johann J. Winckelmann, who praised the noble simplicity and calm grandeur of ancient Greek art. David's style, in its simplicity and strength, seemed the very antithesis of the aristocratic art of the Rococo, and David was adopted as the artist of the developing French Revolution. Not only the style but also the subject of *The Oath of the Horatii* acquired political implications. Three Roman brothers, the Horatii, pledge to fight for Rome against three other brothers, the Curiatii, from the city-state of Alba, to decide which city will rule the other. The wife of one of the Horatii is sister to one of the Curiatii, and one of the Horatii's sisters is betrothed to another of the Alban champions. Fatherland above family was the message carried by the painting. After the Revolution, David became a veritable dictator of the arts. His Neoclassical style was the order of the day, and he was powerful enough to have the Royal Academy abolished. However, David's painting changed in the early years of the nineteenth century. David and others were inspired by Napoleonic history, and Greco-Roman subjects gave way to dramatic contemporary events. The austere rigidity of David's early style softened to suggest more dramatic movement and more detailed accessories. For example, the *Bonaparte Crossing the Alps* (1800, Kunsthistorisches Museum, Vienna) employs unsupported contrasting diagonal forms quite unlike the stable triangular arrangements in David's earlier works. The search for timeless, ideal human form changed to an interest in topical detail, as demonstrated by *The Coronation of Napoleon* (1805, Louvre, Paris). After the fall of Napoleon, David went into exile in Belgium, where he continued to produce portraits and also painted mythological subjects, which he treated in a less dramatic manner than that of his earlier style.

WILLIAM BLAKE (England, 1757–1827).   Blake was an engraver, painter, poet, and visionary. He illustrated his own poems with hand-colored engravings. *The Creation of Eve* (Fig. 17-3), from Milton's *Paradise Lost*, is a watercolor incorporating typically linear, ideal, Neoclassic figures into a very personal vision. A flaming nimbus surrounds the body of Adam, and the light figures are set against a delicate foliage pattern, a black sky, and a crescent moon. His most famous works include 21 illustrations for *The Book of Job* (1820–26) and 102 illustrations for Dante's *Divine Comedy*. Blake's late style became more extraordinary in imagination, more extreme in figure proportions, and less clear in spatial relations. He drew inspiration from Medieval and Renaissance art. Some of his work was based on a mythology of his own, infused with personal mysticism. His art provides a link between Neoclassic form and the subjective dreamworld of many Romantics in the following generations. Blake also influenced Art Nouveau, which developed in the 1890s (see p. 271).

17–3   WILLIAM BLAKE,   *The Creation of Eve,* from the *Paradise Lost* series, (1808). Pen and watercolor on paper, 19¾″ × 15¾″.   90.95, Gift of Subscription, 1890. Museum of Fine Arts, Boston.

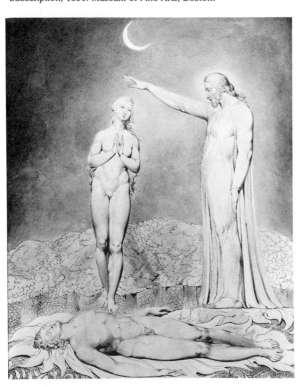

CASPAR DAVID FRIEDRICH (Germany, 1774–1840). Friedrich studied at the Academy of Copenhagen and moved to Dresden in 1798, where he joined a circle that included the Romantic writers Ludwig Tieck and Novalis and the painters Philipp Runge and Ferdinand von Olivier. In 1805, Friedrich's sepia drawings won a prize in a competition judged by Goethe. Friedrich's subjects tend to show a single person or a small group dwarfed by the vastness of nature. He loved grand scale, sweeping vistas, effects of sunrise or moonlight, and a mood of solitude, meditation, or melancholy. He is identified with Romanticism in Germany, as was Delacroix in France, but there are wide differences between the styles of the two men. Friedrich loved precise detail and patterns formed by delicate silhouettes. His *Cloister Graveyard in the Snow* (Fig. 17-4) is typical. The painting evokes a powerful mood of melancholy. Although it has none of the vigorous brushwork and apparent spontaneity of Delacroix's art, it contains a similar suggestion of man's tragic and ephemeral existence.

17–4 CASPAR DAVID FRIEDRICH, *Cloister Graveyard in the Snow.* (1810). Approx. 47″ × 70″. (Now lost.) Staatliche Museen, Berlin.

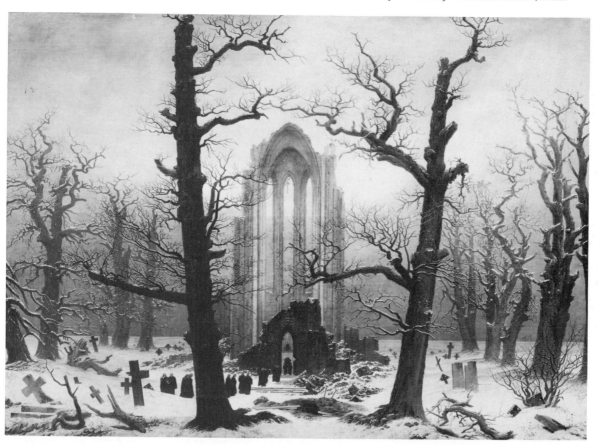

JOSEPH MALLORD WILLIAM TURNER (England, 1775–1851).   Turner was first a watercolorist, adding color washes to drawings by Thomas Girtin, but in the 1790s he began painting landscapes in oil, his major sources of influence being seventeenth-century Dutch landscapes, Claude Lorrain, and Nicolas Poussin. During walking tours of England and France, Turner made thousands of drawings that became the bases for many of his paintings. He worked in two styles: one recorded nature in faithful detail and was the basis for his acceptance by a part of his public; the other, thought of today as the typical Turner, intensified the vast scale of nature and the effects of light and atmosphere (Fig. 17-5). Solid forms dissolve in a shimmer of mist, glowing light, and iridescent color. *Rain, Steam, and Speed* (Plate 18 and Fig. 17-6) exploits rain and the steam of a locomotive for these effects. Sunrise, sunset, storm, and the clearing after a storm were favorite moments for Turner. He frequently used mythological subjects

17-5   JOSEPH MALLORD WILLIAM TURNER,   *Burning of the Houses of Parliament,* (1834). Oil on canvas, 36½″ × 48½″.   The Cleveland Museum of Art, Bequest of John L. Severance.

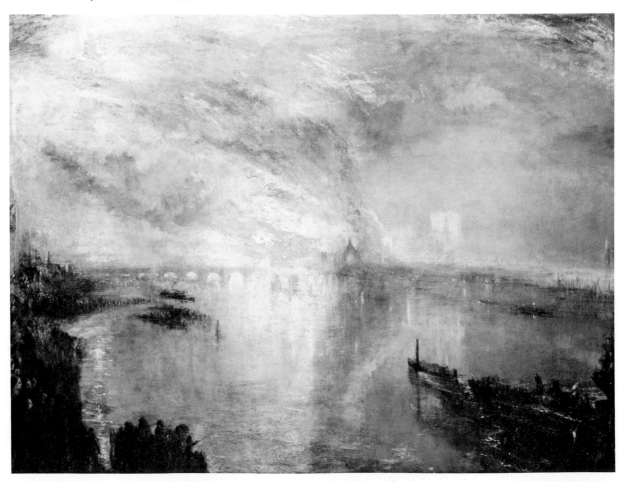

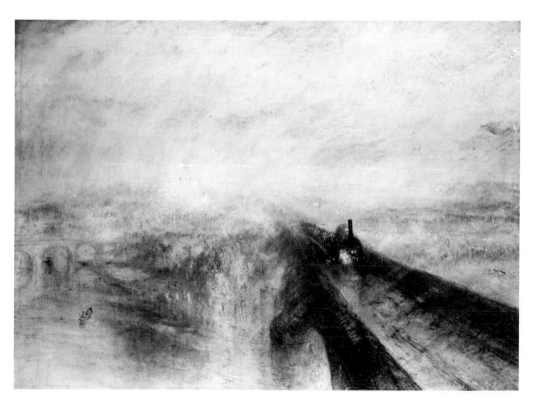

17–6 JOSEPH MALLORD WILLIAM TURNER, *Rain, Steam, and Speed,* (1844). Oil on canvas, 3′ × 4′. Reproduced by courtesy of the Trustees of the National Gallery, London.

or motifs based on actual situations: a slave ship jettisoning its cargo or a grand old warship being towed to the scrapyard by a dirty tug. Because many of his works sacrifice detail for effects of light and color, Turner has been considered a source of French Impressionism, which developed in the latter half of the century. But Turner's more imaginative paintings are visions that magnify the mystery and grandeur of nature; in this respect, they reflect the Romantic attitude.

JOHN CONSTABLE (England, 1776–1837).   Constable began life as the son of a country miller, but in 1799 he was admitted as a student to the Royal Academy in London. His mature style was considered to be crude and unfinished by some critics. *The Hay Wain* (Fig. 17-7), one of his best-known landscapes, was exhibited in 1821. Although considerably more detailed than a full-sized oil sketch of the subject (Victoria and Albert Museum, London), the final work has sparkling color and buttery paint application that create an effect of dewy freshness. The composition reflects the influence of Constable's idols, Claude Lorrain and Thomas Gainsborough, as well as of seventeenth-century Dutch landscape painting. *The Hay Wain* was exhibited in the Paris Salon of 1824. French critics,

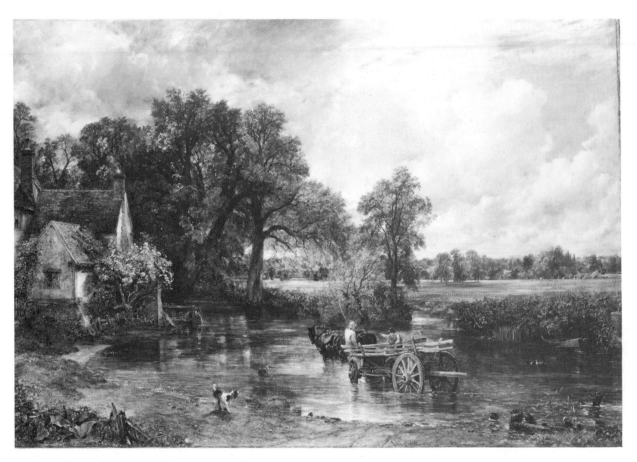

17–7   JOHN CONSTABLE,   *The Hay Wain,*
(1821). Oil on canvas, approx. 4′ × 6′.   Reproduced by
courtesy of the Trustees of the National Gallery, London.

like the English, had mixed responses, but painters were impressed by the vigor and freedom of the execution. Delacroix is said to have repainted the background of his 1824 Salon entry after having seen Constable's painting. Along with Turner, Constable helped to open the way for the freer interpretation of landscape later in the nineteenth century.

JEAN AUGUSTE DOMINIQUE INGRES (France, 1780–1867).   David's successor as leader of academic Neoclassicism did not emerge immediately. The early work of Ingres, a pupil of David, was criticized for the distortions of anatomy and complexities of drapery that the young artist created in the interests of rhythmic line. Ingres was happy, therefore, having won a Prix de Rome with a carefully constructed academic exercise, to leave France in 1806 for Florence and Rome. This first sojourn lasted eighteen years. The *Grande Odalisque* (Fig. 17-8) reveals Ingres's Neoclassic training, his love of Raphaelesque ovoid forms, his use of arbitrary human proportions, his contrast of smooth flesh

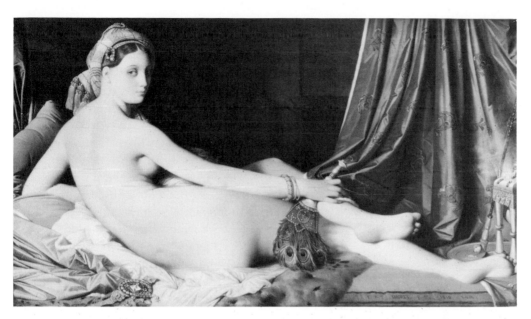

17–8 JEAN AUGUSTE DOMINIQUE INGRES, *Grande Odalisque,* (1814). Oil on canvas, approx. 35″ × 64″. Louvre, Paris

17–9 JEAN AUGUSTE DOMINIQUE INGRES, *Portrait of Count Rodolph Apponayi,* (1823). Graphite and white chalk on paper, $17\frac{13}{16}″ × 13\frac{5}{8}″$. Courtesy, Fogg Art Museum, Harvard University. Grenville L. Winthrop Bequest.

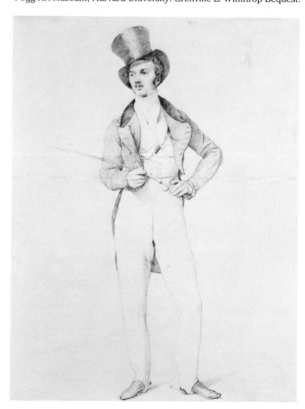

with complex drapery, and his highly finished paint surfaces. His portraits, in paint and in pencil, display great linear elegance (Fig. 17-9). His 1824 Salon contribution, *The Vow of Louis XIII,* was so successful that he returned to Paris as leader of academic painting and became president of the École des Beaux-Arts. Academic teaching under Ingres's leadership was very dogmatic; he insisted that drawing was the basis of art, and he stressed sharply defined contours and smooth finish. He was considered to be the champion of Neoclassicism and the foe of Romanticism; at the Paris International Exposition of 1855, the most lavish representation in the exhibit of French painting was accorded the paintings of Ingres and Delacroix.

THÉODORE GÉRICAULT (France, 1791–1824). The sensation of the Paris Salon of 1819 was a painting of shipwrecked people on a raft. The subject came from the recent wreck of a French vessel and the subsequent abandonment of passengers and sailors by the captain and officers. Géricault prepared by interviewing survivors and drawing cadavers. His respect for factual reality stemmed in part from his youth in the era of Napoleonic wars when French artists painted contemporary scenes with factual accuracy. Yet Géricault did not paint the figures in a realistically emaciated condition. In this, in the undatable vagueness of the clothing, in the grand scale, and in the dramatic lighting, he suggests the general struggle of humanity against nature. The desire to find the universal within the particular is a faint echo of Davidian Neoclassicism. While Géricault carried much of the immediacy of his studies into the final painting, the poses recall the art of Michelangelo and other Italian masters whose work he had studied in Italy. The *Raft of the Medusa* (Fig. 17-10) was exhibited in London, where Géricault lived from 1820 until 1822. There, he drew and made lithographic prints of workers, the poor, and of horses. With humans and with horses, his depictions range from specific studies to monumental scenes of ideal forms. Géricault's late work dealt with lion hunts, the Greek war of independence from the Turks, and character studies. The most striking of the latter are oil portraits of anonymous patients in mental hospitals. Géricault planned large paintings of social themes such as the abolition of slavery, but mental depression and injuries from horseback riding accidents led to his death at thirty-three. He is usually seen as a pioneer of Romanticism, yet he is also significant for the later Realist movement.

17–10 THÉODORE GÉRICAULT, *Raft of the Medusa,* (1818–19). Oil on canvas, approx. 16′ × 23′. Louvre, Paris.

CAMILLE COROT (France, 1796–1875).   Corot was born in Paris and trained by painters of classic

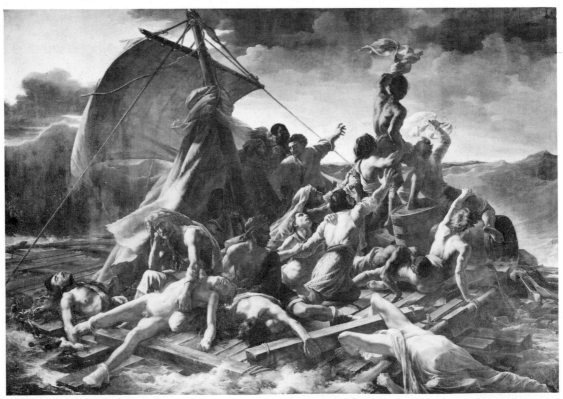

landscape in the tradition of Poussin. During a sojourn in Italy in the 1820s, Corot developed landscapes with bold masses and simplified areas of light and dark, usually grouped around a horizontal or vertical axis, as in *Democritus and the Abderites* (Fig. 17-11). In the 1840s, he turned to the silvery, cloudlike foliage and poetic delicacy typified by *Souvenir de Mortefontaine* (Plate 17 and Fig. 17-12). Small flecks of light-colored flowers float against deep shadows; light filters through the leaves, and hazy banks of foliage step back into space. Although Corot occasionally peopled his landscapes with Grecian nymphs, his scenes are more earthbound than those of Turner. Corot's landscapes are based on a lifetime of outdoor drawing and painting; he was associated with the Barbizon painters. Until the twentieth century, Corot's figure paintings were less appreciated than his landscapes. Most are portraits of anonymous people whom Corot painted in subtle colors and solid forms and with quiet dignity, using some of the broad simple areas of value and color that are typical of his early work. Corot was awarded the Legion of Honor in 1846. His success was such that forgers provided "Corots" to meet a growing demand by collectors.

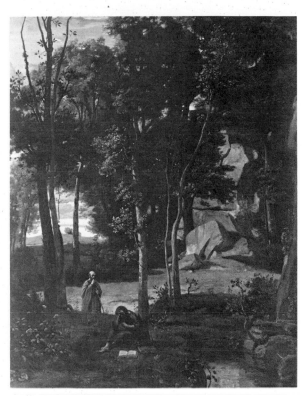

17-11 CAMILLE COROT, *Democritus and the Abderites,* (1841). Oil on canvas, approx. 4'11" × 3'11". Musée des Beaux-Arts, Nantes.

17-12 CAMILLE COROT, *Souvenir de Mortefontaine,* (1864). Oil on canvas, 25¼" × 34½". Louvre, Paris.

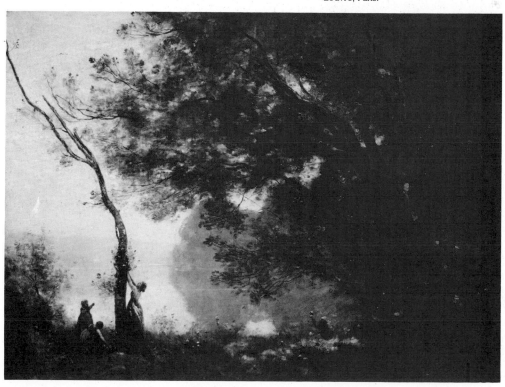

17-13 EUGÈNE
DELACROIX, *The
Lion Hunt,* (1851). Oil
on canvas, 30½″ × 38½″.
Collection of The Art Institute
of Chicago, Potter Palmer
Collection.

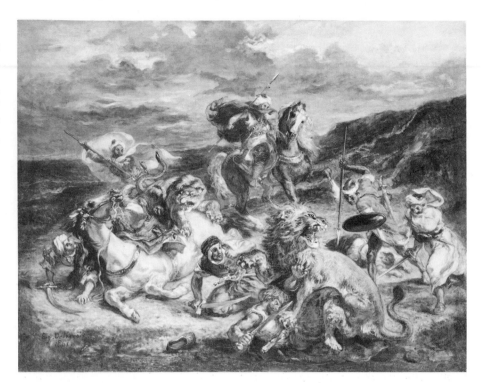

17-14 EUGÈNE DELACROIX, *The Abduction of Rebecca,*
(1846). Oil on canvas, 39½″ × 32¼″. The Metropolitan Museum of Art,
Wolfe Fund, 1903. Catharine Lorillard Wolfe Collection.

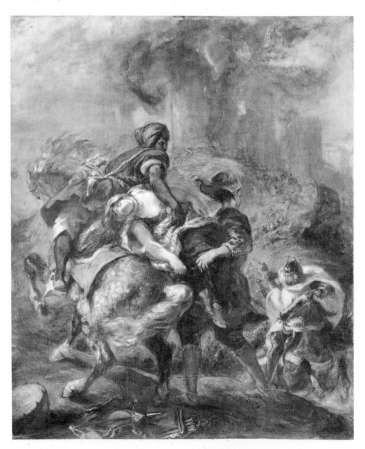

EUGÈNE DELACROIX (France, 1798–1863).   For
Delacroix, the most important qualities in painting
were vitality and the sensuous appeal of color.
Although his teacher was the academic painter
Guerin, his real inspiration was the art of Michelangelo and Rubens; Delacroix was a descendant
of the *Rubénistes*. While his subjects usually came
from literature, as did those of Ingres, Delacroix's
painting seemed violent, crude, and unfinished to
Ingres and his followers. *The Lion Hunt* (Plate 16
and Fig. 17-13) recalls similar subjects by Rubens
and reveals Delacroix's love of dramatic action
and exotic settings; a trip to Morocco in 1832 and
the reading of Byron's *Childe Harold* had fired his
enthusiasm for the Near East. The writhing entan-
glement of hunters, horses, and lions suggests the
eternal struggle between man and his environment, a theme dear to Delacroix and to Romantic
art and literature. *The Abduction of Rebecca* (Fig.
17-14) was inspired by Sir Walter Scott's book
Ivanhoe. The explosive energy of the composition
is organized within an oval of light. The blurred
edges, the *lost-and-found* (discontinuous) outlines, rapid brush strokes, vigorous paint texture,
and touches of bold color all make the action
more convincing. Delacroix did not seek the timeless ideal form and precise sleek finish of Ingres's

painting, nor did he employ the heroic proportions of Rubens's figures. The sense of immediate, everyday reality in Delacroix's treatment of literary themes comes in part from his use of ordinary human proportions, like those of the people in the paintings of Rembrandt. It is not surprising that Delacroix's painting is often described as emotional and that of Ingres as intellectual; yet Delacroix's *Journals* indicate that he had a calculating nature, while Ingres's emotional nature was well known. The apparent freedom and spontaneity of Delacroix's canvases were achieved with deliberation and method. He learned much from the dynamic compositions of his fellow student Théodore Géricault and from the English painter Constable, who often placed colors side by side rather than blending them smoothly together. Delacroix's use of complementary colors to obtain liveliness within shadow areas forecasts the practices of the Impressionists. In spite of official opposition to his work, Delacroix received a number of important mural commissions and was finally granted membership in the Academy in 1857.

HONORÉ DAUMIER (Paris, 1808–79).   Daumier's keen powers of observation and his remarkable ability as a draftsman compensated for his lack of formal training. He earned a meager living as a cartoonist, using woodcuts for book illustrations and lithography for political journals like *La Caricature* and *Le Charivari*. The bourgeoisie, the law courts, and the government all provided material for Daumier, but his main protests were against the shortcomings of human nature on all social levels. His work ranges from brutal caricature to gentle humor and warm appreciation of life (Fig. 17-15). Daumier was essentially an optimist endowed with the grace of liking people in spite of their failings. Unlike Goya, he was realistic without being bitter. Daumier's oil paintings were relatively unknown until his first exhibition, which was in 1878, the year before his death. While the prints rely on line reduced to its most essential and expressive gesture, the paintings depend on starkly simple masses modeled in strong chiaroscuro. *The Third-Class Carriage* (Fig. 17-16) retains the sensitive line characteristic of his lithography; yet the use of light and mass is typical of his oils.

GUSTAVE COURBET (France, 1819–77).   While various aspects of realism are basic to the art of

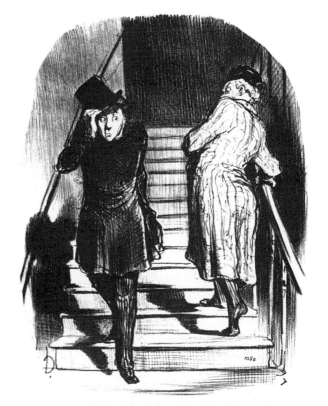

17–15 HONORÉ DAUMIER, *Behind in the Rent,* (1847). Lithograph, $10\frac{1}{8}'' \times 7\frac{1}{2}''$. Courtesy of the Boston Public Library, Print Department.

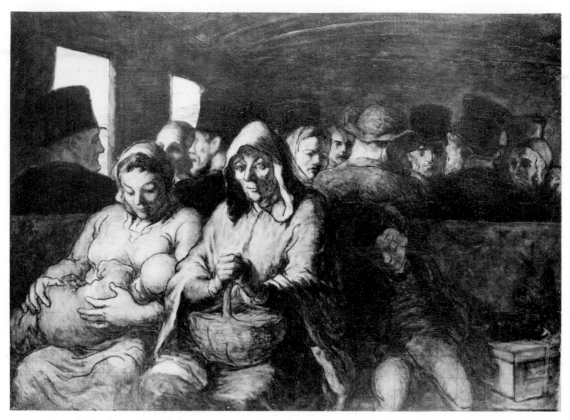

17–16   HONORÉ DAUMIER,   *The Third-Class Carriage,* (*c.* 1865). Oil on canvas, 25¾″ × 35½″.   The Metropolitan Museum of Art, Bequest of Mrs. H. O. Havemeyer, 1929. The H. O. Havemeyer Collection.

Goya and of Daumier, the artist who chose the term *Realism* for his battle standard was Courbet. He came from a farm to Paris and had several of his early works accepted by the Salon. His notoriety and his leadership in French painting began with the Salon of 1850, where his *Rock Breakers* (Fig. 17-17) and *Funeral at Ornans* (Louvre, Paris) were attacked as unartistic, crude, and socialistic. His early works had been admitted to the Salon because their moody chiaroscuro fitted the now acceptable qualities of much Romantic painting. His mature work stresses the physical reality of the everyday world and the artist's enjoyment of paint textures. Neither the polite veil of the acceptable ideal form of Ingres nor the exotic dramatic subject matter of Delacroix appealed to Courbet, who preferred subjects from his own experience and painted them with an obvious enjoyment of the texture of the paint itself, which he applied with brush and palette knife. The epithet "socialistic" came partly from the combination of style and subject that made *The Rock Breakers* look like ragged workers doing a miserable task—the wrong kind of content for a bourgeoisie still frightened by the socialist uprising that occurred after

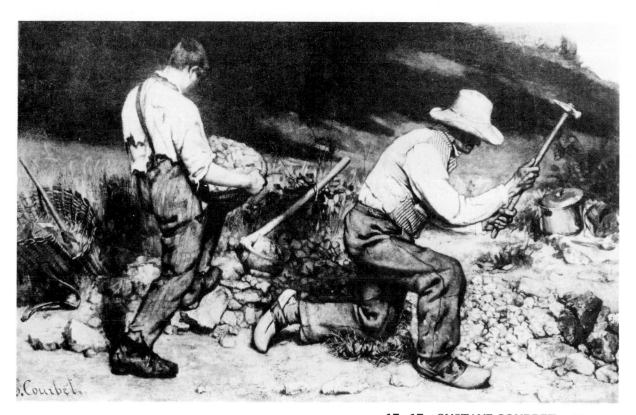

17–17 GUSTAVE COURBET, *The Rock Breakers,* (1849). Formerly in the Staatliche Kunstsammlungen, Dresden (painting lost during the Second World War).

the Revolution of 1848—and partly from the perennial tendency of some critics to ascribe any deviation from conventional standards in the arts to the latest unpopular political movement. Courbet was adopted as a standard-bearer by the socialist philosopher Proudhon, but his painting continued to be a fresh appreciation of the people and the landscape around him. During the International Expositions of 1855 and 1867 in Paris, Courbet built his own pavilions of Realism and held private showings of his work, thus helping to establish the artist's right to have privately organized exhibitions.

ÉDOUARD MANET (France, 1832–83).   The most shocking painting in the Salon des Refusés of 1863 was the *Luncheon on the Grass (Déjeuner sur l'Herbe)* (Fig. 17-18) by Manet. Earlier work by the painter had been accepted; Manet had come from a wealthy family and had studied under the academic painter Couture. He had even won an honorable mention in the Salon of 1861. Neither the subject nor the style of the *Luncheon on the Grass* was considered proper by the public or by many critics. Manet had taken the basic idea from Giorgione (Plate 9) and had borrowed the poses of the

17–18 ÉDOUARD
MANET,   *Luncheon on
the Grass (Déjeuner sur
l'Herbe),* (1863). Oil on
canvas, approx. 7′ × 9′.
Musée d'Orsay, Paris.

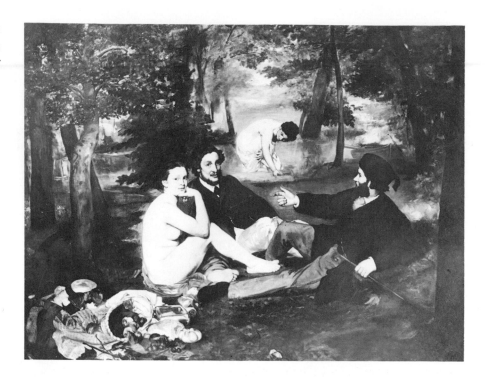

17–19 ÉDOUARD MANET,   *The Bar at the Folies-Bergère,* (1881–82). Oil on canvas, 37″ × 51″.
Courtauld Institute Galleries, London (Courtauld Collection).

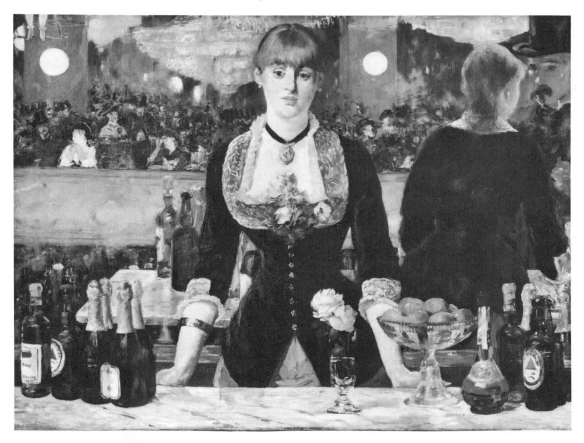

main figure group from an engraving of a Raphael painting of the *Judgment of Paris*, but he had omitted the mythological context and shown a nude woman in the company of two well-dressed contemporary Frenchmen. Further, he reduced the forms to large simple areas of color and value; few highlights or shadows break up the shapes. The brushwork is bold and rejoices in the texture of the paint. Frans Hals and Rembrandt, not to mention Delacroix, had used bold brushwork, but without such drastic simplification of form. After 1874, Manet's style changed; the large forms were broken more and more into small areas of bright color, and he increasingly depicted outdoor scenes and effects of light. His late work is represented by *The Bar at the Folies-Bergère* (Fig. 17-19). Here the intensity of vision is different from that in the early work. The shimmering light and color partially fuse the forms and suggest a momentary glimpse during an ebb and flow of constant change. Manet owed this vision to the young Impressionists.

EDGAR DEGAS (France, 1834–1917).   Manet's friend Degas also came from a family of means. Degas admired Delacroix but idolized Ingres and studied under one of Ingres's pupils. Line was the most natural medium of expression for Degas, but he was not interested in adopting the ideal forms of Neoclassicism. He found his favorite subjects in the streets of Paris, the cafes, races, theaters, and women's boudoirs. The *Foyer de la Danse* (Fig. 17-20) is typical of Degas's unconventional composition and reflects the influence of Japanese prints. An irregular, diamond-shaped spatial disposition is made by the dancer on the far left, the background dancers, the group around the ballet master, and the foreground chair. Architecture supports the figure arrangement through the placement of the arch, the corner of the room, the open door on the left, and the practice bar. The center of the composition contains only the psychological tension between the ballet master's group and the dancer receiving his correction. Such focus of attention helps the lone figure on the

17–20 EDGAR DEGAS, *Foyer de la Danse,* (1872). 12½″ × 18⅛″. Camando Collection, Louvre, Paris.

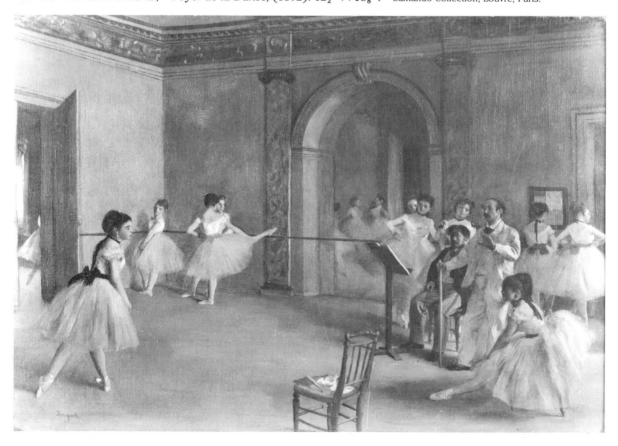

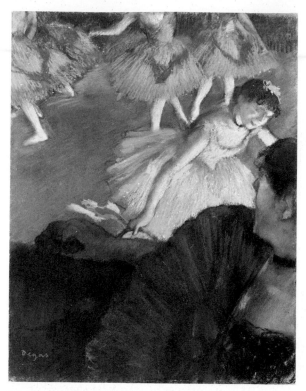

17–21   EDGAR DEGAS, *Ballerina and Lady with a Fan,* (*c.* 1885). Pastel on paper, 26″ × 20″.
John G. Johnson Collection, Philadelphia.

left counterbalance the greater weight of objects on the right. Unlike Manet, Degas often chose to depict the marginal event, the wings of the stage, as though the essential meaning could best be seen in those watching or waiting to perform. It is this "keyhole" vision, inspired partly by Japanese prints, that gives the impression of a momentary glimpse in Degas's particular kind of Impressionism, which differed sharply from that of the Impressionist leader Claude Monet. Degas did not subscribe to the soft form and vague edges in Monet's work until late in his career. While Monet saw human forms merely as objects reflecting light and color, Degas showed strong interest in the character of individuals. In his later work, Degas abandoned oil for pastels; soft light and glowing, broken colors are combined with firm anatomical structure and the softened but ever-present contour (Plate 19 and Fig. 17-21). His relatively traditional use of line enabled Degas to exhibit frequently at the Salon. Although he disliked the term "Impressionism," he participated in most of the eight Impressionist exhibits. Degas modeled wax and clay statuettes of dancers and horses, many of which have expressive poses and rough surfaces that produce multiple highlights, making the sculptures comparable to some of his drawings and paintings.

JAMES MCNEILL WHISTLER (United States and England, 1834–1903).   Whistler's controversial work made him a forerunner of twentieth-century abstraction. Influenced by Japanese art, he simplified shapes, using diffuse light and delicate, almost monochromatic gradations to create art that seems to respect the flat surface of the canvas while suggesting depth, atmospheric effects, and a finely tuned sensitivity to visual harmonies. Musical terms in his titles encourage us to look for such harmonies instead of factual documentation or narration. Compositions came from the Thames River (Fig. 17-22), its harbors, from the coast and sea, from French towns, Venice, and from occasional portraiture. His etchings sold more readily than his paintings, yet critics found all of his work "unfinished." After premixing colors for hours, Whistler did a painting quickly in a few strokes, scraping off, if necessary, and repainting until an effect of effortlessness was achieved. Only in the

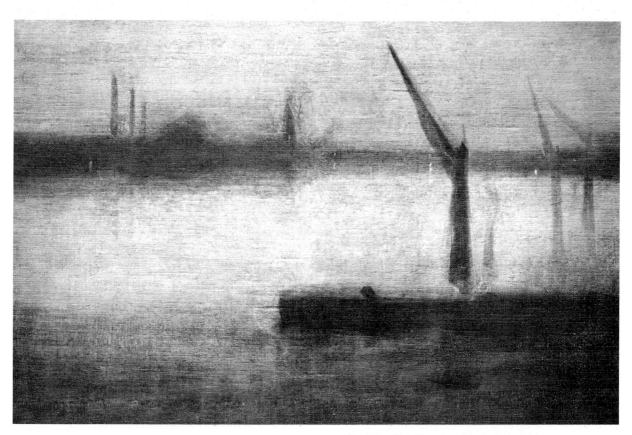

17–22 JAMES MCNEILL WHISTLER, *Nocturn-Blue and Silver-Battersea Reach,* (1870s). Oil on canvas, 19⅝″ × 30⅛″. Courtesy of the Freer Gallery of Art, Smithsonian Institution, Washington, D.C.

1890s was Whistler financially secure. Solo exhibitions and awards increased, and the products of his barbed tongue and lethal wit were published. Although he played the role of self-confident, eccentric genius, Whistler was highly self-critical and destroyed many of his pieces.

WINSLOW HOMER (United States, 1836–1910). Homer's early work in magazine illustration emphasized bold massing of values and incisive characterization. He made a sensational debut as an oil painter with Civil War subjects. His paintings of genre scenes show a keen interest in outdoor light and atmospheric effects. He turned increasingly to elemental subjects of man and nature: the lone hunter, the struggle of boats in rapids, and the violence of the sea. His watercolors range in technique from broad sweeping brush strokes with sparkling transparent washes to small areas of overlapping washes and careful detail. Both in watercolors and in oils Homer subordinated detail to large areas of contrasting values that strengthen the visual impact of the composition. This aspect of his style is exemplified in *The Artist's Studio in*

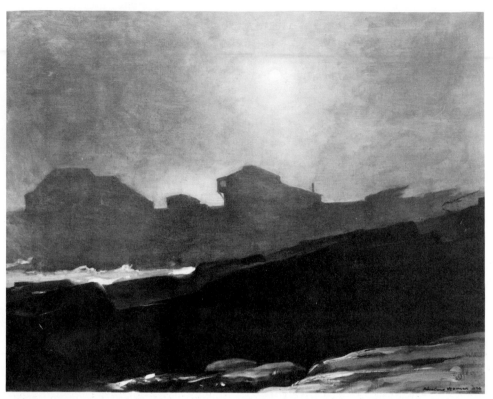

17–23   WINSLOW HOMER,   *The Artist's Studio in
an Afternoon Fog,* (1894).   Memorial Art Gallery of the
University of Rochester, R. T. Miller Fund.

an Afternoon Fog (Fig. 17-23), an oil study in
browns that has satisfying variations in its simple
proportions. Certain angles in the roofs echo the
powerful middle-ground diagonal plane, which
seems to express the conflict of land and sea; this
darkest area is set against the small patch of water
and foam that receives the brightest highlights in
the painting and outshines the veiled sun. Homer's
method of working was apparently instinctive, for
he denied that he modified nature for the sake
of art.

PAUL CÉZANNE (France, 1839–1906).   One of the
most celebrated of the Post-Impressionist painters
was Cézanne, who came from Aix-en-Provence to
Paris and studied at the Académie Suisse, an unusual institution that provided models and working space but no instruction. The young artist admired Delacroix and Courbet but also several of
the academic painters. Cézanne's early work is
characterized by dark values, bold awkward
forms, and thick paint handled in such a way as to
suggest powerful feelings. In the 1870s, he turned
to Impressionist painting and exhibited the *House
of the Hanged Man* (Fig. 17-24) in the first Impres-

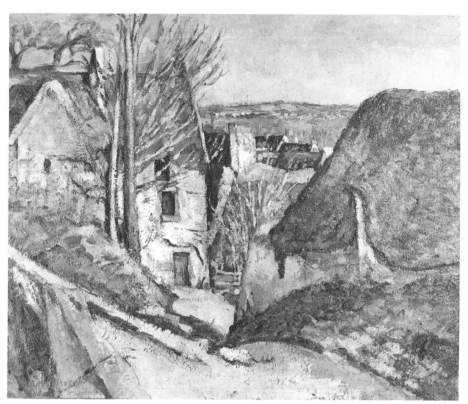

17–24 PAUL CÉZANNE, *The House of the Hanged Man,* (1873–74). Oil on canvas, 22¼″ × 26¾″. Louvre, Paris.

sionist show in 1874. He came to feel, however, that Impressionism sacrificed too much solidity and structure, and in the 1880s he changed to the style for which he is well known today. Cézanne's portraits, still lifes, and landscapes all reduce objects to basic planes and masses that are brought into subtle complementary relationships on the canvas. The *Mt. Ste.-Victoire from Bibémus Quarry* (Plate 22 and Fig. 17-25) is typical in the small groups of parallel brush strokes that suggest massive form in mountain, in foliage, and even in sky. Lost-and-found outlines define the masses but allow them to flow into each other at various points, and the planes and angles of the forms are echoed and modulated throughout the canvas. All the forms acquire a structural unity—a family resemblance—in this way. Roundness is achieved not only with light and shadow but also with advancing and receding colors. Yet all forms are obviously constructed with paint, and there is a paradoxical suggestion of mass and depth and at the same time of a flat painted surface. In contrast to Impressionist painting, Cézanne's mature work emphasizes a static structure that largely excludes motion or the changing effects of light and

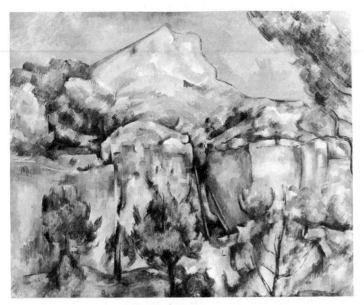

17–25   PAUL CÉZANNE,   *Mt. Ste.-Victoire from Bibémus Quarry,* (*c.* 1898). Oil on canvas, 25½″ × 32″. The Baltimore Museum of Art: The Cone Collection, formed by Dr. Claribel Cone and Miss Etta Cone of Baltimore, Maryland.

weather. His link with the past can be found in the art of Poussin. Cézanne's importance for the future was summed up in his advice to a young painter to paint nature in terms of the cylinder, the sphere, and the cone — that is, the basic geometric forms. This is generally what was done in Cubist art, which began in 1907, a year after Cézanne's death and the same year as his first large retrospective exhibition.

ODILON REDON (France, 1840–1916).   Redon came from Bordeaux to Paris in 1864. He devoted much of his time to charcoal drawings and lithograph albums, but he also worked in oils and pastels. His titles, referring to dreams, the works of Edgar Allan Poe and Goya, the Temptation of St. Anthony, and Baudelaire's *Fleurs du Mal,* indicate his concern with fantasy. *The Cyclops* (Plate 25 and Fig. 17-26) reveals a world of iridescent color and floating forms. His monsters, spiders, and ghostly faces seem more playful or melancholy than frightening. Many of his flower paintings are simply delicate, ethereal bouquets; others contain apparitions of faces. His gentle, mysterious work was discovered by the French Symbolist writers in the 1880s, and Redon was labeled a Symbolist and admired by the painters known as the *Nabis* (see p. 299). Redon's art prefigured surrealism.

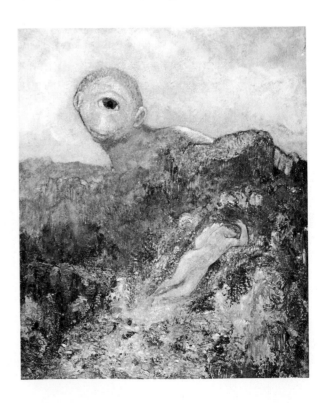

17–26   ODILON REDON,   *The Cyclops,* (1900–1905). Oil on panel, 25¼″ × 20″.   Collection: Rijksmuseum Kröller-Müller, Otterlo, Holland.

CLAUDE MONET (France, 1840–1926).   Monet came from Le Havre to Paris and studied at the Académie Suisse and in the studio of the academic painter Gleyre, where he met Renoir and several other young men who would later participate in the Impressionist movement. In Le Havre, Monet early acquired a love of painting outdoors, partly through the example of his older friends Eugène Boudin and Johan Jongkind. His early style was bold in color and vigorous in brushwork. Large unbroken areas recall the art of Manet; yet the Salons of 1865 and 1866 accepted some seascapes and a portrait by Monet and praised him as a "naturalist." However, as he went further in his studies of the effects of light on color and as his forms became less clearly defined, Monet was continually rejected by juries. In 1874, his *Impression: Sunrise,* a painting similar to that in Figure 17-27, caused the label "Impressionism" to be attached to the exhibition by critics. The smoldering light of the rising sun coming through mist and shimmering on the surface of the water is rendered in loose brush strokes and vague forms, a technique meant to distill the total visual impression of a particular moment. For many critics this appeared to be sheer incompetence. Seeking more subtle distinctions in changing light and color, Monet sometimes worked in series, painting the same subject — a haystack, a railway station, or the Cathedral of Rouen — in various kinds of light. *Rouen Cathedral* (Plate 20 and Fig. 17-28) employs the complementary colors blue and orange in separate brush strokes to create a vibrating miragelike image that sacrifices solid form for intensity of visual experience. The Impressionist process of applying colors separately in order to exploit their effects on each other is called the technique of *broken color.* It suggests a world in constant motion. By the 1890s, Monet's series paintings had met with considerable success; his approach could be appreciated as scientific, although scientific interest is not a satisfactory explanation of his work. There is an intensification or exaggeration of natural color and light effects — typified in Plate 20 — that comes from the artist's sensuous enjoyment of such phenomena. The subject of Monet's last great series, spread over the latter years of his life, was a pond with water lilies. Here the imaginative quality of his art grew more evident, and the paintings became increasingly abstract.

AUGUSTE RENOIR (France, 1841–1919).   Renoir, Monet's friend and fellow Impressionist, began as an apprentice to a porcelain decorator and then he also studied with the academic painter Gleyre.

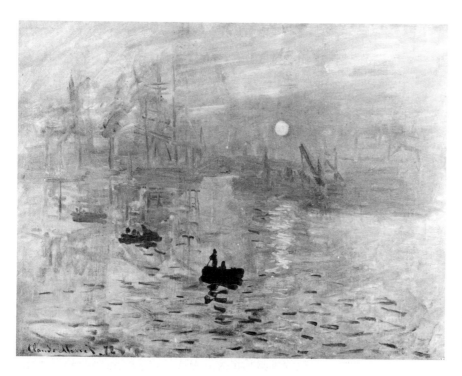

17–27
CLAUDE MONET,
Impression: Sunrise,
(1872). Oil on canvas,
19⅝″ × 25½″. Musée
Marmottan (Collection Donop de
Monchy), Paris.

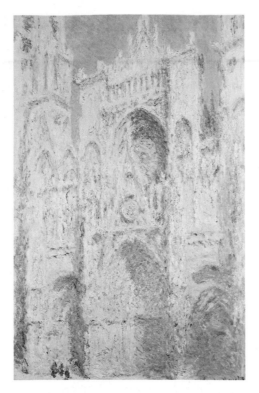

17–28   CLAUDE MONET,   *Rouen Cathedral,* (1894). Oil on canvas, approx. 39¼″ × 25⅞″.   National Gallery of Art, Washington, D.C. Chester Dale Collection, 1962.

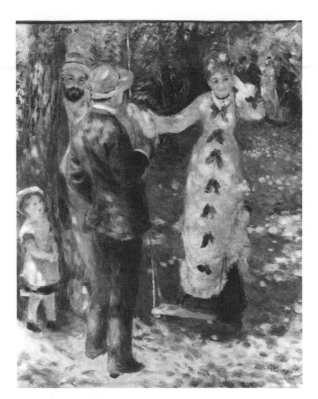

17–29   AUGUSTE RENOIR,   *The Swing,* (1876). Oil on canvas, 35¾″ × 28″.   Louvre, Paris.

17–30   AUGUSTE RENOIR,   *Little Blue Nude,* (*c.* 1880). Oil on canvas, 18¼″ × 15⅛″.   Albright-Knox Art Gallery, Buffalo. Consolidated Purchase Funds, 1941.

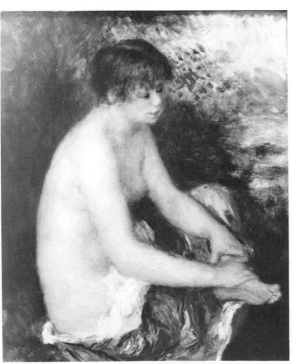

His early work consists of tightly detailed landscapes and earthy, solidly painted nudes that show the influence of Courbet. The Salon accepted Renoir in the 1860s and occasionally thereafter. Like Monet, he turned increasingly to broken color and the evanescent effects of light (Fig. 17-29). He managed to obtain a number of portrait commissions, and these were usually executed with more detail than his other subjects. During his travels in the 1880s, his encounter with Raphael's paintings in Italy led him to return temporarily to sharper outlines and curved forms in flowing, rhythmical relationships. In the work that followed, the interest in curving forms remained, but contours were softened. Woman is the main subject, and Renoir gave her his personal concept of ideal form: soft masses of flesh in delicate, luminous colors. In *Little Blue Nude* (Plate 24 and Fig. 17-30), color and light suggest full volumes while paradoxically dissolving solid form. The impersonal treatment of the human figure in earlier work here gives way to a mystical reverence for woman as a symbol for the fecundity and glory of nature.

MARY CASSATT (United States and France, 1844–1926).   Family affluence enabled Mary Cassatt to study first at the Pennsylvania Academy of Art and then independently in France, where she spent most of her life. Her paintings won acceptance at the official salons in Paris from 1872 through 1876. Then she stopped submitting work to the salons and, at the invitation of Degas, joined the Impressionists. She was the second woman artist to do so, having been preceded by Berthe Morisot. Degas was her lifelong friend and adviser. She shared the Impressionist enthusiasm for the light and color of an ephemeral moment. Her oils and pastels often juxtaposed vibrating colors in loose strokes, but like Degas, she also enjoyed the rhythmic flow of line. Her subjects were family and friends, often depicted in interiors, as part of the calm, orderly, and socially proper world of her daily existence. Cassatt was more interested in character study and human relationships than were most of the Impressionists; she was especially held by the theme of mother and child (Plate 23 and Fig. 17-31). Her interest in printmaking developed after study in Parma in 1871. She often combined soft-ground etching, drypoint, and aquatint. The climax of her printmaking, in 1891, is a set of ten color intaglios inspired by Japanese woodcuts. Cassatt painted a mural for the Women's Building at the World's Fair in Chicago in 1893. While she exhibited in the United States, her career and reputation developed in France. It was there that she received, in 1904, the Legion of Honor.

THOMAS EAKINS (United States, 1844–1916). Eakins first studied at the Pennsylvania Academy of Fine Arts in Philadelphia and then went to Paris in 1866, right after the stormy Salon des Refusés and during Manet's notoriety. Eakins studied with the French academic painter Jean L. Gérôme, however, and his art shows little influence of the young French painters of the day. He seems to have been more sympathetic to the art of Velázquez and Ribera, which he saw during a trip to Spain. Upon his return, Eakins settled in Philadelphia and spent the rest of his career painting the people and the life around him. His major interests were the unique character of a human face, the anatomical structure of the body, and the abundance of textures and details in all things. *The Agnew Clinic* (Fig. 17-32) is typical of his detailed

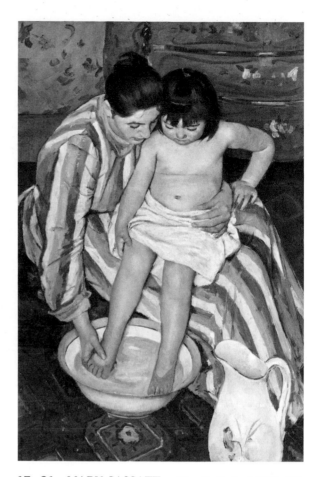

17–31 MARY CASSATT, *The Bath,* (*c.* 1892). Oil on canvas, 39″ × 26″. Collection of The Art Institute of Chicago.

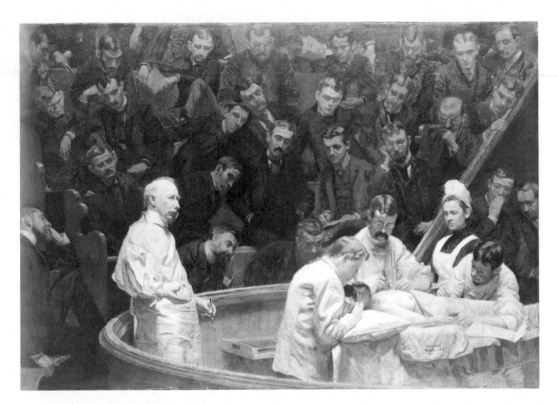

17–32 THOMAS EAKINS, *The Agnew Clinic,* (1889). Oil on canvas, 6′2″ × 10′10″. Courtesy of the University of Pennsylvania Collection, Medical School.

observation of contemporary life. The dramatic focus in the painting stems from sharp tonal contrasts, actual and suggested diagonal forces in the background, the curved rail, and the separated and distinctive figure of the speaker.

PAUL GAUGUIN (France, 1848–1903).   As a young man, Gauguin developed a promising career in a brokerage firm, collected Impressionist paintings, and painted as a hobby. This hobby eventually led him to leave his secure situation and seek a career as a full-time painter. Partly to live less expensively and partly because he was fascinated by primitive societies, he went to Brittany (first to Pont-Aven and then to Le Pouldu). His early work there was Impressionistic; but under the influence of Cézanne, Manet, Japanese prints, and the young painter Bernard's use of flat shapes, Gauguin slowly turned away from broken color and began to use outlines around areas of closely modulated color. The color areas became more closed, suggesting flat textile patterns, and color contrasts became bolder. Several young men joined Gauguin in Brittany and accepted him as their leader. These Pont-Aven artists chose the word *synthesism* to describe their painting. Later the term *symbolist-synthesist* was used frequently as Gauguin became acquainted with some of the Symbolist writers. Two of the Pont-Aven painters joined the *Nabis* (Hebrew for *prophets*), a group that derived some of its symbolism from the mysticism of Theosophy, but Gauguin maintained an independent attitude. His symbolism expresses the mystery and the imaginative life of primitive peoples. In 1891 he traveled to Tahiti, where he produced such works as *The Moon and the Earth* (Fig. 17-33) and *The Spirit of the Dead Watching* (Plate 27 and Fig. 17-34). In the latter work resonant hues of yellows, purples, oranges, and blues join the flat patterns that set off the ponderous, solid body of the frightened girl lying on a bed. The spirits of the dead, represented by small flashes of light, and a ghost, represented by a woman in profile, watch from above and behind. Gauguin's sculptures and woodcuts from this period were influential in early twentieth-century expressionistic art. Gauguin returned to Paris for a short time (1893–95) and rapidly spent a small inheritance. He was soon back in Tahiti, where his health began to fail. His last two years were spent in the Marquesas Islands.

VINCENT VAN GOGH (Holland and France, 1853–90).   Van Gogh was a Dutchman, but most of his painting was done in France during the last four

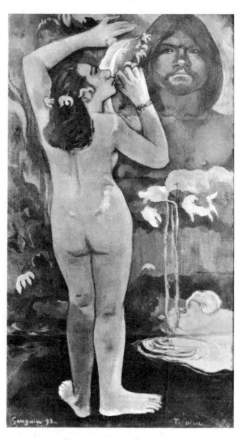

17-33 PAUL GAUGUIN, *The Moon and the Earth,* (1893). Oil on burlap, 45″ × 24½″.   Collection, the Museum of Modern Art, New York, Lillie P. Bliss Collection.

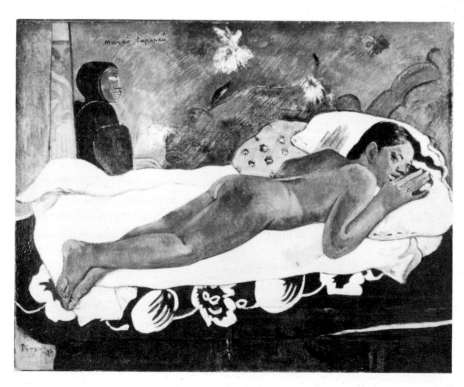

17-34 PAUL GAUGUIN, *The Spirit of the Dead Watching,* (1892). Oil on canvas, 28¾″ × 36¼″. Albright-Knox Art Gallery, Buffalo. A. Conger Goodyear Collection, 1965.

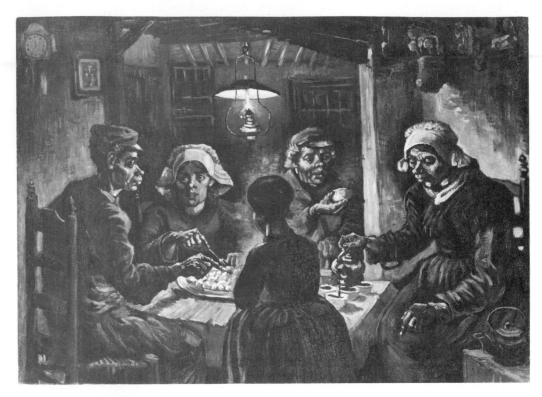

17–35 VINCENT VAN GOGH, *The Potato Eaters,* (1885). Oil on canvas, 32¼″ × 44⅞″. Collection National Museum Vincent Van Gogh, Amsterdam.

years of a short but intense life. After abortive attempts at working for art dealers (in The Hague, London, and Paris), studying theology, and preaching evangelism among coal miners, Van Gogh turned to painting in 1880. Millet, Daumier, and Rembrandt were the idols of his early period; in works like *The Potato Eaters* (Fig. 17-35), poverty-stricken workers are compassionately portrayed with heavy blunt forms and dark brownish color. In 1886, Van Gogh settled in Paris with his brother Theo. Study with the academic painter Cormon soon gave way to enthusiasm for the Impressionists. With the encouragement of Camille Pissarro, Van Gogh's colors became brighter and lighter, and he began to use broken color; yet his brush strokes have a writhing liveliness unlike those in most Impressionist work. While in Paris, Van Gogh became acquainted with Japanese prints, such as those shown in the background of his portrait of *Père Tanguy* (1887–88, Collection of Stavros Niarchos, Athens). In 1888, Van Gogh left Paris for Arles in southern France. His compositions began to employ more powerful colors, often clashing complementaries; thick paint textures that seem to be sculpted with the brush or the palette knife; and shapes whose abruptly changing

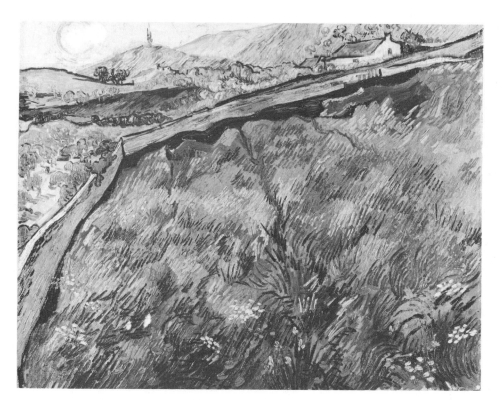

17-36 VINCENT VAN GOGH,
Enclosed Field, (1890). Oil on
canvas, $28\frac{1}{2}'' \times 36\frac{1}{4}''$.   Collection:
Rijksmuseum Kröller-Müller, Otterlo, Holland.

17-37 VINCENT VAN GOGH,   *Portrait of Dr.
Gachet,* (1890). Oil on canvas, $26'' \times 22\frac{1}{2}''$.   Private
collection, U.S.A.

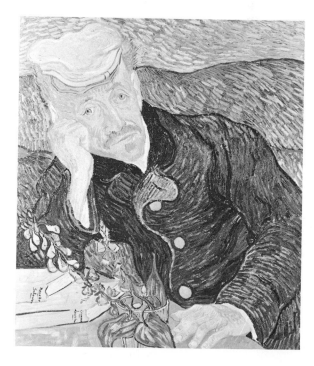

contours express a convulsive energy. Van Gogh was subject to occasional epileptoid seizures, and these led to a year's residence in the asylum at Saint-Rémy. The *Enclosed Field* (Plate 26 and Fig. 17-36) is a work typical of this period in its glowing colors and in the dancing, twitching rhythm that activates earth and sky. Paint is applied in short, choppy strokes that seem to sculpt edges and surfaces. From Saint-Rémy, Van Gogh went to Auvers, near Paris, to receive treatment from Dr. Gachet (Fig. 17-37), a friend of Pissarro, and it was at Auvers that he committed suicide. His imaginative use of color, his expressive distortion of natural forms, and the emotional force of his art made him an important source for many trends in twentieth-century painting, particularly Fauvism and Expressionism. His letters to his brother Theo are, with Delacroix's journal, among the richest documents of modern art.

GEORGES SEURAT (France, 1859–91).   The last Impressionist exhibition, in 1886, was marked by dissension; Monet and Renoir were both absent. A central problem was the new approach represented by Seurat and his followers. Their works were displayed in a separate room and their

17-38 GEORGES SEURAT, *Sunday Afternoon on the Island of La Grande Jatte,* (1884–86). Oil on canvas, approx. 8'9" × 10'. Collection of The Art Institute of Chicago, Helen Birch Bartlett Memorial Collection.

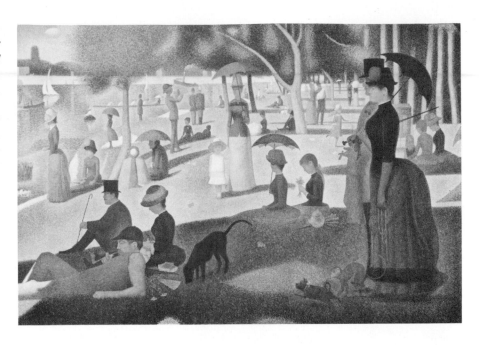

17-39 GEORGES SEURAT, detail showing pointillism from *Sunday Afternoon on the Island of La Grande Jatte,* (1884–86). Oil on canvas. Collection of The Art Institute of Chicago.

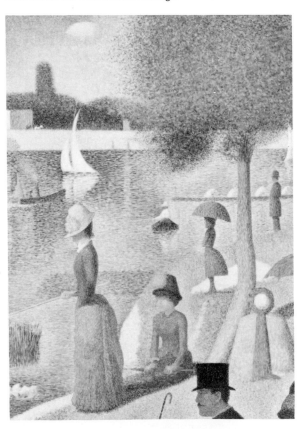

style, generally subsumed under the label of Post-Impressionism, came to be called *Neo-Impressionism.* The intensity of light and color in Impressionist work appealed to Seurat, but he felt —as did Cézanne— that mass and compositional structure had been unduly sacrificed; so he set out to systematize the broken color of Impressionism and to clarify its forms. On the basis of the color theories of Michel Chevreul and Charles Henry, Seurat applied colors in uniformly small dots in specific quantities to control particular effects. Seurat's paint-application technique was called *pointillism* and his use of systematically broken color was termed *divisionism.* The suggestion of constant change and movement found in much Impressionist work was replaced, in Seurat's painting, by more rigid organization and static form. In his *Sunday Afternoon on the Island of La Grande Jatte* (Plate 28 and Figs. 17-38 and 17-39) the shadows, trees, and figures form static horizontals and verticals; the clearly edged and simplified forms become standard rather than individual objects; and there is a quality of geometric order, of inflexible balance, and of calculated method. In 1884 Seurat became one of the founders of the *Salon des Indépendants,* which provided exhibition opportunities without jury selection and thereby answered one of the basic needs that had inspired the Impressionist exhibitions between 1874 and 1886.

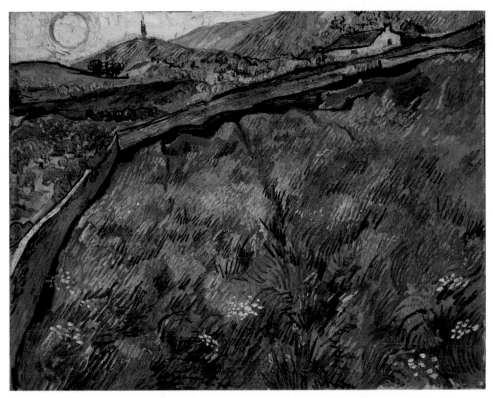

Plate 26

VINCENT VAN GOGH, *Enclosed Field,* (1890). Oil on canvas, 28½″ × 36¼″.
Collection: Rijksmuseum Kröller-Müller, Otterlo, Holland.

Plate 27

PAUL GAUGUIN, *The Spirit of the Dead Watching,* (1892). Oil on canvas, 28¾″ × 36¼″.
Albright-Knox Art Gallery, Buffalo. A. Conger Goodyear Collection, 1965.

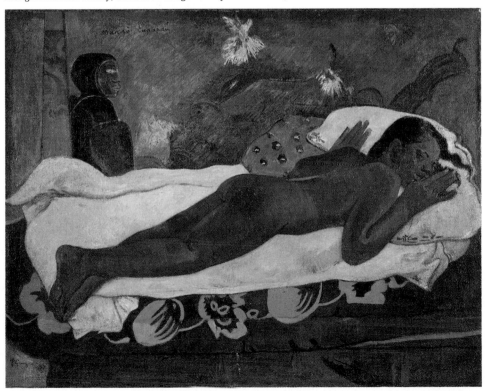

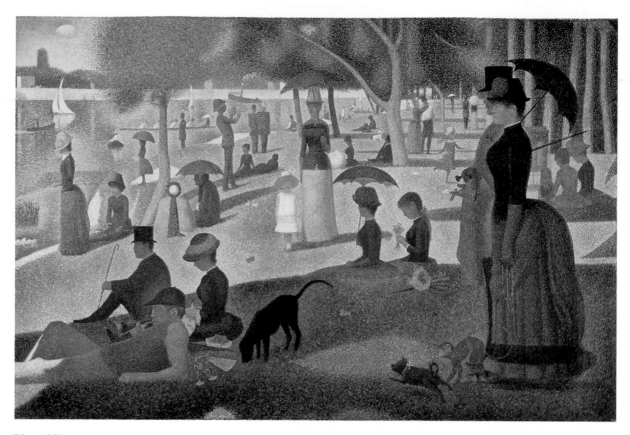

Plate 28

GEORGES SEURAT, *Sunday Afternoon on the Island of La Grande Jatte,* (1884–86). Oil on canvas, approx. 8′9″ × 10′.   Collection of The Art Institute of Chicago, Helen Birch Bartlett Memorial Collection.

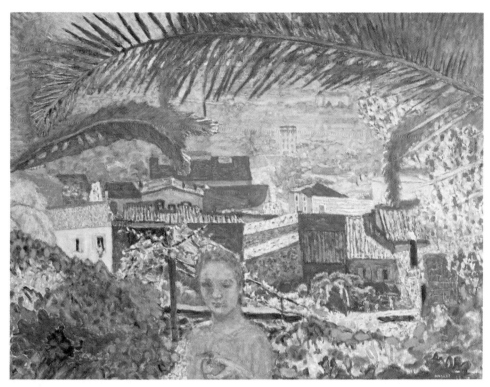

Plate 29

PIERRE BONNARD,   *The Palm,* (1926). Oil on canvas, 44″ × 57¼″.
The Phillips Collection, Washington, D.C.

Plate 30

EMILE NOLDE,   *Christ among the Children,* (1910). Oil on canvas, 34⅛″ × 41⅞″.
Collection, the Museum of Modern Art, New York. Gift of Dr. W. R. Valentiner.

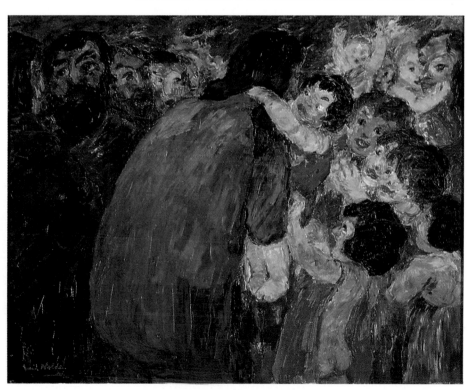

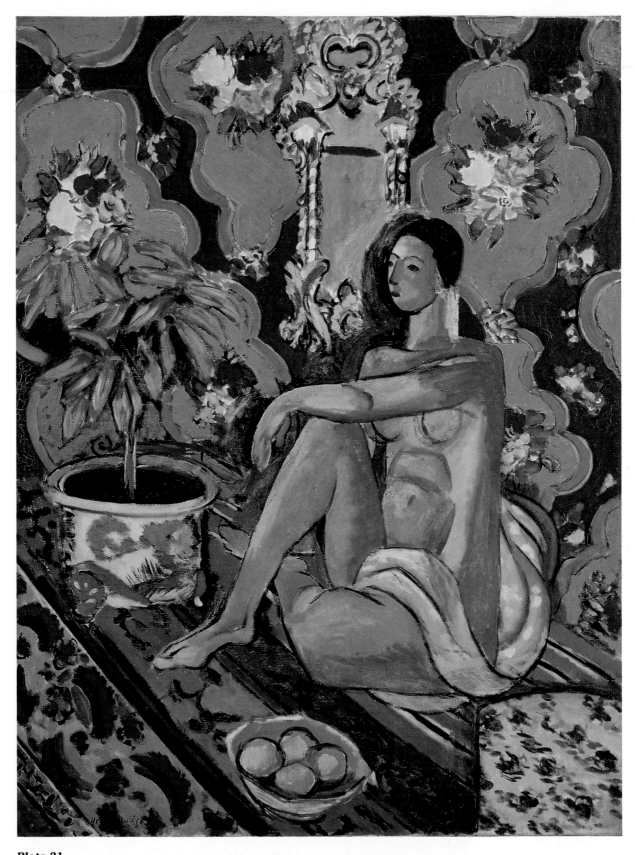

Plate 31

HENRI MATISSE, *Decorative Figure on an Ornamental Background,* (1927). Oil on canvas, approx. 48″ × 36″.
Musée National d'Art Moderne, Paris.

Plate 32

VASILY KANDINSKY, *Painting with White Form, No. 166,* (1913). Oil on canvas, 47" × 54⅜"
Collection, the Solomon R. Guggenheim Museum, New York.

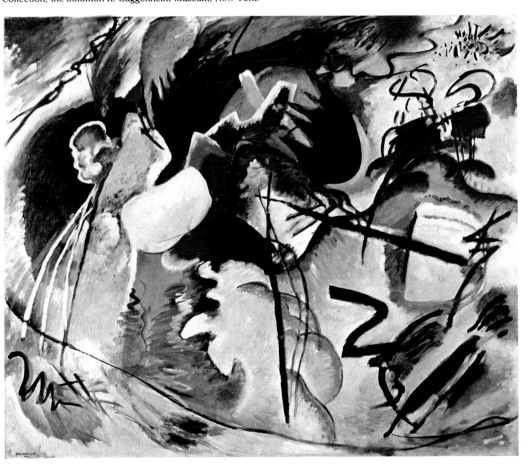

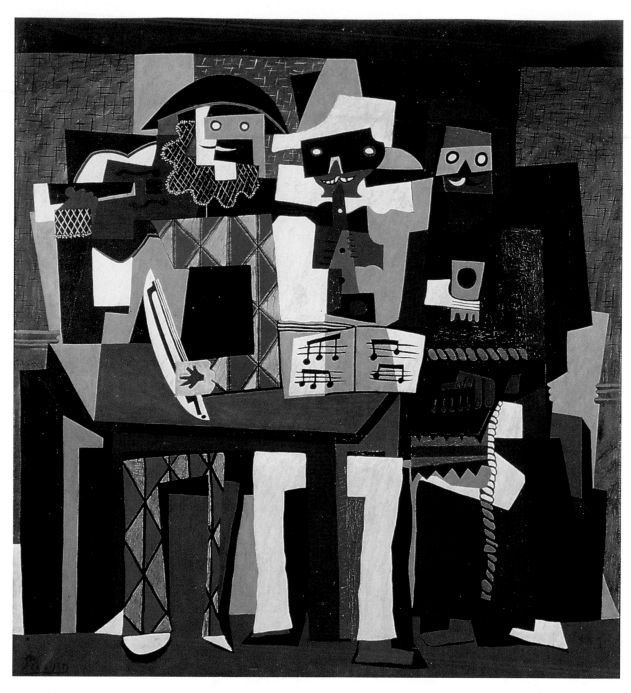

Plate 33

PABLO PICASSO, *Three Musicians*, (1921). Oil on canvas, 80″ × 74″.
The Philadelphia Museum of Art: the A. E. Gallatin Collection.

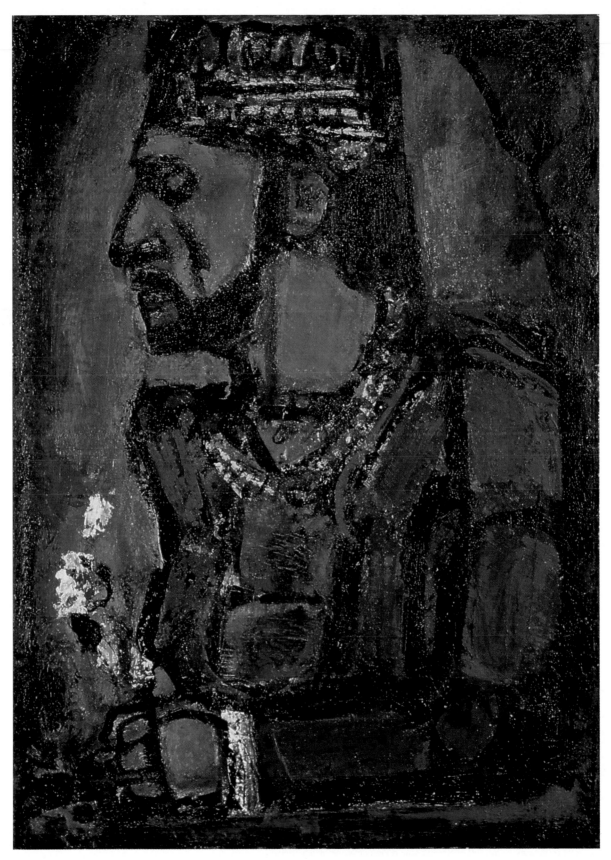

Plate 34

GEORGES ROUAULT, *The Old King,* (1916–38). Oil on canvas, approx. 30¼″ × 21¼″.
Collection, Museum of Art, Carnegie Institute, Pittsburgh. Museum Purchase: Patrons Art Fund, 1940.

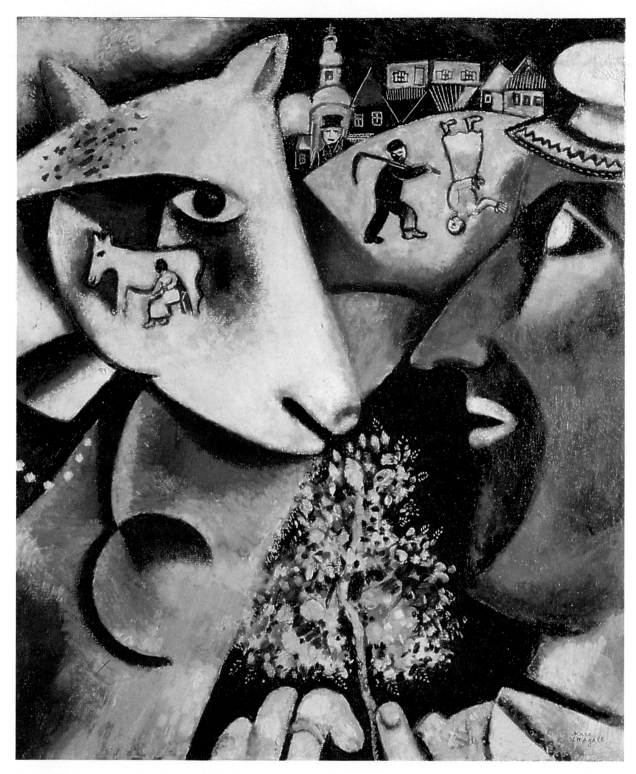

Plate 35

MARC CHAGALL, *I and My Village,* (1911). Oil on canvas, 21¾″ × 18¼″.
The Philadelphia Museum of Art. Gift of Mr. and Mrs. Rodolphe M. de Schauensee.

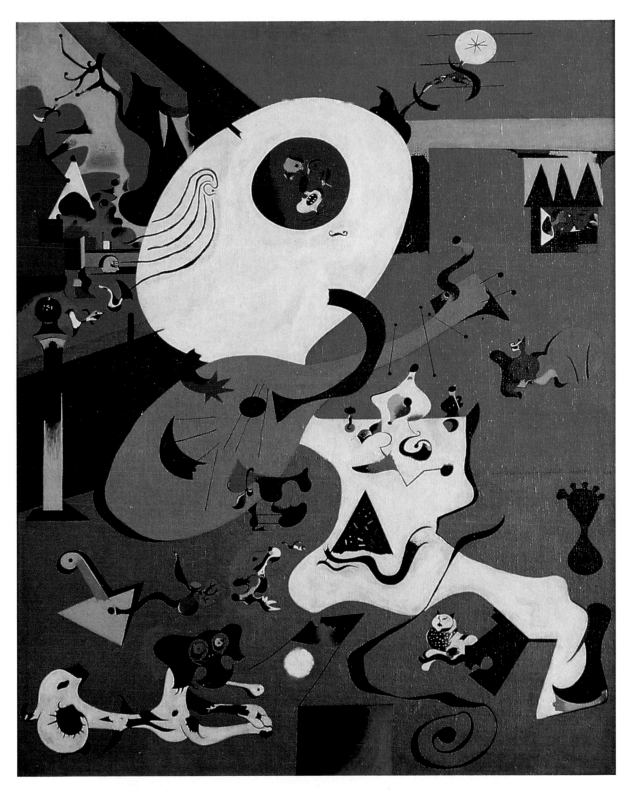

Plate 36

JOAN MIRÓ, *Dutch Interior, I,* (1928). Oil on canvas, 36⅛″ × 28¾″.
Collection, the Museum of Modern Art, New York. Mrs. Simon Guggenheim Fund.

Plate 37

RUFINO TAMAYO, *Woman in Grey,* (1959).
Oil on canvas, 76¾″ × 51″.
Collection, the Solomon R. Guggenheim Museum, New York

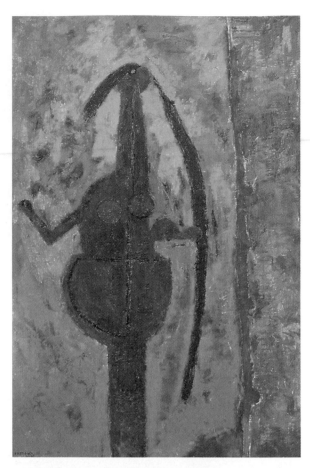

Plate 38

ARSHILE GORKY, *Agony,*
(1947). Oil on canvas, 40″ × 50½″.
Collection, the Museum of Modern Art, New York.
A. Conger Goodyear Fund.

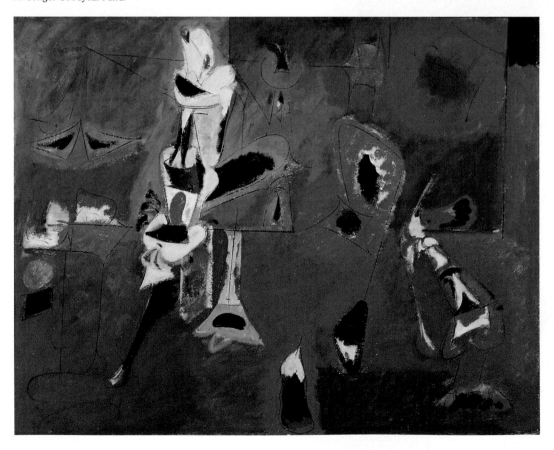

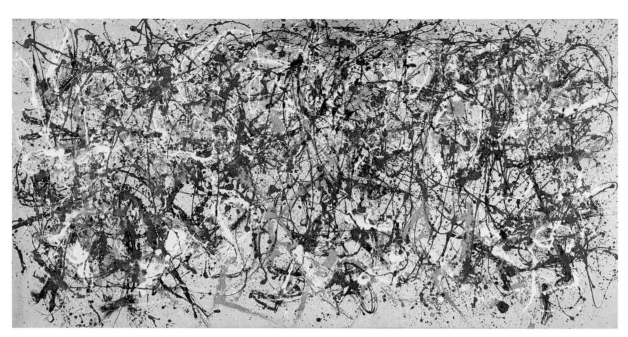

Plate 39

JACKSON POLLOCK, *Autumn Rhythm,* (1950). Oil on canvas, 105″ × 207″.
The Metropolitan Museum of Art. George A. Hearn Fund.

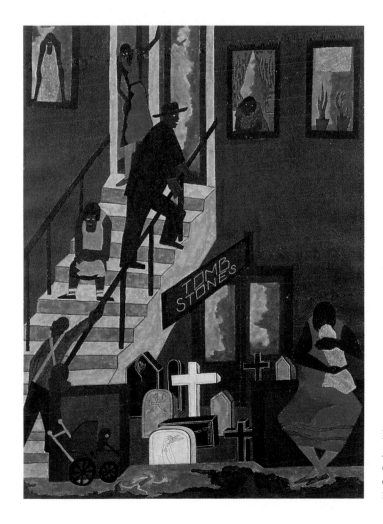

Plate 40

JACOB LAWRENCE, *Tombstones,* (1942)
Gouache, 28¾″ × 20½″.
Collection of the Whitney Museum of American Art.
Purchase.

Plate 41
HANS HOFMANN,
Bird Cage, Variation II, (1958).
Oil on canvas, 60″ × 48″.
Collection of Saul Z. and Amy S. Cohen,
Larchmont, New York.

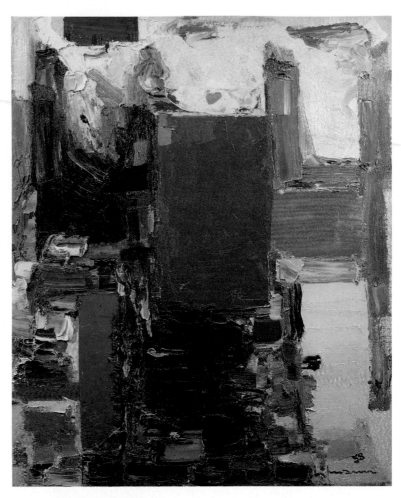

Plate 42

JOSEF ALBERS,
Homage to the Square: Apparition,
(1959). Oil on board, 47½″ × 47½″.
The Solomon R. Guggenheim Museum, New York.

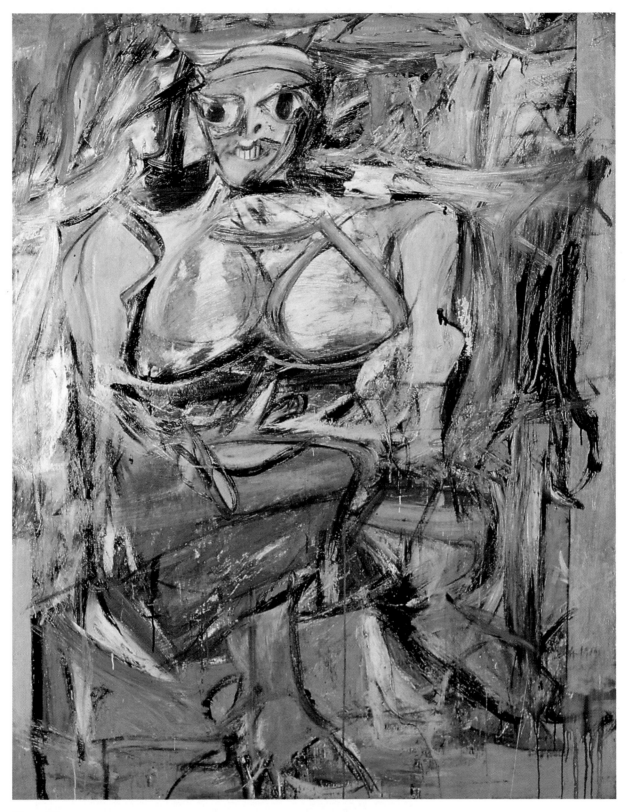

Plate 43
WILLEM DE KOONING, *Woman I,* (1950–52). Oil on canvas, 75⅞″ × 58″.
Collection, the Museum of Modern Art, New York. Purchase.

Plate 44
MARK ROTHKO,
Brown and Black on Plum,
(1958). Oil on canvas,
80″ × 82″.
Private collection, Switzerland.

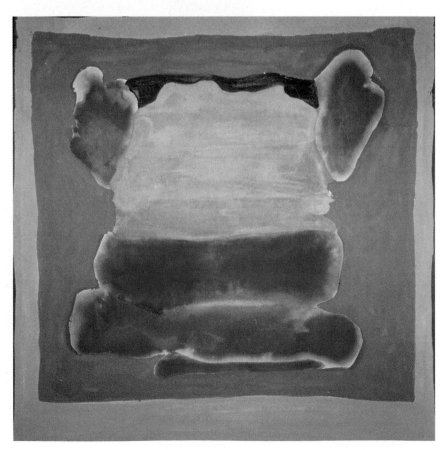

Plate 45
HELEN FRANKENTHALER,
Buddha's Court, (1964).
Acrylic paint on canvas,
98″ × 94″.
Mr. and Mrs. Robert K. Hoffman,
Dallas. Courtesy of the André
Emmerich Gallery.

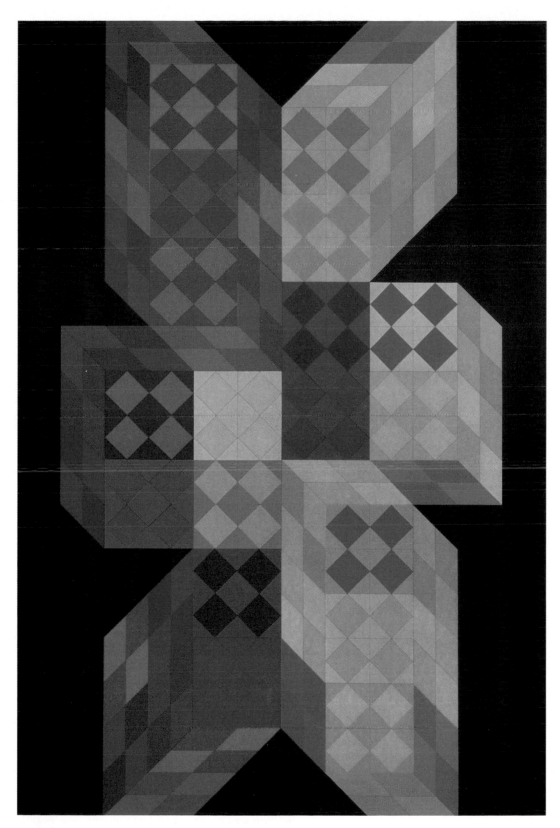

Plate 46
VICTOR VASARELY, *YMPO,* (1970). Acrylic on canvas, 67″ × 99½″.
Private collection.

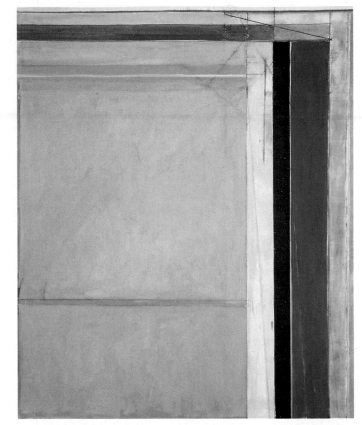

Plate 47
RICHARD DIEBENKORN,
Ocean Park #83, (1975).
Oil on canvas, 100″ × 81″.
In the collection of the Corcoran Gallery of Art. Museum purchase with the aid of funds from the National Endowment for the Arts, Washington, D.C., a federal agency, the William A. Clark Fund, and Margaret M. Hitchcock.

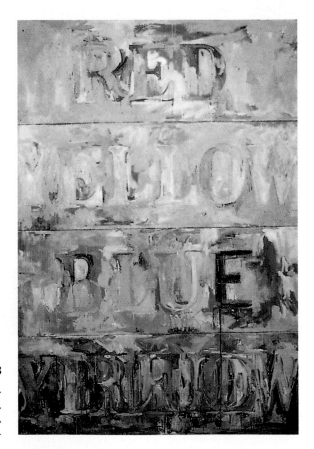

Plate 48
JASPER JOHNS,   *By the Sea,* (1961).
Encaustic on canvas, (4 panels), 72″ × 54½″.
Private collection. Photo courtesy of Leo Castelli Gallery, New York.

HENRY OSSAWA TANNER (United States and France, 1859–1937).   Tanner, a black American, chose France for the development of his career. Paris was a world center for art during his lifetime, and, as such, attracted artists from all nations. His training under Thomas Eakins in Philadelphia and his subsequent study in Paris gave him a thorough technical basis for the glazing of sonorous colors and dramatic value contrasts that mark much of his art. Throughout his career, Tanner suppressed details to heighten the expressive power of larger forms (Fig. 17-40). These forms often acquire special intensity through halation. Tanner was deeply religious, and his major successes came with Christian subjects. Beginning with an Honorable Mention in the Paris Salon of 1896 for his *Daniel in the Lion's Den*, his work gathered awards and praise in France and the United States. He was awarded membership in the Legion of Honor in 1923 and in 1927 was made a full academician of the National Academy of Design in New York. However, like many academically successful artists, Tanner was increasingly eclipsed by the waves of artistic revolutions in the twentieth century. In his late work, colors brightened and brushwork loosened, but this was still conservative to a public involved in the controversies over Fauvism, Cubism, or Surrealism.

JAMES ENSOR (Belgium, 1860–1949).   After studying at Ostend and Brussels, Ensor became a painter and printmaker; he worked with still life, landscape, marine, religious, and mythological subjects, ranging from everyday scenes to frightening grotesqueries involving men, animals, and monsters. His early art employed gentle lighting and subtle colors, although the paint was often applied vigorously with a palette knife. In the course of the 1880s, fantasy invaded his subject matter, and paint application became increasingly nervous and complex. *Masks Confronting Death* (Fig. 17-41) is typical in its combination of delicate color and grotesque subject. It recalls late Medieval prints depicting the Dance of Death. Ensor's etching *The Vengeance of the Hop Frog* (1898) combines cruelty with a Bosch-like imagination. In his most macabre works, Ensor mixed religious and scatological elements; yet at the same time, he continued to paint still life, landscape, and marine subjects like those of his early period. While some

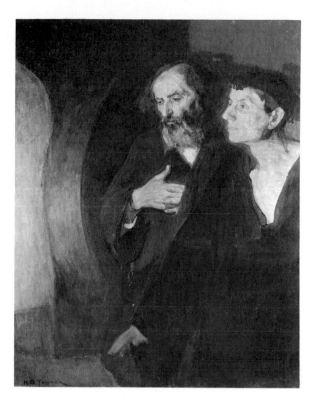

17-40   HENRY OSSAWA TANNER,   *Two Disciples at the Tomb*, (1906). Oil on canvas, 50½″ × 40½″.   Robert Alexander Waller Memorial Collection, Courtesy of The Art Institute of Chicago.

17-41   JAMES ENSOR,   *Masks Confronting Death*, (1888). Oil on canvas, 32″ × 39½″.   Collection, The Museum of Modern Art, New York, Mrs. Simon Guggenheim Fund.

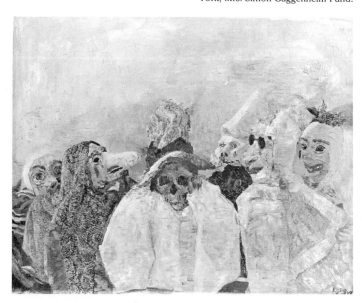

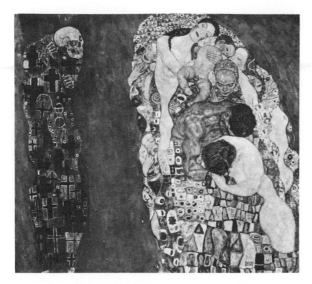

17–42   GUSTAV KLIMT,   *Death and Life,*
(*c.* 1908, reworked 1911). Oil on canvas,
70¼″ × 78″.   Private collection, Vienna.

17–43   EDVARD MUNCH,   *The Cry,* (1893). Oil
on canvas, 33″ × 26½″.   Nasjonalgalleriet, Oslo.

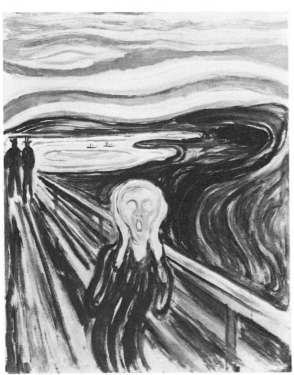

of his more conventional paintings owe much to Impressionism, the highly imaginative compositions are more closely related to the Expressionist art of the late nineteenth and early twentieth centuries.

GUSTAV KLIMT (Austria, 1862–1918).   Klimt both studied and worked in Vienna. In 1897, he became the first president of the Vienna Secession, an organization of artists opposed to conservative art. In *Death and Life* (Fig. 17-42), Klimt used two-dimensional shapes, stressed undulating contours, and exploited intricate, abstract patterns based on geometric and plant motifs for symbolic purposes. His art can be seen as a significant contribution within the introspective and symbolic tendencies of the late nineteenth and early twentieth centuries and within the stylistic trend of Art Nouveau.

EDVARD MUNCH (Norway, 1863–1944).   A government grant for study in Paris from 1889 to 1892 and a controversial exhibition of his work in Berlin in 1892 were major events in the formation of Munch's style and his recognition as a leading figure in Expressionist art. During the Paris sojourn, his style changed from a boldly painted, factual presentation modified by Impressionist light to stronger, simpler, and more arbitrary colors and shapes. Toulouse-Lautrec and Gauguin were major influences. The Berlin exhibit was closed as a result of pressure by conservatives, and Munch became a celebrity among young German painters and an important influence on the *Brücke* group (see p. 318). *The Cry* (Fig. 17-43) employs dissonant colors, undulating shapes, and violent perspective to express the tension and anxiety characteristic of Munch's art. He intended many of his works to be part of a *Frieze of Life,* a series that was never finished.

HENRI DE TOULOUSE-LAUTREC (France, 1864–1901).   The extreme dissoluteness of Toulouse-Lautrec's life, his aristocratic ancestry, and his dwarfed and crippled body have made dramatic material for biographies. In spite of the dissipated life he led, however, his short career was remarkably productive. After training in the studio of an academic painter and working in an Impressionistic vein, he formed a style closely related to that of Degas. His *At the Moulin Rouge* (Plate 21 and Fig.

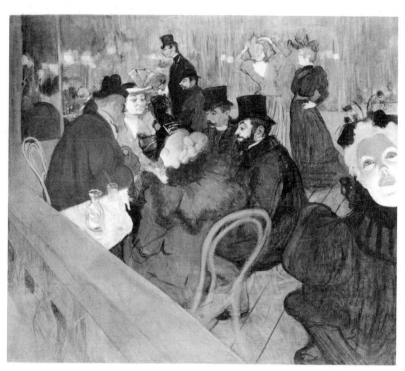

17–44 HENRI DE TOULOUSE-LAUTREC, *At the Moulin Rouge,* (1892). Oil on canvas, approx. $48\frac{3}{8}'' \times 55\frac{1}{4}''$.   Helen Birch Bartlett Memorial Collection, Collection of The Art Institute of Chicago.

17-44) is a casual passing glimpse of the cabaret life that provided many of his subjects. The large areas of color function as bold patterns and reveal the influence of Japanese prints and the paintings of Degas. As in Degas's work, movement is expressed by the contours of active shapes, the sweeping asymmetrical diagonals, and the extension of major figures beyond the edges of the composition. Like Degas, but unlike many of the other Impressionists, Toulouse-Lautrec was interested in human personality. His depictions of Paris dandies and prostitutes show a sensitivity that neither condones nor criticizes but mercilessly reveals the monotony, the frantic efforts to live fully, the cynicism, the lust, and the gaiety of a certain stratum of international society. His famous posters for several of the cabarets are brilliant demonstrations of lithography applied to advertising art. Toulouse-Lautrec never became a member of the Impressionist group; he belongs more properly with the Post-Impressionists.

Sculpture

Nineteenth-century sculpture was less inventive than painting, and stylistic trends are less distinct. After the Revolution, France gave preference to the clear sweeping lines and ideal forms of Neoclassic sculpture. Napoleon supported this preference and commissioned portraits from the Italian Neoclassicist Antonio Canova. The Romantic attitude in sculpture became apparent in the Salons of 1833 and 1834, when rough surfaces, individualized features, and entangled forms were used to accentuate active subjects, as in the work of Antoine Barye and François Rude. The second half of the century saw more precise anatomical and costume detail. The major figure in French sculpture of the late nineteenth and early twentieth centuries was Auguste Rodin, who combined an interest in lively, rippling surfaces with expressions of his subjects' state of mind.

During the first half of the century Italy was the center of Neoclassic sculpture, whose major proponent was Antonio Canova. During the second half of the nineteenth century, the tendency toward increasingly naturalistic or documentary detail was international.

ANTONIO CANOVA (Italy, 1757–1822).   Canova was trained in Venice and developed an early style that combined naturalistic detail with late Baroque composition. When he moved to Rome in 1779, however, and studied Roman ruins and ancient

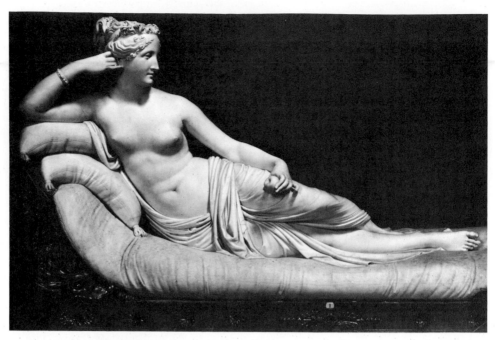

17–45   ANTONIO CANOVA,
Pauline Borghese as Venus,
(1805–1808). **Marble, life
size.**   Galleria Borghese, Rome.

17–46   FRANÇOIS RUDE,   *The Departure of the
Volunteers of 1792,* (1833–36). Approx. 42′ × 26′.
Arc de Triomphe, Paris.

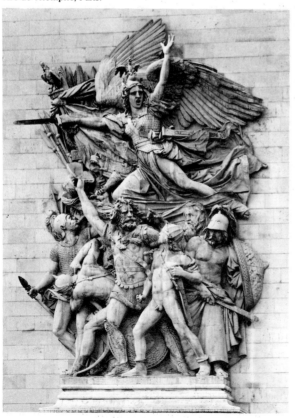

sculpture, his style changed to the simplified anatomy, long sweeping curves, and quiet compositions that became representative of the Neoclassic aesthetic. The *Pauline Borghese as Venus* (Fig. 17-45) presents an idealized portrait of Napoleon's sister in a serene pose with clear stately contours in a static alignment of vertical and horizontal elements. The composition seeks an absolute beauty outside the reach of motion, change, or time.

FRANÇOIS RUDE (France and Belgium, 1784–1855).   Rude studied in Dijon and came to Paris in 1807. After a successful beginning and a twelve-year sojourn in Belgium, he returned to Paris and won the Legion of Honor in the 1833 Salon. Of his many commissions, the best known is *The Departure of the Volunteers of 1792* (Fig. 17-46), a 42-foot-high relief on the Arch of Triumph in Paris. This bristling composition depicts young and old warriors, allegorically dressed in an imaginative version of Roman armor, setting off for battle. Above them, the winged goddess of war surges forward, seemingly in a call to arms. The frantic complexity of the group sets it apart from Neoclassic concepts, and Rude was associated by critics with the furor of Delacroix's Romanticism.

AUGUSTE RODIN (France, 1840–1917).   The Frenchman Rodin dominated Western sculpture in the late nineteenth and early twentieth centuries. He was trained as a sculptor's helper and as a carver of architectural ornament. A voyage to Italy in 1875 opened his eyes to the expressive power of Donatello and Michelangelo; he was particularly impressed by the pulsating life suggested in the rough surfaces of Michelangelo's unfinished work. Exhibited in the 1877 Salon, Rodin's *Age of Bronze* (Rodin Museum, Paris) gains its vitality from surfaces broken into a flickering complexity of highlights while preserving some of the malleability of clay, his favorite material. In 1879, Rodin began planning *The Gates of Hell* for the Museum of Decorative Arts in Paris. Although the project, initially inspired by Dante's *Inferno,* was never finished, the constantly evolving plan for the work served as a source from which Rodin took figures for other sculptures. *The Thinker* (Fig. 17-47) was first conceived as part of the reliefs for *The Gates*

of Hell but gained fame as an individual figure. The bronze presents a convincing muscular and skeletal structure, but details have been omitted, and the surfaces are rippled as well as roughened. Like many of Michelangelo's figures, *The Thinker* implies that physical power does not hold the solution for humanity's most challenging problems. Because of such expressive distortions, Rodin's *Monument to Balzac* (Fig. 17-48) was refused by the society that commissioned it. Rodin also produced stone sculpture, but his style is best seen in his bronzes, which catch the essence of the artist's work in clay; assistants did much of the stone carving. The effect of agitated surfaces in Rodin's work has caused him to be called an Impressionist in sculpture. Such a designation ignores the powerful emotional expression in his art, a quality not basic to Impressionism in painting but most important to French Fauvism and to German Expressionism.

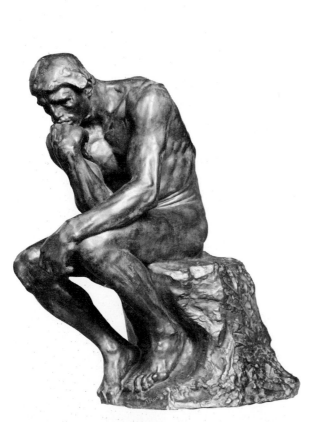

17–47 AUGUSTE RODIN,   *The Thinker,* (1889). **Bronze, 70½″ high including base.**   Metropolitan Museum of Art, New York (gift of Thomas R. Ryan, 1910).

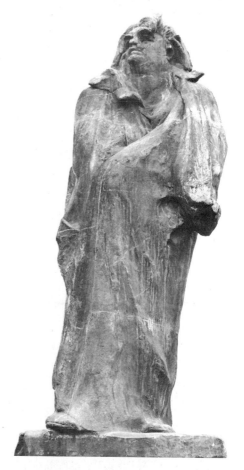

17–48 AUGUSTE RODIN, *Monument to Balzac,* (1891–98). Bronze, 79″ **high.**   Musée Rodin, Paris.

Architecture

Nineteenth-century architecture has been described as the "Battle of the Styles" because of the prevailing tendency to borrow forms from various periods of the past. This eclecticism had begun in the eighteenth century, especially in England, where the work of a single architect would frequently include buildings in the Greek, Roman, Romanesque, Gothic, and Renaissance styles. Eclecticism became international during the nineteenth century, and the word *revival* is often used to indicate the close dependence of a particular style on its historical prototype. Iron could be cast into different kinds of ornamental details, but it could also be used inventively for strikingly new architectural forms such as those of the Crystal Palace, built as an exhibition hall for the London International Exhibition of 1851. In the last quarter of the century, steel frames were used in monuments like the Eiffel Tower and in the development of skyscrapers. During the second half of the century, England developed the so-called *Victorian Gothic* (Italianate Gothic with polychrome stripes) and imported the Second Empire Style from France. The British arts and crafts movement urged efficient, practical design and was an indirect influence on twentieth-century art and theory.

France began the century with dreams of creating an empire rivaling that of ancient Rome. Napoleonic plans provided for vast Greco-Roman monuments, such as the Arch of Triumph and the Church of the Madeleine, many of which were finished long after the Battle of Waterloo. Renaissance revival designs were also popular. The *Second Empire Style*, named for the empire of Napoleon III, is characterized by *mansard* roofs (steeply pitched roofs with a flat or almost flat platform at the top) and highly decorated dormer windows. Walls were treated with ornate sculptural richness, in a style often described as *Neo-Baroque*. French and Belgian architecture of the 1890s spearheaded the international style called *Art Nouveau*, which turned away from eclecticism and exulted in a profusion of irregular, curving, linear ornament inspired by plant life.

Outside of France and England, the revival styles were equally current in Germany, Italy, and the United States. The reaction against eclecticism began with the work of Louis Sullivan and Frank Lloyd Wright.

THOMAS JEFFERSON (United States, 1743–1826). One of the stylistic phases of postcolonial architecture in the eastern United States is often called the *Federal Style*. Thomas Jefferson's home, Monticello (Fig. 17-49), is a fine example of this Roman phase of the Neoclassic. Of the many amateur architects of his day, Jefferson produced some of the

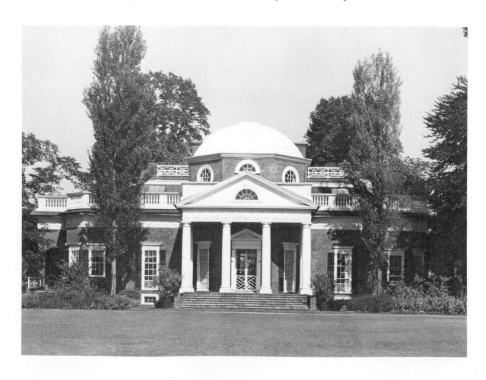

17–49   THOMAS JEFFERSON, Monticello, Charlottesville, Virginia, (1796–1808).

most influential buildings, even while he was engaged in a variety of other activities. Monticello is based on Palladio's Renaissance interpretation of Roman architecture. Jefferson used strict symmetry, a pedimented porch with a semicircular Roman window, Roman-inspired Tuscan columns, a low Roman dome on an octagonal base, severely simple ornament, and the single-story effect of a Roman temple. His designs for the Capitol Building at Richmond, Virginia (1785–89), were based on the Maison Carrée (Fig. 11-2). Jefferson's architecture, however, shows a flexibility and inventiveness in the application of Roman forms that is a refreshing contrast to the more imitative pedantry of many Neoclassic designers.

SIR JOHN SOANE (England, 1753–1837). One of England's most original Neoclassicists was Sir John Soane. During a visit to Italy, he studied the antique world of Piranesi's imaginative prints, actual Roman ruins, and Renaissance buildings. In 1788, he was appointed architect for the Bank of England. He used Roman domes and arches, but instead of the ponderous mass of Roman work, Soane used linear ornament. The total effect, as seen in the Consols Office of the bank (Fig. 17-50), is one of crisp precision with thin, taut surfaces. Soane's house in London — No. 12, Lincoln's Inn Fields (now a museum) — provided more opportunity for experiment. Canopylike cross-vaulted ceilings cover spaces that continue over screening walls that stop short of the ceiling. From low dark spaces, one is drawn toward high, brightly lighted areas. Mirrors help to convey light and to emphasize the continuity of space. The variety of spaces and light effects and the variety of Soane's collection of art objects lead one to expect surprises around every corner. It is here, rather than in the austerely simple surfaces and restrained linear ornament of his larger buildings, that we see Soane's kinship with Piranesi.

KARL FRIEDRICH VON SCHINKEL (Germany, 1781–1841). Germany's leading architect in the first half of the nineteenth century began, like Inigo Jones, as a designer of stage sets. His architecture began as Greek revival and eventually employed Roman domes and arches. A good example

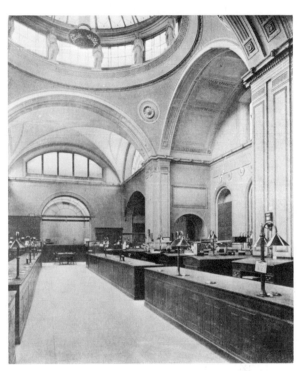

17–50 SIR JOHN SOANE, Consols Office of the Bank of England, London, (1797).

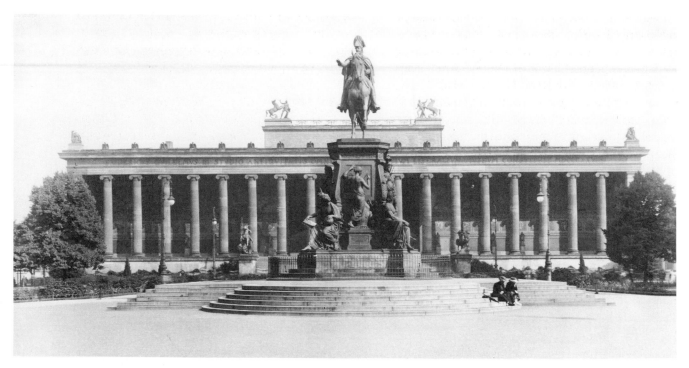

17–51   KARL FRIEDRICH VON SCHINKEL,   Old Berlin Museum, (1824–28).

17–52   SIR CHARLES BARRY and A. WELBY PUGIN,   Houses of Parliament, London, (begun 1835).

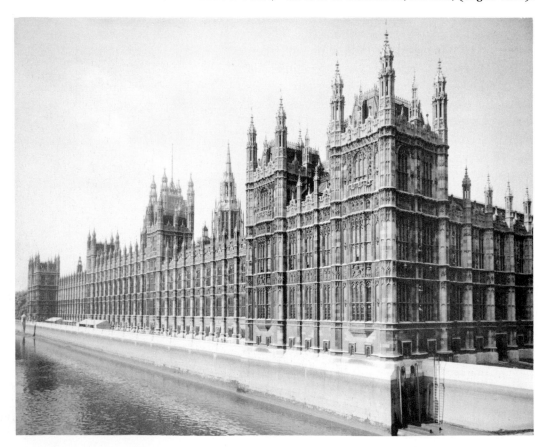

of his early work is the New Guardhouse in Berlin (1816–18), with an authentically proportioned Doric order and the severe simplicity of parts that is characteristic of much Greek revival architecture. His Old Berlin Museum (Fig. 17-51) masks the two-story interior with a huge Ionic stoa and hides the interior Roman dome behind a simple rectangular attic. Von Schinkel was also active as a painter and city planner.

SIR CHARLES BARRY (England, 1795–1860). Barry's career demonstrates the various enthusiasms of nineteenth-century architects and their patrons. Barry began by designing Gothic revival churches but turned to Renaissance revival as his major interest. In 1836 he won the competition for the new Houses of Parliament (Fig. 17-52) with a Gothic design, forecasting the wide popularity of Gothic in the Victorian period. In the same year, A. Welby Pugin's book *Contrasts* appeared, arguing that the Gothic style should be used exclusively. It was Pugin who designed the details for

the Houses of Parliament; late Gothic was used because its more complex ornament was considered to be richer and more picturesque for a skyline as prominent as that of Parliament.

HENRI LABROUSTE (France, 1801–75). Labrouste's masterpiece is the Bibliothèque Sainte-Geneviève in Paris (Fig. 17-53), a design based on Italian Renaissance palaces but handled with sensitivity in its proportions and inventiveness in the application of iron in the interior. The reading room (Fig. 17-54) gains spaciousness from the slender iron columns, which support a ceiling of plaster panels between round arches of perforated iron. Labrouste added a reading room to the Bibliothèque Nationale in Paris (1862–68), where he again used thin iron columns, this time supporting light terra cotta domes. The book-stack areas that he designed for the same building are of iron and glass. With respect to both design and materials, Labrouste was an important leader in mid-nineteenth century French architecture.

17–53   HENRI LABROUSTE,   Bibliothèque Sainte-Geneviève, Paris, (1843–50).

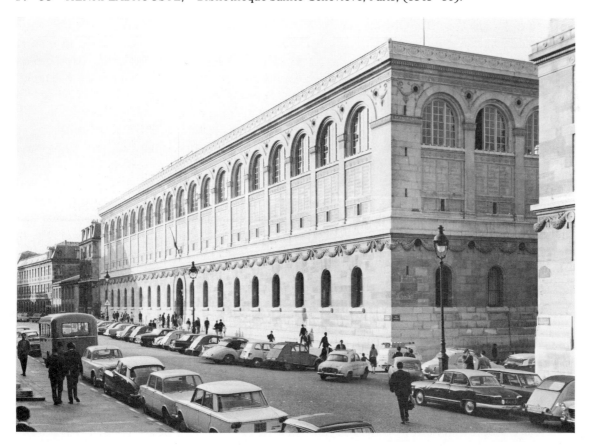

17–54
Reading room of the
Bibliothèque Sainte-
Geneviève.

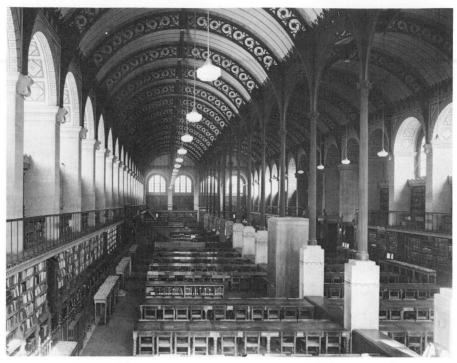

ANTONIO GAUDI Y CORNET (Spain, 1852–1926). After studying architecture in Barcelona, Gaudi made his career there, aided by many commissions from the industrialist Güell. Gaudi's inventive mind utilized Medieval masonry vaults, Moorish forms, and contrasting materials to develop a unique style related to Art Nouveau in its irregular, constantly curving surfaces. His thin, laminated vaults of tile and mortar, his warped surfaces—such as hyperbolic paraboloids (see p. 43)—and his inclined supports all forecast later twentieth-century architecture. The Casa Milá (Fig. 17-55) presents a constantly undulating wall surface of hammered stone. Windows and doors suggest grotto openings, and balcony railings are explosions of foliagelike ironwork. The irregular rise and fall of the roof line and the twisting forms of certain chimneys and ventilators offer a bizarre silhouette. Interior rooms are irregular, with curving walls and spaces that seem flexible and flowing. The building was originally intended to be a base for an enormous statue of the Virgin.

LOUIS SULLIVAN (United States, 1856–1924). America's most innovative architect in the late nineteenth century was Louis Sullivan, who was trained at the Massachusetts Institute of Technol-

ogy and at the École des Beaux-Arts in Paris. At a time when architecture was deriving inspiration from the past, Sullivan insisted on a fresh approach to form and decoration. His concept that *form follows function* (suggested earlier in the century by Horatio Greenough) argued that design should express the use, structure, and materials of a building. Sullivan, a Bostonian, came to Chicago in 1873, and from 1879 to 1895 he worked in partnership with Dankmar Adler. Representative of Sullivan's early work is the Chicago Auditorium Building (Fig. 17-56). In the lower floors, the granite masonry is handled with bold roughness and deep shadows, emphasizing the base and creating an effect of vast scale and strength. Above, the smooth stone façade is unified by tall arches with groups of windows that decrease in size as they approach the final cornice. Sullivan here shows the influence of Henry Hobson Richardson, an earlier architect noted for his sensitive interpretation of Romanesque forms. Other Chicago architects were more advanced than Sullivan in exploring new structural methods and materials, particularly the steel frame, but these new techniques were hidden behind facings of columns and pilasters. It was only in 1890 and 1891 in St. Louis that Sullivan used the steel frame in a design

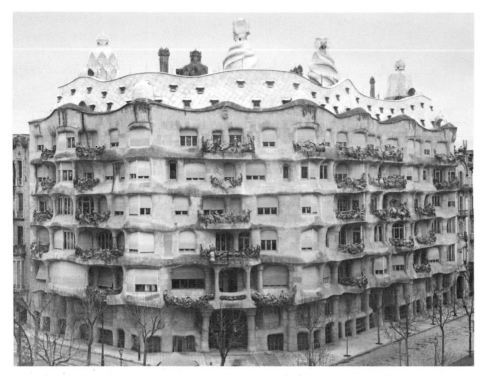

17–55 ANTONIO GAUDI Y CORNET, Casa Milá, Barcelona, (1907).

17–56 LOUIS SULLIVAN and DANKMAR ADLER, Chicago Auditorium Building, (1889).

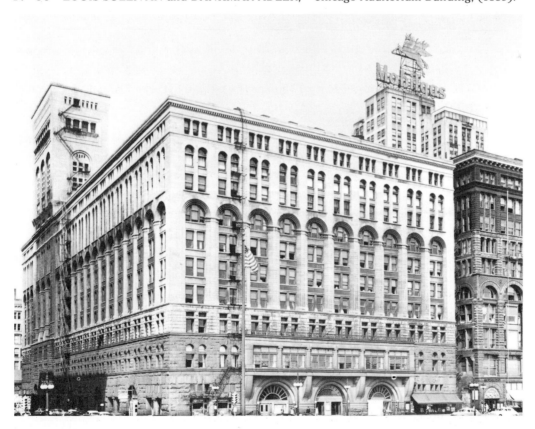

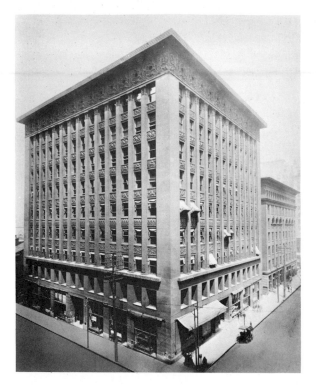

17–57   LOUIS SULLIVAN and DANKMAR ADLER,   Wainwright Building, St. Louis, (1890–91).

independent of past styles. In his Wainwright Building (Fig. 17-57) the idea of form following function resulted in large-windowed shops at the base, a central section of offices treated as a framed area, and a crowning band of floral ornament beneath the projecting cornice. The steel frame is suggested in the large windows and slender brick-covered piers; it is obvious that the steel skeleton, not the walls, supports the building. Sullivan believed that a tall building should look tall, so he made the vertical piers rise through the contrasting horizontal floors with their panels of rich ornament. The ornament is composed of geometric and plant forms in intricate profusion. Though there is no direct reference to past styles, the total effect recalls Celtic art or the looser, more asymmetrical Art Nouveau in Europe. Sullivan's commissions for large buildings declined as eclecticism increased in commercial architecture during the late nineteenth and early twentieth centuries. His ideals gained fuller acceptance after his death, when they were carried on in the work of his former employee, Frank Lloyd Wright.

Suggestions for Further Study

Badt, Kurt. *The Art of Cézanne.* Translated by Sheila Ann Ogilvie. Berkeley: University of California Press, 1965.

Courthion, Pierre. *Edouard Manet* (The Library of Great Painters). New York: Abrams, 1963.

Elsen, Albert. *Rodin.* New York: Museum of Modern Art, 1963.

Fernier, Robert. *Gustave Courbet.* Translated by Marcus Bullock. New York: Praeger, 1969.

Goldwater, Robert. *Symbolism.* New York: Harper & Row, 1979.

Hamilton, George Heard. *Painting and Sculpture in Europe, 1880–1940* (Pelican History of Art), 3rd ed. New York: Penguin Books, 1981.

Hitchcock, Henry Russell. *Architecture: Nineteenth and Twentieth Centuries* (Pelican History of Art). Baltimore: Penguin Books, 1977.

Holt, Elizabeth Gilmore. *The Triumph of Art for the Public: The Emerging Role of Exhibitions and Critics.* Garden City, N.Y.: Anchor Press/Doubleday, 1979.

———. *The Art of All Nations: 1850–1873: The Emerging Role of Exhibitions and Critics.* Garden City, N.Y.: Anchor Press/Doubleday, 1981.

Honour, Hugh. *Romanticism.* New York: Harper & Row, 1979.

Huyghe, René. *Delacroix.* Translated by Jonathan Griffan. New York: Abrams, 1963.

Moffett, Charles, et al. *The New Painting: Impressionism, 1874–1886*. An Exhibition Organized by the Fine Arts Museums of San Francisco with The National Gallery of Art, Washington. Geneva: Richard Burton Publishers, 1986.

Nochlin, Linda. *Realism* (Style and Civilization). New York: Penguin Books, 1972.

———. *Realism and Tradition in Art, 1848–1900* (Sources and Documents in the History of Art). Englewood Cliffs, N.J.: Prentice-Hall, 1966.

———. *Impressionism and Post-Impressionism, 1874–1904* (Sources and Documents in the History of Art). Englewood Cliffs, N.J.: Prentice-Hall, 1966.

Rewald, John. *The History of Impressionism*. New York: Museum of Modern Art, 1980.

———. *Post-Impressionism from Van Gogh to Gauguin*. New York: Museum of Modern Art, 1979.

Rheims, Maurice. *Nineteenth-Century Sculpture*. Translated by Robert E. Wolf. New York: Abrams, 1977.

Rosenblum, Robert. *Jean Auguste Dominique Ingres* (The Library of Great Painters). New York: Abrams, 1967.

Rosenblum, Robert, and H. W. Janson. *Nineteenth-Century Art*. New York: Abrams, 1984.

Rubin, William, ed. *Cézanne: The Late Work*. New York: Museum of Modern Art, 1977.

Schnapper, Antoine. *David*. Translated by Helga Harrison. New York: Alpine Fine Arts Collection Ltd., 1980.

Sullivan, Louis. *Kindergarten Chats and Other Writings* (Documents of Modern Art). New York: Wittenborn, 1976.

18

Modern Art

1900 to 1945

The twentieth century, even more than the nineteenth, has been characterized by international and individual styles and by a diversity that makes generalization difficult. New materials and techniques, as well as a rapidly changing world view, have influenced art since 1900. The increasing importance of the machine seems to be reflected in some styles and reacted against in others, and psychology and physics have reshaped the artist's conceptions of human beings and the physical world. The complex interaction of factors that forms the artist's style, however, does not encourage simple or easy explanations, especially since many artists have embraced a number of stylistic trends.

One widespread tendency in twentieth-century art has been to place the highest value on purely formal qualities — for example, the coherence, variety, subtlety, and uniqueness of forms — rather than to stress the interpretation of subject matter. This tendency accompanied perforce the rise of abstract and nonobjective art, but it has since affected attitudes toward representational art as well. Most artists and critics have used the language of pure form to evaluate the cityscapes of Hopper (see p. 333) as well as the personal revelations of De Kooning (p. 373) and the calculated structures of Mondrian.

Sometimes allied with and sometimes opposed to the emphasis on formal qualities has been a tendency to stress subjectivity, individual reaction to the world, exploration of the realm of fantasy, or creation of new worlds without familiar objects.

More pervasive than either of these characteristics has been the tendency to attack conventional ideas about the nature and value of art, even when such ideas have only recently played a revolutionary role themselves. The *Fauvist* movement asserted the artist's right to reshape the ordinary world according to his or her subjective vision. *Cubism* affirmed the conviction that art was not primarily a representation of the daily world but the creation of a reality with its own system of order—essentially the artist's conception of a new world, which might use parts of the mundane world as building blocks. As early as 1913, Marcel Duchamp challenged the traditional concept of art as a precious object of high taste when he exhibited factory-produced utilitarian articles as art. Duchamp was linked with the *Dada* movement, which, like its successor, *Surrealism*, mocked the rationalist basis of Western civilization.

Painting

Twentieth-century Western painting's first major event occurred at the Paris Salon d'Automne in 1905, when a number of French painters, including Derain, Vlaminck, Marquet, Rouault, and Matisse, exhibited paintings with such expansive shapes, intense color, and free brushwork that a critic called the painters *fauves* ("wild beasts"). Vlaminck's painting (Fig. 18-1) is typical in the simplified and flattened shapes, active contours, and urgent brush strokes. *Fauvism* was a short-lived movement that lasted only about three years and was never formally organized. While its influence was widespread in later twentieth-century painting, only a few adherents, notably Matisse,

18-1 MAURICE DE VLAMINCK, *Portrait of a Woman,* (1905–1906). Oil on canvas, 24⅛″ × 18″. A painting from the Fauve period.   Collection of Mr. and Mrs. Nathan Smooke.

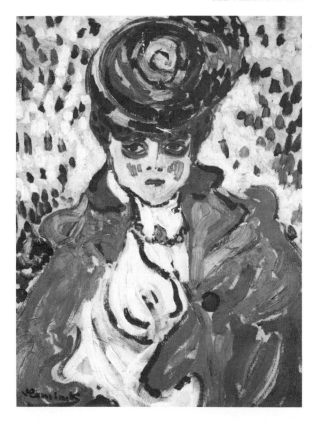

continued to paint in the style. Fauvism's immediate sources were Van Gogh and Gauguin, and its bursting vitality and instinctive spontaneity made it an expressionistic movement.

The year 1905 also marked the first exhibition of a group of German painters that called itself *Die Brücke* ("the Bridge"). The major painters in the group were Karl Schmidt-Rottluff, Emile Nolde, Ernst Ludwig Kirchner, Erich Heckel, and Max Pechstein. It lasted from 1905 until 1913. These men, who headquartered in Dresden, were inspired by the paintings of the Fauves, the Norwegian painter Edvard Munch, and Medieval German woodcuts. They used harsh, brutally simplified forms and strong, often clashing colors in a heavy, expressionistic manner. Some of the members of the Bridge group were absorbed by *Der Blaue Reiter* ("the Blue Rider"), a group formed in Munich in 1911 by Vasily Kandinsky that encompassed a variety of styles, ranging from Kandinsky's gay, buoyant, nonobjective paintings to the moody, geometric abstractions of Franz Marc. The Bridge and Blue Rider groups provided the basis for the broad trend known as *German Expressionism*, which gained new vitality during the 1980s with German Neo-Expressionist art.

Meanwhile, *Cubism* developed in France from 1907 to 1914 under the strong influence of Cézanne. Two notable Cubist pioneers were Pablo Picasso and Georges Braque. The movement's early phase, often called *Analytical Cubism*, sought to reduce nature to its basic geometric shapes, frequently depicting objects from several sides simultaneously. This *simultaneity* of vision implies a summation of visual experience from different moments and different positions in space and suggests an intriguing parallel to the theories of relativity that Einstein was proposing in the same period. Analytical Cubism employed restrained colors, limited space, and a restricted repertory of geometric shapes; it may be understood partly as a reaction to the spontaneous freedom and lively color of Fauvism. The second phase of Cubism has been called *Synthetic*, because it is a more imaginative reconstruction of or improvisation on the forms of natural objects. Color and space are less limited, and shapes are less restricted to basic geometry. Synthetic Cubism often employed *collage*, the pasting of actual objects,

such as pieces of newspaper, to the surface of the painting.

French Cubism influenced the Russian painter Kasimir Malevich, who proclaimed a movement called *Suprematism* in 1915. Malevich considered his art to be supreme in its emancipation from subject matter and in its reduction to a few geometric shapes (Fig. 18-2).

The Russian *Constructivist* movement broke into factions over questions of personal versus public art. Its forms, like those of Suprematism, were often nonobjective and heavily influenced by Cubism. Although the brothers Antoine Pevsner and Naum Gabo did not consider themselves to be Constructivists, their art and their *Realist Manifesto*, issued in 1920, are considered to reflect significant Constructivist ideas. French Cubism also inspired the Dutchman Mondrian to seek even greater austerity in compositions of rectangles and primary colors. In Holland, Mondrian helped form a group in 1917 that is generally known by the name of its magazine, *De Stijl* ("the Style"). Echoes of Cubism also reverberate in the Italian movement called *Futurism* (*c.* 1909–15), which used multiple contours, diagonal lines, and swirling curves to express the dynamism of the machine age.

The tendency to apply a severe geometric system of order to an objective or a nonobjective world has been widespread in twentieth-century art and has produced a wide variety of styles. A very different tendency has developed concurrently since 1916, when *Dada* was founded in Zurich, Switzerland. Dadaism was a nihilistic rejection of rationality and order. Arising from the disillusionment of the First World War, Dada sought to destroy through ridicule the old ideas about the character, aims, and standards of art and to build a new standard using an appreciation of fantasy and the irrational. Dadaists used sculpture, painting, and photomontage (compositions made up of various photos or of their fragments) to present extraordinary combinations of ordinary objects, thereby destroying the conventional meaning of the objects and opening the way for new interpretations by the spectator. Dadaism reflected the growing appreciation of the role of the irrational as revealed by psychiatry. The Dada movement spread quickly to Cologne, Berlin,

18-2   KASIMIR MALEVICH,
Suprematist Composition: White on White,
(1918) Oil on canvas, 31¼″ × 31¼″.
Collection, the Museum of Modern Art, New York.

Paris, and New York, and although its organized life was short (1916–22), its influence can be seen in much contemporary painting and sculpture. Many Dadaists joined the *Surrealist* movement, which announced its aims in a Paris manifesto in 1924 and continues to exert influence on painting today. Some Surrealist works, like those of René Magritte, attempt to depict hallucinatory or dream experiences in which recognizable forms appear in surprising combinations. Other Surrealists, like Joan Miró, produced compositions with lighter, more humorous fantasies. The works of Giorgio de Chirico, who was painting haunting, dreamlike landscapes as early as 1910, were major sources of both Dadaism and Surrealism.

In the 1920s and 1930s, while Surrealism, Expressionism, and various kinds of geometric abstraction developed, many European, American, and Mexican artists were producing works that emphasized social commentary. The cynicism that grew out of the First World War encouraged not only the Dada movement but also a trend that in Germany was called *The New Objectivity (Die Neue Sachlichkeit)*. Here realistic detail was used more specifically than in Dadaism to point out the horrors and corruption of people and society. There were counterparts to the New Objectivity in

other countries. In the United States, the vigorous life of crowded cities, particularly that of the slum areas, provided subject matter for the so-called *Ash Can School*, or *The Eight*, which played an avant-garde role from 1908 until 1913. After the 1913 New York Armory Show, which jolted Americans into awareness of advanced trends in European art, American patrons became more sympathetic to abstract art. A generation of American artists, many of whom had studied in Paris during the crucial years of Fauvism and Cubism, had become pioneers in American abstract painting. However, in the late 1920s there was a tendency to move away from abstraction and to represent aspects of the American scene. The Depression of the 1930s encouraged art that depicted not only the face of America but also the tragedy and suffering caused by economic crisis. In Russia after 1921 the Communists forced into exile those artists who would not turn to a propagandistic realism in support of the government's political ideals. Mexico produced three of the most powerful artists of social commentary in the 1920s and 1930s — José Orozco, Diego Rivera, and David Alfaro Siqueiros — whose mural paintings protest the viciousness of humanity and the oppression of the weak by the strong, especially in Latin America.

VASILY KANDINSKY (Russia, Germany, and France, 1866–1944).   Vasily Kandinsky was born in Moscow but settled in Munich; he became the leader of the Blue Rider group in 1911. Earlier he had abandoned a career in law and had turned to Fauvist painting and, eventually, to increasingly abstract forms. It may have been as early as 1910, depending on the disputed date of a watercolor, that he developed nonobjective art. His treatise *Concerning the Spiritual in Art*, published in 1912, urged that painting can approach the state of pure music — that is, that line, color, and form may be used like sounds to evoke emotional response without the help of subject matter. Kandinsky often used titles such as "fugue" or "improvisation" to stress the correspondence with music. *Painting with White Form* (Plate 32 and Fig. 18-3) is typical of his early nonobjective paintings. Cloudlike forms, rainbow colors, and angular and wavy lines expand spirally from a nucleus of smaller, brighter, denser, and more sharply contrasting parts. The activity is buoyant and spontaneous in effect but carefully controlled within the limits of the picture. From the 1920s on, Kandinsky also composed with rigid, precise, geometric

shapes or combinations of geometric and freer forms. Occasionally, recognizable objects appear in his work. In 1934, Kandinsky settled in Paris, where he spent much of the remainder of his life. His art has been a major influence in twentieth-century painting.

KÄTHE KOLLWITZ (Germany, 1867–1945). Printmaking and sculpture served as the media with which Käthe Kollwitz became a powerful defender of the poor and the oppressed. Her compassion grew from a family background of intellectual idealism and social concern. Although her training at the Berlin and Munich Schools for Women Artists was basically in painting, she turned early to printmaking and exhibited regularly in Berlin. Her reputation came quickly with a series of six lithographs and etchings entitled *The Weavers* (1894–98). The subject, inspired by a play, is the 1844 revolt of underpaid handloom weavers in Silesia. A gold medal was designated for the artist by the jury of a Berlin exhibition; however, the German monarch, Wilhelm II, disliked social commentary and vetoed the medal. Kollwitz won awards shortly thereafter in Dresden

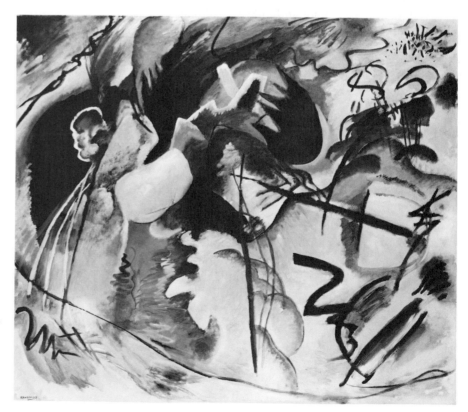

18-3   VASILY KANDINSKY, *Painting with White Form No. 166*, (1913). Oil on canvas, 47″ × 54⅜″.   Collection, the Solomon R. Guggenheim Museum, New York.

and London. *The Peasant War*, a series of seven intaglio prints produced between 1902 and 1908, portrays an unsuccessful revolt of serfs in the sixteenth century. Kollwitz gradually eliminated incidental details and evolved massively expressive forms with striking value contrasts. She stressed this economy of means in her teaching at the Berlin School for Women Artists. Awards and renown came steadily. World War I and the soldier's death of her youngest son strengthened her commitment to social protest and her concern for the suffering of mothers and children. Protest against war and compassion for suffering constitute the content of her *War* series, seven woodcuts from 1920, and of *The Survivors* (Fig. 18-4), a lithograph that was converted into one of her many antiwar posters. In 1919, Kollwitz was the first woman to be elected Professor in the Berlin Academy of Art, a position taken from her in 1933 by the Nazi government. From 1933 until her death, the government tried to efface her presence and her work. Her art is a major example of social commentary and of German Expressionism.

PIERRE BONNARD (France, 1867–1947).   In the 1880s, Pierre Bonnard joined the *Nabis* (see text, p. 299), a small group of French painters who believed that lines, shapes, and colors can evoke within the spectator a certain state of mind. In their view, the real content of the work of art was the spiritual result of its physical forms. Following the lead of the poets Charles Baudelaire and Stéphane Mallarmé, the Nabis spoke of mystical correspondences between the physical and the spiritual worlds and of the possibility of using one sensory experience, such as sight, to evoke another, such as sound or taste (synesthesia). Critics linked the Nabis with the Symbolist movement in literature. In painting, Gauguin was the Nabis's idol; his flattened forms and imaginative colors demonstrated that a painting was an expressive and symbolic object not to be confused with an imitation of nature. They also found these qualities in Japanese wood-block prints. Of the Nabis, Bonnard especially, throughout the 1880s and 1890s, used flat, softly edged shapes with occasional undulating, Art Nouveau curves and muted colors. He therefore was often called "the Japanese Nabi." His works of this period portray people in parks and interiors; the mood is often meditative, almost

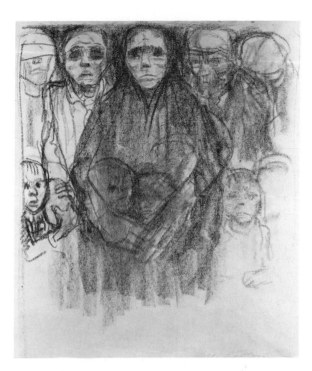

18-4   KÄTHE KOLLWITZ,   *The Survivors,* (1923). Lithograph, 22⅛″ × 27″.   National Gallery of Art, Washington, D.C. Rosenwald Collection.

sacramental. Critics coined the term *intimiste* to describe the emotional tone of his paintings. In addition, Bonnard created lithographic illustrations for *La Revue Blanche* and designed posters, sets, and costumes for Lugné-Poë's experimental Théatre de l'Oeuvre and Paul Fort's Théatre d'Art. By 1911, Bonnard had heightened his palette, using more intense and sometimes dissonant colors sensitively organized on the picture surface. In *The Palm* (Plate 29 and Fig. 18-5), small ovoid color spots produce smoldering contrasts. The drawing seems at first unsure and the proportions clumsy, yet the total composition is very effective. The curves of the palm branches, the colors, and the soft geometry of the houses focus with great intensity on the figure. The result goes beyond Impressionism to suggest a visionary experience. Although he played an avant-garde role in the late nineteenth century, Bonnard's popularity came in the twentieth century, after Fauvism had paved the way for his use of stronger colors. Historically and stylistically, his art links very different movements —Impressionism, Symbolism, and Fauvism.

18-5   PIERRE BONNARD,   *The Palm,* (1926). Oil on canvas, 44″ × 57½″.   The Phillips Collection, Washington, D.C.

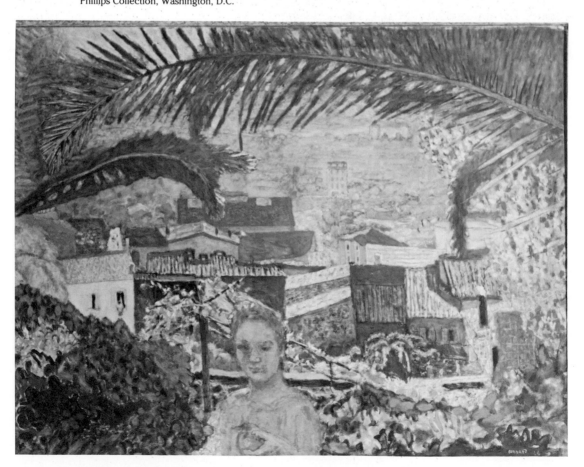

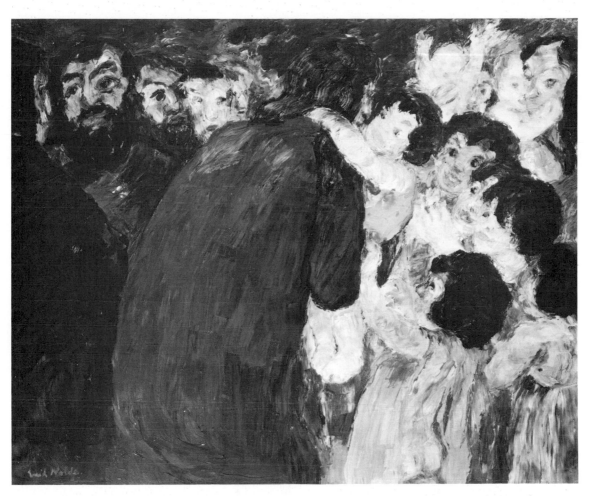

18-6 EMILE NOLDE, *Christ among the Children,* (1910). Oil on canvas, 34⅛″ × 41⅞″. Collection, the Museum of Modern Art, New York. Gift of Dr. W. R. Valentiner.

EMILE NOLDE (Germany, 1867–1956). Although a member of Die Brücke, Emile Nolde was a very independent German Expressionist, unique in his sense of fantasy, his mystical attachment to nature, and in his religious subject matter (Plate 30 and Fig. 18-6). Like the other members of Die Brücke, he admired primitive art and developed a style of violent brushwork, extreme expressive distortions, and arbitrary color. Typically, Nolde used smoldering and contrasting colors to depict emotionally heavy landscapes and seascapes, explosions of flowers, and intense religious images. He made a major contribution to twentieth-century printmaking in etching, woodcuts, and lithography. Nolde was raised in the Danish-German coastal region and returned there during the summers even after his eventual success in Berlin. After 1941, he stayed in the region of his youth, painting secretly. By that time, the Nazi government had branded the Expressionists "degenerate" and had forbidden them to paint.

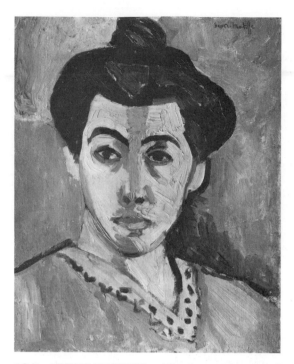

18-7   HENRI MATISSE,   *The Green Line,* (1905).
Oil on canvas, 16″ × 12¾″.   Statens Museum for Kunst,
Copenhagen.

18-8   HENRI MATISSE,   *Decorative Figure on an
Ornamental Background,* (1927). Oil on canvas,
approx. 48″ × 36″.   Musée National d'Art Moderne, Paris.

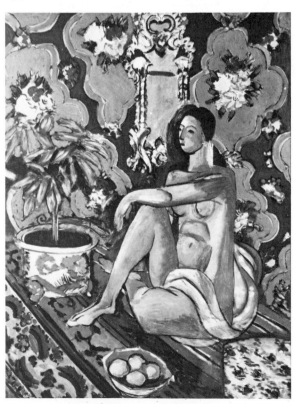

HENRI MATISSE (France, 1869–1954).   The study
of law failed to satisfy the young Matisse, and his
brief period as a student of the academic painter
Adolphe Bouguereau was equally frustrating. He
studied next with the lenient Gustave Moreau. Matisse's early work revealed an interest in Impressionism and in Seurat's pointillism. Matisse then
became enthusiastic about the work of Cézanne
and Gauguin. By 1905 Matisse's art had developed
large areas of relatively unbroken color, often
chosen quite independently of nature, and shapes
manipulated to intensify their directional forces. In
the Salon d'Automne of 1905, Matisse was seen as
the leader of the Fauve group. *The Green Line* (Fig.
18-7), a portrait of Madame Matisse, indicates by
its title the artist's concern with color. Vibrating
complementaries — greens and reds, yellows and
violets — achieve a dynamic equilibrium and a life
of their own. Such gymnastics with color continued to be typical of Matisse's style, but in his later
works he tended to use thinner paint and to create
looser forms. *Decorative Figure on an Ornamental Background* (Plate 31 and Fig. 18-8) is one of
the more tightly constructed works from the
1920s, yet the solid rigidity of the figure contrasts
with the exuberance of the patterns and colors.
The exhilarating effect of ease and spontaneity
masks the continual repainting and the deliberation that went into Matisse's work. In *Notes of a
Painter*, published in 1908, Matisse describes his
dream of an art of balance, purity, and serenity
devoid of troubling or depressing subject matter.
No elaborate theories guided him; he relied on his
instinct as he worked and reworked a composition
according to his conviction that everything —
shapes, spaces between shapes, colors, lines —
should contribute to the total expression. In the
1940s Matisse developed a special technique: *pa-
piers collés*. He painted sheets of paper, cut them
into shapes, and pasted them on a background.
The resulting patterns were crisp and lively, with
striking contrasts of hue and value.

JOHN MARIN (United States, 1870–1953).   John
Marin started his career in painting late, after a
serious attempt at architecture. Following his studies in Philadelphia and New York, he spent most of
the years from 1905 to 1911 in Europe, where he
produced etchings and watercolors and exhibited
in the Paris salons. While in Europe, he began a

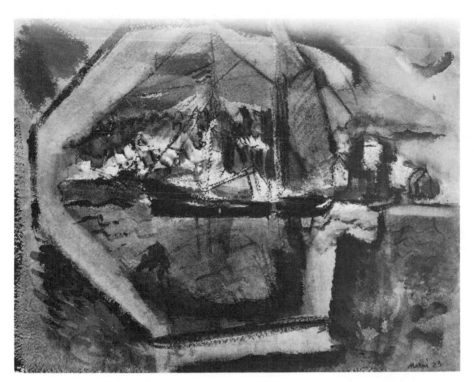

18-9 JOHN MARIN, *Sailboat in Harbor,* (1923). Watercolor on paper, 13½″ × 17″. Collection, The Columbus Gallery of Fine Arts, Columbus, Ohio. Gift of Ferdinand Howald.

lifelong friendship with Alfred Stieglitz. Marin first exhibited in Stieglitz's 291 Gallery (see p. 434) in 1909. Once back in New York, Marin produced watercolors with slashing, angular strokes that expressed his feelings about the dynamism of that city in a style related to Cubism and Futurism. After 1914, his subjects were New York in the winter and Maine in the summer. In landscapes and seascapes, Marin's sense of conflicting forces in nature was realized within a conception of the picture plane as a field of forces. Pencil lines and brush strokes construct intricate geometric shapes that preserve the flat plane of the paper while suggesting natural forms like rocks or water, as in *Sailboat in Harbor* (Fig. 18-9). Dry-brush strokes contrast with watery washes of delicate hues in this watercolor. While the painting may suggest deep space and solid objects in the natural world, it also presents a formal structure with its own laws and drama. Marin is known primarily as a watercolorist; his oils utilized similar forms but exploited the thick textures possible with that medium.

GEORGES   ROUAULT   (France,   1871–1958). Georges Rouault's training consisted of an apprenticeship to a maker of stained glass and the study of painting with Gustave Moreau. By 1905, Rouault was utilizing the slashing brushwork and urgent

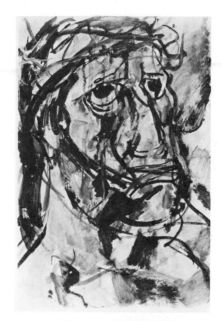

18-10   GEORGES ROUAULT, *Head of Christ,* (1905). Oil on paper mounted on canvas, 38¾″ × 24½″.   Chrysler Museum at Norfolk. Gift of Walter P. Chrysler, Jr.

18-11   GEORGES ROUAULT,   *The Old King,* (1916–38). Oil on canvas, approx. 30¼″ × 21¼″. Collection, Museum of Art, Carnegie Institute, Pittsburgh.

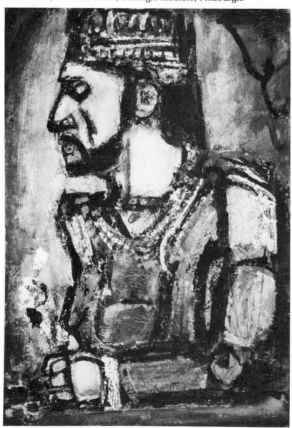

scumblings (see p. 35) seen in the *Head of Christ* (Fig. 18-10). Although his works were not exhibited in the same room with those of the Fauves during the Salon of 1905, he seemed Fauvist in the expressive violence of his forms and was often identified with this movement. Rouault's content, however, which deals more with the pathos, tragedy, and corruption of humankind, links him with German Expressionism. Frequent subjects are prostitutes, sorrowful clowns, evil judges, and the head of Christ. His deep religious convictions owed much to the writings of Léon Bloy; his sense of social justice recalls the art of Daumier. As Rouault's style matured, contours became rigid containers for islands of thick glowing color. *The Old King* (Plate 34 and Fig. 18-11) has the radiance of a stained-glass window or a Byzantine icon. Rouault's genius as a printmaker is revealed in the lithographic and intaglio prints that he executed as book illustrations under the patronage of his dealer, Ambrose Vollard, from 1916 to 1927, and which he eventually published as the *Miserere.*

PIET MONDRIAN (Holland, 1872–1944). Piet Mondrian, even more than Kandinsky, was the exponent of nonobjective painting. Mondrian studied at the Amsterdam Academy and began as a painter of landscapes in bright Fauvist colors. After moving to Paris in 1912, his style was strongly influenced by Cubism and became increasingly abstract. *Composition* (Fig. 18-12) indicates that by 1913 Mondrian was reducing subject matter to intricate flat rectangular systems limited to a few colors. He returned to Holland in 1913 and remained there during the First World War. In 1917, he and a circle of friends founded the magazine *De Stijl,* whose name was subsequently attached to their group. Mondrian remained a major spokesman for the group and the only faithful follower of the strict principles he enunciated, which he termed *Neo-Plasticism.* He stated that the new plastic idea would seek universal harmonies using the pure forms of straight lines and primary colors. He saw subject matter as an impurity that limited the universality of the painting by tying it to a particular time and place. *Composition with Blue and Yellow* (Fig. 3-2) exemplifies Mondrian's mature style; a certain intensity of warm yellow and a certain intensity of cool blue are adjusted in quan-

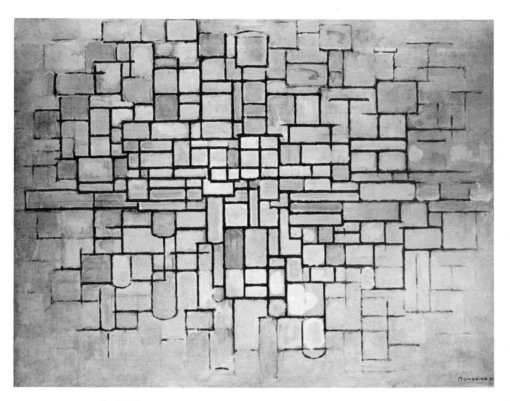

18-12   PIET MONDRIAN,   *Composition,* (1913). Oil on canvas, 34⅝″ × 45¼″.   Rijksmuseum Kröller-Müller, Otterlo.

tity to form an equilibrium within the simple grid-work of black lines. This search for absolute order makes an interesting parallel with the Neoclassic artist's effort to find an absolute beauty that would last through the changes of time and place. In 1919, Mondrian returned to Paris and stayed there until 1938, when the impending Second World War forced him to move to London for two years and then to New York. His art has had a wide influence on painting, sculpture, architecture, and commercial design.

KASIMIR MALEVICH (Russia, 1878–1935).   The Kiev School of Art and the Moscow Academy of Fine Arts provided Kasimir Malevich with his formal training. By the time of his first exhibition in 1909, his art revealed the influence of Vuillard, Bonnard, and Matisse. Between 1911 and 1913, Malevich came under the spell of Cubism and Futurism. The desire to purify and reduce painting to essential elements led him, in 1913, to paint *Black Square* (Russian Museum, Leningrad), a black rectangle in the center of a white canvas. This was followed by other geometric compositions, sometimes in only one color, with simple shapes float-

ing against white backgrounds. Only in 1915 did Malevich announce a name and a program for this kind of painting: Suprematism. *White on White* (Fig.18-2) was the apex of his search for purity; the white square can be distinguished from its white background only through faint value differences. Malevich's Suprematism influenced many Russian artists who became involved with Russian Constructivism, a larger movement, whose geometric and nonobjective forms in painting and sculpture had an international impact.

PAUL KLEE (Switzerland and Germany, 1879–1940).   Paul Klee grew up in Bern, Switzerland, but studied in the Academy at Munich. After traveling in Italy, he painted and did etchings in Bern until 1906, when he moved back to Munich. In 1912, he participated in the second Blue Rider exhibit there. Although his studies included a firm academic grounding in life drawing and perspective, Klee early developed a preference for abstractions done in small scale with subtle color and delicate line. His intellectual attitude was very sophisticated, but his writings show a desire to join adult understanding and experience with the freshness

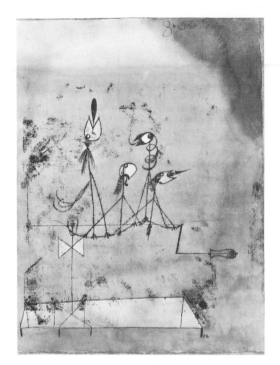

18-13   PAUL KLEE,   *The Twittering
Machine,* (1922). Watercolor and
pen-and-ink, approx. 16¼″ × 12″.
Collection, the Museum of Modern Art, New York.
Purchase.

18-14   ERNST LUDWIG KIRCHNER,   *Street,
Berlin,* (1913). 47½″ × 35⅛″.   Collection, the Museum of
Modern Art, New York. Purchase.

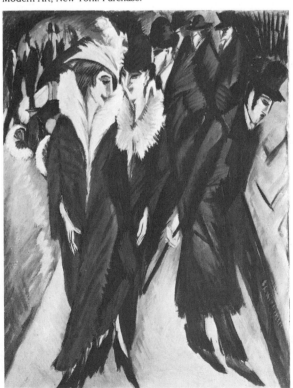

of vision and the delightful fantasy usually left behind with childhood. Many of his landscapes of the 1920s employ delicate rectangles of color and softly emerging shapes of trees and birds. The quality of intimate personal fantasy is all-pervasive. Klee's sly sense of humor and sensitivity of line are evident in such works as *The Twittering Machine* (Fig. 18-13). During the 1930s, his shapes tend to become bolder, the line heavier, and the colors more opaque. From 1920 to 1930, Klee taught at the Bauhaus, the pioneering German school of design. During these years, he published many of his ideas in the *Pedagogical Sketchbook.* After teaching at the Dusseldorf Academy from 1931 to 1933, Klee was dismissed by the Nazi government; he returned to Bern, where he worked until his death. Klee exhibited with German Expressionist groups, but his use of *psychic automatism,* the bringing forth of images from the imagination or from nonrational thought, linked his work as well with Surrealism.

ERNST LUDWIG KIRCHNER (Germany, 1880–1938). In Dresden in 1905, Ernst Kirchner, along with several other young painters, founded *Die Brücke,* a group dedicated to the ''renewal of German art.'' The dating of Kirchner's early paintings and prints is uncertain, but they seem to reflect the character of Art Nouveau and the influence of Edvard Munch. Influenced by Medieval German woodcuts and African and Oceanic art, Kirchner's work became more abrupt, angular, and dissonant. His colors became more brilliant and clashing, and distortions more extreme. In 1911, Kirchner moved to Berlin, where the life of the city provided the theme for a series of paintings and woodcuts. Some of the latter were used in the avant-garde publication *Der Sturm. Street, Berlin* (Fig. 18-14), one of the paintings in the series, demonstrates the conflict of angles, the splintered forms, and the spatial tensions common to Kirchner's work before 1920. From the time of his military service (1914 to 1915) and concomitant nervous disorders, Kirchner's style slowly changed. In the 1920s, shapes began to be more clearly separated and to contain less active brushwork. Kirchner went to Switzerland, where he spent the remainder of his life, and took much of his subject matter from the Swiss Alps. Like many pioneering artists, he was vilified by the Nazis as a degenerate.

This contributed to the discouragement that led to his suicide in 1938.

FRANZ MARC (Germany, 1880–1916).   Franz Marc and Vasily Kandinsky organized the Blue Rider exhibitions in 1911 and 1912 and edited *The Blue Rider Almanac*, a collection of essays on avant-garde theory. Theological and philosophical interests may have led Marc away from his representational student work toward animal paintings with simplified forms, arbitrary colors, and symbolic content. His paintings of horses in landscapes, painted in 1910 and 1911, use undulating Art Nouveau curves in lyrical visions of harmony between animals and nature, a harmony that Marc believed humans had lost. Following Kandinsky, Marc saw painting as an expression of inner necessity, a bridge between spiritual and material life. Through painting, he sought harmony with the universe. Colors were symbolic for him; blue was masculine, yellow was feminine, and red expressed materialistic matter. His pantheistic tendencies and the desire to merge with nature reflect not only the tradition of German Romanticism but also the impact of Van Gogh's art, which Marc saw in Paris in 1907. Another Paris trip in 1912 brought him into contact with Cubism and with the French painter Robert Delaunay, who was painting and arguing for an art that was essentially nonobjective. Marc's images moved slowly toward greater abstraction. In the course of 1912, curves gave way to angular planes with a prismatic effect of color and transparency. This crystalline structure differs from its Cubist sources in Marc's mysticism and symbolism. *Stables* (Fig. 18-15), painted in 1913 and 1914, exemplifies the elusive and intricate spatial environment into which the horses have merged. In 1914, Marc painted a series of works that are apparently nonobjective: *Playing Forms, Broken Forms, Gay Forms*, and *Fighting Forms*. Marc died in the trenches during World War I.

PABLO PICASSO (Spain and France, 1881–1973). After a triumph as a precocious academic student, Pablo Picasso went from Spain to Paris and quickly began experimenting with the revolutionary styles of the recent past. From early attempts at Impressionism, he moved to the first of many personal stylistic developments: his Blue Period (1901–1904), during which he used blues and grays to depict people who seem spiritually and physically exhausted. In 1905 and 1906 he turned to warm tans and reds; circus subjects were frequent in this Rose Period. Slowly the forms stiffened and the faces became masklike. Picasso had become interested in the primitive formal power of African

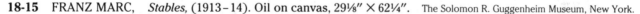

18-15   FRANZ MARC,   *Stables,* (1913–14). Oil on canvas, 29⅛″ × 62¼″.   The Solomon R. Guggenheim Museum, New York.

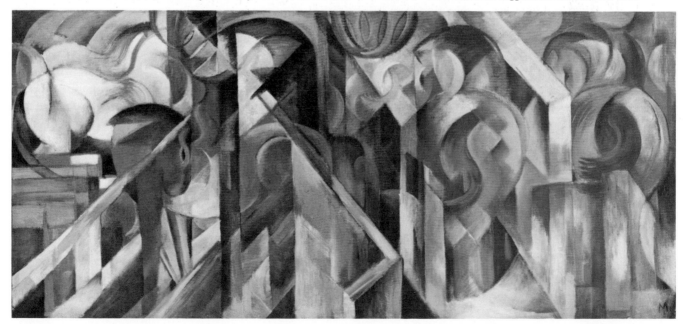

18-16 PABLO PICASSO, *Les Demoiselles d'Avignon,* (1907). Oil on canvas, 8′ × 7′8″.   Collection, the Museum of Modern Art, New York. Acquired through the Lillie P. Bliss Bequest.

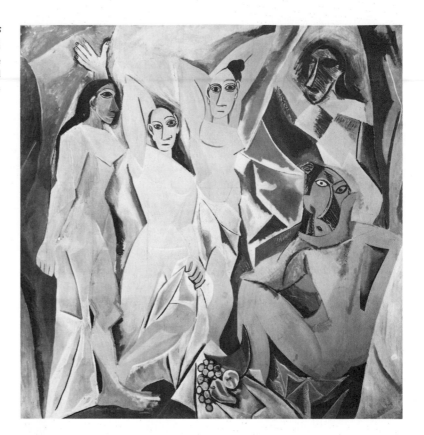

18-17 PABLO PICASSO, *The Aficionado,* (1912). Oil on canvas, 53¼″ × 32⅜″.   Kunstmuseum, Basel.

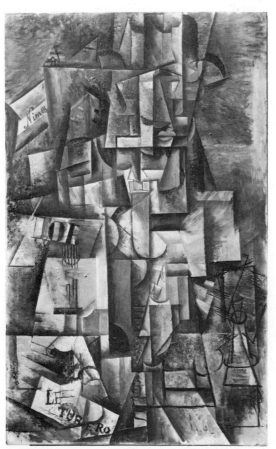

Negro and ancient Spanish sculpture. A major milestone is *Les Demoiselles d'Avignon* (Fig. 18-16), in which five female figures with masklike faces and flat, angular body forms become part of a sequence of splintered planes with lost-and-found edges. The painting is often seen as the starting point for Cubism. An example of Analytic Cubism is Picasso's *The Aficionado* (Fig. 18-17), while Synthetic Cubism is exemplified by *Three Musicians* (Plate 33 and Fig. 18-18), where the effect of collage is produced with paint, and the liveliness of the composition is achieved within a more severe discipline than is found in Fauvist work. The drawing of Dr. Claribel Cone (Fig. 1-1), done in the same period, presents an entirely different stylistic discipline. It employs the massive simplified forms seen in many of Picasso's paintings done mainly during the 1920s. These works have been called Neoclassical because they have some of the qualities of Greek sculpture. From the next decade, the best-known work is the *Guernica* mural, done for the Spanish government building at the Paris World's Fair of 1937. The painting is a violent but controlled expression of the horror

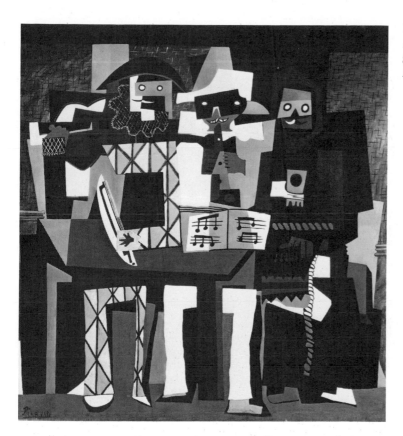

18-18 PABLO PICASSO, *Three Musicians,* (1921). Oil on canvas, 80″ × 74″.   The Philadelphia Museum of Art: The A. E. Gallatin Collection.

18-19 PABLO PICASSO, *Weeping Woman,* (1937). Oil on canvas, approx. 21″ × 17½″.   Private collection, London.

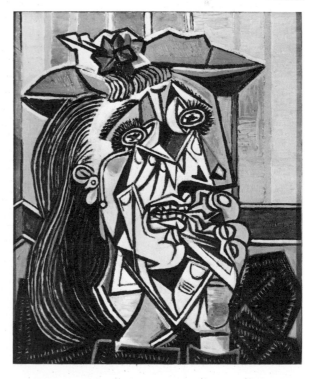

evoked by the bombing of the town of Guernica during the Spanish Civil War. Interest in dissonant forms — shapes with much internal conflict in their directional forces — had been building in Picasso's work before *Guernica* and now became prevalent in his art (Fig. 18-19). The stylistic variety continued, however, and ranged from precise portraits to ebullient patterns in strident colors.

In sculpture, Picasso led the way in Cubism and assemblage. Chicago's Civic Center Plaza contains a late work (1967) in the form of an immense sheet steel head, which recalls African tribal masks.

FERNAND LÉGER (France, 1881–1955).   The Cézanne retrospective exhibition of 1907 opened Fernand Léger's eyes to a new kind of pictorial architecture. By 1910, he was exhibiting Analytic Cubist paintings that contained human figures reduced to cylindrical robots. The *Contrasts of Forms* series of 1913–14 is apparently nonobjective, an approach that he used occasionally until 1925. His mature style combined identifiable and nonidentifiable forms. For years the space was

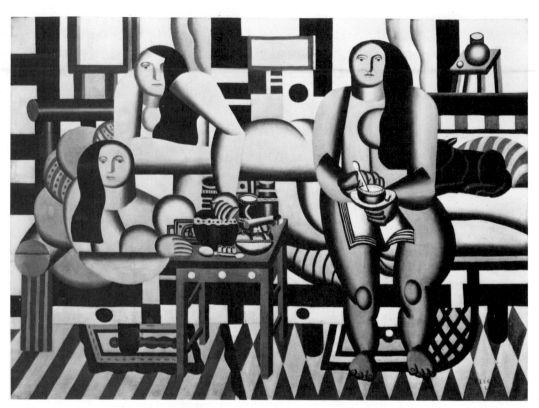

18-20   FERNAND LÉGER,
Three Women, (1921).
Oil on canvas, approx. 6′ × 8′3″.
Collection, the Museum of Modern Art, New
York. Mrs. Simon Guggenheim Fund.

dense, crowded by overlapping geometry (Fig. 18-20). After the 1920s, his style loosens up; objects float freely in an indeterminant space, although interweaving of shapes is sometimes complex. Forms seem tubular, possibly inflated. Their simplification suggests the influence of modern advertising and the tautly pneumatic figures that appear often in Picasso's art from 1917 into the 1920s. Léger said that his arbitrary colors were inspired by neon lights. He created a stocky, expressionless human type that bounces contentedly through an urban-industrial world.

GEORGES BRAQUE (France, 1882–1963). Georges Braque went from Le Havre to Paris and, by 1906, was painting Fauvist works. In the following year he became enthusiastic about the art of Cézanne, and some of Braque's offerings to the Salon d'Automne of 1908 were refused because of his startling use of lively geometric form applied to landscape subjects. The critic Louis Vauxcelles wrote of "Cubism" in describing Braque's work, thus naming for the first time one of the most important movements in twentieth-century art. Picasso had already initiated this trend in 1907, and he continued to provide the inventiveness and drive for Cubism, while his friend Braque went through fewer drastic changes of style and worked more methodically in exploring stylistic possibilities within a limited range. The shallow depth, restrained color, and many-faceted order of Analytical Cubism are evident in Braque's *The Portuguese* (Fig. 18-21). After serving in the military in the First World War, Braque worked in the style of Synthetic Cubism but employed unique, low-keyed, sonorous color harmonies. In the 1920s, he painted a number of nudes with delicate wavering outlines, thin washes of paint, and monumental proportions like those in some of Picasso's figure compositions from this period. Braque simultaneously used the same sensitive modulations of shape, texture, and color in still-life paintings. More playful arabesque curves and lighter colors appear in his work during the 1930s, and during the 1940s he developed a series of compositions on the theme of the *atelier* (studio). These paintings reach a new height in complexity and control; textures, textile patterns, and transparent and opaque shapes move back and forth within labyrinthine spatial relationships.

EDWARD HOPPER (United States, 1882–1967). Commercial art provided Edward Hopper's living for years while he studied painting with Robert Henri and absorbed European art in museums and on trips abroad. From 1908 until his death, he lived in New York and spent summers in Maine. Hopper's subjects include New England houses and coast scenes, but he is best known for paintings of the city. Works like *Early Sunday Morning* (1930, Whitney Museum of American Art, New York) and *Night Hawks* (Fig. 18-22) utilize bold patterns of light, shadow, and color to distill the character of buildings and to express the monotony and the drama of daily life. A poignant loneliness frequently haunts the mute façades. Hopper's paintings of the American scene help us find significance in the commonplace; one senses the isolation of the individual within the group, the ageless cycle of life and death. The drab buildings assume the expressive burden of the human condition. Hopper's view of the American scene was colored by a stern realism and aspects of social commentary. His subjects are treated with compassion but never with sentimentality.

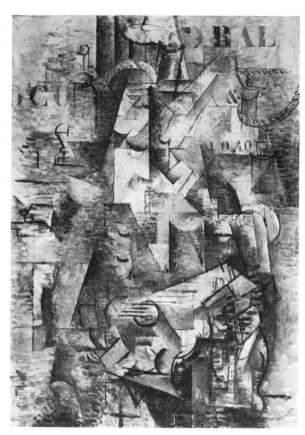

18-21   GEORGES BRAQUE,   *The Portuguese,* (1911). Oil on canvas, approx. 46″ × 32″.
Kunstmuseum, Basel.

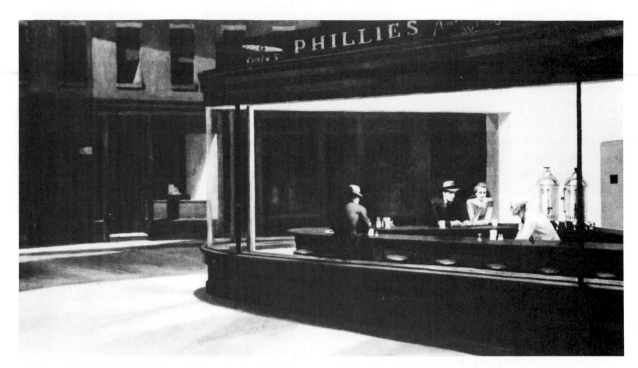

18-22   EDWARD HOPPER,   *Night Hawks,* (1942).
Oil on canvas, 30″ × 60″.   The Art Institute of Chicago.
Friends of American Art Collection.

UMBERTO BOCCIONI (Italy, 1882–1916). Umberto Boccioni's painting drew from Seurat's divisionism but employed featherlike brush strokes that evoke forms in violent motion. Boccioni was one of the authors of the *Technical Manifesto* of Futurist painting in 1910, which stressed the destruction of material bodies by movements and light and called for painting that expressed universal dynamism and metamorphosis. These convictions are powerfully conveyed by *The Dynamism of a Soccer Player* (Fig. 18-23), in which objects sacrifice much of their solidity and take on the appearance of colorful whirlwinds. Boccioni's sculpture, like his painting, evokes a strong sense of violent motion and the interpenetration of mass and space.

JOSÉ OROZCO (Mexico, 1883–1949).   After training in the Academy of San Carlos in Mexico City, Orozco painted murals depicting themes of revolution, pillage, suffering, and cruelty, using huge, massive forms. At the New School for Social Research in New York, he painted the revolution of the proletariat. In the Baker Library at Dartmouth College, he interpreted American history. The Dartmouth paintings include one of the most overwhelming of Orozco's compositions, *Christ Destroying His Cross* (Fig. 18-24). Having lost patience with humankind, Christ has repudiated his

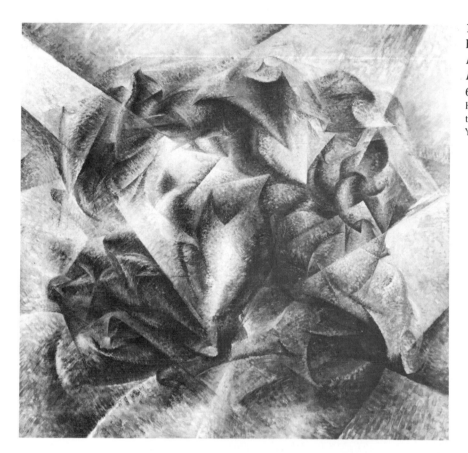

18-23 UMBERTO BOCCIONI, *The Dynamism of a Soccer Player,* (1913). 6′4⅛″ × 6′7⅛″. The Sidney and Harriet Janis Collection. Gift to the Museum of Modern Art, New York.

18-24 JOSÉ OROZCO, *Christ Destroying His Cross,* (1932–34). Fresco. Dartmouth College, Hanover, New Hampshire.

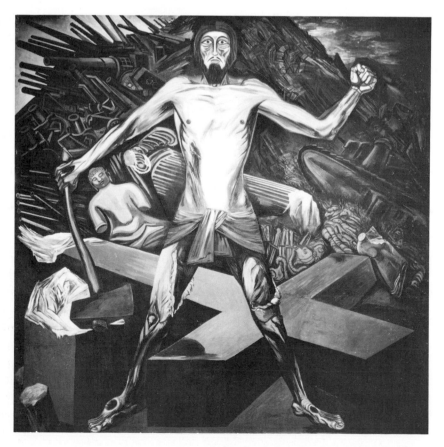

sacrifice and chopped down the Cross. His wrath is awesome as he stands facing us with an ax in one hand and the other hand raised in a clenched fist. He is portrayed with enlarged eyes, blue-shadowed face, reddish beard and hair, a torso of blue, orange, green, gray, and purple, and partially flayed legs. In 1934, Orozco returned to Mexico to paint his most furious condemnations of war in murals for the Palace of Fine Arts in Mexico City and for the University, the Government Palace, and the Hospicio Cabañas in Guadalajara. Orozco was a leader in the Mexican muralist movement, and his work is a thundering example of social commentary.

AMEDEO MODIGLIANI (Italy and France, 1884–1920).   After conventional art training in Italy, Amedeo Modigliani arrived in Paris in 1905 or 1906 and became associated with Pablo Picasso and Constantin Brancusi, as well as other avant-garde artists. By 1908, his painting showed the influence of Fauvist brushwork and the muted colors of Picasso's Blue Period. His subjects were mainly portraits and nudes. Enthusiasm for African sculpture and the sculpture of Brancusi, as well as for the painting of Cézanne, led Modigliani to develop simpler forms and harmonious relationships between the curves and angles in his figures and backgrounds. Contours assumed great importance. In the portrait of Anna Zborowski, the wife of his patron (Fig. 18-25), the diagonal upper body and the contrasting diagonals of her dress and right arm divide the background into three shapes that are highly dynamic. Forming as wedges that thrust against the figure, their dynamism is reinforced by active brushwork. These shapes, as well as those of the dress, hands, neck, and face produce a shallow, flattened space. The overlapping or tilting planes suggest that edges have been lifted slightly from the painted surface, an effect utilized in Cubism during the preceding ten years. Long, graceful curves relate the different parts of the composition. Theme and variations ease the taut conflict of figure and ground. The head is typical of Modigliani's images. Its elongated ellipse is repeated in the eye sockets, eyes, mouth, and neck. Remarkably, the individuality of Modigliani's subject is always retained in these masklike faces. The suave harmony of elliptical shapes contains a faint echo of Raphael's art. Modigliani's colors are

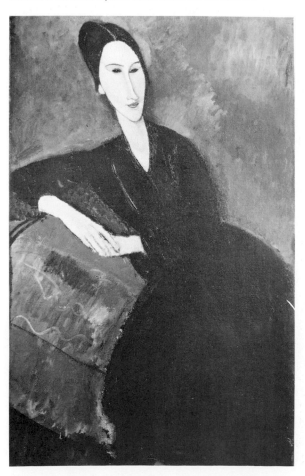

18-25   AMEDEO MODIGLIANI,   *Anna Zborowski,* (1917). Oil on canvas, 51¼″ × 32″. Collection, the Museum of Modern Art, New York. Lillie P. Bliss Collection.

quiet, but there are lush combinations of complementaries, such as terra-cotta reds and oranges against greens and blues, or somber harmonies in tans, red browns, grays, and blacks. Between 1909 and 1915, Modigliani carved masklike heads and *caryatids*—kneeling female nudes supporting a segment of architecture.

MAX BECKMANN (Germany and the United States, 1884–1950).   The Weimar Art School provided training for the young Max Beckmann. During military service in the ambulance corps in the First World War, he developed compositions of great dissonance and intensity, like his *Self-Portrait with Burin* (Fig. 1-2). As a leader in the German New Objectivity movement, he depicted the poverty, corruption, and hopelessness of his era in a harshly expressionistic style. *Departure* (Fig. 18-26) assumes the traditional triptych format of an altarpiece. The harsh angles, the pinched and twisted figures, the conflict of two-dimensional versus three-dimensional forms, and the spatial compression are found, to some extent, in much of Beckmann's work. The side panels depict scenes of torture and of burden-bearing or constraint; the center is relatively tranquil. At one time,

Beckmann said that the woman bound with a man, on the right, symbolized the individual searching through life but tied to the burden of past failures; that the center depicts triumph over the tortures of life and attainment of freedom; and that the title referred to departure from the illusions of life. However, he also said that each spectator must understand the painting in his or her own way. Unlike Medieval symbolism, Beckmann's symbols, along with those of many other twentieth-century artists, are personal and enigmatic, and demand completion by each spectator. Beckmann left Germany for Amsterdam during the Second World War. In 1947 he moved to the United States, where he taught painting in St. Louis and in New York. His art is one of the most powerful expressions of concern for the anguish and suffering of twentieth-century humankind.

OSKAR KOKOSCHKA (Austria and Switzerland, 1886–1980).   African art, Oceanic art, and Japanese woodcuts fascinated Oskar Kokoschka even before his training at the Vienna School of Arts and Crafts. His early paintings (*c.* 1908–10) included many portraits from a circle of friends, among them Arnold Schönberg, Gustav Mahler, and

18-26 MAX BECKMANN, *Departure,* (1932–33). Oil on canvas, triptych central panel 7'¾" × 3'9⅜".   Collection, the Museum of Modern Art, New York (given anonymously).

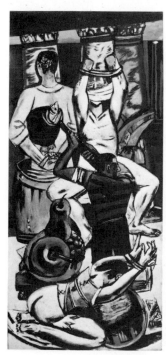
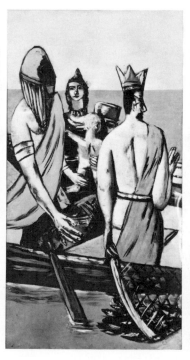
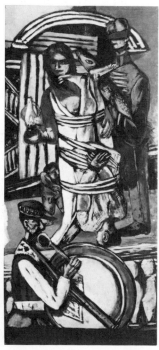

Anton von Webern. Kokoschka scraped and rubbed a thin layer of paint onto the canvas and then often scratched lines into the paint with his brush handle. The worried paint surface, the delicate color, and the gauntness of the figures all suggest a hypersensitive, fragile, anxious world. In 1910, Kokoschka moved toward thicker, darker, and more iridescent paint. By 1914, in *The Tempest* (Fig. 18-27), an expression of the painter's passion for Alma Mahler, the brush strokes are sweeping, and the forms are conceived as active forces. By this time, Kokoschka had sojourned in Berlin, done art work for *Der Sturm*, and influenced some of the Brücke painters there. Between 1938 and 1947, he stayed in England; in 1947 he moved to Switzerland. His style after 1924 tended to combine active line and brushwork with luminous color. Kokoschka was one of the leading Expressionist painters.

GEORGIA O'KEEFFE (United States, 1887–1986). After growing up in Wisconsin, training in Chicago and New York, and teaching art in Texas, Virginia,

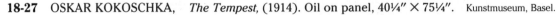

18-27   OSKAR KOKOSCHKA,   *The Tempest,* (1914). Oil on panel, 40¼″ × 75¼″.   Kunstmuseum, Basel.

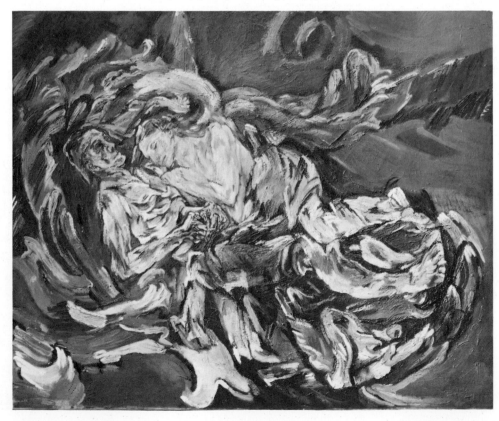

and South Carolina, Georgia O'Keeffe moved to New York in 1918. She was impressed by the towering buildings that loomed darkly against the moon or were punctuated by the flicker of lighted windows and revealed by the glow of streets far below. Geometric patterns were essential for her, but so was the poetry of the moment and the place. While Canadian and New England barns and adobe structures in the Southwest furnished her with subjects, the most important sources were flowers and landscape, especially that of New Mexico. From 1929 on, she spent most of her summers in New Mexico; after 1949, she lived there. The prairies, mountains, and mesas had, she found, a primordial grandeur in their vastness and in the revealed conflict of natural forces (Fig. 18-28). The sky in her paintings frequently is a force arching over the eroded masses of land. The bleached skull of a steer offers delicate complexities of edge and cavity. It also suggests the cycle of life and death in living things that is set within the longer cycles of geological change. The pelvic bone of a steer provided the source for a series of

paintings in the 1940s. Reduction to a few essential shapes has given power to her images, but subtlety remains. Paint is applied thinly and evenly in very gentle value and color gradations. O'Keeffe is perhaps best known for paintings derived from flowers. These too are often done in series, developing from representations of wholes to abstractions of magnified parts. Although her combinations of flowers, skulls, and landscape may recall Surrealist work, she was not interested in irrational thought processes. Instead, she offers an intuitive identification with nature and a sensuous enjoyment of its character.

JUAN GRIS (Spain and France, 1887–1927).   In 1906, Juan Gris came from Spain to Paris and settled in the building that housed Picasso and Braque. From magazine illustration, Gris turned to Analytic Cubist painting. He developed a lushness of value and color and a smoothness of gradation that gave his work a highly finished quality. His Synthetic Cubist painting includes extensive collage (Fig. 18-29). Like Picasso and Braque, Gris

18-28 GEORGIA O'KEEFFE, *Red Hills and Bones,* (1941). Oil on canvas, 30″ × 40″. The Philadelphia Museum of Art: The Alfred Stieglitz Collection.

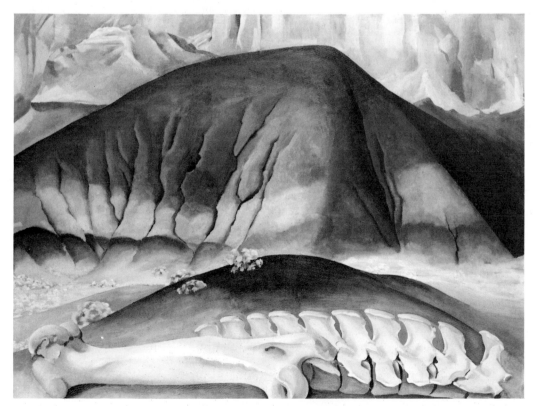

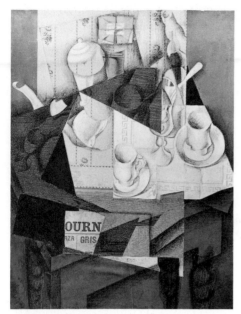

18-29 JUAN GRIS, *Breakfast,* (1914). Pasted paper, crayon, and oil on canvas, 31⅞″ × 23½″.   Collection, the Museum of Modern Art, New York. Acquired through the Lillie P. Bliss Bequest.

18-30 MARCEL DUCHAMP, *The Large Glass or the Bride Stripped Bare by Her Bachelors, Even,* (1915–23). Oil and wire on glass, 34¾″ × 21½″. The Philadelphia Museum of Art. Bequest of Katherine S. Dreier.

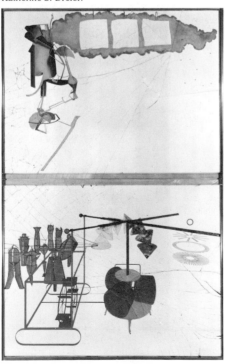

sometimes thickened the texture of his paint with ashes and sand. Unlike them, he was interested in theory, which he explained in lectures and articles. He described his work as flat, colored architecture. While objects in his compositions may be seen from various points of view, they are frequently tipped up and enmeshed in a pattern of vertical, horizontal, and diagonal planes and lines. The shallow but complex layering of space constantly reasserts the flatness of the canvas. The unique harmony of all parts was the advantage of a painting over the real world, yet Gris felt that recognizable objects were necessary. He claimed to work deductively, moving from geometric patterns to recognizable forms.

MARCEL DUCHAMP (France and the United States, 1887–1968).   Marcel Duchamp has been one of the most publicized exponents of the irrational in art. He studied at the Académie Julian in Paris and painted under the influence of Cézanne and then of the Fauves. By 1912, he had formed a personal style and painted the *Nude Descending a Staircase* (Arensberg Collection, Philadelphia Museum of Art), which became the focus of attention in the New York Armory Show of 1913. The concern with motion and its expression through multiple contours or repeated shapes suggests the influence of Cubism, photography, and the Italian Futurist movement. In 1913 Duchamp also produced the first of his "ready-mades," a bicycle wheel mounted upside down on a stool. By exhibiting a common, machine-made article as art, he challenged traditional definitions and values. *The Large Glass or the Bride Stripped Bare by Her Bachelors, Even* (Fig. 18-30) has been the subject of much interpretation. Some critics have restricted their analyses to sexuality, based on the implications of the title; others view the work as an attack on the mechanization of modern man. The composition relates readily to Dada art, and Duchamp was, between 1915 and 1920, the center of a New York group that was Dada in character and, eventually, in name. In the 1920s, Duchamp's activities as an artist gave way to his interest in chess, although he did help to organize the 1942 Surrealist exhibition in New York.

GIORGIO DE CHIRICO (Italy and France, 1888–1978).   A precursor of the Surrealists, De Chirico was trained in Athens and in the Munich Academy, where he grew to admire the art of the Swiss painter Böcklin, the German painter Klinger, and the German philosopher Nietzsche. For De Chirico, Böcklin's fantasies, painted with realistic detail, may have expressed the reality underlying the physical world. *The Mystery and Melancholy of a Street* (Fig. 18-31) exemplifies the style that made De Chirico famous during his stay in Paris from 1911 to 1915. The empty arcades of two buildings, each seen from a different eye level, and a long human shadow provide a disquieting environment for the small girl playing with a hoop. Colors are somber and the paint is applied thinly. There is an almost hypnotic effect of loneliness and quiet. De Chirico's deserted cities, echoing arcades, and vast spaces suggest the world of dreams, and he was later an inspiration to the Surrealists in Paris. After being called into the Italian army in 1915 and stationed in Ferrara, De Chirico found time to paint. He and Carlo Carra, a former Futurist, established the *Scuola Metaphysica*, a small group of painters who were influenced by De Chirico's style. In 1918 De Chirico returned to Rome and changed his style, gradually producing more conventional work in a Neoclassical vein. The Surrealists eventually attacked him for having deserted their camp; the critics lost interest in his work, and De Chirico was reduced, on occasion, to copying or imitating works in his earlier style.

MARC CHAGALL (Russia, the United States, and France, 1889–1985).   Marc Chagall's early style took form during his residence in Paris from 1910 to 1914, when he was introduced to Cubism. Memories of his childhood in Vitebsk, Yiddish folklore, and Cubist geometry are freely combined without regard to time, space, or scale in *I and My Village* (Plate 35 and Fig. 18-32). Back in Russia between 1914 and 1923, Chagall served as Commissar of Fine Arts at Vitebsk and designed murals and stage sets for the Jewish State Theater in Moscow. *Double Portrait with Wine Glass* (Fig. 18-33), from this period, portrays Chagall seated on his wife's shoulders drinking to the future while his young daughter hovers over his head. The monumental figures dwarf the cityscape beneath them, and bright colors combine with sudden angles, rippling curves, and anatomical transformations to produce an ecstatic vision. In the 1920s

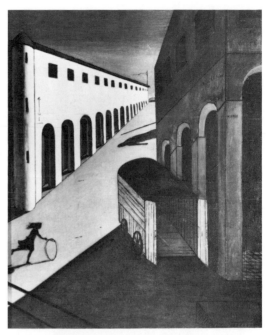

18-31   GIORGIO DE CHIRICO,   *The Mystery and Melancholy of a Street,* (1914). Oil on canvas, 34¼″ × 28⅛″.   Private collection.

18-32   MARC CHAGALL,   *I and My Village,* (1911). Oil on canvas, 21¾″ × 18¼″.   The Philadelphia Museum of Art. Gift of Mr. and Mrs. Rodolphe M. de Schauensee.

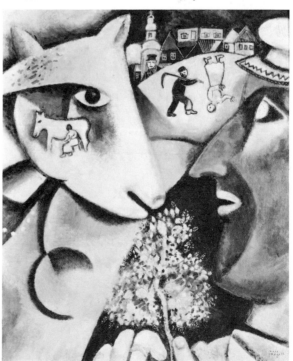

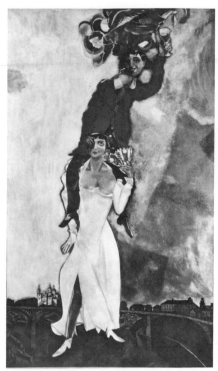

18-33   MARC CHAGALL,   *Double Portrait with Wine Glass,* (1917). Oil on canvas, 91¾″ × 53½″.   Musée National d'Arte Moderne, Paris.

18-34   MAX ERNST,   *Napoleon in the Wilderness,* (1941). Oil on canvas, 18¼″ × 15″.   Collection, the Museum of Modern Art, New York. Acquired by exchange.

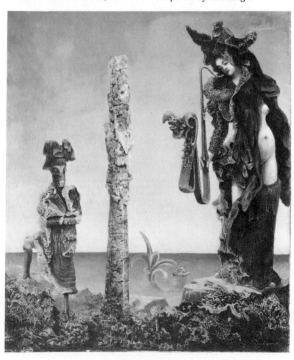

geometric elements faded from his art, and softer, more sensuous shapes appeared. The dreamlike fantasy in his work links it to Surrealism. Chagall designed many sets of stained-glass windows, one of which is in Chicago's Art Institute. National Square in Chicago contains Chagall's monumental mosaic *The Four Seasons* (1974), and two of his largest paintings can be seen in the Lincoln Center for the Performing Arts in New York.

MAX ERNST (Germany and France, 1891–1976). In 1919, Max Ernst, a former student of philosophy, became a leader of Dada art in Cologne. A 1920 exhibition of his work in Paris was a sensation, and he moved there in 1922, joining the Surrealists in 1924. As a child he had been introspective, sensitive, and imaginative. As a young man he was haunted by obsessive images, interested in the art of mental patients, and inspired by the work of De Chirico, Chagall, and Kandinsky. Ernst developed several of the popular Dada and Surrealist devices for exploring the realms of fantasy. One of these devices was psychic automatism. Another was photomontage, including fragments of engravings, which he used as a means to create surprising combinations of ordinary objects that upset rational expectations and stimulated the imagination. He also produced extraordinary images by using rubbings of objects placed under paper (*frottages*) and elaborating on the forms that emerged. Another of Ernst's devices was *decalcomania*, a work of art produced by painting the surface of an object and pressing it onto a canvas to transfer an image. The resulting textures and shapes were then developed by the artist, as in *Napoleon in the Wilderness* (Fig. 18-34). Ernst also scraped, spattered, and smoked the surface of a canvas to produce hallucinatory images of animals, plants, machinery, and persons. After the Second World War, which he spent in the United States, Ernst moved to France. Although he had broken with the Surrealist group in 1938, his work continued to be Surrealist in character. After 1945 his colors were more intense and luminous. Ernst was also a major Surrealist sculptor, combining such forms as snakes, bottles, and horned disks to tempt the observer's imagination.

JOAN MIRÓ (Spain and France, 1893–1984).   Joan Miró was born in Barcelona and trained in the La

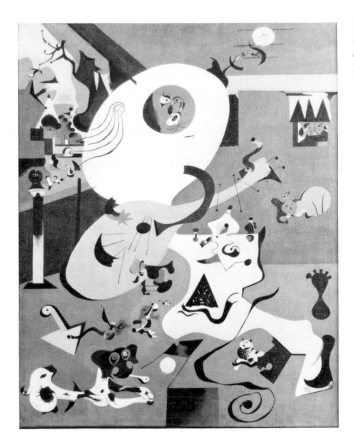

18-35 JOAN MIRÓ, *Dutch Interior, I,* (1928). Oil on canvas, 36⅛″ × 28¾″. Collection, the Museum of Modern Art, New York. Mrs. Simon Guggenheim Fund.

Lonja School of Fine Arts. His early work consisted of landscapes and portraits done in lively colors, patterns of repeated shapes, and occasional delicate detail. After 1919, Miró spent much of his time in Paris, and in 1924 he associated himself with the Surrealists. By that time, his work had developed the combination of reality and fantasy that evoked the quality of dream experience so interesting to the Surrealists. *Dutch Interior, I* (Plate 36 and Fig. 18-35) presents a preposterous collection of brightly colored objects wriggling buoyantly in an architectural interior. Many of Miró's works are more abstract than this (Fig. 18-36), but some identifiable objects are usually present. Frequently, the soft, undulating, amoebalike shapes change color where they overlap. Miró often dribbled or splashed paint onto a new canvas, employing accident to suggest the start of a composition. Renown brought him a number of important mural commissions, such as that for the graduate center at Harvard University (1950–51). After devoting much time to ceramics between 1955 and 1959, he produced two ceramic murals for the UNESCO Buildings in Paris.

18-36 JOAN MIRÓ, *Painting,* (1933). Oil on canvas, 5′8½″ × 6′5¼″. Collection, the Museum of Modern Art, New York. Gift of the Advisory Committee.

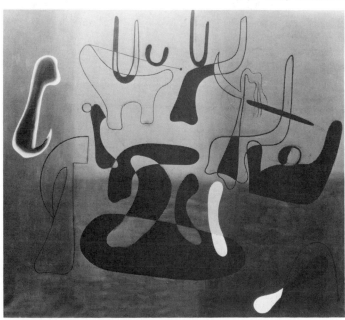

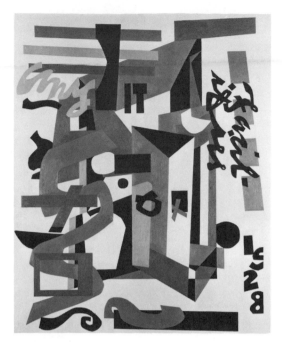

18-37   STUART DAVIS,   *Something on the Eight Ball,* (1953–54). Oil on canvas, 56″ × 45″.   The Philadelphia Museum of Art. Purchased. The Adele Haas Turner and Beatrice Pastorius Turner Memorial Fund.

18-38   RENÉ MAGRITTE,   *Les Promenades d'Euclide,* (1955). Oil on canvas, 64⅛″ × 51⅛″.   The Minneapolis Institute of Art. The William Hood Dunwoody Fund.

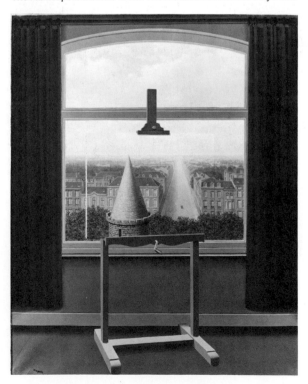

STUART DAVIS (United States, 1894–1964).   Stuart Davis received his early training in New York. The famous Armory Show of 1913 introduced him to Cubist and Fauve painting. During a year in Paris (1928–29), he produced a number of street scenes with delicate lines and rectangular patterns. After his return to New York, his compositions were still lifes, bustling city street scenes with garish advertising, and harbor scenes — all done with the aggressive shapes, jangling colors, and bits of letters or words that have come to characterize his mature style. *Something on the Eight Ball* (Fig. 18-37) is typical in the jerky curves and angles that weave a loose dynamic structure.

RENÉ MAGRITTE (Belgium, 1898–1967).   With the exception of his mother's suicide in 1912, René Magritte's life was remarkably uneventful. His excitement came from mental adventures — the search for mystery in ordinary objects. He studied at the Brussels Academy of Fine Arts and had his first exhibition in 1920. The Cubist character of his early work changed after he saw reproductions of the paintings of Giorgio De Chirico. Magritte's interest in the elusive nature of reality dates from this event in the 1920s. From 1927 until 1930 he lived in Paris and had intermittent contacts with the Surrealists. He was uninterested in the leftist political concerns of their leader, André Breton. Magritte admired Max Ernst but was not interested in Ernst's technical experimentation, in psychic automatism, or in dream experience. *Euclidean Promenades* (Fig. 18-38) invites consideration of the ambiguity between the physical world and representations of it. Magritte used the picture-within-a-picture theme for many paintings; it had been used earlier in De Chirico's art. Occasionally, Magritte made his point by using words within the picture. *The Use of Words I* (1928–29, Collection of William M. Copley) is a meticulously painted image of a pipe above the sentence *Ceci n'est pas une Pipe* ("This is not a Pipe"). Magritte felt that an image, work, or symbol is vastly different from its referent, although the differences are not always clearly understood. This simple point has profound implications for daily life, in which we depend constantly on interpretations of images, words, and symbols. For Magritte, painting was not an end in itself; it was a means of exploring mental processes and of giving images maximum significance. His images acquire a peculiar intensity through their elusive and paradoxical meanings. While most Surrealists have relied upon startling combinations of unrelated objects, Magritte often used related objects but changed their scale relationships (a rose blossom fills a room), their substance (a stone fish lies on a rocky shore), their dependence upon gravity (a rock floats beside a cloud), or their separateness (a pair of shoes turns into feet). Magritte's mature painting reveals little stylistic change. His manner was methodical and meticulous except for two brief periods. During the Nazi occupation of Belgium in the 1940s, Magritte turned to a soft, colorful Impressionistic style that he said was in opposition to the oppressive political situation. In 1947 his *vache* (cow) paintings employed violent brushwork and deliberate crudeness in a parody of Fauvism.

RUFINO TAMAYO (Mexico and the United States, 1899–).   Rufino Tamayo studied at the San Carlos Academy of Fine Arts in Mexico City. After working as a teacher and administrator, he went to New York in 1926. He has divided his career between New York and Mexico City. Unlike the social commentary art of Diego Rivera and José Orozco, Tamayo's themes are less literal and more universal, his style more abstract. While his early work in the 1920s and 1930s presents ponderous, massive female figures, monumental still lifes, or scenes of Mexican folk life, he changed in the 1940s to more fragmented figures that reveal the influence of Picasso, Braque, and pre-Columbian sculpture. Resonant blues, browns, oranges, reds, pinks, and purples come from pigments that Tamayo prepares himself. Paint texture is not heavy, although it seems to be so because of the scumbled overpainting and the frequently granular surfaces. The worn, layered quality of the work often combines with deliberately primitive human images to recall prehistoric rock paintings or tribal icons (Plate 37 and Fig. 18-39). Themes are rarely easy to comprehend; rather, they hint at hidden or long-lost meanings. Titles are usually general: *Dialogue, Couple, Matrimonial Portrait*, or *The Solitary*. Tamayo has said that his themes are usually simple and that they concern humankind confronted by the mysteries and the terror of an inscrutable universe.

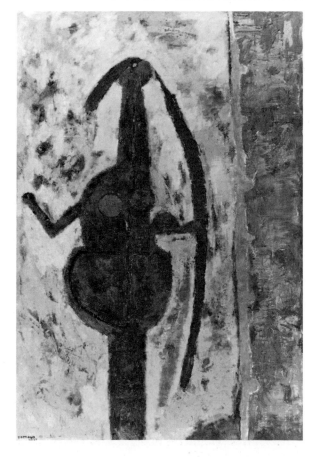

18-39   RUFINO TAMAYO,   *Woman in Grey,* (1959). Oil on canvas, 76¾" × 51".   Collection, the Solomon R. Guggenheim Museum, New York.

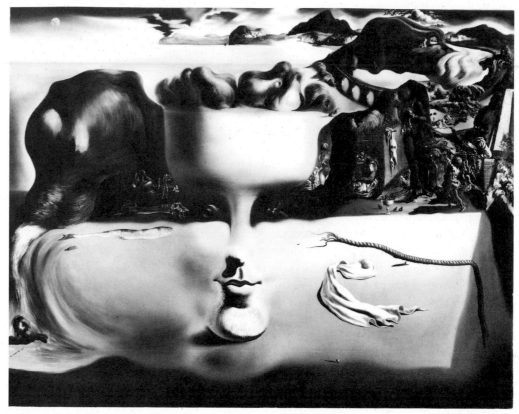

18-40   SALVADOR DALI,   *Apparition of Face and Fruit-dish on a Beach,* (1938). Oil on canvas, 45″ × 57½″. Wadsworth Atheneum, Hartford, The Ella Gallup Sumner and Mary Catlin Sumner Collection.

SALVADOR DALI (Spain, France, and the United States, 1904–).   This most publicized of Surrealist artists was an eccentric child prodigy who was eventually expelled from the Madrid School of Fine Arts for disruptive behavior. He tried various stylistic directions before settling on a dazzling illusionistic portrayal of objects that vary from normal to nightmarish. A startling and irrational combination of images serves Dali's *paranoiac-critical* method, by which he intends to combat reason and release repressed images from the unconscious. Dali believes that the hypersensitive free associations of the paranoid mind are an ideal means of achieving this. He has tried to intensify imaginative activity by the use of multiple images. Landscapes may suggest faces or animals (Fig. 18-40). At other times, Dali only hints at double identities by modifying the normal shapes of things. His images of limp watches, which he has called the Camembert cheese of space and time, won him early notoriety that he has since maintained by technical virtuosity, continually surprising imagination, and shrewdly outrageous behav-

ior. Since the late 1940s, Dali has done occasional paintings of Christian subjects. These seem more traditional in content than his earlier work and they have broadened his audience. However, from the beginning, the exhibition and selling of his work have been no problem. Dali has written books and has made remarkable forays into film, jewelry, stage, and furniture design.

Sculpture

As the twentieth century has unfolded, notable characteristics of sculpture have included (1) a tendency to find inspiration in primitive art; (2) the rejection of mass by many sculptors; (3) the consideration of space as a positive compositional element; (4) the use of actual movement in sculptural compositions (kinetic sculpture); (5) the increasing use of welded metal and a variety of synthetic materials; and (6) the tendency to create sculpture by assembling objects that have been worn out or cast aside by our culture. During the first half of the twentieth century, sculpture often reflected artistic developments that occurred first in painting.

In the early years of the century, the mobile surfaces of Rodin's art were countered by the stable massiveness of Aristide Maillol's work. Revolutionary portents emerged in the simplified forms and aggressive three-dimensionality of sculpture done by the Fauve painter Matisse. Equally expressionistic work was produced in Germany by sculptors such as Ernst Barlach. Cubist sculpture, like Cubist painting, practiced disciplined analysis and free improvisation on natural forms. The Russian, Naum Gabo, produced much nonobjective sculpture, created a pioneering example of kinetic sculpture, and provided a significant statement in the form of the *Realist Manifesto* (1920), which asserted the importance of space and time, rather than mass, as elements from which art should be built. The few pieces of sculpture created by Futurists are important three-dimensional expressions of the artists' obsession with speed and constant change. The Dada movement expanded the technique of *assemblage* that had been initiated by Cubist collage and first realized in sculpture by Picasso in 1912. Dada sculptures, sometimes called objects of nonart by their

creators, were efforts to ridicule the world of convention and reason. The Dada blurring of distinctions among painting, sculpture, and commercially manufactured objects was portentous for later art. Surrealist sculpture has been more methodical in its effort to investigate the nonrational and to stimulate fantasy and free association by creating surprising combinations.

ARISTIDE MAILLOL (France, 1861–1944).   Maillol and Rodin were two major influences in early twentieth-century sculpture. In the 1890s, Aristide Maillol developed a mature style that remained essentially unchanged throughout his career. Unlike Rodin, Maillol preferred ponderous masses and broad simple surfaces; his poses are usually static. In *The Mediterranean* (Fig. 18-41), the back and the raised knee and arm create a large stable triangle that is reinforced by the smaller triangular forms of the raised leg and the arm supporting the head. Geometric stability is strengthened by the simple, massive body forms, but the stony monumentality of the work is softened by slight undulations in contour. This sturdy female body, ranging from blocky hardness to active musculature appears throughout Maillol's work. His art has been described as a form of modern classicism.

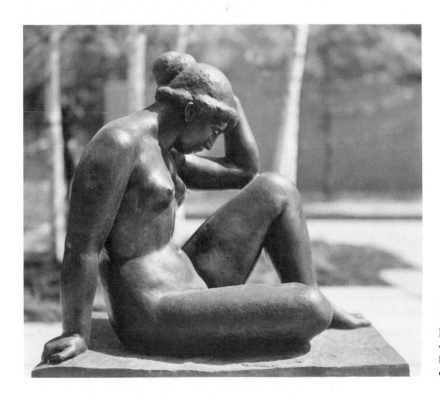

18-41   ARISTIDE MAILLOL, *The Mediterranean,* (1902–1905). Bronze, 41″ high, at base 45″ × 29¾″.   Collection, the Museum of Modern Art, New York. Gift of Stephen C. Clark.

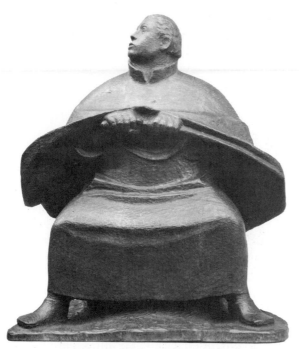

18-42 ERNST BARLACH, *Man Drawing a Sword,*
(1911). Wood, 29½″ high. From the Collection of the
Galleries of the Cranbrook Academy of Art, Bloomfield Hills,
Michigan.

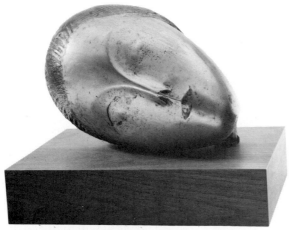

18-43 CONSTANTIN BRANCUSI, *The Sleeping
Muse,* (1910). Bronze, 10¾″ long. Collection, the
Metropolitan Museum of Art, New York. The Alfred Stieglitz
Collection.

ERNST BARLACH (Germany, 1870–1938). The
key to Ernst Barlach's style may be found not so
much in his studies in Hamburg and Dresden as in
an early trip to Paris in 1895, where he saw and
admired the massive peasants in Jean François
Millet's paintings, the expressive force of Van
Gogh's art, and the enduring strength of the
workers sculpted by Constantin Meunier. From
early work in clay, Barlach turned to wood as a
favorite material. He reduced the human body and
its costume to large simple masses, often unified
by a common texture of gouge marks, emphasizing lines of force that express powerful feelings.
His *Man Drawing a Sword* (Fig. 18-42) rises from
the lines of tension in the skirt to the sweeping flare
and bold shadows of the cape, which call attention
to the hands drawing the sword. Tense urgency
and vitality emanate from the simple forms. Barlach is generally considered to be an expressionist.

CONSTANTIN BRANCUSI (Rumania and France,
1876–1957). Constantin Brancusi studied at the
Academy of Fine Arts in Bucharest and, after settling in Paris in 1904, at the École des Beaux-Arts.
His first exhibit in 1906 revealed the influence of
Rodin. By 1908, Brancusi was finding his way
toward greatly simplified forms with slight but important surface variations. A series of heads gains
monumentality from sweeping planes and the reduction of facial features to grooves and ridges.
These works indicate Brancusi's debt to African
sculpture and his influence on the sculpture and
painting of Amedeo Modigliani. By 1910, Brancusi
had pushed simplification still further in *The
Sleeping Muse* (Fig. 18-43). The head is reduced
to an egg shape, with slight ridges for nose, lips,
and ear. This reduction to geometric forms must
be distinguished from that of Cubism; Brancusi
was not interested in a multiplicity of views or a
plane-by-plane analysis. He sought form that
would be both visually exhilarating in its absolute
simplicity and significant in its symbolism. *The
New-Born* (1915, Museum of Modern Art, New
York) is a sleek bronze egg form that is sliced by a
plane and interrupted by a ridge. Where flat surface meets curved surface, the resulting edge gives
a more precise idea of the nature of the curved
surface. In addition to satisfying formal elegance,

the work has subject matter that can be discerned with the help of its title. The egg not only refers to the beginning of life but also suggests the head of an infant, the anonymous face of a child whose personality is yet to be shaped by experience. Brancusi's preference for ovoid form is evident in the series of heads entitled *Mlle. Pogany,* done in many versions over a period of years, or in the versions of the *Fish* (one in the Museum of Modern Art, New York, done 1918–28), where the sleek, blade-shaped form is poised over a flat surface. Polished forms were sometimes set on bases of roughly carved wood. Brancusi's late work included pieces done entirely in wood, with choppy surfaces and abrupt transitions between the parts (Fig. 18-44). These have the character of tribal gods. Brancusi remained aloof from the various groups and movements in twentieth-century art, yet the influence and appreciation of his sculpture have been international.

JEAN (HANS) ARP (France, Germany, and Switzerland, 1887–1966).   When Jean Arp exhibited with the Blue Rider artists in Munich in 1912, he had already studied in Weimar and Paris and had shown an early tendency toward abstraction. From 1916 to 1919 he produced painting, sculpture, and poetry as a member of the Dada group in Zurich. Some of his nonobjective collages seem to have been arranged according to the laws of chance, reflecting the Dadaist rejection of rational order. With the exception of some rectangular compositions, Arp preferred irregular curves that suggested animal life. His shapes were sawed from planks, superimposed in two or more layers, and painted in usually contrasting hues to form polychrome sculpture. His first freestanding sculptures came only in the 1930s. Arp was a member of the Dada groups in Cologne, Paris, and Zurich. When Dada ideas and artists were absorbed into the Surrealist movement in 1924, Arp was in Paris to contribute to their first exhibition in 1925. In all his work, a sly humor is present in the relationships of irregular curves and unexpected angles. The subject of *Aquatic* (Fig. 18-45) eludes clear identification, but in the sculpture lurks the hint of a rollicking seal, or perhaps a penguin that has stumbled. Like Brancusi, Arp sought forms that had broad symbolic overtones and subtle relationships

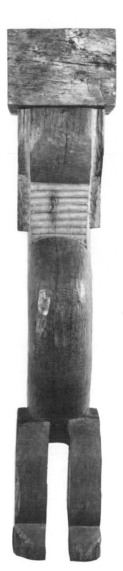

18-44   CONSTANTIN BRANCUSI,   *Caryatid,* (early 1940s). Wood, 90⅛″ high.   Musée National d'Art Moderne, Paris.

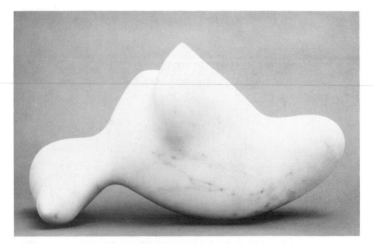

18-45   JEAN ARP,   *Aquatic,* (1953). Marble, 13″ high, 9″ deep, 25½″ long.   Collection, Walker Art Center, Minneapolis.

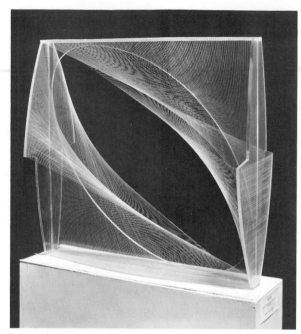

18-46   NAUM GABO,   *Linear Construction,*
(1942–43). Plexiglas, 24¼″ × 24¼″.   The Phillips
Collection, Washington, D.C.

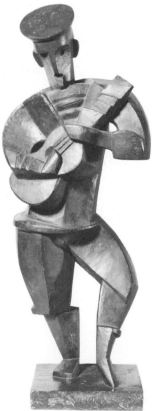

18-47   JACQUES LIPCHITZ,
Sailor with Guitar, (1914). Bronze,
31″ high.   The Philadelphia Museum of
Art. Given by Mrs. Morris Wenger in memory
of her husband.

between the parts, yet Arp's work is more complex and more playful. It seems to be a celebration of the vitality and ceaseless metamorphosis that he perceived in nature.

NAUM GABO (Russia, Germany, France, England, and the United States, 1890–1977).   Naum Gabo's Russian parents sent him to study medicine in Munich, but his interests turned to science and sculpture. Acquaintance with Vasily Kandinsky, travels in Italy, and visits with his brother Antoine Pevsner, then a painter in Paris, all strengthened Gabo's interest in art. He began to use wood, metal, and celluloid to create forms that were open spatial volumes rather than masses. In 1917, Gabo returned with his brother to Russia, and in 1920 they published the *Realist Manifesto,* which called on art to express the new realities of space, time, and motion. Soon the Soviet government became hostile to abstract art, and Gabo and Pevsner were among the many artists to leave Russia. Gabo's *Linear Construction* (Fig. 18-46) is typical of his mature style. Nylon string and plastic sheets form gracefully curving planes that are subtly adjusted to the square edges of the composition and frame a central opening. Light and space permeate the transparent composition, and space participates as a positive element, providing the major theme in the form of the central opening. Gabo's work continued to embody most of the principles of the 1920 *Manifesto.* Using transparent planes, he imposed order on space. Time is organized by motion, but motion is expressed by flowing rhythmic continuity rather than by actual movement. After his first experiment with motorized kinetic sculpture in 1920, Gabo decided that represented movement, rather than actual movement, was more reliable for his sculpture. In 1946, he moved to the United States and continued his career.

JACQUES LIPCHITZ (Lithuania, France, and the United States, 1891–1973).   Lipchitz left the Russian section of Lithuania in 1909 and moved to Paris. His early work shows a tendency toward stolid equilibrium and heavy, simplified anatomy similar to that in the art of Maillol. Soon, however, Lipchitz became involved with the concepts of Cubism. *Sailor with Guitar* (Fig. 18-47) has the cascading sequences of planes found in Cubist painting. Lipchitz's art was to become more open in form. After doing a series of relief plaques in a Cubist style, he began to use freer-flowing curves. A series of *transparencies*, as he called them, abandoned the traditional mass of sculpture for thin perforated planes, straps, and wiry forms. During the 1930s, the forms regained some of their mass and became knotted and muscular. In *Prometheus Strangling the Vulture II* (Fig. 18-48), the forms become convulsive in their energy. Primarily a modeler, Lipchitz makes the malleable clay burst with a life force. He has attempted to exploit the spontaneity of accident by blindly forming a mass of clay and then improvising with the result. He called such works *semiautomatics*. Although most of his subjects can be recognized, their expressive and symbolic character is not always easy to define; the forms seem laden with suggestions of fecund plant and animal life, of male and female elements, and of the mystery of creation. After 1941, Lipchitz continued his career working in the United States.

ALEXANDER CALDER (United States and France, 1899–1976).   Although Naum Gabo experimented with moving, motor-driven sculpture, Alexander Calder is acknowledged internationally as the most important pioneer in kinetic sculpture. Calder was born in Philadelphia; he studied engineering before he enrolled at the Art Students' League in New York. In Paris, in 1926 and 1927, he used wire to create toy circus performers and caricatures. From this, he turned to more abstract compositions of wire, metal shapes, or wood forms that were activated by electric motors or hand cranks. His acquaintance with the work of Mondrian led him to use color on some parts. After 1932, Calder decided that natural air currents were the best means of activating mobile or kinetic sculptures. *Red Petals* (Fig. 18-49) is typical in the lively curved metal shapes attached to the ends of delicately hinged and balanced wires. The flat metal pieces, like those of a weather vane, react to air currents, and the composition bobs and turns. Such sculpture renounces the traditional importance of mass; the open compositions participate actively in time and space. A major work greets visitors to the Greater Pittsburgh Airport. Calder also created many *stabiles*, in which the motionless forms acquire liveliness from the directional forces within the cutout sheet-metal pieces.

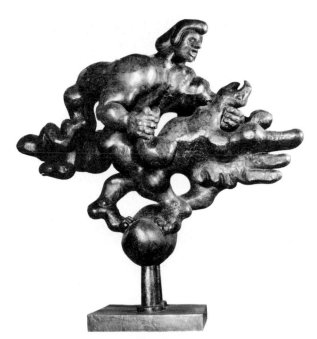

18-48   JACQUES LIPCHITZ, *Prometheus Strangling the Vulture II,* (1949). 7′8″ × 7′9″.   The Philadelphia Museum of Art. Purchased: The Lisa Norris Elkins Fund.

18-49   ALEXANDER CALDER, *Red Petals,* (1942). Painted metal, stabile-mobile, 102″ high, petal span, 3′ × 4′.   Collection of the Art Club of Chicago.

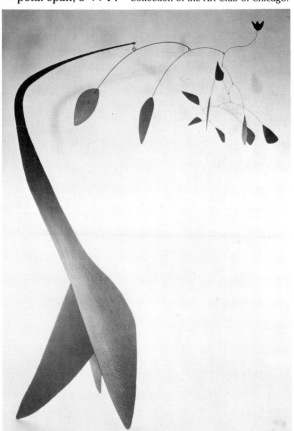

HENRY MOORE (England, 1898–1986). England's most renowned twentieth-century sculptor studied at the Leeds School of Art and had his first one-man show in 1928. Henry Moore's early work is simple, massive, and blocky, reflecting an enthusiasm for ancient Mexican sculpture. By 1932, Moore was piercing the masses with openings treated as shaped spaces. The *Reclining Figure* (Fig. 18-50) has such positive spaces; the female figure acquires the broad undulating hills and valleys of a landscape. As in so many of Moore's reclining figures, there is the suggested symbolism of the great earth mother, source of all life. During the 1930s, Moore executed a number of string figures, in which string is threaded through the masses to form groups of lines that define spaces. Meanwhile, his reclining figures became increasingly open. During the bombings of London in the Second World War, Moore made drawings of Londoners sleeping in subway tunnels; war had driven people back into the womb of the earth. The cavernous openings within the figures suggest a relationship with their cavernous environment. It was also during the war that Moore began his series of *Helmet Heads* (Fig. 18-51), helmetlike metal shells into which one of a number of bony core forms could be fitted. Although very abstract,

18-50   HENRY MOORE,   *Reclining Figure,* (1935). Wood, 19″ × 35″. Albright-Knox Art Gallery, Buffalo.

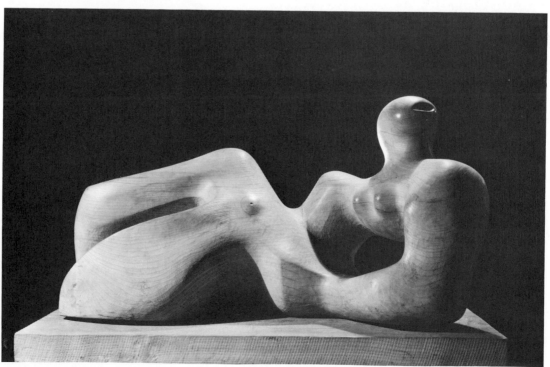

the results produce the uncanny effect of a frightened being looking out of a sheltering helmet. In the 1950s he produced a number of sparse skeletal figures with a regal, if occult, bearing, and several mutilated warriors, timeless expressions of humankind's self-destructive tendencies. Moore's sculptures, like those of Lipchitz, rely not on precise conventional symbols but on forms that suggest partly hidden truths about the nature of humanity and its relation to the universe.

ALBERTO GIACOMETTI (Switzerland and France, 1901–66).   Alberto Giacometti settled in Paris in 1922. His early work was inspired by Cubism, but from 1929 until 1934 he was a member of the Surrealist group and produced such sculpture as *The Palace at 4 A.M.* (1932–33, Museum of Modern Art, New York), a cagelike structure inhabited by skeletal forms. After 1934, he turned to more definite human figures, employing drastically elongated proportions. The fragile, isolated, phantom beings in *City Square* (Fig. 18-52) suggest that human society offers no escape from man's alienation from his fellows.

BARBARA HEPWORTH (England, 1903–75).   One of England's foremost sculptors, Hepworth received her training in England and Italy during the 1920s, when she also held her first exhibitions. Her early sculptures were figures in simplified masses and rhythmic harmonies that reflect the influence of Brancusi and Arp. In 1931 she produced a piece of sculpture in which a hole served as the focus.

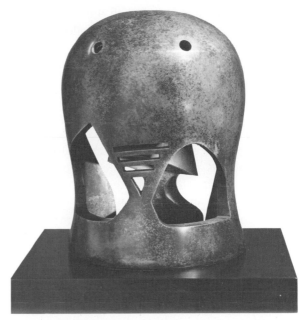

18-51   HENRY MOORE,   *Helmet Head No. 1,* (1950). Bronze, 13½″ high.   The Tate Gallery, London.

18-52   ALBERTO GIACOMETTI, *City Square,* (1948). Bronze, 8½″ × 25⅜″ × 17¼″.   Collection, the Museum of Modern Art, New York. Purchase.

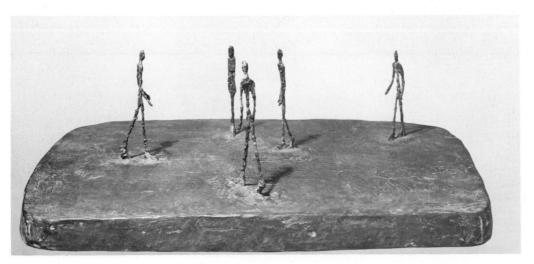

This work led the way, in British sculpture, for the positive use of empty space. The following year Henry Moore moved in the same direction. Subsequently, he used space as a cavernous interior volume, while Hepworth retained the sense of a pierced opening communicating between two sides of a mass. From 1934 on, she turned predominantly to nonobjective forms, preferring for several years a very rigid geometry. During the 1930s, she was a member of the Seven and Five Society, Unit One, and Circle groups, which produced abstract and nonobjective art. Inspiration for this abstract movement came from the temporary presence in England of Gabo, László Moholy-Nagy, and Mondrian. By 1938 Hepworth had returned to freer, more irregular forms. At this time she frequently used paint on the interior surfaces of her sculpture and occasionally used strings to define her open spaces. In *Pendour* (Fig. 18-53), painted blue and white surfaces contrast with the openings and natural color of the wood to produce delicate shadows that delineate the complex movements and rhythms of the forms. In 1950 Hepworth represented England in the Venice Biennale, an international cultural event. In 1956, she began to use metal, first by cutting metal sheets directly and then by working with plaster and wood from which castings were made. Severe rectangles and circles reappeared among the wide repertory of forms in her later work.

ISAMU NOGUCHI (United States, 1904–).   The son of an American mother and a Japanese father, Isamu Noguchi spent most of the first thirteen years of his life in Japan. After one year's training in New York (1924), he was sculpting conventional nudes and portraits with precocious ease. An exhibit of Brancusi's sculpture led him to feel, however, that abstraction was the way to greater depth. In 1927, he worked for Brancusi in Paris. Portraiture provided funds for travel to China and Japan. Japanese primitive mortuary sculpture and garden design impressed him with their elemental symbolic forms and social significance, qualities that Noguchi seems to seek in stage, furniture, garden, and playground design. In this work and in his individual pieces of sculpture, there is often a polarity between basic shapes, between rough and smooth, or boldness and subtlety. The artist argues that polarity is constantly present in the conflict between our inner and outer lives and our idealism and practical demands. His Chase Manhattan Bank Plaza court and fountain (Fig. 18-54) contrasts natural rocks with rhythmic patterns of

18-53   BARBARA HEPWORTH,   *Pendour*, (1947). Painted wood, 10⅜″ × 27¼″ × 9″.   Hirshhorn Museum and Sculpture Garden, Smithsonian Institution, Washington, D.C.

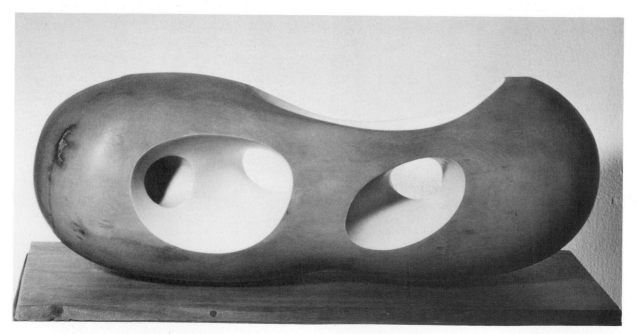

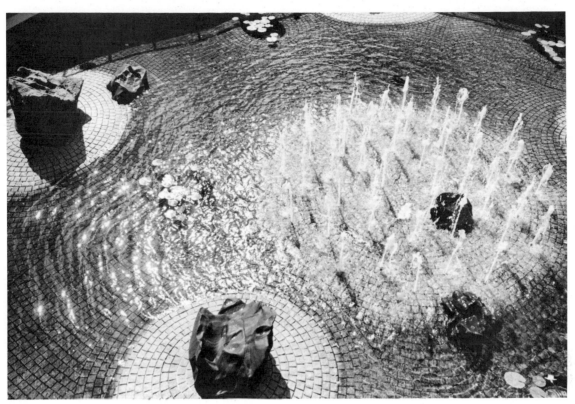

18-54   ISAMU NOGUCHI, Chase Manhattan Plaza Garden, (1961–64). New York City, New York.

paving that echo the raked sand patterns around stones in traditional Japanese gardens. In the Marble Garden of the Beinecke Rare Book and Manuscript Library at Yale University, Noguchi contrasted a pyramid (which he saw as a symbol for the earth), a circle (the sun), and a tipped cube (a die standing for human fate and the unpredictability of life).

Architecture

Twentieth-century architecture has lost almost all vestiges of regional style and has been characterized by broad international trends. Eclecticism and Art Nouveau continued as rival stylistic tendencies in the early years of the century. The relatively new materials—steel and reinforced concrete—were usually disguised by traditional forms in eclectic work; their structural potential was demonstrated more clearly in the organic curves of Art Nouveau. An architectural style that exploited the advantages of reinforced concrete had its beginnings in buildings by the Frenchman

Auguste Perret. The simplicity of Perret's work provided refreshing contrast to the crowded surfaces and self-conscious ornament of both eclecticism and Art Nouveau. Simplification was carried further by several Viennese architects, notably Adolf Loos. After 1910, the severe cubic forms of Loos's work were echoed in other countries and came to be known as the *International Modern Style*. The austere geometric buildings of this style were designed by Walter Gropius, Ludwig Mies van der Rohe, and other architects who worked at the *Bauhaus* (Germany's famous school of design) during the 1920s, and by Le Corbusier in France. A secondary trend developed between 1910 and 1925 in Holland and Germany, where certain architects designed buildings with sudden curves or exaggerated streamlining. Effects ranged from playfulness and whimsy to overpoweringly animated or machinelike forms. This architecture has been described as expressionistic.

In the United States, Frank Lloyd Wright followed his master, Louis Sullivan, in rejecting eclecticism, and Wright's use of uninterrupted interior spaces, asymmetrically expanding plans, long horizontal lines, and interlocking masses influenced the early work of Gropius, Mies van der Rohe, and several of the Dutch architects, all of whom learned of Wright's work through German publications. In place of severe geometric simplicity, however, Wright preferred a proliferation of masses and the enrichment of surfaces with contrasting textures and colors. Wright has had great influence in residential design, while Gropius and Mies van der Rohe laid the basis for modern trends in the architecture of skyscrapers.

The principles of modern architecture and urban planning found their major support in CIAM (Congrès International d'Architecture Moderne, or the International Congress of Modern Architecture), which lasted from 1928 until 1956. CIAM's most influential members were Le Corbusier, Gropius, Alvar Aalto, and José Luis Sert.

FRANK LLOYD WRIGHT (United States, 1867–1959). Frank Lloyd Wright, America's leading architect in the first half of the twentieth century, had two years of engineering training at the University of Wisconsin before joining the Chicago architectural firm of Adler and Sullivan. Unlike Sullivan, Wright designed few large public buildings. He acquired from Sullivan a love of mass, a hatred of imitation, and the convictions that form should be determined by function and that decoration should emphasize structure. The low, widespread, asymmetrical ranch house has its ancestry in Wright's early *prairie houses*, the best known of which is the Robie House (Fig. 18-55). In this house, the asymmetrically arranged spaces are interrupted as little as possible and flow around the central chimney mass (Fig. 18-56). Wright believed that walls should be opened up by large groups of windows to achieve the greatest sense of spaciousness, but he loved to contrast large window areas with unbroken masses of wall. He felt that the exterior should seem to be part of the building's site. The long low lines of the Robie House echo the flat earth plane and were originally punctuated by greenery in planters, so that the house seemed to be a part of nature. The wide overhanging eaves are typical expressions of Wright's conviction that the sheltering function of a roof should be emphasized. Concrete, brick,

18-55 FRANK LLOYD WRIGHT, *Robie House,* Chicago, (1909).

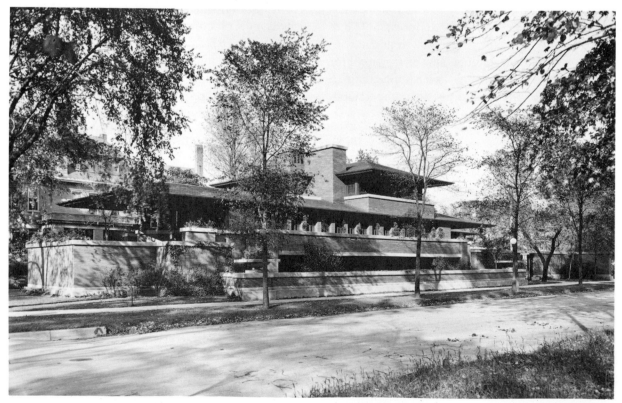

stone, and natural wood were used for contrasts of color and texture. Wright often elaborated on interlocking structures; throughout his work, masses, spaces, and the smallest details interpenetrate to express the unity of the whole. Wright's favorite term for such unity of site, structure, and decoration was *organic architecture.* His designs are remarkably original, though he learned much from Japanese architecture. Some of his more massive buildings reveal the influence of ancient Mayan architecture. His greatest technical triumph was the design of the Imperial Hotel in Tokyo (1915–22), which was planned to be earthquake-proof and was undamaged by the powerful earthquake of 1923. The houses of his later years sometimes employ a polygonal, circular, or triangular thematic shape as a unifying module for floor plans, for built-in furniture, and even for gardens. A circular module was the basis for the most controversial large building of Wright's career, New York's Guggenheim Museum (Fig. 18-57).

ADOLF LOOS (Austria and France, 1870–1933). Adolf Loos was one of the architects who rebelled against both eclecticism and ornament. He spent three years (1893–96) in the United States, and returned to Vienna to pursue a career in architecture, teaching, and writing. The Steiner House

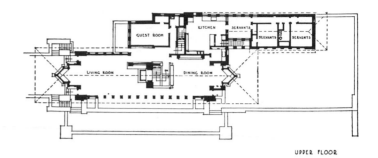

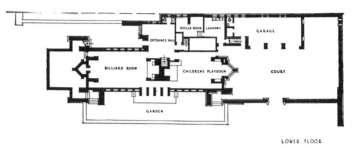

18-56
Plan of Robie House. A small third floor is not shown.

18-57 FRANK LLOYD WRIGHT, Guggenheim Museum, New York, (1946–59).

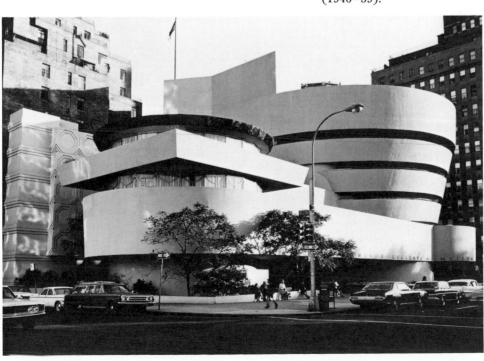

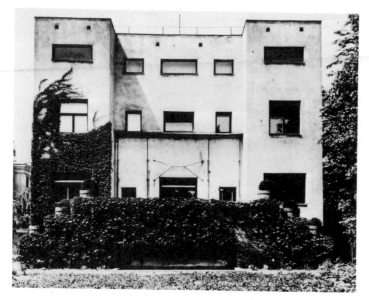

18-58   ADOLF LOOS,   Steiner House, Vienna, (1910).

(Fig. 18-58), built in 1910, illustrates his preference for starkly simple, boxlike geometric forms that rely completely on proportions for their aesthetic effect. Loos first acquired an international reputation through his writing, which was published in Vienna and then republished in Berlin and Paris. His most controversial essay was "Ornament and Crime" (1908), in which he equated ornament with crime and argued that culture advances as ornament decreases. Loos, like many of the International Style architects, was an avid admirer of engineers and machines. After 1923, he was active in Paris.

AUGUSTE PERRET (France, 1874–1954).   Auguste Perret was trained as an architect in the École des Beaux-Arts. He is especially important as a pioneer in the use of reinforced concrete. For his Rue Franklin Apartments (1902–1903, Paris), he used a ferroconcrete framework protected on the exte-

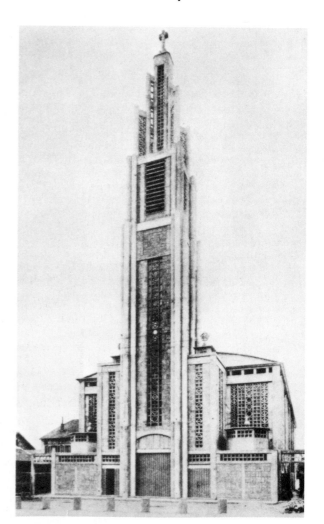

18-59   AUGUSTE PERRET,   Notre Dame Le Raincy, (1922–23).

rior by tile. Dramatic openness was arranged in the Garage Ponthieu (1905–1906, Paris), where the stark concrete frame is filled in with glass. Perret's basilica church of Notre Dame Le Raincy (Figs. 18-59 and 18-60) has canopies of ferroconcrete vaults supported by slender columns (Fig. 18-61). The walls, which are not needed to support the vaulting, consist of concrete blocks perforated with designs and filled with stained glass. The buoyant, light-filled interior thus uses new means to achieve some of the qualities of Gothic architecture. Perret often mixed color aggregates with concrete in order to vary the color and minimize weather staining.

WALTER GROPIUS (Germany and the United States, 1883–1969).   Mies van der Rohe, Le Corbusier, and Gropius were the major leaders in the trend toward austere simplicity in architecture from about 1920 until 1940. Of these, Walter Gropius is the one whose theories have been most influential, through his architecture, his teaching, and his writing. In 1918, after several years of private practice

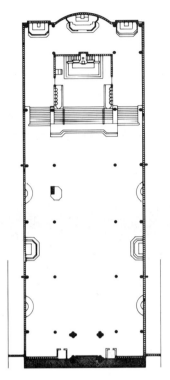

18-60   Plan of Notre Dame Le Raincy.

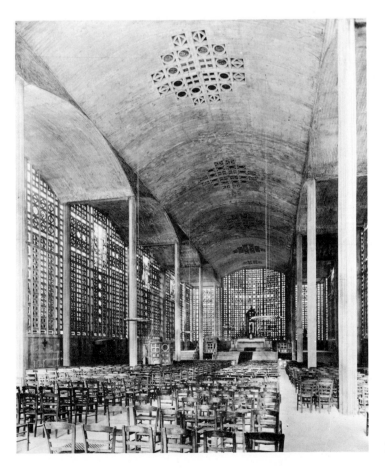

18-61   Interior of Notre Dame Le Raincy.

as a Berlin architect, he was appointed Director of the Grand Ducal Saxon School of Applied Arts and the Grand Ducal Academy of Arts in Weimar. He united the two schools under the name the *Bauhaus* with the aim of joining the creative energies of artists and product designers. Like Loos, Gropius was enthusiastic about the possibilities of the Machine Age and deplored the use of applied ornament as a kind of cultural cake frosting. Gropius's buildings have been consistent with his theory. His first major work (in collaboration with Adolf Meyer), the Fagus Factory, employed steel supports, concrete floor slabs, and screen walls of glass. Gropius used glass curtain walls (nonload-bearing walls that are attached to the building frame) again with dramatic effect in 1926 in the new Bauhaus buildings at Dessau (Fig. 18-62). In the Stuttgart Werkbund Housing Exhibition of 1927, where Le Corbusier and others demonstrated their advanced ideas, Gropius submitted a prefabricated house using a metal frame with asbestos and cork walls. In 1934, Gropius was forced by Nazi policies to leave Germany. He first went to England and, in 1937, came to the United States, where he taught at Harvard and formed TAC (The Architects' Collaborative). In spite of Gropius's hatred of labels, we must see his architecture as part of the International Modern Style.

18-62 WALTER GROPIUS, Bauhaus shop, Dessau, (1925–26).

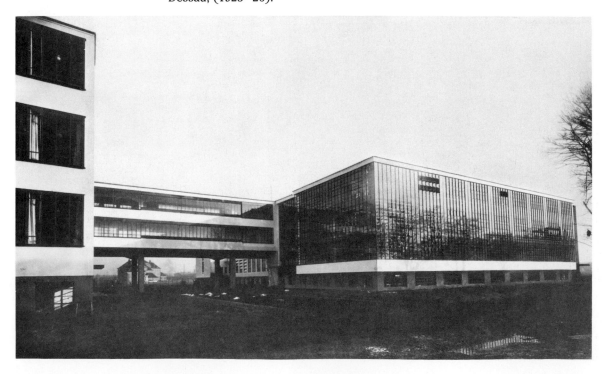

LUDWIG MIES VAN DER ROHE (Germany and the United States, 1886–1969).   Like Gropius, Mies van der Rohe worked with the architect Peter Behrens before starting independent practice in Berlin. The extent of his vision was evidenced in his plans for an office building for Friedrichstrasse in 1919. He proposed a steel frame with cantilevered floors and curtain walls of glass. His design for a brick country house (1923) has low spreading lines, grouped windows, and asymmetrical spaces that suggest the influence of Frank Lloyd Wright. Van der Rohe directed the Werkbund Exhibition of 1927 in Stuttgart. Two years later, for the German Pavilion at the International Exhibition in Barcelona, Van der Rohe produced one of the landmarks of twentieth-century architecture (Fig. 18-63). This small building consisted of marble panels, steel supports, and glass walls. Spaces were defined without being isolated from each other or from the exterior. The spaciousness, the long low lines, the reflecting pools, and the steel, glass, and marble materials all created an effect of serene elegance. These stylistic features were incorporated in the famous Tugendhat House (1930, Brno, Czechoslovakia). The exterior of the house is starkly simple, employing blank walls and

18-63 LUDWIG MIES VAN DER ROHE, German Pavilion, International Exposition, Barcelona, (1929).

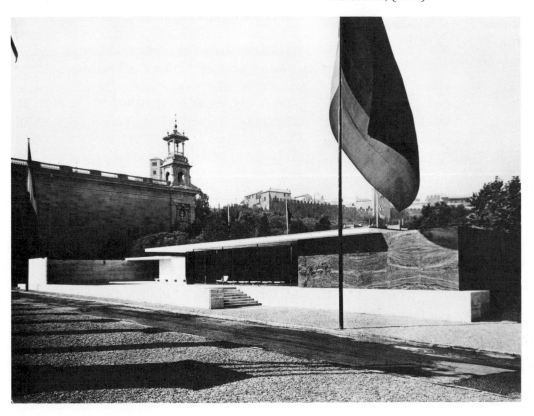

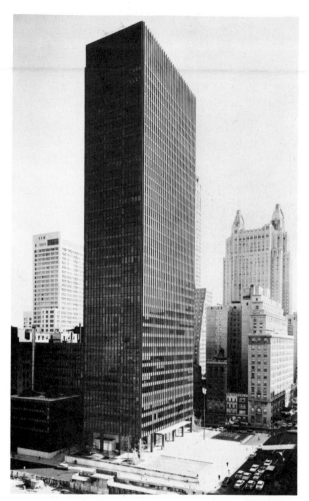

18-64   LUDWIG MIES VAN DER ROHE,   Seagram Building, New York, (1956–58).

translucent glass on the street side and curtain walls of transparent glass on the garden side. Within, slender steel columns support the roof, and the minimal number of dividing walls creates a maximal sense of space. In 1933 Van der Rohe, who was then its director, closed the Bauhaus because of political pressure, and in 1939 he moved to Chicago to head the architectural school of the Armour Institute, which later became the Illinois Institute of Technology. The buildings that he designed for I.I.T. became his manifesto in America. The simple rectangular forms were made of steel cages constructed on a 24-foot module and filled in with brick or glass. The Seagram Building (Fig. 18-64) was planned in 1956. The interior floor space gained by the height of the building enabled the architect to leave a large open area at the base for outdoor pools and gardens set into a pink granite platform, thus relieving the congestion at street level. The amber gray glass and bronze tower that forms the main part of the building extends beyond the steel piers on which it is raised, emphasizing its lightness and openness. The vertical bronze beams, partly structural and partly decorative, stress the soaring height and provide a delicate linear pattern in relief. Van der Rohe's architecture can be seen in the context of the International Modern Style. He was distinctive in his preference for glass curtain walls on steel frames, his austere use of lavish materials, and his demand for perfection in craftsmanship.

CHARLES ÉDOUARD JEANNERET, *called* **LE CORBUSIER** (Switzerland and France, 1888–1965). Charles Édouard Jeanneret, who took the name Le Corbusier to avoid confusion with his cousin, the architect Pierre Jeanneret, was born in Switzerland but pursued his career in France. He studied with Perret, learning about ferroconcrete and inheriting Perret's admiration for engineering and the efficiency of machines. Le Corbusier's Domino multiple housing project, planned in 1914 and 1915 but never built, used ferroconcrete frames that reduced walls to weather screens having no weight-bearing function. The plans for the Citrohan House (1919–22) were a more complete exposition of his aims. Standardized parts were used wherever possible, and the severely simple boxlike form was of plain ferroconcrete, with no effort to vary texture. A wall of windows at one end

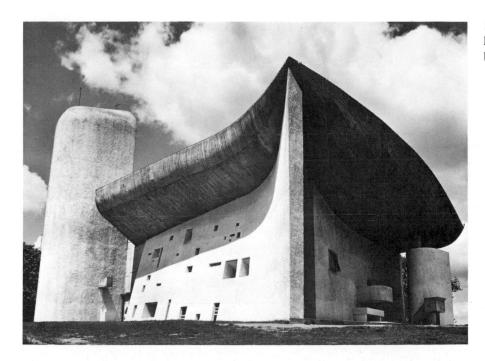

18-65 LE CORBUSIER, Notre Dame du Haut, Ronchamp, (1950–55).

illuminated a two-story high living room; bedrooms were on a balcony and a third floor, and a recreation area was provided on the flat roof. A second version raised the whole house on concrete piers. Like Frank Lloyd Wright, Le Corbusier was a leader in opening up interior space with grouped windows and a minimum of partition walls. Although his houses were criticized as bleak machines, Le Corbusier often sacrificed the practical for the aesthetic — the huge window areas and two-story living rooms, for example, are very costly to heat. Le Corbusier's sense of the beautiful was inspired by machines, and his buildings have the look of machinelike efficiency, but they are designed to satisfy his love of spaciousness and light. Many of his projects were never built, but the Citrohan idea was realized in a house built for the Stuttgart Werkbund Exhibition of 1927. Only in the latter years of his career did Le Corbusier have the opportunity to realize his urban planning theories. The most notable design is that for Chandigarh, the new capital city of the Punjab. Prior to 1940, Le Corbusier's work belongs within the International Modern Style. After 1940, Le Corbusier's architecture developed a very different character. The rigid boxlike forms gave way to irregular curves and deep openings in wall surfaces, producing a more sculptural effect. The church of Notre Dame at Ronchamp (Figs. 18-65 and 18-66)

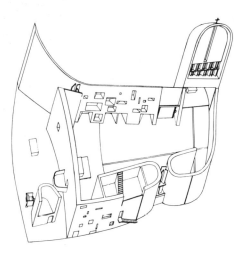

18-66
Plan of Notre Dame du Haut.

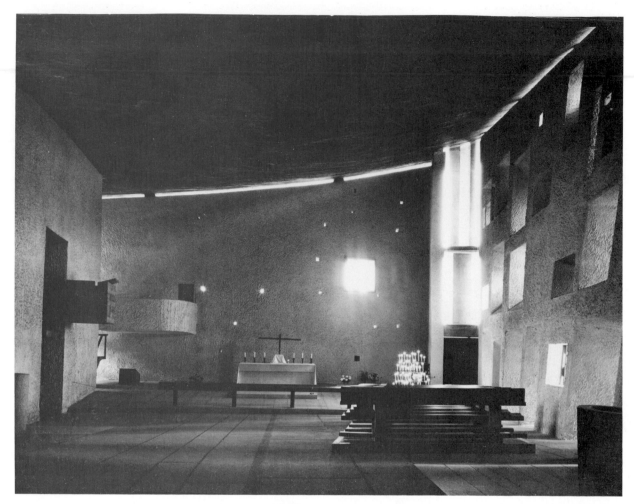

18-67
Interior of Notre Dame du Haut.

is an outstanding example, and it is one of the most controversial church designs of our time. The billowing vitality of the roof, the sweeping curves of the walls punctuated by deep irregular windows, and the spotlighting effects on the interior (Fig. 18-67) dramatize the experience of worship. The massive proportions and rough surfaces in much of Le Corbusier's architecture after 1940 were an inspiration for the international trend called *Brutalism*, which is discussed in the next chapter.

Suggestions for Further Study

Arnason, H. H. *History of Modern Art*, 2nd ed., rev. and enl. Englewood Cliffs, N.J.: Prentice-Hall, and New York: Abrams, 1977.

Barron, Stephanie, and Maurice Tuchman. *The Avant-Garde in Russia, 1910–1930. New Perspectives*. Cambridge, Mass.: M.I.T. Press, 1980.

Blake, Peter. *The Master Builders: Le Corbusier, Mies van der Rohe, Frank Lloyd Wright*. New York: W. W. Norton, 1976.

Breton, André. *What Is Surrealism? Selected Writings*. Edited by Franklin Rosemont. New York: Monad Press, 1978.

Crespelle, Jean Paul. *The Fauves*. Translated by Anita Brookner. Greenwich, Conn.: New York Graphic Society, 1962.

Curtis, William J. R. *Modern Architecture Since 1900*. Englewood Cliffs, N.J.: Prentice-Hall, 1983.

Franciscono, Marcel. *Walter Gropius and the Creation of the Bauhaus in Weimar: the Ideals and Artistic Theories of its Founding Years*. Urbana: University of Illinois Press, 1971.

Golding, John, and Roland Penrose, eds. *Picasso in Retrospective*. New York: Harper & Row, 1980.

Gray, Camilla. *The Great Experiment: Russian Art, 1863–1922*. New York: Abrams, 1962.

Hamilton, George Heard. *Painting and Sculpture in Europe: 1880–1940* (Pelican History of Art). Baltimore: Penguin Books, 1967.

Jaffe, H. L. C. *De Stijl, 1917–1931: the Dutch Contribution to Modern Art*. Cambridge, Mass., and London, England: The Belknap Press of Harvard University Press, 1986.

Kandinsky, Vasily. *Point and Line to Plane*. Reprint of 1926 edition. New York: Dover, 1979.

Neumann, Erich. *The Archetypal World of Henry Moore*. Translated by R. F. C. Hull. Princeton, N.J. : Princeton University Press, 1959.

Norberg-Schulz, Christian. *Intentions in Architecture*. Cambridge, Mass.: M.I.T. Press, 1966.

Read, Herbert, and Leslie Martin. *Gabo: Constructions, Sculpture, Paintings, Drawings, and Engravings*. Cambridge, Mass.: Harvard University Press, 1957.

Richter, Hans. *Dada Art and Anti-Art*. New York: Oxford University Press, 1978.

Rickey, George. *Constructivism: Origins and Evolution*. New York: Braziller, 1967.

Roh, Franz, with additions by Juliane Roh. *German Art of the 20th Century*. Translated by Catherine Hutter. Greenwich, Conn.: New York Graphic Society, 1968.

Rosenblum, Robert. *Cubism and Twentieth-Century Art,* rev. ed. New York: Abrams, 1976.

———. *Modern Painting and the Northern Romantic Tradition. Friedrich to Rothko*. New York: Harper & Row, 1983.

Selz, Peter. *German Expressionist Painting*. Berkeley: University of California Press, 1957.

Seuphor, Michel (Ferdinand Louis Berckelaers). *The Sculpture of This Century*. Translated by Haakon Chevalier. New York: Braziller, 1960.

Taylor, Joshua C. *Futurism*. New York: The Museum of Modern Art, 1961. Distributed by Doubleday, Garden City, N.Y.

19

Modern Art 1945 to the Present

Geographically, the United States became much more important to contemporary art after the Second World War. New York replaced Paris as a creative center, although art has tended toward decentralization, with new developments occurring in Tokyo, London, or Berlin. The movement with which New York seized leadership was *Abstract Expressionism.* In spite of its label, much Abstract Expressionist painting was nonobjective. It encouraged critical and theoretical discourse based on formal analysis. This situation was changed by the sudden appearance of *Pop Art* in the early 1960s. Subject matter drawn from advertising and comic strips invited the accusation that Pop artists were the "new vulgarians." Slick, simplified shapes and smooth surfaces seemed cool and impersonal after the emotional deluge of Abstract Expressionism. Pop Art blurred the distinction between art and mass-media images or mass-produced objects. It challenged Abstract Expressionism's concern with subjective experience and with personal style. So did the very different tendency called *Minimal Art*, a culmination of the reductive inclinations in much geometric abstraction. Equally controlled and precise were the complex geometric shapes in *Op Art*, which produced optical effects of change and motion for the viewer. The rapid proliferation of styles produced yet another surprise with *Photorealism*, which, from the late 1960s, has demonstrated enormous patience, skill, and fascination with the characteristics of photographic images rendered in paint.

The traditional concept of art as a precious object that is merchandised and collected has also been attacked by means of sculpture that destroys itself in a dramatic performance, through some earthworks, and through *Happenings*, artist-directed theatrical events employing crudely made properties and improvised action. Happenings were replaced in the 1970s by *Performance Art*, which is less improvisational and, in turn, has various forms. *Video Art* has documented performances planned specifically for video tape. Categories have overlapped and multiplied in art criticism as a result of the complex and swiftly changing situation. Some trends of the 1960s and 1970s at first scorned the "art establishment" of critics, dealers, collectors, and museums. However, these institutions, as well as a portion of the public, moved quickly to underwrite and absorb new developments whenever possible, and many of the disaffected artists have accepted this encouragement and returned to the fold.

During the 1970s and 1980s, a *Postmodernist movement* developed, in which artists and architects appropriated styles from various movements in the history of art. Surprising combinations of styles sometimes produced irony, parody, or humor. Many Postmodernists question the values of modernist movements, in which originality, the freedom to express personal vision, and formal consistency were given highest priority. Theoretically inclined Postmodernists tend to see art as the product of cultural and socioeconomic conditions. In conjunction with this, art criticism and art history have become more interested in the cultural and socioeconomic context and how this may have affected or determined art. A basic source for this approach is the Marxist interpretation of culture as the product of political and economic forces.

1945–1960

Painting and Printmaking

Between World War II and 1960 an international trend toward abstract and nonobjective art enjoyed dominance. Many European artists were driven by the war to the United States, bringing with them quantities of talent and new ideas. It was in New York, under the leadership of Jackson Pollock, Franz Kline, and Willem de Kooning, that the first major movement in postwar painting developed — Abstract Expressionism. The explosive impact of this work is frequently magnified by large scale. The quality of expressed activity — often cathartic in its violence — led American critics to describe much Abstract Expressionist art as *Action Painting*. A less violent trend within Abstract Expressionism has been called *Color Field* painting because it relies for its impact on large areas of intensely interacting colors. Although the term Abstract Expressionism was applied first to American painting of this type during the 1940s, similar work has been done in other countries. This movement has its ancestry in Fauvism, German Expressionism, and the Surrealist emphasis on instinct and fantasy. More than previously, however, Abstract Expressionist painters produced series of works that were intended to be experienced as a whole. The way was paved for compositions of total environments that were to become common, especially after 1960.

Toward the end of the 1950s, young British and American artists were laying the foundation for Pop Art, which utilized mass-media images. Geometric abstraction also continued. In France, Victor Vasarely was experimenting with the optical illusions that were to become essential to *Op Art* in the next decade.

HANS HOFMANN (Germany and the United States, 1880–1966).   From Impressionist painting produced while a student, Hans Hofmann turned to Cubism during his stay in Paris from 1903 to 1914. After his return to Munich, he quickly gained a reputation as an art instructor. This led to summer

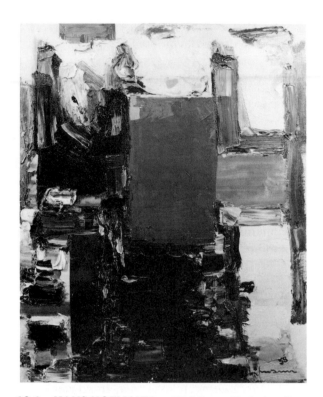

19-1   HANS HOFMANN,   *Bird Cage, Variation II,*
(1958). Oil on canvas, 60″ × 48″.   Collection of Saul Z.
and Amy S. Cohen, Larchmont, New York.

teaching jobs in California and to permanent residence after 1932 in New York, where he taught at the Art Student's League and later opened his own school. His art and teaching form a major link between European Expressionism and New York Abstract Expressionism. In his paintings, he ranged stylistically from free forms done with poured, spattered, or violently brushed paint to hard-edged, rectangular planes. Often the two kinds of forms are combined in one painting, as in *Bird Cage, Variation II* (Plate 41 and Fig. 19-1). Textures in the paintings vary from thin washes to puttylike thicknesses. Hofmann argued that vitality in art arises from movement and tension between opposing elements, which he termed "push-pull." In painting, this vitality comes from the contrasting directions of overlapping planes, the opposing movements of line and the immediate juxtaposition of soft and hard edges, quiet and aggressive brushwork, and — most of all — from advancing and receding colors (see p. 16). The illusionary spaces between colors are charged, he felt, with energy. He wanted to preserve the sense of the flat surface of the canvas even while the illusion of depth was generated by his jockeying of forms in space. The central red-orange plane in *Bird Cage, Variation II* floats forward but is tied to the surface by colors that overlap and diffuse its edges. The green bar in the lower left pulls away from the yellow background at its left edge but is overrun by thick strokes of paint on its right; no area of the composition is allowed to be empty. In Hofmann's theory even the smallest area, active or passive, should have interest or substance. The relatively passive white areas have sparks of color, delicate modulations of value, and textural weight. At the upper left, the variegated whitish mass surges in front of the blue rectangle. For Hofmann, a painting was a field of forces to be controlled and manipulated by the artist in achieving the utmost vitality.

JOSEF ALBERS (Germany and the United States, 1888–1976).   Josef Albers taught in elementary schools and produced lithographs and *linocuts* (linoleum block prints) before entering the Bauhaus as a student in 1920. By 1923, he had become an instructor there, teaching glass painting, which is a form of stained glass. His nonobjective works in this medium were made at first from scavenged bottle-glass of irregular shapes. Then he turned to precise, rectangular forms in milk glass with color overlays. At the same time, he made linocuts and woodcuts, occasionally creating ambiguous spatial effects with overlapping shapes. When the Bauhaus closed in 1933 Albers came to the United States, where he taught at Black Mountain College in North Carolina, at Harvard, and at Yale. He spent his career investigating the perception of line and color. His best-known series, *Homage to the Square* (Plate 42 and Fig. 19-2), painted from 1949 until the end of his life, employs symmetrically arranged squares of pure colors and unvarying textures. With the exceptions of pink and rose, the colors are used directly from commercial tubes of oil paint and noted on the back of each Masonite panel. Colors and proportions are selected to create effects of vibration, translucency, changing saturation, and movement up and down or back and forth in illusionary space. In our perception, color changes according to its environment. Albers's aim was to make us more sensitive to color phenomena; he was a forerunner in the development of Op Art.

DAVID ALFARO SIQUEIROS (Mexico, 1896–1974). Siqueiros's life and art were directed by his dedication to the Mexican Revolution and to laborers worldwide. Under the influence of Marxist theory, Siqueiros's painting and political activities were used as weapons against fascism and the exploitation of the working classes in underdeveloped countries. Having served as a soldier and officer in the Mexican Revolution, Siqueiros was sent by the revolutionary government to Europe to study art and to become an artist of the Revolution. Italian Futurist art, with its emphasis on dynamism and mechanization, impressed the young Siqueiros. He published manifestos in 1921 and 1922 urging artists to make their art monumental, public, and polemical on behalf of the proletariat in the class struggle. Periods of intense political activity, imprisonment, and exile interrupted his artistic career, yet Siqueiros's productivity was staggering.

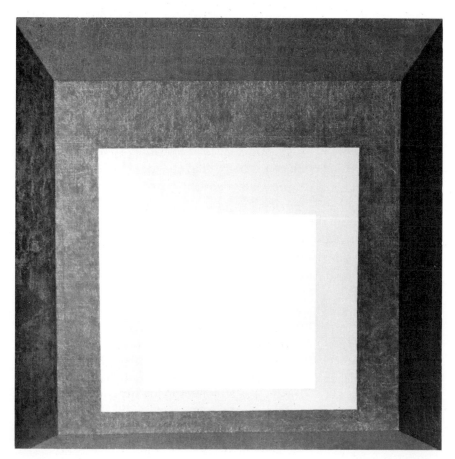

19-2 JOSEF ALBERS, *Homage to the Square: Apparition,* (1959). Oil on board, 47½″ × 47½″. The Solomon R. Guggenheim Museum, New York.

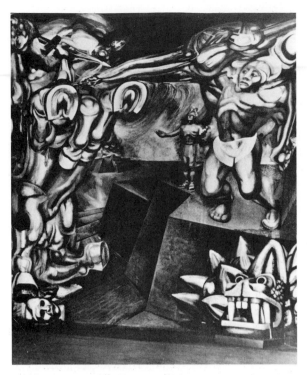

19-3   DAVID ALFARO SIQUEIROS,   *Cuauhtémoc Against the Myth,* (1944). Pyroxylin on celotex, 1,000 sq. ft. Union Housing Project at Tlatelolco.

19-4   S. W. HAYTER,   *Tarantelle,* (1947). Engraving, 550 × 332 mm. Collection of The Art Institute of Chicago.

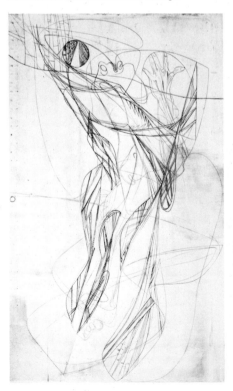

Siqueiros became one of the leaders in the Mexican mural movement with works like *Cuauhtémoc Against the Myth* (Fig. 19-3), originally in a private residence but now in a public housing project. The towering, rearing centaur (man-horse combination) is an allegorical representation of Hernán Cortés, the sixteenth-century Spanish conqueror of Mexico, who raises a dagger in the form of a Christian cross. In the center background, Moctezuma, ruler of the Aztec nation at the time the Spaniards arrived, prays passively to the gods. At the right, Cuauhtémoc, the last emperor of the Aztecs, hurls his spear in defiance of the myth of invincibility that clung to the technically superior Spanish invaders. At bottom right, a painted sculpture by another artist forecasts Siqueiros's later efforts to combine painting and sculpture. The violence of the action is matched by the expressive exaggerations in scale, musculature, and perspective. The style suggests that Siqueiros learned much from Baroque paintings during his 1919 trip to Italy. The theme of the mural runs through much of Siqueiros's art. He saw the history of Mexico and South America as the story of agrarian peoples exploited economically by other nations and, in modern pre-Revolutionary times, by an internal aristocracy. Siqueiros hoped for industrialization in Mexico, and he exhorted artists to set an example by utilizing the newest materials and techniques. He used synthetic pyroxylin paint, an airbrush (spray gun), masonite and aluminum panels, projectors for enlargement, and occasional photographic images in his work. In his later murals, Siqueiros seemed to abandon the Marxist emphasis on a materialistic solution to human needs, and his painting took on a strangely abstract remoteness. Perhaps Siqueiros, the indomitable revolutionary, became disillusioned with political means of establishing universal contentment, but to the end, his work did not abandon the belief, which he shared with the French revolutionary painter Jacques Louis David, that art should electrify the soul of the people.

STANLEY WILLIAM HAYTER (England, France, and the United States, 1901–88).   Stanley William Hayter was a pioneer in the twentieth-century renaissance of printmaking. In 1927, he founded a printing shop in Paris where experienced and beginning printmakers could learn together. This research and teaching center, Atelier 17, was moved to New York from 1940 until 1950. Printmakers who trained there have founded centers in other countries. Hayter's early prints were representational; later, they became abstract, with taut, elliptical, aggressively looping lines, often combined with textured areas from soft-ground etching (Fig. 19-4). Sparkling white relief occurs where holes have been cut out of the intaglio plate. Hayter developed methods of printing numerous colors at once by inking the plate with black and then screening or stenciling colors on the plate before printing. Or, he deeply engraved or etched a plate and then applied different colors in layers before printing. This was done with inks of different viscosities and rollers of different degrees of firmness. An avid sailor, Hayter began in the 1950s to use water patterns in his work. He said that he allowed shapes to be influenced by the dictates of the medium and by his feeling for what ought to happen next. Both method and result imply psychic improvisation, the device of the Surrealists, with whom Hayter exhibited beginning in 1929.

JEAN DUBUFFET (France, 1901–85).   Enraged spectators slashed some of Jean Dubuffet's paintings in 1946 at his second one-man exhibition. Undaunted, he became a leader in the international avant-garde of the 1950s. He used tar, cement, glue, bark, sponges, driftwood, steel wool, and butterfly wings to produce images of startling energy, brute force, and childlike directness of vision. Dubuffet was interested in folk art and in the art of the mentally disturbed, which he collected and exhibited under the title *l'Art Brut* (unrefined art)—a term which has been applied to his own work as well. He tends to produce paintings in series on such subjects as female figures, landscapes, city scenes, tables (Fig. 19-5), and portraits of friends. Even in his portraits, personal features are less important than the suggestion of a type. Often a major form within a composition is so expansive in proportion to the surface area that it threatens to burst the pictorial boundaries. On a technical level, his preference has been to use heavy pastes composed of ingredients like zinc oxide and varnish, which are troweled onto panels. Cut-and-pasted shapes, impressions of kitchen utensils as well as other objects, and incompatible paints all contribute to the wrinkled and lacerated forms of his images. For Dubuffet the crudeness of his materials serves to intensify his forms while providing resistance to the facile recognition of his images. The shock of finding images in such crude materials evokes within the spectator fresh imaginative responses. In his later years, Dubuffet used more delicate textures in such series of works as *Texturologies* and *Beards*. Many of these works have employed shapes like those of jigsaw puzzles. In spite of his anti-intellectual position, Dubuffet's talks and writings are highly sophisticated and articulate.

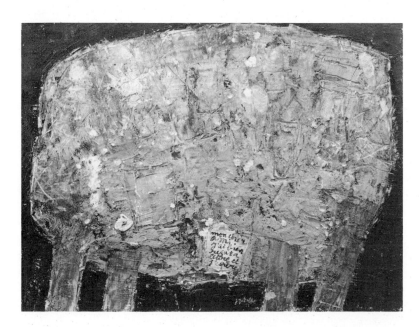

19-5 JEAN DUBUFFET, *Work Table with Letter,* from the Landscaped Table Series, (1952). Oil paint in Swedish putty on composition board, 35⅝″ × 47⅞″. Collection, the Museum of Modern Art, New York. Gift of Mr. and Mrs. Ralph F. Colin.

19-6 MARK ROTHKO, *Brown and Black on Plum,* (1958). Oil on canvas, 80″ × 82″.   Private collection, Switzerland.

MARK ROTHKO (Russia and the United States, 1903–70).   In 1933, at the time of his first one-man show, Mark Rothko was using subtle colors and flat shapes to depict isolated figures in urban settings. In the 1940s, he changed to wide bands of thinly painted color containing delicately drawn forms that suggest plant or animal fossils. By 1950, he had turned to large, nonobjective compositions of several soft-edged rectangles aligned with the canvas surface, as in *Brown and Black on Plum* (Plate 44 and Fig. 19-6). Rothko chose colors that would produce luminous intensity where the rectangles meet. The blurred, resonant edges make the shapes and their position in space elusive. While the forms seem to be absorbed in the canvas surface, they also appear to float in a veiled space, creating a tension between surface and depth. Their power and size tend to overwhelm or engulf the spectator, especially when the work is viewed at close range. Because color is more important than shape in his work, Rothko is considered a Color Field painter.

ARSHILE GORKY (Armenia and the United States, 1904–48).   Arshile Gorky may be seen as a link between Surrealism and Abstract Expressionism in New York (see p. 366). An Armenian immigrant, he changed his original name, Vosdanig Manoog, to that of the celebrated Russian novelist. In addition to brief periods of formal training, Gorky taught himself by submissive study of such masters as Cézanne, Picasso, Miro, Kandinsky, and De Chirico. About 1941, Gorky's painting coalesced into an individual and highly abstract style. However, during the 1930s and early 1940s, the American art-interested public was unsympathetic to abstraction. The Depression had aroused strong political concerns and inspired art that dealt with social issues and the American scene. Gorky played the role of unappreciated genius with fervor. His cubistic abstraction softened to brushy, watery, or spattered shapes and darting lines that hint at plants, animals, viscera, or sexual organs, all floating in a viscous space (Plate 38 and Fig. 19-7). Increasingly open and spontaneous forms may have been encouraged by European Surrealists, displaced by World War II, who had relocated in New York. The Surrealists were impressed by Gorky's apparent psychic improvisation. However, he was less spontaneous than his art sug-

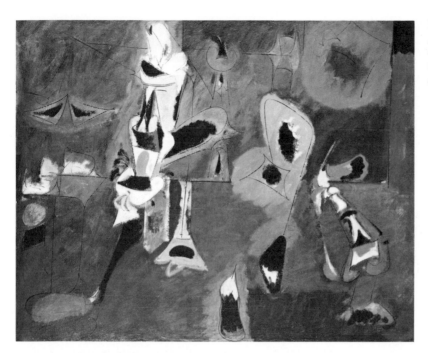

19-7 ARSHILE GORKY, *Agony,* (1947). Oil on canvas, 40″ × 50½″. Collection, the Museum of Modern Art, New York. A. Conger Goodyear Fund.

gests. There are careful preparatory drawings for most of his paintings. Still, the apparently nonrational images forecast the more violent free forms of Action Painting in the late 1940s and 1950s (see text on p. 367).

WILLEM DE KOONING (Holland and the United States, 1904–).   Willem de Kooning worked as a commercial artist during the day and studied art in night classes, first at the Academy in Rotterdam, later in Belgium, and, after 1926, in New York. In 1935, he became a full-time painter, and during the 1940s he made his reputation in New York. His early style, in the 1920s and 1930s, often combined recognizable objects with geometric shapes. Forms are solidly modeled in some parts and flattened in others, and there is a constant shifting from mass to plane and from flatness to depth. Colors develop around pinks, yellows, and light blues, sometimes in vibrating contrasts. In the 1940s, De Kooning produced a series of abstract and nonobjective works in black and white, with sprightly curving planes and active lines. These paintings constituted a major part of his first one-man show in 1948, which immediately established his reputation. During the 1950s, color was added to the slashing brushwork and explosive energy of his earlier works, as is evident in the series called *Woman.* Plate 43 (Fig. 19-8) is typical of this

19-8 WILLEM DE KOONING, *Woman I,* (1950–52). Oil on canvas, 75⅞″ × 58″. Collection, the Museum of Modern Art, New York. Purchase.

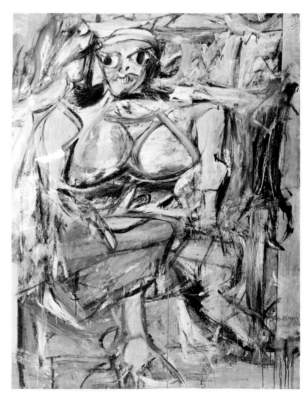

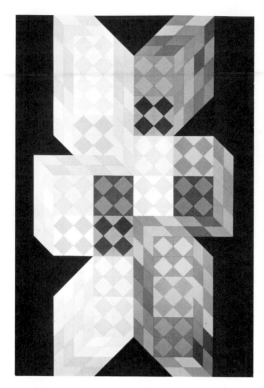

19-9   VICTOR VASARELY,   *YMPO,*
(1970). Acrylic on canvas, 67″ × 99½″.
Private collection.

19-10   FRANCIS BACON,   *Number VII
from Eight Studies for a Portrait,* (1953). Oil
on canvas, approx. 60″ × 46⅛″.   Collection,
the Museum of Modern Art, New York. Gift of Mr. and
Mrs. William A. M. Burden.

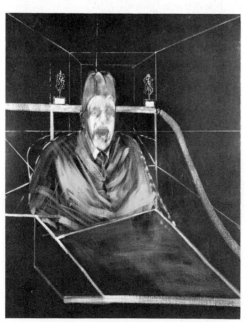

group; the work seems to have emerged from a
violent encounter between the artist and his materials to become a record of action and spontaneous decision. In the late 1950s and early 1960s, De
Kooning painted many nonobjective works; in the
mid-1960s, he began painting the human figure
again, this time with more fluid brushwork than
before. De Kooning was a prominent figure in Action Painting.

VICTOR VASARELY (Hungary and France, 1908–).
Victor Vasarely came to Paris in 1930 after study in
a Budapest school patterned after the German
Bauhaus. For a time he worked as an advertising
designer and did noncommercial designs in his
free time. In 1944 he first exhibited his "free-
graphics" and left commercial art. His early geometric abstractions occasionally used optical illusions of change and movement in patterns and
colors, and after 1955 Vasarely became a pioneer
in the exploitation of these kinetic effects, which
he called *cinétisme.* This technique is exemplified
by *YMPO* (Plate 46 and Fig. 19-9). The physiological explanation for such illusions is retinal fatigue.
Vasarely inspired such groups as NTrc (Nouvelle
Tendence recherche continuelle) and GRAV
(Groupe de Recherche de l'Art Visuel), which developed in the 1960s as part of the international
spread of Kinetic and Op Art (see p. 393).

FRANCIS BACON (Ireland and England, 1909–).
Although Francis Bacon began to paint in the
1930s, painting became his chief activity only in
1945. Even after the violence of the Second World
War, the public was unprepared for the images
Bacon thrust upon it. In a painting from the early
1950s, half-effaced, dislocated, humanoid forms
seem to be screaming through the walls of transparent boxes (Fig. 19-10). Bacon's later works depict even more violent contortions and a sense of
urgent metamorphosis achieved with swirling
brushwork and paint applied with rags or thrown
onto the canvas. Today Bacon feels that portraiture is the most challenging subject. He prefers to
work largely from photographs because it is easier
to do "injury" to the image when the subject is not
watching, although he is not deliberately creating
horror images or commenting on the human situation. Rather, he wishes to record intensely some
aspects of human behavior and to remake images

irrationally. Bacon feels that life is an accident without purpose or reason, but also that one can derive satisfaction from a profound experience and an awareness of different levels of reality. His interest in controlled accident and instinctive or irrational painting is indebted to Surrealism. In this way he evokes a special mood of crisis, of physical and mental vulnerability, that reflects some of the anxiety explored by post-World War II existentialism. Intentionally or not, Bacon's work seems to reveal contemporary humans as changeable, molded by contingency, and possibly self-contradictory.

FRANZ KLINE (United States, 1910–62).   Franz Kline, one of the major figures in Abstract Expressionist Action Painting, was born in Pennsylvania. He established himself in New York in 1938, teaching at Pratt Institute and working as a commercial artist to earn a living. During the 1930s and 1940s, Kline painted portraits, landscapes, and cityscapes. In 1950, the same year of his first one-man show, he saw some of his small drawings enlarged by an opaque projector. The power of the magnified forms inspired Kline to turn to broad, sweeping strokes in nonobjective compositions. For several years he used only black and white, but in the mid-1950s he began to employ color again. Kline did brush drawings on newspapers and the pages of telephone books. These sketches were then framed with different-sized rectangles or cut into fragments. Once the concept was established in this way, it was enlarged on canvas and painted with large brushes. *Le Gros* (Fig. 19-11) is typical in the slashing power of the black strokes, which establish a horizontal shape poised on a vertical one. Prolonged observation, however, calls into question the relationship between the black figure and the white background, for the artist dragged white paint over the black in certain areas to keep the white from being simply empty. It takes little effort to reverse the figure-ground relationship and see the white shapes as positive forms in black space.

19-11   FRANZ KLINE, *Le Gros,* (1961). Oil on canvas, 41⅜″ × 52⅝″.   The Sidney and Harriet Janis Collection. Gift to the Museum of Modern Art, New York.

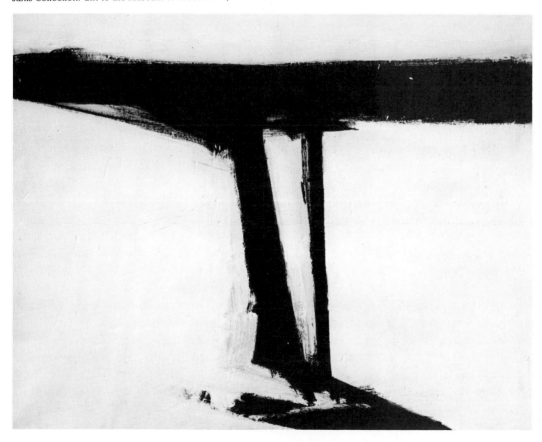

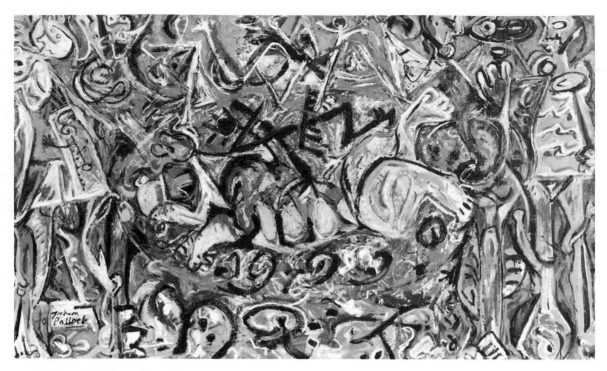

19-12 JACKSON POLLOCK, *Pasiphaë,* (1943). Oil on canvas, 56⅛″ × 96″. Collection, Lee Krasner Pollock.

JACKSON POLLOCK (United States, 1912–56). Jackson Pollock studied in Los Angeles and New York and eventually settled on Long Island. His painting became increasingly abstract after 1940. From convulsive linear shapes that sometimes acquire the character of humans, animals, or cryptic symbols, as in the *Pasiphaë* (Fig. 19-12), he turned by 1948 to intricate, nonobjective networks of swirling, colored line. *Autumn Rhythm* (Plate 39 and Fig. 19-13) is typical of his late works, sometimes called drip paintings because they were done by dripping paints of different thicknesses from cans onto canvas stretched flat on the floor. Pollock's painting career was cut short by his death in a car accident, but he has exerted wide influence as a leader of Abstract Expressionism and Action Painting.

ROMARE BEARDEN (United States, 1914–88). Mathematics and cartoon art were Romare Bearden's major interests at a New York high school and at New York University. He became aware of social comment painting while studying with George Grosz at the Art Students' League during the Depression. An early work, *The Annunciation* (1942), presented simplified forms with strong value contrasts and washes of superimposed colors. By the mid-1950s, Bearden was doing nonobjective pieces in oil. His style moved from slabs of thickly encrusted paint to diaphanous washes and spatters of delicate color. Then subject matter returned to his work, and collage became important. Photographs in magazines were photocopied, enlarged, cut, and reassembled. Images of people, architecture, landscapes, and textural details, such as close-ups of grass or foliage, produce sparkling value contrasts and startling conflicts in scale. Even parts such as hands and faces were fragmented with drastic scale changes between fingers and palms or eyes and mouths. Disjunctions joining the eyes from a photo of a person and lower face from a photo of an African mask may suggest an uneasy combination of present and past. Some of the compositions were done only in black and white, a contrast that for the artist and his friends signified racial conflict. Bearden said that the recurring railroad engine was, for him, a symbol of industrialization and of the encroachment of white civilization upon black culture. Under a general title, *The Prevalence of Ritual,* he depicted such rites as baptism (Fig. 19-14) and funeral. During the 1970s, his work included many

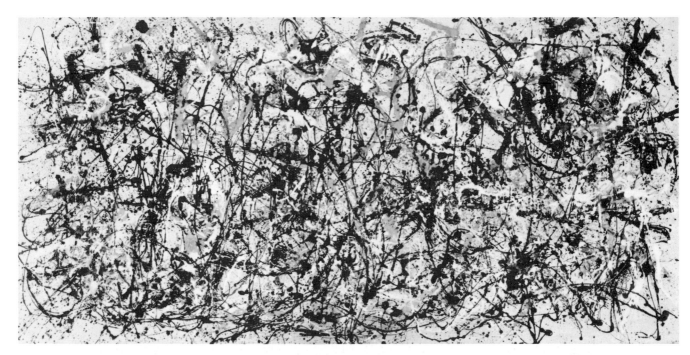

19-13 JACKSON POLLOCK, *Autumn Rhythm,* (1950). Oil on canvas, 105″ × 207″. The Metropolitan Museum of Art. George A. Hearn Fund.

19-14 ROMARE BEARDEN, *The Prevalence of Ritual: Baptism,* (1964). Photomechanical reproduction, synthetic polymer, and pencil on paperboard, 9⅛″ × 12″. Hirshhorn Museum and Sculpture Garden, Smithsonian Institution.

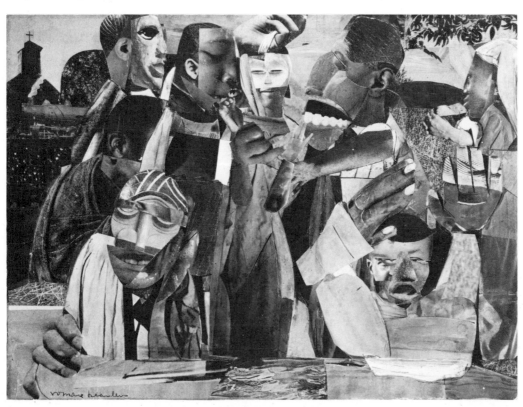

idyllic forest and lake scenes with rich colors, an elaborate variety of photographed textures, and intricate, mosaic patterns. The effect is exotic, but the railroad engine occasionally appears in the background.

ROBERT MOTHERWELL (United States, 1915–). Research on the art theories of Delacroix, Baudelaire, and the French Symbolists prepared Robert Motherwell to appreciate the subjective character of Surrealist art. Motherwell used paint and collage to create large, irregular shapes and areas of texture and pattern in his early work that recall Miro's art in their animation and representational implications. A sweeping oval above tapered legs becomes Pancho Villa; wavering vertical bands and sharply edged rectangles become a Spanish prison. The symbolic potential of psychic automatism or psychic improvisation was important to Motherwell, who knew French Surrealists in exile in New York during the Second World War and whose art was taking form during the early phase of Abstract Expressionism. The major theme of his

career came from childhood memories of news reports about the Spanish Civil War. He began his *Elegies to the Spanish Republic* series in 1949 (Fig. 19-15). Large canvases present threatening oppositions of black with white and of violently brushed verticals with ovoid forms. These ominous polarities suggest symbolic conflicts of life and death or the heavy rhythm of funereal drum beats. Greater automatism is evident in the *Lyric Suite* (1965), a series of compositions made with ink that was poured and spattered on rice paper. The *Open* series (1967–69) developed very different forms. Subtle modulations within a single color hint at the possibility of atmospheric depth on the flat canvas surface. Thin lines suggest a window shape that appears to be more closed than open. These gentle enigmas continued in some work of the 1970s, but there has also been a return to active brushwork and aggressive shapes with bold value contrasts. Automatic forms characterize much of his work in lithography, silk screen, and etching. Motherwell is a major theoretician of contemporary painting; his editing, writ-

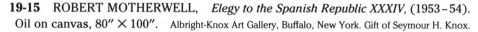

19-15   ROBERT MOTHERWELL,   *Elegy to the Spanish Republic XXXIV,* (1953–54). **Oil on canvas, 80″ × 100″.**   Albright-Knox Art Gallery, Buffalo, New York. Gift of Seymour H. Knox.

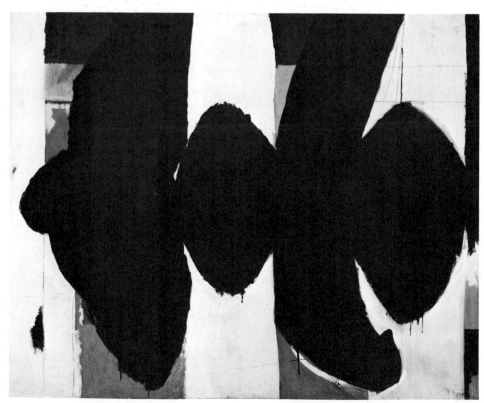

ing, and teaching have made an important contribution to the continuing dialogue about the nature and role of art in the twentieth century.

GABOR PETERDI (Hungary and the United States, 1915–). Although the recipient of many awards as a painter, Gabor Peterdi is best known as a teacher of printmaking whose students have made printmaking an important area in university art departments across the United States. Peterdi began his printmaking in Stanley Hayter's Atelier 17 in 1933. Paris was feeling the tensions of the Spanish Civil War and the approach of World War II. Peterdi believes that this anxiety is reflected in the violence of his subjects and forms during the 1930s. His first portfolio of engravings, *The Black Bull* (1939), includes such scenes as that of a bullfighter being disemboweled by a bull. The swinging, looping, knife-sharp lines of Hayter's style are evident in many of Peterdi's prints and paintings during these years. Peterdi's subjects came more from nature after he settled in the United States in 1939, and the violence subsided to darting, surging, jittery rhythms of tiny strokes (Fig. 19-16). Sky, water, woods, and vast fields of marsh grass all

19-16 GABOR PETERDI, *Angry Sky,* (1959). Etching and engraving, printed in black, plate 22¾″ × 32¹¹⁄₁₆″. Collection, the Museum of Modern Art. Gift of the artist.

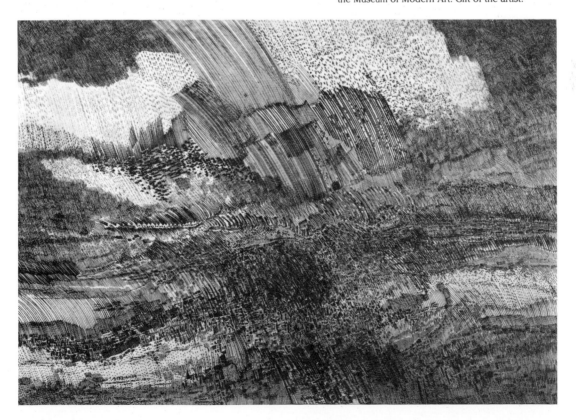

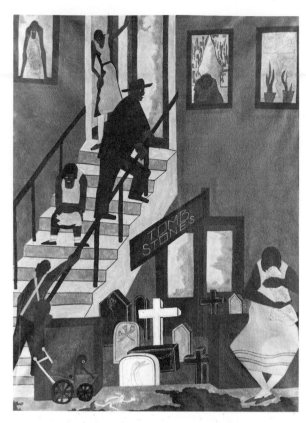

19-17   JACOB LAWRENCE,   *Tombstones,* (1942). Gouache, 28¾″ × 20½″.   Collection of Whitney Museum of American Art. Purchase.

vibrate with intense calligraphic life. The skittering lines of dots and dashes that characterize many of his engravings can be produced by an electric drill with a burr. The variety of marks in the prints and the subtle modulations of color in the paintings offer rich sensuous rewards. Peterdi uses minute parts to construct a model of the vastness and energy of nature.

JACOB LAWRENCE (United States, 1917–   ).   Art classes in a New York settlement house gave Jacob Lawrence his first encouragement. Pattern was the element to which he responded most intensely, and it became the strength of his mature style. During the Depression, he worked for the Federal Arts Project, which provided government commissions and stipends. As a black artist, Lawrence has portrayed leaders, events, and situations in black history. His major media have been tempera and casein-gouache. Often the paintings have developed in series with themes such as *Toussaint l'Ouverture, Frederick Douglass, Harriet Tubman, The Migration of the Negro, John Brown,* and *Harlem.* Unfortunately, many of the series have been broken up by sales to different collectors. Whether Lawrence depicts the hopeless boredom of ghetto life or a child's piano lesson, his paintings are charged with tension, dissonance, and often with crackling activity. The sharply edged flat shapes have abrupt angles that bite into each other and are compressed within larger planes. Linear perspective is ignored, exaggerated, or compressed (Plate 40 and Fig. 19-17). Primary colors, brown, and black produce a resonance that is harsh and urgent. During the 1950s, Lawrence turned to more intricate patterns. Subjects were introspective and allusive. Performance in music or theatre was a frequent theme. The McCarthy era of political turmoil inspired Lawrence's *Struggle* series (1955–56), which stressed revolutionary aspects of American history. Likewise, the civil rights conflicts of the 1960s prompted polemical paintings. In the 1970s, one of his major themes was construction. Carpenters, tools, and parts of houses provided subjects that imply hope for the building of a new and more equitable society.

CHARLES WHITE (United States, 1918–79).   As a black artist, Charles White has portrayed black culture in America. Chicago racial tensions, personal experiences of discrimination, and training during the Depression and the period of widespread social commentary in American art all influenced White's conception of art as a means of revealing suffering and injustice. Study in Mexico acquainted him with the powerful social murals of Rivera and Orozco. Their dramatic composition and simplified, massive, and expressively modified proportions shaped the stylc of White's murals in the United States. He has used etching, lithography (Fig. 19-18) and portfolios of reproduced ink, crayon, and charcoal drawings to reach a wider audience, especially among black Americans. His subjects range from heroes in Afro-American history to anonymous preachers, unemployed workers, or mother-child relationships. His draftsmanship became somewhat less geometric in his later years; his sense of expressive proportion and subtle value gradation continued to develop. This can be seen in his series of oil paintings on the theme of *Wanted Posters*. Nineteenth-century reward posters depicting escaped slaves serve as the basis for superimposed images of black victims, printed laws, Confederate flags, and monetary rewards.

19-18 CHARLES WHITE, *The Prophet, No. 1,* (1975). Lithograph, 69 × 94 cm. Heritage Gallery, Los Angeles.

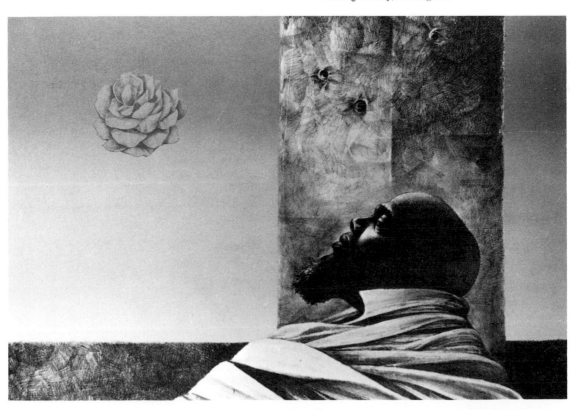

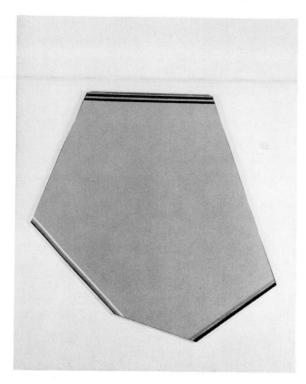

19-19 KENNETH NOLAND,   *Turnabout,* (1978).
Acrylic on canvas, 89″ × 74½″.   Courtesy André
Emmerich Gallery, New York.

KENNETH NOLAND (United States, 1924–).
Helen Frankenthaler and Jackson Pollock provided the influences that led Kenneth Noland to
become a Color Field painter. To assert the pri-
macy of color over shape, Noland, like his former
teacher Albers, used series of paintings based on
simple shapes. His circle, or target, paintings
(1950s) were followed by chevron paintings, diamond paintings, stripe paintings, and, in the
1970s, plaid paintings and shaped canvases (Fig.
19-19). After working with color staining on raw
canvas, Noland began to vary texture and opacity
of paint, sometimes buffing sections or rubbing the
canvas to obtain a soft suede effect. He works
quickly with little preliminary study and rarely re-
paints. His method has been to tack the rectangular canvas to the floor, paint first the large color
fields, then the smaller areas, and, finally, to crop
the canvas and shape its perimeter. Because of the
advancing or receding qualities of colors and of
hard over soft edges, there is frequently a tension
between flatness and the illusion of depth. In the
shaped canvases, he has heightened the tension
between shapes and colors and added tensions
between the interior and perimeter. Since 1968,
Noland has produced welded metal sculpture with
a stylistic affinity to the work of David Smith and
Anthony Caro.

RICHARD DIEBENKORN (United States, 1922–).
The land forms, space, and light of California and
New Mexico have been essential to Richard Diebenkorn's painting. His student work burgeoned
in San Francisco in the late 1940s, a period of
enthusiasm for Picassoesque Cubism, heavy paint
texture stressing pictorial surface, and Matisse's
simplified areas of color. Diebenkorn used rough-
edged, flat, rectangular forms in abstract or nonobjective compositions. After he moved to New
Mexico in 1950, boulder and mesa shapes modified the rectangularity. Colors lightened; lines became more playful and were sometimes detached
from planes. By 1953, Diebenkorn was back in
Berkeley. After two years, he began a more representational period, frequently painting still lifes
and figures in interiors or on terraces. Paint is
scumbled in layers, objects are simplified, and the
architectural forms produce geometrical enclo-
sures, but open windows, clear skies, and large
areas of intense light suggest vast space and free-

dom of movement. This contrast of geometric containment and spatial openness characterizes the more abstract paintings that have constituted Diebenkorn's major work since a move to Los Angeles in 1966: *The Ocean Park Series* (Plate 47 and Fig. 19-20). Linear and planar elements are vertical, horizontal, and diagonal. Luminous and subtle color comes from repeated scraping and scumbling to produce the paradoxical sense of richly reworked surfaces and wind-blown spaces. Diebenkorn's art contains aspects of geometric abstraction, Action Painting, and Color Field.

ROBERT RAUSCHENBERG (United States, 1925–). After trying a variety of approaches, including blank white canvases and compositions in black and white, Robert Rauschenberg turned to assemblages of found objects and objects combined with vigorously brushed painting, such as *The Bed* (1955, Collection of Mr. and Mrs. Leo Castelli), which consists of quilt, pillow, and paint. By 1961, exhibits in New York and Paris had established

Rauschenberg as a daring and prolific talent. *Tracer* (Fig. 19-21) indicates a flattening tendency in that no actual objects are attached to the canvas surface. The work's photomontage profusion was obtained by transfer of magazine images to silk screens that the artist then used to print on the canvas. The energy and scale of the brushwork links such a painting with Abstract Expressionism; the unexpected combinations of common objects recall Dada photomontage.

Sculpture

The sculptural counterparts to Abstract Expressionist painting are rough, jagged forms, often constructed by welding, and given color and texture by chemicals; energetic and spontaneous effects are prized. Assemblages of found objects add to the symbolic and imaginative possibilities of sculpture. An alternative was offered by continuing geometric styles, which suggested strict control and deliberate calculation. New methods of

19-20 RICHARD DIEBENKORN, *Ocean Park #83,* (1975). Oil on canvas, 100″ × 81″.   In the collection of the Corcoran Gallery of Art. Museum purchase with the aid of funds from the National Endowment for the Arts, Washington, D.C., a federal agency, the William A. Clark Fund, and Margaret M. Hitchcock.

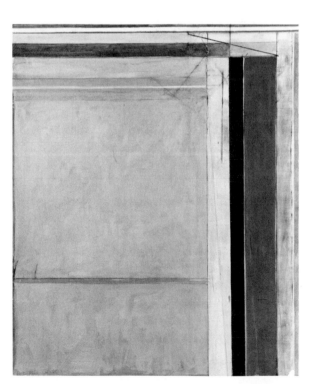

19-21 ROBERT RAUSCHENBERG, *Tracer,* (1962). Approx. 17′9″ × 12′8″.   Collection of Mr. and Mrs. Frank Titelman, Altoona, Pennsylvania.

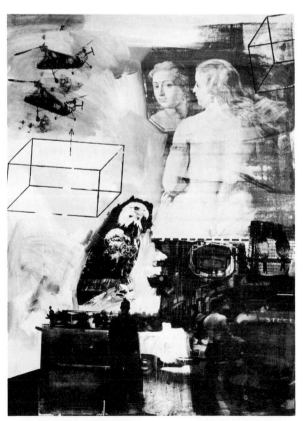

construction have allowed for easier experimentation than did traditional methods such as carving and casting. During the period from 1945 to 1960, sculpture gained a new momentum, which has grown subsequently and given sculpture great importance.

LOUISE NEVELSON (Russia and the United States, 1899–1988).   Louise Nevelson's early work dealt with the human figure treated in simplified cubic masses and lively angles. Bronze, terra cotta, and occasional marble pieces were produced from the late 1920s into the 1940s, but in 1944 she exhibited for the first time her compositions assembled from scrap wood, the type of sculpture that was to make her reputation. These totemic compositions recall Russian Constructivism, with the added wit of Dada and the ambiguity of Surrealism. In the 1950s Nevelson began to create works composed of found objects and scraps of wood assembled in boxes that were then combined in compartmentalized groups that filled whole walls (Fig. 19-22). She then unified the rich diversity of parts in these works by spray-painting each composition a single color; from flat black, she turned to pure white and then to gold. In 1965 Nevelson was one of the

19-22   LOUISE NEVELSON, *Royal Tide II,* (1961–63). Painted wood, 94½″ high, 126½″ wide, 8″ deep.   Collection of Whitney Museum of American Art, New York. Gift of the artist.

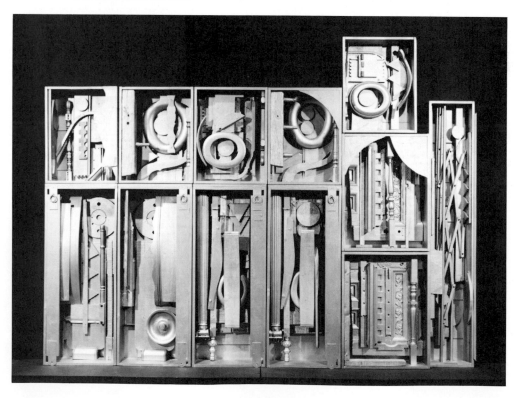

artists chosen to represent the United States at the Venice Biennale. At about the same time she began to use aluminum or Plexiglas to create forms of a precise, machinelike quality. In the late 1960s and early 1970s she produced some pieces from aluminum scraps and weathering steel, which allows controlled rusting for color and texture. Her favorite material, however, continued to be wood, painted black and arranged in compartmentalized structures.

JOSEPH CORNELL (United States, 1903–72).   Max Ernst's work inspired Joseph Cornell's initial collages. Following the lead of Ernst, Marcel Duchamp, Schwitters, De Chirico, and their Dada-Surrealist fascination with unexpected associations of images, Cornell, by 1932, was collecting and making objects and arranging them in glass-faced boxes. He used shells, trinkets, marbles, toys, maps, and clippings from old books and magazines (Fig. 19-23). Informing his search were intense interests in theatre, opera, dance—especially nineteenth-century ballet—and symbolist literature. From these sophisticated resources and a childlike freshness of imagination, he assembled mysteries that tempt our fantasy with a partially revealed symbolism, lavish associational possibilities, and a telescoping of space and time. Cornell sometimes dedicated a box to a favorite performer, and he developed series of boxes around such themes as the Medici family, birds, grand hotels of the past, and earthly and astronomical maps and diagrams.

DAVID SMITH (United States, 1906–65).   David Smith studied painting in Washington, D.C., and New York during the 1920s. In 1931, inspired partly by Picasso's welded sculpture, he began attaching found and shaped wooden objects to his paintings. In 1932 he began making welded sculpture. Rough-edged geometric planes and masses were combined and painted in compositions like *Suspended Cube* (1938, Estate of David Smith). Social comment appears in the *Medals of Dishonor*, silver and bronze reliefs pointing out unjust or inhuman aspects of the Second World War. Smith's inventiveness ranged from such unlikely subjects as *Hudson River Landscape* (Fig. 19-24) and *Banquet* (1952, private collection, New York), both linear steel hieroglyphs in space, to a

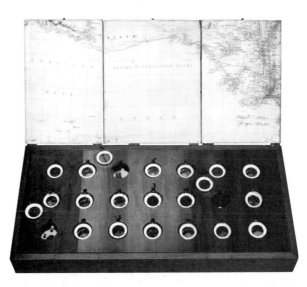

19-23   JOSEPH CORNELL,   *Object,* (1942–53). Wooden box with 21 compasses set into a wooden tray resting on a Plexiglas-topped and partitioned section, divided into 17 compartments containing small miscellaneous objects and a three-part hinged lid covered inside with parts of maps of New Guinea and Australia, 2⅝″ × 21¼″ × 10⅜″.   Collection, the Museum of Modern Art, New York. Mr. and Mrs. Gerald Murphy Fund.

19-24 DAVID SMITH,
Hudson River Landscape, (1951).
Steel, 101¾″ high, 33″ wide,
20½″ deep.   Collection of Whitney
Museum of American Art, New York.

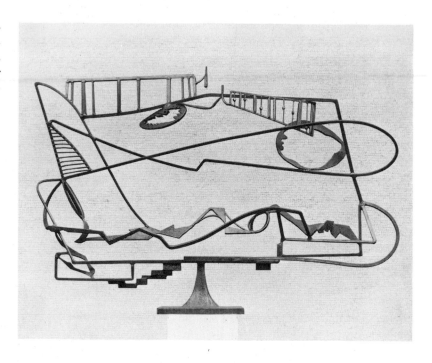

pure geometry of burnished or painted steel in the *Zig* and *Cubi* series. *Cubi XVIII* (Fig. 19-25) is a daring and "momentary" poise of shimmering geometric solids, a visual statement with the authority of a trumpet call.

THEODORE ROSZAK (United States, 1907–81). Theodore Roszak was born in Poland and came to Chicago in 1909. He settled in New York in 1931 and created geometric nonobjective sculpture in the manner of the Constructivists. In 1945 came the stylistic change that led to his mature style, a bristling, explosive combination of jagged, torn forms and rough textures. The *Whaler of Nantucket* (Fig. 4-6) has the elusive symbolism of *Moby Dick.* The welded steel assumes threateningly violent forms that refer obliquely to the snout of a whale, the thrust of a harpoon, and the prow of a boat. Such active, powerful form links Roszak's art to Abstract Expressionism and Action Painting.

19-25 DAVID SMITH,   *Cubi XVIII,* (1964).
Polished stainless steel, 9′7¾″ high.   Museum of Fine Arts, Boston. Anonymous Centennial gift.

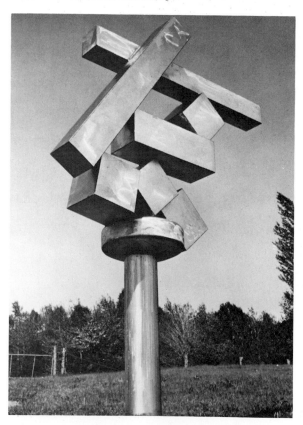

Architecture

The post-World War II period was characterized by extensive rebuilding, expansion, technological progress, and affluence in the industrialized Western countries. Architects and critics, like Lewis Mumford in the United States, became increasingly concerned with the sociological, political, and technological aspects of architecture, sometimes at the expense of aesthetic concerns; city planning became much more important. The prevailing tendency was to destroy existing structures and replace them with tall buildings that allow for high density at the same time that they provide open spaces for the community; in city planning the tendency was to separate activities for maximum efficiency. Opponents of this trend, like Jane Jacobs in the United States, argued that such bulldozer schemes sacrifice cultural roots, diversity, individuality, and human scale; they felt that the old should be selectively restored and that planning should link the past with the future. Restoration and preservation movements ensued. The destruction of existing structures was not necessary for two exciting new cities: Chandigarh, the new capital of Hariana and the Punjab, designed by Le Corbusier, and Brasília, the new capital of Brazil, designed by Oscar Niemeyer. The planners of both cities attempted, with mixed success, to separate social and economic activities.

This period also saw the late work of the "first-generation" leaders: Wright, Gropius, Mies van der Rohe, and Le Corbusier, all but the latter working in the United States. With the exception of Mies van der Rohe's work, the style of these men changed from an early austerity toward a complexity in form and richness in texture and color. Some critics saw this development as "neohistoricism" or "decorated modern," but nevertheless it influenced the second-generation leaders. Mies van der Rohe's expression of structure and Le Corbusier's use of massive, rough concrete were basic to an international inclination toward fortresslike proportions and rough surfaces that has been termed the *New Brutalism*.

LOUIS KAHN (United States, 1901–74).   Louis Kahn received his degree from the Architecture School of the University of Pennsylvania in 1924 and worked as assistant to other architects until 1934. His early work, involving city planning and housing projects, revealed an admiration for Gropius in its flat-roofed, wide-windowed horizontality. In 1947, Kahn joined the architecture staff of Yale University and began to design more buildings that expressed his individual concepts rather than those of a team. Kahn's work emphasized revealed structure and spaces that are more separate than continuous. The Richards Medical Research Building (Figs. 19-26 and 19-27) clearly

19-26   LOUIS KAHN,   Richards Medical Research Building, University of Pennsylvania, Philadelphia, (1957–61).

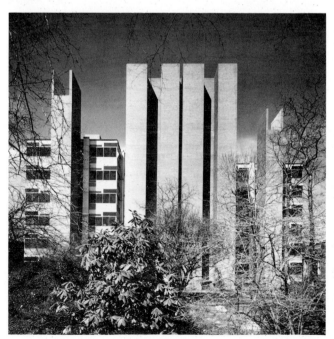

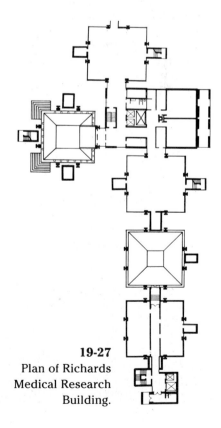

19-27
Plan of Richards
Medical Research
Building.

separates the massive service-utility towers from the glass-walled laboratories. Although the whole form is complex, the stark simplicity of its individual parts and the bold contrast of upright and horizontal, transparency and opacity, projection and recession, give a total effect of variety and monumentality. Stylistically, this, and many other Kahn designs, may be included in the New Brutalism movement.

PHILIP JOHNSON (United States, 1906–).   In 1932, Philip Johnson coauthored *The International Style: Architecture since 1922,* a book that established the International Modern Style in architectural history. From architectural historian, Johnson turned architect, creating the Glass House (Fig. 19-28) under the influence of Mies van der Rohe. Johnson soon grew more interested in

mass, in compartmentalized spaces, and in historical references. His Kline Science Center (1962), at Yale University, is a soaring, massive design stressing the historical motif of the column. His Amon Carter Museum of Western Art (1961), in Fort Worth, Texas, uses the arch form in a nonstructural screen. The determining factors are not utility, but rewarding formal design and meaningful historical reference. The Johnson and Burgee design for the American Telephone and Telegraph Company headquarters (1978), New York, shocked his peers: the skyscraper is topped with a broken pediment. His 1979 design for the Pittsburgh Plate Glass headquarters combined reflective glass and Gothic elements! Johnson has been a leader in the new historicism that is a significant factor in much *Postmodern* architecture (see text on p. 423).

19-28   PHILIP JOHNSON,   Glass House, (1949). New Canaan, Connecticut.

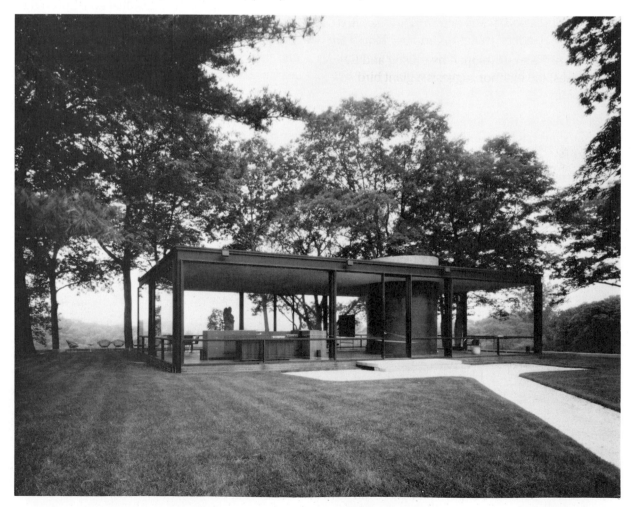

EERO SAARINEN (Finland and the United States, 1910–61). After moving with his family to the United States in 1923, Eero Saarinen studied in Paris and at Yale before joining the architectural firm of his father, Eliel Saarinen. His developing concept of architecture led to a professional disassociation from his father in 1948. Eero Saarinen's firm designed the huge General Motors Technological Center near Detroit (1951–57), using a severely rectangular architecture influenced by Mies van der Rohe. Unlike Mies van der Rohe, however, Saarinen enlivened his forms with red, blue, yellow, and orange walls. From this colorful outgrowth of the International Modern Style, Saarinen, like Le Corbusier, turned to a more complex, animated style. In the University of Chicago Law School (1956–60), he employed glass in vertical accordion pleats as deliberate embellishment. Although his former restraint occasionally returned, his late trend is strikingly exemplified in the TWA Terminal at Kennedy Airport (Figs. 19-29 and 19-30). Here the convoluted ferroconcrete forms are notable for their absence of stabilizing horizontal and vertical lines. The interior space is restlessly enveloped by ebbing and flowing masses; the exterior suggests a giant bird with lifted wings.

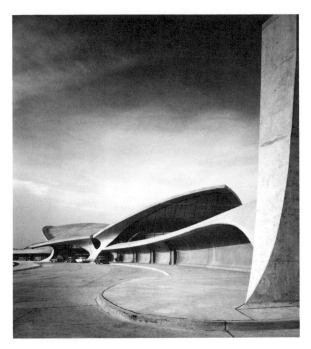

19-29 EERO SAARINEN, TWA Terminal, Kennedy Airport, New York, (1956).

19-30
Interior, TWA Terminal, Kennedy Airport.

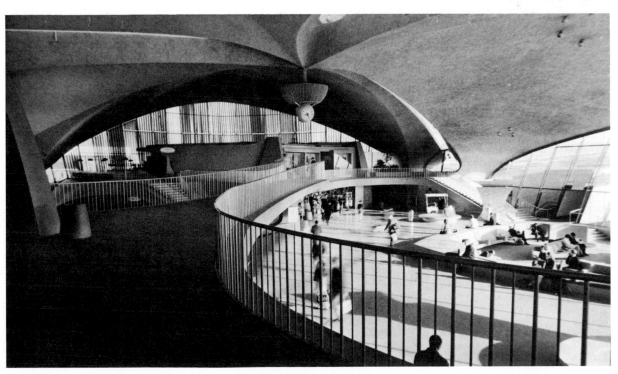

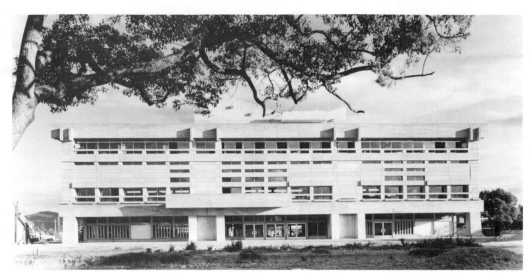

19-31 KENZO TANGE, Kurashiki City Hall, Okayama Prefecture, (1958–60). Façade facing plaza.

19-32 KENZO TANGE, Olympic Gymnasium, Tokyo, Japan, (1961–64).

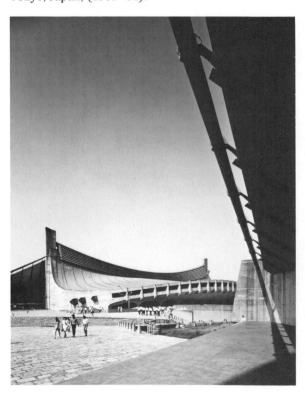

KENZO TANGE (Japan, 1913–). Internationally, Kenzo Tange is the best known of the senior Japanese architects and city planners. He has combined traditional Japanese elements, such as the open post and lintel structure of ancient Japanese temples, with the concrete geometry of Le Corbusier. In the early 1950s, the proportions of his work were slender. The Peace Memorial Museum in Hiroshima is a long box standing high on *pilotis* (piers) with a lattice of concrete sunscreen over its glass walls. It recalls the Rio de Janeiro Ministry of Education and Health (1937–43, designed by Lucio Costa, Oscar Niemeyer, and Le Corbusier) as well as traditional Japanese wood beam architecture. Tange calls this slender concrete work his *Yayoi* style, referring to a Japanese concept of aristocratic elegance. He abandoned this style for more massive proportions during the second half of the 1950s. Designs such as that for Kurashiki City Hall (Fig. 19-31) retain qualities of Japanese wooden architecture reinterpreted in massive rough concrete. For Tange, it was a change toward *Jomon*, the idea of rugged, primitive peasant culture, which he found epitomized in folk ceramics and in massive tile-faced walls in Kurashiki. It is noteworthy, however, that his change to this Jomon character occurred right after Brutalism had been developed as a trend in the West. By the 1960s, Tange was also turning toward more imaginatively expressive forms, often employing sweeping, curved surfaces. His skating rink for the Tokyo Olympics of 1964 (Figs. 19-32 and 19-33) may have been influenced by the

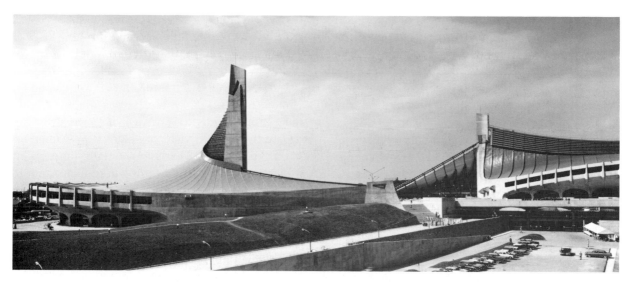

19-33
Aerial view, Olympic Gymnasium, Tokyo.

work in the United States of his friend Eero Saarinen, but it also hints at the curves of Japanese temples or peasant straw hats. Like Saarinen, Tange had come to feel that modern architectural movements had neglected symbolism and imagination. He wanted the rink to evoke and symbolize the excitement and openness of international athletic competition. Technically, the structures were challenging because they used systems of suspended cables on which roof panels were placed (Fig. 19-34). His symbolism became literal representation in the gymnasium at Kagawa Prefecture

19-34
Interior, Olympic Gymnasium, Tokyo.

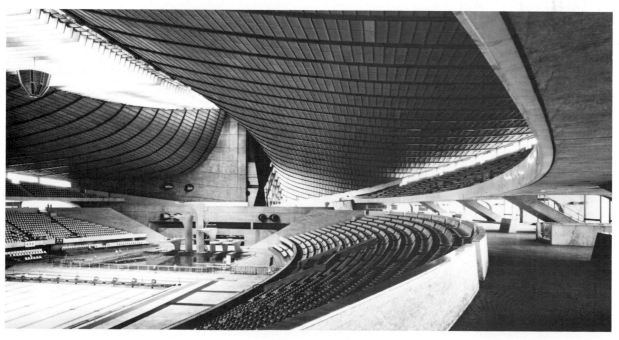

(1964); the building takes the form of a giant concrete boat, in keeping with the proximity of the Seto Inland Sea! Tange participated in the international enthusiasm for *megastructures* (towering and intricate single-building cities) in the early 1960s. The idea of one huge structure housing multitudes of people and catering to all of their physical and social needs was pertinent to the growing concern for the world population explosion and for improvement in urban living. Le Corbusier had been a pioneer in megastructure design, and Soleri was proposing startling possibilities (see the next section). Tange envisioned megastructures in much of his city planning. He saw spaces as conductors of communication and human contact in an informational society. He employed spatial *spines* as pedestrian and vehicular avenues and axial cores. By the late 1960s, such vast schemes were being criticized as inhuman in scale, insensitive to the historical past, and destructive to the environment. Restoration and preservation advocates had gained the upper hand. Few of Tange's urban plans have been realized.

PAOLO SOLERI (Italy and the United States, 1919–).   Paolo Soleri came from Italy in 1947 to join Frank Lloyd Wright's community of architects at Taliesin West in Arizona. He remained there until 1949. After a return visit to Italy, Soleri settled in Arizona, where he has made ceramic and bronze bells to earn a living. His drawing-board projects for visionary cities have gained increasing attention. Evolution occurs through increasing complexity and through miniaturization, Soleri argues; he feels these two principles should be basic to urban planning. His designs for megastructures achieve high population density with minimum energy expenditure for transportation, manufacturing, environmental control, and waste disposal. Automated manufacturing functions are usually located deep in the base of the building near the major energy source; community, business, and cultural areas are in the center; living quarters, sports areas, gardens, promenade decks, and heliports are on the outer surface. *Babeldiga* is designed for 1,200,000 inhabitants and a population density of 665 people per acre. Soleri's theory is called *arcology*, a combination of the

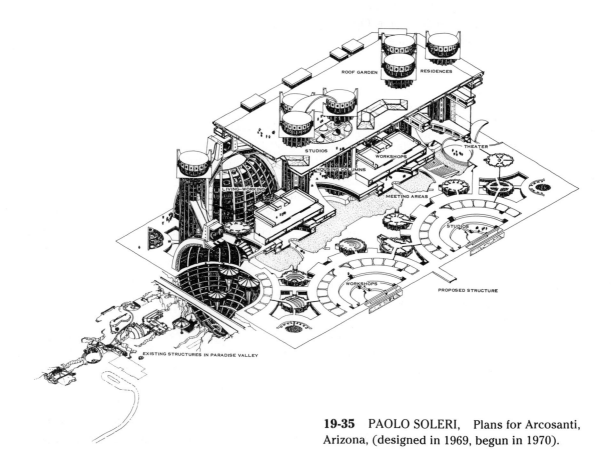

19-35   PAOLO SOLERI,   Plans for Arcosanti, Arizona, (designed in 1969, begun in 1970).

words architecture and ecology. Soleri bases his ideas not only on socioeconomic efficiency, but on a conviction that controlled environments will help humankind attain a more compassionate value system and a more aesthetic life. Architecture students have been flocking to Soleri's Arizona headquarters to contribute volunteer labor in the construction of a small city, *Arcosanti* (Fig. 19-35), that is planned as an experimental model.

1960 TO THE PRESENT

Painting, Sculpture, Art Fabric, Ceramics, and Intermedia

After 1960 the dominance of Abstract Expressionism was challenged by such international trends as Pop Art, Op Art, and Minimal Art. Pop Art first developed in England during the 1950s and then blossomed in the United States in the next decade. Op Art was a development within the broad category of geometric abstraction and nonobjective painting; it employed precise shapes and optical illusions to achieve literally dazzling effects of movement and ceaseless change. Some Op Art works overlap Minimal Art, a movement toward the reduction of a work of art to a few shapes and colors or to a single shape and color.

More ephemeral works were also produced during the 1960s, such as some of the kinetic sculptures of the Swiss artist Tinguely that were designed to destroy themselves by fire and explosion in a predetermined sequence. Similarly unique but temporary occurrences were the Happenings, nondramatic events in time and space, organized by Allan Kaprow and others. Some artists, equally interested in the problems of time in art, have used neon and fluorescent lights to create spatial and temporal environments through which the spectator moves. The terms *systemic art* and *serial art* were applied to some of these neon or fluorescent pieces and to some geometric sculpture and painting that develop elaborate combinations of one or two basic parts or modules. This modular approach to art has been encouraged by systems analyses in socioeconomic studies.

Artists have increasingly exploited modern technology since the 1960s. Some have employed a mixture of several media, such as painting, sculpture, light, film, and sound. These pieces are called *multimedia* or *intermedia*. Electronic technology has become available to the artist and has created vast new possibilities for aesthetic experience. For example, sound can be fed into laser equipment to create three-dimensional projections of colored forms in space, and computers have been used to produce drawings. *Cyborg*, or *cybernetic*, works allow feedback, which is the mutual response of and interaction between the work of art, its environment, and its spectators. Here there is a continuation of the earlier interest in chance or unpredictability. Computer information systems and recent linguistic theories have inspired types of art that explore or demonstrate the processes of human thought and have led to theory and criticism that stresses the communicative rather than the personally expressive aspects of art.

Along with the interest in modern technology is a renewed interest in the individual and society. *Super Realism* or *Photorealism* are both terms applied to a tendency to document minutely the surface effects of a visual experience. In painting, subjects cover the traditional range from landscape to portraiture, but special interest is shown in commercial urban street scenes and interiors. Highly reflective surfaces prevail. Photographs are frequently used by the artists as aids. Photorealism has grown out of Pop Art and has the same mechanical, impersonal nature. In sculpture, life-sized nudes, race riots, or tourists acquire the eerie effect of wax museum counterfeits. Concern for social integration has also stimulated art forms that involve participation in group experiences and the study of relationships among people, between socioeconomic systems, and between people and the environment. Huge, inflated plastic balloons have been used for a variety of purposes: for sound and film projections, and for people to bounce upon. While the balloons could be considered giant playthings, one creator of such *air structures* has said that their aim is to explore individual behavior in groups and to lower social barriers. In addition to the direct concern with social phenomena, an interest in space, time, and constant change has led to *Performance Art*, which can be exemplified by the public gesture of releasing a piece of plastic to float in the wind or by a person lying wrapped in a blanket on the floor of an art gallery. Performance Art owes much to the Happenings of the 1960s. Related to Performance Art is *Body Art*, in which the artist may mark his or her body or place it in jeopardy to demonstrate ideas, processes, or relationships between people, animals, and objects.

Today, art takes many forms and has broken through many barriers. For example, it can create a new environment for the spectator-participant. Interiors much like stage sets have been exhibited with accompanying written descriptions (*scenarios*) of social situations to fit the set. Life-sized mannequins or plaster casts of humans have been combined with actual objects, such as automobiles or lunch counters, in compositions that provide an entire environment. Total floor areas of galleries have been used as compositional frames for fluorescent light arrangements or for *floor pieces* that may be scattered objects or rigidly geometric arrangements of objects. *Earthworks* may be mammoth bulldozer projects in desert areas so remote that only photos are available to spectators, or they may consist of piles of stone on a gallery floor. *Field pieces* are outdoor works that may be permanent or impermanent. Compositions in the "field" have been created by cutting designs in grass or by arranging bales of hay in the countryside. Concrete or steel forms installed in a landscape, however, provide an art form that is more traditionally permanent. The growing awareness of change and interaction between elements has led to *Process Art*. A process artist might expose chemicals to the air so that oxygen acts upon them to produce visible changes. The rebellion against viewing works of art as precious objects culminated in *Conceptual Art*, in which words or graphs may be used to present the idea of a work rather than the finished work itself. This dematerialization of art often leaves little that can be sold or collected, although indefatigable collectors have sought to purchase the ideas or plans for concept pieces.

Some recent developments in contemporary art indicate a concern for extra-aesthetic or nonformal matters. In contrast to the aesthetic attitudes in earlier twentieth-century art, some avant-garde works produced today point to human problems generated by our postindustrial society: the relationship of the individual to a diminished sense of self, the threatening dominance of technology, and the dangers of ecological imbalance. As a result of this new social orientation, there is an interest in modifying or creating complete environments, as well as an impatience with the traditionally rigid divisions between art media and with what is now perceived as a false separation of art and life. Much contemporary art seems to challenge even the most recent conventions and to force a constant reevaluation of our established ideas.

While modern technology, with its emphasis on group production, is exploited for a variety of purposes in much present-day art, other developments stress the uniqueness of individual, handmade objects.

Interest in ceramics, fiber-fabric art, and other media that were originally utilitarian arts and crafts has been growing. Slowly, these have been accepted as expressive arts with the same potential as painting and sculpture. Some artists returned from abstract modes to representational images, as in Super Realism or the Neo-Expressionism that became evident in the late 1970s and early 1980s. By the early 1980s, unabashed decorative painting with lavish patterns experienced a revival. Critics referred to this tendency as "P. and D." (pattern and decoration). A Neo-Expressionist movement became international in the 1970s and 1980s. In the United States, its exponents drew upon Action Painting of the 1940s and 1950s. In Germany, its sources included the painting of Die Brücke. Its frank borrowing from the past marks Neo-Expressionism as one aspect of Postmodernism, whose advocates argue that art has always grown out of its past and that only the modernists tried to deny this. Postmodernists de-emphasize the significance of the individual artist's originality. They see art as a continuum of cultural signs, symbols, styles, and messages that each artist inherits, rearranges, and modifies. Postmodernist artists try to reveal this cultural situation by simulating, imitating, or appropriating from prior art in ways that are intended to push the viewer to question the claims of the modern movements for uniqueness and freedom from the past. Critics call this *deconstructing* modernism. The multifaceted aspects of contemporary art seem to be expanding in accordance with the growing complexity of modern perceptions.

In this section, we depart occasionally from the method of discussing individuals in order of birth so as to consider them in the period of their most important work.

NICOLAS SCHÖFFER (Hungary and France, 1912–   ). Nicolas Schöffer studied at the Budapest Art Academy before coming to Paris in 1936. At the time of his first one-man show in 1948, he was still a painter, but in 1950 he presented an exhibition of kinetic sculpture. In 1954, with the financial and technical aid of the Phillips Corporation, he created his first spatiodynamic tower. The tower was an open metal frame with moving, colored, rectangular blades and loudspeakers emitting taped music composed of electronic and environmental sounds. Since then, other towers have combined sound, light, projected images, and motion, expressing Schöffer's belief that art should utilize the essential elements of space, time, light, and change. *CYSP I* (Fig. 19-36), whose name stands for cybernetic-spatiodynamic construction, was done in 1956, again with the help of the Phillips Corporation. The piece is mobile and sonic. Darkness and silence cause it to move and to produce loud sounds; brightness and noise cause it to become still and quiet; the presence of different colors produces varying degrees of reaction. A ballet was created by Maurice Béjart using *CYSP I*, dancers, and electronic music.

JOSEPH BEUYS (Germany, 1921–86).   Joseph Beuys has been described as the most controversial artist and the most sought-after teacher in Germany. Reflecting the influence of Dada art objects from the period 1916–22, his work employed clay, gauze, fat, and bloodsoaked cloth to suggest decay and the impermanence of organic life. He earned much of his notoriety with *actions* (performances). For one of these, which took place in 1974, he flew to New York, was wrapped in felt blankets before leaving the airport, came directly to his art gallery in an ambulance, and spent three days in a fenced-off area there with the following properties: a live coyote, a stack of *Wall Street Journals* (renewed each day), a pile of hay, a pan of water, a cane, two felt blankets, and a constantly burning flashlight. He played with the coyote, talked to friends, smoked, and occasionally wrapped himself in one of the felt blankets,

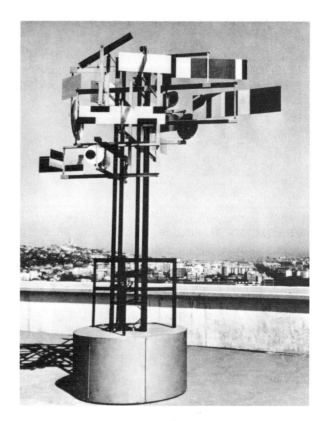

19-36   NICOLAS SCHÖFFER,   *CYSP I*, (1956). Steel and aluminum, 70⅞" × 63". Galerie Denise René, Paris.

with only the cane protruding. After bending and swaying, he would topple over and lie still for a time. Periodically, he would strike a triangle hanging from his vest. This signaled the playing of fifteen seconds of deafening tape recordings of industrial noises. At the end of three days, he departed for Germany in the manner in which he had arrived. In spite of his involvement with nonpermanent art, Beuys repeatedly stressed the importance of the art object as a palpable thing that can provide spiritual nourishment. He also believed that art and life are identical; thus he considered his political convictions as part of his art. Beuys influenced a generation of art students in Germany.

HARVEY K. LITTLETON (United States, 1922–). Harvey Littleton has been a pioneer in developing *studio glass:* one-of-a-kind works of glass art produced with small furnaces in the artist's studio. After training in sculpture and work in various areas of the Corning Glass plant in Corning, New York, Littleton was a successful potter for many years and a leader in the American Craft Council. His interest in creating with molten glass *(hot glass)* intensified after a 1957–58 visit to small glass factories in Italy and to the Paris studio of a former glass artist. In Wisconsin, Littleton put together a glass studio, experimented, lectured, wrote, taught, and exhibited his developing works of glass. His early cut, ground, and polished pieces were followed by blown forms of functional objects, such as vases. He soon transgressed conventional methods to create irregular glass sculptures by exploding the glass (blowing sharply into the blowpipe) and imploding it (drawing in on the blowpipe to collapse the molten blown glass). He would dip the blown piece back into molten glass to add lumps *(prunts)* in chosen areas. Chemicals produced unified or striated colors. The results had the sense of freedom and improvisation of much Abstract Expressionist painting. During the late 1960s, Littleton worked with blown tubes and rods that were allowed to bend, sag, or stretch while still molten. When cold, these were sliced at different angles and combined in groups. They acquired the graceful rhythms of kelp moving in underwater currents. He sliced blown bubbles to make hemispheres that could be nested in graduated sizes. The results suggest eyes. Brass rods

19-37 HARVEY LITTLETON, *Sympathy,* (1978). Barium/potash glass with cased double overlay on lead optic base.   High Museum of Art, Atlanta. Gift of the artist.

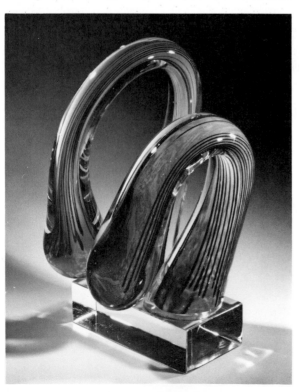

were used as supports for glass planes of partially melted, undulating forms. He cut and sandblasted optical glass discs and joined these to molten glass. In 1978, Littleton began a solid geometry series. These pieces encased layers of clear and colored glass in crisply cut cubes and many-faceted solids. Colored overlays were also used in elegantly sinuous forms (Fig. 19-37). In the 1980s, he devised complex, twisted forms, sometimes cut to reveal cross-sections of layered color. He described these as *topological geometry*, but they have a biomorphic elegance. Always, his art expresses the nature of the material and the processes by which it has been formed. Littleton's recognition has been international.

ELLSWORTH KELLY (United States, 1923–). Ellsworth Kelly's paintings in the early 1950s sought maximum visual impact with stripes, grids, or panels in dazzling black and white contrasts or in a few brilliant colors. By 1955, he had begun to do painted reliefs and freestanding sculpture using simple metal shapes painted in highly saturated colors. In both painting and sculpture, a single intense color often suffices to give one or two shapes great energy. In *Blue-White* (Fig. 19-38), two swelling fields of powerful blue meet in the center, cutting in two the white buffer between them. Though he is linked with the tradition of geometric abstraction, Kelly has been a leader in Minimal Art.

ROY LICHTENSTEIN (United States, 1923–). In 1962, Roy Lichtenstein emerged as one of the leading artists in the Pop movement. His work, like that of other Pop painters, was considered at first to be vulgar and non-art because of his portrayal of ordinary objects, such as tennis shoes, golf balls, food, and scenes from comic strips, in a style of bold flat colors, brash outlines, and simplified images. Lichtenstein's sources were poster and advertising art. He explains that these mass-media, stereotypical images have a compelling forcefulness, which he intensifies by enlargement and further simplification. The abbreviated marks for facial features, shadows, and highlights and the Ben Day dots of commercial printing (used to produce an illusion of tone) are blown up until we are forced to see them as shapes with mechanical,

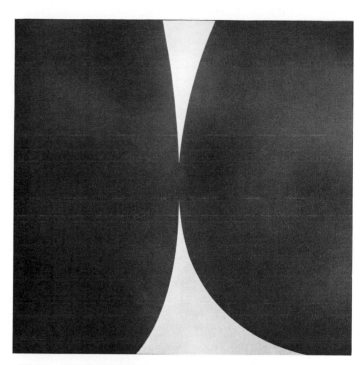

19-38 ELLSWORTH KELLY, *Blue-White,* (1962). Oil on canvas, 8'7" × 8'10". Collection, Brandeis University Art Collection, Rose Art Museum. Gevirtz-Mnuchin Purchase Fund, Waltham, Massachusetts.

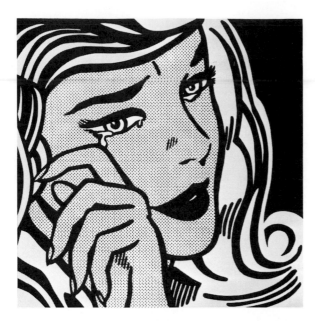

19-39   ROY LICHTENSTEIN,   *Crying Girl,* (1964).
Enamel on steel, 46″ × 46″.   Milwaukee Art Center.
Courtesy of Leo Castelli Gallery, New York.

repetitive, or animated character. Some of Lichtenstein's compositions taken from comics show only part of a face, collar, or hand, thereby denying us a story and pushing us to observe the form rather than a narrative. Yet, implied narrative is important to many of his pieces. In the 1960s, war and romance were often depicted (Fig. 19-39). The artist explains that he wished to show such passions dispassionately and mechanically. He is impressed by the insensitivity and superficiality of our society as it is revealed in comics and advertising. Intimate and personal experiences become anonymous and stereotyped. From the 1960s into the 1980s, Lichtenstein produced paintings that reinterpret the styles of celebrated individuals (Monet, Picasso, Mondrian, Marc) or movements and periods (Futurism, Expressionism, or Art Deco cubist murals of the 1930s). He commercializes these culture monuments with his bright basic colors, sleek flat paint surfaces, and Ben Day dots. He maintains that his parodies are not meant as criticisms of masterpieces. Even such ephemeral phenomena as sunsets and explosions became subjects for series of paintings and sculpture. They are converted to abbreviated, almost hieroglyphic images. Although Lichtenstein claims not to make social commentary his aim, he has admitted in interviews to a concern for the dehumanization of people in our machine society.

MIRIAM SCHAPIRO (United States, 1923–). Miriam Schapiro gained international recognition during the 1970s as an artist identified with the Feminist Movement. She created paintings with collage (her term is "femmage") of lace, quilt fragments, doilies, and images of baby clothes and teapots, all referring to traditional concepts of women's role in our culture. Schapiro wanted to commemorate the homemaker role even while pointing out its restrictive limitations. While this symbolic content fit the rhetoric of the Feminist Movement, Schapiro's complex and lavishly decorative style made her a leader in the Pattern and Decoration movement, which was not usually involved with social commentary. At least one critic wrote that Schapiro's message was weakened by sentiment and prettiness. In the 1950s, Schapiro had painted Abstract Expressionist works. In the 1960s, she had changed, along with many other artists, to hard-edged geometric forms, although there was often symbolic content (such as the egg form) relating to female experience. In 1971, Schapiro and Judy Chicago established the Feminist Art Program at the California Institute of the Arts in Valencia. In the 1980s, Schapiro's art incorporated human figures and the themes of theater and the dance. Within this context, references are autobiographical and deal with the artist's effort to escape traditional female stereotypes and to define her own role as a creative person and as a woman. In *I'm Dancing as Fast as I Can* (Fig. 19-40), the collage and decorative vitality continue. A faceless male with top hat and cane strides confidently offstage to the left. On the right, a ballerina with a face of flowers portrays an accepted role for the gifted female. In the center, a female representing Schapiro, torn between male and female aspirations, dances in frantic gyrations. She has explained that such compositions are autobiographical (often a palette and brushes are included), and that she uses dance and the theater as a metaphor for life. As with her earlier work, she seeks to address, through her own experience, the human condition.

19-40 MIRIAM SCHAPIRO, *I'm Dancing as Fast as I Can,* (1984). Acrylic and foline on canvas, 90″ × 144″. Courtesy of Bernice Steinbaum Gallery, New York.

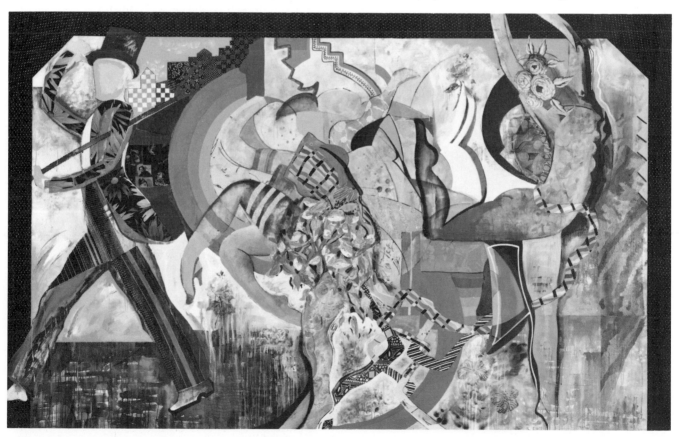

ANTHONY CARO (England, 1924–).   Anthony Caro is the recipient of many awards for his non-objective, welded metal sculpture, which is often described as *constructivist*. His early work, figurative, rough-surfaced, and expressionistic, changed suddenly in 1960 after he saw the work of David Smith. For years, Caro used standard steel I beams, bars, tubes, cylinders, and mesh to create his sculptures, and he painted each work in a single intense color. Only occasionally were ready-made objects evident. Usually, no single form is interesting in itself; the whole composition acquires a unique character that is derived from the tension of directional forces and a precarious balance. The predominently horizontal works inspired critical analogies to sentence structure (Fig. 19-41). Caro has produced a series of pieces designed to hang over the edge of a table. In the 1970s, he dropped the use of color and allowed the natural steel to rust, fixing it with varnish. In the 1980s, he has combined welded bronze with castings from clay and found objects. Although he was represented in the 1966 Primary Structures show (New York) that heralded the growth of the *minimal* art movement, Caro's work is typically more complex than minimal sculpture.

19-41   ANTHONY CARO,   *Early One Morning,* (1962). Painted steel and aluminum, 132″ × 114″ × 224″. Tate Gallery, London.

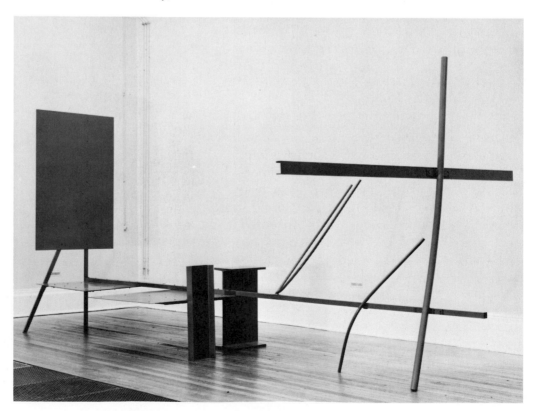

GEORGE SEGAL (United States, 1924–).   The contrast of ghostly white, life-sized, plaster figures with environments of actual assembled objects is characteristic of the sculpture that has earned George Segal an international reputation. The figures seem lost in thought; poses and gestures become a mute body language. Segal has said his objective is a feeling of revelation and psychological truth. In 1959, after twenty years as an expressionist painter, he exhibited plaster figures as extensions of his paintings. In 1961, he discovered that he could use strips of bandage material soaked in plaster to make thin sectional molds of live models. These molds could be assembled, the surfaces reworked, and the resulting figures used as finished sculptures (Fig. 19-42). The surfaces of his works retained much fabric texture until the mid-seventies. Then, he started using the more traditional method of taking positive castings from the molds. The result was more representational surface detail. In 1974, Segal also began doing reliefs, many of which depict only the upper two-thirds of the body or the torso without the head. There is more emotional remoteness, in spite of the more representational surfaces of the positive casts. In the mid-seventies, Segal also began to paint some of the plaster figures in vivid single colors. Acrylic paint was applied in layered glazes of translucent red, yellow, blue, or green. The labels *Pop* or *genre* at first seemed appropriate to Segal's work, but it soon became apparent that his art stood apart from Pop and from the local color of genre by virtue of its intense subjectivity.

PETER VOULKOS (United States, 1924–).   A dynamic personality and violently expressive form have made Peter Voulkos a daring leader in ceramic art during the last thirty years. Beginning with wheel-thrown pieces, he may punch, rip, slash, gouge, and stack these into compositions of intimidating energy (Fig. 19-43). He adds slabs and fills holes with *pass-throughs* of different clay bodies. Paper stencils allow colored slips to be built up around a sheltered shape, which then becomes a sunken area surrounded by color in relief. Wax may serve as a *resist* to shelter selected areas when colored glazes are applied with the freedom of action painting. Voulkos has said that he uses the painted shapes to violate the three-dimensional forms. Dissonance helps Voulkos

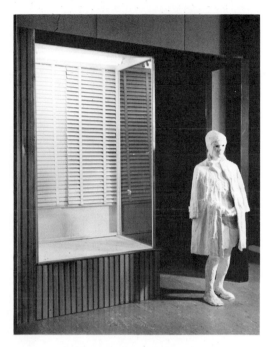

19-42   GEORGE SEGAL,   *The Store Window,* (1969). Mixed media construction: plaster, wood, Plexiglas, aluminum, venetian blinds, fluorescent light, 96″ × 103″ × 39¾″.   Collection of the Milwaukee Art Museum. Gift of Friends of Art.

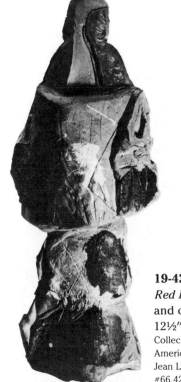

19-43   PETER VOULKOS, *Red River,* (c. 1960). Clay and colored glazes, 37″ high, 12½″ wide, 14½″ deep. Collection of Whitney Museum of American Art. Gift of the Howard and Jean Lipman Foundation, Inc. Acq. #66.42.

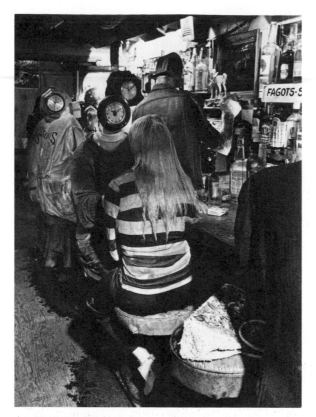

19-44   EDWARD KIENHOLZ,   *The Beanery,*
(1964–65). Mixed media, 22″ × 7′ × 6′.   Stedelijk
Museum, Amsterdam.

19-45   HELEN FRANKENTHALER,   *Buddha's
Court,* (1964). Acrylic paint on canvas, 98″ × 94″.
Private collection, André Emmerich Gallery.

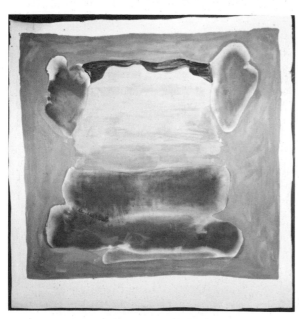

achieve maximum energy, which, for him, as for
Hans Hofmann, brings life to the work. His use of
epoxy paint and his joining of fired pieces with
glue shocked traditional artists but influenced
younger ceramists. Voulkos has been active both
as a painter and as the sculptor of huge bronze
pieces that combine cubes, cylinders, elbows,
domes, and plates. Some of these parts are cast
and some are purchased ready-made from industrial sources. Voulkos stockpiles the basic parts
and welds them together, often on the site, for
exhibition or for commissioned pieces.

EDWARD KIENHOLZ (United States, 1927–   ).
The social commentary implied in many of Edward Kienholz's tableaux may stem from his early
work experiences, which ranged from dance band
manager to mental hospital attendant. Kienholz
settled in Los Angeles in 1953 and by 1959 had
turned from painting to freestanding assemblages.
In 1961, these became life-sized and environmental, in that they seem to invite spectator entry.
The Beanery (Fig. 19-44) represents a well-known
Los Angeles eatery. All the figures except that
of the owner, Barney, have clocks for heads, and
all are stopped at 2:10 except for the clock behind the bar. Kienholz has said that he wanted to
show the escape from time. *The Wait* (1964) presents the loneliness of the aged and the inevita-
ble encounter with death. His *Art Show* (1963–
1977) parodied exhibition openings. He filled a
gallery with clothed plaster casts of art celebrities,
embedding car air-conditioning vents in the faces
and tapedecks in the chests. Thus, all the figures
"spoke," providing the cacaphony of art talk that
characterizes such an event.

HELEN FRANKENTHALER (United States, 1928–   ).
Thin paints poured onto flat canvas produce the
fluid, free forms that have made Helen Frankenthaler's painting internationally known. Her New
York background included training by some of the
major Abstract Expressionists of the 1940s and
1950s. While retaining their freedom of form, she
moved away from impasto in the early 1950s and
used instead thin oil on raw canvas. The resulting
stained, flowing forms seem to unite with the
background into which they are literally absorbed,
yet an ambiguous illusion of deep space often
seems to contradict this unified surface. Fran-

kenthaler's paintings of the 1950s often allude to natural objects. Turning to acrylics after 1962, she later painted in a darker palette, with firmer edges to her shapes, and simpler, quieter, more compact and nonobjective forms. *Buddha's Court* (Plate 45 and Fig. 19-45) was painted shortly after her work began to exhibit these characteristics. In contrast to the traditional respect for the original format of a painting to which the artist adjusts his or her composition, Frankenthaler often crops a work after it is finished, thus composing "after the fact." Her style could be classified between Action Painting and Color Field.

DONALD JUDD (United States, 1928–). Donald Judd studied painting at the Art Students' League and at Columbia University before turning to three-dimensional form. In the early 1960s, he produced reliefs of painted wood and metal and made his first boxlike floor constructions of metal and Plexiglas. Judd states that he wants to rid his art of illusions, compositional relationships, and rational implications; the work should be experienced as a single whole without reference to ideas beyond itself. This position has been taken by other Minimal artists and has been related to phenomenological philosophy. The untitled construction from 1965 (Fig. 19-46) is a series of identical masses and spaces whose reflecting surfaces and complex shadows produce effects of sensuous richness and severe order.

CLAES OLDENBURG (United States, 1929–). After studying English and art at Yale, Claes Oldenburg enrolled at the Chicago Art Institute. His first one-man show, in New York, was in 1959 and consisted of assemblages of street materials painted in gray, white, or black. In 1961, he created an environment of store objects in a rented storefront. After the exhibit closed, the store became "The Ray Gun Theater," where Oldenburg produced Happenings. *The Store* was his first critical success; its second version, in the Green Gallery in 1962, contained an enormous hamburger and a slice of cake, both made of brightly colored stuffed canvas. *The Soft Typewriter* (Fig. 19-47), though modest in size, was produced during this phase. A common object is presented with a change in one basic characteristic — a change that makes the viewer perceive the object in a new

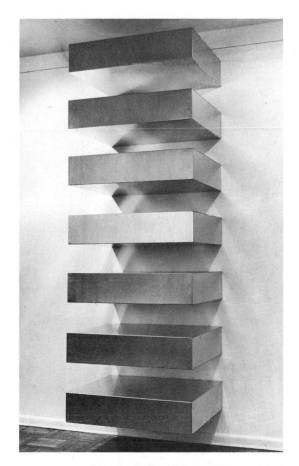

19-46 DONALD JUDD, untitled construction, (1965). Galvanized iron and aluminum, 33″ × 11′9″ × 30″. Leo Castelli Gallery, New York.

19-47 CLAES OLDENBURG, *The Soft Typewriter,* "Ghost" version, (1963). Canvas, kapok, wood, liquitex, 9″ × 27½″ × 26″. Karl Stroher Collection, Darmstadt.

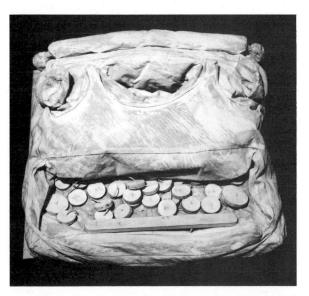

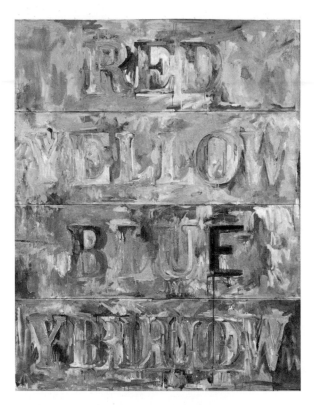

19-48   JASPER JOHNS,   *By the Sea,* (1961).
Encaustic on canvas (4 panels), 72″ × 54½″.   Private
collection, New York.

way. As a major Pop artist, Oldenburg has tended
to depict objects or images from our consumer
culture. In the late 1960s, he planned large public
monuments based on such common objects as
lipsticks. Unlike many Pop artists, Oldenburg
sometimes implies satire; he has said that humor is
a useful tool in a dissolving world.

JASPER JOHNS (United States, 1930–).   Since
his first one-man show in 1958, Jasper Johns has
been a leader in painting and sculpture. His early
work involved stained surfaces, collage, and assemblages in boxes. During the 1950s, he initiated
most of his major themes: targets, flags, numbers,
and letters, all of which came from fixed, conventionally symbolic images. His media have been
encaustic, oil, collage, and sculptmetal (a metallic
plastic), sometimes combined with plaster casts
and actual objects. Clearly defined commonplace
objects and symbols are robbed of their clarity and
dependable meanings, acquiring an ironic allu-
siveness. Johns subverts the usual clarity of his
chosen images by submerging them in collage and
layers of dripping, impetuously brushed paint. For
example, the primary colors—red, yellow, and
blue—have been sabotaged in a series of paintings. In *By the Sea* (Plate 48 and Fig. 19-48), four
separate canvases within one frame present the
words *red, yellow,* and *blue,* and a fourth "word"
that is an amalgamation of the first three. With
word mixing, Johns seems to parody the color
mixing learned by all beginning art students. We
look in vain, however, for a pure red, yellow, or
blue in the composition. Each letter of each word
is produced by a complex and subtle mixture of
the three primary colors. The letters almost lose
their identity and merge with the equally rich surface around them. The entire work was painted
with spontaneous brushwork, eroding the objective clarity of the standard letter shapes and the
three basic colors. The obvious becomes elusive
as Johns uses contradiction, disjunction, and
paradox to throw doubt on our conventional symbols and the logic of language.

MAGDALENA ABAKANOWICZ (Poland, 1930–).
Magdalena Abakanowicz disdains the old concept
of the crafts as minor arts. Her fiber-fabric works
are explosive in texture, value contrast, color,
three-dimensionality, and scale. Horsehair, fine

yarn, sisal, nylon, or fur may be used in sizes extending from thread to hawser (Fig. 19-49). Abakanowicz may work in black and white or in a single vehement red or yellow. She creates not only single pieces, suspended or freestanding on armatures, but also whole environments for exteriors or interiors. One fiber-fabric environment, installed amid sand dunes, was the setting for *Abakany*, a film made in 1969. The indoor environments have consisted of huge woven forms and massive ropes, which swing from the ceiling, gather in mammoth knots, or lie inertly on the floor. Abakanowicz's worldwide exhibitions and many awards testify to increasing public awareness of fiber-fabric as a major art medium.

ANDY WARHOL (United States, 1930–87).   Andy Warhol, one of the best-known figures in the Pop Art movement, was raised in Pittsburgh and trained at the Carnegie Institute of Technology. He began a career in advertising art and window display and later employed the image of advertising in his paintings. After 1961, his subjects included cola bottles, soup cans, Brillo boxes, and the actress Marilyn Monroe. The Brillo boxes are plywood boxes on which labels have been silk-screened; they belong more to the realm of sculpture than do the other subjects, which are depicted on flat surfaces. Repetition is an important characteristic of Warhol's art. Frequently his compositions consist of one subject repeated many times, sometimes with slight variations. Figure 19-50 is one of a group of four Campbell's soup cans that differ from one another only in color. Warhol verbally expressed a conviction that individuality is on the wane; his art celebrates the impersonal nature of a machine-oriented culture.

NAM JUNE PAIK (Korea, Japan, Germany, and the United States, 1932–   ).   Nam June Paik has been an international pioneer in video art. After studying classical music, art history, and aesthetics, he carried forward the explorations of Marcel Duchamp, the Dada movement, and John Cage. Paik used "prepared" traditional musical instruments (instruments altered to produce unusual effects), untraditional instruments, chance, found environments of sound, and audience participation to create video sculpture. His early professional activity occurred in Germany from 1956–64. Against

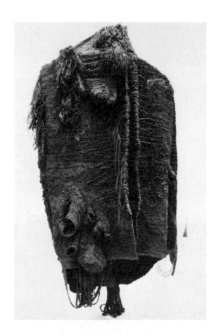

19-49 MAGDALENA ABAKANOWICZ, *Abakan Black Garment,* (1969). Fiber, 310 × 150 × 100 cm.   Stedelijk Museum, Amsterdam.

19-50 ANDY WARHOL, *Campbell's Soup,* (1965). Oil, silk-screened on canvas, 36⅛″ × 24⅛″.   Collection, the Museum of Modern Art, New York. Elizabeth Bliss Parkinson Fund.

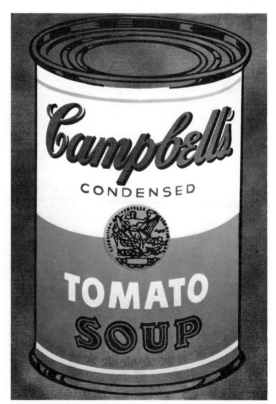

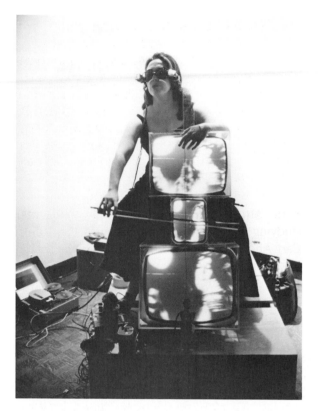

19-51 NAM JUNE PAIK, *Charlotte Moorman with TV Glasses and TV Cello,* (1971). *TV Cello,* collection of Charlotte Moorman. *TV Glasses,* collection of the artist. Photo © 1971 by Peter Moore.

19-52 CHRYSSA, *The Gates to Times Square,* (1966). Welded stainless steel, neon, and Plexiglas, 120″ × 120″ × 120″. Albright-Knox Art Gallery, Buffalo, New York. Gift of Mr. and Mrs. Albert A. List, 1972.

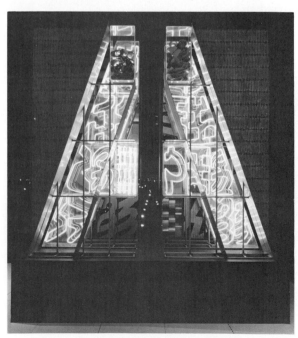

a tape of classical music and newscasts, Paik might throw beans at the ceiling or cut off the necktie of someone in the audience. In 1963, he began using groups of modified television sets in a move to demystify electronic media. Since 1964, he has been in the United States, except for time spent on world tours as video artist and performer. He has served as artist in residence at schools and as researcher/artist in experimental laboratories. A frequent collaborator has been the cellist Charlotte Moorman. Their 1971 performance, *TV Cello,* consisted of television sets arranged to resemble a cello and "played" by Moorman (Fig. 19-51). The TV screens showed her actual performance and videotapes of other cellists. Paik has said that he wants to humanize technology. He often does this through metaphor: the television sets are like a cello in that they can be played upon or manipulated for personal expression. The metaphor may involve audience participation. Paik's *Magnet TV* (1965) allowed a spectator to move a magnet in front of a television set to distort the image. The artist has used a synthesizer to deform the image of the viewer on a closed-circuit television and an arrangement that converts spectator-produced sounds into television images. Paik's international importance has come from his imaginative use of technology as an expressive tool and from his exploration, via electronic means, of the age-old tension between material form and spiritual content in art.

CHRYSSA (Greece and the United States, 1933–). The boisterousness of America as seen in the lights of Times Square has been, for Chryssa, poetic and even Homeric! The information power of letters and words excites her most. After settling in New York in 1954, she created relief sculptures of multiple white plaster letters or single letters formed from variously arranged pegs. Her newspaper paintings and photolithographs employ repetition and variations of news articles, ads, and weather or financial diagrams. Between 1962 and 1966, she produced a major work, *The Gates to Times Square,* incorporating reworked fragments of commercial signs and even preparatory drawings (Fig. 19-52). Various letters or their parts are repeated like motifs in music. Many of her pieces from the 1960s are entitled *Studies for the Gates.* Most use a dark gray Plexiglas box to enclose brilliantly illuminated neon forms turned on and off by a timer. The light-dark alternation recalls the basic rhythm of day and night; the part-by-part illumination of many of the pieces suggests the willful rhythm of human programming. The neon forms, single or double letters repeated in series, are often barely legible because they are simplified and sometimes placed on their sides. In the 1970s, Chryssa returned to plaster letters in white or varied colors. These are scrambled or arranged in rows on plaster backgrounds in box frames. In some, there is no neon; in others, two to four letters are neon, hinting that the other white plaster letters are invested with great potential energy. Chryssa is one of many contemporary artists using light as a medium. She is distinctive in her use of light to express the magic of communication by the printed word.

SAM GILLIAM (United States, 1933–). Sam Gilliam, a black artist working in Washington D.C., began, in 1966, to pour and roll acrylic paint onto unstretched canvas. Folding and repainting produced diagonal linear bands and complex colors. In 1968, he began to drape and hang canvases from walls and ceilings. These suspended paintings acquired swinging rhythms that alternate between billowing openness and knotted constrictions. By 1973, Gilliam was staining canvas, stitching assemblages of canvas pieces, and drap-

ing these over timbers and across the floor. However, he also used stretched canvases, onto which he poured layers of thickened acrylic paint. A final layer of white or black was raked to reveal underlying colors. Subsequently, Gilliam cut some of his paintings into geometric pieces and added these as collage to other works. The results were skeins of spattered and poured colors in shimmering geometric patterns (Fig. 19-53). Gilliam has used irregular canvases with as many as nine sides.

CARL ANDRE (United States, 1935–). After studying painting and filmmaking in the 1950s, Carl Andre traveled abroad and then settled in New York. From poetry and painting, his focus shifted to geometric sculpture in Plexiglas and wood; Andre's major inspiration came from the work of Brancusi. Compositions of rough lumber, notched and stacked, gave way in the mid-1960s to stacks of styrofoam slabs and floor pieces of bricks arranged in rectangular units related proportionally to the room in which they were placed. His *Spill*, consisting of eight hundred plastic blocks scattered from a canvas bag onto the floor, revealed an interest in chance. The *Plain* is one of many floor pieces constructed of commercially made metal plaques. Variations in color and texture are used to create patterns that are often sensuously rich and intricate. In his more recent work, Andre has used rods and bands of industrial

19-53 SAM GILLIAM, *Lion's Rock-Arc,* from the *Red and Black* series, (1981). Acrylic on canvas, 82″ × 191″. Middendorf Gallery, Washington, D.C.

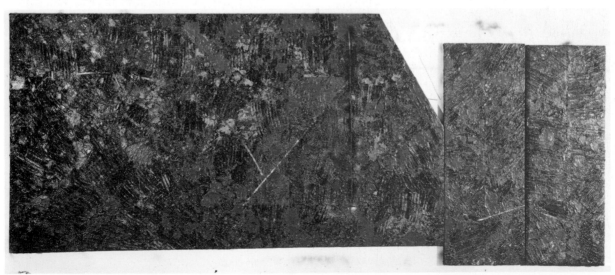

materials such as plastic, steel, and iron in parallel and random distributions. They occupy the room completely, producing an environment filled with multidirectional forces that contrast with the static geometry of the otherwise empty room.

EVA HESSE (Germany and the United States, 1936–70).   A brain tumor cut short Eva Hesse's career. Her mature works, between 1965 and 1970, often utilized obsessive repetitions, yielding flaccid forms, hanging or wandering lines, and bland textures and colors (Fig. 19-54). Critics described them as pathetic, uneasy objects (simultaneously grand, whimsical, sad, humorous, quiet, and nervous) that raised questions rather than proposed answers. Hesse was born in Germany and came to the United States, by way of Holland and England, in 1939. She earned a graduate degree in art from Yale University and presented her first solo exhibition, one of drawings, at a New York gallery in 1963. Her best-known drawings are rows or grids of equal-sized circles in delicate ink wash. In some of these, lengths of string perforate the centers of the circles and dangle uncertainly from their regimented and very "certain" two-dimensional

19-54   EVA HESSE,   *Repetition 19, III,* (1968). Nineteen tubular fiberglass units, 19″ to 20¼″ high × 11″ to 12¾″ in diameter.   Collection, the Museum of Modern Art, New York. Gift of Charles and Anita Blatt.

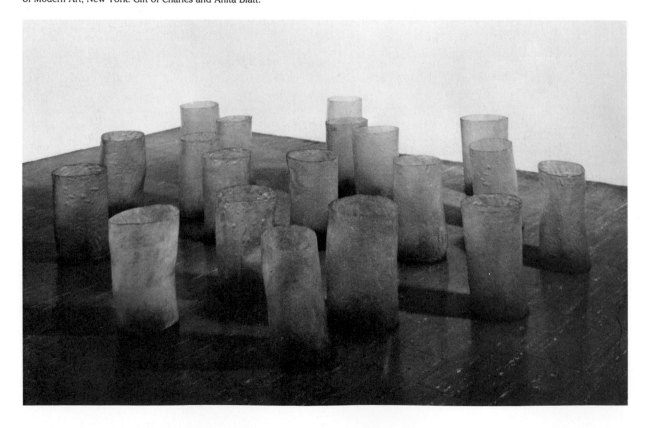

backgrounds. Other drawing series use rough rectangular images in a rich mixture of media, surface, and color effects. However, sculpture became her dominant medium. Hesse used inner tubes and sausage-shaped, partially inflated balloons wrapped in cord or covered with papier-mâché and painted. With fiberglass and latex, she cast wobbly, open-ended, translucent boxes, which she arranged in vertical or horizontal rows, or tubes that she stood casually against the wall. She spoke of the absurdity of life, and she enjoyed this quality in her art. Hesse combined repetition with oppositions and divergencies that produce surprise and awkwardness, important qualities for an artist who wanted to counteract conventional expectations about composition.

RICHARD ESTES (United States, 1936–).   Work experience in advertising and illustration gave Richard Estes the technical background for paintings like *Nedick's* (Fig. 19-55). This work is typical of the Photorealist movement. While paintings such as *Nedick's* are related to Pop Art, they are less concerned with the amplification of simple mass-media images and more obsessed with the literal depiction of surface details. Sharp-focus photography is an influence and a tool. There is a preference for reflective, synthetic surfaces in complex urban scenes. The Photorealists often work from photographs, sometimes projecting them onto the canvas and rendering them with an airbrush. Sharpness of focus is often manipulated by the painter. Estes achieved intensification of physical data by equally sharp focus in foreground and background. Perhaps in reaction to subjective trends in twentieth-century art, the Photorealists, like the Pop artists, value a cool, neutral effect. Estes's painting is so intensely descriptive that the physical character of glass, metal, and concrete acquires an almost hypnotic quality. We are presented with a heightened and immediately accessible physical reality.

19-55 RICHARD ESTES,   *Nedick's,* (1969–70). Oil, 48″ × 66″.   Private collection.

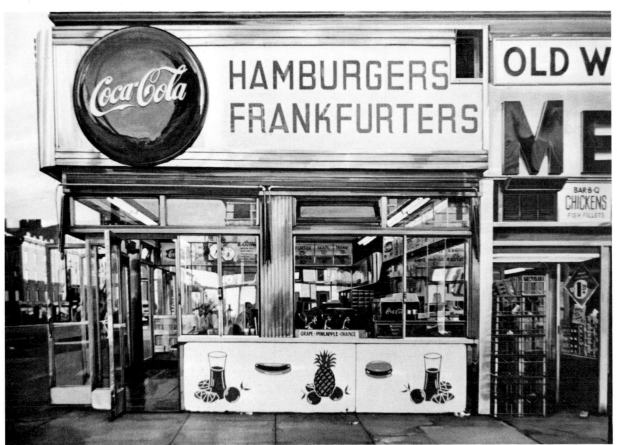

FRANK STELLA (United States, 1936–   ).   At the end of his tenure as a student at Princeton, Frank Stella's painting changed from Abstract Expressionism to forms that soon drew antagonistic but interested reactions from critics. The pieces consisted of wobbly three-inch bands that were almost monochromic and then, from 1959–60, only of black bands separated by strips of bare canvas. Stella said that he wanted to abolish illusionistic space and complex formal relationships, an aim also endorsed by Minimalist Donald Judd. The demanding presence of the large symmetrical black paintings was undeniable, but some critics called them icons of nihilism. In the 1960s, Stella's formats began to change. Rectangular canvases acquired notches that were echoed by the painted bands, establishing a special oneness between perimeter and the forms within. Black was succeeded by equally flat aluminum paint. A series of metallic copper band paintings came in 1960–61. These were in shapes such as U, L, or T. The titles came from Colorado towns. By 1963, canvas shapes were polygonal and trapezoidal, with open centers that revealed the gallery wall. A favorite color was metallic lavender (it has since faded). Concurrently, Stella produced compositions with several vibrant colors in bands that refused to meet in the center. The result was a return to spatial illusionism, but with great tension and ambiguity as shapes buckled and moved in and out through optical illusion. To this disjunctive and nonobjective geometry, Stella added fluorescent colors in the *Protractor Series* (c. 1967–69). Names came from ancient cities in Asia Minor. In the 1970s, Stella did three sets of paintings from forty drawings titled from Polish synagogues that were destroyed in World War II. Set I used paint and collage of felt, paper, and canvas; Set II added masonite and wood to produce low relief; Set III employed tilted planes for very three-dimensional painted sculpture. One of the Polish paintings was done with aluminum, opening the way for the *Brazilian Series* (started in 1974), which was executed on etched and lacquered aluminum. Scumbling with oil sticks created spontaneous linear patterns that recall action painting. The works extended even farther out from the wall. Exotic birds were title sources for another series of similar content. Jarring dissonance and raucous energy come from contrasts of colors and of taut geometric shapes (some taken from the standard plastic French curves used in architectural drafting) with squiggling lines and wild brushstrokes. Drawings and models were the basis for the final pieces, which were fabricated by tooling companies. In the 1980s, the explosive energy and crackling dissonance continued in relief paintings that now included cylinders and cones modeled by precise stripes or wedge-shaped bands (Fig. 19-56).

DOROTHEA ROCKBURNE (Canada and the United States).   Interest in mathematical set theory and proportions such as the Golden Mean (pp. 19–20) has led Dorothea Rockburne to produce compositions that suggest the manipulation of modules within a system. She is a conceptual artist in that her works stress predetermined parameters and process. For years, she used common materials, such as paper, carbon paper, charcoal, grease, staples, and glue, which tended to resist sensuous appreciation and focused on relationships and ideas. She used a series of operations involving layering, hanging, soaking, rolling, and unrolling. Her recent *Egyptian Paintings* employ precisely folded linen triangles and black lines drawn on the gallery wall (Fig. 19-57). Gesso, conte crayon, pencil, and oil paint give to a basically black and white schema a subtle play of textures and shadows, and a tension between the linen and the wall. A sensuous and ethereal quality overlies the conceptual precision of the series.

DAVID HOCKNEY (England, 1937–   ).   International recognition came very quickly to David Hockney, whose paintings and drawings have been largely biographical but still accessible to the public by way of his wit, fantasy, drawing skills, and references to past art. In the early 1960s, his style was childlike in drawing and proportion (under the influence of Dubuffet), fragmented, painterly in its brushy textures, and hieroglyphic in its simplified, schematized imagery. Words and phrases are crudely painted into the composition, and an easy number code (1 = A, 2 = B, 3 = C, and so on) is used to indicate persons depicted or associated ideas. For example, 4.2 stands for D. B. This is *Doll Boy*, a hit song by a popular singer. The numbers 23.23 stand for W. W. or Walt Whitman, a favorite author of Hockney's and a source for some of the artist's pictorial ideas. Much of Hock-

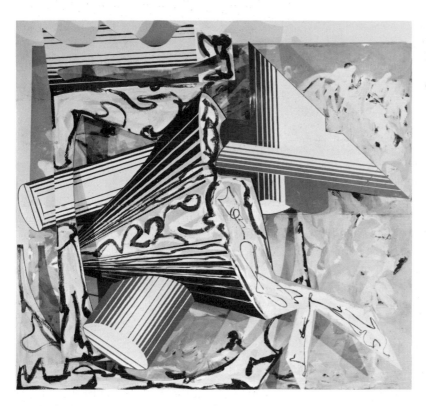

19-56 FRANK STELLA, *Quaquá! Attaccati Lá!,* (1987). Mixed media painted relief, 156⅜″ × 171½″ × 24⅞″. Courtesy of Leo Castelli Gallery, New York.

19-57 DOROTHEA ROCKBURNE, *Egyptian Painting: Scarab,* (1980). Conte, pencil, oil, gesso on linen, 47″ × 28⅜″. Xavier Fourcade Gallery, New York.

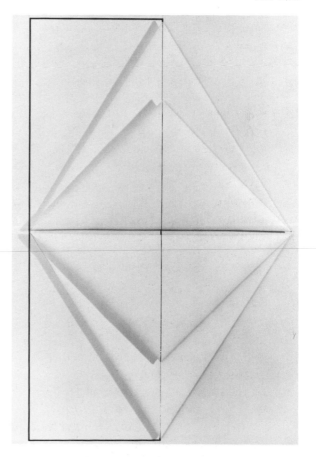

ney's iconography alludes to his homosexual experiences in the gay subcultures of London and Los Angeles. Much of his work contrasts dissimilar elements of line drawing, volumetric modeling, and paper-thin insubstantial surfaces. In doing this, he points out both the flat plane of the picture and the artistic devices used to deny it, such as perspective and modeling. We are constantly reminded that a picture is primarily a human construction of marks. With Hockney, the marks have varied levels of meanings. A tightly representational picture of his friends may echo, in its composition, a famous painting from the Renaissance. This is the case with some of the depictions of his friends in their Los Angeles homes, done in the second half of the 1960s. Hockney had turned to acrylic paint and smooth, simplified surfaces in assertive colors. There is a suggestion of poster art, probably encouraged by the advent of the Pop movement. Hockney's new naturalism is presented with a luminosity and a compositional grid that recall the work of Piero della Francesca. Increasingly, Hockney used photographs to supplement drawings from life as a basis for painting. Some of these drawings were done in closely observed and delicate contours reminiscent

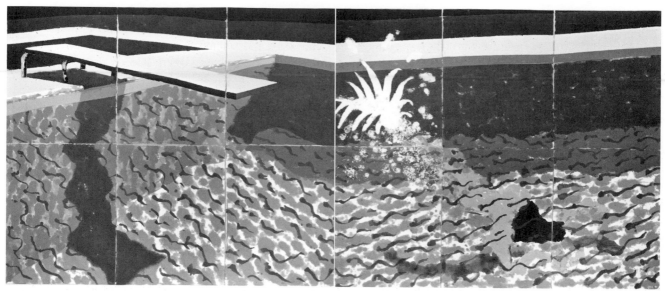

19-58   DAVID HOCKNEY,   *Le Plongeur,* Paper
Pool 18, (1978). Colored pressed paper pulp, 12
sheets, each 36″ × 28″.   Courtesy of Tyler Graphics Ltd.

of one of Picasso's styles. Along with Hockney's
interest in contrasting styles came an interest in
different techniques. Etching was his choice for
illustrations to the poetry of C. P. Cavafy (1967)
and for a selection of Grimm's *Fairy Tales* (1970).
Pressed and dyed paper pulp provided one of his
most luminous images (Fig. 19-58). The plain and
patterned surfaces, the conventionalized treatment of the water, and the fascination with transparency all can be found, but with less intensity, in
his other depictions of swimming pools. Of his
stage set designs, the most impressive may be
those for Mozart's *The Magic Flute*. The thirteen
separate backdrops (1977–78) were set in ancient Egypt and ranged from wild landscapes to
formal gardens and great reception halls. The style
was inspired by early Italian Renaissance painting.
In the 1980s, Hockney's work became more
imaginative again. California landscapes were rendered in resonant colors, thick oil paint textures,
symbolic shorthand images, and compressed
space.

19-59   JUDY CHICAGO,
Reincarnation Triptych - 2 "George
Sand," (1973). Oil on canvas, 5′ × 5′.
Private collection.

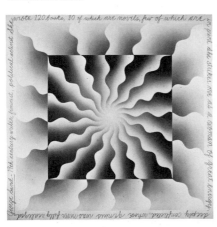

JUDY CHICAGO, *formerly* JUDY GEROWITZ (United
States, 1939–).   Judy Chicago's early work
ranged from minimal sculpture to performances
with colored smoke. In the late 1960s, she turned
increasingly to the problems of women in a male-
dominated society. For her *Reincarnation Triptych* themes, she chose three women of special
accomplishments: Madame de Stäel, Virginia
Woolf, and George Sand (Fig. 19-59). Each com-

position contains a written commentary. In the George Sand piece, the radiating center contained by enclosing squares symbolizes a phase in women's history as well as a phase in Judy Chicago's development. In 1979, Chicago and a group of associates completed *The Dinner Party,* a triangular table (48 feet to a side) with settings commemorating the contributions of women to culture, from early history to the present. The setting consists of 39 fourteen-inch plates, varying from flat design to high relief, each symbolizing a specific woman of great accomplishment. Under each plate is a runner, done in a variety of materials and stitchery techniques, representing the woman's historical role. Utensils and goblets are of porcelain. Beneath the table is a floor of glazed tiles inscribed with the names of 999 women of importance to history.

RICHARD SERRA (United States, 1939–   ). Richard Serra studied sculpture in California and at Yale. In the Documenta V exhibition in Kassel, Germany, in 1972, his interest in structuring complete envi-

ronments was shown in a work consisting of four upright steel slabs arranged in an X, thus dividing a room into four parts. He has chosen an open-air setting and a larger scale for field pieces like *Shift* (Fig. 19-60), a composition of six concrete slabs, each eight inches thick, arranged in two sets, one for each of two hills. The valley between the sets is about 120 feet wide. The directional alignment of each slab corresponds to the sharpest drop of the land, and the downhill end of each slab is beveled to relate to the direction of the next slab. The length of the slabs varies from 90 to 240 feet. Each piece begins flush with the ground and extends horizontally until the ground has dropped 5 feet. Thus, the length and direction of each slab are determined by the topography of the land. Walking into the composition provides a succession of changing views; as the zigzag forms are seen from different angles, they appear to compress or extend space. Their horizontal top edges establish bases for the contours of the land above and behind them, while the bottom of each piece defines and is shaped by the curvature of the hill. Each slab

19-60   RICHARD SERRA,   *Shift,* (1970–72). Six rectilinear cement sections, total length 815′. King, Ontario.

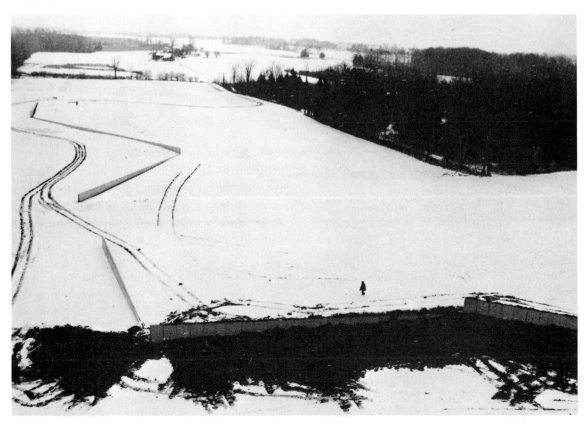

acts as a template to reveal the profile of the earth mass. The geometry of the slabs contrasts with the irregularity of the site. As with ancient monuments, one feels that nature has been modified by the presence of the human mind.

VITO ACCONCI (United States, 1940–   ).   Vito Acconci first gained critical attention in 1970. In work which is often referred to as body art, he has tried to erase the distinction between the artist and the work of art. *Step Piece* (1970) was a work in which the artist stepped up and down on an eighteen-inch stool at the rate of thirty steps a minute beginning at 8:00 A.M. and continuing for as long as he was able without stopping. In *Security Zone* (1971), Acconci's hands were tied and he was blindfolded. He then allowed a stranger to spin him around and let him wander dangerously near the edge of a pier. In this and other pieces, he attempts to make himself vulnerable, to put himself at another's mercy. In this way he seeks to open up closed systems and to break through conventional behavior in order to break down barriers between people.

PAT STEIR (United States, 1940–   ).   The personal, spontaneous, and gestural brush stroke became the keystone of the Abstract Expressionist movement. Pat Steir saw gestural mark-making from a more conceptual and historical viewpoint. This is understandable, since she was maturing as an artist during the 1960s, when conceptual art became prominent. Steir has been fascinated by the way marks on a flat surface change from personal gestures to signs, symbols, and illusions of three-dimensional objects. She uses oil paint, crayon, pencil, and ink for paintings that are fragmented and diagrammatic. They imply physical and mental processes and refer to various movements in the history of art. *Cellar Door* (1972) includes a blackish rectangular field that seems to speak of Minimal Art, yet its dripping paint refers to the process of handling paint and to the immediacy of Abstract Expressionism. A value scale with numbered gradations suggests the process of mixing and modulating paint as well as the procedures for commercial reproductions of images. Tiny rows of vertical strokes have the nature of a printed text, and a crossed-out image of mountains and water seems to propose that representational im-

agery is insufficient. *Lima Being (Being/Been),* executed in 1980 (Fig. 19-61), is a nine-panel piece presenting the various possibilities of marks in a formal system of diamond and square frames. These are bordered by bands of alternating black, white, and colored squares that evoke the late work of the pioneer modern painter, Mondrian. Inside the frames are marks: some gestural and free, others regimented, some flat and abstract, others producing the illusion of three-dimensional objects in space, both abstract and representational. The most representational image is that of a pod of beans. The title appropriately involves word-play. "Lima Being" hints at a philosophical view of the ordinary lima bean, as does the rest of the title: "(Being/Been)." Being and becoming, existence and the development of things within existence, the static moment and change within time are all implied. Steir has said of one painting (*Line Lima,* 1973) that it is about the evolution of a single mark to an image. She is concerned with the meaning of language, the meaning of paint, and the meaning of meaning. For *The Brueghel Series, A Vanitas of Style,* Steir used eighty panels in a twenty by sixteen foot piece that refers to style changes in image making over centuries of the history of art. She chose a flower painting by Jan Brueghel the Elder (Flemish, 1568–1625), dividing it into a grid of square panels and then repainting each panel in the style of a different artist, from the Renaissance to the present. Each part of the same subject reflects a viewpoint of a different person and a different epoch in human experience. Steir has said that such quotations from the styles of previous artists allow her to have a living relationship to art history. She does not see these as the kind of borrowings from the past that are typical of Postmodern "appropriation." Steir's work is distinctive in its calculated, systematic, and conceptual allusions.

ELIZABETH MURRAY (United States, 1940–   ). After a sophisticated education at Chicago's Art Institute and Mills College, Elizabeth Murray developed a kind of painting that seems, on first encounter, to be untrained, crude, awkward, and emotionally explosive. From her earliest work, she was attracted to the animated shapes and narrative elements in popular cartoons. This was probably encouraged by the California paintings called

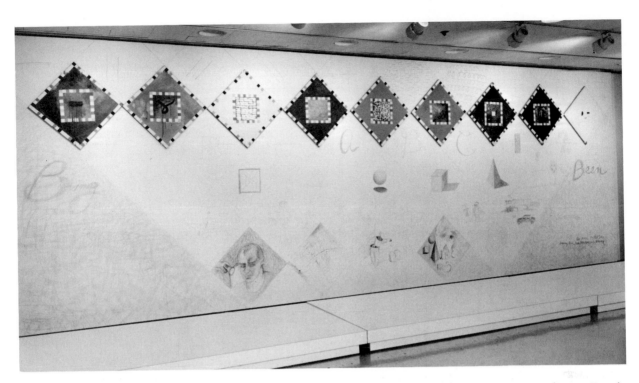

19-61 PAT STEIR, *Lima Being (Being/Been),*
(1980). Oil on canvas, 9 panels, each 24″ × 24″, each
installation with unique pencil wall drawings.
Collection of the Chase Manhattan Bank.

Funk Art, a boisterous, irreverent, and cartoon-inspired movement of the 1960s. After moving to New York in 1967, Murray's work became less obviously narrative; the drama came more from color and shape relations. In 1976, she began using irregularly shaped canvases, or groups of such canvases, whose abrupt angular formats set up violent tensions. Colors were intense, and painted shapes recalled the bulbous, expansive, biomorphic qualities in the art of Miró or Arp. Murray's instinctive imaginative freedom recalls the psychic automatism dear to the Surrealists. The shapes in her work often have a tentative and earnest clumsiness of edge or contour that implies dedicated struggle rather than technical virtuosity. She emphasizes the physical nature of the viscous oil paint and the woven canvas support. The viewer is forced to recognize that the painting is a handmade object of particular materials that have special characteristics of their own. Murray's art history training is revealed by allusions in many of her works to the styles of earlier masters of modern art, such as Picasso or Juan Gris. Her *Open Book* (Fig. 19-62) is typical of her art in the awkward, lunging energy of the edges and in its multiple identities. The openings on each page could be windows that, as a metaphor for book learning, lead us to new truths. They could also be the eye

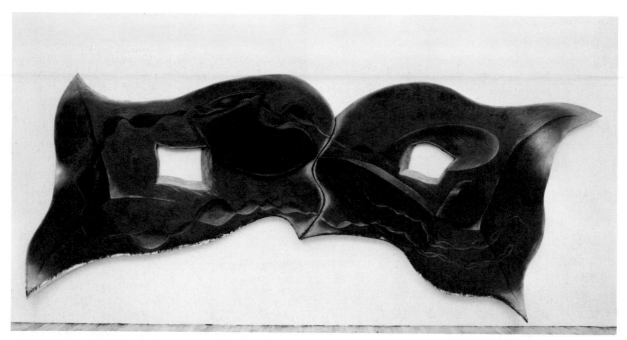

19-62 ELIZABETH MURRAY, *Open Book,*
(1985). Oil on canvas, 2 panels, one 90½″ × 121″ ×
11″ and one 88¼″ × 111¼″ × 9¾″. Collection of
Whitney Museum of American Art, New York. Gift of the Mnuchin
Foundation.

openings of a mask that hides the truth. The piece
is actually a painted relief; three of the central
balloonlike shapes are separate canvases that are
projected in front of the main surface. The apparent urgency and spontaneity of her work have
placed Murray under the broad umbrella of Neo-
Expressionism.

JENNIFER BARTLETT (United States, 1941–).
In 1975, Jennifer Bartlett's *Rhapsody* established
her as a major artist. This mural, spanning 154 feet,
consists of 988 one-foot square steel plates on
which she painted with enamel. It is a diagram of
visual and conceptual language, using variations of
basic lines, shapes, and colors and four motifs:
tree, house, mountain, and ocean. The images
range from mechanical to freehand and from geometric shapes and generic signs to specific representations. The painting implies that the mind handles and generates images in the manner of a
computer and that originality is a rearrangement of
conventional images. *Rhapsody* also forecast the
appropriation of different styles and images that is
characteristic of Postmodern art. In 1979, Bartlett
began to use more representational images and
more sensuously rich color and paint manipulation. *In the Garden,* a series made up of some
200 drawings and numerous paintings of a tree-
bordered pool, explores different stylistic inter-

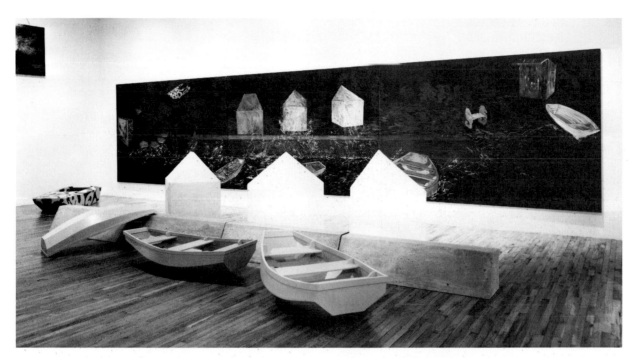

19-63 JENNIFER BARTLETT, *Sea Wall,* (1985). Mixed media painting and sculpture, canvases 7′ × 30′9″ overall.   Courtesy of Paula Cooper Gallery, New York.

pretations and a wide-range of conceptual and emotional content. As in *Rhapsody,* the allusions to different stylistic movements in the history of modern art relate her work to the Postmodernist interest in escaping the restrictions of one stylistic language. During the 1980s, Bartlett combined large paintings with three-dimensional models of motifs within the paintings, such as boats and houses (Fig. 19-63). The models are executed in a variety of materials and in unexpected colors that tend to subvert their mundane identities. It is as though these objects have escaped from the two-dimensional limits of the paintings and invaded our space, bringing with them the irrational freedom of the artist's fantasy. Bartlett suggests in much of her recent work that reality is a mental construction consisting of conventional signs modified by individual subjectivity. The size of her work has been appropriate to commissions from corporations done for specific sites.

MICHAEL HEIZER (United States, 1944–).   In the 1960s, Michael Heizer turned from painting to earthworks. His *Dissipate* (1968) consists of five shallow trenches, each twelve feet long, in a fifty-foot-square area of Black Rock Desert, Nevada. Heizer determined the positions of the trenches by throwing toothpicks on a tabletop. His most publicized earthwork is *Double Negative* (Fig. 19-64),

19-64 MICHAEL HEIZER, *Double Negative,* (1970). 240,000 ton removal on Virgin River Mesa, Nevada, 1,600′ × 30′ × 50′.

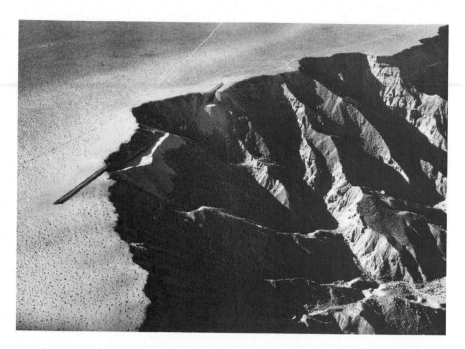

executed in 1969 but reworked in 1970, on the Virgin River Mesa, Nevada. In the 1970 version, 240,000 tons of earth were displaced to produce a trench (1,600 feet long, 50 feet wide, and 30 feet deep); it consists of two parts that notch the sides of an indentation in the wall of the mesa. The straight gouge is a startlingly human mark on the desolate landscape. Heizer prefers relatively inaccessible sites, and his earthworks are known mainly from documentary photographs.

JOSEPH KOSUTH (United States, 1945–   ). Joseph Kosuth studied painting at the School of Visual Arts in New York during the 1960s and became interested in the gap between the physical world and language. His *Table* (1965–67), includes an actual table, an enlarged photograph of the table, and an enlarged photocopy of a dictionary definition of a table. His *Fifteen Locations, Art as Idea* (1969–70), occurred when he published selected entries from a thesaurus in the advertising columns of newspapers and magazines all over the world. The *Ninth Investigation, Proposition 1* of 1972 consisted of looseleaf notebooks containing photocopied pages from philosophical writings on science and linguistics; enlarged photocopies of selections from each notebook were keyed to the work and hung on the facing wall. Drawing inspiration from such contemporary

thinkers as Claude Lévi-Strauss, Ludwig Wittgenstein, Noam Chomsky, and A. J. Ayer, Kosuth believes that works of art are analytical systems with their own logic and no meaning outside the context of art. For Kosuth, a leader in the field of Conceptual Art, the physical art object is little more than a historical curiosity; the actual work of art is the idea.

ANSELM KIEFER (Germany, 1945–   ).   By the late 1980s, influential American critics saw Anselm Kiefer as the most important European artist of the last quarter of the twentieth century and as a leading Neo-Expressionist painter. His youth during the aftermath of World War II and his study under Joseph Beuys probably led him to see art as a means of confronting large issues in human history. His huge paintings of bleak plowed fields and echoing monumental interiors seem desolate, alienated, and tragic. Their titles or painted interior labels make implicit and explicit references to myth, cultural tradition, and political history. *Painter's Studio, Inner Room* (1981) presents the tattered image of Hitler's audience hall, a haunting vision of German history. The title proposes that this is the artist's studio or the historical background in which he must work. *Sea Lion* (1975), the code name for Hitler's planned invasion of England, is the title of a Kiefer piece that depicts warships in a coffin-shaped foreground pool against an expansive background of cityscape and sky. At the top float the livid images of three empty chairs. Kiefer goes beyond invoking the demons of Germany's past, however. *Osiris and Isis* (Fig. 19-65) refers to the Egyptian myth of the god Osiris, who was murdered and dismembered by his brother and then resurrected as King of the Dead. The body parts are represented by pieces of broken ceramic attached to the painting of an immense stepped pyramid tomb. The ceramic pieces are connected by copper electrical wire to a circuit board at the top of the pyramid. The life and death opposition from an ancient Egyptian myth is related to the life and death potential of a modern atomic pile or nuclear reactor. The dramatic power of Kiefer's art comes from its monumental size, recalling the history paintings of the premodern era, and from the rough aggressiveness of the materials: canvas, paint, sand, lead, foil, and straw. While his content seems to be essentially tragic, the urgency and intensity of the work imply that Kiefer retains some hope that his message may play a didactic role in the reform of humankind and the building of a better future.

19-65 ANSELM KIEFER, *Osiris and Isis,* (1985–87). Acrylic, porcelain, and wire on canvas, 360 × 560 × 16 cm. Collection of the San Francisco Museum of Art. Courtesy of Marion Goodman Gallery, New York.

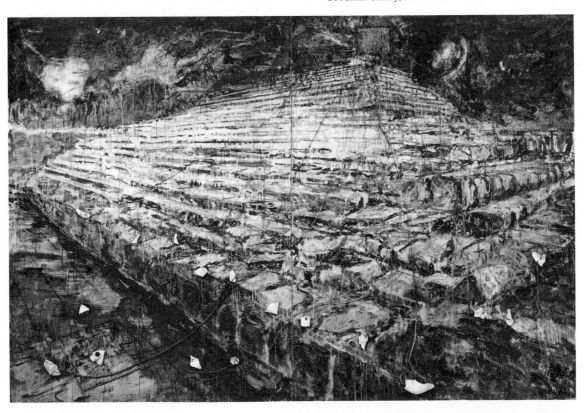

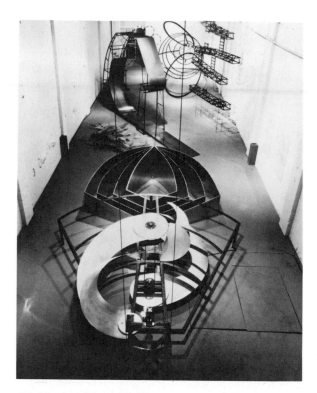

19-66 ALICE AYCOCK, *The Thousand and One Nights in the Mansion of Bliss,* (1983).   Courtesy of the John Weber Gallery, New York.

ALICE AYCOCK (United States, 1946–).   Science fiction and magic seem basic to Alice Aycock's fantastic constructions. In the 1970s, she produced precise architectural drawings that were plans for both realized and unrealized interior environments and exterior field pieces. Spectator participation was invited. The works tempted the spectator to enter into precarious situations: disorienting mazes, high narrow stairs or ledges without handrails, or confined spaces of potential entrapment. Aycock's prime materials were wood and concrete. Drawing from myth, history, archaeology, literature, records of schizophrenic hallucinations, and obsessive childhood fears, she imagined dramas for which these pieces were settings. Aycock has stated that she has never lost the child's sense of the uncertainty of existence in a mysterious and threatening world. During the 1980s, she often excluded spectator participation. The basic material was metal, and she used electric motors for movement. Aycock is fascinated by invisible forces. Electricity, for example, is magical for her. Her series of blade machines (1980s) features vicious knife shapes, referring both to modern technology and to medieval swords. She is attracted to and frightened by these creations and their evocation of both productive and destructive forces. The largest of the group was *The Thousand and One Nights in the Mansion of Bliss* (Fig. 19-66). In writing about her art, Aycock uses the surprising associations of Surrealist psychic automatism. The works have multilayered symbolic and associational content that often short-circuits conventional thought.

JUDY PFAFF (England and the United States, 1946–).   In the late 1970s and early 1980s, Judy Pfaff became known as the creator of seemingly chaotic, violently diverse, multimedia environments, which she described as an editing and splicing of the complex freneticism that she saw around her: ''I wanted to shatter space and then reform it.'' She used paint, plastic sheets, plywood, wire, tree branches, metallic paper, and tubing for these installations. They invaded floors, walls, and ceilings and were usually temporary (Fig. 19-67). Pfaff explained that she liked to surround the viewer so that the piece could not be seen with a single glance. Like the real world, it was all-encompassing. Both the titles and her comments

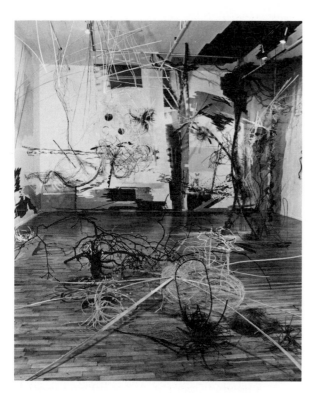

19-67   JUDY PFAFF,   *Deep Water,* (1979–80). Installation, partial view.   Courtesy of the Holly Solomon Gallery, New York.

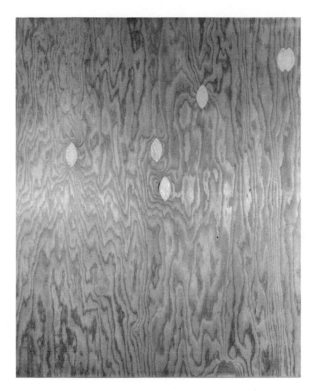

19-68   SHERRY LEVINE,   *Untitled (Golden Knots: 1),* (1987). Oil on wood, 62½″ × 50½″. Courtesy of the Mary Boone Gallery, New York.

about her works suggest that they were symbolic landscapes of vast scale. They were inspired not only by the active character of modern life but also by specific experiences, such as the viewing of a car race, a scuba diving trip, a Japanese film, and news releases about the Falklands War. In the 1980s, Pfaff turned to permanent wall reliefs, which sacrificed the overwhelming power of the environments but retained the same kinetic energy. Steel rods, lattice work, plywood, and vivid colors produced effects of spinning, layered, and conflicting spaces shot through by jittering, whirling, linear elements of wire or tubing. Although the gestural spontaneity recalls Abstract Expressionism, Pfaff's art can be considered as part of Neo-Expressionism.

SHERRY LEVINE (United States, 1947–   ).   During the 1980s, after the many revolutions of modern art, Sherry Levine's work shocked a public that one might have expected could no longer be shocked. She did this by questioning the major criterion of value in all the modern movements, that of originality. Marcel Duchamp had led the

way with his ready-mades early in the century. Levine escalated the attack by exhibiting, as art objects, pictures cut from books and magazines. She followed this with exhibits of photographs that she had taken of photographs by famous photographers. Then she did drawings and watercolors that copied printed reproductions of paintings by the masters of modern art: Mondrian, Miró, Leger, Malevich, and others. In 1986, she showed a series of paintings of vertical stripes in vivid colors and a series of plywood panels with gold-edged knotholes (Fig. 19-68). These two series were representative of two broad categories in twentieth-century avant-garde art: geometric nonobjective painting and the use of found objects. Levine had come to believe that all art has appropriated ideas and images from antecedents, and that the modern era has been naive in its search for unique images. Her art challenges the viewer to reconsider the history of modern art, the insistence on originality as a basis for value, and the art object as a commodity in an economic system. Her questioning of traditional assumptions is an example of the deconstruction typical of Postmodern art.

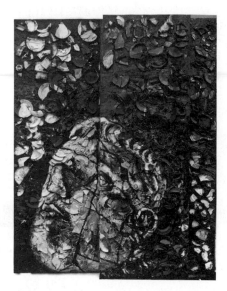

19-69   JULIAN SCHNABEL, *800 Blows,* (1983). Oil, plates, bondo on wood, 108″ × 84″.   Courtesy of the Mary Boone Gallery, New York.

JULIAN SCHNABEL (United States, 1951–).   A jangle of critical discord brought international attention to Julian Schnabel in the late 1970s and early 1980s. He was accepted as a strident leader of Neo-Expressionism in America. Some critics censured his work as theatrical bombast; others declared it to be sensational. He uses oil, encaustic, or plaster to create large, violent images on wood, canvas, sisal carpeting, or velvet. He incorporates such objects as antlers and broken dishes (Fig. 19-69). Schnabel has said that he seeks to evoke an emotional state that will engulf the spectator. His work has sources in the Abstract Expressionism of the 1950s, in Robert Rauschenberg's combines, and in European expressionism from Fauvism and Die Brücke to Dubuffet. The borrowing has been described as Postmodernist appropriation. Yet Schnabel has, with heroic scale and dissonance, managed to shock the art-interested public. This is remarkable, coming late in a century that has witnessed many artistic revolutions and in an era following Conceptual Art, which asserted that all painting was obsolete.

Architecture

Architects, as well as other artists, since the late 1960s have shown an increasing awareness of the problems created by rapid change, social dislocation, and ecological ignorance. As a result, there has been a growing trend toward nonspecialized, multipurpose, easily transformable buildings. In schools of architecture, the traditional concern for individual buildings is now rivaled by an interest in environmental design. Among younger architects, the belief that architecture is a social art that creates environments for human situations has gained wide acceptance. Versatility and flexibility are being sought not only for a changing technology but also for the changing human patterns that go with it. Some architects have pointed to an increasing freedom and variety in life-styles and have argued that environmental design must plan for this. The swift rate of change, especially in cities, has encouraged the argument that aesthetically satisfying buildings are less important than urban structures that can be modified quickly to meet changing needs. Architects have projected cities with movable or changeable parts that plug into a framework that has attachments for energy, water, and disposal systems. There have also been proposals for cities, or city "frames," and energy centers that could move on rails.

Architects who continue to be *modern* in their design have used dramatic or unusual geometric forms, in contrast to the cubelike geometry of the earlier International Modern Style. Colored reflective glass gives buildings a dazzling opacity or an ability to merge ethereally into a reflected sky.

A reaction against *modern* architecture has been linked with renewed interest in the preservation and restoration of old buildings. *Postmodernist* critics and architects argue that architecture, like a spoken language, should not avoid familiar forms, though these may be used in new ways. Postmodern architecture may refer to past styles for symbolic content that is serious, ironic, or playful. Such design has been called *radical eclecticism* to distinguish it from the historical eclecticism of nineteenth-century architecture.

ROBERT VENTURI (United States, 1925–). In 1950 Robert Venturi graduated from Princeton and worked first with Saarinen and then with Kahn. A controversial Postmodernist, Venturi argues that complexity and contradiction suit the richness and ambiguity of modern experience and are necessary to architecture today. He finds most contemporary buildings dull and void of content. As with many innovators, few of his major designs have been executed; an outstanding example, however, is his Lieb beach house (Figs. 19-70 and 19-71). The elevations present jolting contrasts; forms constantly crowd, intersect erratically, or interrupt each other. The plan also contains dissonance and surprise. Although the house appears to be square, the plan reveals it to be trapezoidal. Venturi describes the house as an ordinary shed with conventional elements, such as asbestos shingles with imitation wood grain. Yet the conventional elements behave unconventionally; the forms are blatant on one level and subtle on another. Venturi has maintained that the clutter of mainstreet is almost all right. The elements that others have equated with visual and auditory pollution, Venturi desires for perceptual excitement relevant to an "autoscape." Architecture, for him, is a system of communication, and he feels the iconography and mixed media of roadside commercial architecture provide the "language"

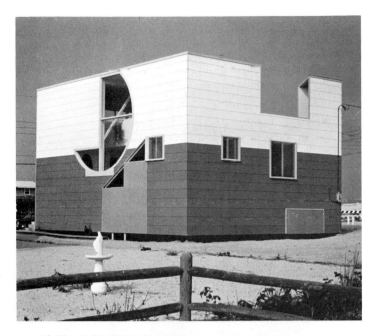

19-70   ROBERT VENTURI and JOHN RAUCH, architects and planners, with the assistance of GEROD CLARK. Residence, Mr. and Mrs. Nathaniel Lieb, Loveladies, New Jersey, (1967).

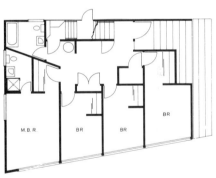

FIRST FLOOR

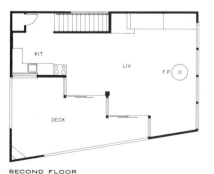

SECOND FLOOR

19-71   Plan of Lieb beach house.

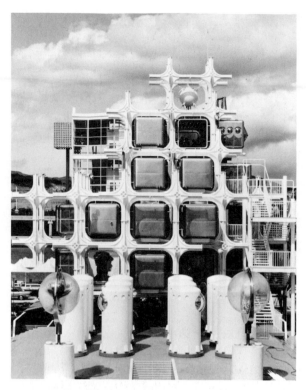

19-72   KISHO NORIAKI KUROWKAWA,   Takara Furniture Group Pavilion, Expo '70, Osaka.

suited to our needs. Popular art forms, he believes, are valid; they are a kind of aesthetic realpolitik. Not surprisingly, Venturi's work has been called Pop architecture.

KISHO NORIAKI KUROKAWA (Japan, 1934–). Kisho Noriaki Kurokawa received his training at the Kyoto School of Architecture and at Tokyo University during the 1950s. He belonged to the *Metabolist* group of Japanese architects, who saw architecture and city planning as life-support systems with aesthetic qualities. Space is thought of as an information network, and information is seen to include people, things, and energy in effective circulation — like nourishment in a bloodstream. Just as the metabolism of organisms involves constant transformation, the Metabolists argued, so architecture must be changeable, with multipurpose spaces and variable components. The Metabolist term "group form" refers to units of many buildings and to individual buildings with many changeable parts. Kurokawa's Takara Furniture Group Pavilion for Expo '70, in Osaka, is a deliberately dramatic presentation of Metabolist theory (Fig. 19-72). Prefabricated, six-armed crosses are bolted together to form a many-celled frame into which rooms can be inserted. The frame is painted white, the display rooms are stainless steel, and the exterior service pipes are painted vivid red and blue. The transformable and expandable nature of the structure is emphasized by its unfilled spaces and the projecting arms that await additions. Kurokawa has also proposed one city in the form of a curving wall and another in the form of a stepped helix. His boldest plans, however, have thus far remained on the drawing board.

RICHARD MEIER (United States, 1934–).   By 1975, the interested public was aware of certain young New York architects who were continuing the tradition of purist geometry in the International Modern Style. Their major source was Le Corbusier's pre-World War II work and his concept of architecture as the magnificent play of light on masses. This group also shared his conviction that architecture should satisfy a basic human need for order and that it should express the highly integrated organization of a technological society. Of the New York group, Richard Meier has been one of the most consistent stylistically. His mature style

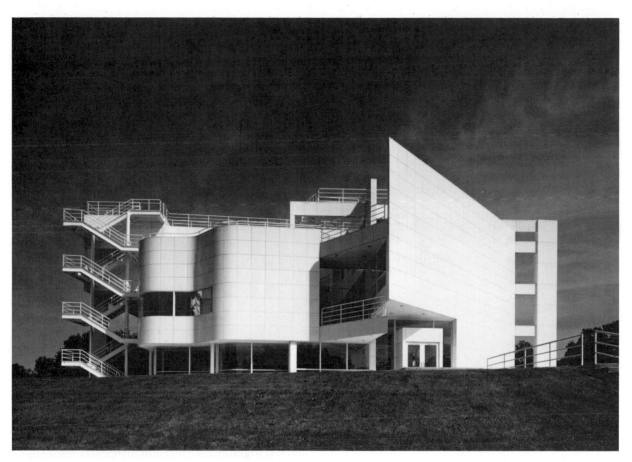

19-73 RICHARD MEIER,   Atheneum, New Harmony, Indiana, (1975–79).

was evident by 1967 in the Smith House, a glowing white cubist structure set amid rocks and trees on Long Island Sound. The three-story waterfront façade is an arresting play of advancing and receding planes of glass and wood that demands prolonged observation to understand its complexity. While its antecedents are clearly in the International Modern Style, this interplay of solids, voids, and transparencies is more polyphonic and dramatic. (The same could be said for much work by other members of the New York group. See Michael Graves, below.) A sequence of Meier's celebrated residential designs led to commissions for public buildings. He began to use steel or aluminum panels for exterior walls. The Atheneum (Fig. 19-73), a community center, is sheathed in porcelain-enameled metal panels. Its walls undulate, push out in acute angles, or frame deep volumes. The changes are breath-taking and continuous as one walks around the structure. The High Museum (Figs. 19-74 and 19-75) exemplifies his use of screen walls and glass to lead us through a sequence of interlocking spaces. Wherever we

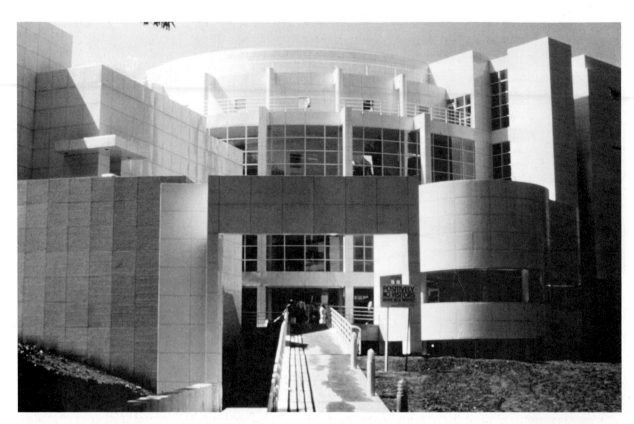

19-74   RICHARD MEIER,   The High Museum, Atlanta, Georgia, (1980–83).

19-75   Drawing, the High Museum, Atlanta.

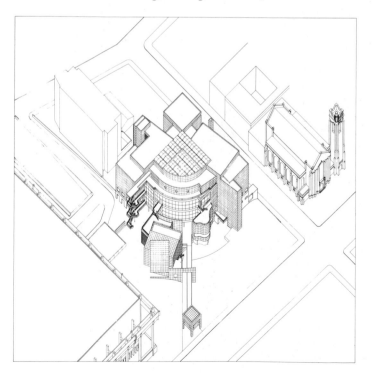

stand, there is a temptation to explore further, as layers of space overlap and unfold before us. This is not to say that such richly ordered environments are always practical. While the exterior enamel may be self-cleaning, the white interiors mark or stain readily (Fig. 19-76), and the pervasive sunlight makes some interior spaces dangerous for art objects. Ultraviolet light can fade colors and destroy wood and cloth. Meier sees his work as a creative continuation of the modern tradition. He criticizes Postmodern design as eclectic application of borrowed bits of history.

MICHAEL GRAVES (United States, 1934–   ).   Postmodernistic and radically eclectic are labels that have been applied to Graves's architecture. His early designs drew mainly from those of Le Corbusier but added greater complexity and ambiguity. An open frame defined a space that was then only partially enclosed. Walls were screens that shaped spaces into layers, yet the actual transition from outside to inside was not immediately clear (Fig. 19-77). Graves invited us to enjoy the possibilities of spatial organization. Within his houses, he painted murals that encapsulate and intensify

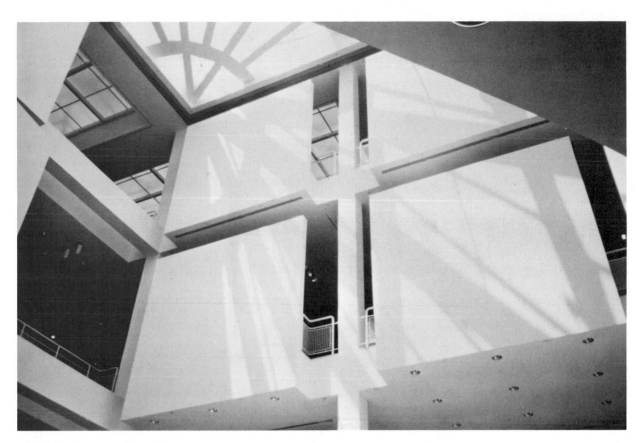

19-76   Interior, the High Museum, Atlanta.

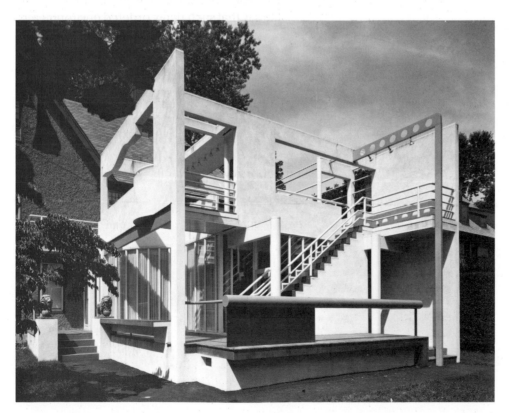

19-77   MICHAEL GRAVES, Addition to the Benacerraf House, Princeton, New Jersey, (1969).

the geometry of the architecture. In the early 1970s, Graves began to use motifs from architectural history. Massive columns may support little or no structure; arches may lack keystones. Surprise and ambiguity recall Renaissance Mannerism or the eighteenth-century delight in the picturesque. Apparently incomplete structures suggest the impossibility of permanent, humanly organized environments in a world of change. This is an architecture that is inventive and multivalent in association, metaphor, and symbol.

Suggestions for Further Study

Alloway, Lawrence. *Robert Rauschenberg.* Washington, D.C.: National Collection of Fine Arts, 1976.

Anderson, Wayne. *American Sculpture in Process: 1930–1970.* Boston: New York Graphic Society, 1975.

Ashton, Dore. *The New York School: A Cultural Reckoning.* New York: Viking, 1973.

Banham, Reyner. *The New Brutalism: Ethic or Aesthetic.* New York: Reinhold, 1966.

———. *Theory and Design in the First Machine Age.* Boston: M.I.T. Press, 1980.

Battcock, Gregory, ed. *Idea Art.* New York: Dutton, 1973.

———, ed. *Minimal Art: A Critical Anthology.* New York: Dutton, 1968.

———. *Super Realism: A Critical Anthology.* New York: Dutton, 1975.

Blake, Peter. *Form Follows Fiasco: Why Modern Architecture Hasn't Worked.* Boston: Little, Brown and Company, 1977.

Burnham, Jack. *Beyond Modern Sculpture: Effects of Science and Technology on Sculpture of This Century.* New York: Braziller, 1968.

Constantine, Mildred, and Jack L. Larsen. *The Art Fabric: Mainstream.* New York: Van Nostrand Reinhold, 1973.

Driskell, David. *Two Centuries of Black American Art.* Los Angeles County Museum of Art. New York: Alfred A. Knopf, 1976.

Henri, Adrian. *Total Art: Environments, Happenings, and Performance.* New York: Oxford University Press, 1974.

Jencks, Charles. *The Language of Post-Modern Architecture.* New York: Rizzoli International, 1977.

———. *Post-Modern Classicism: The New Synthesis.* London: Architectural Design and Academy Editions, 1980.

Lippard, Lucy. *From the Center: Feminist Essays on Women's Art.* New York: Dutton, 1976.

———. *Six Years: The Dematerialization of the Art Object from 1966 to 1972.* New York: Praeger, 1973.

—— et al. *Pop Art*. New York: Praeger, 1966.

Lucie-Smith, Edward. *Late Modern: The Visual Arts Since 1945*, 2nd ed. New York: Praeger, 1976.

Mayor, A. Hyatt. *Prints and People: A Social History of Printed Pictures*. New York: The Metropolitan Museum of Art. Distributed by the New York Graphic Society, 1971.

Meyer, Ursula. *Conceptual Art*. New York: Dutton, 1972.

Motherwell, Robert, ed. *The Dada Painters and Poets: An Anthology* (Documents of Modern Art). Reprint of 1951 edition. New York: Hacker, 1980.

Myers, Bernard. *Mexican Painting in Our Time*. New York: Oxford University Press, 1956.

Rose, Barbara. *Claes Oldenburg*. New York: Museum of Modern Art, 1970. Distributed by New York Graphic Society, Greenwich, Conn.

Rubenstein, Charlotte Streifer. *American Women Artists*. Boston: G. K. Hall, 1982.

Sandler, Irving. *The Triumph of American Painting: A History of Abstract Expressionism*. New York: Praeger, 1970.

Schneider, Ira, and Beryl Korot, eds. *Video Art: An Anthology*. New York and London: Harcourt Brace Jovanovich, 1976.

Torre, Susana, ed. *Women in American Architecture: A Historic and Contemporary Perspective*. New York: Watson-Guptill, 1977.

Venturi, Robert. *Complexity and Contradiction in Architecture*, rev. ed. New York: Museum of Modern Art, 1977.

——. *Learning from Las Vegas*, rev. ed. Cambridge, Mass.: M.I.T. Press, 1977.

Wall, Donald. *Visionary Cities: The Arcology of Paolo Soleri*. New York: Praeger, 1971.

Wallis, Brian, ed. *Art After Modernism: Rethinking Representation*. New York: The New Museum of Contemporary Art in association with David Godine, Publisher, Inc., Boston, 1984.

Wright, Frank Lloyd. *An American Architecture*. Edited by Edgar Kaufmann. New York: Horizon Press, 1955.

20

Photography and Motion Pictures

Photography and motion pictures (film), as we know them, began in the nineteenth century and have grown to special prominence in the twentieth. Initially art forms in their own right, they were later joined with other forms in intermedia works to expand the definition of art.

Photography's greatest initial impact came from its documentary function in recording the likeness of a sitter or of important events and topography. Although photography was occasionally used as an aid by artists, it generally competed with documentary painting and graphics, which had provided artists with ways of earning a living. It was not long, however, before photography began developing aesthetic criteria that were separate from its recording function. As the aesthetics of photography developed so too did its technology. Part of that developing technology was the invention of motion pictures, which in turn generated a new aesthetic involving time as well as space. Eventually, visual images in motion were brought from the public theater into the private living room by means of television.

Visual images engage the viewer more directly and convey information more quickly than does the printed word. Photography and film have surrounded us with visual images, generating in part the information explosion of the twentieth century. Film and television shrink distances and tend to jump language barriers, making possible what Marshall McLuhan has described as the "global village."

Photography

It is no accident that our word *camera* comes from the Italian word for room. The *camera obscura* (dark room) described by Renaissance Italian writers was a darkened chamber with a small hole in one wall. This hole produced an inverted image of a brightly lit exterior on the opposite wall of the darkened room. Later the term "camera obscura" was applied to various kinds of boxes, some of them portable, with ground-glass screens onto which the image was projected and lenses for sharpening the focus. These boxes were used during the seventeenth and eighteenth centuries as an aid to artists in drawing from nature (Fig. 20-1). The desire to make projected images permanent, without the labor of tracing them from a transparent screen, led, after considerable experimentation, to photography — the fixing of images on a surface by means of chemicals sensitive to light or other radiant energy.

In France between 1816 and 1829, the inventor Nicéphore Niépce succeeded in fixing an image on pewter by using bitumen of Judea. He called his process heliography but did not live to perfect it. Photography later became available to the public through the work of Niépce's partner, the painter and showman Louis Jacques Mandé Daguerre, who developed the *daguerreotype.* For these early photographs, copper plates coated with iodide of silver were exposed to light and the resulting image was then developed by mercury and made permanent by a salt or hyposulfite-of-soda solution. A tiringly long exposure was necessary, and there was no negative; the original plate became the sole print (Fig. 20-2). Daguerreotype studios

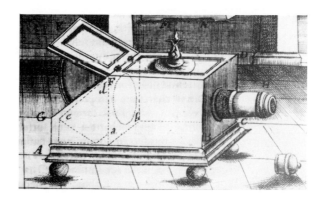

20-1 Camera obscura with reflex lens, Germany, invented by Johann Zahn, 1685.   Gernsheim Collection, the Harry Ransom Humanities Research Center, the University of Texas at Austin.

20-2 PHILIP HAAS, *John Quincy Adams,* (1843). Daguerreotype.

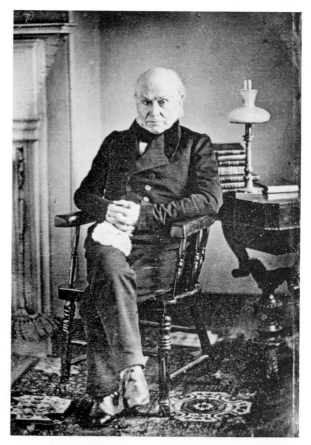

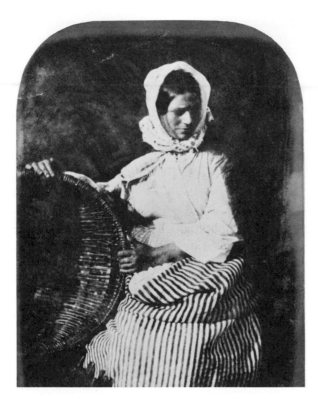

20-3   DAVID OCTAVIUS HILL and ROBERT ADAMSON,   *Fishwife, Newhaven, Scotland,* (*c.* 1848). Calotype.

20-4   NADAR,   *Eugène Delacroix,* (1855). Wet plate, or collodion, print.

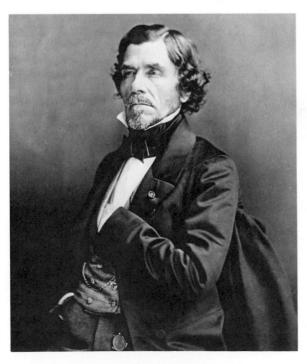

sprang up in many countries after the process was announced in the summer of 1839. At the same time in England, William Henry Fox Talbot produced paper negatives from which any number of prints could be made. His findings were also announced in 1839, and the prints came to be called *calotypes* (Fig. 20-3). They were soft and grainy, lacking the sharp detail of daguerreotypes. In 1851, the Englishman Frederick Scott Archer discovered that the *wet plate,* glass coated with wet collodion and silver nitrate, gave superior results (Fig. 20-4) in less time, though the wet plate had to be developed immediately. By 1878, the *dry plate,* glass coated with a bromide emulsion in gelatin, made possible faster exposures and eliminated the need for immediate developing. After 1889 celluloid was used for roll film. Shorter exposures became possible as more light-sensitive chemical emulsions were made on film, permitting quicker reaction to light.

Progress in film technology was accompanied by improvements in two other vital elements of the camera: the shutter and the lens. The shutter is a windowlike device that opens for a precisely controlled amount of time, such as 1/500 of a second, to allow light to enter the camera and strike the film. Early cameras had simple metal flaps or lens caps that were removed and then replaced after the necessarily long exposures. Later, the flap or cap was replaced by a shutter. In addition to the shutter, an adjustable *diaphragm* was developed to control the amount of entering light (measured in units termed *f* stops). In dim light, fast film, a wide-open diaphragm, and a slow shutter speed are used in order to let maximum light enter the camera. For dim light, the photographer also needs a fast lens. The lens is a single- or multiple-glass assembly that gathers and focuses light. Fast film, fast shutters, and fast (wide, light-gathering) lenses have made possible photographs of fast-moving objects. When a fast lens is used with a wide diaphragm opening and focused on foreground objects, the *depth of field* (range of depth in which objects are sharply defined) becomes shallow. To obtain *deep focus* (acceptable definition in foreground and distant objects), the diaphragm aperture must be reduced and the exposure time lengthened. Early photographers used flash powder for taking photographs in dim light. In 1929, Johannes Ostermeier patented the flashbulb. Today, pocket-sized, rechargeable electronic flash units can be attached to small 35-mm cameras (width of film is 35 mm).

Enlarging is a darkroom process whereby light is projected through the developed film *(negative)* onto chemically-coated photographic paper, thus producing a photographic *print*. A print that is not enlarged but is the same size as the negative is called a *contact print*. Enlarging was difficult until late in the nineteenth century; therefore, camera sizes varied according to the desired size of the finished contact print. Improvements in the enlarging apparatus made possible the popularity of the 35-mm camera from the 1920s to the present.

The lack of color in photography was considered a drawback from the beginning, and some daguerreotypists hand-colored their work. Experiments with color were made continually, however, and, in the 1930s, Kodak in America and Agfa in Germany began manufacturing color film with three layers of emulsions: one for each of the primary colors of light — red, blue, and green. According to the type of film used, either color transparencies (slides) or color prints (opaque color on photographic paper) can be made, and transparencies can be used to produce color prints. In 1963, color film was finally developed for Polaroid cameras, which use special film sheets that develop into finished prints within seconds after exposure.

Early photography was used mainly for city views, landscapes, and — as exposure time shortened — portraiture. At that time the role of photography was thought to be documentary reportage and photographs were, therefore, sharply focused to provide maximum information (Fig. 20-5). As photography progressed, some photographers posed models, arranged sets, and created storytelling, allegorical, and moralizing pictures in imitation of much nineteenth-century painting. In these "artistic" photographs, retouching and *soft focus* (blurred forms) could be used for "painterly" effects, and several negatives might be assembled to make *combination prints*. One of the

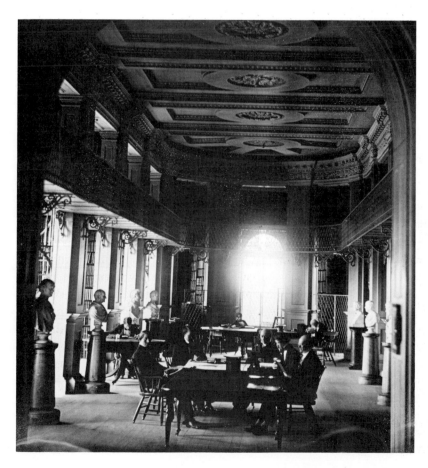

20-5 ALBERT SANDS SOUTHWORTH and JOSIAH JOHNSON HAWES, *The Boston Athenaeum*, (1853).

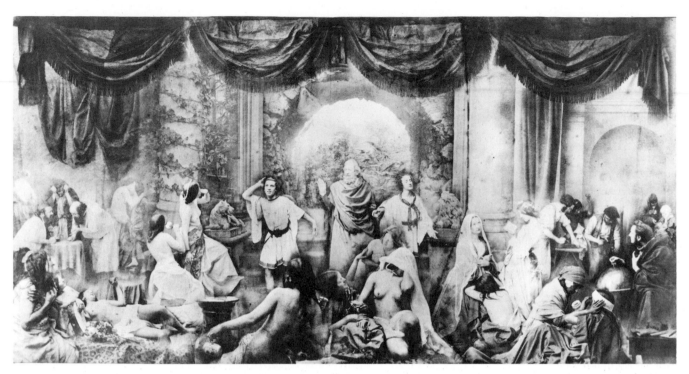

20-6   OSCAR G. REJLANDER,   *The Two Paths of Life,* (1857). Combination print.

most famous of such prints is Oscar G. Rejlander's allegory, *The Two Paths of Life* (Fig. 20-6), which interprets a young man's choice between a life of industry and one of sensual pleasures. This sort of manipulation of subject and form was referred to as *pictorial* photography.

By the 1850s, a heated controversy arose between advocates of pictorial photography and proponents of documentary photography. The major arenas were the annual exhibitions of the Photographic Society of London (founded in 1853), the annual salons of a group called The Linked Ring, which stressed "artistic" (pictorial) photography, and the annual issues of *Photograms of the Year,* a publication begun in 1895. Similar magazines and photographic societies appeared in the major cities of many countries. In New York, Alfred Stieglitz edited *Camera Work* (1902–17), a photographic quarterly open to the avant-garde of all the arts. His 291 Gallery exhibited both direct and manipulated photographs, as well as avant-garde drawings and paintings. As the technology of photography progressed, the distinction between direct and manipulated work became less evident or significant. Today different lenses and filters make possible a great variety of

images in exposure without the need for retouching the negative or manipulating light in printing.

Abstract and nonobjective trends have also developed in twentieth-century photography, but these trends have not become as dominant in photography as they did in painting and sculpture. After 1918, Dada photographers and painters produced *photomontages* (combination prints or cut-and-pasted photographs). They also created photographs without cameras by placing objects on or suspending them over photosensitive paper to create nonobjective compositions. Man Ray, Dada photographer and painter, called these items *Rayographs;* László Moholy-Nagy, a painter-designer who taught at the Bauhaus in Germany, called them *photograms*. In contrast to abstract experiments, the *New Objectivity* movement produced obsessively detailed, recognizable images. This movement arose in photography, as in painting, during the 1920s and spread from Germany to other countries. Social commentary and direct photography of precise detail from the everyday world were stressed, although magnification of small details sometimes resulted in rich patterns but unidentifiable forms. Today, the influence of the New Objectivity style may be seen not only in documentary photography but also in abstract work by photographers who do not believe in altering the image after exposure.

Some recent photography reveals Postmodern characteristics (see p. 394) in that it literally copies the work of other photographers, thus ridiculing or demystifying the concept of originality and uniqueness that has been basic even to the most revolutionary modern art. The photography of Sherrie Levine is a case in point (see p. 421).

Since the end of World War II the range of possibilities for photography have expanded greatly. Extraordinary shapes have been obtained in microscopic photography, while infrared photography has produced unusual dark-light contrasts in black-and-white film and unexpected hues in color film. Experimentation in the darkroom has taken many forms. Images have been broken up and recombined in photomontage; distortion has been induced by tilting the paper under the enlarger or by making the paper concave or convex during enlargement. Photographers have lightened areas of a print by masking them or shading (dodging) them during exposure under the enlarger. High-contrast photographic paper has been used to eliminate details and half-tones, thus producing bold contrasts between major shapes. Negative prints reverse dark and light values and negatives have been modified before printing. For example, partial reexposure of film during its development has resulted in part negative, part positive prints with luminous effects, a process called *solarization* (Fig. 20-7). In the *cliché verre* technique, glass is drawn or painted on and then used as a negative to make photographic prints. A whole new field for photography exists in *holograms*, three-dimensional photographic images projected into space by laser beams.

The following are only a few of the outstanding photographers of the late nineteenth and twentieth centuries.

ALFRED STIEGLITZ (United States, 1864–1946). Stieglitz grew up in New York and went to Germany to study engineering, where he changed his field of study to photography and, after eight years abroad, returned to New York in 1890. As his career developed, he produced photographs of his immediate surroundings that reflected remarkable patience and a subtle sense of tonal values and

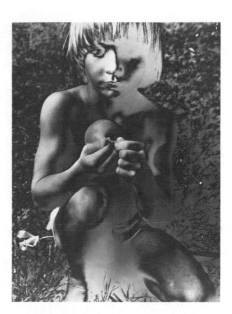

20-7 DOUG PRINCE, Untitled, (1975). Solarization print. Courtesy, Witkin Gallery, New York.

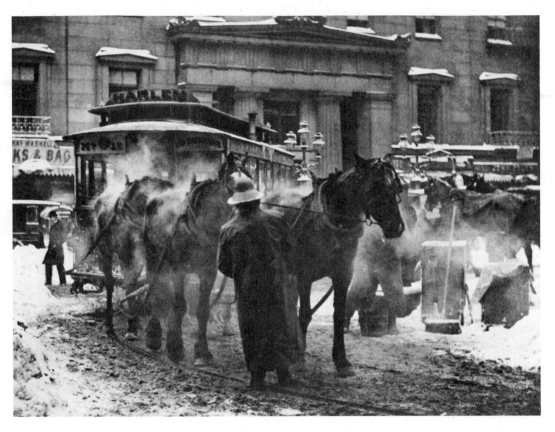

20-8   ALFRED STIEGLITZ,   *The Terminal,* (1893).

design. Although he did not retouch, enlarge, or manipulate effects, Stieglitz defended pictorial, or manipulated, photography because his major interest was in the aesthetic potential of formal elements. Many of his photographs, moreover, convey great sensitivity to the character of a place. In *The Terminal* (Fig. 20-8), an initial sense of numbing cold and steaming horseflesh is portrayed within a subtle range of grays and a design that sets the diagonal of the car and the taut curves of the rails against the white of the piled snow and the angles of the architecture. Through his own photography as well as his editorship of *Camera Work* and his leadership of the 291 Gallery, Stieglitz achieved international importance in the history of photographic art.

IMOGEN CUNNINGHAM (United States, 1883–1976). After studying chemistry in the United States and Germany, Imogen Cunningham turned to professional photography. Returning to the United States, she opened a portrait studio and quickly gained a steady clientele. She continued her portrait photography, on both commercial and artistic levels, for the rest of her life. Always concerned with the carefully designed image, she also photographed people in a wide variety of contexts, plants in tight close-ups, and architectural elements in virtually abstract compositions. Although devoted to the principles of direct photography espoused by the f/64 group (a group of California photographers whose name, f/64, refers to a small diaphragm aperture that produces sharp focus), Cunningham used various techniques to manipulate her images. But the works for which she is primarily noted are straight photographs of people and plants. Her *Self-Portrait on Geary Street, 1958* (Fig. 20-9) combines the several qualities characteristic of her photography. Although an example of direct photography, the picture gives one the impression of being a multiple image created in the darkroom. This is achieved by the discontinuity in spatial relationships created by the vertical mirror. On the level of abstract form, however, there is considerable continuity throughout the image. The verticals of the mirror's edges are paralleled by the verticals of the architectural details, such as the doorways and the supporting post; the rectangles of the back wall are continuous with rectangles reflected behind Cunningham in the mirror; the diagonal edge of her cloak in the mirror echoes the diagonal axes of the panels leaning against the side wall on the porch. An intense awareness of the interaction of light, tone, form, and design is present throughout all her work.

EDWARD WESTON (United States, 1886–1958). From his youth, Edward Weston planned to be a photographer. He earned his living by portraiture, but he established his reputation as an artist with photographs of landscapes and architecture, and close-ups of shells, fruits, and vegetables. Weston first earned awards for soft-focus pictures and then changed to sharp detail during the growth of the New Objectivity movement in the 1920s. His favorite instrument was an 8″ × 10″ view camera (a camera with a removable back that allows the photographer to see on ground glass the image that will be received on the plate of film that is then inserted; the camera also has bellows that are extendable, allowing the use of a wide variety of lenses). Weston worked directly, usually without enlargement. In 1932 he helped found the f/64 group. Between 1937 and 1939, Weston received two Guggenheim grants and produced fifteen

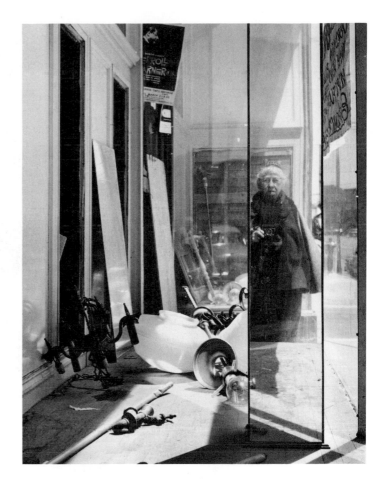

20-9 IMOGEN CUNNINGHAM, *Self-Portrait on Geary Street,* (1958).

20-10   EDWARD WESTON, *Dunes, Oceano, California,* (1936).

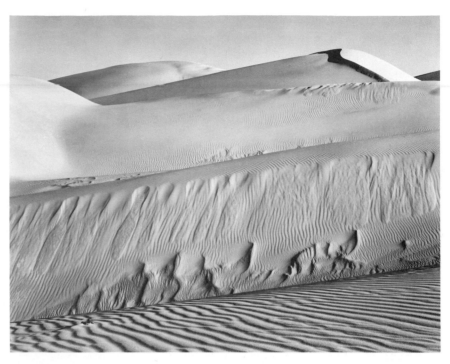

hundred pictures, many of which were later published in *California and the West,* a record of a photographic trip, produced jointly with his wife. *Dunes, Oceano* (Fig. 20-10) is typical of his later work in its rich textural detail, bold patterns, and dramatic rhythmic sweep.

DOROTHEA LANGE (United States, 1895–1965). After studying photography at Columbia University, Dorothea Lange set out at age 20 to work her way around the world as a photographer. She got no farther than San Francisco, however, where she opened a portrait studio in 1916. Photography became for her a means of understanding human beings in specific situations, a way of enticing the viewer to appreciate the lives of others. During the Depression in the 1930s, Lange and the economist Paul Taylor were employed by the State of California, and later by the federal government, to report on the living conditions of American workers. Their published reports and photographs of the unemployed and dispossessed awakened the sympathy of the country. *Migrant Mother* (Fig. 20-11) conveys anxiety and maternal concern without posing or dramatic lighting. Lange was able to catch people in naturally expressive moments and to demand that viewers of her photographs consider the fate of her subjects as human

20-11   DOROTHEA LANGE, *Migrant Mother, Nipomo, California,* (1936).   Dorothea Lange Collection, The Oakland Museum.

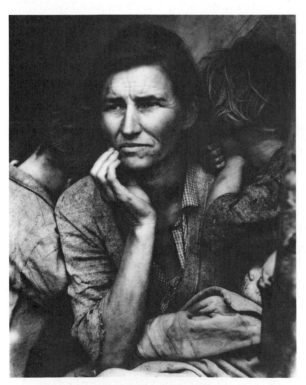

beings. She tried not to pose or to influence her subjects, and she sought a sense of place and time. Her factual and masterful work reveals rather than preaches. She is among the best photographers in the documentary tradition.

ANSEL ADAMS (United States, 1902–1984). Ansel Adams put aside a promising career as a concert pianist after publishing successful portfolios of photographs between 1923 and 1930. His favorite subjects were the people and the landscapes of California and the Southwest. In 1932 he helped to establish Group f/64 and exhibited his work in a one-man show in the De Young Museum in San Francisco. Alfred Stieglitz was enthusiastic about Adams's work and exhibited it in New York in 1936, a year after Adams published his first book on photographic technique. In *Sierra Nevada from Lone Pine, California* (Fig. 20-12), the delicate trees and the horse emphasize awesome scale. Contrast in values and contours expresses the grandeur of the peaks; the dark, softly curved hills mediate between the frozen, jagged heights and the fertile, life-supporting valley.

20-12 ANSEL ADAMS, *Sierra Nevada from Lone Pine, California,* (1944).

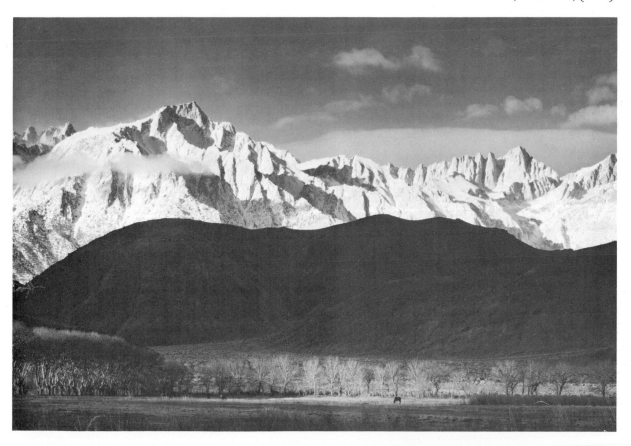

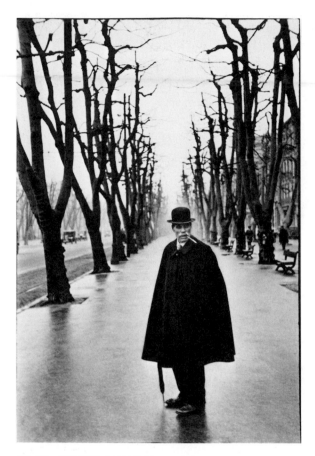

20-13 HENRI CARTIER-BRESSON, *Allée du Prado, Marseilles,* (1932).

HENRI CARTIER-BRESSON (France, 1908–). Cartier-Bresson gave up painting for photography in 1930. Traveling throughout the world, he searched out representative human situations. He uses only a 35-mm camera, eschewing flash equipment, any form of posing or manipulation, and unusual angles. This severe limitation of means allows his sure sense of design and subtle recognition of the expressive moment full play. The *Allée du Prado, Marseilles* (Fig. 20-13) exploits symmetry and perspective to focus attention on the man's head and reinforce the formal dignity of his bearing. The man's simple silhouette presents a marked contrast to the jagged trees and, with its forceful impact, suggests the power of his personality. Cartier-Bresson also made documentary films of the Spanish Civil War and served with a French army film unit during World War II. After the defeat of France he was imprisoned by the Germans and escaped after three attempts to work with the underground, for which he organized a photographic unit that took pictures of the occupation and the retreat of the Nazi armies. His exhibitions and books of photographs have earned him an international reputation.

DUANE MICHALS (United States, 1932–). "Everything is quite extraordinary but we use all our energies to make things ordinary," Duane Michals has said. Like some Surrealist painters, he wants to reveal the mystery of common objects and events. He turned to photography in 1960 after having worked as a free-lance designer in New York. The portrait photographer, he argues, should never impose his own personality upon that of the subject; technique should be simple and geared only toward capturing the most telling qualities of the subject. To express the character of our environment, Michals photographed a series of generally well-populated places that were empty of people, including a subway car, a barbershop, an office, a bus, a theater, and a laundromat. In 1968 he began to use groups of photographs in narrative sequences. In *The Human Condition* (Fig. 20-14), the first two scenes show a young man standing on a subway platform; the second two show him dissolved in an aura of light; and the last two are views of the heavens, which suggest that the individual has been absorbed into the vastness of the universe. Michals's images repre-

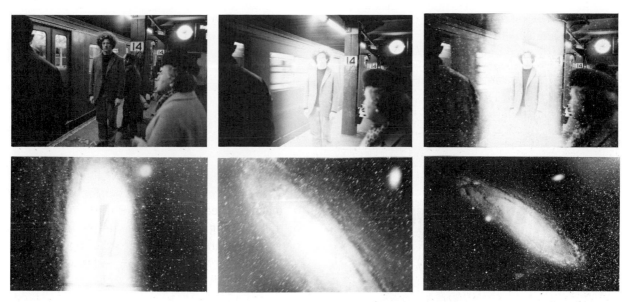

20-14 DUANE MICHALS, *The Human Condition,* (1969).

sent an interior reality dealing with the unusual in life and the mystical in death. His recent works voice social and political criticism. *Christ in New York* (1982) is a series of six black-and-white photos with text. Jesus returns to the earth, observes sadly that humankind has made little moral progress, and is murdered in New York, all without being recognized.

JERRY N. UELSMANN (United States, 1934–   ). Superimposed images have been the primary device in Jerry Uelsmann's photography. With them, he entices the viewer's imagination by way of symbolic associations. People grow out of stones, the earth, water, the trees, or the landscape. Trees grow out of people. The part is contrasted with the whole: foreground seedpods are set against trees; the earthly globe hovers over the land; the ceiling of a room becomes the sky. We sense the relatedness of all things and the fecundity of the universe. Ambiguity and mystery abound. In a dark countryside, a simple little white church stands behind a huge pool that resembles a keyhole. Is this a reference to the key to salvation? Not exactly, for the pool has no discernible water surface; it might be a pit! Uelsmann's method is intuitive. He does not plan an idea and then search for images to illustrate it. Rather, he surrounds himself with hundreds of prints and then tries out various combi-

nations until one seems to work. He rarely uses titles, for he believes that they limit the observer's responses (Fig. 20-15). His work has often been called Surrealistic. The ambiguity, dreamlike aura, and hovering objects often found in Uelsmann's photos certainly recall the painting of Dali or Magritte, but Uelsmann does not use psychic automatism nor does he employ esoteric personal images such as those of most Surrealists. Uelsmann's symbolism is more accessible to us. Formally, the work is a feast for the eye. Patterns, textures, spatial modulations, and a range of values from glowing whites through elegant grays to velvet blacks are all seductive, and all are in black and white. Uelsmann has rarely used color. His reputation has grown rapidly since a 1967 exhibition at The Museum of Modern Art in New York. Articles and books have interpreted his art, and he has presented workshop demonstrations in various parts of the world.

CINDY SHERMAN (United States, 1954–   ). Cindy Sherman has established her identity as a photographer of self-portraits. In the late 1970s, her pieces echoed film stills, the single-frame shots often used to advertise a movie. While the person in the photograph was always Cindy Sherman, the expression, costume, and context implied that observers were seeing an actor in very different roles

20-15   JERRY UELSMANN,
Untitled, (1983).

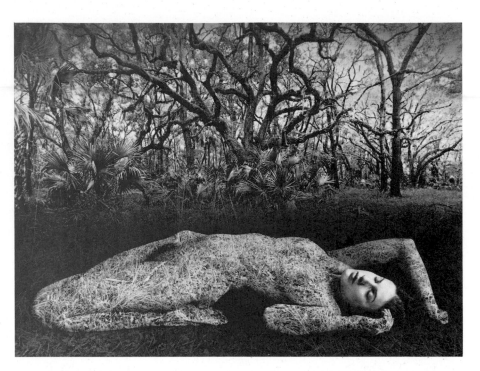

20-16   CINDY SHERMAN,   Untitled, (1985).

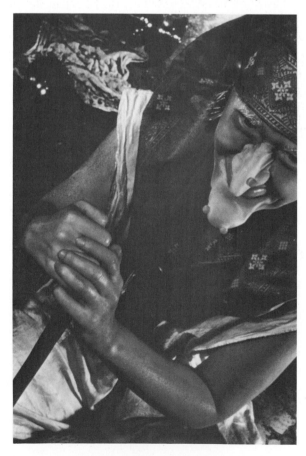

and in the midst of some story. Viewers were tempted to speculate about the narrative and to recognize the role-playing that we all do in our daily lives. Sherman especially seemed to be pointing critically to the typecasting that is prevalent in filmmaking, television, and advertising. This demystifying or parodying of media stereotypes is a kind of dismantling or *deconstruction* of ideas and techniques that are considered to be outworn, desensitizing, and dehumanizing. Deconstruction is an aspect of Postmodernist art (see p. 394). Recently, Sherman has moved to more elaborate settings, costumes, and makeup or masks. The results have been increasingly imaginary. In 1985, she was commissioned to do a series of photographs inspired by fairy tales, such as *The Arabian Nights* (Fig. 20-16). The self-portraits became quite demonic and almost life-size. Hags, witches, or beauteous sorceresses look out from bizarre or sinister contexts. While it is not possible to identify exactly the events being acted out, the implied narrative is more demanding than ever.

Motion Pictures

The most distinctive, typical, and influential art form of the twentieth century is the motion picture. Film employs visual images in time and space, elements that imitate more closely than the traditional art forms our common experience of reality. Because the viewer is seated in a dark interior before a screen and a vast range of visual and auditory effects, film is less vulnerable to distractions and more completely absorbing than many other arts. While any art form can become infinitely complex, film has complexities derived from the elements of the other arts, such as plot development, pictorial composition, acting, music, and dance. The filmmaker must integrate these elements and anticipate the contributions of the camera operator and film editing as he or she attempts to visualize the finished work.

The basic structural units of motion pictures are the *shot*, an uninterrupted camera view that may be close up, medium, or long, and the *sequence*, a combination of shots that is produced by *editing* (cutting and splicing). The camera angle can evoke the emotional overtones of a character or a setting (see the discussion of perspective angles on pp. 7–8). *Framing* (composing) the shot within the rectangle of the film involves many of the pictorial elements and design functions discussed in Part One of this book, but with the complicating addition of actual movement. The use of the wide screen has made vast scale possible but has produced problems in framing. These problems are prominent when one or two characters are shown on a wide rectangular screen that includes a large amount of setting. In such situations, soft focus can be used to keep the background from competing with foreground action. The motion-picture camera may be stationary during a shot, or it may be attached to some form of *dolly*, a mobile platform that can be as simple as an extension arm on a tripod, or as complex as a wheeled platform on tracks with a boom (a platform device on a truck-attached fire ladder), which allows the camera operator to hover over the subject. A dolly shot can, for example, follow a group traveling through a landscape, or can move toward or away from a subject to express isolation or intimacy. A *pan* (sweeping) shot is effective for panoramic vistas.

The expressive content of a film depends on effective editing as well as on camera work. An editing sequence may develop around a *scene*, during which action occurs in one time and place or it may take the form of a *montage*, which is a rapid succession of images and/or sounds, often used to build emotional intensity. Because of edit-

ing, filmmakers are able to shift time and space, move back and forth between past, present, and future, or alternate between reality and unreality. Editing may also abbreviate narrative, suggest connections between events, and show different points of view. Many of these effects are achieved by various types of *cutting*—changing from one shot to another. *Cross cuts* are rapid switches from one scene to another to present simultaneous actions, as with alternating views of the pursued and the pursuer. A shot may *fade out* (slowly disappear from the screen), sometimes to be replaced by another. A *dissolve* simultaneously superimposes the new shot as the former image fades. Fade-outs are often used to conclude a film. When cuts make large jumps in space and time, the filmmaker must ensure against spectator confusion—unless ambiguity is desired. Transitions between narrative events are sometimes needed: cutting back to previous events (a technique termed *flashback*) can supply the necessary connections and is often used to provide exposition or background information for a film. Transitions can also be achieved by use of similar shapes or sounds: an oval-shaped face might dissolve into the oval of a baseball stadium; a thundering waterfall might merge into the sound of stampeding horses. By manipulating shots, as in accelerating or slowing the experience of time in a sequence, the editor can create rhythm, gradation, and climax in a film.

Other elements that affect the expressive content of a film are makeup, costuming, set design, lighting, color, and sound quality (volume or harshness). Each of these elements can utilize the design functions—repetition, theme and variation, gradation, and climax—that were discussed in Part One.

Film's ancestry goes back to the magic lantern, a primitive slide projector invented in the seventeenth century. By the 1830s, a number of toys had been invented that produced the illusion of moving images. In one of these, a series of figures in varied poses was painted around the outside of a disk, the circumference of which was notched with slots (Fig. 20-17). The user held the painted side toward a mirror, spun the disk slowly, and viewed the reflected figures through the slots. Rather than a blur of forms, a distinct image was seen in apparent motion. By the 1850s, a magic

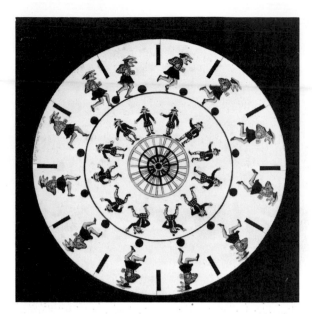

20-17   Phenakistiscope.

lantern was used to project such images onto a wall. In the 1870s, two experiments advanced the analysis of motion through photography: Eadweard Muybridge arranged a row of cameras along a racetrack and produced a series of photos showing the sequential positions of a galloping horse, and the movement of the planet Venus was recorded by the French astronomer Pierre Jules César Janssen, who used a clockwork photographic device to take pictures at intervals *(chronophotography)*. In the 1890s, motion pictures were projected from film by inventors in France, the United States, Germany, and England. By passing film — consisting at first of hundreds, then later of thousands, of still photographs *(frames)*— through a projector, the illusion of motion was produced on the screen. Although each frame occupies the screen for only a fraction of a second, the image is retained somewhat longer by the retina of the eye, causing each image to merge with the next. Since the position of a moving object is slightly different in each frame, the rapid sequence of merged frames produces the sensation of moving objects.

Borrowing tested plots from the popular stage, early directors created films characterized by violent action, exaggerated pantomime, strong contrasts in emotions, and polar contrasts of good and evil. The result was melodrama. Live music, usually provided by a piano, was added in the theater to accompany a film and to stress action and mood. Early silent films were made with a stationary camera recording uninterrupted action, like that of a stage play. The narrative time of the film was confined to the actual time it took to photograph the scene. Such early films were only several minutes in length and recorded special events or provided amusement with pantomimed comic episodes. As technical improvement occurred, directors freed themselves from the space-time and static-spectator limitations of the early films and developed the expressive potential of a mobile camera and film editing. Changes in narrative time and space were pioneered by the French director Georges Méliès in his science-fiction films *The Vanishing Lady* (1896) and *A Trip to the Moon* (1902). In America, Edwin Porter began to alternate close-up and medium shots, as well as interior and exterior scenes, to build his stories in *The Life of an American Fireman* (1902) and *The Great Train Robbery* (1903).

The greatest early filmmaker was the American D. W. Griffith, who toned down overacting, used electric lighting for dramatic effects, employed double and triple exposures, tinted his film, and made camera work and editing as expressive as acting. Simultaneously, Charles Chaplin was directing and acting in comic masterpieces of his own creation. Somewhat later, documentary films were introduced in America with Robert Flaherty's *Nanook of the North* (1922), which explored the life of the Eskimo.

One of the trends in German filmmaking after the First World War was *Expressionism,* a cinematic style that bore some resemblance to German painting, poetry, and drama identified by the same label. *The Cabinet of Dr. Caligari* (1919–20), by Hans Janowitz, Carl Mayer, and Robert Wiene, depicted various states of mind by employing artificial light, abstract sets designed by German painters, unusual camera angles, sudden shifts of scene, stylized acting, and a complex plot (Fig. 20-18). Germany and Austria, however, also produced a *Realistic* film trend that, although related to Expressionism, dealt with simple, ordinary situations involving individual and social tensions. *The Joyless Street* (1925), directed by G. W. Pabst, portrayed the economic and moral decline of the Austrian middle class during the inflationary period following World War I. The Realistic film movement paralleled the New Objectivity movement in photography and in German painting during the 1920s.

In marked contrast to German and Austrian cinema, Russian films of this period combined epic scale and social commentary. Russian development began right after the October Revolution of 1917 and was led by Sergei Eisenstein, who used editing to create powerful contrasts and symbolic parallels between nature, objects, and people. His actors were often nonprofessionals. Each shot was carefully composed to exploit the affective relations of masses, shapes, and values; narrative conflict was frequently reinforced by contrasting movement in the images of successive shots. Eisenstein's primary cinematic device was montage, which he used to heighten the dramatic intensity, symbolic force, and ideological persuasiveness of

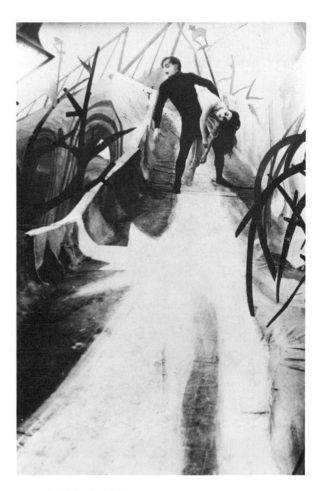

20-18 HANS JANOWITZ, CARL MAYER, and ROBERT WIENE, *The Cabinet of Dr. Caligari,* (1919–20).

his films. The small Russian film industry was put under government control after 1919, and thereafter films served a propagandistic function.

After 1919, significant film experiments were undertaken in France and Germany by proponents of the *Dada* movement, which lasted from 1916 to 1923, and the *Surrealist* movement, which began in 1924. These movements, largely in literature, painting, and sculpture, were inspired by the Freudian theory of the unconscious and by an increasing appreciation of nonrational thought processes and of the subjective nature of reality (see Chapter 18). Dada and Surrealistic films employed surprising combinations of images to reproduce the effects of dream experience in order to stimulate the viewer's imagination. Leaders in Germany were Hans Richter and Raoul Haussmann; in Paris, they were the American painter-photographer Man Ray, the French artist Marcel Duchamp, the Spanish filmmaker Luis Buñuel, and the Spanish painter Salvador Dali. Their films pioneered the use of sudden, disjointed contrasts in images, and their influence is important in contemporary cinematography.

After more than thirty years of experiment with synchronized records and other devices, sound tracks for film became available in the 1920s. The first major sound film in America was *The Jazz Singer* (1927). Initially actors had to stay close to a microphone in sound films and the noisy camera had to be enclosed in a soundproof booth, resulting in severe restriction of movement. Greater freedom came with the development of quieter cameras and of more sophisticated microphones suspended on booms (cranes) near the actors.

Sound was exploited immediately in the animated films made by Walt Disney. Animated films are made by photographing thousands of drawings, each one with slight variations in the position of the object to be represented in motion. When film shot in this way passes through the projector, the illusion of movement is produced in the same way as with frames photographed with living actors.

Color use was attempted early in film history. Monochromatic tints were used at the outset: for example, green for landscapes, red for dramatic violence. By 1935 a wide range of colors was available to filmmakers, but for some years these colors were often garish and lacking in nuances. Today

filmic color can provide a subtle display of nuances in hue and tone. The serious filmmaker is now able to use either color or black and white, according to his aesthetic needs.

During the 1930s and 1940s, filmmaking in Hollywood became big business, resulting in huge studio organizations that deprived the director of total control by interposing special departments for music, sound, writing, producing, directing, and editing. Artistic quality often suffered as a result. In its place, dependable formulas for box-office success were developed for musicals, westerns, comedies, detective stories, and fantasies. Good usually triumphed over evil, and daydream over reality. Both inside and outside these Hollywood formulas good works were produced when depth and subtlety of content or strength of cinematic technique rose above stereotypes. Among war films, Lewis Milestone's *All Quiet on the Western Front* (1930) was a deeply moving antiwar statement that benefited from its compelling episodes and effective editing. Alfred Hitchcock's mysteries, such as *The Thirty-Nine Steps* (1935), were original in their mixture of suspense, surprise, and whimsy. John Huston's *The Maltese Falcon* (1941) was unusually strong in its combination of humor, tension, violence, and surprise. Filmmaking landmarks included Orson Welles's *Citizen Kane* (1941), brilliant in its sociological interpretation, compositional complexity, and technical innovation (Fig. 20-19), and John Ford's *Grapes of Wrath* (1940), wherein fine acting and editing did justice to John Steinbeck's powerful novel about the tragedy of the dust bowl. In comedy, outstanding acting overcame unimaginative or stereotyped plots in Charlie Chaplin's *The Great Dictator* (1940) and other films, and in films by W. C. Fields during the 1930s.

In France during the 1930s and 1940s filmmakers learned from the Surrealist experiments of the 1920s and from powerful psychological studies such as Carl-Theodore Dreyer's *The Passion of Joan of Arc* (1928). René Clair's *À Nous la Liberté* (1931) combined fantasy with harsh comment on the dreary lives of mass-production workers. Visual metaphors, creative use of sound, and symbolic action in that film are outstanding. Moral decadence in the French upper class furnished the theme for Jean Renoir's *The Rules of the Game* (1939), while Marcel Carné and the poet Jacques

Prévert collaborated on films such as *Port of Shadows* (1938), which explored the problems of individual freedom within a social system. The union of aesthetic subtlety and social realism caused the term "poetic realism" to be applied to these films.

England also experienced a great expansion in film technology, audience support, and organization within the filmmaking and film-distributing industry in the 1930s and 1940s. Alfred Hitchcock directed mystery films, and Anthony Asquith's *Tell England* (1931) was the first effort to interpret World War I with historical perspective. Along with a wealth of documentary films on such themes as weather warning systems and sea rescue, there were realistic dramas like Carol Reed's mining story, *The Stars Look Down* (1939). The English film industry, which was relatively small even in its period of greatest expansion, produced many elaborate costume epics based on historical figures such as *Catherine the Great*, directed by Paul Czinner in 1934, and on literary classics such as Shakespeare's *As You Like It*, directed by Czinner in 1936. The further development of British films was interrupted by World War II from 1941 until 1945.

German films of the 1930s suffered under restrictive Nazi pressures. After an imaginative mountaineering film called *The Blue Light* (1932), director Leni Riefenstahl turned her efforts to the filmic glorification of Hitler in *The Triumph of the Will* (1936). G. W. Pabst scorned the heroics of militarism in *Westfront, 1918* (1930) and was forced to flee to Paris. Max Ophuls also incurred the wrath of the Nazi regime with his *Liebelei* (1933) and left Germany in 1933.

Government control continued to hamper the creativity of Russian filmmakers in the 1930s and 1940s; nevertheless, impressive films were produced. Eisenstein believed that sound should not be used merely to record the speech of the actors but also to add a distinctly different and often opposing element, which is evident in parts of *Alexander Nevsky* (1938). The Soviet government film control committee felt that Eisenstein was too esoteric for the masses and accused him of "formalism." Similarly accused was Vsevlod Pudovkin, a leading director of Soviet films (*Deserter*, 1933), who preferred smoother, less abrupt editing than that of Eisenstein. Stunning composition

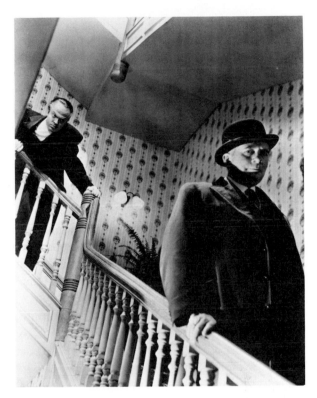

20-19 ORSON WELLES, *Citizen Kane,* (1941).

within the frame and a sense of fantasy characterize the work of Alexander Dovzhenko (*Ivan,* 1932). The Soviet leader in documentaries was Dziga Vertov (*Three Songs of Lenin,* 1934).

The Second World War resulted in a significant hiatus in the history of serious film. After the war, many countries needed years to regain lost momentum. Moreover, postwar television changed the role of movies and the nature of movie audiences. In the United States, especially, television, and more recently, videotapes have partially supplanted moviegoing.

Postwar French films continued their earlier emphasis on elaborate formal structure at the expense of naturalness. Surrealist experimentation inspired the writer Jean Cocteau to make films. Having fled Germany, Max Ophuls made his major films in France during the 1950s. His works minimize narrative and use a series of situations to comment on conflicts between sexual obsessions and social mores. Jacques Tati's few but carefully made films established him as a brilliant comedic director and actor. The most distinctive postwar French movement was *la Nouvelle Vague* (the

New Wave), which began in 1958. The films of this movement were stylistically identifiable by ambiguity, surprise, and abrupt changes in space, time, and mood. Among the important proponents of New Wave cinema, Alain Resnais used the most calculated effects. His *Last Year at Marienbad* (1961), from the script by Alain Robbe-Grillet, retains a slow, contemplative pace while blurring distinctions between past, present, and future (Fig. 20-20). François Truffaut employed more spontaneous leaps in time and space in conjunction with abrupt changes in shooting style, ranging from long nostalgic shots to abruptly comic ones, as in *Jules and Jim* (1961); Jean-Luc Godard switches from rational to irrational actions and encourages the viewer to remain detached from filmic illusions.

Contemporary with the New Wave were films striving for great realism and owing much to the documentary tradition. Directors such as Jean Rouch often used nonprofessional actors and filmed outdoors without elaborate sets. This *Cinema Verité* trend was often concerned with socioeconomic and political questions.

20-20   ALAIN RESNAIS,   *Last Year at Marienbad,* (1961).

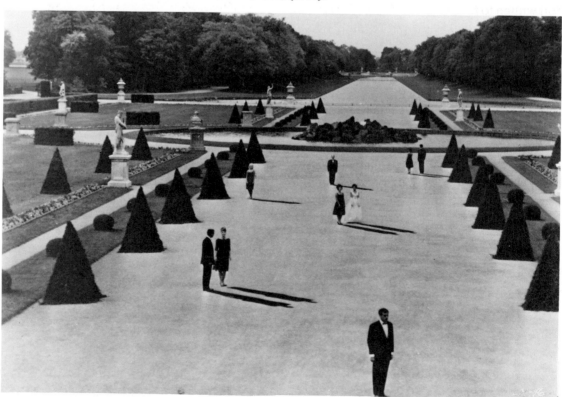

Other directions have also been explored since the 1950s. The Swedish director Ingmar Bergman employs elaborate symbolism and allegory to deal with life, death, and human strivings. England's postwar films have included polished adaptions of literary classics, elegant Robert Hamer comedies for Alec Guinness, "Angry Young Men" portrayals of life at various levels of British society—especially the working class—and suspense films of military or political conflict.

In reaction against the technical slickness and banality of films made during the late 1930s and 1940s, especially those produced in Hollywood, the postwar moviegoing public found special satisfaction in the loosely plotted, commonplace dramas of survival presented by Italian Neorealist films such as Roberto Rossillini's *Open City* (1945) and Vittorio De Sica's *The Bicycle Thief* (1947). These films, which often used nonprofessional actors, expressed the ideas of one person, the filmmaker, and led, in Europe, to the "auteur" (author) approach to film criticism, which developed in the mid-1950s and treated the film as a work of art expressing the views of the director rather than those of a group, as in Hollywood. The auteur approach is less suited to big Hollywood films, which are often the product of a collective effort written to fit the talents of specific stars, and motivated by economic interest first and by artistic interests secondarily.

Two of the most influential Italian filmmakers of the 1960s and 1970s, Michelangelo Antonioni and Federico Fellini, produced their early works in the Neorealist style. Antonioni has moved from the effects of social situations on individuals to evocations of states of mind. Fellini has developed toward lavish richness and multiplication of images loosely connected by a narrative line. He portrays bodily frustration and spiritual decay in a corrupt society.

Revolutionary political content characterizes many of the contemporary films made in Cuba, South America, and the communist or socialist countries of Eastern Europe. The most creative work, however, is usually less specific in its political message and more involved with the broader aspects of human experience. In spite of a strong nationalistic trend, Cuban films have shown imagination, humor, and versatility; Tomás Gutiérrez Alea and Manuel Octavio Gomez have been the important directors. In Brazil, Glauber Rocha has written on film theory and directed experimental films that combine folklore with urgings for social reform.

In Eastern Europe, the state is often the sole producer and distributor of films. This discourages criticism of the status quo. However, in recent years, some socialist and communist countries have allowed more freedom in the arts. Criticism can be general, such as an expressed frustration with a disinterested bureaucracy, or it may be metaphorical. The filmmaker may reveal social problems indirectly, through psychological studies of individual characters. Hungarian director Miklós Jancsó's films, such as *Silence and Cry* (1968), often deal with the confusion that follows a war, with arbitrary acts of cruelty, with shifting political power, and with opposing groups that are neither good nor bad, right nor wrong. His style consists of long shots taken by a constantly moving camera; cuts are used mainly to show a change of time or place. The films of the Hungarian István Szabó have stressed metaphorically the intertwining of politics and art. In Yugoslavia, Dusan Makavejev used brilliant editing in his *WR: Mysteries of the Organism* (1971) to unite a kaleidoscopic array of materials into a hilariously erotic political comedy. Miloš Forman was a prominent director in Czechoslovakia before moving to the United States. In Poland, Andrzej Wajda and Roman Polański are recognized as original and accomplished filmmakers. Polański emigrated to the United States but now works in France. East European filmmakers tend to emphasize the impurity of all motives. For American audiences, their work seems heavy in cynicism, irony, alienation, antiheroes, and tragedy. A study of the historical background makes this attitude easier to appreciate. The Marxist dialectic of struggle between socioeconomic classes may be basic to the world view of even those who are thoroughly disillusioned with communist governments.

In India, the films of Satyajit Ray have portrayed tensions between traditional social forms and modern developments in society by focusing on individuals and select details. Ray's major work has been the Apu trilogy: *Pather Panchali* (1954), *Aparajito* (1956), and *The World of Apu* (1959). In Japan, Akira Kurosawa has been a leading filmmaker for the past thirty years. Although he has been influenced by such Western authors as Dostoyevski, Kurosawa addresses himself primarily to social and human issues within the distinctive context of Japanese culture. His films *Rashomon* (1950) and *Seven Samurai* (1954) made Western viewers aware of Japanese filmmaking. In *Rashomon,* he used tracking shots with great effectiveness to express moods, personalities, and the uncertainty of perception. In *Seven Samurai,* intercuts, panning shots, and zoom shots were used to create the illusion of frantic action and the terror of battle (Fig. 20-21). Kurosawa's carefully composed frames have been praised as poetic and powerful. *Seven Samurai* has an international reputation as one of the best postwar films.

In America, Neorealism had some impact on works such as Stanley Kramer's and Fred Zinnemann's *High Noon* (1952), Otto Preminger's *Exodus* (1960), and Elia Kazan's *On the Waterfront* (1954). Arthur Penn's *Bonnie and Clyde* (1967) went further than earlier films in using sudden changes in mood, abrupt contrasts of humor and brutality, and antiheroes. Imagination and vast scale were joined in Stanley Kubrick's *2001: A*

Space Odyssey (1968) and George Lucas's *Star Wars* (1977). *Bonnie and Clyde* and Kubrick's films utilize ambiguity, but the space-time and causal relationships generally remain more conventional than in the most pioneering films of Fellini, Antonioni, or Resnais. More recently, American filmmakers have depended on the occasional successes of massive efforts, such as Francis Coppola's *Apocalypse Now* (1979). Often, they have tried to aim at audiences with special interests. Theater design reflects this in smaller auditoria grouped so that several films may be shown simultaneously in one building. Earlier restrictions on violence and sexual activity in film have been relaxed or eliminated, partly because of changing societal attitudes and partly in an effort to attract audiences. Underground films, however, have been the freest vehicles of experimentation in America. Some directors, such as Andy Warhol, reverted to simple, even crude, methods and equipment, using a static camera to portray an almost eventless scene or a continuous shot to study explicit sexual behavior. Other underground filmmakers use hand-held cameras, while still

20-21   AKIRA KUROSAWA,   *Seven Samurai,* (1954).

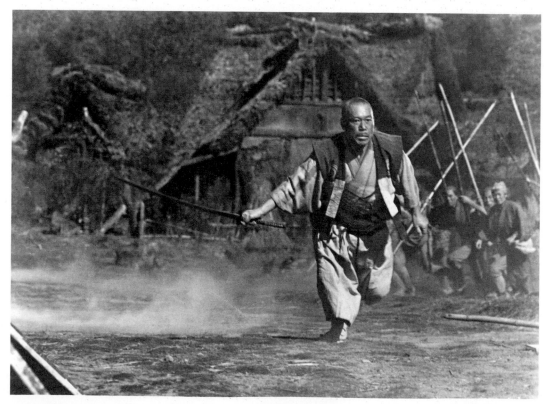

others use complex equipment. Stan Brakhage, for example, produced dizzying superimpositions of astronomical, anatomical, and microscopic images in *Dog Star Man* (1959–64).

The avant-garde films made since World War II have tended to express the uncertainty of our experience of reality, especially our inability to distinguish illusion from reality. They reject or modify traditional narrative sequences and causal relationships. These films present emotional states or responses to the environment by means of random, often disconnected episodes. Transitions between scenes may be minimized for effects of jarring discontinuity, as in some contemporary poetry. Dialogue and background music have sometimes been reduced or entirely eliminated. Avant-garde films have revealed a human need to defy traditional rules and values, a need also seen in the other arts — painting, literature, music, and dance. They demand a fresh vision, heightened awareness, and continuous sympathy from their limited audience. Above all, avant-garde filmmakers have sought freedom to use all aspects of the human experience in their work.

The following directors represent a very incomplete list of outstanding talents in twentieth-century filmmaking.

DAVID WARK GRIFFITH (United States, 1875–1948). After a childhood in Kentucky, D. W. Griffith went to New York, where he acted in Edwin S. Porter's films. By 1908 Griffith was directing short melodramas for the rapidly multiplying nickelodeon theaters. Between 1908 and 1913 he experimented with camera and editing techniques in these short, innovative films. His insistence on rehearsals, an extravagance in the eyes of his employers, led to improved acting. Griffith's films always had a melodramatic quality, in part because he was a moralizer who stressed the virtues of peace, courage, motherhood, fidelity, home, and family. In 1914 he produced his first epic, *The Birth of a Nation*, based on Thomas Dixon's novel *The Clansman*, which concerns the South in the periods before, during, and after the Civil War. The racist portrayal of blacks mars the film, but its stupendous scale, innovative camera work, and imaginative editing made it a commercial success

20-22 DAVID WARK GRIFFITH, *Intolerance,* (1916).

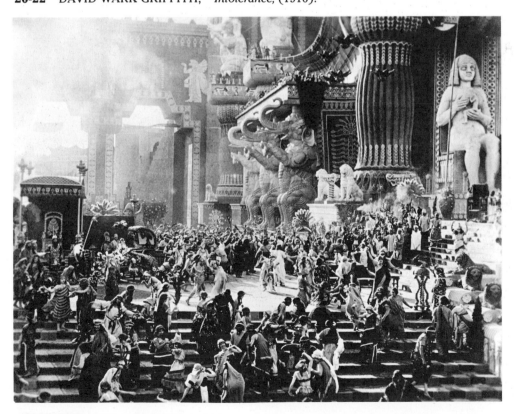

and an object of international study. Griffith's next spectacle was on an even grander scale (Fig. 20-22). *Intolerance* (1916) was intended as a rebuke to those critics who had censured *The Birth of a Nation* for its bigotry. The basic theme of the later film is that narrow-mindedness results in evil. *Intolerance* was not a commercial success and Griffith's moralizing and his melodramatic compulsions eventually made his films seem old-fashioned. After 1931 he ceased making films and spent his last seventeen years watching others develop an art in which he had been a pioneer.

ROBERT FLAHERTY (United States, 1884–1951). The documentary films made by Robert Flaherty are a form of realism dealing with the human battle for survival against nature. Flaherty's first use of a movie camera was to document an exploration of Hudson Bay in Canada. In 1920 he persuaded a French fur company to sponsor him in producing a film about one year in the lives of a typical Eskimo family. For sixteen months he shared that family's precarious existence and returned with *Nanook of the North* (1922). The camera was stationary, using only pans and tilts, and the editing was simple, but the frames were effectively composed and the stark presentation was impressive. Unlike Griffith or Eisenstein, Flaherty used very simple and direct techniques in his early works. Despite this simplicity of method, he led viewers to understand his subjects and their values. *Man of Aran* (1934), filmed in the stark Aran Islands off Ireland, also centered on the life of a representative family wresting a meager living from the land and the violent sea. Bolder dark-light contrasts were used with increased sophistication in editing. Flaherty's documentaries ignored modern influences in the lives of his subjects. He wanted to record their primitive customs even when some of these had to be relearned and staged for the camera. Such staging raises questions about the truth that documentaries seek.

CHARLES CHAPLIN (England and the United States, 1889–1977).   In 1913 Charles Chaplin was lured from vaudeville by the Keystone Studios, where he was directed by Mack Sennett. Sennett, however, emphasized superficial silliness, and Chaplin, who had spent two years of his boyhood in a workhouse for the poor, wanted to use comedy to re-

veal human aspirations and weaknesses. He therefore left Keystone for Essanay so that he could write and direct his own films. In works like *The Tramp* (1915) and *The Gold Rush* (1925), he portrayed a tragicomic loner, excluded from most human fellowship and from the good life — at least until the climactic scenes of the film. Through his character types, especially his clown figure, the Little Tramp, Chaplin commented on social values. He was also ingenious in exploiting objects as instruments of comedy and using variations on themes to unify his plots. His early sound films, such as *Modern Times* (1936), used synchronized scores but not speech (Fig. 20-23). His later works contain much pathos and social comment. *Limelight* (1952) revives the circus theme, which Chaplin had used earlier in *The Circus* (1928), to present clowns as symbols of the tragicomic duality of human behavior.

JEAN RENOIR (France and the United States, 1894–1979).   Renoir, the youngest son of the renowned painter, wrote his first script and directed his first film in 1924. The financial failure of his early works forced him to produce conventional, commercially viable films during the rest of the silent film era. With the advent of sound in films, however, Renoir began to create works that were both artistically significant and profitable. International attention came with *La Grande Illusion* (1937), which uses a World War I prison to reveal stratification and change in European society. In microcosm viewers are shown the decline of aristocracy and the rise of the working and middle classes. *The Rules of the Game* (1939) depicts the corrupt and ritualistic behavior of the upper class. Here Renoir was a pioneer in the use of deep focus to contrast foreground with background actions for purposes of tension. Tracking shots of long duration contrast with the fast action of the plot, which develops during a weekend house party at a country estate. Conventional behavior patterns are seen to apply to adultery as well as to a brutal hunt. Much of the film's power derives from parallel action. The hunt of the animals by the weekend guests is echoed in the "hunt" of the women by the men and the hunt of an "enemy" by a jealous husband. Rhythmic editing and subtle use of the camera help express the moods of the characters and the world they inhabit; comic touches abound. The film was banned by the French government. Renoir spent the years of the Second World War working in the United States. His post-war films, among them *The Golden Coach* (1953), were more abstract in allegory, more delicate in image, and lighter in mood than his earlier work. Protest gave way to benevolence.

SERGEI M. EISENSTEIN (Russia, 1898–1948). Viewing Griffith's *Intolerance*, Sergei Eisenstein changed his interest from stage to screen, and his first picture, *Strike*, was made in 1924. A scarcity of camera film is thought to have led Russian directors to use sequences of brief shots that imply much more than is actually shown. Under the tutelage of film teacher Lev Kulshov, and through study of Griffith's work, Eisenstein learned to use editing to build narrative, suggest ideas, and evoke emotion. In his films, shots jump ahead, flash back, or crosscut to represent simultaneous actions. Parallel shots of a priest tapping his crucifix and an officer tapping his sword in *Potemkin* (1925) suggest the oppression of the people by church and state. In the same film, a shot of a sailor smashing plates forecasts a mutiny. Far more subtly than for Griffith, editing works for Eisenstein in several ways to create mood: (1) tonally, by moving gradually or suddenly from light to dark; (2) rhythmically, by varying the length of shots to suggest slowing or quickening of tempo; (3) formally, by exploiting the difference or similarity of shapes for unity or contrast; and (4) directionally, by repeating or contrasting movement. A textbook demonstration of such devices can be found in *Potemkin*, an interpretation of a mutiny that is supported by the people of the Russian port city of Odessa and, in Eisenstein's hands, becomes an epic representation of the Russian Revolution. Eisenstein did not use professional actors for his films, choosing instead untrained local people to fill all roles. His process of selection reflected his interest in social groups and types rather than in individuals. As his career developed, Eisenstein wrote many books on film theory that provide unusual insights into the creative process of filmmaking.

RENÉ CLAIR (France, 1898–1981). Clair came to filmmaking by way of acting and film criticism. His first film established the character of his style. *Paris qui dort* (1923), or *The Crazy Ray*, deals with

20-23 CHARLES CHAPLIN, *Modern Times,* (1936).

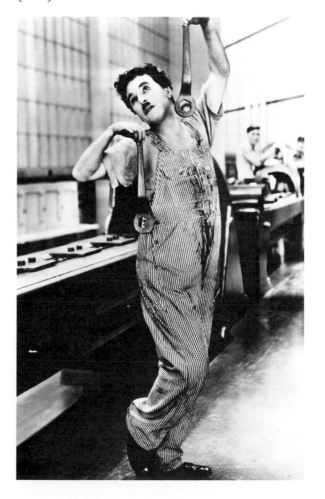

the effects of a ray that puts the Parisian population to sleep, paralyzed in the midst of their activities. When the ray is turned off, action is first frenetic and then depicted in slow motion. The narrative line of *Entr'acte* (1924) is less logical. The film ranges from fantasy to slapstick and reveals the influence of Dada and Surrealist art. Cinematic trickery abounds. *The Italian Straw Hat* (1927), usually considered the best of Clair's silent films, adds satire of bourgeois manners to wild whimsy. The economic crisis of 1930 may, in part, explain the harsher social comment in *À Nous la Liberté* (1931), in which two escaped convicts find that neither management nor labor has freedom in a production-oriented society. Parallel shots of prison and factory activities are effective. The pessimism of the message is lightened by bits of Chaplinesque humor. During the Second World War, Clair worked in Hollywood and made a number of elegant films.

ALFRED HITCHCOCK (England and the United States, 1899–1980).   After being influenced by Hollywood films during the 1920s and 1930s, Alfred Hitchcock left England to become part of American filmmaking and a significant influence on European — especially French — films after mid-century. He is known as a master of suspense dramas involving crime. Although he usually based his scripts on novels or plays written by others, Hitchcock's unique interpretations made him a pioneer in auteurism. He manipulated audience emotions rather than inviting puzzle-solving analysis. For this, he found it effective to use ordinary people — persons with whom viewers easily identify — for heroes and villains. Suspense is orchestrated by letting the audience know the source of evil before it is known to participants in the film. Audiences then tend to sympathize with the film's characters and to fear for future events. Nevertheless, there are surprises for viewers, as well as episodes of delightful humor in most of Hitchcock's work. Hitchcock's training was thorough, beginning with the design of credits and titles for silent films and continuing with film direction in England and Germany. Silent films pushed him to rely on effective visual narrative rather than dialogue, although he produced the first successful "talkie" in England in 1929. His *The Thirty-Nine Steps* (1935) and *The Lady Vanishes* (1938) were

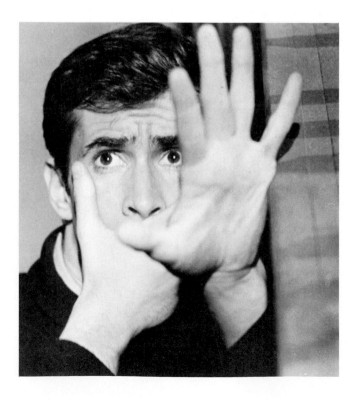

20-24   ALFRED HITCHCOCK,   *Psycho,* (1960).

classic "chase" thrillers. The latter won the New York Film Critics Award. In the following year, 1939, Hitchcock moved to the United States. His first U.S. film, *Rebecca* (1940), won an Oscar award for best picture of the year. *Spellbound* (1945), *Dial M for Murder* (1954), and *The Birds* (1963) were among the works that cemented Hitchcock's reputation. There is often a keen interest in psychology in his films. *Psycho* (1960) reveals a murderer (Fig. 20-24) whose domineering mother caused him to develop a split personality or double identity. He assumes the identity of the mother and kills young women to whom he is attracted. In films and television, Hitchcock achieved international acclaim. Shortly before his death, he was knighted by Queen Elizabeth.

LUIS BUÑUEL (Spain, United States, Mexico, and France, 1900–83). Luis Buñuel's disapproval of the Spanish government led him to move to France in 1925. *Un Chien Andalou* (1927) and *L'Age d'Or* (1930), made by Buñuel and Salvador Dali, are early classics of Surrealist cinema. Shocking in their illogical contrasts, sexual references, and sadistic violence, these films represent a world subject to the chaotic demands of the subconscious. *Un Chien Andalou*, for example, contains an unforgettable shot of a razor slicing the eye of a young woman (Fig. 20-25). Buñuel used a more documentary approach in *Los Hurdes* (1932) and *Los Olvidados* (1950) to show the degradation of extreme poverty in Spain and Mexico. The intensity of action and image makes a powerful, pessimistic statement about society. While Buñuel's repertory includes comedy, his dominant themes emerge from a sardonic view of human weakness. *Belle de Jour* (1967) presents a typically jolting contrast of beautiful photography and brutal action and a blurring of distinctions between the worlds of reality and fantasy. A young doctor's wife, through boredom or frustration, becomes a daytime prostitute in a brothel. After erotic adventures with a wide range of clients, she is so desired by one that he shoots and cripples her husband, whom the wife then apparently nurses. The closing scene, however, suggests that much of the preceding story might have been fantasy. The film's light touches do not soften Buñuel's basic view of human nature as ambivalent and easily corruptible.

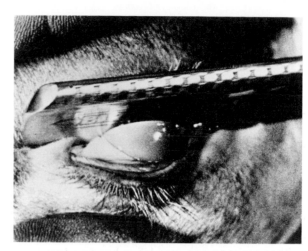

20-25 LUIS BUÑUEL and SALVADOR DALI, *Un Chien Andalou,* (1927).

VITTORIO DE SICA (Italy, 1902–74). A well-known actor in the 1930s, Vittorio De Sica turned to directing in 1939. His films were the inspiration of the Neorealist movement between 1944 and 1952. His most admired work, *The Bicycle Thief* (1948), involves the search by a father and son for a stolen bicycle that is necessary to a newfound job (Fig. 20-26). In desperation the father finally steals a bike but is caught and shamed before his son. De Sica's filming of all scenes on location rather than in the studio, his use of nonactors for major roles, and his emphasis on demeaning social conditions are typical of Neorealism. Simple editing and use of medium shots support an effect of objectivity that reinforces the realism of the film.

AKIRA KUROSAWA (Japan, 1910–). Internationally the best-known of Japanese filmmakers, Akira Kurosawa began directing in 1943, using subjects from the martial arts and medieval Japan. After World War II, he explored postwar Japanese society and the problems of readjustment. International fame came with *Rashomon* (1950), a story of rape and murder told by conflicting witnesses.

Realistically, viewers are left to wonder which of the witnesses, if any, were truthful. The plot, acting, photography, and sound track overwhelmed Western audiences. Equally popular was *Seven Samurai* (1954), in which seven feudal warriors are hired to defend a village from recurring plunder (Fig. 20-21). The sudden changes from shot to shot and the intensity of the sound effects underscore the primitive brutality of the action. It is memorable violence. Kurosawa has also taken narratives from Western literature and put them into Japanese contexts. Examples include *Idiot* (1951), from Dostoyevski, *The Lower Depths* (1957), from Gorky, *Throne of Blood* (1957) and *Ran* (1985), from Shakespeare's *Macbeth* and *King Lear* respectively. Kurosawa's methods are exacting. He paints pictures of major scenes for planning purposes. He will wait weeks for the appropriate filming weather and he is demanding in every detail. Understandably, he often exceeds his budget. Financial backers have been frightened away. He found Russian patronage for *Dersu Uzala* (1976), based on a Russian autobiography and filmed in the USSR. The film, an account of the

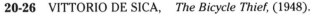

20-26 VITTORIO DE SICA, *The Bicycle Thief,* (1948).

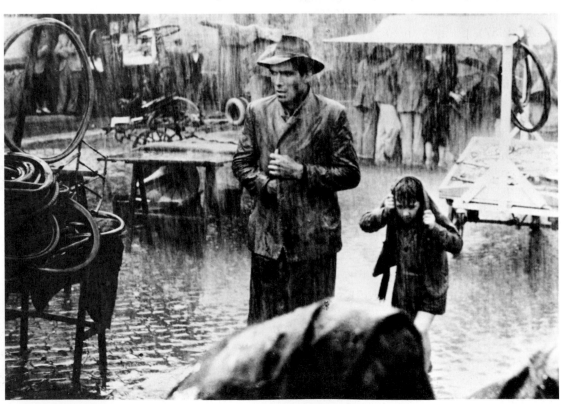

friendship of a Russian army surveyor with a reclusive mountain dweller, has great subtlety in photography and sound. It was popular with critics but not with a wide public audience. *Kagemusha* (1980), the tale of a sixteenth-century Japanese ruler, met with the same mixed reaction. Although not a box-office success, the film, financed by American and Japanese backers, was awarded a grand prize at the Cannes Film Festival. Ten years of scriptwriting and searching for financial backing preceded the filming of *Ran.* Its eleven-million-dollar budget provided for much of the epic sweep and thundering battles that Kurosawa loves. Toward the end, as the old king dies melodramatically, Kurosawa's philosophical message is enunciated by two actors: humans have always been power hungry and willing to betray each other. Indeed, the nature and uses of power have been basic questions examined by many of Kurosawa's films.

MICHELANGELO ANTONIONI (Italy, 1912–). Antonioni's early films were documentaries. His first full-length picture, *Cronaca di un Amore* (1950), contains elements of his later films: special emphasis on women and a tendency to emphasize his characters' feelings more than the events of his stories. This film, like *Le Amiche* (1955) and *Il Grido* (1957), portrays frustrated, isolated lives and allies itself with Neorealism. A change is evident in *L'Avventura* (1960), the film that won its director international acclaim (Fig. 20-27). During an excursion a girl disappears; she is never found, but, in the process of searching for her, her fiancé and friends experience complex changes in their relationships to each other. Transitions between scenes are slow, and the meager narrative events are overshadowed by Antonioni's study of their mental consequences. As in earlier films, the human situation is characterized by boredom, self-centeredness, ambivalence, and loneliness; yet in this work some communion is finally apparent between the two main characters. The end of the film suggests a trace of hope for the future. Alienation is also a major theme in the two films that followed: *La Notte* (1961) and *Red Desert* (1964). In Antonioni's films, the human problem is to break out of one's solitude, to communicate with others. This theme is evident in *Blow-Up* (1967), which in its fast action, jumpy editing, and

20-27 MICHELANGELO ANTONIONI, *L'Avventura,* (1960).   Courtesy Janus Films.

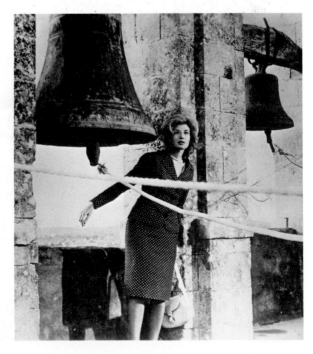

blurring of fantasy and reality is related to the New Wave films in France. In *Zabriskie Point* (1970), shot mainly in Death Valley and dealing with American youth, Antonioni develops greater looseness of narrative links between beautifully photographed kaleidoscopic parts than he had previously.

INGMAR BERGMAN (Sweden, 1918–). Bergman began writing and directing professionally for stage, radio, television, and films in 1944, after studying at Stockholm University and working in amateur theater. International recognition came in the 1950s with three films: *The Seventh Seal* (1956), *Wild Strawberries* (1957), and *The Magician* (1958). The first film uses moody symbolism to explore the human quest for meaning in a brutal world. A disillusioned knight returns home from years of crusading to find Sweden ravaged by the plague and by moral corruption. The figure of Death appears, and the knight challenges him to a game of chess in order to gain time to seek knowledge of God and to do some worthy act. The knight, who seeks God, and his squire, a cynical, practical materialist, are contrasted in their sophistication with a family of young actors whose simple love is unburdened by profound questions or the cynicism of worldly experience. The knight

distracts Death, losing the chess match but saving the lives of the actors, and thus accomplishing a positive moral act. At the end of the film all but the actors are forced to join Death in a dancing procession that moves out along a high ridge silhouetted against the sky (Fig. 20-28). The basically simple plot is complicated by the symbolic overtones of every action and detail. Bergman treated theological questions within an allegorical framework, yet the power of his presentation and the universal import of his message appeal to a wide modern audience. Although his editing is not unusual, his composition within each frame is striking and has gained him wide acclaim. *Persona* (1966), a title taken from the Latin word for an actor's mask or the Jungian term for the role an individual plays in life, is freer in narrative style and cinematic technique than Bergman's earlier films. Attention is called to the film medium itself when cinematographer and director are photographed and when, at a moment of great tension, the face on the screen dissolves as the film is burned away. Bits and pieces of consciousness are presented from different and uncertain points of view in time and space, as the film seems to portray a struggle for identity between a nurse and her patient as well as the conflicts between dream and reality, life and art. Equally concerned with aesthetic distance,

20-28 INGMAR BERGMAN,   *The Seventh Seal,* (1956).   Courtesy Janus Films.

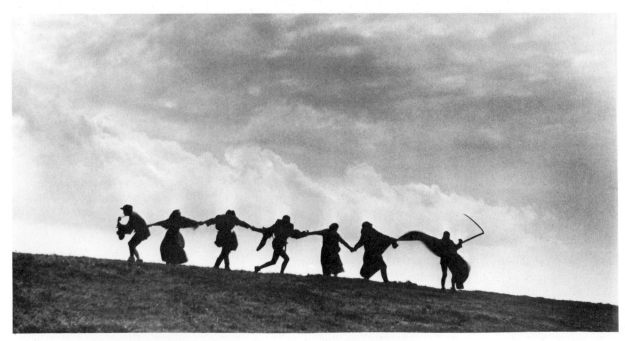

The Passion of Anna (1969) explores psychological conflicts and the search for love. The film has a complex structure that uses interviews with actors to promote viewer detachment. Sound, color, and composition within the frame are remarkably expressive.

FEDERICO FELLINI (Italy, 1920–).   Fellini is concerned with alienation from a moral point of view. Neorealism is evident in *I Vitelloni* (1953). By 1954, with *La Strada*, Fellini's insistence on private feelings represented a break with Neorealism. The success of *La Strada* opened the way for *La Dolce Vita* (1958–60), a vast, convoluted, fragmented work that became the subject of international controversy (Fig. 20-29). Fellini wanted to show the moral condition of humanity and the rootlessness of modern culture. He has stated that autobiographical material was used in this film and in *8½* (1962), where divisions between reality and illusion are less distinct. In this work, a film director goes to a health spa to rest, and the arrival of first his mistress and then his wife (Fellini's spouse) triggers memories and fantasies in a lavish profusion of images. Dialogue is relatively unimportant. In *Satyricon* (1969), the orchestration of forms and colors reaches a zenith. The source of the film is a fragmented work of literature attributed to Petronius, a Roman of the first century A.D. The original story consists of a series of episodes, often disconnected in time and space and rarely complete in themselves, that occur in the life of a beautiful youth. His adventures run the gamut of sexual perversities and debauchery in a Roman society that has lost its faith, values, and stability. Fellini hewed closely to the episodic structure of the original, created an astounding variety of grotesque human characters, and added a mélange of languages. Action is sometimes recounted in dialogue rather than being shown; at other times, dialogue is hardly more than background sound to the action and images. Fellini has said that he wanted *Satyricon* to suggest the idea of fragments excavated from the debris of the past. He also intended an analogy with society today.

ALAIN RESNAIS (France, 1922–).   In 1959, *Hiroshima, Mon Amour* won prizes at the Cannes Film Festival and brought Alain Resnais world recognition as a New Wave filmmaker. The film, written by Marguerite Duras, poses a daring contrast

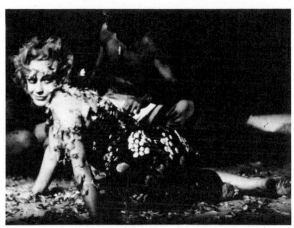

20-29 FEDERICO FELLINI, *La Dolce Vita,* (1958–60).

between a banal love story and its setting in Hiroshima, a city of global tragedy in World War II. *Last Year at Marienbad* (1961), written by Alain Robbe-Grillet, strengthened the perception of Resnais as a chilly intellectual whose films did not allow the audience to become sympathetically involved with the characters (Fig. 20-20). *Marienbad* blurs present, past, imagination and reality with fragmented and discontinuous shots. The acting is formal and ritualistic; the total effect is that of a dream. In 1961, the editing seemed revolutionary. Resnais's later films (he directed only seven feature-length films between 1959 and 1978) incorporate more emotional content. In *Muriel, a Time of Return* (1963), memories and renewed encounters from World War II and the French-Algerian War provoke tensions between characters in a modern French setting. Viewers are forced to piece together an understanding of the situation from discontinuous shots, sometimes connected by a sound track that overlaps from a previous shot into a new scene. *Stavisky* (1974) was written by Jorge Semprun and based on the true story of a fraudulent financier whose speculative pyramiding led to the resignation of the French government in 1934. The film is less the history of the scandal than a study of the complex character of Stavisky and his public image, but it was a commercial success. Resnais's self-reflective and self-conscious attention to the nature of the film medium is best seen in *Providence* (1977). Three-fourths of this film deals with an old writer's imaginings of various story possibilities during a long sleepless night. His characters, drawn mainly from family, change roles, behave inconsistently, and utter trite lines, as the author's mind criticizes and rearranges. On the day after the long night, viewers meet the real characters as they celebrate the old man's birthday. The film was written by David Mercer in English. It is a comedy of great subtlety and depth, one that sustains Resnais's reputation as a complex intellectual filmmaker.

STANLEY KUBRICK (United States, 1928–). After experience as a staff photographer for *Look* magazine and as director of two documentaries, Stanley Kubrick started making feature films in the 1950s. *Paths of Glory* (1957) was an antiwar state-

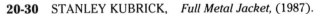

20-30   STANLEY KUBRICK,   *Full Metal Jacket,* (1987).

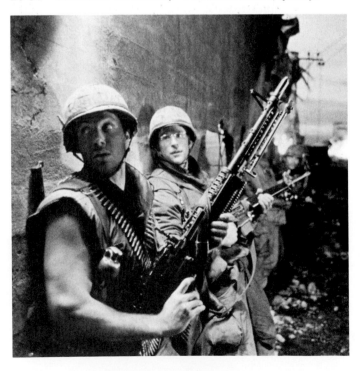

ment dealing with World War I. *Spartacus*, an adventure epic with Kirk Douglas as a Roman gladiator and leader of a slave revolt, was released in 1960. A sequence of heroically conceived and budgeted successes followed. *Dr. Strangelove: Or, How I Learned to Stop Worrying and Love the Bomb* (1964), from a novel by Peter George, has been described as a nightmare comedy and a brilliant satire on incompetent and irresponsible military leadership. The film *2001: A Space Odyssey* (1968), based on a novel by Arthur Clarke, is a mind-boggling visual experience of science fiction. *A Clockwork Orange* (1971) is a frightening vision of a chaotic future. In spite of box-office success, these films received mixed reviews from critics, some of whom felt that the plots and acting were weaker than the visual fireworks. *Full Metal Jacket* (1987) is a film about the Vietnam War. The title refers to the armored cartridge used by the marines in that conflict. Viewers follow one platoon through its training and combat (Fig. 20-30). The training, aimed at brutalizing and desensitizing men as preparation for killing the enemy, is described vividly and accompanied by a numbing chorus of shouted obscenities. The combat scenes are unforgettably realistic, from the devastated land to the explosion of blood at the impact of a bullet. The overall character of the film is consistent with many of Kubrick's films. He pushes the audience to recognize the inhumanity of war, the ignorance, irresponsibility, or insensitivity of some leaders, and our nation's entrapment by its bureaucracies and by history.

JEAN-LUC GODARD (France, 1930–).   Godard's first major film, *Breathless*, appeared in 1959 as part of the New Wave in France (Fig. 20–31). His films are self-conscious comments on reality rather than imitations of it; they constitute a director's philosophical statement rather than a revelation of characters. The audience is never allowed to lose itself in a story. Sudden jumps, shifts, digressions, fragmented images, and editorial comments are used to create distance between the audience and the filmed events. Like many twentieth-century painters and sculptors, Godard wants his spectators to appreciate the art medium not as an imitation of life but as a separate though related world. The mystique of the woman and the

20-31 JEAN-LUC GODARD,   *Breathless,* (1959).

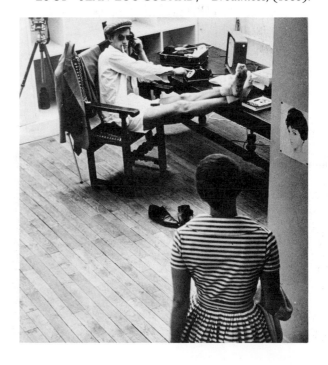

individual's involvement in violent human relations and class politics are basic themes developed with increasing complication in films ranging from *Le Petit Soldat* (*The Little Soldier,* released in 1960) to *The Weekend* (1968). After the French student revolts of 1968, Godard withdrew from the established film industry and joined the *Dziga Vertov* group, named after a Soviet documentary filmmaker, to direct indoctrination films for political-action organizations. In 1972 Godard returned to making films meant for commercial distribution with *Tout Va Bien (All's Well),* which investigates the role of the intellectual in the revolution of the working class. In this film, Godard points to a lack of leadership and coordination in the various aspects of the class struggle. Both the Communist party and the New Left are presented as inadequate. The audience is left to ponder the sources of new leadership and the tripartite social division between workers, bourgeoisie, and intellectuals. Godard's film style has been described as illogical, careening, and anarchic, yet he is considered one of the most important innovators of the 1960s.

FRANÇOIS TRUFFAUT (France, 1932–84). Truffaut's success and his reputation as a warm and faithful friend might not have been predicted from his childhood. He was expelled from schools and sent to a reformatory. Autobiographical material is frequent in his work, especially in *The 400 Blows,* issued in 1959 (Fig. 20–32), and in the five films of the Antoine Doinel series (1959–78), which trace Antoine's life from his childhood through his marriage and eventual divorce. *Small Change* (1976) is an episodic collage of childhood situations stressing that of an alienated and parentally-abused boy. A teacher's impassioned plea for greater concern and justice for children is a clear presentation of Truffaut's feelings. His most adventuresome film is perhaps *Shoot the Piano Player* (1959), based on a novel by the American David Goodis, and made into a personal statement. In this and his other films, Truffaut used comedy, melodrama, unexpected changes in mood, and allusions to American films and film personalities. He was fascinated by American films of the 1930s and 1940s and by the work of Alfred Hitchcock. Truffaut's humor was accessible to a wide audience, while his allusions invite more complex readings by sophisticated viewers. In some of his later works, Truffaut's desire to entertain pushed him to contrived situations and slapstick caricature. His rigorous film criticism, published in *Arts* and *Cahiers du Cinéma,* urged the

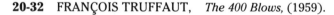

20-32   FRANÇOIS TRUFFAUT,   *The 400 Blows,* (1959).

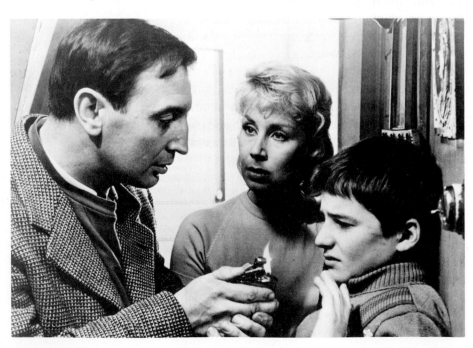

auteur theory. In 1958, he published a plea for the use of natural light, outdoor settings, and natural —even improvised— dialogues. This plea has been considered as a manifesto for much New Wave cinema. Truffaut was not a great technical innovator. His contribution came from a fine sympathy for human beings, a sparkling sense of humor that softens a romantic but pessimistic world view, and an exceptional ability to control audience expectations.

LINA WERTMULLER (Italy, 1932–). Wertmuller's international reputation developed suddenly in the 1970s. She had written scripts and directed for television, theater, and short films before 1963, when Federico Fellini chose her to assist him with his film *8½*. He had previously helped her find financial backing for her first full-length film, *The Lizards* (1962), which won an award at the Locarno Film Festival. Her films show the influence of Fellini's overwhelmingly profuse imagery and of Italian Neorealism. Although she has been described as belonging to the New Left, Wertmuller's films cannot be described as political propaganda; they deal with individuals trapped and denied by social systems of all types. *All Screwed Up* (1973) portrays young people forced into dehumanizing roles in order to survive in an urban situation. *Swept Away* (1974) is a modern treatment of an old theme: the reversal of roles when master and servant are shipwrecked on a deserted island. A wealthy woman behaves arrogantly to a deckhand on her yacht only to become his slave and mistress after they are marooned. In *Seven Beauties* (1975), a petty hoodlum employs a wide range of survival techniques when he counters a murder conviction with a successful insanity plea and maneuvers from a mental hospital to the Italian army in World War II and finally to a German concentration camp (Fig. 20-33). There, he turns in desperation to the seduction of the camp commandant, a frozen-faced Nordic amazon. Wertmuller's penetrating interpretations of human relationships gain vitality from fast-paced, rich, explosive sequences of images. She has explained that she does not have a clear concept of a film until the parts are composed in the editing room. Comedy, vulgarity, cruelty, humanity, and contradictory behavior are all part of her fascinating pattern.

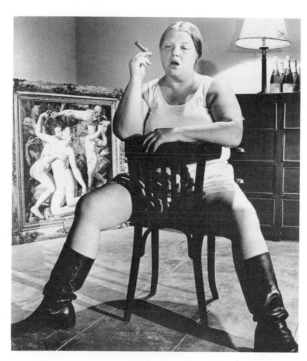

20-33 LINA WERTMULLER, *Seven Beauties,* (1975).

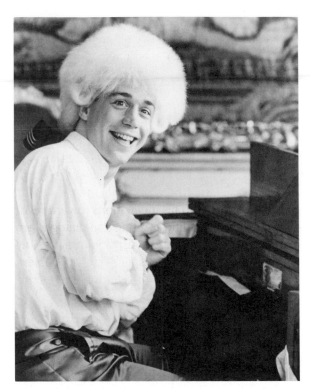

20-34   MILOŠ FORMAN,   *Amadeus,* (1984).

20-35   ROMAN POLAŃSKI,   *Tess,* (1979).

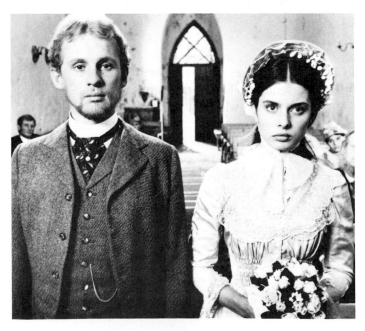

MILOŠ FORMAN (Czechoslovakia and the United States, 1932–).   Growing up under first Nazi and then Stalinist repression, Miloš Forman was primed to become a leader in Czech New Wave filmmaking and an advocate of freedom. After training at the Prague Film Academy, he co-directed *The Puppies* (1957), revealing one of his basic interests: tension between adolescents and their parents in a changing society. A related theme appears in *Competition* (1963), where Forman exposes the self-deception of participants in an amateur talent contest. *Loves of a Blonde* (1965) studies the generation gap and the distortion of reality in young love. Humor, irony, and merciless objectivity are combined in the film, which earned Forman a prize in Venice, a twenty-two-week run in New York, and an international reputation. *Firemen's Ball* (1967) is a hilarious exposé of very human good intentions and incompetence. Such revelations of the discrepancies between official image and actuality are normally proscribed by authoritarian governments, and *Firemen's Ball* was banned in Czechoslovakia. Forman said that his move to America was for professional rather than political reasons. It is, of course, hard to separate the two arenas. In the United States, Forman's budgets and technical facilities have been more lavish, and he has used professional actors more often than he had previously. *One Flew Over the Cuckoo's Nest* (1975) was a commercial and critical triumph. The underlying theme, developed in the setting of a mental hospital, continues to be the director's striving to get beneath appearances. Comedy and tragedy conjoin, but Forman has softened the irony and ambiguity for American audiences. *Amadeus* (1984) was Forman's contribution to the box-office successes of the 1980s (Fig. 20-34). In this dazzling portrayal of Mozart's musical genius and personal immaturity, Forman's debunking of heroes continues. While his dispassionate observation has become less cruel in the American films released thus far, Forman's great strength has been to show us as we are.

ROMAN POLAŃSKI (Poland, the United States, and Europe, 1933–).   *Rosemary's Baby* (1968) was a very successful horror film based on a novel by Ira Levin about a pregnant woman surrounded by people whom she believes to be witches. It was directed by Roman Polański when he was working in the United States. He was admirably suited for the job, having established a reputation with films that exploit violence, sex, psychological stress, and a sense of the ominous in all things. Polański had trained in a Polish film school and became widely known in 1961 with the release of *Knife in the Water*. In the plot, an affluent Polish couple picks up a young hitchhiker and takes him for an overnight cruise on a small sailboat. From the beginning, the older man berates the younger and attempts to dominate him, although there is an obvious ambivalence of attraction and competition between them. Petty incidents during the slow-moving cruise lead to a struggle; the boy falls overboard and hides behind a buoy. The couple believe that he has drowned and quarrel about what to do. The man abandons the wife and swims to shore. The young man comes out of hiding, boards the boat, and is seduced by the wife, who then leaves him on shore and sails back to the marina and the distraught husband. She attempts to tell her husband that the boy is not dead and that she has been unfaithful. The husband refuses to believe her, and the film ends as they sit in their car at a crossroads trying to decide whether or not to drive to the police station. After leaving Poland, Polański worked in France and England. One result was *Repulsion* (1965), the story of a beautiful young woman who goes mad and murders two people. Here, the slowly moving camera dwells obsessively on objects, eyes, and faces. The hypnotically slow pace in the first half of the film picks up only slightly as ghastly events begin to occur. The effect is that of a slow-motion nightmare. Polański's later films, *Macbeth* (1971) and *Tess* (1979), had problems with casting and inadequately understood historical context (Fig. 20-35). Polański's dark world view may owe something to his youth as a Polish Jew during the Holocaust and a childhood incident in which he was almost killed by a bicycle thief. Later, his wife was murdered in California. He has apparently used tragic experience as a source for creative productivity.

RAINER WERNER FASSBINDER (Germany, 1946–82). Cocaine and sleeping pills brought a premature end to Fassbinder's turbulent, productive, and controversial career as director, writer, and actor. He wrote most of the screenplays for his forty films. The prevailing pessimism and alienation came, in part, from a lonely childhood, made viable only by constant attendance at movies. Most of these were American. Fassbinder's early films (1965–71) used the American gangster genre as a vehicle for very personal, often autobiographical content, even though he liberally borrowed his characters from favorite novels. There is constant criticism of German middle-class society, its smugness, prejudice, and conventional restraints. Fassbinder worked with the *Antiteater* group, which shared his inclinations toward revolutionary art and politics. Acting and dialogue are often artificial and ritualistic, especially in his early films. Actors sometimes speak to the camera rather than to each other. Thus the audience finds it hard to identify emotionally with any of the characters. An analytical response is encouraged. Fassbinder wanted the audience to reconsider its views of human relations and of the film medium in the light of his convictions. His characters are shaped in his own image, that of an outsider. They try vainly to escape the existential situation that holds them. Social problems are the core of many of Fassbinder's scripts. *The Bitter Tears of Petra von Kant* (1972) describes dependency and exploitation in a lesbian friendship. *Fear Eats the Soul* (1973) deals with the love of a middle-aged German housemaid and a younger Moroccan imported worker. Imported workers in Germany, as in England and the United States, have experienced intense problems of assimilation into the new culture. *Effie Brest* (1974) came from a novel about adultery and consequent tragedy. *The Fox and Friends* (1974) portrays gay society in Germany, while *Mother Küsters Goes to Heaven* (1975) presents a failure of the German Communist party to help a widow, who then turns anarchist and is eventually shot. Like many of Fassbinder's films, this is loosely based on another filmmaker's work: a 1929 film with a socialist point of view. Surviving in occupied Germany after World War II is the theme for *The Marriage of Maria Braun* (1978), a significant commercial success that spread Fassbinder's name (Fig. 20-36). Maria's new husband disappears on the Russian front during the war. She takes a black American soldier as her lover. Her husband's return causes a fight, during which she kills the American. Her husband takes the blame and goes to prison.

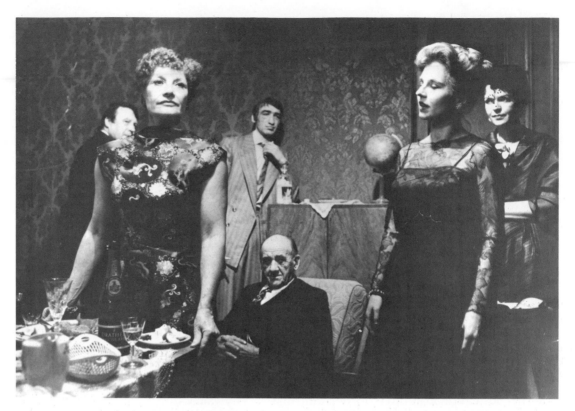

20-36   RAINER WERNER
FASSBINDER,
The Marriage of Maria Braun, (1978).

Maria, with his knowledge, becomes the mistress and indispensable business assistant to a wealthy man. The husband is eventually released but disappears for a period of time in order to find himself. She continues her relationship with the wealthy businessman until his premature death. At this point, the husband reappears. She discovers that in a prearranged payment for his absence, the businessman has left half of his fortune to the husband and the other half to Maria! The reunited couple plan their affluent future only to die the same day in the explosion of a gas stove. Appended are pictures of German political leaders since World War II, a device meant to encourage us to see an allegorical relationship between Maria and her husband's willingness to sell themselves for security and Germany's postwar economic success sponsored by the United States. Fassbinder's clear intention of social commentary is sometimes indicated in a prologue to a film. His *The Third Generation* (1979) concerns terrorism. His prologue describes it as a comedy about social games intensified by suspense, excitement and logic, horror and insanity. This description seems to serve as well for Fassbinder's view of life.

Suggestions for Further Study

Dudley, Andrew. *Concepts in Film Theory*. Oxford and New York: Oxford University Press, 1984.

Gernsheim, Helmut, and Alison Gernsheim. *The History of Photography from the Camera Obscura to the Beginning of the Modern Era*, 2nd ed. New York: McGraw-Hill, 1969.

Jeffrey, Ian. *Photography: A Concise History*. New York: Oxford University Press, 1981.

Metz, Christian. *Film Language: A Semiotics of the Cinema*. Translated by Michael Taylor. New York: Oxford University Press, 1974.

Monaco, James. *How to Read a Film: The Art, Technology, Language, History, and Theory of Film and Media*, rev. ed. New York: Oxford University Press, 1981.

Newhall, Beaumont. *The History of Photography from 1839 to the Present*, rev. and enl. ed. New York: The Museum of Modern Art. Distributed by the New York Graphic Society Books, Little, Brown and Company, Boston, 1982.

Newhall, Nancy. *Ansel Adams: The Eloquent Light*. New York: Harper & Row, 1980.

Paul, David W., ed. *Politics, Art, and Commitment in the East European Cinema*. London: Macmillan Press Ltd., 1983.

Pollack, Peter. *The Picture History of Photography*, rev. ed. New York: Abrams, 1970.

Robinson, David. *World Cinema, A Short History*, 2nd ed., rev. and enl. London: Eyre Methuen, 1981.

Sandford, John. *The New German Cinema*. London: O. Wolff; Totowa, N.J.: Barnes and Noble, 1980.

Sarris, Andrew. *Interviews with Film Directors*. Indianapolis: Bobbs-Merrill, 1967.

Scharf, Aaron. *Art and Photography*. Baltimore: Penguin Books, 1974.

Shipman, David. *The Story of Cinema: An Illustrated History*. 2 vols. London: Hodder and Stoughton, 1982.

Simon, John. *Ingmar Bergman Directs*. New York: Harcourt Brace Jovanovich, 1972.

Sitney, P. Adams. *Visionary Film: The American Avant-Garde*, 2nd ed. New York: Oxford University Press, 1979.

Solomon, Stanley J., ed. *The Classic Cinema: Essays in Criticism*. New York: Harcourt Brace Jovanovich, 1973.

Steichen, Edward. *A Life in Photography*. Published in collaboration with The Museum of Modern Art, New York. New York: Doubleday, 1963.

Glossary

Words in definitions that appear in *italics* are also defined in the Glossary.

aerial perspective   The softening of *value* contrasts, the muting of colors, and the blurring of contours and details to give the effect of distance.

agora   Hellenistic urban assembly areas.

alla prima   Refers to painting in which only a single layer of paint is used.

ambulatory   Broadly, a covered walkway. Specifically, an aisle around the interior *apse* of a Christian church.

amphora   A tall vase with two handles.

apadana   A rectangular or square *hypostyle* hall.

apse   A semicircular exterior projection or interior concavity in the wall of a Roman basilica or the altar end of a Christian church.

apses in echelon   Apses placed beside a main apse or on the arms of a transept.

aquatint etching   Etching technique in which powdered resin is sifted onto a heated copper plate. Acid attacks the plate between the particles of resin. The pitted surface produces a sandy or speckled effect on prints.

architrave   The lowest horizontal division of the *entablature* resting immediately on the *capital* of a column (see Fig. 9 – 6).

arcology   A term coined by visionary designer Paolo Soleri: a combination of architecture and ecology.

armature   The internal wire, wood, or pipe frame that supports or reinforces a sculpture.

Art Nouveau   An international stylistic trend that flourished in the 1890s and brought a preference for flat shapes and undulating, vinelike contours into art and product design.

assemblage   Sculpture that is assembled from scrap materials or from worn-out and castaway objects.

atelier   French for "studio."

atmospheric perspective   See *aerial perspective*.

atrium   The receiving hall of a Roman house. There was often an opening in the ceiling to allow rain to fall into a centrally placed pool.

baldacchino   A canopy on columns, often over an altar.

barrel vault   See *tunnel vault*.

basilica   A Roman building used as law court, public hall, and audience chamber, consisting of a rectangular structure with an *apse* at one or both ends and entrances in the sides or at one end. Under Christianity, the Roman basilica was adopted for church architecture.

battered   Sloping.

bays   Sections of a vault.

binder   The substance in crayons, *pastels*, and paint that holds pigments together and makes them adhere to a surface.

blind arcades   Arcades in walls for decorative or buttressing purposes; not openings.

broken architrave   An *architrave* interrupted by an arch.

broken color   A painting technique of juxtaposing small strokes of colors to exploit their visual interactions; used especially in Impressionist work.

buon fresco   A painting technique in which paints with a water *binder* are painted onto wet plaster, usually on a wall, and become an integral part of the plaster.

burins   The cutting tools used in *wood* and *metal engraving*.

buttressing   Supportive bracing used in architecture.

cancel   To "x" out, with lines, the printing surface after an *edition* has been produced.

cantilever   A structure, anchored at one end, that extends out into space beyond its supports.

cantorie   Gallery for singers in churches.

capital   The enlarged top or crowning element of a column.

caprice   Imaginary scenes in painting.

cartoon   A full-size preparatory drawing that will be transferred to another surface for a finished work.

caryatid   A structural column in the form of a human figure.

catacombs   The underground passageways with niches used for burial by early Christians.

cathedral   Derived from the word "cathedra," which was the throne of the bishop. The throne was placed in the main church in the bishop's diocese.

ceramic glaze   A glass or fine clay coating that is *fired* onto a clay work.

chiaroscuro   The gradations of light and shadow that suggest three-dimensional forms in the two-dimensional surface of a drawing or painting.

clerestory   A windowed section of a building that overlooks lower roofs of the same building.

cliché verre   A photographic technique in which glass is drawn or painted on and then used as a negative to make photographic prints.

closed form   A *form* with an unbroken or uninterrupted contour. The term applies to sculpture, architecture, and especially painting.

codex   The form of books as we know them today, in which pages are turned; compare to *rotulus*.

coffering   An excavated grid effect or waffle pattern, seen in Roman vaults.

colonnade   A row of regularly spaced columns, usually supporting an *architrave* or a roof.

color   The combination of *hue, saturation,* and *value*.

colossal orders   Columns or pilasters more than one floor high.

combination prints   The combining of several *negatives* to make one *photographic print*.

complementaries   The colors opposite each other on a color wheel that have the effect of intensifying one another when placed side by side; they tend to produce a neutral gray or brown when mixed.

consular diptychs   Two-part ivory plaques celebrating election to the office of consul.

contact print   A photographic print that is the same size as the *negative.*

contrapposto   A classic pose in which the body is relaxed, with the weight on one leg and the hips at a different angle than the shoulders.

cornice   A terminal molding, or group of moldings, that projects from the top of a wall or building.

cross-cuts   Rapid *cutting* from one *scene* to another in motion pictures to present simultaneous actions.

crosshatching   Intersecting sets of parallel lines used to create a sense of shading.

crossing   Space in Medieval Christian churches where the transept crosses the nave.

cross vault   The crossing of two vaults at right angles which distributes the load to four legs and allows the sides of the structure to be opened up (see Fig. 4-14).

crown   The top of a vault.

crypt   A vaulted underground space for tombs and relics found under the *apse* or choir of a Medieval church.

cutting   In motion pictures, changing from one *shot* to another.

cybernetic art   Works of art that are in a dynamic state, responding to their environment and their spectators, as much as the latter respond to the work itself.

cyborg   An object with *cybernetic* qualities.

daguerreotype   A silver-iodide-coated copper plate that was developed into a photographic print; invented by Louis Daguerre in the 1830s.

De Stijl   The name of a magazine created in 1917 by a group of Dutch painters typified by Piet Mondrian; De Stijl became the name of their movement, even though they preferred the term "Neoplasticism."

decalcomania   A technique in which a painted object is pressed onto a canvas to transfer the image.

depth of field   In photography, the range of depth in which objects are sharply defined.

Der Blaue Reiter   German for "The Blue Rider"; an early twentieth-century group of German painters that absorbed some members of the *Die Brücke* group; the group included a wide variety of styles.

diaphragm   An adjustable opening used with a photographic lens. The diaphragm determines the amount of light that will strike the film.

Die Brücke   German for "The Bridge"; an early twentieth-century group of German painters who used harsh, simplified forms and strong colors in an expressionist manner.

directional editing   *Editing* that utilizes repeated or contrasting movement.

dissolve   In motion pictures, the technique of superimposing a new *shot* as a *fade-out* disappears from the screen.

divisionism   The systematically broken color found in the *pointillism* of Seurat.

dolly   A mobile platform used in filming motion pictures.

dolly shot   In motion pictures, a *shot* in which the *dolly* follows, moves toward, or moves away from the action.

double-ender   A structure with *apses* at both ends of the nave.

dromos   A stone-lined approach to Cycladic tombs.

drypoint   An *intaglio process* in which a sharp point is used to scratch lines into a soft copper plate.

editing   The cutting and splicing of motion-picture film to create a *sequence* from a series of *shots.*

edition   The total number of *prints* of a given work.

elevations   An architectural drawing that shows the side of a room or building without perspective distortion.

empathy   Identification with, and sympathetic response to, an image or object.

encaustic paint   Paint in which the *binder* is refined beeswax with additives.

engaged columns   Columns carved in relief in such a way that they appear to be partially buried in a wall.

entablature   The structure above the *capital* of a column and below the roof.

entasis   The slight outward curving in the sides of the shaft of a Doric column.

etching   A process in which acid is used to eat lines into a metal plate. These lines are filled with ink, the high surfaces are wiped clean, and prints are made by putting paper on the inked plate and running it through a press.

ex-votos   Small figurines used as offerings of thanks for cures.

fade-out   A motion-picture *shot* that slowly disappears from the screen.

faïence   Low-fired clay covered with opaque colored glazes.

fete galante   A special category of subject matter typified by the paintings of Antoine Watteau and other Rococo painters, portraying the aristocracy at leisure in a landscape.

firing   The process of baking natural clay in a *kiln*.

fixative   A thin varnish sprayed on a *pastel* or chalk drawing in order to keep it from smearing.

flashback   In motion pictures, cutting to a scene or image that belongs to an earlier time in the story.

flask   An iron holder used in the *sand-mold* process.

floor pieces   A modern art form that utilizes a floor area as the compositional frame for a piece of art.

fluted   Vertical channels or grooves carved all the way around column shafts.

flying buttresses   The arched segments carrying the thrust from vaults to vertical *buttresses* on the exterior of a structure.

foreshortening   Portraying an object as extending diagonally into space toward the viewer.

form   *Shape, mass,* and structure, considered in the broadest sense.

formal editing   *Editing* that exploits the difference or similarity of shapes for contrast or unity.

forum   The civic center of a Roman town.

frames   The individual still photographs that, by the thousands, compose a motion picture.

framing   The composition of a motion picture *shot* within the rectangle of film.

french sand   A mixture of clay, silica, and alumina used in *sand molds*.

fresco-secco   Painting on a dry plaster surface using a variety of media.

frieze   A horizontal band of designs or carvings.

frottage   A technique of creating an image by rubbing (with graphite or crayon) paper that has been placed over an object or over a textured surface.

gable   The triangular area formed at the end of a building by a pitched roof. When framed by moldings it becomes a *pediment*, as at the end of a Greek temple.

genre subjects   Scenes from everyday life.

glaze   A transparent layer of oil paint.

gouache   Opaque watercolor.

Greek key or fret   A geometric pattern that resembles a row of key ends standing upright.

grog   *Fired* and ground-up clay.

groin   The exterior indentation where vaults meet in a *cross* or *groin vault*.

groin vault   See *cross vault*.

ground   In painting, the immediate surface that receives the paint. In printmaking, the acid-resistant material used in *etching*.

ground line   The horizontal bottom edge of a composition.

half-timber   A kind of construction made of a joined wood frame, filled with mud, plaster, brick or *wattle-and-daub* panels.

high relief   Sculpture in which the forms project boldly from a background slab (as opposed to freestanding sculpture).

hue   The name of a *color;* the property that distinguishes one color from another.

hypostyle   A hall with a roof supported by columns.

iconoclasm   The controversy between the *iconophiles* and the *iconoclasts*.

iconoclast   One in Byzantine times who believed that representations of divinities were sacrilegious idols.

iconography   The study of conventional symbols, often religious, as they appear in the people, objects, and events depicted in a work of art.

iconology The study of factors that cause changes in *iconography* and the interpretation of those changes within the history of thought.

iconophile One in Byzantine times who wanted religious images.

impasto Thickly applied paint.

intaglio process A printmaking technique in which a metal plate is cut or eaten into with acid. The lowered parts, rather than the relief parts, hold the ink and transfer it to the paper print under the pressure of a press. *Etching* is an intaglio process.

jambs The layers of a splayed opening.

Jugendstil The German counterpart of Art Nouveau.

kiln The high-temperature oven used to fire natural clay.

kore Young woman. Statues of young women found in Greece from the seventh and sixth centuries B.C. Plural: korai.

kouros Young man. Statues of young men found in Greece from the seventh and sixth centuries B.C. Plural: kouroi.

lancet A bullet-shaped window.

linear perspective A means of creating an illusion of depth on a flat surface. Parallel lines appear to converge at a *vanishing point* on the horizon line, or on a line perpendicular to the horizon line.

linoleum cuts A printmaking technique in which linoleum mounted on wood is cut into a *relief* printing surface.

lithography A printmaking process that employs grease-containing crayons, pencils, or inks on a limestone or metal surface to establish the design. The block is then chemically treated to reject ink except over the grease design.

local color The basic *color* an artist gives an object in a painting.

low relief Sculpture in which the forms project slightly from a background slab.

mansard roof A steeply pitched roof with a flat or almost flat platform at the top.

mass Three-dimensional *shape* and *form*, in actuality or illusion.

mastaba A type of Egyptian tomb formed by a rectangular block with sloping sides and more *mass* than enclosed space.

medium of expression A particular material, and a technique appropriate to it, used to produce a work of art.

megaron A rectangular hall with a central hearth, anteroom, and pillared porch.

metal cut A printmaking technique in which metal is cut or etched into a *relief* printing surface. Engraving tools, metal punches, or acid can be used.

metal engraving An *intaglio process* in which *burins* are used to cut out the metal from the plate in order to produce lines that hold ink.

modeling To mold in sculpture or in two-dimensional art, to make forms appear three-dimensional with variation in *value* or *color.*

monotype A printmaking technique that yields one print. Ink or paint is applied to a smooth glass or metal plate; paper is then pressed against the plate and lifted off as a print.

montage A rapid succession of images and/or sounds that is part of, or that composes, a motion-picture sequence.

multiple-point perspective The use of more than one *vanishing point* in *linear perspective.*

narthex A porch or vestibule of a church, generally *colonnaded.*

negative Developed photographic film.

obelisk A pillar in the shape of a tapered shaft with a pointed tip.

oculus A round skylight-opening in the center of a dome.

one-point perspective The use of a single *vanishing point* in *linear perspective.*

open form A *mass* or *form* that includes or is penetrated by open space.

optical mixing An effect created when individual strokes of color in a painting are seen from a distance so that they seem to blur and are thus "mixed" by the eyes of the viewer.

order   The column and *entablature* considered as a unit.

Palladian Revival   Eighteenth-century architectural movement in England that favored a revival of simpler Roman architectural forms as found in the sixteenth-century Italian architecture of Andrea Palladio.

pan   In motion pictures, a sweeping *shot* that moves from one side to another.

pass-throughs   A term used by Peter Voulkos for a plug of clay that is pushed into an opening in the side of a clay vessel.

pastels   Colored drawing sticks made from a mixture of pigment and glue.

patina   The color acquired by bronze sculpture as a result of acid baths and heat treatment.

patineurs   The workers who apply *patina* to bronze sculpture.

pediment   The triangular *gable* at the end of a building.

pendentives   The curved triangular infills in the corners at the top of a square room that convert the square to a circular base for a dome.

peripteral   Surrounded by a *colonnade.*

peristyle   A covered *colonnade* that surrounds a building or court.

pharaohs   The kings of ancient Egypt.

photogram   A photograph created without a camera by placing an object on or over light-sensitive paper, exposing the paper, and then developing it as a print.

photographic print   The finished product of photography; a chemically treated surface onto which the *negative* image has been transferred.

photomontage   Cut-and-pasted or superimposed photographs, or *combination prints.*

pilaster   The flattened column shapes that project in *low relief* from a wall.

plate drapery   Folds of clothing represented in a manner that suggests overlapping plates of armor.

plate mark   The indentation left on print paper by the *intaglio process* metal plate.

pointillism   A method of paint application used by Seurat that utilizes uniformly small dots of paint in the techniques of broken color and optical mixing.

pointing machine   A device that transfers proportions from a small model carving to a larger block.

porcelain   A very hard and usually translucent ceramic ware made from a special clay *fired* at a high temperature.

primary hues   *Hues* that can be mixed to produce most other hues. With colored light, the primaries are red, green, and blue-violet. With pigments, magenta-red, yellow, and turquoise-blue are the traditional primaries.

priming   A preparatory first coating of paint or *size* to prepare a surface for painting.

print   A work of art produced by a transfer from another surface. Sometimes called a multiple original, a print is considered an original rather than a reproduction because it is the deliberate end product.

psychic automatism   The bringing forth of images from the imagination or the "unconscious"; a device used by Surrealist and Dadaist artists.

putti   Sculpted figures of cupids or cherubs.

pylon   A massive sloping façade.

quadriga   A chariot pulled by four horses.

quadripartite   A *ribbed cross vault* that is composed of four separate sections.

quoins   The bold stonework used to emphasize the corners of a building.

radical eclecticism   Postmodern architecture that refers to past styles for symbolic content.

rayograph   See *photogram.*

reflected light   The light reflected onto a shadowed area from a directly illuminated surface.

registration   In printmaking, the accurate placement of colors printed by a sequence of different printing surfaces, as when a colored *woodcut* is printed by a succession of blocks, one for each color.

relief   A form of sculpture in which the background is cut away to leave raised images.

relief process   In relief process, the artist

cuts down parts of a block. The part that is left raised is inked, and the ink is transferred to paper from the raised or relief parts.

relieving arch   An arch that protects the lintel below it from the weight of a dome.

reliquaries   Elaborate containers for sacred relics.

resist   A substance that isolates or protects an area on a work of art from coloring matter applied to surrounding areas. Rubber cement, for example, can be put on parts of watercolor paper to protect it from colored washes. Then it can be rubbed off to expose the untouched white paper.

rhythm (visual)   A recurrence of similar or identical elements, such as *shapes, colors, masses,* or spaces, that suggests order and continuity.

rhythmical editing   Motion-picture *editing* technique that varies the length of shots to suggest slowing or quickening of tempo.

ribbed cross vault   A *cross* or *groin vault* with *ribs.*

ribs   The moldings that emphasize the boundaries of a vaulted *bay* or the *groins* of a *cross vault.*

round arch   A semicircular arch.

rotulus   A book or document in scroll form.

rustication   The bevelling of the edges of stones in masonry to emphasize the joints between them, in order to give a bold rustic effect.

sand mold   *French sand* pressed around a plaster form to make a mold for bronze sculpture.

saturation   The purity or vividness of a *color.*

scene   A motion-picture *sequence* that occurs in one place and time.

schiacciato   A kind of subtle *low-relief* sculpture used by Donatello.

scumbling   In painting, opaque color that is dragged or rubbed over previously applied colors to modify without obscuring them.

sequence   A combination of motion-picture *shots,* produced by *editing.*

serigraphy   See *silkscreen.*

sexpartite   A *ribbed cross* vault with a *transverse arch,* so the structure is composed of six separate sections.

shade   A color made darker by the addition of black or a *complementary* color.

shape   An area or plane with identifiable boundaries.

shot   In motion pictures, an uninterrupted camera view.

silkscreen   A printmaking technique that pushes ink or paint through porous silk or synthetic fabric onto the print surface. The design is created by blocking the pores of the silk except for the shape of the design; the fabric thus becomes a stencil.

simultaneous contrast   The intensifying and brightening effect of *complementary* colors or contrasting *values,* when placed side by side.

sizing   A substance used in painting to limit the absorption of the base material (particularly when the base material is wood or canvas).

soft ground etching   This process uses an especially soft *ground.* Paper, fabric, or other materials can be pressed onto the ground; when the material is lifted off, it pulls the ground with it to expose the plate to acid.

solarization   A photographic technique in which film is partially reexposed during its development.

splayed openings   The doorways or windows formed by layers of increasingly smaller arches, producing a funnel effect.

springing   The beginning of the curve of an arch.

squinch   An arched infill that converts the corners at the top of a square room to a circular base for a dome.

staffage   Figures that staff or people a landscape, providing literary content and a means of establishing scale or creating nostalgia.

star vault   Multiple ribs suggesting superimposed star shapes; sometimes used over the crossing of a Gothic church.

states   The different stages of composition during the making of a print.

stele   An upright slab or pillar, usually carved or inscribed for commemorative purposes.

stoas   *Colonnaded,* open-fronted sheds used in city centers as promenades and shopping areas.

stoneware   A very hard ceramic ware made from a special clay body and *fired* at a high temperature.

stop out   An acid-resistant varnish used to seal off areas of an etching plate while other areas are being *etched* more deeply.

strapwork   In painting, flat decorative bands resembling cut leather.

stringcourse   A horizontal band or molding.

stucco   A fine plaster or cement used for covering walls or for decoration in the form of cast designs or figures.

support   The basic material (wood, canvas, and so forth) underneath the *ground* in painting, when the ground is *sizing* or *priming*.

synthesism   The term used by the followers of Gauguin to describe their painting movement.

tabernacle   A devotional center in a church ranging in size from a small plaque to a large wall niche.

tempera   Paint in which the *binder* is an emulsion (mixture of water and oil).

tenebristi   The followers of Caravaggio's tenebroso style.

terra cotta   The term loosely used to refer to all clays that can be *fired*, but more accurately a brown-red unglazed clay.

thermae   The Roman public baths.

tholos   A circular building; also, a round tomb.

throwing   The process of forming vessels on a potter's wheel.

tint   A *color* that has been highly diluted with white.

tonal editing   *Editing* that moves from light to dark, or dark to light.

tooth   The relative texture of a drawing paper.

tracery   Intricate stone carving within a window.

transept   Part of a church that crosses the nave at right angles, giving the plan the shape of a cross (see Fig. 4–15).

transverse arches   Arches perpendicular to the length of a vault that have the appearance of, and sometimes function as, reinforcements.

trial proof   The trial *print* made during the preparation of printing surfaces in printmaking.

triumphal arch   A freestanding commemorative structure with inscriptions and relief sculpture. A common type of Roman monument.

trumeau   The center post of a double door.

tufa   An easily worked stone that hardens when exposed to air.

tumuli   Earthen mounds, especially burial mounds.

tunnel vault   An extension of the round arch that requires *buttressing* along its sides.

Tuscan order   A Roman derivation of the Greek Doric order.

tympanum   The framed surface over a door.

value   The lightness and darkness of an area or a *hue*.

vanishing point   In *linear perspective*, the point or points at which parallel lines appear to converge.

vedute   Paintings of views of a city.

vellum   Calfskin or kidskin prepared as a surface for painting or writing.

volutes   Carved spirals, especially in the capitals of Ionic columns.

wagon vault   See *tunnel vault.*

wash   A transparent layer of watercolor paint.

wash drawing   The dilution of watercolor or ink with water to create transparent *washes*. Only one or two *colors* are used, thus it is called a "drawing," rather than a painting.

waste mold   A plaster mold that is chipped away and destroyed in order to free the cast piece inside.

wattle and daub   A structural process using woven saplings plastered with mud.

westwork   A high, blocklike enlargement in church architecture that gives the effect of a west *transept* that contains a *narthex* at ground level and a chapel above.

wheel window   A round window divided into sections by stone elements that radiate from the center like the spokes of a wheel.

woodcut   A printmaking technique in which a block of wood is cut into *relief*. Plank grain (grain running parallel to the board) is used.

wood engraving   A printmaking technique in which the end grain (grain at a right angle to the surface) of the wood block is cut into *relief;* working with the end grain allows greater detail than does the plank grain of woodcuts.

Picture Credits

Castelli Gallery, New York; 387, left, Malcolm Smith Studio; 388, Courtesy Philip Johnson; 389, top and bottom, Ezra Stoller © ESTO; 390, top, Photo by Fumio Murasawa, courtesy Tange Assoc., Tokyo; 390, bottom, and 391, top and bottom, Photos by Osamu Murai, courtesy Tange Assoc., Tokyo; 395, Courtesy Nicolas Schöffer; 398, Photo by Rudolph Burkhardt, courtesy of Leo Castelli Gallery, New York; 399, Courtesy, Bernice Steinbaum Gallery, New York; 402, top, © A. J. Petersen, Amsterdam; 402, bottom, Courtesy, André Emmerich Gallery, New York; 403, bottom, Photo by Geoffrey Clements, Staten Island; 404, Photo courtesy of Leo Castelli Gallery, New York; 405, top, Artur Starewicz, Warsaw, ul. Swietojerska 16m3, Poland; 409, Courtesy, Alan Stone Gallery; 411, top, Photo by Dorothy Zeidman, courtesy Leo Castelli Gallery, New York; 411, bottom, Courtesy of the artist; 412, top, Produced and published by Tyler Graphics, Ltd. © David Hockney/Tyler Graphics, Ltd.; 412, bottom, © Judy Chicago 1973; 413, Photo courtesy of Leo Castelli Gallery, New York; 417, Courtesy, Paula Cooper Gallery; 418, Gianfranco Gorgione; 419, Courtesy, Marion Goodman Gallery, New York; 420, Courtesy, John Weber Gallery and the artist; 421, left, Photo by Julius Kozlowski. Courtesy, Holly Solomon Gallery, New York; 421, right and 422, Courtesy, Mary Boone Gallery, New York; 423, top, Venturi, Rauch and Scott Brown; 424, Shashinka Photo; 425, Ezra Stoller © ESTO; 427, bottom, Photo: Laurin McCracken

CHAPTER 20 p. 431, bottom, The Metropolitan Museum of Art, New York, Gift of I. N. Phelps Stokes, Edward S. Howes, Alice Mary Howes, Marion Augusta Howes, 1937; 432, top, George Eastman House, Rochester, New York; 432, bottom, Bibliothèque Nationale, Paris; 433 and 434, George Eastman House, Rochester, New York; 435, Courtesy of the Witkin Gallery, New York; 436, The Alfred Stieglitz Collection, Art Institute of Chicago; 437, The Imogen Cunningham Trust, Berkeley, California; 438, top, © Arizona Board of Regents, Center for Creative Photography; 438, bottom, Courtesy of the Dorothea Lange Collection © the City of Oakland and the Oakland Museum; 439, Photograph by Ansel Adams. Courtesy of the Ansel Adams Publishing Rights Trust. All Rights Reserved. 440, Magnum Photos; 442, top, Jerry N. Uelsmann; 442, bottom, Courtesy, Metro Pictures; 444, George Eastman House, Rochester, New York; 445, The Museum of Modern Art/Film Stills Archive; 447, RKO Radio Pictures, a division of RKO General Inc./photo courtesy of the Museum of Modern Art/Film Stills Archive; 448, 450, 451,

453, The Museum of Modern Art/Film Stills Archive; 454, Paramount Pictures Corporation; 455, The Museum of Modern Art/Film Stills Archive; 456, © 1985 Richard Feiner and Company, Inc.; 457, 458, 459, The Museum of Modern Art/Film Stills Archive; 462, Zenith International Pictures; 463, Cinema 5 Ltd.; 464, top, Orion Pictures © The Saul Zaentz Company; 464, bottom, Columbia Pictures; 466, New Yorker Films

COLOR SECTIONS Plates 1, 3, 4, 8, 10, 11, Scala/Art Resource; Plate 2, By permission of the Board of Trinity College, Dublin; Plates 9 and 14, Art Resource/ Giraudon; Plate 16, © 1987 The Art Institute of Chicago, Potter Palmer Collection, 1922; Plate 17, Réunion des Musées Nationaux de France; Plate 21, © 1987 The Art Institute of Chicago, Helen Birch Bartlett Memorial Collection; Plate 23, © 1987 The Art Institute of Chicago, Robert Waller Fund; Plate 28, © 1987 The Art Institute of Chicago, Helen Birch Bartlett Memorial Collection; Plate 31, Photographie Musée National d'art Moderne, Centre Georges Pompidou, Paris; Plate 33, Photo by Alfred J. Wyatt; Plate 35, Philadelphia Museum, given by Mr. and Mrs. Rodolphe M. de Schauensee; Plate 37, Photo by David Heald; Plate 40, Collection of the Whitney Museum of American Art, Purchase; Plate 41, Photo by Malcolm Varon, New York; Plate 45, Courtesy of André Emmerich Gallery, New York; Plate 46, Courtesy of Victor Vasarely; Plate 48, Photo courtesy of Leo Castelli Gallery, New York

© ARS New York/SPADEM, 1989 for the following: Plates 20, 29, 31, 33, 34, 36. Front cover. Pp. 5; 28; 295; 296, top right; 324, top and bottom; 326, top and bottom; 330, top and bottom; 332; 340, top and bottom; 342, bottom; 346; 347; 363, top; 374, top

© ARS New York/ADAGP, 1989 for the following: Plates 23, 32, 35, 36. Pp. 303, bottom; 333; 338; 341, bottom; 343, top and bottom; 348, bottom; 349, top and bottom; 351, bottom; 353, bottom; 371

© ARS New York/Pollock-Krasner Foundation, 1989 for the following: Plate 39. Pp. 376; 377, top

© CNNHS/ARS New York/SPADEM, 1989 for the following: Pp. 101, top right; 172; 264

©ARS New York, 1989: Page 411, top

©BILD-KUNST, West Germany/VAGA New York, 1989 for the following: Pp. 5, top right; 321; 337

©SIAE, Italy/VAGA New York, 1989 for the following: Page 341, top.

©BEELDRECHT, Amsterdam/VAGA New York, 1989 for the following: Page 327.

© The Artist/VAGA New York, 1989 for the following: Pp. 378; 382; 383, right; 386, top and bottom; 405, bottom; 406, bottom; 413

Illustrations

Pp. 54; 81, top and bottom; 98, top; 112; 125, bottom; 134; 152, right; 153, bottom; 155, bottom left; 156, middle left; 158, bottom; 159, bottom; 165, right; 166, top; 167, bottom right; 211, top; 236; 263: From *Gardner's Art Through the Ages,* Eighth Edition, edited by Horst de la Croix and Richard Tansey © 1986 by Harcourt Brace Jovanovich, Inc. Reproduced by permission of the publisher.

Pp. 56; 69, top; 74, bottom; 196, left: © 1975 The Royal Institute of British Architects and the University of London, by permission of the Athlone Press.

P. 59, top: From R. Ghirshman, "Village perseachemenide," *Mem. de la Mission Archéologique d'argent à l'époque achéménide,* Athèna, 1956.

P. 73, top: Reproduced in *History of Art,* by H. W. Janson. After N. de Garis Davies.

Pp. 80; 141, bottom left: Hirmer Fotoarchiv, Munich.

P. 102, top: Reproduced in *History of Art,* by H. W. Janson. After F. Krischen.

Pp. 233, top right; and 234, top left: From Rudolf Wittkower, *Art and Architecture in Italy: 1600–1750* (Pelican History of Art, 2nd revised edition, 1965), pp. 119, 157. Copyright © Rudolf Wittkower, 1958. Reprinted by permission of Penguin Books, Ltd.

P. 248, bottom left: The Wren Society.

P. 359 top: From Henry R. Hitchcock, *Nineteenth- and Twentieth-Century Architecture,* 2nd edition, Penguin Books, Ltd., 1963.

P. 392: Reproduced by permission of Cosanti Foundation, Scottsdale, Arizona.

P. 423: Venturi, Rauch, and Scott Brown.

P. 426: Richard Meier.

DRAWINGS Felix Cooper, Vantage Art, Inc., Ira Graboff, Bert Schneider.

Index

Page numbers in *italics* indicate illustrations.